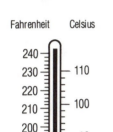

Fahrenheit | Celsius

Fahrenheit	Celsius
240	
230	110
220	
210	100
200	
190	90
180	80
170	
160	70
150	
140	60
130	
120	50
110	
100	40
90	
80	30
70	20
60	
50	10
40	
30	0
20	
10	
0	−10
−10	
−20	−20
−30	
−40	−30
−50	−40
−60	
−70	−50
−80	−60

Metric to English

Approximate Conversions from Metric Measures

Symbol	When You Know	Multiply by	To Find	Symbol
Length				
mm	millimeters	0.04	inches	in
cm	centimeters	0.4	inches	in
m	meters	3.3	feet	ft
m	meters	1.1	yards	yd
km	kilometers	0.6	miles	mi
Area				
cm²	square centimeters	0.16	square inches	in²
m²	square meters	1.2	square yards	yd²
km²	square kilometers	0.4	square miles	mi²
ha	hectares (10,000 m²)	2.5	acres	
Mass/Weight				
g	grams	0.035	ounces	oz
kg	kilograms	2.2	pounds	lb
t	tonnes (1000 kg)	1.1	short tons	
Volume				
ml	milliliters	0.03	fluid ounces	fl oz
l	liters	2.1	pints	pt
l	liters	1.06	quarts	qt
l	liters	0.26	gallons	gal
m³	cubic meters	35	cubic feet	ft³
m³	cubic meters	1.3	cubic yards	yd³
Temperature (Exact)				
°C	Celsius temperature	9/5 (then add 32)	Fahrenheit temperature	°F

Inches

Centimeters

SEVENTH EDITION

SCIENCE IN ELEMENTARY EDUCATION

Peter C. Gega

Professor Emeritus
College of Education
San Diego State University

Macmillan Publishing Company
New York

Maxwell Macmillan Canada
Toronto

Maxwell Macmillan International
New York   Oxford   Singapore   Sydney

Cover photos: © David Young-Wolff, PhotoEdit
Editor: Linda James Scharp
Production Editor: Jonathan Lawrence
Art Coordinator: Peter A. Robison
Photo Editor: Anne Vega
Text Designer: Jill E. Bonar
Cover Designer: Russ Maselli
Production Buyer: Patricia A. Tonneman
Illustrations: Academy ArtWorks, Inc.

This book was set in Goudy and New Baskerville by Carlisle Communications, Ltd., and was printed and bound by R.R. Donnelley & Sons Company. The cover was printed by Lehigh Press, Inc.

Macmillan Publishing Company
866 Third Avenue
New York, NY 10022

Macmillan Publishing Company is part of the
Maxwell Communication Group of Companies.

Maxwell Macmillan Canada, Inc.
1200 Eglinton Avenue East, Suite 200
Don Mills, Ontario M3C 3N1

Library of Congress Cataloging-in-Publication Data

Gega, Peter C.
      Science in elementary education/Peter C. Gega.—7th ed.
         p.   cm.
      Also published in two separate volumes: Concepts and experiences in elementary school science (2nd ed.) and How to teach elementary school science (2nd ed.).
      Includes bibliographical references and index.
      ISBN 0-02-341302-6
      1. Science—Study and teaching (Elementary)   I. Gega, Peter C.
   Concepts and experiences in elementary school science. 1994.
   II. Gega, Peter C. How to teach elementary school science. 1994.
   III. Title.
   LB1585.G4 1994
   372.3'5'044—dc20   92-43308
                                                                                                          CIP

Printing: 1 2 3 4 5 6 7 8 9   Year: 4 5 6 7

CREDITS

Chapter 1 opener: Michael Siluk; Chapter 2 opener: Barbara Stimpert; Fig. 2-18: Education Development Center; Chapter 3 opener: Barbara Stimpert; Chapter 4 opener: Robert Finken; Chapter 5 opener: Barbara Schwartz/Macmillan; Fig. 5-1: Michael Houghton/Studiohio; Fig. 5-2: Bausch and Lomb; Fig. 5-3: Ken-A-Vision Manufacturing Co., Inc.; Chapter 6 opener: Jean-Claude Lejeune; Fig. 6-7: Barbara Schwartz/Macmillan; Fig. 6-8: Copyright Optical Data Corporation, 1987; Chapter 7 opener: Barbara Schwartz/Macmillan; Chapter 8 opener: Barbara Stimpert; Chapter 9 opener: Robert Finken; Fig. 9-3: U.S. Department of Energy; Chapter 10 opener: Robert Finken; Fig. 10-2: Spencer Grant/Stock, Boston; Fig. 10-3: Courtesy Department of Library Sciences, American Museum of Natural History; Chapter 11 opener: Robert Finken; Chapter 12 opener: Robert Finken; Chapter 13 opener: Mary Jane Porterfield; Chapter 14 opener: Anne Vega; Fig. 14-5: High Spencer; Fig. 14-6: Bruce Roberts/Rapho/Photo Researchers; Chapter 15 opener: Barbara Schwartz/Macmillan; Fig. 15-1: Tumblebrook Farms, Inc.; Fig. 15-4: Runck Schoenburger/Grant Heilman; Fig. 15-5: Raymond L. Ditmars/Department of Library Sciences, American Museum of Natural History; Fig. 15-6: Carolina Biological Supply Company; Fig. 15-8: Courtesy Department of Library Sciences, American Museum of Natural History; Fig. 15-13: Carolina Biological Supply Company; Fig. 15-14: Runck Schoenburger/Grant Heilman; Chapter 16 opener: Jean-Claude Lejeune; Chapter 17 opener: AP/Wide World Photos; Fig. 17-1: General Biological Supply House; Fig. 17-3: U.S.D.A. Soil Conservation Service; Fig. 17-4: U.S. Dept. of Agriculture; Table 17-1: pumice: H. Stearns/U.S. Geological Survey; volcanic breccia: Mackay School of Mines, University of Nevada; obsidian: C. Milton/U.S. Geological Survey; basalt, granite, conglomerate, sandstone, slate, quartzite: Courtesy Department of Library Services, American Museum of Natural History; shale: W. Bradley/U.S. Geological Survey; limestone: F. Calkins/U.S. Geological Survey; marble: A. Heitanen/U.S. Geological Survey; Chapter 18 opener: AP/Wide World Photos; Fig. 18-3: ESSA (a & b), NOAA (c); Fig. 18-5: Courtesy of Qualimetrics, Inc., Sacramento, CA; and Chapter 19 opener: NASA.

Preface

This book combines practical methods, subject matter, and activities on how to teach science to children, ages 5 to 12. It has two complementary parts.

Part I takes up why science education is basic to children's schooling and explains the foundations that give it form and substance. Each of its seven chapters develops a broad competency or a cluster of related teaching skills through step-by-step descriptions and use of many real-life examples. (Incidentally, all the examples reflect my personal teaching experiences or firsthand observations with elementary schoolchildren.) The chapters and several included follow-up exercises should enable you to

- Decide what science is basic, useful, and learnable for children.
- Recognize and assess differences in children's thinking.
- Use closed-ended and open-ended teaching activities.
- Improve children's thinking in several ways.
- Locate and use a variety of resources to teach science.
- Arrange and manage learning centers, microcomputer centers, and projects.
- Organize and assess science teaching.

Part II has 12 chapters of subject matter, broad investigations, and activities—all designed with three purposes in mind. First, it helps you apply in teachable ways the skills developed in Part I. For example, the questioning methods and the open-ended and closed-ended strategies in the early chapters are shown in hundreds of in-context examples. This is also true of suggested thinking processes. Early sections on learning centers and projects show how to quickly and easily convert many investigations in Part II for those uses. So following through on these and other methods is strongly emphasized.

Second, Part II gives you hundreds of lively and interesting concrete experiences to use with children. These are in two forms: activities and investigations. The *activities* offer firsthand experiences through which children may learn concepts and procedures. The *investigations* offer chances for you and your pupils to inquire, as co-investigators if you wish, into open-ended problems and topics. Both kinds of learning experiences use every-day, easy-to-get materials and can also enrich school science programs. (A complete inventory of investigations and activities follows the Contents.)

The third purpose of Part II is to give plain talk explanations of subject matter that can help you where you may feel lacking in background. These are tied to the learning experiences and give useful, everyday examples of science concepts and principles at work. Of course, you can build a good subject-matter background as you investigate with children. But I believe you'll also find that the explanations will make it easier for you to guide children confidently and creatively.

Thanks are owed to many people in the preparation of this seventh edition of *Science in Elementary Education*. I especially appreciate the help given to me by Christine Ebert, University of South Carolina; John P. Huntsberger, University of Texas—Austin; Linda Cronin Jones, University of Florida; Ernest W. Lee, University of North Carolina—Greensboro; and Nedra C. Sears, East Central University. I believe that their many practical suggestions have notably increased the value of this latest edition.

Peter C. Gega

Contents

7 How to Organize and Assess Science Teaching   160

II Subject Matter, Investigations, and Activities   191

How Part II Can Help You   192

8 Light Energy and Color   194

9 Heat Energy   240

INVENTORY OF INVESTIGATIONS & ACTIVITIES

13 Simple Machines and How They Work   389

14 Plant Life and Environment   431

15   Animal Life and Environment   481

16   Human Body and Nutrition   522

19 The Earth in Space 658

I

HOW TO TEACH ELEMENTARY SCHOOL SCIENCE

Science in Elementary Education

When you were a child, you and all the other girls and boys wanted to know a great deal about the world around you. Children still do. Sooner or later, they will ask questions like

Why doesn't a spider get stuck in its web?

How does a bird get in the egg?

How can you tell the difference between a boy tree and a girl tree?

and

Where does the dark come from?

What makes the wind blow?

Where do the people on TV go when you turn it off?

If you had asked these questions as a child, how thoughtfully would your teachers have handled them? Would you have been able to explore some of your own interests? Or was learning more restricted? Were you guided to think through some problems for yourself? Or were answers always given?

How your teachers worked with children reflected their notions about science teaching and how they thought it could benefit their pupils. The same applies today with you. Your school or district office can give you some instructional materials. But your concepts and values about science teaching will strongly affect what children actually learn in your classroom.

Notice the contrasting approaches taken by several teachers—one pair each at the primary-, middle-, and upper-grade levels—as they prepare to introduce a hands-on activity.

In two separate primary-level classrooms, the children are supposed to experience the same listening activity. They have brought in empty shoe boxes and numerous small objects: marbles, jacks, crayons, paper clips, pencils, and the like.

Teacher 1 explains what to do. Each child will work with a partner. One child will secretly place an object in the box and replace the lid. The partner will try to identify the object by tilting the box back and forth, listening with an ear held close to the box. The teacher then says, "Will you be able to

guess what your partner put into the box? After you do, take turns."

Teacher 2 has asked her class to bring, besides shoe boxes, *matching pairs* of small objects. Each child will also work with a partner. Each child is to display six different objects in a row before her or his partner, then secretly select from the matching objects one that matches a displayed object. This is to be put into the box and lid replaced. The teacher says, "See if you can figure out which one of the six objects in front of you matches the object secretly placed in your box. Listen to the noises the object inside makes as you tilt it back and forth. Also look carefully at the objects in front of you. Which one is most likely to make the sounds you hear?"

Here we have two very different notions of what the lesson is about. The first teacher sees the activity as a fun way to engage the children in a listening experience that is little more than a guessing game. The second teacher sees the activity as an interesting chance for children to make observations that require them to use their minds. Visibly displaying concrete objects enables the children to connect the *appearance* of objects with their probable *sounds*. This teacher also realizes that she has to limit the number of objects displayed to avoid confusing her young pupils. If six objects prove to be too many for some to consider, she is ready to reduce this number at any time. Among other things, this teacher shows knowledge of how children learn science and a sensitivity to what's possible at their developmental level.

In two separate middle-level classrooms, pupils are going to make magnets out of common iron nails. Each teacher has some nails, paper clips, and several magnets for the activity. Both intend to use the same activity described in the textbook:

Can you make a magnet out of a nail?

Materials: magnet, iron nail, paper clips

1. Place one end (pole) of the magnet on the nail near its head.

2. Rub the whole nail's length with the magnet in one direction. Then lift the magnet off the nail.

3. Do steps 1 and 2 again. Rub the nail 10 times, always in one direction.

4. Touch the nail to some paper clips. What happens?

Teacher 1 directs the children to do the activity as written. The children find that the nails attract from two to four paper clips. A monitor quickly retrieves the materials and the class begins a related reading assignment in the science textbook. After the reading, pupils write answers to questions posed in the book.

Teacher 2 also conducts the activity as written, then says, "Wait a minute. How do we really know that rubbing the nail with a magnet made it a magnet? Maybe it was a magnet *before* you rubbed it." Protests and a lively discussion follow until it dawns on the children that they are operating solely on faith. They decide it makes sense to first check any nails for magnetism before rubbing them with a magnet. Maybe nails have a "little bit" of magnetism to start with, some say. Now that things are loosened up, further questions are raised by pupils and teacher: Why did some nails pick up more clips than others? What would happen if you rub the nail more, or fewer, times? In *both* directions? How long will a nail hold its magnetism? Can you make a nail lose its magnetism? My nail lost most of its magnetism—what's wrong? What would happen if you cut the nail in half? Would it be only half as strong? And so on. The teacher invites pupils with questions to write them on the chalkboard. Most can be answered by experimenting with the materials on hand. A few questions may call for locating and carefully reading reference materials, or conferring with people who are most likely to have valid knowledge about magnetism.

The first teacher in this example is willing to provide a concrete experience for pupils, but subordinates it to getting general information about magnetism through routine and unfocused reading. What's missing is an understanding of the nature of science, and how to get children thinking in purposeful, scientific ways.

Teacher 2 takes an otherwise humdrum activity and uses it to provoke curiosity, generate real experiments, critically examine procedures and assumptions, and think carefully about exactly what to read or whom to confer with for further information students need to answer *their own questions.* The children's minds are opened to further possibilities for investigation in ways that resemble how intelligent and educated persons, including working scientists, operate.

In two separate upper-level classrooms, two teachers are scheduled to teach the same three lessons. Here's how each begins each lesson:

Teacher 1: Does cold air hold less moisture than warm air?
Teacher 2: Why do our lips and skin seem so dry today?

Teacher 1: Does air have weight? What is air pressure?
Teacher 2: When you drink pop through a straw, what makes the liquid go up the straw?

Teacher 1: Can sunlight cause a chemical change in things?
Teacher 2: How many of you have seen colored clothing that has faded?

Maybe you're aware that the first teacher in each case has simply stated the science principle that will be taught in the form of a question. So in the first lesson, for example, the children will learn that *cold air holds less moisture.*

Teacher 2, in contrast, begins with an *application* of the principle. She tries to begin (and end) most lessons by referring to children's everyday experiences. To her, the most significant, understandable, and unforgettable science is what students can apply in their lives. Science principles, or *generalizations* as we'll refer to them in this book, typically have many real-life applications. When we begin and end lessons with applications, it enables children to reflect on their experiences.

It's easy to see that the second way of teaching in each example is likely to be more interesting and productive than the first way. This kind of teaching is exhilarating. You feel a growing sense of excitement, competence, and fulfillment as your pupils respond enthusiastically and grow. Yet if you're like most persons who select elementary teaching as a profession, science is not likely to be your strongest subject. So it's only natural to wonder if you are up to the job.

Perhaps you'll be surprised to learn that my university colleagues and I have observed many student teachers, as well as experienced teachers, using methods like those in the better examples you have just read. Generally, these persons have taken only the few science courses required for graduation, plus a course on the teaching of elementary school science. What they *do* have, in abundance, is good judgment. An internal set of guidelines enables them to judge between what science is basic and what is trivial, what is useful and what is ornamental, what is learnable and what is obscure.

An effective way to develop sound judgment in any subject is to study its *imperatives*—the powerful, essential ideas and processes that give the subject its value. When we heed and work in tune with clear imperatives, good results are likely to come our way. When we ignore them, the opposite result is likely no matter how hard we try.

There are three sources of imperatives in science education: those that come from science as a discipline, those that reflect society's needs, and those that reveal how children develop and learn. Your keen study of these imperatives can enable you to judge what is basic in science, what science is useful to nonscientists in our society, and what sci-

ence children can learn. This can also help you to put into perspective the specific teaching methods of following chapters and gain confidence from seeing the big picture.

SCIENCE IMPERATIVES

The imperatives from science as a discipline are found in *how* scientists go about finding out—*process;* and *what* scientists have found out—*knowledge.* Although the two in practice are inseparable, it will be convenient now to look at each separately. Let's consider knowledge first.

Knowledge

You and I try to explain, predict, and control our experiences by generalizing about the patterns or regularities we observe:

Muscles get sore when overworked.

Quality and price go together.

Actions speak louder than words.

Knowing the generalization about sore muscles may cause you to say, "I overworked yesterday, that's why I'm sore!" (explain) or, "I'm probably going to be sore tomorrow" (predict) or, "I'm not going to overwork today" (control). Can you see how you might also use the other two generalizations for these three purposes?

Scientists, too, observe patterns and generalize about them. But they usually do so with far more precision and reliability. This is a big reason nonscientists can profit from the study of science and its methods.

Scientists use an ingenious array of tools and organized ways to search for patterns in objects and events. The generalizations they invent to explain what they observe may look like these:

Plants have adaptations that enable them to survive changing conditions.

Fossil remains show that some life forms have become extinct.

Eclipses happen when the earth, sun, and moon are aligned.

However, few scientists pretend to fully "explain" or understand natural events. What they do is to *describe* natural events and, when they can, to predict or control them. What they may call "explanations" (concepts, generalizations, principles, laws, theories) are really descriptions—often brilliantly conceived and useful, but descriptions after all. How well a description enables them to "explain," predict, or control events becomes the chief measure of its worth.

Consider the concept of mammal, for example. Like other concepts, this one stands for a class of things with similar properties. Suppose a small whale gets tangled in a fishnet below the ocean's surface. Can you predict what will soon happen to the whale? You might think: "Whale—that's a mammal. Mammals are lung breathers. It will probably drown." Notice how the concept of whale as mammal brings up a property (lung breathing) associated with all mammals. This enables you to make a reasonably certain prediction. Or if a friend asks, "A whale *drown*? How?" you can explain by using the same property. Your understanding of the concept might also prompt you to influence or control the event, by swiftly cutting the net, for instance.

The generalizations of science help us in a similar way. The statement "Most matter expands when heated and contracts when cooled" interrelates several concepts. This generalization enables us to relate and explain a number of apparently different events: a sidewalk that cracks and buckles in hot weather; telephone wires that sag in summer but do not in winter; why we can loosen a tightly screwed jar lid by running hot water over it; the reason rocks rimming a campfire break apart when we douse the fire (and rocks) with water; and so on.

The learning of key concepts and generalizations invented by scientists is imperative in science education because it dramatically increases brainpower. Notice that in Figure 1-1 a large variety of animals could be classified as mammals. But only a comparative handful need be studied to get a handle on the concept.

Once we understand the physical properties of mammals, it's easy to classify even unfamiliar animals found in zoos, stories, or on television. Despite not knowing their names, we already know a great deal about them.

A similar transfer of learning happens with properly learned generalizations. Although few events may be studied to learn the generalization (Figure 1-2), many more may be applied. This explains why persons who organize their thinking into concepts, generalizations, sequences, and other patterns broaden and deepen their understanding throughout their lives. In contrast, persons who study unrelated facts quickly forget what they have been taught.[1] Learning the patterns of nature allows us to continually apply, or transfer, these learnings to new objects and events. The new facts collect and stick to well-learned patterns almost like iron filings to a magnet. This is not to say that teaching for transfer is easy. Pupils must often see applications made within a variety of contexts and at increasingly complex levels. Still, everyone reaps benefits from the cumulative work of scientists of today and years past, for only the relatively short time it takes to learn about that work.

---

[1]Robert F. Biehler and Jack Snowman. *Psychology Applied to Teaching.* 5th ed. (Boston: Houghton Mifflin, 1986), pp. 427–28.

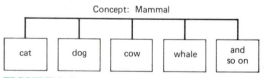

Concept: Mammal

| cat | dog | cow | whale | and so on |

FIGURE 1-1

Concepts stand for a class of things with similar properties.

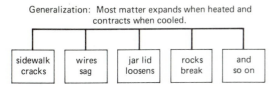

FIGURE 1-2
Generalizations enable us to relate and explain apparently different events.

Incidentally, have you already inferred how you might test to see if concepts and generalizations can be applied by pupils? You'll want to ask questions that contain examples of objects or events that have *not* been studied. If the child can link *unstudied* examples of a studied concept or generalization, chances are that transferable learning has occurred.

Scientists search for patterns, but they also look for inconsistencies in the patterns. Under certain conditions, for example, plants may *not* adapt and survive. The occasional deviation from the usual allows scientists to sharpen their generalizations and theories. In the same vein, we may find when shopping that quality does not always accompany higher prices. Figuring out under what conditions this happens improves our previous notion and makes us cagier shoppers.

Children, too, can learn to refine their generalizations. A second-grade class placed various small objects in water-filled pans to see which would sink or float. Some children summed up what they had learned by saying, "Light things float and heavy things sink." On hearing this, the teacher had them compare on a balance the weights of some things that had floated and sunk. A few objects that floated were heavier than some that had sunk. This made everyone look at the objects more carefully. Still, no one seemed to know what to say. When the teacher drew attention to the objects' sizes, the children soon concluded, "Things that are light for their size float. They sink when they are heavy for their size." Not bad, considering that the children had to think about two variables together, size and

weight. (More on this mental operation in Chapter 2.)

It is hard when dealing with natural events to foresee all the conditions that might cause them to change. This is why scientists see their generalizations and theories as *tentative*—always subject to change with new data. It also explains why generalizations may be stated in *probabilities,* a frequent practice when dealing with living things: "Persons who eat fatty foods run a greater risk of heart attacks than those who do not."

Parsimony.   Scientists may offer competing explanations or theories to account for a natural phenomenon. This is likely when the phenomenon can only be observed indirectly (the makeup of the earth's core, for instance), or has happened in the distant past (extinction of the dinosaurs, for example), and so cannot be fully tested. When competing theories account for the data equally well, scientists prefer on principle the simplest one. This principle of *parsimony*—literally, the word means the quality of being stingy or miserly—helps to keep the scientific enterprise more manageable and economical than it would be without it.

In an upper-grade class I visited recently, the teacher was well acquainted with the principle of parsimony. Several children were reporting their explanations of hidden electric circuits they had tested. They had connected a battery-operated circuit tester in various ways to wires hidden in a cardboard folder and inferred the locations of the wires. (You'll find a similar investigation on page 357 of this book.)

One child explained how three hidden wires connected in a certain pattern would account for the times the circuit-tester bulb had lit up. Another pupil showed how only two hidden wires could give the same results. Although both explanations were "correct," the class quickly saw the wisdom of preferring the simpler one when the teacher brought up the point. Later, the teacher told me that the pupils themselves had cited the principle of parsimony within several further discussions during their instructional unit on electric circuits.

Spiral Approach. If you switch to a higher grade after several years of teaching, don't be surprised if a previously taught generalization shows up again in your curriculum guide. Because a science generalization consists of several concepts and accounts for many facts, it usually takes more than one exposure for pupils to learn it well. So curriculum developers may plan for children to study the generalization several times, at increasing levels of complexity and abstraction, and in different contexts, during grade levels K–6 or K–8.

Consider, "Heat is a form of energy that is transferred in several ways." It may be studied in one of the primary grades as simple heat conduction from the source through solid materials, such as metal, plastic, wood, and cloth. The question, Why do people use cloth pot holders? and other matters dealing with safety around hot objects may be emphasized. (Children are especially vulnerable during the primary years.) In one or two of the intermediate grades, radiation and convection might be introduced, besides a more refined treatment of conduction. Upper-grade pupils, in turn, may tackle heat as molecular energy. Each of the experiences and smaller ideas contribute to the overall generalization about heat transfer.

Figure 1-3 shows how this generalization may be scheduled in a science curriculum that spans grades K–8. Notice how the generalization "spirals" up through nine grade levels but is substantially taught only three times. In curriculum development, this is known as an *interrupted spiral approach* to teaching concepts and generalizations. The approach embodies the need to restudy ideas at higher levels of complexity while it avoids needless repetition.

Not every curriculum treats these ideas in this way. Some may address a major idea at almost every level. Others may be more sparing. But at least two general practices seem clear: Most curricula are organized around

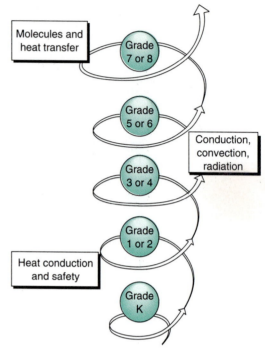

Generalization: Heat is a form of energy that is transferred in several ways.

FIGURE 1-3
An interrupted spiral approach to teaching concepts and generalizations.

the major concepts and generalizations of science, and study of these ideas is developmental. That is, children will study the broad ideas more than once, and with increasing complexity, during the several elementary grades. You can see how important it is for teachers from all school levels—elementary, junior high, and senior high—to plan together in selecting or constructing a curriculum.

Following are main points from the preceding pages on science as knowledge:

■ It is natural for people, scientists and nonscientists alike, to generalize about the regularities they observe.

■ Science is an organized search for regularities or patterns and inconsistencies that may occur in them.

- Scientists invent concepts and generalizations to explain the patterns they observe and, when possible, to predict and control objects or events that fit the patterns.
- Learning science concepts and generalizations increases intellectual power because we can apply this knowledge well beyond the facts studied to learn them.
- Varying conditions may produce inconsistencies in the patterns scientists observe; so the generalizations they invent may be stated as probabilities and change with new data.
- When competing generalizations or theories explain an event equally well, scientists use the principle of parsimony to select the simplest one.
- The learning of concepts and generalizations is ongoing and integrative; so science curricula present them at least several times, with increasing refinement and complexity, within the elementary grades.

One purpose in Part II of this book is to identify and develop in teachable ways many of the key concepts and generalizations used by scientists. You'll also find most of these ideas within the elementary science curriculum you teach. The knowledge that comes from science as a discipline is a powerful force in shaping the modern curriculum.

Process

Although the basic concepts and generalizations of science are always subject to change with new data, their high quality generally makes them last a long time. The quality is no accident. The processes and attitudes scientists use in seeking regularities have been screened over many years to get the best results. Scientists realize the futility of trying to construct immutable laws or truths. But they also understand that the quality of their knowledge is linked to the quality of the processes used to produce it. So scientists continually try to sharpen their observations and how they think about them.

Such an approach breeds deeply a continuing curiosity, the willingness to listen to others' ideas, the caution to suspend judgment until enough facts are known, the readiness to try innovations, and many other qualities we collectively label "scientific attitude." This attitude does not come from some special quality of nobility or goodness in scientists, of course, but from their constant awareness that their thinking can probably be improved. The next several pages present principles that guide their thinking and attitudes. As you'll see, these can also benefit nonscientists, both children and adults.

If the scientist's question *"What* do I know?" is linked to *knowledge,* "*How* do I know it?" reflects the habits of mind and attitude called *process.* At the heart of process is the nature of acceptable *evidence.* Science itself is often defined as a search for *observable* and *reproducible* evidence.

Observable Evidence. In guiding children, help them to understand that only data that can be detected by the senses is "observable evidence." Sometimes the senses must be extended by instruments. The microscope allows us to see organisms too small for the unaided eye. A radio permits us to detect silent radiations from a broadcasting tower. But however aided, the senses must confirm that something tangible exists.

Reproducible Evidence. Scientists assume that, under the same conditions, natural events are "reproducible." That is, they will recur either naturally or, if conditions are the same, in the laboratory. Any qualified scientist should be able to observe or produce the event if the necessary conditions are made public. In the same vein, your pupils should be able to reproduce each other's findings when questions arise about data. You can see how this and the preceding test make it harder for thoughtful children to be misled by questionable data or, later in life, to accept the abracadabra of self-appointed spiritualists and psychics.

Interacting Objects. For a further test for evidence, envision a room where you live. Is the air temperature near the ceiling warmer or cooler than that near the floor? You probably will say warmer. Why? A common explanation we hear is that "warm air rises." Think about it. Does it go up all by itself? Is it immune to gravity? A more acceptable answer is that something is pushing it up. Cooler, heavier air displaces warmer, lighter air. In a confined space such as a room, the warm air is pushed up because there is nowhere else for it to go. Children can learn that this is the reason we may leave a window partly open at both top and bottom to have fresh air. Fresh, colder air enters at the bottom and pushes warmer air out the top. (Outdoors, colder air displacing warmer air is the primary cause of winds.)

What we have is a cause-and-effect relationship between two interacting objects: cold air and warm air. (In science, any material substance—solid, liquid, or gas—may be considered an "object.") Children can find evidence of the interaction by first measuring air temperatures near the floor and ceiling. Then they can close and open the window, each time holding strips of tissue paper at the top and bottom of the window, to observe directions of air flow.

To establish a cause-and-effect relationship, then, acceptable evidence must describe interacting objects. What most people call science "explanations" are typically descriptions of interacting objects. In science, the most powerful tool to discover cause-and-effect relationships is the experiment.

Correlation and Causation. Does breaking a mirror bring bad luck? Most schoolchildren have had experiences with common superstitions, claims of magic, astrology, and the like. These practices offer many chances to teach the difference between a genuine cause-and-effect connection and mere *correlation without causation*. For example, because two events—

breaking a mirror and then badly stubbing a toe—happen closely together, there is no logical reason to assume that one event caused the other.

One reason people outside the scientific community adopt seemingly plausible but untrue ideas comes from their concept of authority. To the nonscientist, an "authority" may simply be someone who by personality, position, or unsubstantiated eloquence attracts much attention. But in science, what counts is tested evidence. Any ballyhoo of untested ideas gets a fishy eye whether it comes from a distinguished veteran or a novice.

Nature of "Proof". Is it better to "test" hypotheses or to "prove" them? In elementary science, it's wise to avoid the term *prove*. Seldom can we experimentally prove anything in an elementary classroom. More important, the idea itself is antiquated. The modern view is that well-designed experiments and observations yield powerful data that lend power to the ideas behind them. Poorly designed experiments and slipshod observations yield less-powerful data and theories. Since all forms of evidence may be improvable, how can any corresponding hypothesis or theory be finally "proved"?

It is also wise to avoid saying to children that they are right or wrong when they give ideas and explanations. This behavior sets us up as an arbitrary authority who accepts or rejects proposals. Instead, we can simply ask, What is your evidence? This invites everyone to examine the data. Which of these two ways do you prefer?

"Failure" as Evidence. The perseverance of scientists is well known. Many grind on fruitlessly for years to find evidence that will support a hypothesis or solve a problem. Where is the reward? Their tenacity almost seems contrary to human nature. The makeup of science as an organized discipline helps us to see why this happens.

For the most part, science is a cooperative enterprise whose practitioners are expected to share their findings with others through publications and meetings. Persons who spread the results of careful work save time, money, and energy for everyone else with a common interest even when they announce no breakthroughs. This narrows the search and so benefits all. Also, careful work—the pursuit of plausible hypotheses with acceptable procedures—continually impels researchers forward because of its potential. As a scientist friend of mine says, "If you keep making a decent effort, sooner or later something good might happen." Besides this, recognition, promotion, and grant money often flow to researchers who share careful work. Although success is preferred, intelligent "failure"—which is the far more frequent outcome of investigation—is rewarded, too.

In your science teaching, you'll often find it useful to organize pupils into small groups that work independently to test a hypothesis or solve a problem. At times, some groups may report that they have failed to find supporting evidence for their ideas. Here, you might do what many effective teachers do: recognize their shared efforts as positive contributions, as well as the work of more successful groups. Commend them when possible on the intelligence of the methods they used, and discuss how to improve those processes. This raises morale and shows everyone a core value in science. It also resembles in a way what happens when scientists report research at their conventions.

Science Processes and Objectivity. The quality of the evidence we collect usually depends on the quality of the thinking processes we use and how objectively they are applied. The processes used by scientists (detailed in Chapter 4) as they seek and work with data include the following:

- Observing
- Classifying
- Communicating
- Measuring
- Inferring and predicting
- Experimenting

"Objective" persons use such processes in an impersonal manner—without bias, without allowing their desires and expectations to influence the process or outcome. Probably the chief way that scientists promote objectivity is to require that all reported findings be achievable by others under the same conditions. Procedures within each process can help make such replication possible.

For example, consider a "double blind" medical experiment in which a drug is being tested. The experimenters set up the test so that neither they nor the patient groups sampled know who is receiving the drug or who is being given the placebo. (An independent third party keeps track.)

Of course, objectivity is much harder to get with children than with highly educated adults. One common tendency you may have already observed, especially with primary-level pupils, is the subjective way they may view nonhuman objects. The child's environment often promotes fantasy over reality. Children commonly read stories or see TV cartoons in which animals talk, the sun smiles, and steam locomotives suffer pitiably as they huff and puff up a steep mountainside. Giving human characteristics to nonhuman objects is called *anthropomorphism*. Children usually have no trouble deciding whether such events are true or fictional. But sometimes they make anthropomorphic inferences without realizing it. These can take several forms.

Children may be quick to imbue some animals with human personality traits. But is a lion truly "braver" than a mouse? A fox "sly"? A wolf "nastier" than a dog? This is *personification*. No doubt some movies children see contribute to this form of anthropomorphism.

Sometimes children ascribe a conscious purpose to nonhuman things. Do plant roots really "seek" water? Do female birds find food for their young because "they don't want them to die"? This is *teleology*.

A third form of anthropomorphism, especially common in young children, is to endow almost any object with life and human feelings. I've had several primary-level pupils tell me it rains because "the clouds get sad and cry." Others, responding to the question, "Where is the sun at night?" have said, "It's tired and goes to sleep." This is *animism.*

Science educators today view anthropomorphic statements in the context of children's early attempts to explain their world. As children grow, these statements decrease and also become more easily correctable. Anthropomorphism in all its forms can be overcome by pupils when they learn how to make proper inferences from their observations. How to teach all the science processes and apply them objectively are described in detail in Chapter 4. The processes are also applied in every investigation in Part II. Marginal notes show where each is used, so you can observe in context how they are applied.

The Importance of Processing Data. Much
factual material may be learned by children from books and other ways of being told about it. But to learn the science processes, they *must work with data.* For instance, pupils may be told how the period of a pendulum (to-and-fro motion) is determined, and some may understand and remember this. But pupils who are given a few materials and guided to figure this out for themselves will soon be counting the number of swings per minute (measuring), trying various possibilities to change the swing rate (experimenting), taking notes of what they did (communicating), making graphs (more communicating), and drawing conclusions from their findings (inferring). They are also more likely to remember and apply the principle of pendulums throughout their lives (clocks, playground swings, metronomes, oscillating water sprinklers, and so on).

Perhaps what makes processing data so effective in improving children's thinking is that they can actually observe the consequences of good and bad thinking. The objects they work with will usually "tell" them if

they are on the right track: snails will eat only what they are adapted to eat, toy boats will sink like real boats when they are not buoyant, green plants will die when deprived of light, and so on. Science is a good subject in which to demonstrate observable consequences because it presents so many opportunities to test ideas with concrete materials.

Interactive Nature of Process and Knowledge. Process thinking is typically neglected
in science education. One reason is that many teachers are unsure about how to teach it. In reaction, some curriculum writers press process teaching so hard they neglect subject-matter content. This approach runs against the inseparable nature of process and knowledge.

The science processes are not like computational skills in arithmetic. Nor are they like decoding skills in reading, which, once learned, may be applied in any subject-matter context. Cognitive psychologists say that the quality of the science processes we use is "domain specific." That is, *our ability to apply a process in a situation is strongly linked to our understanding of the organized field of subject matter that pertains to the situation.*[2] A physician's observations of subtle weather signs are likely to be no more useful than a meteorologist's observations of subtle disease symptoms, if each tries to do the other's work. Their subject-matter background of concepts and generalizations is what gives purpose, meaning, and significance to what they observe in their chosen fields. Background knowledge is inseparably mixed with the process of observation. The same can be said of the other processes they use in their work.

This means that a curriculum must give children continual opportunities to learn thinking processes within a wide variety of subject-matter areas and conditions if the processes are to be generally useful. So the

---

[2]Ellen D. Gagné. *The Cognitive Psychology of School Learning* (Boston: Little, Brown, 1985), pp. 145–150; and Barry K. Beyer. *Practical Strategies for the Teaching of Thinking* (Boston: Allyn and Bacon, 1987), p. 164.

trend today is to guide children to apply thinking processes in all the school subjects. Because process and subject-matter concepts are open-ended, pupils can get better at processing data and learning concepts throughout their lives. An effective science curriculum gives chances to teach process thinking within all topics at all grade levels. How you can identify and maximize these opportunities is an important objective of this book.

Following are the main points of the preceding pages on science as process:

- Science is a search for publicly observable and verifiable evidence.
- Evidence must describe interacting objects to establish cause-and-effect relations.
- Correlation is not the same as evidence of causation.
- Acceptable evidence is always subject to change with new data; so nothing is finally "proved."
- "Failure" gives evidence that narrows the search for further evidence.
- The search for evidence requires the objective use of science processes.
- Knowledge and the science processes are interactive; so effective curricula present opportunities to teach the processes within all topics and grade levels.

You can see that the imperatives of science as an organized discipline can set the foundation and tone for a quality science program. But there is much to choose from, and very few of our pupils will become scientists. What's likely to be useful for most people within our society?

SOCIETAL IMPERATIVES

As you saw on page 4, you are likely to teach better and stimulate more interest and appreciation in lessons when you apply science learning to everyday life. It's fun for pupils to learn how eyeglasses work when they study light energy and the eye. And it's interesting when studying electrical energy for them to make their own flashlights from simple materials. A well-planned curriculum usually contains many of these everyday applications.

At the same time, there are many broad concerns, problems, and changes that continually crop up in our society. Coping with them raises the need to educate people and change attitudes. It's only natural to look to the schools for help. Is it important for future adults to learn that the survival of many plant and animal species is threatened by humans? That our supply of safe, drinkable water continually decreases? That science-related careers are possible for women and men of all races, ethnic groups, and national origins?

The growing awareness of how *science, technology, and society* (STS) interrelate has generated an STS movement in science education. This causes numerous science programs to embody an "applications first" policy—to keep foremost how science impacts our lives. Science education today typically reflects many of society's concerns, including cultural literacy, energy and environmental problems, the ever-growing importance of technology, and career awareness for students at all levels.

Science and Cultural Literacy

Every society wants its contributing members to be culturally literate, that is, to have enough background knowledge and ability to communicate, produce, and improve the general welfare. When the culture of a society is primitive, knowledge is limited and fixed. People are self-sufficient. They can continue for many years doing the same things in the same self-sufficient ways.

In advanced societies such as ours, knowledge must multiply quickly. Interdependence increases as people develop narrow specialties to earn their way. Under such conditions, people need a common core of knowledge. How else can they efficiently communicate with one another, and address matters of public policy? The challenge compounds because of our country's large population and the cultural differences of persons who have settled here from many lands.

The need for cultural literacy arises at every hand. Turn on a TV and find references to toxic waste dumps, test-tube babies, AIDS, nuclear power, and artificial hearts. Pick up a newspaper and read stories about vaccines, fossil fuels, sonic booms, ozone depletion, radiation, and gene splicing. Shop for a new automobile and consider horsepower, fuel injection, disk brakes, and quadriphonic radio systems. Employers expect even more background knowledge. You can see that our functioning in this society, and even our well-being, are linked with cultural literacy.

Science literacy is the part of cultural literacy that enables us to live intelligently in a society that leans heavily on science and technology. It is not gained overnight. The student who is achieving science literacy is gradually

1. Developing positive attitudes about science and taking an active interest in natural phenomena and technological achievements.

2. Learning fundamental concepts of science and how the applications of these concepts affect our daily lives.

3. Learning techniques that compose the scientific methods to validate knowledge and to develop thinking skills for lifelong learning.

4. Using attitudes and knowledge about science to live as an informed citizen in a technologically advanced nation.[3]

All children need a rich array of firsthand experiences to grow toward a full measure of science literacy. It's especially important for disadvantaged children to have such experiences at school. They are less likely than advantaged children to have other opportunities for such growth. Quality science programs can expand their horizons and benefit other chil-

dren as well. Possibilities increase for advanced study later that can lead to many occupational choices and benefits to society.

Energy and Environmental Education

Most thinking persons now realize that we must continue to move from a position of exploiting the environment to conserving or using it wisely. Not only are resources of the planet limited, but almost every year we see a greater demand on these resources from other nations. The immensity of the changes needed in the United States as we shift to environmental awareness is revealed in our yearly consumption of energy. With five percent of the world's population, the United States recently used *twenty-five percent* of the world's energy.

The history of material progress everywhere closely parallels a rise in energy use. More and more demand has been made on the earth's dwindling energy *stocks;* in modern times, these have been mainly the fossil fuels. As such fuels disappear, more attention will be turned to tapping into the relatively inexhaustible energy *flows:* solar, wind, and tidal energy, and the heat energy trapped beneath the earth's surface (geothermal energy). Material progress and swelling populations have also brought air, water, and land pollution and growing problems with managing solid wastes.

Education in environmental awareness is critical for massive changes to happen, especially in a democracy. Uninformed people are not ready to support essential research and development, to use less, to recycle materials, or to alter long habits that harm the environment. What is needed now as never before are people who understand that the earth is a closed system with natural self-renewing cycles. These cannot be overloaded without harm to the earth's inhabitants.

Working harmoniously with nature does not mean that the quality of life *must* go

---

[3] *Science Model Curriculum Guide, K–8* (Sacramento: California State Department of Education, 1987), p. 1.

down. Creative, imaginative people should continue to solve (or resolve) energy and environmental problems. But cooperation and common objectives among many persons are needed to apply solutions.

Nobody properly expects children to take on and solve such worldwide problems. However, the kinds of habits and understandings to effect major changes are best begun early and then reinforced over a number of years.

Many useful activities and information on energy and environmental education may be found integrated into several physical science chapters (8, 9, 12) and environment-related chapters (14, 15, 17, 18).

Technology and Career Awareness

Solutions to energy and environmental problems will flow in good part from applied science or *technology*. So will advances in health care, business, communications, agriculture, and many other areas.

As you saw earlier, scientists invent ideas to explain, predict, and *control* phenomena. Technology is the branch of science that is mainly concerned with controlling, or managing, objects and events in improved ways.

Where will the people come from to fill the many technical jobs that will be available? Only a tiny percentage of people can become research scientists. But many thousands can become professional engineers or skilled technicians with satisfying careers and substantial pay. The need for engineers' useful inventions and creative solutions to technical problems should continue indefinitely. So should a strong demand for technicians to conduct laboratory tests, treat waste water and solid wastes, service and program computers, repair electronic devices, operate medical equipment, and the like. Far more technical workers will be needed in the future.

Traditionally, women have avoided many jobs in technology. Sex-role stereotyping is still deeply etched into our culture. But attitudes are changing. Elementary school science programs can contribute to this change.

Science textbooks and other teaching materials now show women and men in a variety of science-related jobs and describe what they do. Becoming aware of a variety of occupations and having realistic role models open up a broader range of choices for pupils when the time comes to make career decisions.

Technology and the Curriculum

Some old notions about teaching science die hard. Don't be surprised to hear remarks like these in the school lounge:

> *"Even a new science textbook is dated by the time it's distributed."*

> *"No science curriculum should be adopted for more than four years."*

> *"I can't teach science. Who has time to keep up with it?"*

People who talk like this have the wrong idea about teaching *elementary school* science. Contrary to their view, the basic ideas and processes we need to teach usually last a long time. As you know, scientific thinking may change with new information. But many ideas we use today—gravity, motion, adaptation, interdependence, rules of evidence, and the like—can last for generations in unchanged or only slightly altered forms.

Where, then, are fast changes likely to happen? In *technology* (from copper telephone wires to fiber optics); in specific *facts* (from 186,198 miles per second for the speed of light to 186,282 miles per second); and in the thinking of scientists engaged in *frontier research* (from few subatomic particles to many).

Basic concepts and generalizations in effective science programs are often linked to technological applications: aeronautics, rocketry, telecommunications, electric circuitry, soil conservation, food processing, and the like.

Learning about these applications helps to keep study alive and interesting. It can also change the ways children view many of the useful gadgets around us. Children who see some everyday devices as understandable and interesting develop different self-concepts than those who see them as mysterious and bewildering.

Yet a worthwhile *elementary* curriculum will probably always be rooted in the basic ideas and processes of science because it yields a bigger payoff: pupils understand more basic science and so more applications, including technology.

If you are concerned about teaching technology, please remember that its complex forms are typically reserved for junior high school and beyond, where teachers are subject specialists. Let the textbook or curriculum be your guide. Most authors are sensitive to what young children can understand. And the simple applications they present are likely to be both interesting and well grounded in basic science.

CHILDHOOD IMPERATIVES

Science as a discipline and as applied to society's concerns comprises the bulk of what makes science education valuable to most persons. But we are dealing with the very young. How do we match what there is to be learned with what children actually need and can do?

Perhaps you have heard the expression, "To a child who's discovered the hammer, all the world is a nail." It captures nicely the broad curiosity and inner need of children to try things out for themselves whenever they are free to do so. Science education is of great value to children because it richly enhances these and other attributes that loom so large in their development. But the nature

of childhood also makes us recognize several other realities.

For example, because broad generalizations and skills are so useful in science study, it is tempting to increase their scope so they apply to more and more phenomena. When we deal with children, though, there is always the question of when to stop. Explanations become continually more abstract and remote from common experience as their "mileage" increases. As a generalization or process approaches the most advanced scientific model, it is less likely that children can learn it or will even want to. To persist is simply to have them bite off more than they can chew. So teaching generalizations about molecules in the primary years, for example, or insisting that *all* variables be controlled in upper-grade experiments is likely to be self-defeating.

It is important for children to understand and see the purpose of what they are doing. Also, they need to reach short-range goals as they head toward those farther away. To do otherwise cuts down pupil interest and personal significance in what is taught. Because children are relatively inexperienced and intellectually as well as physically immature, they usually learn best when working with concrete and semiconcrete materials, limited generalizations, and the here and now. This is most obvious and necessary with younger pupils, as primary teachers are quick to tell us.

So science and applied science as practiced by adults usually must be modified to fit what we know about children's capacities. Ideas and processes need to be simplified, known interests and needs of children considered, and their physical coordination and dexterity weighed. What they can apply now must be assessed, as well as complementary learnings from the other goals of early general education.

It is unlikely that any publisher or curriculum office can develop a program in advance that suits every child or class. To bring a suitable match between pupils and curriculum requires our intelligent intervention.

This, in turn, requires us to understand in some detail the imperatives of childhood, particularly how children learn science. The whole second chapter is given to that important objective.

HOW SCIENCE CONTRIBUTES TO WHOLE LEARNING

So far you've examined some imperatives to help you judge the good and bad in science teaching. But your work as an elementary-school teacher goes far beyond the teaching of science. No subject in the curriculum stands alone. After all, we want to provide a basic *general* education in the elementary school. What can science give to meeting objectives in other subjects? How is this done? Now is a good time to put science, with its exciting potential for enriching your overall teaching, into perspective.

It is only common sense to realize that learning in science often calls for skills from other parts of the curriculum to be applied. When pupils look up information about caves in an encyclopedia, they are reading. When they measure and graph changes in a growing plant, they use mathematics. They use language skills to organize and report their findings in experiments and observations. When children plan and draw a large panel picture to illustrate conservation practices, this is art. Such integration of subjects is both desirable and usually necessary if you want to promote useful, whole learning.

There are also times when several content subjects or parts of subjects are integrated with science. Energy and environmental education, and topics in social studies, health, and safety are the most likely areas of the curriculum to be treated in this fashion. Drawing on content from several subjects

makes it easier for cohesive, whole understandings to form in pupils' minds when they study such questions as Where do we get our water? What can people do to conserve energy? Why did they build Megalopolis City in that location?

A main responsibility of the elementary school has been and is to teach pupils skills in reading, language, and mathematics. From time to time over the years, some of the public and even some educators have taken a narrow view of how to do this. In many schools, pupils are being saturated and bored by an isolated approach to these skill subjects.

There *is* probably some need to study each subject separately and sequentially, particularly in the early stages. But this approach by itself does the job only partway. It ignores how the skills are applied and learned in the world outside the classroom. There, the three Rs are used far more flexibly and broadly. They are needed in varied ways and in many different subject-matter situations. A curriculum that allows children to apply these skills in several areas reflects that fact.

There are several reasons some people cling to a narrow view of the three Rs. Consider reading instruction, long regarded as the most important of the elementary school subjects. When pupils' reading scores on tests decline or do not advance at an acceptable rate, a commonsense remedy is to give more time to the subject. This often comes at the expense of science and social studies. But the remedy prescribed can speed *decline* in reading scores after the primary grades rather than advance them.

Why? Reading consists of decoding (phonics, structural analysis, and so on) and comprehension. Decoding instruction is distinct, linear, progressive, and above all, limited. The skills can be mastered by most primary pupils so that further instruction, once the elements are learned, is unlikely to do any good. Comprehension, though, is unlimited or open-ended. No one can "master" it because it largely depends on the quality and extent of one's world knowledge.[4] Most of the general reading material in the world reflects concepts from science, social studies, and literature. So an important way to improve reading comprehension is to increase the time and quality of instruction in these content areas rather than in reading alone. Still, good results do not come right away.

The teaching of decoding during the primary grades usually raises pupils' reading test scores immediately when decoding is sampled because there is a high correlation between what is taught and what is measured. But gains in reading *comprehension* test scores from increased content teaching are likely to appear slowly, be cumulative, and show occasional inconsistencies at different grade levels. Why? Test items must be drawn from a far larger pool of possibilities. In time, though, the probability of significant gains in reading comprehension is high.

Increasingly, top organizations in education are throwing their weight behind subject-matter content as a way to boost performance in the three Rs, and to push up overall literacy. The California State Department of Education explains its view in this way:

> The shift of emphasis from mastering basic skills to understanding thoroughly the content of the curriculum is intentional. Research indicates that children will learn more—and more effectively—if teachers focus lessons on content and the connections among subject areas. Students learn to apply skills by reading, writing, and discussing curriculum content. The essential learnings emphasize central concepts, patterns, and relationships among subject areas and reinforce inquiry and creative thinking.[5]

Science and other content areas give more than just chances to apply the three-R skills. Subject-matter content also supplies situations from which appealing, natural *purposes* for the three Rs arise. The skills by themselves lack these situations. So purpose has to be artificially supplied from the outside by the teacher ("For practice today, do all the division problems on page 151 of our math book."). Or, purpose is contrived within the textbook. Consider some word problems you have seen in mathematics textbooks ("Terry wants to find out how much more the larger wagon costs") and tired examples in language textbooks ("Pretend a friend is in the hospital and you want to write a letter").

Some of the foregoing is fine, but you can see that a steady diet of this alone soon pales. That's why an elaborate system of extrinsic rewards—gold stars, Happy Face stickers, and other reinforcers—often must spice up a strongly-focused three-R curriculum.

The need to apply three-R skills arises more naturally within a science program. Sometimes this happens incidentally ("You can find some answers to your questions about satellites in this book" and "You might write Dr. Thompson to see what she thinks"). Or, it is usually easy to slant science activities toward the skills you want reinforced—experience charts for beginning readers, metric measurements and calculations for math concepts, and so on.

The research[6] on science as a vehicle for helping children learn the basic skill subjects is massive and convincing. Science programs based on manipulative materials are espe-

---

[4]Jeanne S. Chall, *Stages of Reading Development* (New York: McGraw-Hill, 1983), p. 8; and *What Works—Research About Teaching and Learning* (Washington, D.C.: U.S. Department of Education, 1986), p. 53.
[5]*Science Model Curriculum Guide, K–8* (Sacramento: California State Department of Education, 1987), p. vii.

[6]See, for example, Ruth T. Wellman, "Science: A Basic for Language Development," in *What Research Says to the Science Teacher,* Mary Budd Rowe, ed., vol. 1 (Washington, D.C.: National Science Teachers Association, 1978), pp. 1–12; and Sandra R. Kren, "Science and Mathematics: Interactions at the Elementary Level," in *What Research Says to the Science Teacher,* vol. 2, Mary Budd Rowe, ed. (Washington, D.C.: National Science Teachers Association, 1979), pp. 32–49.

cially helpful in building reading and language readiness levels in primary pupils. Firsthand experiences in science expand pupils' vocabularies and reading comprehension at all levels. Similar growth is found in mathematics as children work with various geometric forms and measure real objects and events.

Good science teaching develops in children the kinds of attitudes, ways of thinking, and a solid knowledge base that promote success in the real world. Devoting too much time to the three Rs traps children into a narrow and superficial outlook that reduces their capacity to learn further and solve real problems. Fortunately, increasing numbers of educators and parents see the consequences. That's why in recent years there has been a steady growth of more balanced and integrated approaches across the curriculum, including various forms of "whole-language" teaching, that evoke personal meaning in what is learned and an I-can-think-when-I-try feeling in learners.

How to integrate science and other subjects, with emphasis on the three Rs, is detailed in Chapters 4, 5, and 6. Units of instruction, described in Chapter 7, offer an ideal and systematic way to integrate into science as many experiences in the three Rs or other subjects as you judge best.

SUMMARY

Your view of science teaching makes a big difference in what pupils actually experience, even when you and fellow teachers supposedly teach the same curriculum. Three compelling influences can improve your teaching as you learn more about them: science as a discipline, society's needs, and the characteristics of children. Understanding these imperatives enables you to judge what is basic, useful, and learnable.

Science is an organized search for patterns or regularities. Scientists construct concepts and generalizations to explain the patterns they observe and, when possible, to predict and control objects and events within the patterns. Nonscientists also do this, but usually with far less precision and reliability. Evidence in science is acceptable only when it is collected and processed under objective rules generally agreed to by the scientific community. To conduct scientific investigations requires an integrated knowledge of process and content in the topic of study.

When problems and changes emerge in a society, coping with them raises the need to educate people and change attitudes. Some recent matters that affect science education are society's increased concern for science literacy, energy and environmental education, and technology and career awareness.

Science as a discipline, and the science that adults find useful in our society, must be modified to suit children before we can expect them to learn it. Ideas and processes need to be simplified, known interests and needs of children considered, and their physical coordination and dexterity weighed. What they can apply now must be assessed, as well as complementary learnings from the other goals of early general education, if the science curriculum is to be appropriate for children.

Effective teaching often combines science study with opportunities to integrate and apply the other school subjects. It fosters whole learning in children—the attitudes, ways of thinking, and integrated knowledge base that transfer successfully into the larger world.

SUGGESTED READINGS

American Association for the Advancement of Science. *Science for All Americans, Project 2061.* Washington, D.C.: AAAS, 1989. (One of the most authoritative descriptions of science literacy.)

Cole, K. C., "The Essence of Understanding." *Discover* 5 (4):57–62 (April 1984). (What does it mean to "understand" something from a scientific point of view? A thoughtful and interesting essay.)

Kronholm, Martha, and John Ramsey. "Issues and Analysis." *Science and Children* 29 (2):20–23 (October 1991). (An example of how to approach science-related social issues.)

Penick, John E., ed. *Focus on Excellence: Elementary Science Revisited.* Washington, D.C.: National Science Teachers Association, 1988. (Thirteen of the best school science programs in the country and how they developed.)

Waks, Leonard J. "The Responsibility Spiral: A Curriculum Framework for STS Education." *Theory Into Practice* 31(1):12–18 (Winter, 1992). (How educators can identify, select, organize, and sequence learning activities to promote effective science/technology/society education.)

Yager, Robert E. "A New Focus for School Science: S/T/S." *School Science and Mathematics* 88 (3):181–90 (March 1988). (Describes the interrelations of science, technology, and society for school programs as conceived by leading science educators.)

How Children Learn Science

Let's look again at two of the children's questions with which we began the first chapter:

Why doesn't a spider get stuck in its web?

and

Where do the people on TV go when you turn it off?

Compare the levels of sophistication behind these questions. The child who asked about the spider, for example, is mulling over an interesting discrepancy. If a fly gets stuck on a sticky web, then why not the spider itself? This is high-level thinking. But what of the question about television? Do some children of school age—remember, they may have more than a thousand hours of viewing experience—really believe there are tiny people inside a television set? Surprisingly, some do, in a hazy half-conscious way. At the primary level, it's not rare at all.

There is a wide range of thinking ability among elementary school children. You'll find large differences even within a single class of children of the same age. The ability to assess and understand children's thinking can help you to teach anything, but especially science and mathematics.

CONTRIBUTIONS OF PIAGET

What can children learn in science? And how does their ability to reason grow? Jean Piaget, the world-famous Swiss developmental psychologist, is the researcher who has given most for our understanding of children's thinking. His books[1] and research suggest

---

[1]Among others, *The Language and Thought of the Child* (New York: Harcourt, 1926); *The Psychology of Intelligence* (London: Routledge and Kegan Paul, 1950), *The Construction of Reality in the Child* (New York: Basic Books, 1954). Also, Barbel Inhelder, *The Child's Conception of Space* (London: Routledge and Kegan Paul, 1956), and *The Early Growth of Logic in the Child* (London: Routledge and Kegan Paul, 1964).

that the ability to think develops in several noticeable "stages." Please understand that the idea of *stages* is solely a convenient theoretical construct. Improvement in thinking tends to be gradual and incremental, rather than abrupt and massive, as children move from one stage to the next. All children normally go through the earlier stages in the same fixed order. But not everyone moves from one stage to the next at the same time or achieves all stages in every field of study. A child may think in one stage for some things and a different stage for others. This is why it's preferable to label a specific sample of an individual child's *thinking* as being representative of a stage, rather than the child. However, when describing the typical behaviors of a large group of children within the usual age range of a given stage, it's customary and convenient to label the children as belonging to a certain stage.

As teachers, our concern is with children at the *preoperational stage,* from about 2 to 7 years old; *concrete operational stage,* from about 7 to 12 years old; and *formal operational stage,* from about 12 on.

Preoperational means that children in this stage are not yet able to do certain kinds of thinking Piaget calls *operations.* (Details shortly.) The latter part of the stage, which lasts from about four to seven years, is known as the *intuitive thought substage.* Since this is the time when most children begin school, we'll start our study of children's thinking at the intuitive period of their mental development.

"Intuitive thought" captures well how four- to seven-year-olds think. They typically use their sense impressions or intuition rather than logic in forming judgments. They also find it hard to remember more than one thing at a time.

Concrete operational children, on the other hand, can do much logical thinking. Their handicap is that the ideas they consider must be tied to concrete materials they can manipulate. Or, at least, they must have had some firsthand experience with the materials to think about them.

In the stage of formal operations, children are able to think much more abstractly; there is far less need to refer to concrete objects. With experience similar to adults', they can handle formal logic, that is, use the same mental operations as many adults.

As an elementary school teacher, your work is mainly with children who are in the intuitive and concrete operational stages of mental growth. It will be worthwhile for you to study in some detail how they grow from intuitive thought, to concrete thought, and to the beginnings of formal logical thought. Learning how children think can give you some fascinating chances to reflect on what they do or say. It can make you more sensitive to individual differences. Best of all, it can help you to guide each child in learning science. The next section will describe, in order, typical behaviors of intuitive thinkers, concrete thinkers, and formal thinkers.

Intuitive Period Behaviors

What can you expect of many children ages four to seven? We'll consider their thinking in four related areas. (The same four areas will also be examined later in describing the concrete thinker and formal thinker.) We begin with intuitive children's notions about causes of events.

Cause-and-Effect Thinking.   The logic of intuitive children as to causes can be unpredictable. They may think nothing of contradicting themselves to "explain" some event. If you ask them why an object sinks in water, they may say it is "too small" to float. Another time, it is "too large." If you point out this inconsistency, the typical child may shrug and say, "Well, it is."

Four- to seven-year-olds often give magical explanations for events: "The sky is held up by angels." Or they may suppose that lifeless objects have conscious awareness and other human qualities. Clouds move because they "want to." There is thunder because "the sky is angry." Natural events may happen to serve a human need or purpose: "It rained because the farmers needed it."

Relative Thinking.   Of special interest is the self-centered view of intuitive children. This affects how they relate to other people. Ask them to point to your *right* arm when they are face-to-face with you and they point to your *left* arm. They find it hard to put themselves in another's position. The same problem with orientation may come up when they put on clothing. Left arms are often thrust into the right sleeves of coats and jackets.

This egocentric quality also surfaces in their language. They take for granted that everyone understands (and is interested in) what they are saying. They assume that words mean the same to others as they do to them. If the listener gets confused, intuitive children may simply repeat the original message more loudly. The idea has not yet developed that we need to say things in certain ways to communicate clearly.

Their egocentrism may also affect their perception of objects. So the moon and sun follow *them* as they walk. It doesn't occur to them that others also see the same apparent motion.

Four- to seven-year-olds find it hard to interrelate several ideas at one time. Take time, distance, and speed. If two model windup cars start together on a path, you know the faster will travel farther in the same time. But intuitive children cannot properly interrelate the time/speed/distance variables. Unless they have seen one car overtake and pass the other, they focus on the stopping points. When asked to explain the different end points, they typically say that one car must have traveled longer than the other. The other possibility seldom occurs to them.

The relative nature of other physical properties also dawns slowly in this stage. Some objects are always "heavy," others are always "light." Some are always "large," others are always "small." Little by little, properties of objects such as size, texture, hardness, volume, thickness, and the like are viewed in relative terms: "Peggy's tall, but short next to her Mom."

Classifying and Ordering.   The abilities to classify and arrange objects or ideas in some logical order are basic to thinking in both science and mathematics. By analyzing likenesses and differences, we can make more sense out of our environment.

Intuitive thinkers usually learn to sort objects well. But they are limited to considering only one property at a time. They can put all the objects of one color in a pile and those of another color in a second pile. They can also go on to subdivide these objects by using another descriptive property.

In Figure 2-1, for example, the objects shown have two different colors and two different shapes. An intuitive child has sorted the objects by color, blues and nonblues (reds). The child can also go on to subdivide the blues by shape. This means he or she might sort out the blue circles from the larger group of blue circles and blue triangles. You will find such skill is fairly common even at the lower primary level.

Is this true classification? Piaget would not think so because the intuitive child cannot keep the part-whole relationship in mind. Let me explain further. If you ask, "Are all the blue objects triangles?" the child will say, "No." This, of course, is true. There are blue circles as well as blue triangles. But if you ask, "Are all the triangles blue?" the intuitive child is likely to say "No" again, which is wrong. The notion of class inclusion is too abstract to grasp at this stage.

Intuitive children don't see that the blue triangles are included as a part of a larger class of blue objects. How can all of a smaller group be at the same time only a part of a larger group? This is too abstract to grasp. Similarly, it's hard for them to realize that they can live at the same time on a street *and* in a town *and* in a county *and* in a state *and* in a country.

The ability to order or arrange objects in a series—small to large, thick to thin, and so on—grows fast during the intuitive stage.

Let's consider how these children might seriate different-sized sticks from smallest to largest. Four- or five-year olds may only be able to order at random a few sticks in some consistent sequence. Six-year-olds usually do better, but they rely on trial and error. They will continually size up each stick with the next, then replace each as seems needed, perhaps several times. Only during the last part of the intuitive stage, around age seven for many children, is trial and error replaced by a more systematic attack. These children may look first for the largest and smallest pieces, then arrange the others with the end objects always in mind. Again, the key to success is the ability to hold two or more things in mind at the same time.

Conservative Thinking.   Perhaps the most widely known findings of Piaget are the intuitive child's notions of *conservation*. By "conserve" Piaget means the ability to realize that certain properties of an object remain unchanged or can be restored even though the object's appearance is changed. Take a paper bag, for instance. Even if you crush it, you realize that it still weighs the same and can be opened again to its original capacity. The informed adult, of course, has little trouble with most conservation concepts. But the reasoning of intuitive children can be surprisingly different. Examine next the ways in

FIGURE 2-1

An intuitive child can sort objects by color (blues and reds).

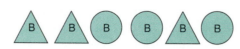 

which they may fail to conserve number, length, amount, area, weight, and volume—each important for science and mathematics understandings.

The conservation of *number* is easily tested. If you put a dozen checkers in two matched rows, these children are quite sure each row contains the same number of checkers. That is because they see a one-to-one correspondence between the checkers. But spread out one row or bunch it together and the children become confused. Now it will seem that there are comparatively more (spread-out row) or fewer (bunched row) checkers in the altered group.

The ability to conserve *length* is necessary before you can ask children to measure meaningfully. Intuitive thinkers will agree that two identical strings are the same length when laid out together. But move one ahead of the other, and they may now say it is longer. This is not simply a misunderstanding of the term "longer." It literally seems longer to them.

Their thinking shows the same limits when they are tested for the conservation of *liquid substance.* If you show intuitive children two identical glasses filled with water, they will probably say each contains the same volume of water. But suppose you pour the contents of one glass into a taller, narrower glass. They are likely to say now that the taller glass contains more water than the remaining filled glass.

These pupils also show the same perception with conservation of *solid substance.* Suppose you show them two identical balls of clay. They will agree each is made up of the same amount of clay. Now flatten out one into a large disk, and they probably will say the disk has more clay than the clay ball. It seems larger to them.

Appearance again fools intuitive children when they are asked to conserve *area.* Two toy buildings side by side on a paper lot seem to take up less space than when the buildings are placed far apart.

Similarly, they cannot conserve *weight.* They believe a solid object weighs more after it is cut up in the form of several smaller pieces. Or, if a soft plastic ball is compressed into a smaller ball, they feel that it now weighs less.

Intuitive children also believe that changing an object's form affects its overall size or *volume.* A clay object submerged in a half glass of water causes the water to rise to a level that equals the volume of the clay object. They do not realize that no matter how the object is reshaped in solid form, it will displace the same volume of water.

Do you see the common thread in these ways to check on the child's conservation of number, length, substance, area, weight, and volume? All give the learner a choice between a perceptual impression and logic. Intuitive children usually choose their perception.

They fail to conserve because of two reasons. When an object's appearance is changed in several dimensions, they center on one and ignore the other. It is too hard to consider more than one thing at the same time. They cannot compensate for the changed dimension. The taller glass of water means to them that there is more water. But you and I see that the taller glass is also narrower. We can compensate for one dimension by thinking of the other at the same time.

The second reason some children fail to conserve these key concepts is that they cannot reverse their thinking. You and I know that what is done can be undone, at least mentally. We can easily change directions in our thinking and imagine a reversed or restored condition. But intuitive children lack this flexibility as they focus on the object's present appearance. In short, they are tied to their perception.

The inability of preoperational children to compensate when an object's appearance changes and to reverse their thinking are the chief reasons they cannot perform "operations" in the Piagetian sense. Let's see next some mental operations that are possible in the *next* stage of development.

Concrete Operational Behaviors

What thinking can you expect of many children ages 7 to 12? A comparison of the child in the stage of concrete operations with the intuitive thinker reveals many differences. Consider again the four areas mentioned before: cause-and-effect thinking, relative thinking, classifying and ordering, and conservative thinking.

Cause-and-Effect Thinking. Unlike intuitive children, concrete operational pupils usually avoid contradictory explanations for events. If a contradiction is pointed out to them, they try to straighten it out. They don't ignore it or otherwise show unconcern as younger children may.

Natural events are no longer seen to happen through magic or to fit some human convenience or purpose. The concrete thinker sees the need to make a physical connection between an effect and its cause. So natural objects or events are influenced by other natural objects or events.

The improvement in thinking is only slight at first. For example, they may now say "the wind comes from the sky" rather than "the wind comes to keep us cool." And a bicycle goes "because the pedals go around" rather than "because a bicycle can go." But notice the linking of physical objects in the first of each of these paired statements. This is a key difference in logical growth that first appears at the early part of the concrete stage.

In the last part of the concrete stage, the child uses explanations that reflect what you and I call "good common sense." They may not always agree with scientific evidence, but they do make sense. The explanations are logical and show judgment. For example, a 10-year-old may say to you, "It's colder in winter because the earth is farther away from the sun." This is entirely logical even though it is wrong. (The earth-sun distance is actually less when the United States has winter. The earth's tilted axis is basically responsible for seasons.)

Relative Thinking. The egocentric quality found in intuitive pupils changes significantly in the concrete stage. Now children are much more aware of viewpoints that differ from their own. And they are more concerned with what others think. So they try to get evidence to support their ideas and spend time attempting to convince their peers.

Concrete thinkers can mentally put themselves in another's place. They realize that someone opposite to them will see direction in an opposite way. Also, the relationship between time and distance as a ratio that determines speed begins to form at this stage.

They can do experiments, but they are usually aware of only a few of the changeable conditions (variables) that might affect the results. The relationships they consider still must be linked to concrete or pictorial objects before they can deal effectively with them. Take this problem, for example:

Bill is shorter than Jane.

Bill is taller than Mary.

Who is the tallest of all?

The concrete operational thinker typically must draw stick figures to get the answer.

Classifying and Ordering. The first true classification appears in the concrete stage. These children recognize the class-inclusion principle. They understand that if all *robins* disappear, there still would be other *birds* left. But if all *birds* disappear, there would be no *robins* left.

However, classifications that require increasingly abstract organizations are beyond them. Suppose you show them some objects that have several properties and ask them to classify them. They may easily organize them into four groups according to four different properties. But if you ask them to classify the four groups into three groups and logically justify the new groupings, this is harder. Forming the three groups into two groups is still harder. This ability usually appears only by age 15 or so, in the formal operations stage.

The concrete child's ability to order (seriate) objects is fairly systematic now, but continues to grow and is by no means complete. It takes until about age nine or later before one can consistently place in series objects of different weights. And the ability to seriate objects by the volume of water each displaces, or to seriate by viewing solid objects, is not consistent until the formal operations stage.

The concrete thinker's improved ability to seriate objects means he or she can better follow a succession of steps or changes in some process. The intuitive child tends to see each step as a separate entity, but the concrete thinker is aware of and understands the connection between the steps. So the steps in making ice cream, or developing a photo, for instance, are much more meaningful to the concrete thinker.

Conservative Thinking. Perhaps the most obvious and dramatic difference that appears in concrete thinkers is their ability to conserve number, length, and so on. This is because, unlike intuitive children, they can consider more than one thing at a time. They can reverse their thinking and hold in mind a sequence of changes. But the ability to conserve develops gradually.

Table 2-1 shows the usual sequence of children's concept development. However, the ages shown may vary somewhat when the same children are tested by different testers, since test procedures, children's responses,

TABLE 2-1
Usual sequence of concept development.

Conservation Concept	Age of Conserver (Years)
Number	6–7
Length	7–8
Substance (solid and liquid)	7–8
Area	8–10
Weight	9½–10½
Displaced volume	12–15

and interpretations of responses may not be wholly uniform. Notice that the displaced volume concept is not conserved until the stage of formal operations. This is probably because, of the concepts shown, it is the most abstract. It incorporates something from most of the others.

Formal Operations Behaviors

Some children begin to show evidence of formal operations at about age 12 or even earlier. But they are not likely to be classifiable as formal operational until they are 15 or 16. Even then, few students can operate consistently at the formal level, particularly when the material to be learned is new to them. This is also true of adults. *Probably most adults and adolescents think at the concrete operational level most of the time.* What the schools can do about this is a matter for much research.

The chief difference between the concrete operational child and the formal operational child is the latter's superior ability to deal with abstractions. Like a skillful checkers player, the formal thinker can think through several moves ahead without touching a checker. A concrete thinker, on the other hand, is limited to considering one move at a time. Even then, this child may need to physically move about the checkers into one tentative position or another before deciding what to do.

Cause-and-Effect Thinking. The beginning formal thinker thoroughly enjoys developing theories or hypotheses to explain almost any event. At the same time, the child is developing the skill to separate the logic of a statement from its content. Consider, for example:

The moon is made of green cheese.

Green cheese is good to eat.

Therefore, the moon is good to eat.

The logic of this proposition is sound. However, we cannot say the same for its factual assumption! The concrete thinker would reject this proposition outright because of its content. ("That's silly!")

Another critical difference between the concrete and the formal thinker is the way each considers the various conditions (variables) that may affect an experiment. Suppose a child is presented with five jars, the liquid contents of which may be mixed in any combination.[2] Only one combination of three jars produces the desired yellow color. The concrete thinker tends to combine two liquids at a time. But then the child may stop or just dump together at random three or more liquids. The formal thinker, however, typically thinks through all the combinations in a systematic way before starting. First come the pairs, then the triple combinations, 1 + 2 + 3, 1 + 2 + 4, 1 + 2 + 5, and so on.

It is during the formal operations stage that children can control variables by holding them constant in mind. This enables them to do quick "thought" experiments. "If all things are equal except . . . , then . . . " becomes a convenient way to appraise hypotheses. This is not typical of concrete thinkers.

Relative Thinking. Children in the formal operational stage become able to understand relative position and motion to the point where predictions become possible. So, for example, a study of the interactions of various bodies in the solar system is meaningful. These boys and girls also understand higher-order abstractions—they can define concepts with other abstract concepts. ("Light energy is the visible part of the electromagnetic spectrum.") They can also explain concepts with analogies and similies. ("An orbiting satellite is like a ball on a string that you whirl around your head.")

Interestingly, the beginning formal thinkers' vigorous habit of using logic to organize and explain everything in the physical world brings out again an egocentric quality in their relations to others. They cannot understand at first why everyone is not as logical as they. "If pollution is ruining the cities, then why isn't the gasoline engine outlawed now? The government is *crazy* if they let this go on!" They are still years away from the adult's perception of reality found in the French proverb, "To understand all is to forgive all." Later they will combine their commendable idealism with a knowledge of what is possible.

Classification and Conservation. You may recall that the formal thinkers are able to reclassify grouped objects in a way not available to concrete thinkers. That is, they can recombine groups into fewer but broader categories with more abstract labels. Also, they can classify things in a hierarchical way. In other words, they are able to form subgroups right down to the individual members and keep the interrelations in mind. This is much more difficult for concrete thinkers.

Here's an example. Suppose some formal thinkers have tested six white powders to learn more about their properties. They might arrange their data as in Figure 2-2.

Besides the ability to conserve the displacement of volume mentioned before, formal thinkers can also conserve solid volume. They realize that a building twice as high as another needs only half the base to equal the overall size of the other building.

Notice that this concept is like the conservation of solid substance concept usually achieved at age seven or eight. Yet the conservation of volume comes unexpectedly late. This shows the value of finding out what is really going on rather than simply following what others assume.

For a summary of children's thinking within the Piagetian stages, please see Appendix E.

Next is the first of several activities within this and the following chapters. They are intended to help you gain further useful knowledge, sharpen skills, and apply key principles. The length of the first exercise—it is by far the longest in the book—reflects its importance.

---

[2]The prototype of this experiment is described in Jean Piaget's and Barbel Inhelder's *The Psychology of the Child* (New York: Basic Books, 1969), p. 134.

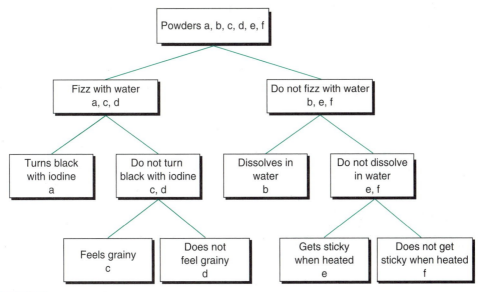

FIGURE 2-2
Formal thinkers are able to classify things into subgroups and keep the interrelations in mind.

EXERCISE 2-1

Assessing Thinking Through Piagetian Tasks

Your understanding of children's thinking can be greatly improved if you try your hand at assessing some of their ideas. You can start by discovering where they are in forming the important concepts of number, length, solid and liquid substance, area, perimeter-area relationship, weight, and volume. Your growing skill in interpreting how children think about specific concepts will be far more useful than merely labeling their general stages of mental growth.

The methods suggested here will be like those developed by Piaget and associates. The tasks described take too long to use with more than a few children. However, the experience you will get in administering these tasks will help you later on to use more informal everyday techniques as you work with pupils.

If your time with and access to children are limited, and you are interested in primary-level teaching, try at least two younger children of different ages (five and eight, for example) with any three of the following tests: conservation of number, length, solid substance, liquid substance, and area.

For minimal upper-level testing, try two older children of different ages (9 and 12, for example) and any three of these tests: conservation of perimeter-area relationship, weight, displaced volume A, and displaced volume B.

You will need to work with each child separately. Everything in each task should be done directly by the child or, when necessary, by you in full view of the child.

The usual sequence of development in conserving a concept is this: First, the child depends almost completely on perceptions in forming judgments. Then, there is a transition period when the child shifts uncertainly between perceptions and logic. Finally, the child is sure of his or her logic—thinking controls perceptions. With this in mind, after administering each task, decide whether the child is a nonconserver (N), in a transitional state (T), or a conserver (C) as to the concept involved. Before you begin, it will be helpful to read, "How to Evaluate Your Task Administration," found at the end of this exercise.

Conservation of Number

Materials: eight red and eight black checkers (or paper disks or buttons).
Procedure:

1. Arrange eight black checkers in a row. Leave some space between each (Figure 2-3).

FIGURE 2-3

2. Ask the child to make a row of red checkers by putting one red checker next to each black one (Figure 2-4). Ask if now there are as many red as black checkers or fewer and why the child thinks so. If the child establishes equivalence, continue. Otherwise, stop at this point.

FIGURE 2-4

3. Next, move the red checkers farther apart from each other. Ask if there are now more black or red checkers, or if there is the same number (Figure 2-5). Then, ask why the child thinks so.

FIGURE 2-5

4. Finally, bunch the red checkers close together and repeat the same questions (Figure 2-6).

FIGURE 2-6

Note: The child who answers consistently that the number of checkers remains the same and satisfactorily tells why each time is a conserver (C) as to this concept. The child who says that the total number changes with each shift is a nonconserver (N). The child whose answers are inconsistent or who fails to give a satisfactory reason for each statement is in a transitional (T) stage. A similar appraisal can be made for each of the following tasks as well.

Conservation of Length

Materials: two identical soda straws (or strings or pipe cleaners).
Procedure:

1. Place the two straws together as in Figure 2-7. Ask the child if they are the same or different length, then why she thinks so. If the child says they are the same, continue. If not, stop the activity here.

FIGURE 2-7

2. Move one straw ahead about one-half length as in Figure 2-8. Repeat your questions.

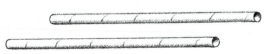

FIGURE 2-8

3. Bend one straw into a Z shape (Figure 2-9) and repeat again the questions. To clarify, you might ask if an insect would have to crawl the same or a different distance on each straw.

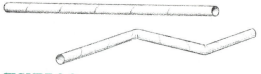

FIGURE 2-9

Conservation of Solid Substance

Materials: two ball-shaped identical pieces of clay; knife.
Procedure:

1. Ask the child if the two clay pieces have the same amount of clay (Figure 2-10). If the child thinks not, have him remove some clay from one until they do seem equivalent. If equivalence cannot be established, discontinue the activity.

FIGURE 2-10

2. Let the child flatten one ball. Ask if both clay pieces contain the same or different amounts of clay, then ask why he thinks so (Figure 2-11).

FIGURE 2-11

3. Have the child shape the flattened clay back into ball form and reestablish equivalence.
4. Tell the child to roll one clay ball into an elongated "snake" form (Figure 2-12). Ask the same questions as in step 2 above.
5. Again, have the child shape the distorted clay back into a ball shape. Reestablish equivalence.
6. Now cut in half one of the clay balls. Point to the ball, then to the two pieces. Ask if the ball is made up of more or less or the same amount of clay as the two pieces. Find out why the child thinks so.

FIGURE 2-12

7. You may want to continue cutting one clay ball into smaller and smaller pieces. Ask the same questions as in step 6, but be sure you reestablish equivalence before each cutting.

Conservation of Liquid Substance

Materials: two identical drinking glasses; also one tall narrow glass; also one glass of greater diameter than the others; pitcher of water; food coloring; medicine dropper. Procedure:

1. Put a drop of food coloring in one of the paired drinking glasses. Pour water into both glasses exactly to the same level, about three-fourths full (Figure 2-13). Ask the child if both glasses contain the same volume of water, then why she thinks so. If the child does not think they are equivalent, she may add water with the medicine dropper until satisfied. Continue only after equivalence is established.

FIGURE 2-13

2. Let the child pour the colored liquid into the tall, narrow glass. Ask if this glass contains the same or a different volume of water as the glass of clear water, then why she thinks so (Figure 2-14).

FIGURE 2-14

3. Have the child pour back the colored water into the original glass and observe the paired glasses. Reestablish that the volumes of colored water and clear water are equivalent.

4. Now let the child pour the colored water into the wide-diameter glass (Figure 2-15). Ask again the same questions posed in step 2.

FIGURE 2-15

Conservation of Area

Materials: two identical sheets of green construction paper; eight small, identical wood blocks or white paper squares.
Procedure:

1. Place the two green sheets side by side. Tell the child to pretend that these are two fields of grass on which cows feed. Ask if there are the same or different amounts of grass on the two fields for the cows to eat. Be sure the child believes the fields are equal before continuing.

2. Put a wood block or paper square on the lowest left-hand corner of each field. Explain that each block represents a farm building. Ask the same questions as in step 1. Establish equivalence again before continuing.

3. Place a second block next to the first block on one sheet, but on the other sheet place another block far from the first block (Figure 2-16). Ask the same questions as in step 1.

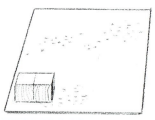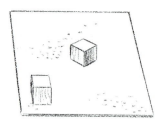

FIGURE 2-16

4. If the child establishes equivalence, add one block at a time to each green sheet. On one sheet, place each block to form a row. On the other sheet, the blocks should be scattered. Ask the same questions as in step 1. Be sure the child establishes equivalence each time before you add blocks and ask the questions.

Conservation of Perimeter-Area Relationship

Materials: two identical 12-inch strings whose ends are tied to form two separate, identical loops.
Procedure:

1. Put one loop on top of the other, so the child sees that the loops are identical.

2. Have the child arrange the loops into two identical circles, side by side. Be sure equivalence is established: Is the first circle as big around as the other? Is there just as much space inside?

3. Now pull the second loop into a narrow, oval shape. Ask: Are the two circles still as big around, or is one smaller than the other? Why do you say that? Is the space inside still the same or does one have less space? Why do you say that? (The perimeter stays the same in each case, but the area changes in the second case. The oval shape has less area inside. This can be checked by placing the loop over graph paper and roughly checking the number of blocks enclosed by the loop in both cases. Interestingly, intuitive thinkers often do better on detecting the larger area than concrete thinkers, who may allow their logic to overcome their perception.)

Conservation of Weight (Mass)

Materials: two identical balls of clay; knife; equal-arm balance.
Procedure:

1. Place the two clay balls before the child. Ask him if the balls are equal in weight. The child may use the balance as needed until agreeing that the balls weigh the same.

2. Let the child flatten one ball into a pancake shape. Ask if the weights are now the same or different, then why he thinks so. Afterward, the child may use the balance as desired to discover the equivalence. If equivalence can be established, continue.

3. Cut the pancake-shaped piece into two pieces. Ask if the weight of the two pieces together is the same or different from the weight of the unchanged clay ball. Then, ask why he thinks so. Afterward, if needed, the child may use the balance as desired to discover the equivalence. Listen for any comments as this is done.

Conservation of Displaced Volume

Note: This concept may be tested in two ways. In Example A, two clay objects of the same weight but apparently different volumes are used. In Example B, two film cans of the same volume but different weights are used.

A. Materials: small clay ball; knife; tall, narrow drinking glass half-filled with water; rubber band; spoon.

Procedure:

1. Place the glass of water before the child. Have her gently submerge the ball in the water and notice that the water level rises. The glass can be encircled with the rubber band exactly at the water line to mark the level (Figure 2-17).

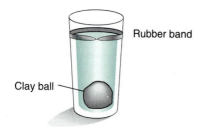

Rubber band

Clay ball

FIGURE 2-17

2. Remove the clay ball with a spoon. Hold the wet ball briefly over the glass, so if it drips, the water will go into the glass. Now let the child flatten the ball. Be sure, however, that it is still small enough to be submerged again in the water. Ask the child to what level the water will rise when the object is placed again in the water. Then, ask why she thinks so.

3. If equivalence is established, cut the flattened ball into two pieces. Ask to what level the water will rise when the two pieces are placed in the water. Then, ask why she thinks so.

B. Materials: two identical plastic film cans (fill one with pebbles, the other with pennies; both cans must be sinkable); tall, narrow drinking glass half-filled with water and encircled with a rubber band; spoon.
Procedure:

1. Have the child inspect and then heft the two film cans in his hands to note comparable sizes and weights. He should conclude that the cans are identical except for weight.

2. Let the child fully submerge the lighter can. Have him adjust the rubber band so it marks the water line. Then, remove the can with a spoon.

3. Ask him how high the water will rise compared to the rubber band if the heavier can is submerged. Ask why he thinks so.

4. Now let the child fully submerge the heavier can. How can he explain this finding? (A conserver will say that the volume or size of the can, not weight, affects the rise in water level.)

How to Evaluate Your Task Administration

It's very possible for two persons to get widely different results when administering the tasks to the same child. Please keep in mind that the tasks are not like a standardized test. They are best suited to a clinical interview setting. Here, the interviewer may use similar questions with different children to begin a task. But follow-up questions must be varied to best get at what each child seems to be thinking at any time. So exactly what questions to ask after you begin is a matter of intelligently following the child's lead.

The language used in an interview must be meaningful to the child if you want worthwhile results. It helps to keep all directions and words as simple and short as possible. If you are not sure the child will understand some terms or directions, try to clarify these before you begin. Some persons continually elaborate on words or procedures during the task. This extra talk often adds to the child's confusion and makes it harder to respond naturally.

In most of the conservation tasks two sets of materials are compared, both before and after a change is made to one set. It's necessary that the children you test believe by themselves that the paired sets are equivalent before a change is made. Otherwise, the whole point to the change is destroyed. So you'll want to avoid leading the children into making this judgment. It's all right to help children tell you what is on their minds, but they must decide for themselves if equivalency exists. For the same reason, it's important for the children to manipulate the materials whenever possible.

The tasks are best done in a relaxed, gamelike setting conducted by someone with an accepting, uncritical, but neutral manner. Avoid saying "Good," or "That's right." To acknowledge an answer, just repeat it or say, "Thank you." Children are also quick to pick up subtle cues about how to act given off by grown-ups. A frown, sigh, change of pace, or voice inflection may cause the child to react to you and not the materials. There is no one correct answer in these tasks. The purpose is to find out where the children are—what is on their minds. Their natural unguided responses are the best clues to their understanding. (Incidentally, you may find that all these points are helpful to keep in mind *whenever* you want to discover what children are thinking.)

A good way to evaluate your task administration is to make a videotape or audiotape of your performance. The following questions can help you to analyze what happened. They are based on the preceding paragraphs.

1. What in the interview shows that your words and directions were clear and brief?

2. What shows that the child established that the paired materials were equivalent before the change was made?

3. What shows that you tailored your follow-up questions to the pupil's responses?

4. What shows that you reacted to pupil responses in an accepting and nonevaluative (avoiding praise or criticism) way?

APPLYING PIAGET'S THEORY TO CLASSROOM SCIENCE

Piaget and colleagues have dealt chiefly with tracing the course of mental development. They have not tried to find how best to teach school subjects to children, but the ideas shaped from their research have strongly affected modern science programs. Three of their most persuasive ideas follow. More and more educators agree that they are essential for helping the child grow in scientific thinking.

1. Schoolchildren in all stages need to share their experiences with others, consider other viewpoints, and evaluate these social interactions thoughtfully.

2. Children need to explore the physical properties of a wide variety of objects. Not to do so in the early years of schooling is wasteful and crippling in later stages of mental operations. *Some effects are likely to be permanent,* because further chances for such explorations may not appear or may be avoided later in life.

3. Besides handling objects and exploring their properties, children must perform mental operations with them. That is, they need to change objects or events for some purpose, organize the results, and think about these operations as much as their development allows.

The Benefits of Sharing Experiences

Children who are exposed to various viewpoints will evaluate their own more realistically. Of course, this is not as likely with the typical five-year-old as with an older child. Yet one's egocentricity takes a beating from others at any age if it is clung to unreasonably. Children who work in groups containing boys and girls of different abilities learn much from each other. The intuitive thinker sees the concrete thinker as an influential model. And children who sometimes demonstrate formal thinking stretch the minds of the concrete thinkers.

How do the more advanced pupils benefit from these interactions? Explaining one's ideas in clear, understandable language is an excellent way to improve thinking. It forces analysis and organization, and exposes what one needs to work on.

Pupils sometimes do a better job of explaining things than teachers. A pupil who has just caught on to some process may remember the reasons for an earlier state of confusion. This may make the child more able than the teacher to communicate to another child who is confused.

So let children work together often when you teach science—in pairs, small groups, and occasionally as a whole class. And don't hesitate to have children of different ability levels work together. We'll take up in some detail how to do this in following chapters.

The Need for Many Concrete Materials

Words—spoken or written—are helpful to most children only to the extent that they are based on concrete materials. Children who are allowed to "think with their hands" are doing what comes naturally. The intuitive and concrete thinkers *must* work with real materials before they can grasp abstractions. It is the only basis from which they can think, if the findings of Piaget and others mean anything.

One of your most important jobs is to arrange for a wide variety of materials children can manipulate. "That's easy to say, but hard to do," is the reaction I get from some people after making this point. Part of the problem is a misunderstanding of what is needed to teach elementary science successfully. Test tubes, expensive microscopes, Bunsen burners, and the like have little or no place in the activities suggested by most science educators today. Instead, we use materi-

TABLE 2-2
Readily available concrete materials.

Disposable pie pans	Wire clothes hangers
Flashlight batteries and bulbs	Mirrors
Buttons and beads	Marbles
Paper clips	Empty cereal boxes
String	Bottle caps
Paper cups	Plastic bags
Milk cartons	Clothespins
Popsicle sticks	Drinking straws

als such as those listed in Table 2-2. Every one of these materials, and much more, are available from around the home and school, and usually just for the asking.

Another part of the job is organization. How can your class help gather the materials? How can they be stored so they are neat, yet easily checked in and out? And what about inventory and replacement? We will take up details of these and other important points in Chapter 5.

Perhaps the really troublesome part of the materials problem is not knowing how to get the most out of the materials you have. Children in some classes go through materials so fast that their teachers are run ragged trying to keep up. The next chapter will help you to avoid this common problem.

The Need to Think While Doing

Everyone knows that children "learn by doing." But Piaget would put it somewhat differently: They learn by *thinking* about what they are doing. Because intuitive, concrete, and formal thinkers differ in how they operate mentally, we must arrange experiences that fit what they can do.

In general, this means that primary-level children learn best when their science activities stress perception. Intuitive thinkers can use all their senses to help them describe and organize in simple ways the properties and interactions of living and nonliving things. Children in the middle grades (ages eight and nine) usually work well with problems and ideas that refer them to concrete materi-als. Upper-grade children (ages 10 on) still need a concrete base to work from, but are often able to develop some abstract ideas (transfer of energy, interdependence, water cycle, and so on) from their experiences.

How necessary is it for us to stick to these guidelines? Can the several stages of mental growth be accelerated? These questions occur to many teachers, but the answers are unclear. Piaget says that we should link the learning environment to the child's present stage. This gives the child a firm footing for each succeeding stage. The child should then slip back less often and should operate more successfully than peers who have had a less complete background in each preparatory stage.

Some American psychologists are more optimistic about acceleration than Piaget. Jerome Bruner thinks it is possible through good teaching to "tempt" children into the next stage.[3] Robert Gagné would move children along more quickly by analyzing and breaking down each desired behavior into smaller, more easily learned subbehaviors.[4] In a well-designed study, Richard Anderson found that an above-average group of first graders performed some mental operations usually associated by Piaget with the formal operations stage.[5]

---

[3]Jerome S. Bruner. *The Process of Education* (Cambridge: Harvard University Press, 1960).
[4]Robert M. Gagné. *The Conditions of Learning* (New York: Holt, Rinehart and Winston, 1977).
[5]Richard C. Anderson. "Can First-Graders Learn an Advanced Problem Solving Skill?" *Journal of Educational Psychology* 56 (1965): 283–94.

Despite some favorable results shown by these researchers and others, no one knows how broadly learning transfers to new situations when children's thinking appears to be accelerated.

Since children learn best by working with concrete materials, thinking about what they do, and sharing these experiences, the teacher's role needs to be compatible. This means we need to do less telling and more listening, for example. A classroom geared to "hands-on" learning activities offers a variety of chances to find out what children are really thinking. It also gives us many chances to guide children in helpful and understandable ways. It is during these times that Piagetian theory is valuable in interpreting what is going on. Read this description of a class of seven-year-olds written by an insightful observer:

As part of a unit about sand, second graders were asked to put an assortment of empty containers in order from largest to smallest. The containers varied in size and were of regular and irregular shapes. After much argument as to which container was bigger, most agreed that height (tallness) could be used to establish an order.

They then were asked whether or not there was a good way to order them when the containers were turned on their sides. The children thought that now they would have to change the order.

Then the class looked for ways to make an order for biggest that would work standing up or lying down. A few thought the biggest container would hold the most sand. How to find out which this was and which was next biggest and so on was a problem. [See Figure 2-18.]

Each youngster's approach was quite individual. One child started filling containers and overturning the contents on trays to compare the size of the piles. Another youngster measured how many handsful of sand were in a container. Another took a tiny cap and found out how many capsful it took to fill a small cup.

Then a girl thought of pouring the sand from one container to another. Her enthusiasm was contagious, but most of the others could not follow her idea because it was so

FIGURE 2-18
Discovering how to measure capacity.

different from their own thinking. A few children did follow her example. They would pour the sand confidently from one container to another, but with no regard for the overflow of sand. When asked which of two containers held more sand, sometimes one was singled out, sometimes another.

From an adult's standpoint it would seem that pouring sand from one container to another would be the easiest way to compare volumes. However, it appeared that unless children have had a great deal of experience—through water play, balancing volumes of materials, or other activities—this is an unknown strategy to them.

It took the children a long time to sort out what mattered, and in what way it mattered. In trying to solve the problem children said things like:

"I poured sand into the jar from the full vase and it didn't come up to the top. Does that mean the vase is bigger because it was full? Or, is the jar bigger, because I could put more sand in it?"

"If the sand flows over that means there is lots of sand, so maybe the container is the big one. If the sand doesn't fill the jar, the amount of sand looks smaller, so maybe that jar is smaller."

"If I pour sand from one container to another and some sand spills, I don't know whether or not I did it right or whether the spilled sand means these are different-sized containers."

"I poured all the sand from this tall one into the pail and didn't even cover the bottom."

When pouring from container to container it appeared to the children that the volume of sand changed as well as the size of the container. They observed the sand and the container as a single thing; when the sand looked too small, that meant the container was too small; when there was a lot of sand, that implied that the container was big. The notion of *too much* was not available to them because everything was changing.

It took a great deal of practice, talking, and thinking before the children realized that in each case of pouring, the amount of sand remained the same. What looked like less sand meant really that there was more container space.[6]

Although the foregoing describes a class at work, you can see that the teacher was actually observing and working with *individuals*. Reaching each child is another important application of Piaget's theory. But you cannot sit down with every child and administer a battery of tasks to find out what each is thinking. So you need to rely on activities that allow you to circulate around the room, first observing, then guiding, individuals at work. It also means that the children themselves should have some freedom to pick and plan activities.

CHILDREN'S CONCEPTS AND MISCONCEPTIONS, AND CONSTRUCTIVIST THEORY

Piaget's theory continues to be a powerful tool in understanding how children's thinking changes over time. In recent years, cogni-

tive psychologists and science educators have added much to Piaget's work. The new contributions show more specifically how learners process subject-matter information and how teachers can tune into the process. What follows is a blending of ideas from Piaget and more recent findings.

Underlying both bodies of research is the notion that all people normally try to make sense of their world. While most of us operate with far less precision than scientists, we still seek to explain, predict, and control our experiences.

In this view, children do not simply receive or absorb incoming information as presented by the teacher or textbook. Nor do they "discover" concepts just by manipulating hands-on materials. Instead, when children are challenged by something they want to learn, they try (with varying degrees of success) to consider any incoming data in the light of whatever related information is already stored in their long-range memories from previous experiences. In other words, they *construct* new knowledge and derive meanings by combining incoming information with what they already know. This view of learning, called *constructivism,* explains why two pupils may get different meanings from the same written paragraph or even the same concrete activity.

Each child may be using a slightly different mental schema, a theoretical concept developed by cognitive psychologists. A *schema* is a remembered network of related information organized around a familiar topic, event, or procedure. When we observe a situation that is even slightly familiar, we draw upon the schema to help us interpret the situation. To link this definition to a word, think of *context.* A schema is what we know, or can apply, in a given context.

Suppose you read, "He rose trembling before the commencement audience, stumbled to the microphone on rubbery legs, then awkwardly tucked his instrument under his chin." No one has to tell you directly about stage fright here or that graduation

---

ceremonies often feature solo performers. And you are unlikely to perceive this person as a polished professional or mistake his instrument for a piano. Will he overcome his fear and do well, or will his performance be a disaster? What will happen to his self-confidence in either case? Will the effects be temporary or permanent? How will his family react? You could go on and on. Drawing on your contextual knowledge about such an occasion allows you to glean a lot from only a little given information.

If you were able to infer much about the case of the hapless musician, chances are you used more than one schema. A schema may be linked to others and form a larger network of related knowledge to draw on. A well-organized memory may have thousands of *schemata* (plural form) combinable in more thousands of ways. This enables us to interpret and act on a huge assortment of experiences.

When confronted with something new, we try to make sense of it by seeing how well it fits into an existing, relevant schema. In other words, we try to use what we already know. This is *assimilation*. If the new experience will not fit a present schema, we must modify the schema or develop a new one. This is called *accommodation*.

Here's a familiar example. Suppose you want to examine a new book in some bookstore. A book-related schema stored in your memory causes you to expect to read each page from left to right and the book itself from front to back. This happens as expected and so you assimilate the experience.

But let's say you observe someone nearby examining another book. She apparently is reading pages from *right to left*, and the book from *back to front!* You cannot assimilate this into your present book-related schema unless it provides for the several foreign languages that are written in that way. Instead, you may fruitlessly search your memory structure for other schemata that will explain what is happening, and seek confirming behavior:

Maybe she is joking. But why doesn't she smile? Maybe she's browsing. But she looks *like she's reading.*

And so on. Suppose the woman, seeing your puzzlement, explains her behavior. This causes you to modify or accommodate your previous book-related schema. The next time you see a similar event, you'll easily assimilate it.

Assimilation and accommodation work together in learning. We adapt our behavior from new information that jibes with our present schemata and that which causes us to revise our thinking.

No child begins school with a blank mind. Schoolchildren have been busily constructing concepts and related schemata since infancy. Some of what they pick up comes from formal schoolwork, of course, but their schemata are chiefly based on their everyday experiences and common sense. The result is a mixed bag of valid and invalid understandings. Several things about this state of affairs are especially important to understand.

One or several concepts usually make up the core of a schema. If a child's concept is wrong, the associated information that collects around the concept is also likely to be wrong or wrongly applied. What's more, children may hold hard to their concept.

During 10 years of writing elementary school textbooks, I received many letters from children. Here's one from a sixth grader, exactly as written:

Dear Mr. Peter C. Gega,
*   I am a student at Junction Aveneu School and I would like to tell you something on page 72 in the first paragraph in Exploring Science Red Book. It says that a bee is an animal, but it isn't, it is an insect. I would like you to correct this page with the proper word.*
*   Sincerely, Mike H.*

Another pupil in Mike's class wrote: "I have read that a bee is an insect but *not* an animal."

Sixth-grade children are usually well able to understand that a small group of objects can belong, at the same time, to other larger groups. So, unlike intuitive-level pupils, they are not baffled by the class inclusion concept. What's going on here is different.

It's more likely that our two letter-writers have picked up from early, everyday experiences an incomplete concept of animal and have long acted accordingly despite school instruction. They are not alone. Children commonly expect an animal to have four legs, be larger than insects, live on land, have fur, and be able to make noise.[7] All in all, do you suppose the second writer actually read that "a bee is an insect but *not* an animal"?

Pupils are especially likely to cling to their commonsense schemata when there is no way to directly observe what is being taught. This often happens when we try to teach abstract concepts— ideas pupils cannot verify for themselves by using their senses—such as potential energy, light waves, molecule, atom, and photosynthesis.

Consider photosynthesis. Children learn early that living things need food to live. They often care for pets and may tend houseplants. They may even hear adults casually remark, "Let's feed this plant some fertilizer."

It's easy for children to infer that green plants *get* their food from water, soil, and fertilizer. This notion can prevent them from understanding that plants *make* their own food, using water, carbon dioxide, and sunlight in the chemical process of photosynthesis.[8] Even after pupils have engaged in hands-on activities—covering leaves with black paper to block sunlight, for example—the old notion may persist. There is no direct way for them to observe photosynthesis. Unless the teacher is aware of their misconception and is skillful, the children may simply assimilate what they experience into their present commonsense schemata and draw the wrong conclusion.

When we help pupils to form a new schema (accommodate), it may have no effect on another, apparently related schema. This is frequent at the primary level.

Young children typically perceive the earth as generally flat, and gravity as vertically down. They know well that, when something falls, it goes down to the ground and stays there. With careful instruction about the shape of the earth using globes, photographs taken from satellites, and so on, you can help many pupils achieve a more realistic concept of the earth's shape. However, if you ask them where people live on the earth (globe), don't be surprised if many say, "On top." Why not also on the sides and bottom? "Because they would fall off."[9]

Children's schemata are usually consistent with their Piagetian level of cognitive development. When they are asked to explain something that is beyond their level, they can only respond with ideas that make sense to them now.

I was once working with a fifth-grade class when the question came up, How does a ship captain know when the ship crosses the equator? (Receiving timed radio signals from three space satellites or measuring relative positions of three stars are two methods. Understanding either, except in the haziest way, requires some formal operational thinking and technical knowledge.) Some of their explanations are shown in Figure 2-19.

One child thought that maybe there was a long rope tied to floats strung across the ocean. (Did the child use his "swimming pool" schema here?) Of course, there would have to be openings to let the ships through.

[7]Roger Osborne and Peter Freyberg. *Learning in Science* (Auckland, N.Z.: Heinemann, 1985), p. 30.

[8]Edward L. Smith and Charles Anderson. "Plants as Producers: A Case Study of Elementary Science Teaching," Research Series No. 127, Michigan State University, Institute for Research in Teaching, East Lansing, Mich., 1983.

[9]Joseph Nussbaum and Niva Sharoni-Dagan. "Changes in Second Grade Children's Preconceptions About the Earth." *Science Education* 67: 99–114 (1983).

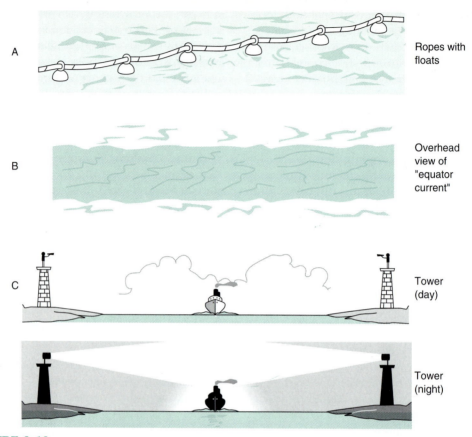

A — Ropes with floats

B — Overhead view of "equator current"

C — Tower (day)

Tower (night)

FIGURE 2-19

How does a ship's captain know when the ship crosses the equator? Fifth graders may offer different explanations, depending on their personal schemata.

Another pupil thought she had read that there was a narrow ocean current at the equator. Perhaps the "equator current" would be a visibly darker green band of water in a lighter-green ocean.

Some children felt it would be possible to have two very tall towers on opposing points of land. Lookouts with telescopes could spot when ships crossed the "line." Then they could radio the ship's captain to announce the event.

How about at night? Well, if the ship's lights were on, the tower lookouts could still see the ship. Or a big searchlight mounted on each tower could be switched on. That way, the ship's officers themselves could tell when they crossed the line.

And if the weather was bad? Hm-m-m. Then they couldn't tell at all.

Notice the thoughtful intelligence behind the children's hypotheses. Although all are operating at a concrete level, they are using their limited schemata for all they are worth.

Would "proper" instruction at this time help? Not much. Interestingly, one boy's father worked on a tuna clipper, which had a radio/satellite navigation device. The child had observed it in action several times, with explanations from his parent. The boy was able to describe the device's appearance, its purpose, and even a bit about how it was operated. But he couldn't satisfactorily tell how it worked. He got confused and soon gave up.

As teachers, what are we to make of these and other examples of children's thinking? How can we apply the powerful ideas of schema theory with Piagetian theory to sharpen our teaching and benefit our pupils?

1. Remember that most pupils are likely to have formed some ideas about objects and events before you teach them. This may influence what they learn for better or worse. So it is good practice to probe their ideas before you teach *and* when they form conclusions about what they have learned. At both times, children need to do most of the talking if you want to find out what they have assimilated or accommodated.

2. If you want your teaching to stick, instruct in ways that help pupils to *construct* schemata and enrich or reshape their present schemata.[10] Teaching that guides pupils to build organized structures of knowledge—concepts, generalizations, patterns, sequences, classification systems, and the like—does this. Well-organized schemata allow more usable information to be stored in memory, then efficiently retrieved and applied as needed.

3. The quality of pupils' thinking—including problem solving—is strongly related to the subject-matter information they can apply to a situation.[11] Children can only intelligently work with objects or events that they can relate to their schemata. They do well when challenged with problems at their cognitive level. And they work well when their lessons begin and end with references to their world of experiences and interests.

Let me add a note to paragraph three for you to consider. Almost any top-notch teacher will tell you that children *love* to use their minds when they are often successful. It

makes them feel competent, confident, "grown up." They *love* to be around a teacher who arranges experiences that foster such feelings. And there's more. They have much incentive to *cooperate* when given these experiences. A curriculum that pupils see as worthwhile is likely to be the best discipline system you'll ever have and promote worthy self-images as well. Praise, reward, recognition, and most of the other positive behavior management techniques we learn as teachers are needed and have much merit when properly used. But nothing comes even close to the internal satisfaction, real competence, lifelong motivation for learning, and self-discipline that come from frequent success at using one's own mind.

ASSESSING CHILDREN'S KNOWLEDGE OF CONCEPTS AND CAUSES OF EVENTS

How can you find out about pupils' common-sense concepts and schemata? One good way is to informally ask them about familiar objects and events: animals, plants, air, clouds, rain, thunder, and so on. If the children have misconceptions, you can be reasonably sure that these do not result simply from lack of first-hand experiences.

To assess for concepts of an object, it's often effective to ask for a definition, then examples, and then nonexamples. Here is an interview I did with a six-year-old:

Q: What do you look for to tell if something is a *plant?*
A: Well, it's green and stuck in the ground. It can be stuck in a pot, too. A plant has leaves. And it grows bigger if you water it.
Q: What are some examples of plants you have seen?
A: Plants in my house and bushes and flowers in my Mom's garden.

---

[10]J. D. Bransford. *Human Cognition: Learning, Understanding, and Remembering* (Belmont, Calif: Wadsworth, 1979).
[11]Lauren B. Resnick. "Mathematics and Science Learning: A New Conception," *Science* 220 (April 29, 1983): 477–78.

Q: Anything else?

A: No.

Q: Is there anything that grows in the ground that is *not* a plant?

A: Yes.

Q: What grows in the ground and is *not* a plant?

A: Grass.

Q: Why isn't grass a plant?

A: It doesn't look like a plant. Grass is grass.

Q: Anything else that grows in the ground that is *not* a plant?

A: I don't know.

Analysis: If this child is consistent (intuitive children often are not), a plant will need to be green, have leaves, be stuck in the ground or a pot, and grow to be classified as a plant. His concept is incomplete, rather than wrong. Especially revealing is his answer that grass is not a plant because "It doesn't look like a plant." His list of plant attributes is composed of objects that look reasonably alike. General appearance is very important to intuitive thinkers in organizing objects. (Note: For the same reason, it's hard for young children to perceive a porpoise as a mammal when it "looks like a fish.")

Considering this child's limited and perception-bound attributes for a plant, we may be able to make some predictions. What do you think this child would say if you presented him with pictures of an untrimmed carrot, a cabbage, and a seed?

Beverly F. Bell, a researcher in New Zealand, discovered that almost one-half of 29 children, at the relatively advanced ages of 10 to 15, thought that a carrot and a cabbage were vegetables but not plants. More than one-half said that seeds were not plant material.[12]

Children's explanations about *causes* of objects and events are particularly interesting. An early book by Piaget offers fascinating views of what many children believed a half century ago about the causes of rain, lightning, and so on.[13] Much of what children today believe is surprisingly similar.

To assess for children's understandings of cause-and-effect relations, it is again helpful to ask for a definition of the object or event. This can clarify what the child is thinking about. Next, you can ask about the cause. If the child immediately launches a causal explanation, though, a definition may not be needed. Here is an interview with a bright eight-year-old girl:[14]

Q: What do you think *thunder* is?

A: It's a big loud boom in the sky.

Q: What do you think makes thunder happen?

A: Well, in space there might be friction between two meteorites.

Q: What is friction?

A: When two things rub together real fast. The meteorites make sparks from the friction.

Q: Is that what thunder is?

A: No! That's the lightning! Sometimes when it rains we have lightning and thunder.

Q: Well, what makes the thunder?

A: You have a big boom when the two meteorites smash together.

Q: Must it rain to have thunder and lightning?

A: No, it only has to be cloudy.

Q: Are there meteorites in the clouds?

A: No, they're in space.

Q: But you have to have clouds for thunder and lightning?

A: Yes.

Analysis: Unlike younger or less able pupils who might see thunder as suiting some human purpose or happening through magic,

---

[12]Roger Osborne and Peter Freyberg. *Learning in Science* (Aukland, N.Z.: Heinemann, 1985), p. 7.

[13]Jean Piaget. *The Child's Conception of Physical Causality* (New York: Harcourt Brace Jovanovich, 1930). For a more recent printing and a companion volume, see *The Child's Conception of Physical Causality* (Totowa, N.J.: Littlefield, Adams, 1972) and *The Child's Conception of the World* (Totowa, N.J.: Littlefield, Adams, 1975).

[14]Based on an interview by Terry Williams.

this girl aptly describes two interacting objects. Even though she is wrong about the causes of thunder and lightning, she is using a previously stored schema and some logic to build what she thinks is a plausible explanation. Also, notice her apparent confusion between correlation and causation at the end of the interview. She believes that clouds must be present for thunder, even though she says that thunder is caused when meteorites collide in space.

EXERCISE 2-2

Interviewing Children for Concepts and Causes of Events

Following is a list of some natural objects and events about which elementary-age pupils have probably formed some notions. To learn more about children's thinking, you might interview two or more who are several years apart in age. As you listen to what they say, compare their conceptual understanding to what educated adults believe. State each suggested question below in language that makes sense to the child, if it does not now. Also, let the child's responses influence your follow-up questions. To avoid guiding responses, be noncommittal and accepting, not directive or reinforcing.

Concepts About Natural Objects and Events

The questions below have children define concepts and give examples. There are four concepts. To avoid confusion, select and work with only one concept, or one concept at a time if you do more. Note each child's responses. Clarify your thinking by writing a short analysis, like that on page 46, for each child you interview.

animal
plant

1. What does the word *animal* (plant) mean to you? What do you look for to tell if something is an *animal* (a plant)?

2. What are some examples of *animals* (plants)?
   [At this point it is often revealing to also ask specific questions, such as Is a snail (earthworm, spider, bird, goldfish, butterfly) an animal? Why or why not?
   Is grass (a tree, a bush, a carrot, a potato, a bean seed) a plant? Why or why not?]

3. What are some living things that are not *animals* (plants)?
   [If you have asked specific questions after 2, it may be more appropriate to begin 3 with, What are some *other* living things that are not . . .?]

air

1. What does the word *air* (energy) mean to you?

energy

2. How can you tell if there is such a thing as *air* (energy)? What do you look for?

Cause-and-Effect Relations

The questions below have children begin by first defining a concept, and then thinking about cause-and-effect relations. To avoid confusion, select and work with only one concept, or one at a time if you do more. Clarify your thinking by writing a short analysis like the one on page 46 for each child you interview.

cloud

mountain

1. What do you think a *cloud* (mountain) is? What do you look for to tell if something is a *cloud* (mountain)?

2. How does a *cloud* (mountain) get to be a *cloud* (mountain)?

3. What makes *a cloud move in the sky?*

thunder

1. What do you think *thunder* (rain) is?

rain

2. What do you think makes *thunder* (rain) happen?

Although we must carefully heed the work of researchers, a little theory—good theory, that is—goes a long way. It's time for specific methods. What *activities* can we use to boost children's learning, now that we have some key principles in mind? The next chapter tackles that question.

SUMMARY

How effectively we teach science to children is linked to our understanding of children's characteristics, including how they learn. Jean Piaget's theory proposes that elementary schoolchildren go through three intellectual stages as they grow: intuitive, in which children are ruled by their perceptions; concrete operational, in which their thinking is tied to concrete experiences; and formal operational, in which abstract thinking becomes a practical possibility. (A larger summary of Piaget's theory can be found in Appendix E.)

Research in human learning continues to verify and augment Piaget's research. According to constructivist theory, based on this combined research, people continually develop personal explanations to make sense of their experiences by reflecting and constructing on

what they already know. Children as well as adults appear to derive meaning from an experience by referring to a schema—a body of related information stored in the long-range memory from previous experiences. Learning proceeds by fitting new information into a schema (assimilation), and modifying or forming a new schema (accommodation). Existing schemata may help or hinder new learning; so teachers should be aware of such knowledge to plan suitable lessons. Teaching that helps children to build organized structures of related information in their memories improves their ability to retrieve and apply the knowledge.

SUGGESTED READINGS

Chaille, Christine, and Lory Britain. *The Young Child as Scientist: A Constructivist Approach to Early Childhood Education.* New York: Harper Collins, 1991. (How younger children construct knowledge.)

Eggen, Paul D., and Donald P. Kauchak. *Strategies for Teachers.* 2d ed. Englewood Cliffs, N.J.: Prentice-Hall, 1988. (Gives a detailed information-processing approach to teaching content and thinking skills across the curriculum.)

Hyde, Arthur A., and Marilyn Bizar. *Thinking in Context.* White Plains, N.Y.: Longman, 1989.

(Shows the inseparable connection between content knowledge and thinking skills in reading, mathematics, science, and social studies.)

Neale, Daniel C., et al. "Implementing Conceptual Change Teaching in Primary Science." *Elementary School Journal* 91(2): 109–131 (1990). (How eight primary teachers changed pupil misconceptions to valid understandings.)

Roth, Kathleen J. "Science Education: It's Not Enough To 'Do' or 'Relate.' " *American Educator* 17 (22): 46–48 (Winter 1989). (A thoughtful essay on three approaches to teaching conceptual understanding.)

Saunders, Walter L. "The Constructionist Perspective: Implications and Teaching Strategies for Science." *School Science and Mathematics* 92(3): 136–44 (March 1992). (A detailed analysis of constructivism in science teaching.)

How to Use Closed-Ended and Open-Ended Activities

Children can learn science in several ways. But generally the most effective way is through hands-on activities, on which we'll concentrate in this chapter.

There are two basic kinds of activities you can use to meet the wide variety of individual differences and objectives faced in classrooms today—*closed-ended* and *open-ended* activities. For a quick view of what each is like, see these two problems:

$$3 + 3 = ?$$
$$? + ? = 6$$

Notice that the first problem has only one correct answer. The second has many answers. Closed-ended problems and activities lead to a single, or narrow, response. They foster *convergent* thinking. Open-ended activities and problems lead to a wide variety of responses. They produce *divergent* thinking. Both types of activities and thinking are needed in learning and solving problems.

In Part II of this book and elsewhere in science programs, you'll find that closed-ended activities tend to be short and tightly focused. Open-ended activities are usually longer, and branch out to many related questions besides the beginning problem focus. To make it easy for you to identify each kind of experience in Part II, I've labelled the closed-ended type *activities* and the open-ended type *investigations*.

Closed- and open-ended activities also differ in other ways. To see how, let's consider each kind in turn. We begin with some common closed-ended examples involving children 5 to 12 years old. In each case the children are active—they do things.

CLOSED-ENDED ACTIVITIES

In a primary class children are learning that vibrations are needed to make sounds. It is obvious that a guitar string moves to and fro when plucked. But what vibrates when a drum is struck? A child is directed by the teacher to sprinkle some sand lightly on the drumhead of a toy drum. The child next strikes the drumhead with a stick. The sand is seen to bounce up and down briefly as the drumhead vibrates. The harder the drumhead is struck, the louder the sound. This also makes the sand bounce higher.

In a middle-level class some children are learning that limestone is a common rock that can be detected by putting acid on it. The acid bubbles when it contacts the rock. A few pieces of limestone have been borrowed from the school district's materials center. Several children put these rocks into small cups of vinegar, which is a weak acid. Nothing happens at first. Moments later they see streams of tiny bubbles rising from the submerged rocks.

In an upper-level class some children are learning about air pressure. One child reads how to use unequal air pressure to crush a metal container. To demonstrate this, the teacher heats a clean, uncapped metal can (such as that used to hold fluid for duplicating machines) for a few minutes on a hot plate. The air inside warms and expands. Some of this heated air escapes through the uncapped opening. The can is then removed from the hot plate, the cap quickly screwed on, and the can allowed to cool. As the air inside the can cools, it requires less space than before because some air has escaped; so it exerts less pressure inside. The children delightedly watch the can slowly cave in as the stronger outside air pressure exerts its force.

Notice that each of these closed-ended activities illustrates some idea or procedure with concrete materials. Everyone can participate if there are enough materials or if pupils take turns. Working with concrete materials helps the children to form realistic concepts or learn useful techniques. Therefore, these activities are often found in science textbooks and the curriculum. Sometimes they are presented as teacher or pupil demonstrations. Here are more concrete but closed-ended examples you will run into from time to time.

Primary Level. Children learn that their bodies give off heat. They are told to feel the heat radiating from their faces by holding the palms of their hands close to each cheek.

Middle Level. Children read that the echo-chamber effect of sounds in an empty house disappears when soft drapes are added. They experience a similar effect when they speak into a solid metal wastebasket before and after lining it with a soft cloth.

Upper Level. Children learn how to tell directions by using the sun, a pencil, and a wristwatch. The pencil is pushed into the ground upright. The wristwatch is placed so that the pencil's shadow covers the hour hand. The hour hand is pointed away from the sun. The pupils are told that north is exactly halfway between the hour hand and the numeral 12.

For further examples of closed-ended activities, turn to the "Inventory of Investigations and Activities" at the front of this book. Notice that *activities* are separately listed. Pick some of interest to you in several different subject-matter chapters to get a sense of how they are organized and what they can do.

Once a closed-ended activity has made its point, there is little need for one to go on with it, at least in its beginning form. So the activity comes to a close, and the child goes on to something else.

Closed-ended activities, when taught well, help children to construct a solid subject-matter background that is rooted in experience. But these activities are not enough for the whole job. As you have seen, the scope in each activity tends to be limited. Outcomes are predictable and specific. Children follow someone else's ideas or procedures—those of the teacher, book, film, or other authority source. To boost children's thinking pro-cesses, independence, and creativity, you need to offer open-ended experiences.

OPEN-ENDED ACTIVITIES

Most good teachers encourage children to try their own ideas about how to investigate and organize objects or events. This allows children to discover or find out things for themselves and opens up the scope of study. It broadens study because children usually come up with their own suggestions. Some suggestions lead to others, so there is almost no end to what may be investigated or organized.

Objects and events in science are described and compared by their observable properties—weight, shape, hardness, resistance to rust, location, speed, order of appearance, and so on. Open-ended activities allow pupils to study objects and events in two very useful ways. Pupils can (1) observe similarities and differences in the *properties* of things, and (2) discover *conditions* that can produce or change properties.

Note the contrast in each pair of these questions you might ask your pupils:

1. What materials will rust? (Observing a property.)
2. In what ways can you get some objects to rust? (Discovering conditions.)

1. How fast does water go up the stems of different flowers?
2. How can you speed up (or slow down or prevent) water rising in flower stems?

1. What things does a nail magnet pull (attract)?
2. How can you make your nail magnet stronger (or weaker)?

1. On what things do molds grow?

2. What conditions must be present for molds to grow?

1. Which objects can be charged with static electricity?

2. What's the longest time you can keep an object charged with static electricity?

1. How long do different cut flowers stay fresh if you keep them in water?

2. How can you lengthen the time a cut flower will stay fresh?

1. What foods attract ants?

2. In what ways can you attract the most ants?

1. In what places can we find sow bugs?

2. In what conditions do sow bugs best live?

1. How many single pulleys can you find around the school?

2. How can you rearrange single pulleys to make work easier?

1. Which juices contain vitamin C?

2. How might a juice lose its vitamin C?

Now that you have compared both kinds of questions, here are a few details to better understand their uses. When children examine the present properties of comparable things, they learn that properties usually exist in varying degrees: some magnets are more powerful, water rises faster in some plant stems, some juices have more vitamin C, molds grow more easily on some materials, and not all places where sow bugs are found are exactly alike.

As pupils inspect these variable examples of things, they may observe, describe, contrast, measure, and classify them according to specific properties. They may also use a procedure and tool—slitting open a plant stem with a pin to see what is inside, for instance—along the way. Even so, they just want to find out what the existing properties are like. *This feature makes open-ended investigations of things with comparable properties very suitable for intuitive-level pupils, and others who lack experience with the materials being examined.*

But when pupils investigate the *conditions* that might produce or change a property of an object or event, their intent is different. Now they seek cause-and-effect connections. *This feature makes investigations of conditions that may produce or change properties more suitable for pupils at or beyond the concrete operational level.* As you saw in Chapter 2, younger children have trouble with cause-and-effect relations.

Naturally, even older elementary school-children cannot seek causes in the strict ways of scientists. Adult researchers must isolate critical variables to invent, test, and modify scientific theories. Instead, children simply try to find out what changes result when they perform one-at-a-time operations on objects. Both younger and older children do this. However, the operations younger pupils perform to cause change are often just hit-or-miss. Older pupils are more apt to use a concept or schema to guide their operations.

We can teach pupils to state such operations as narrow questions. For instance, if you ask, "What can you do to make a nail magnet weaker?" it's natural for children to say things such as

Drop it on the sidewalk.

Heat it.

Leave it alone for a while.

With a little coaching from you, pupils can change these statements into narrow operational questions:

Will dropping a nail magnet on a sidewalk make it weaker?

Will heating a nail magnet make it weaker?

Will a nail magnet get weaker if you just leave it alone?

This does three things for children: they do the thinking, the purpose of the upcoming activity is clear to them, and so is the general procedure. If a few more details are needed in the procedure—who gets and does what, for example—these can now be easily added.

This method does something for you, too. It puts in your corner the greatest science authority in the universe. The only one, in fact, that never makes a mistake. It's a pleasure to teach in ways in which *nature* supplies the answers to children's questions.

To nail down the difference between questions that guide pupils to observe the variable *properties* of comparable things and questions that guide them to discover *conditions* that may produce or change a property, try Exercise 3-1. Find answers at the end in a section entitled "Comments."

EXERCISE 3-1

Which Open-Ended Questions Are for Observing Property Variables? Discovering Condition Variables?

1. What flat materials will magnetism pass through if you put them one at a time between a magnet and a paper clip?
2. How can you make your string telephone work better?
3. What can you do to get a liter of liquid as warm as possible with 30 minutes of sunshine?
4. What foods does a land snail eat?
5. What is the longest time you can keep brine shrimp alive?
6. How much liquid do different kinds of apples contain?
7. In what ways can soil be prevented from eroding?
8. What materials conduct electricity?
9. What do you think will make plants grow faster?
10. Which objects can you identify just by touch?

Comments

Questions 1, 4, 6, 8, and 10 now invite children to inspect comparable examples of objects for variable properties. Here's how they might look if rewritten for pupils to discover variable conditions that might produce or change properties:

1. How can you prevent magnetism from going through objects?
4. How can you get a snail to eat food it usually won't eat?
6. Under what conditions might apples have less liquid than usual?
8. In what ways can you make conductors of electricity nonconductors?
10. In what other ways besides touch can you identify these objects?

Questions 2, 3, 5, 7, and 9 now invite children to find conditions that might produce or change properties of objects. Here's how they could be rewritten to have pupils simply study examples of objects with comparable properties:

2. What different examples of string telephones can we find?

3. How warm will different objects, including liquids, get if we put them in the sun?

5. How long will brine shrimp from different places live?

7. In what places is the soil eroding?

9. How fast do different plants grow?

How to Develop Open-Ended Investigations with Questions

If you want children to come up with their own ideas, ask *broad* questions that will cause them to state what specific points they want to tackle. Broad questions are designed to put as much responsibility for thinking as possible on the pupil—where it belongs. At the same time, we can never be sure of what a pupil's responses will be. This unpredictable, divergent quality in the responses to broad questions is what makes them so interesting.

What happens when youngsters cannot come up with their own ideas? Then we need to help them by asking *narrow* questions—those that zero in on only one example or condition.

The key to knowing how to ask broad and narrow questions in an activity is to identify *which* examples of objects or *which* conditions pupils might vary. To illustrate, let's begin with a typical primary-level, closed-ended activity found in science textbooks:

Find out about rusting. Get an iron nail. Wrap it in damp newspaper. Wait one or two days. What happens to the nail?

This activity shows simply and concretely what rust is. But it is too restrictive in its present form for either good concept building or to sharpen pupils' thinking skills.

The property of rusting is centered here on only one example, a nail. What are some *other examples* of objects young children might want to try, using the same damp newspaper test? Consider some everyday items—safety pins, comb, spoon, penny, and so on—made of aluminum, plastic, steel, copper, rubber, and so on. Let the class gather them.

If the class has done the closed-ended activity, to open it just ask:

What other things do you think will rust if wrapped in damp newspaper?

If no one responds, direct one or two narrow questions to some objects brought to class that might be tested:

Will these aluminum (or plastic, or steel, etc.) objects rust in damp newspaper?

Or you might specifically name some objects:

Will these safety pins (or pennies, or hair curlers, etc.) rust in damp newspaper?

After pupils gain more experience, repeat the broad question:

What other things do you think will rust if wrapped in damp newspaper?

Now, more responses are likely. If not, simply shift down again to one or two narrow questions that focus on further specific objects. As your pupils build a broader concept of the properties of "rustable" objects with more experience, they will be able to make more of their own suggestions.

Another way to open up the activity is to consider some *other conditions* that might produce rust besides wrapping the objects in damp newspaper. (Remember, though, that exploring causative conditions may be hard for younger pupils. So stay sensitive to what they can handle.) Pupils could try to produce rust or to speed up rusting by putting objects in hot or cold tap water, salt water or other liquids, or in damp soil or sand. To prevent rusting, pupils could try covering objects with oil, grease, Vaseline, or different paints or leaving them in different locations. To get pupils to propose operations like these, you could ask any of these broad questions:

> *How else can you get things to rust besides wrapping them in a damp newspaper?*

or

> *How could you make objects rust faster?*

or

> *How could you keep objects from rusting?*

When pupils cannot respond because of limited experience, just shift down to one or two narrow questions that reflect the specific operations you have thought of:

> *Will a nail rust if it is under water?*

or

> *Can salt water make an object rust faster?*

or

> *Do things rust if they are painted?*

Your modeling of these narrow operational questions, and a little coaching, should help pupils state their own. After pupils gain some experience, you can again try opening up the activity with one of the broad questions posed before:

> *How else can you get things to rust . . . ?*

After you have posed many broad questions to stimulate children to test conditions,

you may notice patterns in the ways the questions begin. Here are some beginning phrases that teachers are likely to use when they challenge children to test the conditions of change:

> *How can you . . .*
>
> *How else can you . . .*
>
> *What will happen if . . .*
>
> *What conditions are best for . . .*
>
> *What could you do to . . .*
>
> *What else could be done to . . .*
>
> *What ways could be used to . . .*
>
> *In what ways could . . .*
>
> *In what other ways could . . .*

Helping children to work with property and condition variables is like riding a bicycle with changeable gears in hilly terrain. When the going gets tough, you need to gear down (ask narrow questions on single variables). When the going gets easier, you can gear up (ask broad questions that embrace multiple variables).

Realize that when asking questions you take cues from pupil responses. So the process is interactive and responses are somewhat unpredictable. That is why it's hard for authors of a text or curriculum to provide in advance exactly what to do or say in an open-ended activity. They are generally tied to a narrower, sequential approach that presumes certain pupil responses to closed-ended activities. This is no fault of the authors; it just goes with the medium.

"But what if I can only think of one or two variables?" teachers ask me sometimes, "Can I still open up activities?" Usually, yes. Most children can generate other variables *they* want to explore after being helped with just one or two narrow questions. Or if they already have some background, you can often fruitfully *begin* with a broad question.

Please understand that pupil suggestions for variables to test need not be "correct." We want to find out what they are now thinking and improve it if needed. Children who believe that certain objects will rust and who discover they will not, or who unsuccessfully try other ways to cause rust, are learning to sharpen their future ideas and actions. To use Piaget's term, they are learning to "accommodate."

Broad, open-ended questions typically require much thinking, and it's essential that children have enough time to do so. Mary Budd Rowe has found that many teachers ask questions and react so quickly to silence that pupils are unable to thoughtfully respond.[1] But teachers who ask a question and wait about five seconds for a response (Wait Time I), and wait again about five seconds after the first response before reacting to it (Wait Time

II), get improved results. The quality and length of pupil responses increases, and they listen and react more to each other's statements rather than only to the teacher's comments.

To get similar results in your classroom, use wait time and make remarks like these before you ask thought-provoking questions:

I'm going to give you time to think before calling on anyone.

Before you raise your hand, think carefully for a while about what you might say.

Now for some practice in asking broad and narrow questions. Exercise 3-2 on sprouting bean seeds is almost identical to the previous rusting activity. If you have trouble forming your own questions, just reread the rust-activity section on pages 55–56.

---

[1] Mary Budd Rowe, *Teaching Science as Continuous Inquiry.* 2d ed. (New York: McGraw-Hill, 1978), pp. 273–83.

EXERCISE 3-2

Forming Broad and Narrow Questions

Here's another typical closed-ended activity found in children's textbooks:
Find out about sprouting seeds. Soak a bean seed overnight in water. Plant it in soil. Keep the soil damp. Wait five or six days. What happens to the seed?

1. What broad question can you ask to open up this activity so pupils can explore further examples of objects with comparable properties? (Hint—"What other . . .")

2. Despite your broad question, your pupils cannot think of more objects to try. What narrow questions can you ask that focus on single objects to try? (Hint—First think of further examples of objects like the one tried in the beginning activity.)

3. You now want pupils to explore several conditions that might produce or change the property (sprouting) studied in this activity. What broad question can you ask to do this? (Hints—"How else can you . . . ," "In what other ways can you . . .")

4. You find that your pupils still lack enough background to ask operational questions about conditions. What narrow questions can you model that will include operations they might try? (Hint—First think of some single-condition variables.)

Comments

1. Some broad questions to explore further examples:

   What other seeds will sprout in this way?

   What, besides a bean seed, do you think will sprout like this?

2. Some narrow questions to focus on further examples to try:

   Will *sunflower* seeds sprout in this way?

   Will *radish* seeds sprout in this way? And so on.

3. Some broad questions to explore various conditions:

   How else can you get seeds to sprout besides planting them in damp soil?

   How can you speed up (slow down) the sprouting of seeds?

   How can you prevent seeds from sprouting?

4. Some narrow questions to test single-condition variables:

   Will bean seeds sprout under water?

   Will an *unsoaked* bean planted in damp soil take longer to sprout?

   Will half of a bean seed sprout in damp soil?

Learning about the variable properties of many different objects helps pupils to build a conceptual background and organized data base. That is, it helps them to *construct* schemata. Trying to discover the conditions of change requires pupils to *use* their schemata to solve problems. In doing so, they often find that they also need to pick up more data. The new data are then assimilated or accommodated, depending on what they presently know. The result is improved and additional schemata, which allow your pupils to become even better problem solvers.

Combining Knowledge of Properties with How to Produce or Change Them

When children lack background, finding out about the conditions of change is difficult. After all, they must learn what properties of objects exist before they can discover how they or nature may produce or change the properties. It's a good idea to have children study properties first and then explore whatever conditions of change they can handle. Often, study of one aspect naturally leads to the other.

For example, after two of your pupils demonstrate a tin-can string telephone, you might say to the class, "How many different kinds of string telephones can we make? Don't worry now about how well they are going to work." This will prompt them to use a variety of substitute materials. As children try out each other's phones, some will obviously be more effective than others. Now you can ask, "How can you make your string telephone work better?" and have some assurance that the class has enough background for intelligent problem solving. Pupils could instead build background through reading or consulting some other source of information. But they are likely to find answers rather than raw data they can process for themselves. Which way seems better to strengthen their ability and confidence in problem solving?

When pupils do have background, you may be able to launch an immediate investigation into conditions that produce variation or change. Suppose your class reads the following activity in a textbook:

Find out how much dust falls on your desk top through the day and week. Tape a piece of sticky tape upside down on a small white card. Place it on a corner of your desk. Observe just before you go home each day how much dust sticks to the tape. A magnifier will help you see.

Chances are concrete operational pupils will already know enough about dust to respond intelligently (but not necessarily correctly) to open-ended questions such as

Where do you think you might collect the most dust in this classroom? The least dust? Where in the school? Where on the school grounds? When do you think there would be the most dust? The least dust?

Forming specific operational questions (Will more dust collect by a closed or open window? Will more dust collect on the floor or on top of the tall cabinet? Will more dust collect by the air vent or away from it? etc.), keeping careful records of locations and times tested, and carefully comparing sticky strips would give pupils enough data to answer all these open-ended questions and more.

Experimental and Nonexperimental Activities

You can see that varying a condition to produce or change a property in an object or event tends to be experimental, whereas examining existing properties tends to be nonexperimental or observational. However, children may do more than simply "observe" existing properties. As pointed out earlier in this chapter, they may also group, order, describe, measure, and compare the properties, for example. This can be just as interesting and challenging to pupils as experimenting to discover the conditions of

change. Note the following nonexperimental situations.

In a primary-level classroom three different kinds of open-ended activities in science are going on. In one corner some pupils are sorting leaves by their properties—size, shape, veins, edges, and so on. The teacher then invites them to play a game:

Sort your leaves into two groups according to some property. Will your partner be able to tell which property you used? Take turns. Try a different property each time.

In another part of the classroom other primary pupils are exploring the property of shape with a "feely box." This is a medium-sized cardboard box that has a hole cut in each side for a child's hands. Matched pairs of small objects (for example, blocks, jacks, different-sized Cuisenaire rods, toy soldiers) have been brought in by pupils and supplied for the activity. One of each pair is displayed outside the feely box. The rest are inside the box. A child reaches into the box and tries to find, solely by touch, the mate of an object that a partner points to. When found, it is removed and compared to the outside object. Occasionally the "used-up" objects are replaced by other paired objects to provide a continued challenge.

Still other primary children are working with small milk cartons, containing varying amounts of sand, to explore the property of weight. The cartons are in sets of three; each set is painted in a different color. The children are trying to put in order, from lightest to heaviest, three cartons of each set. They check their work with a simple balance. After stopping by and observing for a while, the teacher says:

How can you pour some sand out of each carton and still keep the same order? How can you check your work?

In the middle-level class some pupils are classifying rocks according to the property of hardness. They are using the scale listed in Table 3-1. The teacher says:

TABLE 3-1
Scale of hardness.

Hardness	Test
Very soft	Can be scratched with your fingernail.
Soft	A new penny will scratch it. Your fingernail will not.
Medium	A large iron nail will scratch it. A penny will not.
Hard	It will scratch glass. A nail will not scratch it.

TABLE 3-2
Users of fossil fuels.

Buildings	Machines
Schools	Trains
Movie theaters	Airplanes
Government offices	Ships
Factories	Private autos
Hospitals	Trucks
Churches	Taxicabs
Houses	Buses
Apartments	Motorcycles

How much will someone else agree with the way you grouped your rocks? How could you check?

A discussion follows on possible procedures. Pupils exchange rocks with partners but do not reveal their test results until the partners themselves have tested the same rocks. Then, both sets of findings are compared. Partners try to iron out differences by retesting, arguing, and describing more carefully what they mean. Some children even try to refine the scale. More rocks are introduced as needed to broaden experiences still further.

In an upper-level class pupils learn that our country must depend on a dwindling supply of fossil fuels for some time before other forms of energy become fully available. But what happens if we begin to run out of fossil fuels sooner than expected? Or, what if pollution in some places gets too bad to continue using such fuels at the present pace? If fossil fuels must be cut back, where should the cuts be greatest? (This highlights the *value* given to the properties of some objects—automobiles, trains, and so on.)

With the help of the children, the teacher makes a list of some buildings and machines that use fossil fuels (Table 3-2). The teacher says:

Let's each arrange these in order from the ones you would cut least to those you would cut most. Also be ready to say why you ordered each in this way. Then, let's discuss our choices and see how they compare.

Themes and the Scientific Search for Patterns

It is easy to feel snowed under by a world stuffed with variable properties and conditions of change everywhere you look. How do you make sense of it all? Or, as one teacher said, "How do you find your way without being an Einstein?" People who feel this way are not likely to seek open-ended science experiences. What's needed is a way to help them see a "forest" every here and there, rather than only trees, trees, trees. Here is where *themes* can be useful.

Themes are large, overarching ideas designed by science educators to cut across content subjects, and so unify what may appear at first to be unrelated facts. They can make understandable and economical what otherwise is confusing and overwhelming. For some examples of themes, please see Table 3-3.

Thematic teaching has become both popular and varied in recent years. For clarity, we need to distinguish the science themes of Table 3-3. which are conceptual, from the *topical* themes that some teachers use to apply and integrate several subjects across the curriculum. "Whales," for example, is a

TABLE 3-3
Some widely used conceptual themes in science.

properties	matter	systems and interactions
change	diversity	patterns of change
order	interactions	material objects
cycles	systems	energy transfer
ecosystems	energy	stability
energy sources	balance	evolution

theme that some teachers use to integrate a high-interest science topic with elements of reading, language, mathematics, art, and music. "Indians of the Southwest" is an even broader topical theme. It allows teachers to select and integrate parts of the entire curriculum so pupils can gain a broad understanding of several Native-American cultures.

Don't expect children to quickly grasp all conceptual themes in science, especially younger pupils. They may need some time and instruction to make broad connections. But most teachers, with just a little experience, can readily use themes to help students see the big picture. You'll find about six in most programs. They also make it easier to locate many possibilities for open-ended explorations across the science curriculum.

Although themes in science programs are devices to guide teachers and students, scientists also invent them to guide their thinking. Three of many themes that scientists and educators alike work with—properties, interactions, and energy—can show you the right direction. Authors of textbooks and curriculum guides also steer by these themes. So knowing them can also better your understanding of how these teaching aids are organized. We've already touched on several of these ideas in earlier chapters. What's needed now is to see how they work together.

Let's begin with what you may be most familiar with—*properties*. Scientists realize that, although individual objects and events vary greatly, many have much in common when viewed collectively. So scientists continually search for *patterns* among the properties of objects and events. This makes it far easier

to keep track of single things. For example, individual rocks vary greatly, but most rocks can be classified as sedimentary, igneous, or metamorphic from common properties in each group. (Because classification is so useful it is often a central objective when scientists observe properties.)

You know, too, that properties of objects change. Yet, as you saw in an earlier example with warm air "rising" (page 10), nothing can change by itself. Scientists realize that any change in an object is evidence that one or more other objects have *interacted* with it. A rounded rock found in a stream bed shows signs that it was tumbled by the stream and rubbed against its bed. To be confident that this happens generally, scientists search for a *pattern of interactions* in similar situations. Or, if needed, they experiment when possible to change other rocks of that type in the same way they think it happens naturally. The experiments are repeated by others to check for the same pattern of results.

Finally, scientists realize that *energy* is needed to change or preserve an active balance in living and nonliving things. Gravity is the force that moves the stream that tumbles the rock. Tracing how energy drives interactions allows scientists to better describe the conditions for change.

In science education, as in science, the variable properties, interactions, and energy sources of objects are carefully observed and changed (when possible) to find out about them. Pupils' knowledge of these three kinds of variables usually improves with additional examples to observe. Their ability to change the variables depends on their learning the conditions of change.

Patterns in properties, interactions, and energy—or similar themes—thread through modern elementary science programs, even when they are not clearly identified. The usual sequence is to begin with properties of objects and events, then move to interactions that change or produce properties, then trace energy sources behind the interactions. (To remember the sequence is as easy as P–I–E.)

The sequence may appear at any grade level. But it is not always complete, nor is each pattern equally treated. Properties are stressed at the primary level. Study of interactions happens more often after the primary grades because it's harder for younger pupils to make cause-and-effect connections. Energy in interactions, being abstract, is studied most intensely in the upper grades.

See next how the three themes cut across the entire curriculum of life, earth/space, and physical sciences. Patterns of properties, interactions, and energy crop up repeatedly as you look for them. These patterns represent much of what the subject matter of elementary science is all about. So getting a feeling for them can truly help you to "find your way."

P–I–E Themes and Some Common Patterns of Variables

In the *life sciences,* children observe the variable properties of living things with all their senses but find that each sense detects only some properties. Touch is useful to detect an object's texture, for example, but not its color. They learn how to group similar body parts, foods, plants, and animals. They see that plants have many uses, that animals develop in several ways. Living things interact with their environment as they respond to light, touch, heat, or cold. Certain needs must be met to stay alive, such as proper temperature, clean air and water, light, food (animals), soil materials (plants), and adequate space. Living things interact with each other in predator–prey and food web connec-

tions, in communities and ecosystems. Energy from the sun makes all of this possible.

In the *earth/space sciences,* children discover the variable properties of earth materials— soil, rocks, air, and water. The earth has a certain size and shape; it rotates and revolves and is part of a solar system whose members share only some properties. Earth materials interact, as when moving air and water erode rocks and soil. Other regular interactions occur at a distance among objects in space and cause predictable eclipses, moon phases, and tides. Gravity and sunshine are seen as the main energy sources behind the interactions.

In the *physical sciences,* children explore energy more directly. They find it has several accessible forms—light, heat, sound, magnetism, and electricity. Each form has some unique and some common properties. Each may be converted through an interaction into another form, as when sunlight strikes a table top and warms it. Energy can trigger physical and chemical changes in matter, as when ice cream melts and wood burns. Children also learn how to send a flow of energy from one object to another, and how to vary or even prevent the energy flow, as they work with batteries and bulbs, everyday sound and heat insulators, mirrors, and string telephones.

Broad questions based on the foregoing variables can generate hundreds of open-ended experiences for children, as you will find in Part II of this text.

Open-Ended Activities and Piaget

In Chapter 2, you saw three important ways in which teachers are trying to apply Piaget's research. According to Piaget each way is essential for helping the child grow in scientific thinking. Look again at these points and consider some added comments:

1. *Children need to explore the physical properties of a wide variety of objects.* It's possible for this to happen with both open- and closed-ended activities, but with which is it likelier to happen?

2. *Children need to perform mental operations as they work with science materials.* That is, they need to change objects or events for some purpose, organize the results, and think about these operations as much as their development allows. Isn't it plain that open-ended activities are well suited to these functions?

3. *Schoolchildren in all stages need to share their experiences with others, consider other viewpoints, and evaluate these social interactions thoughtfully.* From what you have seen so far, which are more likely to do this, open- or closed-ended activities?

The benefits work for both you and your pupils. Multiple approaches to problems allow you to cope more easily with individual differences. A single activity can serve children at several ability levels because they view it in different ways. Children's attention is held longer because the more they dig, the more they find. Fewer activities overall are needed because pupils get more from each experience, and the scramble for materials is reduced.

Even when many materials are called for, getting them is less of a problem. Probably the child's improved motivation is responsible. In following authority, most people feel it is up to the authority figure to get what is needed to put across what they are supposed to learn. But it is different when people go after their own purposes. Children *want* to search for materials that will test their position or their ideas. How far interested girls and boys will go in their searches can be very impressive.

EXERCISES
3-3 to 3-6

How Well Can You Identify and Develop Open-Ended and Closed-Ended Activities?

Most science programs offer a mixture of closed-ended and open-ended activities. However, the number of closed-ended activities far outweighs the other kind. This does not mean that closed-ended activities are bad. As you have seen, they can be valuable in constructing concepts and learning procedures. But used alone, they are very limited in improving children's thinking and ability to function independently. So it will be to your advantage, and the children's, to correct the imbalance. One way to do this is to know where to find open-ended activities. We will discuss this shortly. Another way is to be able to spot the limited activities that have the potential to be expanded.

Almost any activity can be made into an open-ended investigation. However, we are dealing with children. Some activities are easier to work with, have more appeal, and offer more possibilities to improve thinking than others.

Try the following exercises, which include descriptions of six useful but closed-ended activities. Only three have broad open-ended *potential*. The exercises are designed to help you spot and then develop these three activities by practicing what you may have learned so far in this chapter. You will need paper and a pencil. Compare your ideas with the comments that appear after each part of the exercise.

3-3 Which one in each of the three following pairs of closed-ended activities is more likely to be made into an open-ended investigation? (Remember that an open-ended investigation offers many variables to consider, either in the form of observing existing properties or changing them.)

Primary Level

1. Children place an object in water to see whether it will sink or float, to learn something about buoyancy.
2. Children make an outline of their bodies and draw where they think some main bones are, to start learning the bones' locations.

Intermediate Level

3. Children make artificial rocks with plaster of paris and portland cement, to learn more about how some rocks are formed.
4. Children observe how long it takes for an ice cube to melt, to learn more about how heat energy is transferred.

Upper Level

5. Children touch the pulse point on their wrists and count the number of pulses for one minute, to learn how fast hearts beat.
6. Children examine and manipulate a working model of the human heart, loaned by the school's instructional materials center, to learn how the heart works.

Comments

For the primary level, (1) has many more possibilities than (2), which is very limited. There is only one correct answer for where bones are located in the normal body.

For the intermediate level, the better choice is (4). Making rocks with plaster or cement (3) involves following a recipe provided by an authority. There is not much children can vary without fouling up the procedure. If things do go wrong, children can only guess as to why, and this may have no relation to how real rocks are formed.

For the upper level the better choice is (5). Learning how the human heart works (6) is valuable, but it does not generate variables children can manipulate. Other kinds of hearts could be examined—sheep and cow hearts, for example. However, dissection and comparative anatomy are better reserved for later study in properly equipped laboratories with skilled biology teachers.

3-4 Consider now the three *potential* open-ended investigations just identified. What variables for each can you think of that can be tested by children at their level? Hints are given to help you begin.

Primary Level

Children place an object in water to learn whether it will sink or float. (You want to vary the objects and water.)

Intermediate Level

Children observe how long it takes for an ice cube to melt. (You want to change the melting time of ice. What can you vary to do this?)

Upper Level

Children touch the pulse points on their wrists and count the number of pulses for one minute. (You want pupils to observe and produce variations in pulse rates.)

Comments

Primary Level

Some sink and float variables: sizes of objects; kinds of materials objects are made of (plastic, wood, metal, rubber, glass); how pliable the objects are for small hands to shape or change; depth and kind of water (fresh, salty, muddy).

Intermediate Level

Some variables that might change the melting times of ice: still air versus wind; immersion in different liquids and volumes of liquids (fresh, salt, muddy water; alcohol, etc.); air temperature; wrapping the ice in foil or other materials; crushing the ice; changing the shape of the ice (by freezing water in various molds made from kitchen foil).

Upper Level

Some variables to learn how fast hearts beat: children or adults of the same and different age, weight, height; sitting versus standing position; before and after eating or exercise; different times of day; adults before and after smoking.

3-5   It's good to remember variables such as the foregoing while you work with children. If they need help, you have some ideas to supply. These are often best given as narrow operational questions.

Are you able to state a narrow question for each variable children might try? Use the foregoing "Comments" variables in Exercise 3-4 for your narrow questions. Some examples follow to help you start:

Variable: Size of objects. Narrow question: Will the big or small object float, or will both float?

Variable: Medium that ice melts in: air, water, etc. Narrow question: Will an ice cube melt faster in air or water?

Variable: People's height. Narrow question: Do people of the same height have the same pulse rate?

Comments

As you look over the following narrow questions and compare them to yours, please also refer back to the "Comments" variables in Exercise 3-4 that were used to form the questions. There's no need for you to pose exactly the same questions as mine. What we're after is the basic method.

Primary Level

Will more of these plastic or wood (metal, rubber, glass) objects float? Will squashing the foil into a small ball (or other manipulation) make it sink? Will making the water deeper make some things float that sank before? Will more things float in fresh or salt water?

Intermediate Level

Will a fan blowing on an ice cube change its melting time? Will putting a cube in salt water make it melt slower (faster) than it would in fresh water (muddy water, alcohol, etc.)? Will a cube melt faster in warm or cold water (in sun or shade)? How much longer will a cube last if you wrap it in foil (wax paper, newspaper, etc.)? Will a crushed cube melt faster than a regular ice cube? If you refreeze the water from a melted ice cube into a thin pancake shape, will it melt faster than a regular ice cube?

Upper Level

Do people of the same age (weight) have the same pulse rate? Does sitting give a different pulse rate than standing? Is your pulse rate the same before and after eating (exercise)? Is your pulse rate different at different times of the day? Is an adult's pulse rate the same before and after smoking?

3-6 Besides narrow questions, it's useful to ask broad questions. A broad question, you'll recall, is often easy to ask after pupils have explored a narrow question:

> Will magnetism go through paper? (Narrow.) What else besides paper will magnetism go through? (Broad.)

This sequence may be worthwhile when children are very young or inexperienced with the materials they will use. When they are on more familiar ground, you may find it better to open up a lesson right away with broad questions.

Consider again the three potential open-ended experiences we began with:

Primary Level

Children place an object in water to see whether it will sink or float.

Intermediate Level

Children observe how long it takes for an ice cube to melt.

Upper Level

Children touch the pulse points on their wrists and count the number of beats for one minute.

What broad questions can you pose that might make these activities open-ended investigations from the beginning? Please state one or two for each activity now.

Comments

As you compare your broad questions with mine, think of the responses children might make to the questions. Are they likely to come up with some of the same kinds of variables and narrow questions you have seen in Exercises 3-4 and 3-5? This is a better test of the quality of your questions than simply how well they match mine.

Primary Level

Which objects do you think will float? How can you sink the things that floated? How can you make float the things that sank?

Intermediate Level

What could you do to make ice melt faster? In what ways can you slow down the melting of ice?

Upper Level

How might the pulse rates of different people compare? What is there about people, or what they do, that might affect their pulse rate? What are some things that might affect a person's pulse rate?

Did you find it easier to identify the potential open-ended activities than to develop them? That's to be expected now, so don't be discouraged. The ability to develop these activities thoroughly takes some firsthand experience with the materials involved and some understanding of the subject matter. We will take up how to get this background shortly.

The Relativity of "Openness"

Many activities found today in science books and curricula cannot be properly categorized on an either/or basis; that is, they are neither totally closed- nor open-ended. Many authors realize the need for children to extend or apply what is learned, and they know how to ask broad (open-ended) and narrow (closed-ended) questions. Does this mean the two categories are useless? Far from it. However, it does mean that many activities are likely to be closed or open only in a relative sense.

As you saw in Exercises 3-3 to 3-6, some activities can generate a wide variety of variables, and some can generate far fewer. Even with relatively closed-ended activities, it is often possible and desirable to ask broad as well as narrow questions. One type sets up the other. Your ability to do this can boost children's learning, regardless of what kind of hands-on experience you offer.

HOW TO PRACTICE

To improve your ability to develop questions and hands-on learning experiences, examine the investigations and activities in Part II of this book. The investigations typically have a broader scope than the activities and are more open-ended. Check how broad questions are often used to open up the discovery part of each investigation. Notice how narrow questions are used to zero in on single variables as needed. Study, too, how the child is guided to explore materials or a procedure *before* the broad and narrow discovery questions are posed. This experience is usually required before children (and many adults) can see possible chances to observe or manipulate variables. You will find it worthwhile to go through the investigations yourself if you lack background in either the materials or content.

Examine and try the activities, also. They often include broad as well as narrow questions. Some of the activities are relatively open-ended. They could easily become full investigations depending on pupil responses.

Finally, try some investigations and activities with children. Note how they respond to the questions. You may want to amend some or come up with many of your own questions as you interact with pupils. This might bring the best results.

SUMMARY

Science is a purposeful search for patterns among objects and events in the physical world. In searching for patterns, scientists uncover numerous facts, many of which at first seem unrelated. To help organize facts, especially from several different science areas, scientists and educators invent conceptual *themes*. Three such themes are *properties, interactions,* and *energy.* The use of themes also enables teachers to see many chances for open-ended investigations. To find patterns among the variable properties, interactions, and energy sources of material objects, scientists thoughtfully observe and experiment with (when possible) the variables. They develop theories to support their findings and guide further searches. Their purpose is to explain, predict, and control phenomena.

Our purpose is to teach the patterns that scientists discover, and their ways of thinking, that children are most likely to understand and use in our society. To do so, we set up closed-ended and open-ended learning activities. Closed-ended activities are appropriate to directly teach specific subject-matter ideas and procedures through demonstration and illustration. Their scope is limited, and exact outcomes and pupil responses are often predictable. Open-ended activities are best used to discover, through investigative and indirect teaching methods, a broader scope of variables. Children are much more likely here to learn scientific ways of thinking as well as subject matter, but their responses and exact outcomes of lessons are less predictable.

In science education, as in science, the variable properties, interactions, and energy sources of objects are carefully observed and changed (when possible) to find out more about them. Pupils' knowledge of property variables usually improves as we give them additional *examples* to observe. Their ability to change the variables depends on their learning the *conditions* of change.

Varying a condition to change or produce a property in an object or event is usually experimental. Experiments require a higher level of operational thinking than intuitive-level and early concrete-operational children can independently demonstrate. So seeking causes of changes in properties through experiments is done more often beyond the primary grades. Examining existing properties is nonexperimental or observational. Activities in which pupils observe and compare properties are ideal for younger children, and others who may lack experience with the properties of the objects and events being studied.

To guide children's learning, we ask narrow and broad questions. Narrow questions focus their thinking on single variables and will dominate in closed-ended activities. Broad questions open their thinking to multiple variables and will dominate in open-ended activities. A combination of both kinds of questions ordinarily works best in learning activities, whether closed- or open-ended.

SUGGESTED READINGS

Birnie, Howard H., and Alan Ryan. "Inquiry/ Discovery Revisited." *Science and Children,* April 1984, 31–33. (How to vary the open-endedness of inquiry activities.)

Blosser, Patricia E. *How to Ask the Right Questions.* Washington, D.C.: National Science Teachers Association, 1991. (Many helpful ideas in this monograph, including closed and open questioning techniques.)

Hawkins, David. "Messing About in Science." *Science and Children* 2 (February 1965): 5–9. (One of the developers of a national curriculum project describes an open-ended approach to learning science. A classic.)

McCormack, Alan J. *Inventor's Workshop.* Belmont, CA: David S. Lake, 1981. (Clear examples of using variables to "open-end" activities.)

Shaw, Jean M. "A Model for Training Teachers to Encourage Divergent Thinking in Young Children." *Journal of Creative Behavior* 20 (2): 81–88 (1986). (Ways to use questions that promote divergent thinking in primary-level children.)

Wasserman, Selma. "Teaching Strategies: The Art of the Question." *Childhood Education* 67(4): 257–59 (Summer 1991). (Four guidelines for using questions to improve class discussions.)

4

How to Improve Children's Thinking

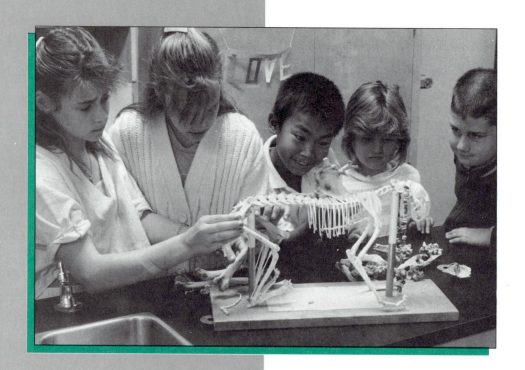

The last chapter sets the stage for this one. You've just seen how to help children observe or change objects and events by asking broad (open) and narrow (closed) questions. Such questions can stimulate children to think—to process data. But to use questions well you need more details. There are several kinds of processes used in science. You can learn how to ask broad and narrow questions that are right for each kind. This chapter presents the processes and the kinds of questions and experiences that spark children's thinking.

Recall that for children to grow in their thinking, they need to explore many objects and events and share their experiences. Most important, they need to perform *mental operations* as they do these things. Everyone is for improving children's "mental operations," just as everyone is for health, happiness, and Friday afternoons. But this can mean anything unless we pin it down. Just what is it that we do to help pupils think within different activities? Must we learn entirely new ways of thinking to help children?

No educated person begins teaching with a blank mind. Over the years you've probably picked up more good thinking habits than you're aware of. You now use many of the thinking processes children need help with, just as you now practice most of the three-R skills they need. This chapter can help you to build on what you do already and apply it to teaching.

The science processes we'll take up are observing, classifying, measuring, communicating, inferring and predicting, and experimenting. Before we examine the processes in detail, it's important for your understanding to put them into perspective. Here are some relevant points from previous chapters:

1. Remember that the basic mission of scientists is to construct *knowledge* about how the world works, so they can explain, predict, and control phenomena. Science processes are the means by which scientists seek data and construct knowledge. A similar outlook works well in science teaching. Regard the processes as tools that enable children to gather and reason about data to make better sense of their world. Little is gained overall unless children's use of processes also results in improved conceptual knowledge.

2. The processes are most productive when guided by a valid conceptual framework. In other words, quality process thinking and accurate knowledge of subject matter are interactive—one helps, and also depends on, the other.

3. The ability to use science processes tends to be "domain specific" when applied to real world problems. Being a good problem solver in one field doesn't guarantee that you will be so in another. So process thinking needs to be groomed across the science curriculum and in all the academic subjects.

4. To learn process thinking requires pupils to work with raw (unprocessed) data. Probably the best learning experience to promote such thinking in children is the hands-on, open-ended investigation, as guided by a knowledgeable teacher.

Open-ended investigations usually give the chance to teach a variety of science processes. But in some investigations, one process will dominate. Following each introduction to a process are several titles of investigations from Part II of this book in which you can see the process applied. To quickly find where a process is used, just look at the marginal notes on the pages indicated.

Now let's consider the processes, one by one.

OBSERVING

The process of observing is the taking in of sense perceptions. It is the most basic and broadest of the processes. In a way, all the others simply refine it. Our job is to help children to

- Use all of their senses when they observe objects or events.
- Notice how things may be alike or different.
- Become aware of changes.

Pupils can learn that each of the senses is a gateway to observing different properties of objects. *Seeing* allows them to notice properties such as sizes, shapes, and colors of objects and how the objects may interact. *Hearing* makes knowable properties of sounds such as loudness, pitch, and rhythm. *Touching* teaches the meaning of texture, and is another way to discover sizes and shapes of objects. *Tasting* shows how properties such as bitter, salty, sour, and sweet can be used to describe foods. (At the same time, pupils can learn not to taste an unknown substance, since it could be harmful.) *Smelling* calls for associating objects with odors because odors are otherwise hard to describe. So something smells "like perfume," "like a lemon," "like cigar smoke," and so forth.

Properties, children find, enable them to compare and describe likenesses and differences among objects. This leads to explorations that require several of the other processes, such as classifying and communicating, which we will examine in other sections.

You can ask broad and narrow questions to guide learning in observing or any of the other science processes.

In a primary-level class children are examining bean seeds that have been soaked to make them easy to open. The teacher gets everyone to observe by saying:

What do you notice about your seed?

Later, some narrower questions are posed:

How many parts did you find?
How does the seed feel to you without its cover?
What does it smell like?

In a middle-level class pupils are raising tadpoles in a large jar. On Monday morning,

they rush to the jar as soon as the classroom opens and see a small sign that reads:

What changes do you observe since Friday?

During sharing time everyone learns what the pupils have noticed. Then, the teacher asks a narrow question to zero in on an interesting change that has been missed:

How has the water level changed since Friday?

In an upper-level class children are comparing plastic but real-looking cat bones and rabbit bones from a kit. The teacher says:

In what ways are the two sets of bones alike?
Different?

The need for a few narrower questions comes up later during a discussion:

How do their back leg bones compare?
How do their skulls compare?

For some examples of *observing* applied in investigations, see:

Your Side Vision and Color (p. 236)
A Way to Generate Electricity (p. 374)
Mealworms and What They Do (p. 489)
The Filtering of Polluted Water (p. 618)

CLASSIFYING

We have already seen in Chapter 2 how children at different developmental stages handle the process of classifying and its variation—arranging objects or events in order according to some property. (It will help to review pages 24, 26, and 28.) Our concern now is to see what happens in classrooms.

Most intuitive thinkers can select and group together real objects by some common property, such as color, shape, and size. They can use a different property each time they make a new group.

In a primary-level class some children remove from bags small objects they have brought from home. The teacher says:

Think of one property, such as a certain shape. Sort all the objects that have that property into one pile. Leave what's left in another pile.

Later, to open up the activity, the teacher says:

What other properties can you use to sort your objects?

Other children in the primary classroom are grouping pictures according to whether they show living or nonliving things. Later, they will be asked to take the pictures of living things and group them into animal and plant categories.

Many middle-level children can classify an object into more than one category at the same time and hold this in mind.

In a middle-level class some children have classified animal pictures into three groups with two subgroups each: mammals, birds, and fishes have each been divided into meat eaters and plant eaters. They have done this in response to their teacher's question:

How can you group these animals by kind and by what they eat?

Some upper-level students can do the foregoing and can also reclassify according to other properties that fit their purposes.

In an upper-level class several pupils have a large collection of animal pictures. They start off by dividing them into groups such as mammals, birds, fishes, and so on, but then decide that this will not further their purpose. They want to alert people to animals of different locations that are threatened with extinction. How to do this?

After talking with the teacher, they decide to classify their pictures according to the animals' natural homes or habitats: woodlands, grasslands, marshlands, and so on. These pictures are then subgrouped into endangered and nonendangered animal cat-egories. Later, they subdivide further for instate and out-of-state animals. Only classmates with similar advanced classifying skills and knowledge will fully understand their request for more pictures:

Can you bring in ones that show animals that are dying out in different environments in our state or other states? We're really short on grassland reptiles.

This example hits a major point about classification: It is done to fit a purpose. What works to fulfill the intent of the classifier is what counts. Objects can be classified in many different ways.

There is a second point worth remembering when we go to classify things: We can think of a property as being present or not present, but we can also think of it in a quantitative way. Consider age, for example. If we think of people as young or old, we have put everyone into two groups. But we can also arrange people in order, from young to old, according to years. It is when we think of a property in a quantitative way—that is, by the *amount* of the property present—that we can arrange objects in some order.

So, younger pupils may group magnets by shapes. They may also arrange several magnets in order by how powerful they are. Older children may group materials as to whether they conduct or do not conduct electricity. They may also test how well some materials conduct electricity by checking the varying brightness of a flashlight bulb used in the test. The materials then may be ranked in order from the worst to the best conductor.

For some examples of *classifying* applied in investigations, see:

A Bottle Xylophone (p. 307)

How to Measure Bulb Brightness (p. 366)

Some Common Levers (p. 392)

The Properties of Rocks (p. 587)

MEASURING

Thinking about properties in a quantitative way naturally leads to measuring them. To measure is to compare things. At first, at the primary level, children may be unable to compare an object with a standard measuring tool, such as a meter stick or yardstick. Instead, they find out who is taller by standing back to back. They find out which of two objects is heavier by holding each object in their hands. They measure how far a soap bubble traveled by stretching a string between the bubble blower and the wet spot and marking the string.

There is good reason to start off measuring in this way. Remember that intuitive thinkers *do not conserve* several concepts that deal with quantity. Changing the appearance of an object still fools them. Children who think that merely spreading out some material gives them more, for example, have to be treated differently from children who conserve quantity. (Now is a good time to review pages 24 and 25.) This means that most young children cannot work meaningfully with standard units of measurement such as centimeters, inches, and so on until about age seven.

Intuitive thinkers can build readiness for working with standard units by using parts of their bodies or familiar objects as arbitrary units to measure things. A primary child may say that "The classroom is 28 of *my* feet wide." Or, "The classroom is 10 of *my* giant strides long." The child also may say, "The mealworm is one paper clip long." Or, "It moved as far as three spelling books during science time."

Pupils' Natural Interest

Children's observations in almost any science area can be sharpened by measuring things. But experienced teachers will tell you that children are not interested in measuring for its own sake any more than they are interested in the other science processes as such. Pupils are more interested—*much* more interested—in the physical activity and its outcome than in the processes they use.

Children get bored when a process is emphasized for its own sake. The teacher who announces, "Today we are going to improve our ability to measure weights," is seldom greeted with foot-stamping enthusiasm and shouts of joy. Things go better if the children hear, "We're running out of hamster food. How much do we need to buy for a month's supply?" *So deal with measurement and the other processes as natural ways to answer questions that come up in investigations.*

Concrete Referents

One way to improve the ability of children to measure and estimate accurately is to have in your classroom many concrete objects they can refer to when needed. Meter sticks, yardsticks, and trundle wheels are useful for thinking about length. Containers marked with metric and English units are good for thinking about liquid volumes.

Similar things to refer to are needed for other concepts involving quantity. A kilometer may be a round trip from the school to the police station; a mile, from the school to the post office. Meanings associated with time can be developed by many references to water or sand clocks (containers with holes punched in the bottom) and real clocks. Temperature differences become meaningful through using several kinds of thermometers.

Improvising Tools

By the time they leave elementary school, many children have had some experience with a variety of measuring instruments: ruler, meter stick, yardstick, balance, clock, thermometer, graduated (marked) containers, protractor, and wind gauge, to mention the more common ones. When possible, children themselves should choose the right measuring tool for the activity under way. Sometimes they can make their own tools when they need them. Inventing and making a measuring instrument can be as challenging and interesting as other activities.

Consider some fourth graders who are trying to figure out how to measure wind speeds during a unit on weather. They have fastened a small cardboard flap to the side of a wind vane so that the flap swings freely. When the wind blows hard, it pushes back the flap more than when there is a light breeze. But how can it be marked to show speeds?

Someone whose bicycle has a speedometer gets the idea to check the flap positions while holding the vane and riding at different speeds. Another child points out that this had better be done on a windless day. A few others say the bike can be ridden in several directions and the "middle" (average) flap positions noted. They are not sure how to figure averages, so the teacher helps them.

Some Advanced Concepts

Children can even begin to learn sophisticated concepts when these are approached in simple ways.

In a primary class several children estimate the number of objects a small jar may hold. Each child first fills the jar with beans and then with marbles. Of course, the beans are not exactly alike. Each time a child tries, it takes a slightly different number of beans to fill the jar. But when identical marbles are used, the number is always the same. The teacher helps the children understand one way that *variations in measurement* comes up by asking:

Why do you get a different number of beans each time? Why is the number of marbles always the same?

In a middle-level class the idea of *sampling* comes up in a plant unit. The seed box

directions show that 90 percent of the seeds should grow under proper conditions. After making sure the children understand that not all the seeds in the box are likely to grow, the teacher says:

We'll be planting only some of these seeds. Some of them are bad, but you can't tell by looking at them. Maybe most of the bad seeds are in one part of the box. How might we avoid picking too many bad seeds?

Sometimes there is a need for *scaling* in elementary science activities. In an upper-level class several pupils want to make a model solar system. After they read the sizes of the planets and the distances between them, the teacher helps the children realize that only planet sizes *or* distances between—not both—can be shown in a classroom model. Because of the huge distances involved, for the model to fit within the classroom, some planets would have to be made too small for easy viewing. The pupils therefore decide that size alone will be scaled in their model. Proper planet distances, according to the scale, will be written neatly in black ink on a sign placed by the model. "That puts Pluto downtown by the bus depot!" the pupils report to their astonished classmates.

Measurement and the Mathematics Program

Measurement is often used in combination with other mathematical skills in practical situations, both in and out of school. Is there a cook or carpenter anywhere who measures and only measures?

Learning how to apply mathematical skills in science teaches a more useful understanding of science and lays the groundwork for further study in later schooling. These experiences can enhance mathematics education as well. You can use science investigations to reinforce certain mathematical skills, give practical contexts to use the skills, and motivate pupils to learn more mathematics.

Understanding the foundations of the mathematics program allows you to grasp the kinds of quantitative thinking pupils can apply in their science experiences. Most programs are developed around a half-dozen or so conceptual strands, such as the following:

- Basic operations
- Measurement
- Problem solving
- Relations and functions
- Tables and graphs
- Geometry
- Probability and statistics

Not all strands are treated equally at every grade level. The basic operations strand generally threads through all grades, while the study of probability and statistics may begin at grade five or beyond. Also, the strands overlap. Seldom can one solve problems, for example, without using skills from the other strands as well.

It is usually sounder to have children apply a skill that has already been introduced in the mathematics program than to introduce it through science activity. The mathematics program is likelier to have a carefully designed sequence of subskills that makes the skill's introduction more understandable.

Following are brief descriptions of common strands in mathematics programs that complement measurement, with some examples of how skills within the strands are applied in science situations. Most of these applications, and others, may be found in the investigations of Part II of this book.

Basic Operations. This is the dominant strand in elementary mathematics programs. It includes counting, tallying, and the four basic processes—addition, subtraction, multiplication, and division. Examples include

- Comparing the power of several magnets by counting the number of paper clips attracted.

- Finding the average air temperature over three days.
- Counting pulse beats for 15 seconds, then estimating beats for 1 minute, hour, day, week, and year.
- Calculating one's weight on various planets by multiplying that weight by ratios supplied in a reference book.

Problem Solving. Problems may range from a simple situation that requires a single calculation to open-ended situations that call for observing, gathering data, making inferences and testing them. Skills from any or all the strands may be needed. Examples include

- Will an adult blue whale fit into our classroom. How can we find out?
- What balanced meals can you plan of no more than 1000 calories?
- How much weight will it take to balance a 40-kilogram person if the fulcrum is 2 meters from the end of a 6-meter board?
- How can you make a string pendulum swing 60 times per minute?

Relations and Functions. Here, the apparent association of one variable with another is revealed. Examples include

- Observing that lowering the water temperature reduces the breathing rate (gill movements) of a goldfish, while raising it increases the rate.
- Finding that the number of times a bike pedal revolves compared with the rear wheel changes with the sizes of gears one uses.
- Learning that the power of an electromagnet varies with the number of turns of wire around its core.
- Observing that changing the slope of an inclined plane varies the force needed to pull up an object.

Tables and Graphs.   The ways data are displayed in tables and graphs make them useful for several purposes. They help pupils to make sense of numerical data and clearly communicate the data to others, to make predictions, to see relationships between variables, to hypothesize about changes in data, and to draw conclusions. You'll see several examples of how to use tables and graphs in parts of following sections on communicating, inferring, and experimenting. Some further examples are

- Making a table and graph of air temperatures over several days.
- Making a table and graph of the effect of practice on writing backward (mirror writing), as measured by the number of times the writing goes outside a narrow border, timed over five trials.
- Graphing the heights reached by several bounced balls and predicting further heights of bounced balls from the data.
- Graphing the loss of vitamin C in orange juice over time as measured by the number of drops of juice required for a blue fluid indicator to lose its color.

Geometry.   Early experiences in applying geometry can build a number of skills, including pupils' spatial and aesthetic judgment, the ability to better describe objects, and the skill to make more technical measurements. Examples include

- Locating everyday objects that demonstrate geometric forms—litter can (cylinder), ice cream cone (cone), hopscotch area (squares), boat sail (triangle), shoe box (rectangular prism), ball (sphere), dice (cube), wheels (circle), church steeples (pyramid), and so on.
- Reading directions in degrees on a magnetic compass to find an object.
- Measuring angles to make a sundial.
- Using coordinates and scale to draw maps and give directions.

Probability and Statistics.   This is a minor strand at the elementary level and is seldom introduced before grade five. The approach is to seek a practical awareness of probability in pupils rather than basic proficiency, which requires a formal operational level of thinking. Examples include

- Recording frequencies of seeds that sprout under varied conditions.
- Tossing a coin to simulate chances for inheriting a trait, as presented in a unit on heredity.
- Learning that a 70 percent chance of rain means a comparison of present conditions to past conditions that produced rain.
- Learning not to generalize about a whole population from measuring a sample unless the sample is representative of the whole.

Measurement and the Metric System

Gradually, the United States is joining the other countries of the world that have replaced the English measurement system with the metric system. School districts now teach both systems. Scientists everywhere have long used the metric system because it is simpler and faster; all of its units are defined in multiples of 10, as in our money system.

The three basic units most commonly used in the metric system are the *meter, liter,* and *gram.* A meter is a little longer than a yard (about 1.1 yd) and is used to measure length. The liter is a little larger than a quart (about 1.06 qt) and is used to measure liquid volume. The gram is used to measure weight or mass and weighs about the same as a paper clip.

Strictly speaking, the terms *mass* and *weight* mean different things in science. Mass is the amount of material or matter that makes up an object. Weight is the gravitational force that pulls the mass. On the moon, for example, an astronaut's weight is only about one-sixth of what it is on earth. But the astronaut's mass stays unchanged.

Prefixes are used in the metric system to show larger or smaller quantities. The three most common prefixes and their meanings are

- *milli*   one-thousandth (0.001)
- *centi*   one-hundredth (0.01)
- *kilo*   one-thousand (1,000)

Let's see how the prefixes are used in combination with the basic units.

Length 1 meter (m) = 1,000 millimeters (mm) or 100 centimeters (cm). 1 kilometer (km) = 1,000 meters (m). A millimeter is about the diameter of paper-clip wire. A centimeter is slightly larger than the width of a formed paper clip. A kilometer is about nine football fields long, or about six-tenths of a mile.

Volume 1 liter (1) = 1,000 milliliters (ml) or 100 centiliters (cl)[1]. 1 kiloliter (kl)[1] = 1,000 liters (l). A milliliter is about one-fifth of a teaspoon; a liter is slightly over a quart.

Weight (Mass) 1 gram (g) = 1,000 milligrams (mg) or 100 centigrams (cg)[1]. 1 kilogram (kg) = 1,000 grams (g). Notice that a milligram weighs only about one-thousandth of a paper clip. A kilogram is a little more than 2 pounds (about 2.2 lb).

Temperature in the metric system is commonly measured by the Celsius (C) thermometer, named after its inventor, Anders Celsius. It has a centigrade scale—that is, one marked into one hundred evenly spaced subdivisions. Zero degrees begins at the freezing point of water, and 100 degrees marks the boiling point of water at sea level.

If you have available only a Fahrenheit (F) thermometer, you can convert it to also read in the Celsius scale. Cover one side of the present scale with masking tape. Mark on the tape the points where water freezes (32°F) and boils (212°F). Then subdivide the distance between into 100 evenly spaced parts.

Before your pupils use different metric standards, have them consider the right standard for the job. The kilometer is good for measuring long distances, as when traveling by automobile or taking a long bike ride. The meter is fine for measuring the size of the playground or classroom. A book or desk top is easily measured in centimeters, while the millimeter should be reserved for very small objects.

Children usually discover that the metric system is easier to use than the English system. Yet some adults find this statement hard to believe. Why? They are often victims of poor teaching. Generations of high school students have had to memorize details of the several metric units with little exposure to concrete materials. With only sketchy practice in using or referring to real materials, what was "learned" was soon forgotten.

Another widespread practice was to present the metric system as something that needed to be *converted* into the English system. This led to dreary and confusing lessons to learn formulas for changing one set of measurements to another.

You can profit from these past mistakes by simply doing the opposite. If your curriculum calls for work with both metric and English measures, give pupils much practice with concrete materials when working with both systems. Also, treat each system separately, instead of shifting back and forth. After much practice, children become able to *think metrically*. At that time, pupils are naturally able to compare units of both systems without confusion.

Despite the proven effectiveness of teaching both systems separately, occasionally you may wish to convert a measurement from one system to the other. For example, your pupils may want to record their body weights in kilograms. But you may have only a scale that reads in pounds. Or, if you are now unfamiliar with some metric unit, it may help briefly

---

[1]Seldom used in elementary school science.

to know the English equivalent until you have had a chance to practice some yourself. For this reason, conversion tables are provided for you on the inside front cover of this book. If you use a hand calculator, conversions are swiftly attained. After a while, once you, too, think metrically, conversions will be largely unnecessary.

For some examples of *measuring* applied in investigations, see:

Echoes (p. 299)

The Volume of Air You Breathe (p. 540)

How Water Sinks into Different Soils (p. 581)

An Earth–Moon Model (p. 673)

COMMUNICATING

In elementary science, communicating means putting the data (information) obtained from our observations into some form another person can understand. Of course, we, too, should be able to understand our data when we reexamine them at a later date.

Children learn to communicate in many ways. They learn to draw accurate pictures, diagrams, and maps; make proper charts and graphs; construct accurate models and exhibits; and use clear language when describing objects or events. The last of these activities is usually stressed in elementary science.

The test of success in communicating is how closely the other person interprets what you say or do with what you have in mind. So it is important to say things or to show data in the clearest ways possible. We can help children learn these ways by giving them many chances to communicate and helping them to evaluate what they have said or done.

In a primary-level class some pupils are seated on a rug. They face a bulletin board on which many pictures of vehicles are pinned. Each picture has a number, so the pictures can be quickly located. The teacher has suggested a game: A child describes the properties of a vehicle ("I'm thinking of a green object. It has four wheels. It is small enough to fit in my garage," etc.) and the others try to identify the object ("Is it number four?" etc.). The child who identifies the object first gets to be the new describer. The original describer is rewarded by getting the picture. Wild guessing is discouraged by reminding the children to consider the data. After each identification, the teacher asks questions such as

What did Maria say that helped you to find the picture? What else would be helpful to say? Did anyone get mixed up? How do you think that happened, Tommy?

In a middle-level class two children are working with a simple balance that has a pegboard-type (perforated) beam. They hang iron washers from opened paper clips hooked to different parts of the beam. They are working out problems written on problem cards. After a while, the teacher says:

What problem cards of your own can you make? Will your partner understand your directions? If not, try to figure out why.

In an upper-level class pupils want to find out the warmest time of the day. Temperature readings are made on the hour from 10 A.M. until 3 P.M. for 5 days in a row and then averaged. They decide to record their results on a line graph but don't know whether to put the temperature along the side (vertical axis) or the bottom (horizontal axis) of the graph. Is there a "regular" way?

The teacher helps them to see how graphs are arranged in their mathematics text. The change being tested, called the manipulated variable by scientists—in this case, time—is usually placed along the bottom axis. The change that results from the test, called the responding variable—in this case, temperature—is usually placed along the vertical axis.

Defining Operationally

Defining operationally is a sub-process of communicating, usually introduced after the primary grades. To define a word operationally is to describe it by an action (operation) rather than just by other words. Maybe you recall the example in Chapter 3 (page 60) in which some children classified rocks according to hardness. The test for "very soft" was, "Can be scratched with your fingernail." This action, then, is the operational definition of "very soft," at least for those children. This definition is clearer than saying, "very soft means not hard," for instance. Here is another example.

Suppose you invite some pupils to hold an evaporation contest: Who can dry water-soaked paper towels fastest? They begin to speculate excitedly. But there is just one thing they will have to agree on before the fun begins. How will everyone know when a towel is "dry"? This stumps them, so you pose another open question that hints at *actions* they could take: What are some things they could *do to the towel* to tell if it is dry? Now, they start coming up with operations (actions) to try:

Squeeze the towel into a ball and see if water comes out.

Rub it on the chalkboard; see if it makes a wet mark.

Tear it and compare the sound to a dry towel you tear.

Hold it up to the light and compare its color to an unsoaked towel.

See if it can be set on fire as fast as an unsoaked towel.

Put an unsoaked towel on one end of a balance beam; see if the other towel balances it.

The children agree that the last operation is easiest to observe and least arguable. It is stated as an operational definition: "A towel is dry if it balances an unsoaked towel from the same package." Activity begins.

Had the open question not worked, one or two narrow questions (How would squeezing the towel show if it is dry? etc.) could have been posed, followed later with a broad question (What else could you do to the towel to tell if it is dry besides squeezing it?)

When operational definitions are not used, it is easy to fall into the trap of circular reasoning: What is the condition of a *dry* towel? It contains no moisture. What is the condition of a towel that *contains no moisture?* It is dry. Or, to borrow from children's humor, consider this example:

He is the best scientist we've ever had.

Who is?

He is.

Who is "He"?

The best scientist we've ever had.

There are some predictable times when the need for operational definitions will come up. Watch children's use of relative terms such as tall, short (How tall? Short?), light, heavy, fast, slow, good, bad (What is "bad" luck?), and so on.

Recording Activities

This is another sub-process of communicating. When activities require time to gather data (e.g., growing plants over many weeks), or when there are many data to consider (e.g., discovering how much vitamin C many juices contain), it is often sensible to make a record of what is happening. Without a record, it is harder to remember what has happened and draw conclusions. In a way, recording can be considered communicating with oneself, besides others. Many teachers ask their pupils to make records in a notebook or *data log*. Records can be in picture or graph form as well as in writing. But whatever way the data are recorded, they should be clear.

In a primary-level class some children are recording the growth of their plants with strips of colored paper. Every other day, they hold a new strip of paper next to their plant and tear off a bit to match the plant's height. They date the strips and paste them in order on large paper sheets. A growth record of the plants is clearly visible to all.

Other children in the class have drawn pictures of their plants at different stages, from seed to mature plant. These they make into record booklets at the teacher's suggestion. They describe each picture for the teacher, who swiftly writes their short statements on paper slips. The children paste these beneath their pictures. The result is a "My Plant Story Book" for each child, who can proudly read it—unassisted—before impressed parents.

In a middle-level class there are five groups at work with narrow strips of litmus paper. (This chemically treated paper changes color when dipped into acidic or basic liquids.) The children want to find out which of five "mystery" liquids in numbered jars are acidic, basic, or neutral. Each group has a recorder, who records the findings on a data sheet. At the end of the work session, the teacher asks how the results of all the groups should be recorded on the chalkboard. It is decided as outlined in Table 4-1. Notice that by having a code (A: Acid, and so on) written to one side, the teacher cuts down on the time needed to record the findings. The data are now compared, differences noted, and possible reasons discussed. Careful retesting is planned to straighten out the differences.

In an upper-level class some children want to find out if there is a pattern to the clouds passing over the city in the spring. They have made a chart that has three columns, one each for March, April, and May. In each column is a numbered space for each day of that month. Next to about half of the days the children have drawn the weather bureau cloud symbols for the main cloud cover, if any, on those days. Even though the record chart is only partly completed, a sequential pattern is taking shape. After the chart is completed, the children will compare it to data gathered by the local weather bureau office for the same months in previous years.

For some examples of *communicating* applied in investigations, see:

The Properties of Leaves (p. 448)

Snails and What They Do (p. 497)

How Practice Improves Learning (p. 527)

The Sensitivity of Your Skin (p. 534)

INFERRING AND PREDICTING

The usual meaning of inferring is to interpret or *explain* what we observe. If Carol smiles when she greets us (observation), we may infer that she is pleased to see us (explanation). The accuracy of our inferences usually improves with more chances to observe. Several like observations may also lead us to *predict* that the next time we see her she will smile (observation) because she will be pleased to see us (explanation). For convenience, then, view the process of inferring as having two forms: We may make an *inference* from what we observe, and we may predict an *observation* from what we infer (observation ⟶ inference, inference ⟶ observation). Let's now look at children *explaining* observations, then later, in another section, *predicting* them.

Inferring as Explaining

There are at least three common ways we can help children to infer properly from observa-

TABLE 4-1
Acidity of mystery liquids.

GROUP	1	2	3	4	5	
Jane	A	B	N	B	A	
Bill	A	B	N	B	A	A: Acid
Kathy	A	A	N	A	A	B: Base
Robin	A	B	N	A	A	N: Neutral
Joe	B	B	N	B	B	

tions. However, expect intuitive-level pupils to have very limited overall understanding of this process.

First, we can get them to distinguish between their observation and inference.

In a middle-level class two children are looking at a picture of shoeprints in the snow. One set of prints is much smaller than the other (observation). One child says, "One of these sets of shoeprints must have been made by a man and the other by a boy" (an inference). The other child says, "That's true" (another inference). Hearing this, the teacher asks an open question to make them aware of other possibilities:

In what other ways could these prints have been made?

They think for a moment and come up with other inferences: Perhaps two children made the prints—one wore his father's shoes; or maybe it was a girl and her mother; or it could have been a girl and her older brother; and so on.

The teacher points out that what they observe is still the same. But there is more than one way to explain the observation. If the children look at the tracks closely, they may *conclude* that one of their inferences is likelier than the others. A *conclusion* is simply an inference in which one has the most confidence after considering all the evidence.

A second way to help children infer is to let them interpret their observed or recorded data. In the preceding section on recording data, recall that pupils used litmus paper to identify mystery liquids. When the several groups recorded their data, they noticed that some data were inconsistent. Some liquids were labeled both acidic and basic. The children inferred from this that the litmus test was done incorrectly by some group. After the tests were redone, all the data became consistent. So the children inferred that their final labeling of the mystery liquids was probably correct.

Also in the section on recording was the cloud data study. The sequential pattern the children saw, when they examined their data, was an inferred pattern. Later, when they compare their pattern with the weather bureau's, they will be able to evaluate the quality of their inference.

A third way to help children infer is to let them observe and interpret only indirect evidence or clues. Scientists must often depend on clues rather than clear evidence in forming possible inferences. For example, no scientist has visited the middle of the earth, yet earth scientists have inferred much about its properties.

In the everyday world we, too, often use clues to infer about objects or events. Sometimes we go wrong. When the boss at long last praises us, we may be quick to infer that the superior quality of our work has finally been recognized—until we are asked to work late that night. When the headwaiter calls us by name at a fancy restaurant, we may infer that we're special—until we observe everyone else getting the same treatment. We need to be cautious when we infer, as do scientists.

Children can learn to make inferences from incomplete or indirect evidence and also learn to become wary of hasty conclusions.

In a primary-level class some pupils are working with two closed shoe boxes. One box contains a round (cylindrical) pencil. In the other box is a usual, six-sided pencil. The children's problem is, which box has which kind of pencil?

They tip the boxes back and forth and listen intently. They then infer correctly the contents of the two boxes. When the teacher asks them what made them decide as they did, one child says, "You could feel which one was the bumpy pencil when it rolled." The other child says, "The bumpy one made more noise."

Later, the teacher puts into the boxes two pencils that are identical except for length. The pupils now find that correct inferring is harder, so they become more cautious. What observations must they rely on now?

In the middle and upper grades children can do an excellent job of inferring the identity or interactions of hidden objects from indirect observational clues. In science this way of inferring is called *model building*. (The second of the following four listed investigations is mainly devoted to model building.)

For some examples of *inferring* in which children basically make explanations, see these investigations:

How to Keep Heat in and Out (p. 271)

Hidden Parts of Electric Circuits (p. 357)

Making Casts of Animal Tracks (p. 487)

Why We Have Seasons (p. 666)

Predicting

To *predict* is to forecast a future observation by inferring from data. As with regular inferring, the more data that are available the more confidence we can have in the prediction; the reverse is also true. We can be very confident that spring will follow winter, but not at all confident that spring fashions this year will be exactly like those of a year ago. Without *some* data, we can only guess about future observations; to predict is impossible.

When pupils put their data in graph form, there are usually many chances to predict.

Upper-level children measure and record on a graph the time candles burn under inverted glass jars. After they have recorded the times for a 100-, 200-, and 300-milliliter jar, the teacher says:

> *How long do you think the candle will burn under a 250-milliliter jar?*

Notice that predicting the time for a 250-milliliter jar would require pupils to read the graph *within* the present data—they have the times for a 200- and a 300-milliliter jar. This is called *interpolating*. If the teacher asked pupils to predict the candle-burning time of a 400-milliliter jar, the children would need to go *beyond* the present data. This is called *extrapolating* from data. Even though a straight-line graph won't result in this case, using these

data to predict is likelier to be more accurate than guessing.

Going much beyond observed data when extrapolating can be misleading. If you are measuring how far a spring or rubber band stretches each time you add a uniform weight, eventually you'll reach its elastic limit. Whatever reading you get beyond that point will be out-of-line with previous results. Likewise, a marathon runner who cuts his finishing time in half in the first year of training can't realistically expect to keep doing so year after year.

Children often need assistance when predicting. Simple diagrams can help them to reason through data. Also, if they cannot calculate precise predictions, just asking them to predict the direction of change is useful. Primary-level pupils might be asked, Will *more* or *less* water evaporate when the wind blows? Middle-level children might be asked, Will a *higher, lower,* or the *same* temperature result when these two water samples of different temperatures are mixed? You can see next in detail how all of these techniques can be applied.

For some examples of *predicting* applied in investigations, see:

The Mixing of Hot and Cold Water (p. 260)

Inclined Planes (p. 389)

Wheel-Belt Systems (p. 404)

Evaporation (p. 635)

EXPERIMENTING

To a child, experimenting means "doing something to see what happens." While this is overly simple, it does capture the difference between experimenting and the other six science processes. In experimenting, we *change* objects or events to learn how nature changes them. Objects and events are usually left unchanged when we use the other process skills. This section is about how children can discover the various conditions of change. You may recall that open-ended investigations, in which pupils explore condition variables, were introduced in the last chapter. Now we'll take up some refinements.

Experimenting is often called an "integrated" process, because it may require us to use some or all of the others: observing, classifying, inferring and predicting, measuring, and communicating. That is one reason some curriculum writers reserve this combined process for upper-grade activities. But experimental investigations, like others, can vary in difficulty. With guidance, even intuitive thinkers can do some limited experiments.

This does not mean any hands-on investigation can properly be called experimenting. Many educators say that two criteria must be met:

1. Children should have an idea they want to test. That is, they should vary the object or event for some reason. The act of forming an idea to test is called *hypothesizing*.

2. Children should vary only one condition at a time. When needed, they should also compare the varied object with a matching object that is left unchanged. This is called *controlling variables*.

How strictly we interpret the two criteria determines how hard it is to do an experiment "properly." To many educators almost any investigation is experimenting *if the child changes an object for a purpose and can compare its changed state to the original one.* This is also the position taken in this book. The stricter view of other educators means that only children near or in the stage of formal operations can properly do experimenting. More on this shortly.

Hypothesizing

How do we get pupils to form ideas they want to test—to hypothesize—before they manipulate objects? Perhaps you realize that a section of the last chapter ("How to Develop Open-Ended Investigations with Questions," page 55) addresses that question. This and the next section will extend the earlier information.

You saw there several ways of getting children to state operations that they wanted to try. For elementary pupils, stating operations as questions—Will dropping a magnet make it weaker? Does adding salt to water make things float higher?—is a clear and easy way for them to state hypotheses. It makes them focus on what they want to do to produce some effect, or on what effect to observe to connect it to a cause.

In adult science, a hypothesis is often stated in an if-then manner: *If* I do this, *then* I believe so and so will happen. Or, stated impersonally: *If* a magnet is dropped, *then* it will get weaker. *If* the acid content of rain increases, *then* more plant species will die. You may want to use the if-then form with older pupils. But for most children, stating a hypothesis as an operational question is easier and more understandable.

As you saw before, letting pupils explore the properties of real objects stimulates them to suggest their own ideas for changing them. Their curiosity usually prompts them to state operations they want to try, or to be receptive to broad and narrow questions you ask for that purpose. Notice how this happens next.

In a primary-level class some children have been making and playing with toy parachutes. They tie the four corners of a handkerchief with strings and attach these to a sewing spool. Some release their parachutes while standing on top of the play slide and watch them fall slowly to the ground. Others simply wad the cloth around the spool and throw their parachutes up into the air.

A few children have made their parachutes from *different* materials. They are quick to notice that some parachutes stay in the air longer than others. After they go back to the classroom, they discuss their experiences. Then, the teacher says:

We have plenty of materials to make more parachutes on the science table. How can you make a parachute that will fall slower than the one you have now?

The children respond in different ways: "Make it bigger," "Smaller," "Use a lighter spool," "Make it like Martha's," and so on. These are the children's hypotheses. Some children say nothing, but peer intently at the materials. They are hypothesizing also—nonverbally. The children's ideas need testing, so what works can be found out. Now the children have purposes for doing further work with parachutes.

Where did the children's hypotheses come from? When the children first observed their parachutes in action, they did much inferring ("Jimmy's parachute is bigger than mine. It stays up longer." "Corinne has a big spool. Her chute falls fast," and so on.) It is natural for people to be curious about the quality of their inferences. *Hypotheses are simply inferences that people want to test.*

Exploring the properties of concrete materials provides the background that most children need to think. They cannot offer broad explanatory hypotheses to test concepts or theories. This calls for the deeper background and concept-seeking mind of the formal operational thinker. This is the reason some "why" questions are hard for children to handle: Why does dew form on the grass? Why does a ship float? Why are there earthquakes? Instead of broad, generalizable hypotheses, concrete thinkers are likely to offer limited hypotheses, best phrased as operational questions, that are tied to the objects they have observed or manipulated.

Intuitive thinkers also do this, as you saw in the foregoing example. But they are far more limited in this ability than concrete thinkers. Their teacher wisely provided more real materials to think about during their discussion instead of relying on talk alone. Even so, many children will need the teacher's personal attention to follow through in a meaningful way. Most intuitive thinkers can only think about one variable at a time. This limits the experimenting they can do, because they are un-

likely to control other variables that might affect the outcome. *So primary-level investigations usually lean more heavily on the other six science processes.*

Controlling Variables

To find out exactly what condition makes a difference in an experiment, we must change or vary that condition alone. Other conditions must not vary. In other words, they must be controlled during the experiment.

Suppose you think that varying the size of a parachute will affect its falling rate. A good way to test the variable would be to build two parachutes that are identical in every way except for size. These could then be released at the same time from the same height. After repeated trials, you could infer if size did make a difference in your test.

But don't expect intuitive thinkers or early concrete thinkers to reason in this way. They will not think of the many variables (conditions) that can influence their experiment. They may unwittingly change several variables at the same time—thickness *and* the length of string, for example. Their intent is simply to make a parachute that will fall slower than another, not to isolate variable conditions. On the other hand, young children will grasp the need to control some variables. Typically, they will insist on releasing their parachutes from the same height and at the same time. Otherwise, "it won't be fair," they will tell you. (Are they applying here schemata constructed from play experiences, such as foot races?)

The parachute experiment is more than just a trial-and-error activity. The children have observed parachutes and have done some inferring about their observations. The changes they try will reflect thinking we can call hypothesizing. And although they may not think of controlling all the possible variables, they are conscious of some. This is the nature of experimenting with children. How well they do and how fast they progress are influenced by how skillful we are in helping them. Here are more examples of teachers helping their pupils to experiment.

In a middle-level class the children have worked with seeds and plants for about two weeks. The teacher says:

> We've done well in getting our plants started. But suppose we didn't want our seeds to sprout and grow. Sometimes in nature seeds get damaged, or conditions are not right for seeds to grow. What could you do to keep seeds from sprouting and growing?

The children begin suggesting operations to try, as shown in Table 4-2. These are their hypotheses; at this point they need not be framed as operational questions. The teacher writes them on the chalkboard, silly or not. The teacher then gets them to screen the hypotheses for those that may have possibilities:

> With which conditions might the seed have some chance to live? Suppose Jimmy squashed his seed just a little. Would the seed sprout? Would the plant look squashed? Would this happen with any kind of a seed? How about some of the rest of these conditions?

This mixture of broad and narrow questions is posed slowly to give the children time to think. The pupils discuss a number of possibilities. After a while, the teacher says:

> How can we test our ideas?

It soon becomes obvious that some children are going to do several things at one time to their seeds, so the teacher says:

> Suppose Beth squashes her seed and also freezes it. How will she know which one stopped the seed from growing?

The children decide to change just one condition at a time. Pairs of pupils quickly form operational questions from hypotheses they want to test: Will squashing a bean seed keep it from sprouting? Will cutting a bean seed in half keep it from sprouting? and so on. Interest is high as experimenting begins.

In an upper-level class the children are working in pairs. They are testing their reaction time by catching dropped rulers. In each pair, one child holds the ruler just above his partner's hand. When he releases the ruler, the partner catches the ruler (the flat part—not the edges) between his thumb and forefinger. The ruler number closest to the top of his pinched fingers is recorded. This is his "reaction time number." After a few minutes of this activity, the teacher asks the pupils to give their reaction times. He writes these on the board as shown in Table 4-3. Table 4-3 is a histogram, a type of graph. It is used to classify data in a way that encourages thinking about the differences in the data.

After a few moments to discuss with the children how the scores are distributed, the teacher says:

> Suppose everything and everyone were the same in our experiment. How would the histogram look? Well, what differences were there that may have given us these results? What conditions might affect reaction time?

The children start forming hypotheses: "Not everybody did it the same way," "Some

TABLE 4-2
Things that may keep a seed from growing.

Squashing it	Cutting it in half
Chewing it	Not watering it
Freezing it	Watering it with salt water
Boiling it	

TABLE 4-3
Reaction time numbers.

1	2	3	4	5	6	7	8	9	10	11	12
				X							
				X							
				X							
			X	X							
				X	X	X	X				
		X		X	X	X	X				
		X		X	X	X	X	X	X		
X		X		X	X	X	X	X	X		X

people have faster reaction times," "Some kids have more practice," "I was tired today," and so on. After a discussion to narrow down and clarify different ideas, the teacher says:

How are you going to test your ideas?

The children state their ideas as operational questions. Will people have the same reaction time if they do the experiment in exactly the same way? Does practice give you a faster reaction time? Do people who feel "tired" (defined as having less than 8 hours of sleep) have slower times than when they don't feel tired? and so on. Everybody agrees that they must do the experiment in the same way each time to control the test variables. Then, each question is tested separately under the controlled conditions.

For some opportunities for *experimenting* in investigations, see:

The Melting of Ice Cubes (p. 255)

A String Telephone (p. 294)

How Salt Water and Other Liquids Affect Plants (p. 442)

How to Train Goldfish (p. 484)

The Need to Consult Authority

It's important to realize that children will seldom be able to consider and control *all* of the relevant variables in an experiment. Nor will they always want to do so. People who still believe in the tooth fairy or who cross their fingers for luck while taking a test are not likely to fully appreciate scientific methods. Failure to control variables, of course, may lead to faulty conclusions. Even research scientists will sometimes err in controlling significant variables. A continual source of argument at science conventions is the quality of experimental design.

So guide pupils to limit their conclusions. Let them verify and extend their findings by checking authority in some form: textbook, encyclopedia, film, and the like. This can be done gracefully, without diminishing children's efforts: Let's see if scientists agree with us. . . . What have scientists found out about . . . ?

If verifying results is necessary, you may say, why even bother with experiments? Our teaching purpose gives an answer. Few elementary school pupils can design and conduct scientifically defensible experiments. Yet they can be taught some investigative methods with good results. Children's experiments are an effective teaching tool to improve their thinking and have them gain some solid knowledge through concrete experiences.

Pros and Cons of Class Data

Consider getting data from the entire class when experimenting and using the other science processes. Individuals or small groups can all work on the same investigation, pooling and cross-checking their data. This gives the pupils more to go on when making inferences. In contrast, the individual experimenter or small group that works alone often must repeat experiments before getting enough data to infer properly about what is being tested. This can take much time. Also, the individual experimenter or small group may keep repeating mistakes, unless you are watchful. Another benefit from the whole class investigation is that a greater variety of ideas will arise for children to mull over when data differences are analyzed.

But we must also be careful with the whole-class approach. Perhaps the most serious problem is that we may think of the children as a class, rather than a collection of individual persons. In designing an experiment, for example, we may get comments here and there from class members. We may then put these comments together ourselves, or lead one child to do so, and then assume everyone knows what is going on. We can be fooled into thinking that what the child can do as a member of a class, he can do independently. This is one reason why many teachers today use individual and small-group experiences besides working with the whole class.

TEXTBOOK EXPERIMENTS

In many elementary schools a children's textbook series makes up the science program. Such books contain many activities for children to work with. Their usual purpose is to illustrate in concrete ways ideas presented in the books. Teachers sometimes call the worst of these activities "cookbook experiments." That is, because the problem, materials, directions, and even conclusions at times are furnished, there is little chance for children to think. All that needs to be done by them is to follow the recipe. Criticism of this kind is waning, because today's books are better than ever before. More authors now use activities that require thinking. And conclusions for activities are now usually tucked safely into the accompanying teacher's manual, rather than right there on a page of the pupils' textbook for all to see.

But authors are restricted by the book format. Working well with children in an experiment typically calls for an interactive process. What we do or say depends much on what the children do or say. If we simply follow the book, there may be little chance for interaction. Yet a good textbook—and there are many—contains much material we can use to begin and move along the interactive process.

In examining a textbook experiment, especially notice the way in which the author leads into the activity and the comments following it. Usually, a question is posed just before the experiment, with extending information following the experiment. This means you can use the author's questions to introduce the experiment and the book's information to extend the children's learning after the experiment is completed. The activity may be done with individuals, small groups, or the whole class. (Ideas about individualizing instruction are dealt with mainly in Chapter 6.)

But start the experiment with the pupils' books closed. The time for reading is after the experiment is finished or at least planned. The book, rather than the children, should serve as the checkup source. "It's fun to find out the book agrees with me," a little girl once said to me. And it's also far more thought-provoking, one might add.

Now consider a contrasting example of two ways to use a text experiment. We begin with an unimaginative method.

Today, we will have a chance to do the experiment on page 161. Let's read the directions carefully so we will know exactly how to set it up.

The pupils follow in their books silently while someone reads orally:

Activity Does planting seeds in different positions change how roots grow?

Materials Ink blotter; wide-mouth glass jar; paper towel; water; bean seeds.

What to Do Place the blotter around the inside of the jar. Wad the towel and stuff it into the jar. This will hold the blotter against the glass. Put seeds in different positions between the blotter and glass. Add an inch of water to the jar to keep the blotter wet, and as needed later to keep about the same water level. Observe for two weeks.

What Did You Find Out? Did all the roots grow downward? Roots grow in this way no matter how seeds are turned. This is because they, like you, are attracted by gravity.

The teacher selects from a thicket of waving hands two volunteers to set up the activity. Daily observations are made to see if the results are like those in the book.

In another class, the same activity comes up. This teacher says:

No need for our books yet, people. We'll be starting with experiments again. Has anyone ever seen some plant roots that were dug up? Which way did the roots seem to grow? What might happen if they didn't grow that way? Well, here's a problem, then. If you plant seeds in different positions, in which direction or directions will the roots grow?

The children respond. The teacher then asks:

How can we test these ideas?

Pupils suggest planting seeds in different positions in soil. Various soil containers are mentioned—paper cups, small milk cartons, quart milk cartons with one side cut out for planting several seeds in a row, and so on. Because the teacher has a box of bean seeds bought at a supermarket, everyone can do the activity. The planning includes procedures to water and then to dig up groups of seeds at staggered times. The teacher says:

It would help to actually see the roots while they are growing. What are some ways this could be done?

Pupils divide into groups to "brainstorm" ideas, but they get nowhere. Seeing this, the teacher places on a table the materials described in the book and says:

Maybe these materials can give you some ideas.

Several suggestions are made by pupils. These are evaluated: How will they tell if the water, rather than gravity, affects the roots? Someone suggests planting a sprouted seed at one end of a cut open quart milk carton placed on its side and watering only the opposite end. Will the roots grow toward the water or straight down, "the way they're supposed to"? Will it work with other seeds? and so on.

Later, the teacher asks the children to compare their findings with those of the scientists, as found in the text. They are pleased with the comparison but find a variable (soil) they forgot to control. Next time, they vow, they will be more careful.

NARROW AND BROAD QUESTIONS FOR SCIENCE PROCESSES

By now, you've seen many examples of teachers asking broad and narrow questions for children to use the science processes. Perhaps you're wondering, Where did the questions come from?

Notice that following this section is a summary of the processes. Each is operationally defined. This means you can see children do the operations listed within each process. Each operation can trigger broad or narrow questions. Let's use "observing" for our example and consider, one by one, each of its three listed operations. Children are observing when they

Identify properties of objects such as color, size, and shape by using any or all of their senses.

A broad question such as, "What do you notice about these objects?" should get this operation from the children. If it does not, you can shift down and ask a narrow question that focuses on a single variable: "What *color* do you see?" or "How *big* are they?" or "What *shape* is it?" and so on. After one or two of these questions, you can shift back to the broad question, "What else do you notice about . . . ?"

State noticeable changes in objects or events.

"What changes do you notice?" can serve here as a broad question. If narrow questions are needed, just focus on a specific change: "How has the *water* changed? How have the polliwogs' *gills* changed?" and so on. Later, "What other changes do you notice?" will serve as a broad question to shift the burden back to your pupils.

State noticeable similarities and differences in objects and events.

"How are they alike? different?" are appropriate broad questions. "How do their *sizes* compare? *shapes* compare? *colors* compare?" are possible narrow questions. "In what other ways are they alike? different?" gets you back again to the broad category.

Knowing how to ask process questions, then, is largely a matter of knowing what operations pupils can do in each process. You'll find a broad question suggested for every listed operation within the processes summary. Narrow questions are not given for the most part because their exact nature depends on the subject matter studied. The best place to see narrow questions used in this book, in combination with broad questions, is in Part II. Consult the summary for operations and turn them into questions, like those suggested, as you work with children. Applying them often in your teaching will enable you to soon learn the operations.

SUMMARY OF THE SCIENCE PROCESSES

The following summary of science processes, with pupil operations you can observe, is the basis for every broad and narrow process question found in Part II. Further operations could be added to each of the listed processes, since they are open-ended. But if your pupils act in any of the ways summarized here, you can be reasonably sure they are doing process thinking.

Observing. Children are observing when they

- Identify properties of objects such as color, size, and shape by using any or all of the senses. (What do you notice about these objects?)

- State noticeable changes in objects or events. (What changes do you notice?)

- State noticeable similarities and differences in objects or events. (How are they alike? Different?)

Classifying. Children are classifying when they

- Group objects or events by their properties or functions. (In what ways could we group these objects?)

- Arrange objects or events in order by some property or value. (How could we put these objects in order?)

Measuring. Children are measuring when they

- Use standard tools such as the meter stick, yardstick, ruler, clock, balance, and protractor to find quantity. (What standard measuring tools could you use to measure this?)

- Use familiar objects as arbitrary units to find quantity. (What everyday things could you use to measure this?)

- Make scale drawings or models. (How could you make a scale drawing or model of this?)

- Use simple sampling and estimating techniques. (How could we get a good sample or estimate of this?)

Communicating. Children are communicating when they

- Define words operationally—through some action—when needed. (What needs to be defined here?)

- Describe objects or events. (How can you describe this . . . so someone else knows what you mean?)

- Make charts and graphs. (How can you make a chart or graph to show your findings?)

- Record data as needed. (How can we keep track of our observations?)

- Construct exhibits and models. (How can we show someone how this works?)

- Draw diagrams, pictures, and maps. (What can we draw to explain what happens? What map can you draw so someone else can find the place?)

Inferring.   Children are inferring when they

- Distinguish between an observation and an inference. (What do you observe, and what does this tell you about . . . ?

- Interpret recorded data. (What findings go together?)

- Interpret data received indirectly. (How can you tell what's inside?)

- Hypothesize from data. (What do you think makes this happen?)

- Draw conclusions from data. (From this information, what have you found out about . . . ?)

- Predict events from data. (What do you think will happen?)

Experimenting.   Children are experimenting when they

- State a hypothesis or operational question to test. (What do you think makes this happen? or, Will fanning the water make it evaporate faster? Remember that an operational question—the second question here—is typically narrow and describes an observable action.)

- Design a procedure in which variables are controlled. (How can we find out?)

Remember that many teachers will accept a less rigorous definition for experimenting: A child changes an object for some purpose and compares the changed condition to the original one.

When shown a list like the foregoing, one teacher said, "How on earth am I going to remember *and* get my kids to do all of those processes?" The reaction is common and understandable, but the job is easier than it first appears. For one thing, the science curriculum carries the main load in developing process thinking, as it usually does in developing concepts. Also, the list sums up in one place most of the processes that might be present in a modern science program. Probably only a few advanced pupils could demonstrate all of them well.

While the listed processes are typical of those in modern programs, they may not be identical. How people think can be organized in many ways. The important thing is for you to find the science processes meaningful. If so, you should have little trouble with teaching processes in any modern curriculum. You should be able to shift from one program to another, as school needs may require.

The teacher who understands and appreciates science processes has far more capacity to help children think than one who does not, even when both use the same curriculum guide. Following a curriculum guide can take us only so far. Teaching for process is often done best through the flexible, immediate tactics used in "teachable moments." *These times come up continually if children are allowed to think for themselves.*

An acronym (COMIC-E) can help you remember the science processes during these and other times:

Classifying

Observing

Measuring

Inferring and predicting

Communicating

Experimenting

A mental picture can also jog your memory. Figure 4-1 may help you to remember two things: the acronym itself and that experimenting is supported and complemented by the other processes.

Another way to remember the processes is through practice in recognizing them. All of the investigations in Part II of this book have marginal notes that identify the science processes used. You might cover the notes with a narrow slip of paper as you read questions in an investigation. Try to identify the process used in each case and then move the paper down to reveal the note. See if we agree. You can get some idea of how much practice you need by doing the following exercises.

FIGURE 4-1

Experimenting (E) is supported and complemented by classifying, observing, measuring, inferring and predicting, and communicating (COMIC).

EXERCISES
4-1 to 4-5

How Well Do You Know the Science Processes?

Try the following exercises. They are designed to help you practice what you may have learned so far in this chapter. You'll need paper and pencil. Compare your ideas with the comments that appear after each exercise. Also, refer to the summary of processes on page 90 as needed.

4-1 You can ask questions to start children thinking about any of the processes. Notice the accompanying list of processes and seven clusters of questions. Each question cluster goes with one of the processes, but the clusters are now out of order. Are you able to match each question cluster with the proper process?

Process	Question Clusters
[a] Observing	[1] Which soap did the better job? What did you find out? What story do the smaller footprints tell?
[b] Classifying	[2] How could you find out? In what ways could you test your idea? What could you do to be more sure the wind is responsible?
[c] Measuring	[3] How could you put these objects together? In what groups do they belong? How could these things be put into some order?
[d] Communicating	[4] What do you notice? How are these objects alike? Different? How does this compare to how it was before?
[e] Inferring	[5] How heavy (light, fast, slow, tall, etc.) is it? What could you use instead of a meter stick? How can you estimate how many peas are in the jar?
[f] Predicting	[6] What do you mean by "blond" hair? How can you show your findings on a chart? How could you keep a record of your plant work?
[g] Experimenting	[7] Where do you expect the most erosion to take place? If we do this, should the mixture get cooler or warmer? What do you think will happen, judging from your graph?

Comments

Process (a) goes with question cluster (4), (b) with (3), (c) with (5), (d) with (6), (e) with (1), (f) with (7), and (g) with (2). If some questions seem misplaced, please review the summary of science processes.

4-2   The teacher's guide for a program may not identify the processes to be taught in different lessons. If you do not have time to teach everything (a usual problem), you need to choose your lessons carefully. Of course, you can choose more wisely if you are aware of what processes are developed in suggested lessons. Following are some passages from a teacher's guide. Are you able to tell what process needs to be used in each quoted passage? A sample answer is given for the first passage to help you start.

Activity	Process Used
[a] Have the children use the line or bar graphs to roughly tell how high the plants might be on the weekend.	Predicting
[b] Because at least a week may be needed for definite findings, help the children write and attach to their experiments the purpose of each.	

Activity	Process Used
[c] Encourage pupils to think of ways to test the effect of temperature on the bean plants.	_____
[d] Invite them to inspect the plant parts carefully and point out similarities and differences.	_____
[e] Have the children line up the sprouted plants according to size, if possible at this time.	_____
[f] Leave the materials on the table. The children may be able to invent several ways to tell how much larger the leaves have grown.	_____
[g] Let the children check their findings. What makes it seem likely that the light was responsible?	_____
[h] This would be a good time to ask the pupils: How could the materials be used to find out if plants grow toward the light?	_____
[i] The seeds could be divided according to how they travel—water, air, by land animals, and so on.	_____
[j] Suggest that each child make a map for his partner that shows where he found the weed. Will his partner be able to find the weed in that place?	_____

Comments

The process needed in activity (b) is communicating; in (c) experimenting; in (d) observing; in (e) classifying; in (f) measuring; in (g) inferring; in (h) experimenting; in (i) classifying; and in (j) communicating. If some process labels seem misplaced, please review appropriate sections in this chapter, as well as the summary of the processes on page 90. Remember, you will also find it helpful to examine the investigations in Part II of this book. The processes used in each are identified in the margins.

4-3   Operational definitions are often needed when language is unclear. If you define a word by what someone or something does—an observable operation—it usually becomes clear. Please <u>underline</u> the word(s) in each sentence that most needs to be operationally defined. Then complete the second sentence to include the operational definition. An example:

You will need a <u>powerful</u> hand lens to see the insect's eyes. By <u>powerful</u> I mean <u>a lens that magnifies three or more times normal size.</u>

1. What is the least distance it takes you to stop when riding a fast-moving bicycle?
   By _____ I mean _____ .
2. Will this detergent get clothes clean?
   By _____ I mean _____ .
3. Add water until the sponge is saturated.
   By _____ I mean _____ .
4. From these, pick out only the truly hard rocks.
   By _____ I mean _____ .
5. Becky is 10 years old, weighs 70 pounds, and has long hair.
   By _____ I mean _____ .
6. Remove the leaf from the pot soon after the water boils.
   By _____ I mean _____ .

Comments

Acceptable answers will be generally like the following:

1. By <u>fast moving</u> I mean <u>more than 10 miles per hour.</u>
2. By <u>clean</u> I mean <u>remove coffee stains from a white cloth napkin, so I cannot see them, after a normal wash cycle in my washing machine.</u>
3. By <u>saturated</u> I mean <u>cannot hold any more water without dripping.</u>
4. By <u>truly hard</u> I mean <u>cannot be scratched by an iron nail.</u>
5. By <u>long hair</u> I mean <u>grown below shoulder length.</u>
6. By <u>soon after</u> I mean <u>before 10 seconds have passed on our classroom clock.</u>

4-4   The purpose of a broad question is to open up a discussion to a variety of responses. But you may get only a yes/no or other limited response if you unintentionally state the question in a narrow form. An example:

What differences can you find? should draw many answers.

Can you find differences? might draw only a yes or no answer.

Sometimes children will sense that you want multiple responses even when a broad question is narrowly stated. When they do not, a follow-up question must be asked. You can learn to avoid this inefficient method with a little practice on how to state broad questions.

How can the following questions with yes/no or limited answers be changed to broad questions with multiple answers?

1. Are the two objects alike?
2. Is there anything you notice about this?
3. Can you think of how this might happen?

4. Do you remember anything else from the chart?

5. Are there other ways to do it?

6. Has it changed? (Assuming observable changes have occurred.)

7. Can you put these objects in order?

8. Do you think something else could make a change here?

Comments

Acceptable answers will generally be like the following:

1. How are the two objects alike? (Or, In what ways . . .)

2. What do you notice about this?

3. How do you think this might happen?

4. What else do you remember from the chart?

5. In what other ways can you do it?

6. How has it changed? (Or, In what ways . . .)

7. How can you put these objects in order? (Or, In what ways . . .)

8. What else do you think could make a change here?

4-5 In investigations, broad and narrow process questions are best used in combination. Narrow questions typically build background in pupils, which allows them to respond successfully to the broad questions. Examine the investigations in Part II of the text whose discovery problems are on pages 295, 350, 405, 437, 576, and 636. Read each discovery problem. Notice where broad questions are used to open up possibilities for exploring many variables. Find where narrow questions are used to focus on single variables. *Please consider all the questions and information that may be contained within each discovery problem, then decide whether the overall problem is broad or narrow in its intent.*

You may find this a convenient way to record your decisions:

p. 000	N	B
A	____	____
B	____	____
C	____	____
D	____	____

Comments

Page 295: A is narrow; B, C, D broad.

Page 350: A is broad; B calls for narrow, either-or-responses; C, D are broad.

Page 405: A is narrow because it refers to the limited choices in the figure. B, C are broad because several possibilities exist.

Page 437: A, B, C, D are narrow because each considers only one variable. (However, A can lead to plantings of many different-sized pieces.) E is broad.

Page 576: A is broad; B, C, D, E are narrow because each considers only one variable; F is broad because it attempts to apply learnings to many variable examples.

Page 636 A, C, D, E are narrow because each suggests limited or single variables to try. B, F, G are broad.

Teaching for process development is serious business. The science processes are vital in learning new concepts, how to attack new problems, and how to construct new knowledge—in learning how to learn, we might say. No wonder all the modern programs include experiences to promote children's thinking.

SCIENTIFIC ATTITUDES

"I can't talk to him. He's closed minded." How often have you heard this said about someone who is unwilling to consider or accept new ideas? This attitude can be annoying when shown by a friend. But it would be a colossal setback to science if scientists were to feel that way.

The processes of science work best when the adults or children who use them are disposed to act in harmony with the processes. Since dispositions are rooted in feelings, they are called attitudes. What favorable attitudes should we look for and encourage as we teach science? The developers of one widely respected program, the Science Curriculum Improvement Study, say this[2]

We have identified four major attitude areas that are part of scientific literacy. The four areas are (a) curiosity, (b) inventiveness, (c) critical thinking, and (d) persistence. Here are definitions and examples of various kinds of behaviors associated with the four areas.

(a) Curiosity. Children who pay particular attention to an object or event and spontaneously wish to learn more about it are being curious. They may give evidence of curiosity by

■ Using several senses to explore organisms and materials.

■ Asking questions about objects and events.

■ Showing interest in the outcomes of experiments.

(b) Inventiveness. Children who generate new ideas are being inventive. These children exhibit original thinking in their interpretations. They may give evidence of inventiveness through verbal statements or actions by

■ Using equipment in unusual and constructive ways.

■ Suggesting new experiments.

■ Describing novel conclusions from their observations.

(c) Critical Thinking. Children who base suggestions and conclusions on evidence are thinking critically. They may exhibit critical thinking largely through verbal statements by

■ Using evidence to justify their conclusions.

■ Pointing out contradictions in reports by their classmates.

■ Changing their ideas in response to evidence.

[2]Reprinted with permission from *Organisms Evaluation Supplement,* written and published by the Science Curriculum Improvement Study. Copyright © 1972 by The Regents of the University of California.

(d) Persistence. Children who maintain an active interest in a problem or event for a longer period than their classmates are being persistent. They are not easily distracted from their activity. They may give evidence of persistence by

- Continuing to investigate materials after their novelty has worn off.
- Repeating an experiment in spite of apparent failure.
- Completing an activity even though their classmates have finished earlier.

Can you imagine the state of science research if scientists did not continually show curiosity, inventiveness, critical thinking, and persistence?

We are dealing here, though, with the teaching of children. Maybe your reaction to the foregoing list of attitude behaviors is like that of a beginning teacher who said, "It's good to know some attitudes to work toward. But *recognizing* positive attitudes isn't my problem. How to *develop* these attitudes is."

What do you do to develop positive attitudes within the four areas as you teach science?

I've often put this question to teachers who do a good job with attitudes. Their responses vary widely, of course, but an interesting thing happens when you boil down their answers. Most use at least one common approach within each of the four areas. Each of these four approaches seems essential. Let's see what they are.

Curiosity

"To be a child is to touch, smell, taste, and hear everything you can between the time you get up and when your parents make you go to bed. I don't have to *teach* curiosity. It's there already."

The kindergarten teacher who said that echoes many of her elementary school colleagues. Yet in some classes it's possible to see girls and boys who lack interest in science. What kills this natural disposition in children?

For an eye-opening answer, walk into two adjoining classrooms, one with a hands-on science program and another where pupils just read and do worksheets during science time. Handing concrete materials to children is like giving catnip to a kitten, rowing downstream, cycling with the wind at your back. Making children sit still and be quiet for long periods is like caging an eagle, rowing upstream, riding into the wind. You can do the latter things, but they are best avoided. Children will lose a lot of their curiosity—at least in school—unless they are allowed to do what comes naturally.

How much time should you give to hands-on experiences? About 40 to 50 percent of the science period seems right to many teachers. This leaves enough time for discussions, explanations, and getting things organized. The exact percentage will vary with the subject.

Teachers who maintain or spark pupils' curiosity also do other things. Most apply science learnings to everyday life as often as possible. Most use textbook experiments, but they often start them with the book closed. Children read the book later to compare their ideas and findings with those in the book. These teachers also use at least several open-ended investigations during a teaching unit—which brings us to the next attitude area.

Inventiveness

To be inventive is to solve problems in creative or novel ways. This contrasts with simply taking a known solution and applying it to a problem at hand: It's good to apply what you know about a car jack to change a flat tire, but what do you do when there's no jack? Inventive people may apply their knowledge to solve problems much as other persons do. But they are more likely to show *fluency, flexibility,* and *originality* in their thinking.[3]

Fluency refers to the number of ideas a child gives when challenged with a problem.

---

[3]John A. Glover and Roger H. Bruning. *Educational Psychology* (Boston: Little, Brown, 1987), pp. 261–64.

We can promote fluency by asking open-ended questions such as

> *In what ways can you prevent this nail from rusting?*
>
> *What objects can be charged with static electricity?*
>
> *What conditions might make orange juice lose its vitamin C?*

Creative persons produce a *larger number* of hypotheses (or operational questions) in such cases. It's helpful for all children to consider a number of possibilities before they try to solve a problem.

Flexibility is the inclination to shift one's focus from the usual—to get out of a rut. Suppose children respond to the rust question with

> *Paint it with silver paint.*
>
> *Paint it with red paint.*
>
> *Paint it with green paint.*

And so on, in that vein.

Primary-level children, in particular, are prone to this. To promote flexibility, you can simply ask, In *what other ways* besides painting the nail can you prevent it from rusting?

Chances abound for flexible thinking when there is a need to improvise or substitute different materials. Questions such as

> *What can we use in place of . . . ?*
>
> *What else can we find to do this . . . ?*
>
> *How could you use _____ to . . . ?*

will prompt children to think of substitutions. To be flexible when substituting one object for another pupils should think more about the present *properties* of the objects, rather than their present *functions*. That's exactly what children do when they convert drinking straws into peashooters.

Originality is shown when pupils generate ideas that are new to them. We can promote it by encouraging them to use their imagination, to combine others' ideas in new ways (most inventors do this), and by withholding evaluative comments until all ideas are in. Pupils need a psychologically safe environment to be original.

Children who are challenged to demonstrate fluency and flexibility will often—but not always—be original. So encourage them, when needed, to give their own ideas as well.

Precisely how creative persons get to be that way is still debatable.[4] Regardless, children can profit much if you expose them to a wide variety of possibilities in problem solving. You probably realize by now that most of the material in Chapter 3 on open-ended activities can do just that. Experiences like these are a sure-fire way to involve your pupils in creative problem solving. The teachers I know who do the most with inventiveness are convinced of this.

Critical Thinking

Ask two people to define "critical thinking" and you're likely to get divergent and uncomfortable replies. Few terms beg more for clarification.

To think critically is to evaluate or judge whether something is adequate, correct, useful, or desirable. A judge does this when she decides if there is adequate evidence of guilt. An editor does this when he determines the correctness of a writer's grammar. Exasperated parents do this at the dinner table when they yell, "Mind your manners!" at Junior or Sis. In each of these cases someone has a *standard* in mind against which a judgment is made. This, then, is a key to critical thinking: Know the accepted standard of behavior and decide whether or to what degree it is being met.

A problem we face as teachers of elementary-age children is that there are nu-

---

[4]Robert Weisberg, *Creativity: Genius and Other Myths* (New York: W. H. Freeman, 1986), pp. 51–69; and Ellen D. Gagné, *The Cognitive Psychology of School Learning* (Boston: Little, Brown, 1985), p. 144.

merous standards of behavior in science. And many are highly sophisticated. Let's see if we can reduce them to a manageable few and restate them on a level that makes sense to young minds.

There are three overall standards for critical thinking in science that most children can gradually understand and learn to make decisions about: *open-mindedness, objectivity, and willingness to suspend judgment until enough facts are known.*

The open-minded person listens to others and is willing to change his or her mind if warranted. An objective person tries to be free of bias, considers both sides in arguments, and realizes that strong personal preferences may interfere with the proper collecting and processing of data. Someone who suspends judgment understands that additional data may confirm or deny what first appears. So looking for further data improves chances for drawing proper conclusions. Children can learn to judge when they themselves, as well as others, do and do not demonstrate the three standards of behaviors.

It's easy to set up such situations. Just have several groups work on the same activity, then report and compare findings. When data from several sources are being considered, it soon becomes obvious when people refuse to listen to others, push their own ideas, and jump to conclusions before all groups have their say.

Frequently, it is also possible in such discussions for you to detect correlation without causation, anthropomorphism, and the need for operational definitions. Once in a while you may even have need to apply the principle of parsimony. This is most likely when older or gifted children give their theories about how something works but cannot directly observe the action.

Critical and creative thinking go hand in hand. It's artificial to keep them separate. When problem solving or experimenting, for example, children should be encouraged to generate a number of possibilities (fluency), rather than just consider the first idea suggested. You also want them to critically appraise all the ideas at one time so that they can immediately tackle what looks most promising. Controlling variables in experimenting gives pupils another chance to generate many suggestions. But they must also think: Will these controls do the job? Later, if groups come up with different findings, critical thinking is again needed to answer why. Perhaps one or more variables were not controlled after all. You can see that creative and critical thinking are different sides of the same coin.

When pupils seek information, there are really *only two sources* available to them: they themselves—in the form of personal observations and experiments; and authority—in the form of printed matter, audiovisual materials, and knowledgeable persons.

Don't be discouraged if it seems hard for children to appraise the merits of authority used in schools. There are several reasons for this.

Perhaps an obvious reason is that elementary-school children just do not know enough yet. Also, they have less logical ability than they will have later. Another reason is that materials used in the schools are likely to be reasonably accurate and reliable. After all, instructional materials must usually run the gamut of editorial supervision, numerous selection committees of educators, and other sources of appraisal. What survives is likely to be quite acceptable. If not, it is hardly likely that children will have the skill and knowledge to detect error or otherwise evaluate critically.

Certainly, children can be cautioned to check copyright dates and agreement with what is known, to consult more than one source, to note the occasional conflict in fact, and the like. But the possibilities for critical appraisal of authority are relatively few, largely because of children's lack of background, limited logical capacity, and few appropriate materials. Therefore, we typically spend little time on critical analysis of materials. Instead, we help children learn the sources of authority that exist, ways to consult these sources efficiently, and to understand what the sources say.

There are many more chances to teach critical thinking in the experiments and observations that children themselves make during science study. These activities are close to the raw, unadulterated facts—information minus the "editorial filter" already supplied when the usual school resources are consulted. Pupils must provide their own intellectual filter, with our guidance when needed, if the data are to be trustworthy.

Persistence

Most elementary science activities can be completed within a short time. But some require a sustained and vigorous effort. This can be a problem when you are dealing with children.

To do our best work—the product we look to with pride, the memory of achievement that motivates us to try even harder on future occasions—often takes persistence. You and I know this, but children lack the background of experience that continually impels adults to stick with a worthwhile goal.

Primary-level pupils, especially, want instant results. Their short attention span and need for physical activity can easily convert into impatience. Some older children are not much better. How do many experienced teachers combat this natural inclination of children? They arouse or use children's *interests*.

What we've considered already, hands-on, open-ended investigations, are powerful vehicles you can use. They allow you to offer pupils a broad array of choices to investigate and the freedom to choose. They also can bring up the need for pupils to commit to specific operations or observations as part of a group effort. Learning centers and personal

projects, which we'll take up in Chapter 6, give other ways to spark and lock onto interests.

When things don't go as desired in long-range activities, pupils may become discouraged and give up. This is the time to help them figure out why and to explain the scientist's positive approach to failure. Then they, too, may view such results as bringing them closer to their goals.

Early learning of attitudes begins with imitation and later comes from experiencing the consequences of having or not having the attitudes. This means that your pupils will probably look to you as a model as they begin to learn scientific attitudes. And they may learn even more from the experiences you provide.

People continually furnish models for our behavior. The more we like and respect them, the more likely we are to model our behavior after theirs. The open-minded, accepting, nonthreatening teacher who reflects positive attitudes is more likely to influence pupils in positive ways than one who lacks these qualities.

But even more important, in a science program where children use science processes, attitudes can develop as they do with scientists. You simply help pupils compare the consequences of having or not having scientific attitudes. The activities—especially those that are open-ended—bring out the consequences at every turn. Success is very much bound up with curiosity, inventiveness, critical thinking, and persistence. So children learn, in a more limited way, the same habits of mind as scientists and other reflective people. Their self-esteem grows as they continue to successfully practice these attitudes.

Such practice is best continued throughout all subjects of the curriculum. Attitudes are the broadest of all learnings, and they are mostly well learned over the long haul. They can be valuable whenever we tackle a problem or make a decision. Educated people use them in every subject, and so can your pupils. The advantage of introducing such attitudes through *science* comes from the many consequences that pupils can literally see for themselves. Just remember,

- For curiosity—use hands-on experiences.
- For inventiveness—use open-ended investigations.
- For critical thinking—use standards.
- For persistence—use interests.

And, best of all, use them in combination as often as you can.

SUMMARY

Science processes are tools that enable children to gather and think about data for themselves. They include observing, classifying, inferring and predicting, measuring, communicating, and experimenting. To teach the processes, we have pupils investigate a variety of subject-matter contexts with concrete materials and guide their thinking with broad and narrow questions pointed to each process.

In *observing*, pupils learn to use all of their senses, note similarities and differences in objects, and be aware of change.

In *classifying*, pupils group things by properties or functions; they may also arrange them in order of value.

Measuring teaches them to use nonstandard and standard units to find or estimate quantity. Measurement is often applied in combination with skills introduced in the mathematics program.

Communicating teaches pupils to put observed information into some clear form that another person can understand.

In *inferring*, children interpret or explain what they observe. When pupils infer from data that something will happen, usually the term *predicting* is used. When people state an

inference they want to test, usually the term *hypothesizing* is used. So predicting and hypothesizing are special forms of inferring.

In *experimenting*, we often guide pupils to state their hypotheses as operational (testable) questions and help them to control variables within their understanding.

The processes of science work best when the persons who use them have attitudes that harmonize with the processes. Four major attitude areas that are part of science literacy are curiosity, inventiveness, critical thinking, and persistence. Teachers can effectively promote curiosity through hands-on experiences, inventiveness through open-ended investigations, critical thinking through use of accepted standards, and persistence through pupil interests.

SUGGESTED READINGS

Beyer, Barry K. *Practical Strategies for the Teaching of Thinking.* Boston: Allyn and Bacon, 1987. (Comprehensive array of methods to teach thinking skills in most school subjects.)

Funk, H. James, et al. *Learning Science Process Skills.* Dubuque, Iowa: Kendall/Hunt, 1985. (Sixteen skills are developed step by step in a workbook format.)

Kyle, Jr., William C., et al. "What Research Says About Hands-on Science." *Science and Children,* April, 1988, 39–40, 52. (Science attitudes of Texas schoolchildren improved far more in a hands-on program than in a book-centered science program.)

Ostlund, Karen L. *Science Process Skills.* Menlo Park, CA: Addison-Wesley, 1992. (Ways to assess each of the science processes, with material lists and reproducible worksheets.)

Ross, John A. "Learning to Control Variables." *Journal of Research in Science Teaching* 27 (6): 523–39 (September, 1990). (Two methods to improve the ability of upper-grade pupils to control variables in experiments.)

Weisberg, Robert W. *Creativity: Genius and Other Myths.* New York: W. H. Freeman, 1986. (Separates research from popular but shaky education folklore on creative problem solving. An absorbing eye-opener.)

5

How to Use Different Resources to Teach Science

The kind of science program you have in your classroom will much depend on what materials you have to teach with. Some school districts or schools furnish total packaged programs. These may include detailed lessons and the equipment and materials needed for each lesson. (Several such programs are described in Chapter 7.) However, in other situations a set of texts is the program and few, if any, materials are purchased to go with the text.

Will this be a big problem for you? Not likely. Most school districts have a variety of resources teachers can draw from to teach science, even though the resources may not be specifically tied to the science text or other programs adopted in the district. This chapter should help you learn many sources of materials commonly available and ways to use them.

GETTING EQUIPMENT AND SUPPLIES

Despite inadequate funds for science supplies, some teachers seem to have no trouble getting many materials to teach science. Often they achieve this happy condition just by turning loose sixty or more volunteers eager to help—pupils and their parents. They then supplement these materials with a few others from commercial sources. Let's see how these methods can help you to get supplies.

Children and Parents As Resources

Most of the materials used in elementary science programs are simple and easy to get—the kind found around the home, school, in local stores, or other convenient places. Pupils themselves often can get what is needed for hands-on learning experiences. It's a good idea to let them do so.

When everyday materials are brought to school and used by children, they can continue the experience at home if necessary. That is common with open-ended investigations. Also, pupils are likely to have a hand in planning the experience. This usually makes its purpose clear and develops in them a commitment to follow through. And by having more materials, more children can participate.

Of course, not all pupils are equally resourceful or reliable. Many primary-level children (and older ones, too) quickly forget what they so eagerly volunteered to bring the day before. So give them notes, remind them of what they will bring the next day, and let several children volunteer for the same item. It is also good for public relations to let parents know that nothing is *required*, to counter the children who may say to them, "We *have* to bring . . ."

The best materials to request are reusable or no-cost items: foam cups, empty shoe boxes, old string, wire hangers, small boxes of soil, and so on. Children should clearly understand that permission of parents is required before any items are brought to school.

Parents can be especially helpful in acquiring materials if you contact them directly. One of the best times to request their help is at the beginning of the year during Parents' Night or some other introductory meeting. Consider passing out a photocopied list of inexpensive or no-cost items needed for the year.

How to get such a list? It is probably already prepared by the publisher of your science program. If so, just duplicate it. Check the teacher's edition of your grade-level guide. Many publishers make two lists of things needed for each chapter or instructional unit: materials supplied by the publisher in kit form, and a list of low-cost or discardable materials usually found around the home and school. Parents are concerned about the quality of education for their children. Most respond well to specific and reasonable requests for commonly found materials. In economically disadvantaged neighborhoods, parents may be able to donate only a few throwaway items. Look for federal and state supplemental funds in these cases.

Parents' Night is also a good time to ask for qualified parent (and grandparent) volunteers who might give special help in one or more instructional units. Be specific. You might want someone to help set up a photo-developing center or a classroom garden; to give an eyewitness account of an earthquake or some other natural phenomenon; or to share information about a science-related occupation, such as laboratory technician, airplane pilot, electrician, meteorologist, and so on.

Commercial Sources

It would be hard for us to rely on children or parents for everything needed in a science program. Commercial sources need to be used: science supply houses, hardware stores, drugstores, and department stores, for example. Many school principals keep a petty cash fund for small purchases or will do so if you ask. The more expensive items can be bought through a science supply house.

Science supply houses provide catalogs that describe available materials and how to order them. A usual practice among several school districts is to circulate periodically to teachers and administrators an equipment and supply list that is at least partly based on the items found in supply house catalogs. After items on the list are checked, the district representative then orders for everyone at one time. All benefit from the usual price discount that accompanies large orders.

Some general supply companies have developed special elementary school catalogs. These make it easier to select materials suit-

able for children from the innumerable items intended for research or education at more advanced levels.

You can find information about general equipment and materials for elementary science in Appendix C.

Science Kits

What kind of science kit should you have if given a choice? Some elementary schools provide self-contained science kits. These consist of a durable box or chest with a teacher's manual and a wide array of materials stored inside. The science kit provides for many activities without most of the storage and distribution problems that accompany the ordering of individual supplies.

The gain in convenience, though, is offset by several disadvantages. The kit is likely to be more expensive than items gathered separately. Also, there is the natural tendency to want to use fully what has been bought. The materials tend to dictate the program, rather than the other way around. Finally, the program is likely to consist more of demonstrations, with materials for only one person, than inquiry experiences.

Many publishers have also developed kits, sometimes called "science labs." These contain equipment and supplies to accompany their science text series or other program. Some labs contain basic materials for all the activities at a given grade level. Others may provide materials for a specific unit of instruction or module (Figure 5-1). Publishers' kits hold several advantages over the general variety. They contain multiple items for hands-on experiences, and so they allow most of your pupils to participate individually or in small groups. Another advantage of the publisher's kit is that it is correlated with a curriculum. You can more easily extend and enrich the concepts taken up because the materials and program go hand in hand.

FIGURE 5-1
This science lab contains materials for a specific module.

Some teachers also make *shoe box kits* to hold materials. These usually complement, rather than take the place of, the publisher's kit. Each shoe box contains one or more sets of materials for a single activity or lesson. Materials inside are listed on the box for quick reference. A collection of shoe box kits is a handy way to package materials for whole-class instruction, learning centers, and individual or group projects.

READING MATERIALS

If you believe that children need to explore many materials firsthand to learn science, you have plenty of company. Most educators do. But some topics and questions that come up in science programs are hard or impossible to handle that way:

What makes a volcano erupt?

Where do comets come from?

How do scientists know about the dinosaurs?

Also, it takes far too much time to sample firsthand all the things pupils need to know. So educators see a need to teach some science through indirect sources, including books and other printed materials. At the same time, they want pupils to apply their reading skills to continually become better all-around readers.

Let's look at some reading materials you are likely to find in your classroom and see how to work with them. Science education offers four main sources for reading:

- Textbooks
- Trade books
- Reference materials
- Language experience charts

Textbooks

In many schools, a coordinated series of textbooks is the science program. Table 5-1 details some of the differences that exist between these science books and reading books through which children learn to read.

Observe how the properties of science textbooks all point to reading as a thinking process. When reading a reader, the child who does not recognize certain words can usually proceed with understanding after decoding and pronouncing them. But with the science textbook, the real problem with many words may be not knowing their meaning *after* they have been recognized. You can see how this is with the following example:[1]

> The batsmen were merciless against the bowlers. The bowlers placed their men in slips and covers. But to no avail. The batsmen hit one four after another with an occasional six. Not once did a ball look like it would hit their stumps or be caught.

Did you find the meaning of this paragraph hazy at best? If so, you have probably never experienced the British sport of cricket. But note that the lack of meaning does not come from the strangeness of the words. Nearly all are simple and quite recognizable when considered in isolation. Instead, the problem comes from *the unfamiliarity of the context.* Recalling the section in Chapter 2 on information processing, it can be said that you lack a suitable schema to which you can refer.

This is one reason you cannot depend on reading formulas when you check the difficulty level of a science or social studies textbook. Most formulas have you count the lengths of words and sentences, and some-times the number of words that appear on familiar-word lists. While of some help, these measures do not go far enough.

A more valid estimate of readability in the content areas raises questions that require judgments about things a reading formula might miss:

- How abstract are the ideas for intuitive-level or concrete-level pupils?
- How heavy is the load of abstractions presented?
- How familiar to children are the contexts in which the ideas are presented?
- How clear is the syntax—the ways in which the words are put together?

Probably the best way to estimate clarity is to give a *Cloze* (derived from "closure") test. Here, children typically read a typed 250-word passage from the beginning of a chapter. Every fifth word is deleted—every tenth word for a smaller primary-level passage—and its space left blank. Pupils write a word in each blank that makes the most sense to them as they read the passage. A score above 55 percent correct usually indicates that the reading material is at an instructable level.

Vocabulary and Meaning.   Take care not to rush into reading activities. The ability to understand words relates directly to our experiences. When children explore problems and the environment before they read, they begin to acquire percepts, ideas, and a vocabulary. All are needed to understand the printed material. In other words, when needed, we should provide concrete experiences first, then the words to label them. This practice is especially helpful for slow readers and pupils with limited English-speaking ability.

The difficulty of words can fool you. Consider this question, for instance. Which is harder for a child to read: "tyrannosaurus rex" or "energy?" If you chose the first item, by "read" perhaps you mean being able to

---

[1]Robert J. Tierney and P. David Pearson. "Learning to Learn from Text: A Framework for Improving Practice." In *Reading in the Content Areas,* edited by Ernest K. Dishner, et al. Dubuque, Iowa: Kendall/Hunt, 1981, p. 56.

TABLE 5-1
Differences between reading books and science texts.

Reading Books	Science Textbooks
Purpose—learn to read	Purpose—read to learn
Stories in narrative form	Information in expository form
Mostly common words	Many technical words
Everyday references	More remote references
Simpler concepts	More complex concepts
Graphic aids simple	Graphics more complex
Readability at grade level or lower	Readability harder than it seems

decode and pronounce words. A choice of the second word may mean that to read is to comprehend. You can easily supply the first term to a child, and he may never forget it. What child wouldn't like to go around the neighborhood babbling "tyrannosaurus rex?" It is much more impressive than "king of the dinosaurs" or "terrible lizard." On the other hand, "energy" is an elusive, difficult concept that builds slowly in the child's mind only after many firsthand experiences. To read in the full sense of the term, of course, a child needs to decode *and* comprehend. Still, it is important to understand the distinction.

It is easy to equate glibness with understanding. Pupils who rattle off big words and memorized definitions may be only hazily aware of what they are reading or talking about. Ironically, pupils who "read" less well may have minds that are well stocked with intuitive concepts. They may simply lack verbal labels to pin to what they already understand.

Remember that the names of objects are much easier to learn than concepts. Identify the *Celsius thermometer* in your classroom by its proper name right away and children will quickly do the same. But they may need a sequence of planned experiences to truly understand the differences between the concepts of *temperature* and *heat*.

You'll generally run into three kinds of vocabulary problems when children see a key word in print that they do not recognize. (1) The word is not recognized, but it is in the children's oral vocabulary and is understandable. (2) The word is not in the children's sight or oral vocabulary, but they understand the concept. (3) The word is not in their sight or oral vocabulary, nor do they grasp the concept. You can handle the first two problems through discussion. But the third may require your pupils to have some firsthand experiences before they can understand the word (concept).

Reading for Meaning. Just as you may need help to get more meaning from the paragraph on cricket, children often need help to understand what they read in science textbooks. You can give such aid before, during, and after they read. Here's how.

Before Reading [about 5 minutes, excluding item 1]

1. Furnish real or vicarious experiences before reading, with vocabulary, if your pupils have little or no background with the concepts to be learned. Experiments, demonstrations, a study trip, displays of real objects, and audio-visual materials will lay the foundation for successful reading. (Chapter 7 gives details.)

2. Relate what your pupils are about to read to what they have studied or otherwise experienced before. This assists them in link-

ing ideas presented in the textbook to the mental schemata they already have. ("Who remembers what a food chain is? That sums it up nicely, Rosa. Well, today we're going to see how living things in several food chains may be connected in a *food web.* How do you think that might happen?")

3. State some clear purposes for reading. ("Your ideas are interesting! You'll find out more about them as we read. Also look for answers to these two questions I've put on the chalkboard as we read pages 105 to 110 in our science books: What is the difference between a food chain and a food web? and, What kinds of food webs might you find in and around our town lake? Be ready to use some facts from the book to back up what you say.")

4. Briefly introduce a few vocabulary words you have selected from the text, to help pupils recognize them in print. Write each word on the chalkboard, pronounce and define it, and use each word in a sentence that parallels its use in the text. ("Before we read, let's take a quick look at these two words on the chalkboard that you'll also see in your book. *Predator.* What does it mean? Good try, Nancy. A predator is an animal that eats another animal. A hawk is a predator that feeds on mice and other small animals. *Prey.* What's that? Almost, Jason. *Prey* is an animal that is eaten by another animal. A mouse may be the prey of a predator, such as a hawk. Let's read now. If you finish early, remember to use your library books to look up some other examples of food webs, especially in and around a freshwater lake.")

During Reading [about 5 to 15 minutes]

1. Have pupils read silently and adjust their pace to suit their purposes. They might skim when looking for specific facts, for example, but slow down when attention to detail is important to understand a process or idea.

2. Move around the room to aid pupils as needed, but instruct them to use self-help first when they meet unknown words, as follows:

   a. Pass over the word and finish the sentence; use context clues and any accompanying graphics to grasp the meaning.

   b. If needed, analyze the word for familiar roots, prefixes, and suffixes.

   c. If needed, use the text's glossary or a dictionary, being careful to select the definition—if several are given—that makes the most sense.

   d. If needed, ask for your aid.

3. Have pupils who finish early switch to self-selected library books on the topic, or reference books, to find additional information on the questions raised.

What to do if pupils cannot read the textbook independently? Read to them aloud as they follow in their books, but do it in an *interactive* way. That is, have them participate enough for you to check whether they can keep up with you and understand what is being read.

Check whether your pacing is all right by occasionally omitting an easy word and having a child supply it *without breaking your rhythm,* if possible. Move around as you read and signal who will supply the word by lightly tapping someone on the arm a second or so before you omit the word. Or check your pacing by noting how children move down a colored marker (a strip of 1-inch by 6-inch paper) under each line as you read.

To monitor understanding, every paragraph or so ask a low-level factual question and invite brief responses. (Which living thing is eaten first? Which animal is the last predator in this food web?) A few such questions might already be in the text. Some textbook authors routinely write in low-level questions to keep the reader's mind active and so promote comprehension from one paragraph to the next. You want pupils now to understand the details as they go along. Later, they will recall and put together this information to answer the one or two main questions you posed at the beginning of the reading session. Pupils will feel encouraged if you periodically remind them through appreciative comments that *they understand well what they are reading.* Interactive reading can change a frustrating failure experience into an encouraging success experience.

Instead of your "live" reading, you could tape the passage for later playback on a cassette player. But pupils are likely to learn more when you interact with them. You can also help less able readers by pairing them with compatible partners who read well.

Above all, avoid round-robin reading, in which children routinely take turns reading aloud sections of the text while the others supposedly follow along. This is boring and ineffective, for several reasons. Children typically read—and should practice reading—much faster silently than orally. Few children read well orally unless they are familiar with the material. Also, the oral reader, preoccupied with the mechanics of the job, understands less than when she reads silently. The situation differs when you read orally because you are likely to do it smoothly, interact with pupils as you go along, maintain a pace that children will follow, and limit the practice to times when children cannot go it alone.

After Reading [10 to 15 minutes, excluding item 2]

1. Have pupils respond to the main purposes or questions first posed. (What is the difference between a food chain and a food web? What food webs might be in and around our town lake?) They may silently skim or reread some sections to find information that supports their responses. If needed, this may be a good time to have a few children read aloud informative excerpts of one or two sentences. If the chapter ends where the present reading assignment ends, you might also have pupils answer the text's chapter-summary questions to find out more about what they have learned.

2. Many text programs supply activity worksheets, for children to extend and apply their learning, at the ends of sections or chapters. You might want to distribute these now. This can also be a good time to invite pupils to do independent or small group projects on activities suggested by the teacher's manual or on topics of children's personal interest.

Summary of Text Reading for Meaning. Children will usually understand well what they read in their textbook if you do the following before, during, and after they read:

Before

1. If pupils have no background on the subject, do something concrete first.

2. If they have background, relate it to what they will read now.

3. State one or two clear purposes or questions for the reading.

4. Briefly introduce a few unfamiliar vocabulary words, if needed.

During

1. Have pupils read silently with purpose(s) in mind.

2. Help them with words only if they first cannot help themselves through ways you have taught.

3. Have pupils who finish early switch to further references.

4. Read aloud in an interactive way with children who cannot read independently.

After

1. Have *all* pupils—able and less-able readers alike—respond to the purpose(s) or question(s) first posed.

2. Extend the learning through follow-up activities, if warranted.

More Textbook Uses. As you'll find in Chapter 7, treating the text as an important tool within a unit of instruction will offer the most possibilities for a variety of worthwhile uses. Here are some extra ways you can profitably use a science text and its accompanying teacher's manual:

- *As a source of investigations, activities, problems, and basic science principles.* ("Before we open our books for help, can you figure out the answer to this problem on the chalkboard?") When used for these purposes, the children's books may be closed at first; the textbook author's ideas are used by the teacher.

- *As a check-up source for experiments and ideas.* ("Let's see if the scientists agree with us.") In these cases, the book may serve as a check for the children to compare the completeness and accuracy of their ideas and activities with those in the book. The book is opened for verification or comparison only after the initial thinking and doing have taken place. Slow readers are helped individually or in small groups.

- *As an information source.* ("You'll find answers to some of your questions in our science book.") Now the book may be consulted for details to address children's questions or purposes. In a primary text consisting mostly of pictures, the pictures may be examined in detail.

- *As a source of additional examples to reinforce a previous activity.* ("For more examples of mammals, let's open our books to page 74.") Study of open-ended experiments, principles, or concepts can be enhanced by learning of additional examples. Frequently, such examples are either mentioned or illustrated in the text.

- *As a summary of important ideas in units of instruction.* ("See if you can sum up the three main ways rocks are formed after you read pages 55–60.") The clear, careful organization of subject matter typical in modern texts is ideal to summarize firsthand experiences within important segments of a unit or even the entire unit itself. The additional filling in of detail and seeing previously studied material in a new context through summary reading provide reinforcement and more completeness in learning.

Trade Books

Even the best of textbooks cannot always do an ideal job in each of the five uses just mentioned. They would soon grow too heavy to carry and too expensive to buy. However, you can turn to other printed materials for help. Children's *trade books,* commonly called library books, are excellent for additional detail. Trade books were so named because, intended for general readership, they are sold through retail trade outlets, such as bookstores, which is not so with textbooks. Often developed around one topic, such as simple machines, weather, soil, or electricity, trade books give richness in depth difficult to put into a textbook chapter. Most schools now have instructional resource centers that contain good collections of trade books. (For examples of titles in different content areas, see each chapter end in Part II of this book.)

Some school districts prepare collections of books, or at least bibliographies, to accompany scheduled instructional units. Local libraries may permit up to 30 or more trade books to be checked out to teachers for a limited period. Children can go to the local library, also, and find books that can help them investigate problems or topics. An advantage in self-selection is that children usually choose books that they can read.

Trade books are probably the best means we have of providing for individual differences in reading. If a variety is available, it almost ensures that able readers will have challenging materials. Less-able readers, also, will usually have at their disposal books that are both interesting and within their more limited capabilities.

Children's trade books are not just limited to interesting expository treatments of science topics. They also include biographies, autobiographies, diaries, reports of major scientific events, and science fiction. Children often find these books inspirational and exciting. They are also an excellent means to stimulate creative writing.

Creative Writing.   Here are some ideas for creative writing that you can use repeatedly with different trade books.

Diary.   Write an entry from an event in the life of George Washington Carver, Marie Curie, and so on. ("February 18, 1897. Is it impossible? I have now tried dozens of ways to . . .")

Letter to a Famous Scientist from the Past or Present.   ("Dear Dr. Einstein:")

Interview with a Famous Person.   (" 'What was it like being an astronaut, Mr. Glenn?' 'It had its up and downs, Sally,' he said with a grin.")

Future Autobiography.   ("An exciting page from your life in the field of _____ !")

TV or Radio Script: "You Are There!"   Reenactment and report of the first landing on Mars, first colony on the moon, development of the first human clone, first successful brain transplant, peaceful visit to earth by creatures from another planet, discovery by junior scientists from Room 6 of the languages used by dolphins, chimps, dogs, and so on, and what they have been waiting so long to "tell" us.

Finding the Best Trade Books.   Many trade books and other books are printed every year. It could be a continual problem just to keep up with what is published, much less pick out quality material. Fortunately, we have several places to which we can turn for help. Among the more useful sources is the annotated bibliography "Outstanding Science Trade Books for Children" prepared annually by the National Science Teachers Association and the Children's Book Council. The listing is published in the March issue of *Science and Children,* a practical magazine for elementary school teachers. For details, write to *Science and Children,* 1742 Connecticut Avenue, N.W., Washington, DC 20009.

Another carefully screened review is "Science Books and Films," published by the American Association for the Advancement of Science, 1776 Massachusetts Avenue, N.W., Washington, DC 20036.

Also very helpful is "Appraisal: Children's Science Books," Children's Book Review Committee, Boston University, 36 Cummington Street, Boston, MA 02215. This publication uses specialists to independently appraise the literary quality of the trade books as well as their scientific validity.

Reference Books and Other Reading Matter

How useful are *encyclopedias* for children? They do provide additional information. But most are hard for younger children to read without some help. Above all, discourage the usual practice of simply copying information out of the encyclopedia. When this happens, comprehension may reach the vanishing point. Help the children interpret information when necessary. If needed, read short segments aloud so individual pupils can jot down in their own words facts they wish to report or know.

Encyclopedias are best used when pupils want to find an answer to a specific question, rather than to see what they contain about some general topic. For the second purpose, try trade books.

"What's this bug?" "Is that bird a robin?" Children like to name and find out more about what they observe. From time to time you might need to use *identification books* in the classroom. These references classify, name, and usually give interesting information about living and non-living things. It is important to have books that are well illustrated. Most pupils rely more on matching pictures than on the use of keys for identification. An excellent and inexpensive shelf of books with color illustrations is the *Golden Guides* series. It is available in inexpensive paperback or cloth editions at many bookstores and from the publisher, Western Publishing Company, 1220 Mound Avenue, Racine, WI 53404. Titles include *Birds, Flowers, Trees, Insects, Stars, Reptiles and Amphibians, Rocks and Minerals, Fishes,* and *Seashores.*

Besides reference, trade, and text reading materials, many teachers discover that magazines, newspapers, charts, workbooks, catalogs, almanacs, bulletins, and the like are worthwhile for seeking information. You'll find that using a variety of reading matter often has double benefits. Not only do children get better at locating and learning science information, but they also improve their ability to find and learn information in other curriculum areas.

Language Experience Charts

"How can children read *science* material if they can barely read at all?" This lament is a familiar one in some schools. But rather than overwhelm beginning readers, science can readily be made to serve their needs.

It is natural for young children to learn new vocabulary words when they have first-hand experiences in science. At the same time, they are more likely to organize and remember these experiences if they summarize and record what they have learned. The making of a language experience chart prompts them to describe their experiences in a form that can be written down. This steps up their oral language development, science learning, and ability to read. The technique is well suited to primary-level pupils, or to older children who read poorly or not at all.

In a first-grade room, the teacher suggests that the class make a chart to tell parents about a just-finished chick-hatching activity. A general discussion follows about the events and their sequence to aid pupils' recall of events and vocabulary. The teacher lists some key words on the chalkboard as they come up: Mr. Simpson, incubator, turned over, hatched, shells, fluffy.

At this point, many experienced teachers refer to the key words to establish a sequence: What happened first? Next? and so on. Once the sequence is determined, individual pupils are then invited to dictate what happened. Some primary teachers *also* feel the need at this time to better control what the children say. They believe, quite correctly, that they are now acting like a text author who is writing something that all the class—not just one child who is contributing a sentence—should be able to read. They claim better results when they state narrow questions to which individual pupils respond: Who gave us the six chicken eggs? What did we do with them? How often did we turn them? and so on. Depending on the teacher's method, then, each child called on in our first-grade example either describes one event or responds to one narrow question about an event.

The teacher now carefully writes what is said on a sheet of large lined paper but tries to keep each sentence short and clear, so everyone can read it. He says each word aloud as he writes, then reads the whole sentence aloud, has the dictating child do so, and then the whole class in unison orally reads the sentence. He moves his hand from left to right each time to guide pupils' reading. This emerges:

Mr. Simpson gave us six chicken eggs.

We put them in an incubator.

We turned them over every day.

Three chicks hatched after 21 days.

They broke the shells and got out.

They were wet.

Then they got dry and fluffy.

The class next reads aloud the entire chart in unison, paced by the teacher's moving hand. Then, individual volunteers each read a line in response to some questions: "Which line tells how the chicks got out of their shells?" "Which line tells who gave us the eggs?" and so on. A title is agreed on—"Our Three Chicks"—and written above the first line.

Being aware of individual differences, the teacher asks the children to copy as few as four to as many as all seven lines of the story on lined paper and circulates to help as needed. Pupils also copy several words of their own choosing onto their individual word lists, for later use.

Children with sparse prereading and early reading backgrounds probably would find the preceding language experience chart too hard. To make it easier, ask narrow questions, keep the chart message limited to fewer lines at first, use shorter sentences, more word repetition, and furnish beginning sentence patterns, when you can, as follows:

"How many eggs did we get?"
  We got six eggs.
"Where did we put the eggs?"
  We put the eggs in an incubator.
"What did we do with the eggs every day?"
  We turned over the eggs.
"How many chicks hatched?"
  Three chicks hatched.
"What is this story about? What short title can we give to this story?"
  Our Three Chicks

Regularly summarizing pupils' experiences on charts rapidly improves their sight vocabulary of commonly spoken words. So it becomes easier for them to read longer sentences and focus on new science words as successive charts are read. This also makes them more able to write and read their own charts about their science experiences. These individual writings usually have longer sentences than group-made charts and embody each child's unique style. Since each is read mainly by the author and a few adults, readability for other children is of less concern.

NONREADING MATERIALS

What nonreading resources can you expect to find in most schools today? They may include:

still pictures

films and filmstrips

slides

models and constructions

microscopes and microprojectors

televisions

videocassettes

microcomputers and related equipment

Strictly speaking, even these materials may require some reading—captions in films, descriptions of pictures, directions for using a microcomputer program, and the like. (We'll consider in Chapter 6 how to use microcomputers and related equipment in science instruction.) As with books, you'll do better if you select and use each resource for a specific purpose.

Pictorial Materials

Let's begin with pictures, films, filmstrips, and television. You can use each of these resources in three general ways:

1. To introduce or overview lessons and raise problems.

2. To help answer questions or explain difficult ideas.

3. To summarize or extend with more examples what has been studied.

Illustrations, or pictures, are probably among the most common aids used in elementary science, perhaps because their sources are so accessible. There are many magazines in which suitable illustrations may be found. Let children help locate these pictures. Books also may contain numerous helpful photographs or drawings. Sometimes you can get valuable pictures from old or discarded books. District and local libraries frequently furnish collections of pictures to interested teachers. A large supply is also obtainable from free and inexpensive commercial sources. These are listed later in this section.

After only a short time of collecting illustrations, the need for a handy way to file them becomes obvious. You can solve this problem by first mounting the pictures on tagboard or stiff paper backing of uniform size, and then filing the pictures upright in an orange crate or a cardboard box of the right dimensions. Almost any careful system of cataloging should assist in retrieving desired illustrations. A system that seems to work well is to file illustrations first by unit titles and then according to specific concepts or ideas within units. Be sure to use cross-filing notations on any pictures that can be used with more than one topic.

Motion pictures can make available in the classroom vicarious experiences that are otherwise difficult, hazardous, or impossible to realize firsthand. Through the technique of animation, motions of bodies in space are seen and understood better in dynamic form. Microphotography enables children to see cell division, rare and active microscopic life, and body defenses reacting to invading germs. Time-lapse sequences enable the movements of developing plants to be recorded. Slow motion permits the leisurely analysis of swift and complex movements. Photography also makes possible the repeatable, safe viewing of solar eclipses, volcanoes, and other natural events. These are just a few examples of techniques and applications available in educational films.

Filmstrips are helpful in that they can show a process or develop an idea in a sequential step-by-step way. In addition, you can stop at specific frames and discuss them as long as needed. *Slides* enable you to do all of this and also arrange the order of presentation.

Growing numbers of teachers are using *videodiscs* (Figure 6-9) in place of still pictures, films, filmstrips, and slides. Even so, the large inventory of these latter materials in many schools, and their continued worth, means they are unlikely to vanish anytime soon.

Television programs in science are now regularly scheduled in many school districts, sometimes over a closed circuit arrangement and sometimes over a public broadcasting station. Schedules and teaching guides are distributed to teachers. The teacher typically presents an overview of the lesson, raises some questions or points to consider with the pupils, and acts as a discussion leader after the telecast is over.

When a *videocassette recorder* (VCR) is available, programs may be taped for showing at convenient times.

Teachers often prefer videocassettes over films, even though the pictures displayed are slightly less sharp and limited to the size of the TV monitor at hand. The cassettes are easily inserted into the VCR, machine noise is absent, and you can more easily rewind or advance the tape to find a scene that needs to be reviewed. Videocassettes also cost less than films, so the present trend toward declining use of films should continue.

Many elementary science TV programs are now available on videocassettes. The nation's largest disseminator of instructional television, the Corporation for Public Broadcasting, allows schools limited copying privileges for numerous shows. One of its best programs for elementary science, *3-2-1 Contact,* includes more than 140 30-minute broadcasts on a broad variety of topics. It's likely that your county, regional, or state instructional television authority has this series and many more.

For a free comprehensive listing of CPB programs correlated with the most used elementary science programs, write to: Corporation for Public Broadcasting, Office of Education, 1111 Sixteenth Street NW, Washington, DC 20036.

MICROSCOPES AND MICROPROJECTORS

"Let's see what the grasshopper's mouth looks like!" Sometimes children want to see a small object more clearly than is possible with the naked eye. For the most part, a hand lens or magnifier is sufficient, especially for primary-level children. From about grade three on, a *microscope* may also be helpful.

Children typically want to see the highest possible magnification of a specimen. The result is usually unsatisfactory. It may be hard to focus the instrument properly. The field of observation may be too narrow to locate the desired area on the specimen. Minor movement or shifting of the slide is greatly exaggerated when viewed through an eyepiece. It is also possible that children will not understand what they are observing. For these reasons, well-built microscopes of lower power—and lower cost—are satisfactory for elementary schools. (See Figure 5-2 for an example of an inexpensive model.)

Because we can seldom be sure of what children are viewing, and since it is likely that only one or a few microscopes can be available for use at one time, many teachers prefer the *microprojector* (see Figure 5-3). With this instrument, it is possible to project an enlarged image of the specimen onto a screen, much like other visual projectors. It is convenient when instructing a whole class because everyone can view together what is taking place. Some science supply houses sell an inexpensive microscope that can quickly be converted into a microprojector, with a filmstrip or slide projector as the light source. (See Appendix C to request science catalogs.) Although the quality is less than that of

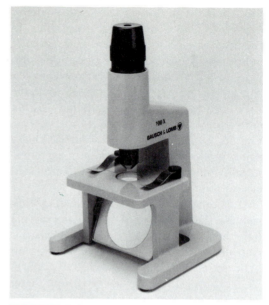

FIGURE 5-2
A suitable microscope for elementary schools.

the more expensive models, elementary school teachers are often pleased with the results. When microscopes and a microprojector are available, you may find microscopes more convenient for individual viewing projects.

Here are some examples of things children are likely to view with microscopes or microprojectors: compound eyes of the housefly, various other insect eyes; fiber structure of wool, cotton, and other cloth materials; penetration of inks and dyes into several materials; newly laid insect, frog, and snail eggs; anatomy of the mosquito and bee; composition of human hair, several kinds of body cells; crystals of salt and sugar; algae, freshwater protozoa; effects of disinfectants on protozoa; composition of mold growth, bacterial colonies; parts of a flower, leaf, seed; onion, root, stem, leaf cells; root hairs; capillary action with colored water; circulation of blood in the tail of a goldfish; heartbeat of a water flea; mouthparts of harmful insects; fiber structures of various kinds of paper.

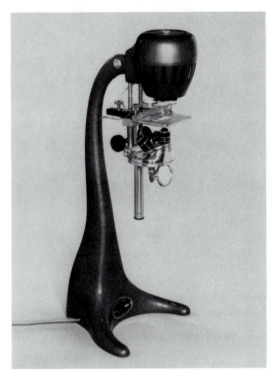

FIGURE 5-3
A microprojector.

Constructions and Models

School and district instructional media centers often have models you may borrow for instruction. These may range from the familiar globe model of the earth to a model skeleton that may be taken apart and assembled again.

In many classrooms, time is also given to constructing models and apparatus. The best kinds of constructions are *functional;* that is, they work by teaching an idea, a process, or helping to gather data. Working constructions such as telegraphs, weather instruments, electric circuit boards, and so forth usually involve thoughtful planning on the part of children.

Less useful are constructions that might be called props—materials that are more decorative and atmospheric than functional: a spaceship made out of cardboard, a paper glacier, a chicken wire and papier-mâché di-

nosaur, a model volcano that shoots up sparks and ash when a chemical is ignited, and so on.

This is not to say that such materials are useless. They may have a worthwhile purpose in dramatic play or art-centered activities, for example. But weigh whether the limited time for investigating basic ideas and processes should be largely used up in this way.

Free and Inexpensive Materials

You can borrow or permanently get many instructional aids from commercial and institutional sources through request only or at low cost. Films, filmstrips, slides, charts, pictures, booklets, samples of raw or processed materials, models, posters, recordings—all these and more are available to supplement science programs.

But before you write for these aids, check the policy of your school district about such materials. Many commercial, institutional, and other donors in the past have used free and inexpensive materials as an advertising or propaganda medium. Educators have been forced to restrict their use.

The supply of donated materials you get by mail is notoriously unreliable. It is wise to use current and reliable listings in making requests. The following compilations of sources are revised yearly. Efforts are made to edit out those sources that either have misrepresented their materials or have otherwise proved unsatisfactory.

Educators Guide to Free Science Materials (films, filmstrips, slides, tapes, transcriptions, pamphlets, and printed materials)

Elementary Teachers Guide to Free Curriculum Materials (pamphlet, picture, and chart materials for elementary and middle school levels)

Guide to Free Computer Materials (films, videotapes, pamphlets, charts, disks, and more)

The guides are often found in university and school district curriculum libraries. All are available at reasonable cost from Educators Progress Service, 214 Center Street, Randolph, WI 53956.

Be sure to use school stationery whenever you request free supplementary materials from sources in the guides. You are more likely to receive them.

SCHOOL AND COMMUNITY RESOURCES

It is possible to get so engrossed in acquiring materials for first-hand experiences, books, and other instructional aids that we forget there is an out-of-class environment for science exploration. The school building itself is a good place to start.

School and Surroundings

Objects and events introduced in science programs become more understandable when they show up as real-life examples in familiar places: Why are there cracks in the masonry and plaster? How do the automatic fire sprinklers work? Why are the stairs worn in the middle and not at the sides? What is making some of the paint outside peel? How is the school heated? How many simple machines does the school custodian use?

Things are also happening on the school grounds. Why are they planting ground cover on the hill? What makes the hot asphalt on the playground "steam" after the cloudburst? How does the seesaw work? What are the names of the birds around the schoolyard, and where do they nest? What makes the shrubs planted on the north side grow more slowly than those on the south side? Why is snow still on the roof of the main building when it has melted on the other roofs? What makes shadows longer in the afternoon?

Study Trips

Where can your pupils see science-related objects and events in their community? There might be many places to explore: a zoo, wooded area, garden, nursery, greenhouse, pond or brook, pet store, bird refuge, observatory, natural history museum, road cut, stone quarry, vacant lot, construction site, waterworks, sewage treatment plant, dairy, airport, and weather bureau. All these and more are rewarding places for elementary school pupils to visit.

Before you take a study trip, some preparation will help make it worthwhile. A school district catalog of suggested places to visit in the community may be available. This can furnish the necessary details for educational trips. In general, however, you will want to keep the following points in mind:

1. Be clear about the purpose for leaving the classroom. A common reason is to stimulate interest and problems at the beginning of a unit of study. Sometimes a study trip is helpful to give additional topical information or see applications of principles.

2. Check with the principal for school policies. Chances are, several procedures will need to be followed—notification and permission of parents, a phone call to the site to be visited, a transportation request, and so forth.

3. Visit the site yourself. It is much easier to make plans when you actually know what conditions are present.

4. Plan with the children what to look for. A list of questions or purposes, and some background, may be needed to enable them to observe intelligently.

5. Develop with the class some behavior and safety standards to be remembered. A buddy system can be used in which each child helps to keep track of another. Less reliable children can be placed at the head of the line. Several parents or moni-

tors at the end of the line can prevent straggling.

6. At the site, make sure everyone can see and hear adequately and ask questions if desired. If the class is large, it may be necessary to divide it into smaller groups.

7. After returning to the classroom, help pupils evaluate the trip. Did they achieve their purposes? Were safety and behavior standards observed?

When it is impossible to arrange visits away from the school, resource persons from the community may be able to visit your classroom. Many districts compile lists of informed persons who are willing to volunteer some of their time and talent for the education of children. As with study trips, maximum benefits from a classroom visit are likelier to happen if there has been some preplanning.

RESOURCES FOR TEACHING PUPILS WITH SPECIAL NEEDS

Stand outside almost any urban school today at dismissal time and watch diversity stream out the doors: girls and boys of different colors, ethnic and cultural origins, religions, economic levels, and abilities—physical and mental. Such differences have always been present in the schools, but never to the degree we see today. What's more, some pupil conditions once thought to require a special education are now expected to be handled in the regular classroom. How do you teach children who need some special provisions in your science teaching? What help can you expect?

Working with Handicapped Pupils

Once, handicapped children were routinely placed in special classrooms. Now federal law requires that handicapped pupils in schools be assigned to the "least restrictive environment" that seems best for their development. This means that some handicapped children who were formerly placed only in special education classrooms may spend some or all of their time in regular classrooms—the "mainstream" of education.

Mainstreaming presents both opportunities and challenges to people in schools. Mainstreamed children learn to live and work in settings that are more likely to develop their potentials to the fullest. The other children profit from a heightened sensitivity and a greater capacity to live and work with individual differences.

The challenges largely come from the diversity of handicaps found in special education. It's natural to ask the question, "How do I deal with them?" On examination, the situation is less difficult than it seems at first. For one thing, each handicapped child is likely to be much more like other girls and boys than unlike them. Each who comes to your classroom is identified as a teachable child. To help ensure this, you share in the placement decision.

The disabled who require the most change in the science curriculum—totally blind or deaf children, for example—are rare. *For most handicapped pupils, a solid hands-on program gives the multisensory experiences they need to learn science well.* So much of what you know and can do now will serve nicely.

Also, realize that an Individualized Education Plan (IEP) is developed for each child by a *team* of persons. Included on the team is at least one person qualified in special education. With a team, you are able to draw on more skills, information, and ideas than by working alone. Responsibility for the child's progress is shared by the team. In many states, the IEP is also accompanied by whatever special instructional media and materials the team believes are essential to meet objectives.

What kinds of handicapped pupils are you likely to teach? What are some of their characteristics? How can you generally help them?

What resources can you draw on that apply specifically to science?

There are many kinds of handicapped children. For our purposes we'll limit the review to four: the visually impaired, hearing impaired, orthopedically impaired, and mentally handicapped.

The Visually Impaired.[2] The problems of visually impaired children may range from poor eyesight to total blindness. Nearly all mainstreamed pupils will have partial sight. A basic problem with the pupils is a lack of firsthand experience with many objects, which is reflected in their language. Vocabulary and descriptive capacity therefore need considerable strengthening.

Some ways to help a child are

1. Use concrete, multisensory experiences to build a greater store of needed percepts.
2. Give plenty of time to explore and encourage the use of descriptive language during explorations.
3. Tell the child what you are doing as you do it.
4. Use tactile cues with materials, such as a knotted string for measuring.
5. Walk the child through spaces to demonstrate barriers and tactile clues.
6. Encourage the use of any remaining vision.
7. Avoid vague phrases, such as "over there," "like that one," or any descriptions that require vision.
8. Be tolerant of, and prepared for, spilled or scattered material.
9. Use oral language or a recorder for instructions and information.
10. Pair the child with a tactful, sighted partner.

The American Printing House for the Blind (see page 122 for address) produces several current elementary science series in large print and braille. Illustrations and graphs are often in the form of touchable raised-line drawings.

The Hearing Impaired. The hearing of these children may range from poor to total deafness. Most wear a hearing aid and have partial hearing. Communication is aided when the child can read lips and certain facial movements, and when sign language is used. Retarded language development is common.

Some ways to help a child are

1. Use concrete objects, pictures, sketches, signs, and the like to get across ideas.
2. Seat the child close to you.
3. Give clear directions and face the child as you speak.
4. Speak with usual volume and speed.
5. Model, rather than correct, pronunciations for the partially deaf child.
6. Wait longer than usual for responses.
7. Make sure you have the child's attention; use direct eye contact.
8. Use gestures and body language, but don't exaggerate these.
9. Avoid speaking for the child.
10. Talk with the child frequently about what she is doing.

The Orthopedically Impaired. Orthopedically impaired children typically have gross or fine motor malfunctions that cause problems in locomotion, coordination, balance, and dexterity. One of the most common impairments is cerebral palsy. Orthopedically handicapped pupils may use walkers, wheelchairs, crutches, braces, or other aids. Like the visually and hearing impaired, they often do about as well academically as the nonhandicapped when proper conditions are present.

---

[2]Many of the suggestions in this section are based on information supplied by Gilda Servetter and Anne McComiskey, Department of Education, San Diego County, CA.

Some ways to help a child are

1. Encourage some participation in all activities.
2. Modify activities to avoid frustrations.
3. Encourage the use of limbs to the fullest ability.
4. Find alternative methods to manipulate things.
5. Allow alternative methods for the child to respond.
6. Keep traffic lanes clear in the classroom.
7. Acknowledge and deal openly with feelings of frustration.
8. Have someone ready to help the child move to where the next activity is if needed.
9. Promote the child's confidence and independence whenever possible.
10. Use activities that foster problem solving and growth in thinking skills.

The Mentally Handicapped.
Mentally handicapped pupils show significantly subaverage abilities in thinking and often in motor development. They are likely to have problems in learning, remembering, problem solving, and everyday skills. Other frequent characteristics are short attention span, confusion, and minimal ability to make choices.

Some ways to help a child are

1. Use direct, closed-ended, concrete teaching methods and materials.
2. Be sure you have the child's attention before you give directions.
3. Demonstrate and model as you give simple directions; speak slowly.
4. Break tasks down to simple, step-by-step parts.
5. Outline expectations clearly for the child before work begins.
6. Review and summarize ideas and procedures frequently; let the child repeat experiences.

7. Give positive reinforcement immediately after each small success.
8. Give responsibility within the child's limits; let the child observe and assist in a role before giving her responsibility.
9. Apply learnings frequently to everyday experiences.
10. Begin instruction with what the child knows and build on that.

Additional Considerations.

Helping. Disabled children are much more likely to have a poor self-concept than other children. Many adults realize this but overprotect the disabled in order to compensate. Unfortunately, this inhibits development and confidence. Disabled children, in turn, often learn and accept overdependence, so a cycle develops that feeds on itself. What to do?

1. Consider when help is necessary, rather than convenient.
2. Except for obvious need, get consent from the child before giving help.
3. Don't persist if the child declines help; let the child discover if help is needed.
4. Offer help matter-of-factly.

The Disabled as Individuals. There are many other kinds of disabilities found in mainstreaming: the learning disabled (children with neurological and emotional handicaps that interfere with learning); the speech/language impaired; the health impaired; the multiply handicapped; and so on. Be aware that entire books are devoted to each one of these and the previously described handicaps. Fortunately, there is no need to become an overall expert in special education to help a specific mainstreamed child. Although it is nice to have some general knowledge about a handicap, *it is far more important to know how that handicap affects a particular child.* You learn this by working with the child.

Disabled girls and boys are individuals, with as many personalities and variables as other children. Making an Individualized Education Plan with the IEP team soon after you receive a disabled child will give you a good start. But be prepared to continually modify the plan as you get to know the child better. By considering and working with handicapped pupils individually, you are most likely to help them learn.

Resources for Science Teaching.   There are several sources that offer programs and information to better teach the mainstreamed handicapped child. An excellent and well-tested program is *FOSS*, the *Full Option Science System*. Designed for *both* handicapped and nonhandicapped pupils in grades K–6, it was developed at the Lawrence Hall of Science, University of California, Berkeley. FOSS is an outgrowth of earlier projects at Lawrence to improve science education for visually impaired and physically disabled pupils. Several modules at each grade level include lesson plans in the earth, life, and physical sciences. Extension activities include work in language, computer, and mathematics applications. The developers worked hard to match activities with pupils' ability to think at different ages. Further work was done to make the program easy to instruct and manage. The commercial distributor of FOSS is the Encyclopedia Britannica Educational Corporation, 310 South Michigan Avenue, Chicago, IL 60604.

Some further sources that can help you plan lessons for children with different disabilities are

Alexander Graham Bell Association for the Deaf, 3417 Volta Place, N.W., Washington, DC 20007.

American Printing House for the Blind, P.O. Box 6085, Louisville, KY 40206.

Center for Multisensory Learning, Lawrence Hall of Science, University of California, Berkeley, CA 94720.

ERIC Clearinghouse on Handicapped and Gifted Children, 1920 Association Drive, Reston, VA 22091.

National Center on Educational Media and Materials for the Handicapped, Ohio State University, 154 West 12th Avenue, Columbus, OH 43210.

Lewis, Rena B., and Doorlag, Donald H. *Teaching Special Students in the Mainstream.* New York: Merrill/Macmillan, 1991.

Shulz, Jane B., *et al. Mainstreaming Exceptional Students.* Boston: Allyn & Bacon, 1991.

Working with Limited English Proficiency Pupils

Not long ago, only a few cities in the United States contained significant numbers of schoolchildren whose native language was other than English. Today they are present in nearly every school. Foreign-born pupils who do not speak English may be placed in bilingual classrooms and taught by someone who is facile in both English and the foreign language. As the pupils acquire some English proficiency, they are mainstreamed for larger parts of the school day. In other schools, they are taught in all-English classrooms. As a regular classroom teacher, expect to have at least some pupils of limited English proficiency (LEP) from time to time. How can you best help them to learn science when their English is still subpar?

Many LEP pupils experience some culture shock, since what they observe now may differ radically from their earlier environment. They may be reluctant to speak because they are afraid to make mistakes. Your warm acceptance and frequent praise will boost their confidence. Whatever you can do to reduce anxiety, to increase meaning of content studied, to model good English, and increase chances to informally interact with English speakers will benefit them. Here are some things that can work for you, based on what many effective teachers have learned from helping LEP pupils.

1. Use a listening–speaking–reading–writing sequence in teaching whenever possible. Listening lays the foundation for the

other language skills. It's easier to speak what we have first heard, read what we have spoken, and write what we have read.

2. Use multisensory, hands-on teaching methods whenever you can. Concrete materials, investigations, demonstrations, audio-visual media, graphs, diagrams and so forth, are more likely to foster meaningful learning than studying printed matter. One great advantage of hands-on science over most other subjects is that the actual doing demands little verbal ability. Most speaking occurs before and after the event.

3. Pair LEP pupils with bilingual partners who can supply brief translations as needed. But coach these partners to focus on teaching English words and phrases for actions taken or objects observed during investigations. For a good pattern, have them say the word or phrase referring to an action or object, and have the LEP child immediately repeat it.

4. Place LEP pupils in cooperative learning groups to increase chances for frequent, low anxiety, informal interactions with other children. (See page 128 for a description of cooperative learning in science.)

5. Speak slowly, use short sentences, and rephrase what you say if a child seems unsure rather than repeat what you have said. Use body language, props, pictures and sketches to clarify your words.

6. Check more specifically whether a child understands by asking questions answerable by yes or no, or by having the child do something you can observe, such as point to an object.

7. Avoid idiomatic expressions; they can be confusing when taken literally: "It's as easy as pie." "Please take your chair."

8. Make whatever you refer to as concrete as possible—what you know the children have done or observed in the past. Give observable examples in the present as

well: "The handle of this pencil sharpener is also a lever."

9. To help pupils build schemata, write key concepts and vocabulary used during a lesson on the chalkboard. Often make a concept map to outline what is to come in a lesson or to summarize the content of a lesson. (See pages 186–87 for concept mapping.)

10. Emphasize and repeat key words of the lesson as you teach. This cues the child about what to remember and how the words sound.

11. For the easiest and most meaningful reading, make language experience charts. Try interactive reading as well. (Pages 109, 113.)

Pupils who are becoming proficient in English require some extra time and attention, but they can also enrich the curriculum by bringing multicultural knowledge and perspectives to what is studied. For many children, bilingualism and bicultural knowledge should enhance their opportunities for academic, social, and economic success throughout life. Others, though, may not be as fortunate.

There is a well-known relationship between socioeconomic status and success in schools.[3] Poverty diminishes the chances for success in a large percentage of immigrant children of minority heritage who come from less-developed countries. This is also true of many native-born children. Pupils from middle- and higher-income homes of all races and ethnic groups are more apt than their poorer classmates to enjoy benefits that help them to achieve at school. Among the benefits are these: (1) They are more likely to have many cultural, travel, and educational experiences outside the school that enrich and extend their knowledge; (2) to have parents who are functional English-speakers and

---

[3]Daniel Levine and Robert Havighurst, *Society and Education,* 6th edition (Boston: Allyn & Bacon, 1984).

able to guide them academically; and (3) to meet or know of a wide variety of persons who may serve as role models in occupations that require higher levels of education.

Curriculum writers are well aware of these advantages and have built into many of the newer science programs factors to enrich the education of all children both at school and home. Besides containing a wealth of materials for hands-on investigations, most published programs offer many multimedia resources you can use to provide vicarious experiences for pupils. For example, choose among videotapes that bring the wonders of barrier reefs, hot air balloons, and giant cave explorations to children. Use videodiscs and bring further sights and sounds into your classroom. Find computer simulations that invite pupils to decide how best to preserve a deer population or plan a town in an earthquake-prone area. You may also discover audiotapes your LEP or other pupils can use to practice saying new words or to review further by themselves what they have studied.

For the home/school connection, look for letters to parents—often in Spanish as well as English—that tell them what science their children will study and how they may help at home. Your program may also include concept summaries and glossaries of key words, printed in some half-dozen languages, that you can send home with pupils. Check to see if science activities are also suggested in which parents and children can explore together concepts being studied at school.

If you leaf through a teacher edition of almost any newer program, you'll probably see places marked to show opportunities for multicultural learnings. You may also find suggestions about how you may locate and invite into your classroom appropriate role models from the community to enrich your instructional units. In the pupil texts, observe how biographies, descriptions, and photos of persons in science and technology reflect diversity in race, ethnicity, gender, and age.

If your school district has a culturally diverse population, chances are it has a long-standing department and materials that can help you to work with LEP pupils. Should more support be needed, sixteen regional resource centers for bilingual education in the United States give training and technical support services to schools. For the center nearest you, call or write The National Clearinghouse for Bilingual Education, 1118 22nd Street, N.W., Washington, DC 20037 (Telephone: 1-800-321-6223). These references from the National Clearinghouse can also further your work with LEP pupils:

Hamayan, Else and Perlman, Ron. *Helping Language Minority Pupils After They Exit from Bilingual/ESL Programs: A Handbook for Teachers,* 1990. ($2.50)

Short, Deborah J. *Integrating Language and Content Instruction: Strategies and Techniques,* 1991. ($2.50)

Working with Gifted Pupils

What can you expect from mainstreamed pupils classified as "gifted" by your district? Gifted children display many of the same developmental qualities as most children. What is different is the greater *degree* to which, and the *speed* with which, these qualities develop. In kindergarten, for example, gifted pupils may perform like second graders. By their senior year in high school, they typically outperform average college seniors on academic tests.[4] From their ranks will come many leaders and most of our future scientists and other high-level professionals.

What are some of their attributes? Compared to other pupils, the gifted child is much more likely to

1. Tolerate ambiguity and complexity.
2. Have a longer attention span.
3. Be a highly curious and sharp-eyed observer.

---

[4]James J. Gallagher, *Teaching the Gifted Child,* 2d ed. (Boston: Allyn and Bacon, 1975), p. 69.

4. Be a top-notch reader who retains what is read.

5. Have a well-developed speaking and listening vocabulary.

6. Have learned well the basic skills.

7. Understand complex directions the first time around.

8. Be imaginative and receptive to new ideas.

9. Be interested in broad concepts and issues.

10. Have one or more hobbies that require thinking.

Gifted pupils who show all or most of these attributes are often placed in a full-time special class or a "pull-out" program for part of the school day. But many are totally mainstreamed. How can we help these children? By working in harmony with their attributes.

A common problem with having gifted children in regular classrooms is that the curriculum is restrictive and unchallenging for them. *One way to "take the lid off," and yet have the gifted manageably working with other children, is to use many open-ended investigations and activities.* This stimulates the kind of creative, divergent thinking gifted pupils need to grow toward their potential. Fortunately for us as teachers, these and other experiences described next also work well for most of the nongifted.

A second important way to help the mainstreamed gifted is to encourage them to build a large knowledge base. This is usually easy because of their broad curiosity, strong ability to locate and understand information, and ability to remember what they find out. A wide variety of open-ended science investigations stimulates them to try multiple observations and experiments and to read for background. Gifted children readily sense how a broad array of knowledge feeds their creative and problem-solving abilities. This motivates them to learn even more.

A third way to help the gifted is to let them manage their own learning through individual *and small group projects, including those done for school science fairs.* (See Chapter 6.) The investigations in Part II of this book can be valuable here, as well as those found in references at the end of this section. Independent study is also fostered when we show pupils how to locate and use references, trade books, and other instructional materials in the school library.

A fourth way to help gifted pupils is by exposing them to persons in science and other professions who can serve as information sources and future role models. This is particularly important for pupils who come from economically disadvantaged backgrounds. Gifted children have the interest and quickly develop the capacity to correspond with knowledgeable adults, interview them by phone or in person, and understand much of what they see and hear. The adults, in turn, are almost always delighted and stimulated from their interactions with these precocious youngsters. Many schools keep on hand a file of adult professionals in science and technology who live in the community and are willing to meet occasionally with children.

We can also help the gifted by attending to their social skills as they interact with other children. Not only are these skills needed for success in many professions but for personal happiness as well. A central objective for mainstreaming the gifted is to help them communicate and get along with persons of all ability levels.

The following references can help you work with the gifted and the nongifted, too:

Alfred De Vito and Gerald H. Krockover. *Creative Sciencing.* Glenview, IL: Scott Foresman (Goodyear), 1991. (A broad spectrum of creative activities to explore concepts.)

Alfred De Vito. *Creative Wellsprings for Science Teaching.* W. Lafayette, IN: Creative Ventures, 1989. (Imaginative projects and puzzlers.)

Alfred E. Friedl. *Teaching Science to Children: An Integrated Approach.* 2d ed. New York: Random House, 1986. (Activities include many discrepant events—those that are unusual or unexpected—which gifted children find particularly interesting.)

MANAGING HANDS-ON ACTIVITIES

The new science coordinator who strongly praises discovery learning at the district's first in-service session is apt to hear this impatient cry for help: "It's all right for you to talk about discovery because you can put 30 sets of materials in the hands of 30 children. But what about those of us who can't? What I want to know is, how do you get everyone involved when you only have a few things to work with?"

It would be ideal if every child could always manipulate materials individually or with a partner. But for the present, this is something only a few programs have been able to achieve—at substantial cost. We can

often solve the problem through learning experiences that use everyday materials, such as those in Part II of this book. But this is not always possible. At these times, what's a teacher to do?

Whole-Class Teaching

One way you can handle the problem of a shortage of materials is to work with the entire class at one time. This is not ideal, but a proper seating arrangement and a mixture of broad and narrow questions addressed to individual children can be fairly effective. The idea is to have everyone close to the action and able to see what is going on. Also, it's important for individual children to have quick access to the materials when called on or when they want to do something to find out what happens.

Figure 5-4 shows how this is done. A low table is placed near a chalkboard, and movable chairs are arranged before it in a semicircle. Half the children sit on chairs, and

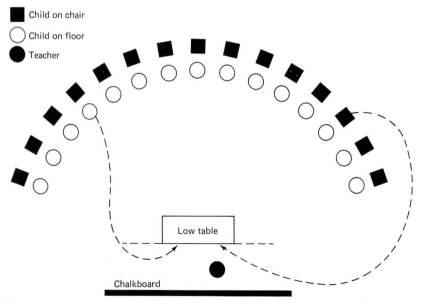

FIGURE 5-4
This arrangement makes it easy to either view or participate in an activity before the whole class.

half sit cross-legged on the floor in front of the chairs. Everyone is close to the table. No one's view is obstructed. There is ready access to the table as individual children are called on to participate. With some reminding, participating pupils will remember to stand *in back of* the table so that everyone can see what is happening. An arrangement of this kind is especially needed with younger children. It is easy for them to lose interest or become distracted when seated some distance away from the activity source. A nearby chart holder or a chalkboard in back of the table can serve for any needed recording.

After the activity is over, put the materials on a science center table so pupils can do the activity on their own during free periods.

The semicircular pattern is also convenient at other times. If a candle flame, hot plate, or other potentially hazardous item is needed in an activity, you can demonstrate the activity in a safe setting. You can also set standards with pupils for small-group activities and assign areas of the room for working. After the several groups or committees have completed their work, you can reassemble them into the initial seating pattern for easier reporting or discussion.

With older children there is less need for this type of seating arrangement. Short attention spans and distractions are less of a problem. The regular grouping of desks and chairs may serve for most occasions, but keep the materials table reasonably close to all the children when experiments and demonstrations are done before the entire class. There is usually no trouble with class control when everyone can see what is happening. If class desks are permanently fixed to the floor, use a higher than usual table for adequate viewing. It may be necessary to let some children change seats or move to a satisfactory location.

Group Teaching

When more materials are available, you can organize the class into smaller groups of two,

four, or six pupils each. Many activities need two people, so even numbers usually work best. Suppose, for example, you have five sets of materials for one activity. This is common when a kit goes with a textbook. You can divide the class into five groups, and have each work with one set. (With primary children, you might have cross-age tutors, parent volunteers, or aides assist the groups.)

You can do much the same thing with one set of materials for each of five activities. Here, the children rotate from one table or learning station to the next after a designated time (Figure 5-5).

When the school provides a kit for every classroom, you may be able to have even more materials by borrowing the kit of another teacher at the same grade level. This is easier to do when units are scheduled at different times and activities don't require consumable supplies. Of course, you'll want to replace all materials well before your colleague needs them, then return the favor.

A further way to stretch materials is to use learning centers, which we'll consider in the next chapter.

Keeping Everyone Involved

Many teachers find that their pupils work better in groups when each has a specific job.

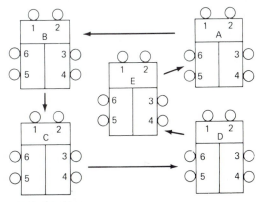

FIGURE 5-5
This arrangement shows how children might move from one learning station to the next after a designated time.

This is easy to arrange, especially from about grade three on. Try the following procedure, which works well in most classrooms.

Cluster the children's tables into islands of two or three each, depending on how many sets of materials you have. Most science kits contain one item for every four to six pupils. Each child sits at a numbered place—one to four or one to six—at the island, which bears the group's letter or name. (See again Figure 5-5.) Children take turns doing the steps of an activity, one step each. All the children in each group take their own notes during the activity, then together at the end they assemble a group report. Each day, a different-numbered child orally gives the report for the group when it's time to discuss results with the whole class. Others in the group add their ideas as well.

A different-numbered child each day picks up and returns the materials. This materials monitor is responsible for making sure everything not consumed is returned, and for reporting in writing what needs to be replaced.

With brief training, group materials monitors can smoothly pick up or return materials set out on a table in *less than* a minute. Notice in Figure 5-6 the inefficiency of *A*. Each monitor waits while the one ahead picks up a materials tray. In *B*, they move almost as one person to a tray, pick it up, and go back to the group. Set a high but realistic performance standard for monitors soon after beginning activities. Stick to it every day, but avoid competitive haste. Children delight in meeting such challenges.

A Class Science Committee

To manage materials, especially if you have a science kit, it will help to appoint a class science committee of about three pupils. (One person for each two groups works well.) Have them prepare trays of materials for the groups, put back the materials where they belong when returned by the group monitors, and check that everything has been

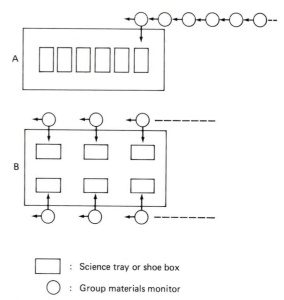

FIGURE 5-6

Arrange science trays or boxes so that group materials monitors can pick them up and return to their groups quickly and efficiently.

returned. Discarded shoe boxes or Styrofoam pizza covers make good trays.

For efficiency, keep the committee small and staffed by children who are rarely absent. Make it a permanent or long-range job, and replace no more than one person at a time. It takes a while to learn where everything goes in a kit, and more than just a few pupils will get in each other's way. Train the committee to collate the daily reports of what, if anything, must be replaced and hand you the list weekly, or as needed.

Cooperative Learning and Managing Group Activities

You may know the story of two stone masons at work. When asked what they were doing, one said, "I'm fitting stones together." The other said, "I'm building a cathedral."

The degree of cooperative behavior, responsibility, and achievement you get from a group is often linked to your outlook—which sooner or later becomes plain to pupils. Some teachers, for instance, view clean-up time at the end of an activity as something to be endured or even dreaded, as room control may get out of hand. Other teachers see it as a chance to develop cooperative skills, build self-esteem, and raise the level of personal responsibility in class members.

Some of the most effective ideas about managing groups stem from the work on cooperative learning by Roger T. Johnson and David W. Johnson.[5] Pupils generally achieve more science learning when they work cooperatively, and learn to better accept one another as well.[6] More and more teachers today are noticing the ability peer groups have to ignite active learning in children. They also see the value of diversity come alive as each child applies unique prior knowledge and perspective to group tasks. In their view, multicultural, racial, socioeconomic, gender, physical and mental differences enrich and broaden education. After all, these teachers say, for what society are we preparing children? Following are six cooperative learning practices I've observed in classrooms that reflect to some degree the Johnson model.

1. *Each group is made up of a cross section of class members.* New groups are chosen by the teacher every few weeks. This insures a balanced spread of talent and exposes pupils to a mix of persons to work with. A group usually consists of two to four members, with as many as six if materials are scarce. Two pairs of pupils work well as a group when enough materials are at hand. One pair consults with the other to iron out problems, share results, and prepare a report. At the primary-grade level, two-person groups are common.

2. *Everyone shares leadership responsibilities.* This includes taking turns doing the steps of an investigation and assuming a specific job for the day. Some useful jobs are *materials monitor,* who gets and returns materials; *checker,* who checks to see if everyone knows what to do, reminds people to stay on task when necessary, and asks the group to decide whether completed work meets expectations; *spokesperson,* who asks the teacher or a spokesperson from another group for help if the group gets stuck, and then conveys the information back to the group; and a *coach,* who notices and praises anyone who uses a newly-introduced social skill, or reminds someone when the skill would be useful. Pupils rotate jobs each day.

3. *Group members depend on each other when doing an assignment.* The group members have a common task, materials are shared, and a group report is prepared. Each group is accountable for working up to a standard rather than having its work compared to that of other groups.

4. *Each person is individually accountable for learning.* It's critical in group work for each person to learn and do his or her fair share. Teachers try to motivate each child to participate and learn in several ways: (a) by randomly picking someone from each group to report group findings at discussion time; (b) by randomly selecting one child's paper or other finished product from each group to represent each group's work; (c) by randomly asking a child in each group to describe what she is learning; (d) by making brief notes periodically about the quality and extent of each child's participation; and (e) by giving tests to individuals on the assigned material.

5. *Each group learns to largely govern its own behavior and learning.* Questions and problems that pupils have are first directed to

[5]See, for example: David W. Johnson and Roger T. Johnson, *Learning Together and Alone: Cooperation, Competition and Individualization* (Englewood Cliffs, N.J.: Prentice-Hall, 1991).

[6]Roger T. Johnson and David W. Johnson. "What Research Says About Student-Student Interactions in Science Classrooms." *Education in the 80's: Science,* Mary B. Rowe, ed. (Washington, DC: National Education Association, 1982), pp. 25–37.

each other, before the spokesperson calls the teacher or confers with another spokesperson. If help is needed, other group members stay at their station and continue to work quietly as well as they can until help arrives.

6. *The children are introduced to and practice a variety of social skills.* Courtesy and the Golden Rule are modeled as much as possible, starting with the teacher. Only one person speaks at a time, with a soft voice. The teacher also teaches group members to share ideas, encourage one another, and to seek agreement by weighing evidence rather than by unsupported argument. Many experienced teachers prefer to observe groups in action before they introduce more than just a few starting skills, to identify needs. Social skills or their lack can make or break cooperative learning, so they are taught as needed along with academic objectives.

Learning experiences can go very smoothly when cooperative learning is given a chance to flourish. Here are some things that effective teachers usually consider when they manage group work. Their planning includes advance preparation for the lesson and what to do at the beginning, middle, and end of the lesson. (We'll focus here on the mechanics of management. Chapter 7 stresses planning for subject-matter and process learning.)

Advance Preparation. Try to select an interesting and worthwhile activity or investigation. What materials are needed that you have on hand or that must be brought in? Are there enough materials for pairs, fours, or sixes? When children work in pairs, it's still desirable to have them consult and form a group report with others at their table cluster.

Some time before the science period—shortly before school, at recess, during free time, for example—have the science committee prepare trays or shoe boxes of materials for each group. At the primary level, this may be done by an aide, a parent volunteer, or a cross-age tutor.

Beginning/Introduction. Look at the situation from the children's viewpoint. You have the "toys." They are itching to get their hands on them. So make the introduction as brief as you can. However, don't hesitate to introduce social skills if needed.

Earlier in the year you may have several times gotten into group work with them in some other subjects as well as science. You may have set such standards as: take turns, speak softly, and only one person in a group speaks at a time. Also, when you give a "stop" signal—bell, piano chord, both hands raised, lights off and on, or the like—everyone stops, is silent, and all eyes are on you.

If you want to introduce a new social skill to the children, now is a good time. Suppose you want to stress the importance of *being a good listener.* Some teachers would begin by role-playing good and bad examples with a child. You could also start by asking,

What do the words "good listener" mean to you? How do you feel when you speak with someone who is a good listener? a bad listener? What does a good listener look and sound like?

After discussing the questions one by one, list on a chart or chalkboard what children reply to the last question; add a few ideas of your own if needed:

A Good Listener

Lets the person speak.
Keeps eyes on the speaker.
May nod head.
May ask questions.

You might briefly model each behavior, to clarify.

Encourage your pupils to especially practice listening today. They can check the list for reminders as needed. Ask them to look for times when the skill is used, to compliment the good listeners, and to remind persons if they forget to use the skill. Tell them you will do that, too.

To summarize, whenever you want to teach a social skill: (1) establish the need, (2) clearly describe and model the skill, (3) provide the practice, and (4) monitor to evaluate, correct, and reinforce the skill.

If the standards are well known in this beginning part of the lesson, you mainly pose the activity problem, rapidly but clearly work out procedures with the pupils, and announce the time period they will work. To avoid distractions, only you have materials at first—to show as needed.

Ask someone to repeat the directions for the class *while* you have the group monitors quickly pick up the materials trays. This prevents dead time. Children go to work immediately on getting the materials. If one or two pupils still have questions, their group tries first to answer them.

It's a good idea to say *everything* you need to say before the whole class gets down to work. Some teachers habitually interrupt the class with further directions and other afterthoughts. This distracts the children, wastes time, and often requires more effort than expected.

Middle/Work Period.   Walk around to different groups to observe how they are doing. Try to spend no more than a minute with one group so you can keep attentively circulating. Stand when possible where you can see all groups as you assist one group. Simple eye contact with a child who starts to get off task quickly stops most misbehavior at the easiest stage. Encourage pupils to help themselves as much as possible. Notice how well they listen, take turns, speak softly, practice courtesy, encourage one another, and do their assigned jobs. Quietly praise helpful behavior as you notice it. If there is a problem, give the group time to work it out and return later. When the lack of a social skill is the trouble, calmly model what to do rather than criticize unhelpful behavior. Make a few brief notes about helpful behavior or any other

matter you may want to bring up later with the whole class.

If your pupils can write, have *everyone* record what's done in the investigation or task. (Use the format of the text activity or one like it. Most published programs now routinely provide individual lab sheets for recording.) This keeps everyone busy and on track. It also allows members to put together a group report in several minutes, and save their own work for personal folders.

If a group finishes early—this seldom happens with *open-ended* investigations—find out how well it did the task before it begins another. Ask broad and narrow questions to learn how well they applied science processes and constructed concepts. If weaknesses show up, most children will readily redo or restudy with purpose. When groups do finish early, have on hand trade books and other references pupils can use to extend their knowledge of the problem or concept being investigated. Children who give interesting new facts in discussions gain status and enrich learning for everyone.

When it is time, give the signal for cleanup alert. Everyone stops and makes eye contact with you. You then tell the class to go ahead. If you prefer, add the time-keeping chore to one of the group job assignments—materials monitor or checker, for example. Be sure, though, that all groups begin and end cleanup at about the same time. Efficient cleanups over the school year can add hours for more hands-on science.

End/Cleanup and Discussion. Everyone pitches in to place materials back on the trays just as received. All stay in their seats and work quietly. This should seldom take more than a minute and can take even less time. The materials monitor makes sure everything is present, then quickly takes the tray back to the materials table. The science committee checks in the materials. (If some things need cleaning, this may be done at a later time.) Meantime, group members at each table cluster quickly compare their notes, using soft voices, and agree on a group report. You might allow about three minutes for this.

Select at random one person from each group to give a report on their work. Help pupils compare findings, resolve disagreements among groups, and make valid inferences.

If you have introduced a social skill, have the reporters mention a few behaviors in their group that reflected the skill. Praise the children for their successes. If they did a super job, have them pat themselves on the back, applaud, shake hands with one another, or give a "high five" to each group member. If a similar behavior problem came up in several groups, ask the group reporters to describe what happened without giving names. Guide the class to suggest effective ways to handle such problems. This is a powerful way to correct and prevent unproductive behavior, especially with older children.

You might now also mention before the whole class several helpful comments or courtesies—whatever positive behaviors you want to reinforce—that you observed in some groups. (Here's where previous note-taking is handy.) There's no need to mention individuals, just the group. Recognize the group before the class, and its members will appreciate and welcome these contributions from their peers even more. Of course, you'll want to tell the helpful child sometime that you are talking about her, if there is any doubt.

The teaching of social skills takes time, particularly when children receive little instruction at home, but experienced teachers know its value. "The time I spend during the first ten weeks or so is more than made up during the rest of the year," one twenty-year veteran recently told me. "And I enjoy teaching the kids a *whole lot* more!"

SUMMARY

The quality of your science program is strongly influenced by the teaching resources you select. Most elementary programs use common, everyday materials. So they are ordinarily easy to gather, especially if you ask others to help. Motivated children can bring to school many free or discardable materials. Parents are also usually willing to help. Other items are best supplied by the school through commercial sources.

Both reading and nonreading classroom materials are needed to teach science. Reading materials include textbooks, trade books, reference materials, and language experience charts. All are more understandable when you provide concrete experiences and develop vocabulary before using them.

Nonreading materials include kits, free and inexpensive items, constructions and models, microscopes and microprojectors, and visual aids—pictures, videotapes, and the like. Each is well suited for particular teaching purposes. Outside the classroom, remember that the school and nearby environment may illustrate concrete examples of objects and events introduced in the science program.

Some special resources and ways to use them are needed for mainstreamed exceptional pupils. A school advisory team is likely to meet with you to compose an individualized educational plan (IEP) for each handicapped pupil. You can best help pupils of limited English proficiency by reducing their anxiety, increasing content meaning, modeling good English, and giving them many chances to informally interact with English speakers. Gifted and talented children thrive on open-ended, divergent investigations and activities.

When few materials are available, hands-on learning experiences require more planning. Arrange the class so it can easily observe several pupils perform activities, then later place the materials where more children can manipulate them at convenient times. You can also divide the class into groups and rotate them among several table clusters that contain materials for single activities.

When you have a class materials kit, have a small committee set out and put back the materials and report what needs to be replaced.

The handling of materials is easier to manage if you routinely follow the mechanics of what to do before, during, and after the lesson. Try cooperative learning for an effective way to enlist the aid of the whole class in managing first-hand learning experiences.

SUGGESTED READINGS

Brandwein, Paul F. and Harry A. Passow, editors. *Gifted Young in Science.* Washington, DC: National Science Teachers Association, 1989. (Advice from 34 scientists, teachers, and scholars on how to develop learning environments that encourage the precollege gifted at all levels to reach their potential.)

Ellis, Susan S. and Susan F. Whalen. *Cooperative Learning—Getting Started.* New York: Scholastic, 1990. (A small and practical handbook, based on research by D. & R. Johnson.)

McCloskey, Mary Lou, and Lorene Quay. "Effects of Coaching on Handicapped Children's Social Behavior and Teacher Attitudes in Mainstreamed Classrooms." *Elementary School Journal* 87(4):425–35 (March 1987). (Exposes several difficulties in changing social behaviors of some handicapped children in grades one through four.)

Romance, Nancy and Michael R. Vitale. "Sealable Science for Busy Teachers." *Science and Children* 28(5):24–26 (February 1991). (How to efficiently organize and package some science materials.)

Russell, Helen Ross. *Ten-Minute Field Trips.* Washington, DC: National Teachers Association, 1990. (How to take advantage of the immediate environment with quick visits for specific purposes.)

Saul, Wendy and Sybille A. Jagusch, Eds. *Vital Connections: Children, Science, and Books.* Portsmouth, NH: Heinemann, 1992. (A comprehensive look at the place of science literature in the lives of children.)

Scarnati, James T. and Cyril J. Weller. "The Write Stuff." *Science and Children* 29(4):28–29 (January 1992). (Explains four purposes for writing assignments in science.)

6

How to Arrange and Manage Complementary Experiences

Should the children in your class all study the same topics and activities, or should there be some variations among individuals and small groups? A class of 30 or so pupils will display a wide range of abilities and interests. Thoughtful teachers often see a need to complement the basic science program with further, more individualized activities.

Many educators say that children should have some choice in what and how they learn. They find that different children learn best in several ways and through varying interests. Allowing some choices can boost morale and whet lifelong interests. Many teachers use individualized activities to cultivate a more open form of inquiry and independent learning. They use them to enrich a teaching unit, or to permit some pupils to pursue their science interests if science is not scheduled in the school district curriculum throughout the year. They use them to stretch few materials among more pupils. Teachers may also employ individual or small group teaching approaches with computer-assisted instruction.

No child learns science solely from classroom activities. Each brings to school concepts and attitudes that are shaped by home and other influences. How can parents complement what their children learn at school and further support your science teaching?

This chapter shows three ways of using individual or small group experiences to complement basic instruction—learning centers, microcomputer centers, and projects—then suggests ways to enlist parents' aid in enriching what their children learn.

HOW TO MAKE SCIENCE LEARNING CENTERS

A classroom learning center is a place where one or several pupils at a time can do activities independently through materials and directions found at that place. A learning center may be arranged so children may choose the activities they can do, or are interested in, and work at a pace that is right for each person. Some teachers also permit children to select the times they go to a center and partners to work with, if any.

An example of a science learning center for a combination second- and third-grade class is shown in Figure 6-1. The topic is the growth and development of frogs. The center's purpose is enrichment. That is, the center allows children to explore independently an area of high interest and develop a background that they may use in a variety of ways. About four children could use this center satisfactorily at one time.

Notice the stored activity cards and worksheets. The cards suggest different things to do. The worksheets go with some of the cards. Children use these to write down data or make drawings as suggested on some cards. Completed worksheets are placed in the left pocket on the background board for later examination by the teacher. Just below that spot is a record booklet in which each child records completed activities.

Observe some other features of this center. An attractive background shows the topic and invites children's attention. Simple overall directions tell how to work at the center. A large aquarium containing frogs' eggs and tadpoles allows firsthand observation of their growth and development. Stories with pictures are available for reading by able children. Those who cannot read may hear these stories through earphones connected to a tape recorder.

Notice the teacher-made game in the foreground called "Ribbet." The title, chosen by the children, mimicks the sound made by frogs. Each lily pad on which a player lands contains a question about frogs' stages of development. To advance, a player must be able to answer the question correctly. Contro-

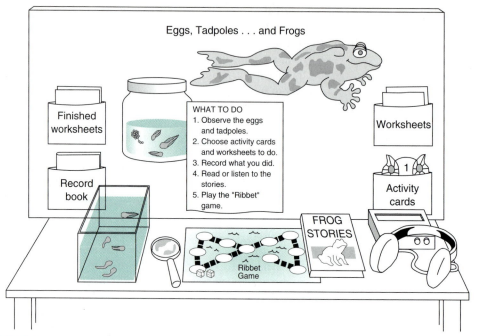

FIGURE 6-1
A science learning center.

versies are resolved by observing the aquarium's contents and looking up information in the stories.

To construct this center, the teacher considered these matters:

- Purpose and objectives.
- Activity cards and worksheets.
- Materials and their resupply.
- Record keeping and evaluation.
- The physical setup.

See now how each of these matters affects the making of a learning center.

Deciding Purpose and Objectives

The first thing in making a science learning center is to decide its purpose. Do you want it for general enrichment? While this is the most common purpose, center activities may also be used to complement an instructional unit[1] or present an entire unit when materials are few. For instance, unit activities may require microscopes, but only several may be handy. The best way to teach the unit, or at least furnish some complementary activities, might be to schedule several children at a time into the science learning center at staggered intervals.

Some topics are best left for whole-class unit instruction. For example, you may want considerable group interaction with overall class data before children generalize about their work. This is particularly important in biology, because variations in organisms—plant and animal—are always present. Also, some topics may call for children to work mostly outdoors. Other areas of investigation may require room darkening. Some activities

---

[1]An instructional unit is a series of related lessons, usually organized around a topic, problem, or set of objectives.

may be quite noisy or involve much movement. In these cases, judge whether a learning-center approach is appropriate. Center activities must be compatible with everything else going on in your classroom.

As a rule, avoid activities whose outcomes take more time to happen than you assign pupils to be at the center. Children want action and they want it *now*. There are, though, occasional exceptions to the rule. In the activity shown in Figure 6-2, taken from a "Things That Change" learning center, pupils start a "changes" jar. They put in materials they believe will deteriorate and will view these slow changes (away from the center) over the course of a month or longer. But the

other change activities at this center happen much faster: Ice cubes melt, liquids evaporate, mixtures fizz, and so on.

When center activities are unit related, you can state objectives for knowledge and process as you do with a unit.

Developing Activity Cards and Worksheets

How can you communicate activities in the most understandable and appealing ways? The directions on activity cards must be simple—what to get and what to do—so independent work is possible. Use short sentences and easy words. Draw pictures beside key words if the cards are intended for less able readers (see Figure 6-2).

Despite your best efforts, some children may not be able to read your directions. What to do? Pairing the child with a good reader will help. In some schools, the policy is to have multiage grouping for classes. Other schools have active cross-age tutoring programs in which older pupils may volunteer to assist younger ones. In such schools, it is relatively easy to help the slow reader or nonreader. Of course, in schools where teacher aides or volunteer parents are available, they can give assistance.

A few teachers find that recording directions on a tape recorder works satisfactorily. However, the children must learn how to use the machine. Teachers of primary-level children usually find that they must briefly introduce each new activity to the entire class before most children can do the activity by themselves.

Try to make the design of your activity cards appealing and different for each topic. To do this, you might design the cards to go with the topic. For example, with the topic "The Melting of Ice Cubes" make each card look like an ice cube. For "Air and Weather" make cloud-shaped cards. Above all, make the cards as childproof as possible. Cut them from heavy paper or tagboard. Avoid having

FIGURE 6-2
A "changes" jar begun at a center allows children to continually observe, away from the center, slow changes.

thin, easily bendable parts, and laminate the cards, or cover them with transparent contact paper.

Include as many open-ended activities as you can that have possibilities for process-skill development. These will also make it more possible for children to suggest additional activities, which they enjoy doing.

Worksheets are a convenient way to know what the child has done, if you cannot directly observe the child at work. A worksheet may be simply a plain sheet of paper on which the child has made a drawing or recorded some data after an activity-card suggestion.

Some teachers like to have a worksheet for every activity. Other teachers reserve worksheets only for activities in which data recording is necessary for the activity to make sense—graphing temperature or other changes, keeping track of results from testing different materials, drawing a conclusion from a number of facts, and so on. Sometimes worksheets are called "laboratory sheets," or "data sheets," along with other titles. See Figure 6-3 for an example of an activity card and its accompanying worksheet.

Several published science programs have activity booklets designed to go with the texts. Usually, these are for grade three and beyond. The detachable activity sheets in these booklets may serve as both activity cards and worksheets for a science learning center.

Providing, Storing, and Resupplying Materials

In your center it is good to have activities that can be done with everyday materials. The children may be able to bring in most of what

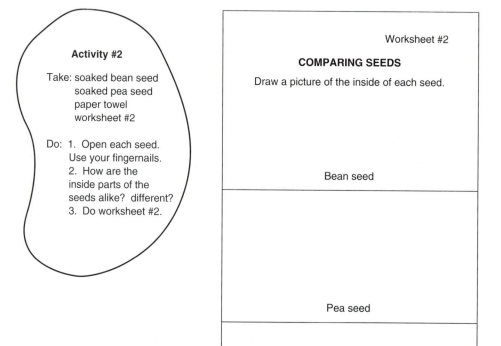

FIGURE 6-3
An activity card and its accompanying worksheet.

is needed. Also, this may dispel the idea of some children that science is a strange enterprise conducted with expensive and mysterious objects.

Use printed and audiovisual materials as well as experiments. Items loaned by museums and collections can be a real help. And motivated children have been known to cut out, mount, and organize extensive picture collections in an hour or less.

How can you package and store your materials? Shoe boxes numbered for each activity card can work well. Tape a list of the contents of each box on the front end. Number both the box and its lid. Some teachers tape one activity card to each shoe box lid so a separate list of contents is not needed. This is fine when one activity requires one box of materials, but sometimes it may be more convenient to have one shoe box of materials for several activities.

You may set up shelves for storing materials from wooden boxes obtained free at some food stores. Or arranging shelves from boards supported by cement blocks may be more convenient.

If your activities require consumable materials, a list should be made of things that must be replaced. It can be displayed by the materials shelves. Beyond the primary grades, materials monitors can be appointed to keep track of such needs.

Record Keeping and Evaluation

Observing children in action is the best way to learn what they need help with and what they can do. Yet if many activities are going on, it's hard to keep track of everything each person has tried.

One way to record pupil progress is to have a master list of all the center's activities or objectives with the children's names written to one side. If each activity has a worksheet, these can be filed by the child in a folder at the center. Check the worksheet against your master list. The worksheet will show what activity was performed. It will also reveal something about the quality of the performance. Develop your own code system for recording the quality of the work and indicating what is incomplete, what should be done over, and so on.

It may be impractical to have a worksheet for each activity. A record booklet of the center can be used by the children to check off the activities they have completed. However, this may cause a few children to make critical comparisons between their work and that of others. ("Ramon did four activities. I only did two.") So it may be better to have a record system in which the child refers only to his own work.

To do this, some teachers give each child who uses a center a record sheet containing only activity numbers. (See Figure 6-4.) A space is left at the top for any center title to be written in. A line is drawn under the last

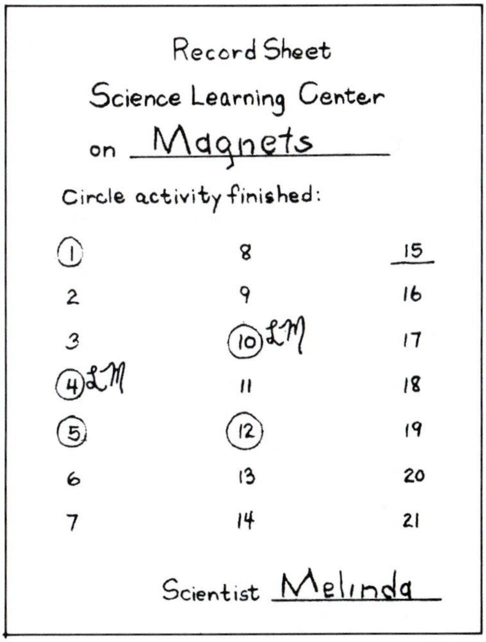

FIGURE 6-4
A record system in which each child refers only to his own work prevents children from making critical comparisons of each other.

number that equals the named center's total activities. On completing an activity, the child circles the activity number on her or his sheet. This record sheet is kept handy for the teacher to review during informal or scheduled conferences. The teacher's initials may be written next to selected activity numbers if the child appears to have accomplished the appropriate objectives. To save time, only the more important objectives may be sampled. The record sheet is filed in the child's science folder along with worksheets and other work products.

Keep an eye on how successful your center is in meeting your objectives and holding the children's interest. What is there about the activities that appeals to the children and gets the job done? Why are pupils avoiding or doing poorly with other activities? Ask the children to give their views, also. Together you can continually improve the quality of your different centers' learning opportunities.

Schedule individual conferences periodically to learn more about each child's accomplishments. Make some brief notes for future reference as needed. Ask questions when you want to evaluate concepts or principles. Invite the child's reactions to the activities performed.

Can the child profit from further, deeper study in the form of an independent project? (See page 153 for details.) Such a project can be particularly valuable with the able and older child. This may be the time to set up a "contract" between you and the child. Or, the child may make a preliminary study before deciding with you on the exact topic, time, and goals for the contract. A worthwhile project may be shared with the class in a report or exhibit. Older children might even construct a simple learning center based on a limited topic or problem.

Arranging the Physical Setup

Where is the best place to put a science learning center? How should it look? What are some ways to cut down the work in setting up new centers? These are some things worth thinking about.

Rule number one, if you listen to experienced teachers, is put the center where you can always keep an eye on it. This alone can do more than anything else to ensure that it gets used properly.

Some science topics require water. In these cases, consider placing the learning center next to a water source and sink. Carrying water to and from a distant sink can be messy, especially with young children. If audiovisual equipment is required, there should be an electrical outlet handy.

How will children move into and out of the center? Locate the center where it will not interfere with other activities. Or, establish a traffic pattern so children working on other activities won't be bothered. Will wall space be needed? Take this into account also.

It is helpful to make a rough sketch of a proposed center. As you draw the sketch, think about where you will put the things that have been mentioned in the preceding paragraphs. Try to have a colorful and eyecatching background that reflects the center's topic.

You can draw enlarged background pictures by using an opaque projector (or make a transparency by putting a picture through a copying machine and then projecting the transparency with an overhead projector). This is a help to anyone and an indispensable tool for the artistically untalented. With it, you can enliven your center's background (or classroom bulletin boards) with familiar comic strip or story characters for child appeal: Dr. Doolittle, Peanuts, Snoopy, and Dr. Seuss' menagerie. It's also interesting to use mystery, surprise, oddities, contrast, and drama in captions or pictures.

For durability, many teachers use a pegboard background as shown in Figure 6-5. The two pieces of pegboard are painted to match the wall color and are joined by sturdy

FIGURE 6-5
One easy, versatile way to assemble a learning center is with two or three pieces of pegboard.

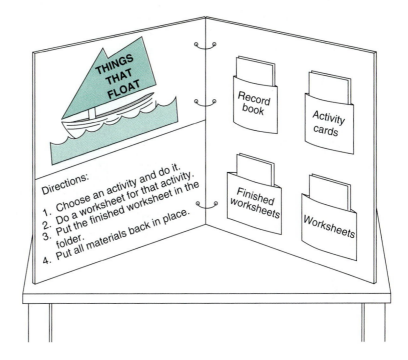

duct tape or metal rings. A three-panel pegboard set also works well. Extra-long paper fasteners are used to secure the four folded-paper pockets, directions chart, and the theme-setting picture.

What if the teacher wants to change the topic of this learning center? The boat is quickly replaced by another theme-setting cutout, and new activity cards and worksheets are placed in the pockets. Everything else is permanent. If the center is no longer needed, the pegboard background is easily folded and stored.

A disadvantage of pegboard is its heaviness. Matte board, chipboard, and corrugated cardboard cut from large cartons are less durable but also work well. Poster board is too flimsy and is best avoided.

Colored matte board is the most convenient of these substitute materials to use for the background. It does not need to be hinged, painted, or covered, and can last for years. A 36-inch by 42-inch sheet (sold in art supply stores) will make two centers that are com-pact and easily fitted into many smaller, underused spaces. To construct a center:

1. Cut the longer dimension into two equal parts with a sharp knife. This will give you 2 background pieces, each 21 inches high and 36 inches wide. For stability, a background board should be wider than it is tall.

2. Consider one piece now. It needs a fold in the middle, so it can stand without toppling. Score it lightly down the middle of the back or uncolored side with an ice pick or nail. Now it should fold easily. Each side of the fold will be 18 inches wide when open and standing.

3. To reinforce the folding part, first completely fold the board. Then stick a wide strip of masking tape evenly down the length of the fold.

4. Open the board and attach a picture, directions, and pockets as with a pegboard-type background. Make holes with an ice pick or nail, and secure the items with ½-inch-long paper fasteners.

If you use extra-large pockets for holding paper or cards, only two may fit on the right front panel. If so, just fasten one or two additional pockets for finished worksheets and record booklet on the *back* of the panel.

Timesaving Shortcuts: Converting Investigations into Centers

Probably the easiest way to make a learning center is to convert one or more of the open-ended learning experiences described in this book. Most of the investigations in Part II can be readily changed into centers, as well as some of the more open-ended activities found there. To select them, use the criteria suggested on page 146, especially the following:

Can children work inside the classroom?

Can children work without interfering with others?

Do activity outcomes happen at the center during the allotted times?

Are most of the learning experiences open-ended?

Examples of investigations that meet the criteria are

Makeup of colored liquids, 227.

Wheel-belt systems, 404.

The properties of leaves, 448.

Snails and what they do, 497.

Examples of those that do *not* meet the criteria are

A bottle xylophone, 307.

The growth of seeds, 433.

How to train goldfish, 484.

Wind erosion, 576.

Can you see why the last four investigations do not belong in a learning center? The first is distracting to other pupils, the next two take much time, and the last needs to be done outdoors.

Figure 6-6 shows a center made by a teacher from an investigation in Part II, on

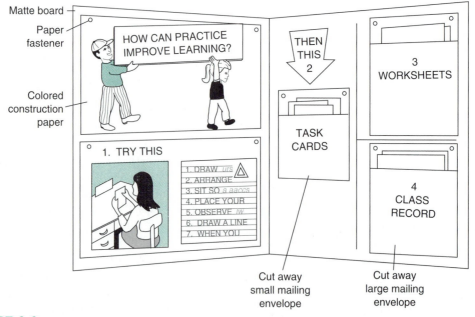

FIGURE 6-6

Many science investigations can be readily made into learning centers.

page 527. Table 6-1 shows where the parts come from.

Instead of having a separate "Try This" section, some teachers make this feature the first activity card. To save more time, you can photocopy the discovery problem section as a whole and glue it to a card rather than copy it one problem to a card. Make duplicate cards if more than two children use the center at one time.

Some teachers save further time by not tying the center title and drawing to a specific topic. You can, for example, simply entitle the center, "Science Center," and attach an appropriate picture (child inspecting some object with a hand lens, or holding up a test tube, or netting a butterfly, for example). Now all you need to change are the activity cards and hands-on materials as you change to further learning experiences. While a "generic" center like this may not look as fresh and interesting to your pupils as one whose theme frequently changes, you may feel that the time saved is worth the trade-off.

To introduce the center to a class, simply use the introduction to the investigation. For sample objectives, background, and so on, see the "Teaching Comments" section of the investigation.

Even converting a Part II investigation into a center takes some time. But because it is simple and straightforward, an aide, a volunteer parent, or an older pupil can do much or all of the task with some supervision.

Seek ways for pupils to help you plan, gather, and prepare materials for centers. It will mean more to them than if you do everything yourself. Also, your centers may be set up in less time with more and better materials. A well-organized teacher who enlists the aid of pupils is usually far ahead of one who does not. This is likely at all levels, but especially so beyond the primary level. Pupils then are more skillful at cutting out things, applying contact paper, writing contents cards for shoe boxes, and so on.

Parents, too, are usually eager to contribute many ready-to-discard but usable items, as well as occasional volunteer service. Volunteer work is more likely to be offered by parents of primary-level children.

MANAGING THE SCIENCE LEARNING CENTER

How will you schedule children into the center? How can you introduce the center and keep things running smoothly? It's hard to describe precisely what will be instantly useful in every situation. Schools and individual classrooms vary so much.

In many schools, there is an instructional materials resource center to complement materials and activities in the classroom. In some classrooms, several persons work together as a team—a teacher, a student teacher, teacher's aide, one of several volunteer parents, and an older child from another class who

TABLE 6-1

Parts of a center may be derived from an investigation.

Center	(Comes from)	Investigation
Leading question		Exploratory problem
Try this		Try this section
Picture		Traced from page 528
Activity-card problems		Discovery problems

serves as a cross-age tutor. An open-space classroom may contain 70 to 100 or more children, with a team of 3 to 5 teachers working together. However, in most instances, a single teacher still works with about 30 children in a self-contained classroom. Let's assume this is your situation.

Scheduling the Center

If you have never worked with learning centers, start with a modest plan within a familiar topic. After you learn the ropes, you can become more creative.

Reserve a large block of time from which a segment can be used for work at a learning center. For example, many teachers reserve a two-hour block daily for the language arts. Suppose you have 32 pupils divided into 4 groups: A, B, C, and D. You rotate these groups daily through several different language arts activities. Table 6-2 shows how you can adapt this organization to schedule a science center.

The block is divided into four half-hour segments. In the first half hour of the block, group A works with you in the literature book. Meanwhile, group B does creative writing. Group C does individualized spelling activities.

During the same half hour, the eight pupils of group D are evenly divided between a language assignment and a science learning center. Four pupils work on activities such as poetry writing, vocabulary development, dictionary use, alphabetizing games, and punctuation practice. (This can be done at their desks or a language development center.) The other four pupils of group D are at the science center doing different open-ended activities of their choice. Both sets of four pupils in D switch assignments after two days. On Friday, all eight pupils of group D work on language activities during the first half-hour period. No one is assigned to the science center.

During half-hour periods two, three, and four, each group rotates into a new assignment as shown. At the end of each daily two-hour block, all four groups will have experienced four different assignments. Usually by Thursday, all the children will have had one hour of work at the science learning center.

If you want more time for science, consider skipping the language center for a while. That way, everyone will have two hours a week at the science center by Thursday. On Friday, reserve some time to summarize and evaluate as a class what has been learned at the center.

Here is a second plan you may want to try. Start with a free period that all the children receive at the same time, for example, 30 minutes. During this time, the children are free to go to the school library or materials resource center, do recreational reading in the classroom, play educational games, and so forth. Of course, some pupils could go to the science center at that time. How about the rest? Each time you plan to teach the class anything that has a follow-up seatwork assignment of about 30 minutes, schedule 4 or more pupils into (or let them choose) the science center. To serve more pupils, add more centers. The seatwork assignment is made up in the next free time period. This is a trade-off most children are delighted to make for science activities.

Free periods also give you time to confer with pupils. Here is where children's records of what they did, and completed worksheets, can be used to extra advantage.

TABLE 6-2
Rotating schedule for small groups.

1	2	3	4	Daily Two-Hour Block
A	D	C	B	Literature book (teacher)
B	A	D	C	Creative writing
C	B	A	D	Individualized spelling
D	C	B	A	Language or science center

Chances are your experience with science learning centers will be as successful and rewarding as that of many teachers. If so, consider a more flexible arrangement that uses additional centers in several subjects. Some teachers reserve mornings for the three Rs and unit teaching. Afternoons are for individualized enrichment and skill-building activities at different learning centers, such as the following:

Science or social studies center

Fine arts center

Hobby center

Literature center

Writing center

Speaking and listening center

Math center

Work at the centers may be either assigned or optional. This setup allows you freedom to vary time and other considerations, and to assist and confer with individuals. You and each child can cooperatively decide on ways to pursue interests, knowledge, and skills. The best learning usually happens when children themselves take an active part in planning their learning.

Introducing Science Learning Centers

Give your pupils a thorough introduction to the science learning center. It will prevent most problems from arising. Describe carefully:

What to do at the center.

How to get and return materials.

Where to put completed work.

How to get help, if needed.

Also show them a general directions chart containing this information displayed at the center. After a while, the chart will no longer be needed.

Introduce one or two activities to whet their interest. The most practical activities will be open-ended ones. At the primary level, you may need to introduce one or two new activities a day. Most young children will not be able to read activity cards satisfactorily.

During the first few days, try to have a parent volunteer or an older child present at the center to help with the activities. If that is not possible, start off with a few of your most able pupils and let the other children consult these able pupils if help is needed. Of course, if you have independent work going on, or several centers operating, you'll be free to give such help yourself. You may try taping some directions, but this can become complicated for young children if multiple activities are involved, and it may require a lot of your time.

How much is "too much" noise? Be sure to work out some obvious signal to alert pupils at the center if their noise level interferes with the work of others. Also, discuss the least-disturbing traffic pattern for going to and departing from the center.

Show the schedule, if any, for using the centers. You might use a pocket chart with pupil's names and times on it. If you start with the rotating schedule described earlier, you can announce to the class when to shift assignments.

To make sure your class understands the setup, take a few minutes to "walk through" the pattern. After a few trials, most children should learn what they need to do.

HOW WELL CAN YOU CONSTRUCT AND MANAGE SCIENCE LEARNING CENTERS?

As with most teaching, actually making and managing a science learning center is a surer way to become able than by merely reading about it. If you do go ahead, it will help to have some guidelines by which you can judge the adequacy of your plan. Following are some questions you might use for the job. They are organized under the same categories used in this chapter and reflect most of the points mentioned. Parenthetical remarks are used to help you recall these points. Look over the list carefully. You may want to omit some questions and add some of your own. You may also want to arrange some order of priority among the questions. Concentrate at first on what you think is most important. In revisions, work on other points. It takes a lot of practice to do *everything* well.

Choosing the Right Topic

1. What is the purpose of the center? (Enrichment, support of text, complement unit, whole unit.)
2. What are the objectives? (Performance, especially if unit connected.)
3. Can children work inside the classroom?
4. Will children be able to work without interfering with others? (Room darkening, noise, movement.)
5. Do activity outcomes happen at the center during the allotted times? (Some activities with long-range outcomes could be started at the center.)

Activity Cards and Worksheets

1. Are most of the learning experiences open-ended? (For process development, individual differences, children's possible contributions.)
2. Do the cards give simple directions? (Materials needed, what to do.)
3. Are the cards interesting? (Design reflects topic, large size, colorful.)
4. Can the cards be read easily? (Simple words, short sentences, drawings, pair

child with a good reader, taped directions.)
5. Are they reasonably childproof? (Laminate or contact paper, sturdy design.)
6. What, if any, worksheets are needed?

Materials, Storage, and Resupply

1. What local materials are available that go with the activities? (Also, printed materials, audiovisual materials, museum loans, collections.)
2. What is a good way to package and store the materials? (Shoe boxes, wooden-box shelves, cement-block and board shelves.)
3. How will you know when to resupply? (List, inventory monitors.)

Record Keeping and Evaluation

1. Do you have a master list of activities and objectives on which you can record pupil progress?
2. Does the child have a record sheet or record book to keep track of progress?
3. Can you observe center activities on a regular basis?
4. Are you able to have informal and scheduled conferences with the children?
5. Are you able to view children's work products? (Worksheets, constructions, reports, drawings, child's science folder.)

Arranging the Physical Setup

1. Where is the best spot to locate the center? (Water and sink, electric outlet, wall space, traffic flow.)
2. How can you make it attractive? (Cartoon character background, color, furniture arrangement, fabrics.)
3. How will the center look? (Sketch, materials needed.)

Managing the Center

1. Who will use the center and at what times? (Rotational assignments, need basis, optional signups.)

2. What do the children need to know to work at the center? (Schedule, what to do, how to get and store materials, where to leave completed work, behavior standards.)

3. What can be done to avoid problems when a new center is introduced? (General directions chart, walkthrough practice, use able pupils as consultants, cross-age or parent or other helpers.)

MICROCOMPUTER CENTERS

"I've never seen kids or parents so excited about an innovation," a principal told me a decade ago, after a successful schoolwide drive to buy a single microcomputer. How times change. More recently her school had two in every classroom and thirty more in the school's instructional materials center. What *hasn't* changed is children's enthusiasm for computer-assisted instruction (Figure 6-7).

At their beginning, school microcomputers served mostly for drill and practice in math and language. But now they are also being used to teach broader applications, simple programming languages, and aspects of the content subjects. With more machines has come improved chances for us to apply them in complementary science activities and for occasional whole-class teaching.

Setting up a microcomputer center for science study, whether in your classroom or school instructional materials center, raises some of the same questions that arise with other learning centers: What do you want to accomplish? Are other means of instruction better? Who will use the center and when?

FIGURE 6-7
Students are enthusiastic about computer-assisted instruction.

What will they need to know? How can you best introduce the center? Answers here parallel those with regular centers.

And there are more matters to weigh. What kinds of programs and computer-directed materials are available? How can you best use them? Consider now the three broad kinds of programs you are likely to see in your school.

Different Kinds of Programs

Microcomputer programs, called *software,* usually appear on small plastic disks that are inserted into the machine. Pictures or words are stored magnetically on the disks. The pictures show on the screen of a TV-like monitor when coded instructions are typed on an accompanying keyboard. Software is available to teach both science processes and knowledge in three loosely defined formats: *tutorials, educational games,* and *simulations.*

Tutorials may teach vocabulary, facts, topical information, or skills—usually in small bite sizes. Questions follow each chunk of presented information, and pupil responses trigger what appears next. The computer may also record responses for evaluation. Tutorial materials and subjects vary widely. Topics include simple machines and their applications, why the oceans are important for survival, how the human heart works, how to classify animals, common constellations, and properties of rocks, to name just a few.

Educational games employ an appealing chancy setting as a device for drill and practice, or to teach processes and knowledge. Programs are designed to sift pupil responses, keep score, and sometimes compete to spur pupil effort. Increased learning may enable children to row a cartoon-style boat farther, climb higher on a mystical mountain, or receive screen-flashed token awards and a rousing musical salute. With reinforcers like these, who wouldn't get excited? This is why some sort of game is often integrated into tutorials.

Simulations give pupils roles in situations that can approximate real events and squeeze years into minutes. The players decide what to do when given certain data, and the computer instantly feeds back good or bad news. In one program (*Geology Search,* McGraw-Hill), small teams compete to find the best places to drill for oil. Success is linked to how well they learn mapping skills and geologic features. In another program, *SimAnt* (Broderbund/Maxis), pupils take on roles of ants. They learn ant behaviors, including how to communicate with one another and how to avoid being done in by fierce red ants, ravenous spiders, and heavy human feet. Using scientific information, pupils develop strategies to survive, increase the size of their colony, and finally reach the ultimate reward—a nearby home with a lavish food supply.

Simulations are excellent to present science phenomena that otherwise are too remote, dangerous, complex, costly, or time consuming. They teach the consequences of real-life decisions yet allow pupils to escape from actually bearing them. Who could ask for anything more?

Computers as Research Tools

How do scientists use microcomputers? Can children use these machines in similar ways? Science educators and computer specialists are digging deeply into both questions. The software and other materials coming from their efforts get children into the heart of science: the gathering, organizing, and sharing of real data.

The software of several programs for pupils have accompanying hardware called *probes.* These are sensing devices that are connected through a cable to the computer. When used with the proper software, probes can measure temperature, light, sound, heart rate, acidity of substances, motion, force, pressure, and other properties of objects.

Several probe-type lab programs (also called microcomputer-based labs) have had much use in elementary schools from about grade three on. The *Bank Street Laboratory* (Holt, Rinehart and Winston) gives pupils chances to record and analyze graphs of temperature, light, and sound data. *Science Toolkit* (Broderbund) has rugged, easy-to-use probes for measuring light, temperature, time, and distance. Data can be organized into tables, charts, and graphs. Probe labs make it easy to gather much data over short or long time periods and then instantly convert the data into analyzable forms.

Further software has been developed that allows pupils to share their information with others through a huge computer network. Children in variously placed schools gather data, transmit the data to a central computer, and share findings with other schools.

In one unit of a popular science program, children in schools scattered around the nation measure the acidity of rain in their local areas and send the data by modem—a telephone/computer linkage—to a scientist collaborating with the program. The data are then pooled through a central computer, organized on charts and maps, and sent back to the pupils. (For more on this project-developed program and others, please see the *National Geographic Kids Network* in Appendix B.)

Accessing Multimedia

"A real fish doesn't look like *that!*" says a child seated at a microcomputer. The reaction is understandable. Visual displays of software material are often only a crude version of the real thing. This is one reason teachers may complement some software with video-cassettes, films, and the like. But a big drawback of these aids is the difficulty of interacting with them. Also, they store only a limited amount of material.

The *videodisc* (also called *laserdisc*), solves both problems. This is a thin aluminum plate, usually about the size of an old long-playing record, sandwiched between two layers of plas-

tic (Figure 6-8). Each side may contain thousands of recorded still pictures and numerous film clips with sounds and narration—often in both English and Spanish.

A computer linked to a videodisc player can access the recorded material in any order within a few seconds and display it on the computer monitor. A laser sensor in the player head flits on command from one place to another on the disk and "reads" the material. You can also display the material *without* a computer by connecting the player to a separate video monitor. In this case, you control the material through the player with either a hand-held remote controller or a bar code reader.

How do you know what's on the disk? A teacher's guide usually comes with it. Each photo frame or sequence, organized under topics, is given a number and bar code identification. With the remote controller, you punch in the numbers of your selection to activate the player. Using the bar code reader

FIGURE 6-8

Videodiscs store audio and visual information that can be displayed on a computer screen or video monitor.

is even easier. You lightly rub one end of the reader across the code, point the other end at the player and push a button.

Most nationally-published science programs today employ videodiscs to some degree—from a centerpiece role to enrichment. Teacher guides may include both whole-class lessons with the disk and ways to put it to work in an individual or small group setting, such as your microcomputer learning center. With the center, for example, you might select frames and animated sequences to follow up a lesson on earthquakes, then arrange bar code stickers or numbers in a sequence to guide pupils. Some science programs provide pupil worksheets with bar codes of the extending material already printed on them. In both cases, pupils may also interact with the material in any way they prefer. Older pupils might also search out material by themselves to integrate into small group or individual reports to the class.

The *CD-ROM* (compact disc, read-only memory) is another way to bring a vast amount of computer-controlled audiovisual material into your classroom. About half the size of a videodisc, you insert it into a CD-ROM drive that is connected to a computer. The material is accessed through the keyboard and viewed on the computer screen. The CD-ROM is simply a variation of the familiar audio compact disc. It's been used mostly for storing reference information, as in encyclopedias and dictionaries, but this function is expanding to others as well. One version of Compton's Encyclopedia (Jostens) includes on a single CD-ROM many thousands of photos and other illustrations, sixty minutes of speech, music, and sounds, an interactive world atlas, and many other features besides the entire printed text. You can see how all this could make the material more meaningful, attractive, and quickly accessible to children than the usual bound books.

If you want your pupils to use your classroom computer center for word-processing science reports and the like, consider attaching a *scanner* to your microcomputer. Like a photocopier, it allows the user to copy photos or drawings and incorporate them directly into a written report or other product produced on the printer.

Should you or a pupil want to deliver to the whole class a presentation on the computer screen, it may be hard for all to see what's displayed. Here's how you can project an enlarged display for easy viewing. Place an *LCD* (liquid crystal display) *projection pad* on the lighted bed of an overhead projector, attach the pad to the computer, and project on a large screen what's on the computer monitor. Of course, you can also use this system whenever you want to introduce new software or otherwise instruct the whole class on how to work with the computer. Figure 6-9 shows some of the microcomputer equipment used in schools.

Advantages and Some Problems

You've already seen some ways computer-assisted instruction can benefit you and your pupils in both learning centers or larger settings. Let's look at several more advantages and then address a few concerns.

It takes only brief experience with computer-assisted instruction to see how much children delight in this medium. The immediate feedback to their responses prompts them to learn more quickly and surely. Slow or fast learners can go at their own pace with an infinitely patient teacher. When they respond incorrectly, a good program branches them into a remedial sequence that reteaches the material in simpler steps. When they respond correctly, a good program moves them quickly into harder material. This truly individualizes instruction.

Perhaps the greatest promise for computer-based instruction lies in simulations. The computer-controlled videodisc and other resources offer all kinds of opportunities for making decisions and solving problems in realistic settings. Any airline pilot can tell you that what's seen through the cockpit wind-

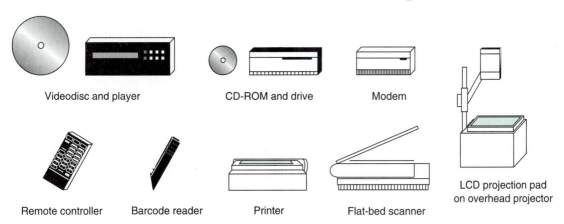

Videodisc and player   CD-ROM and drive   Modem   LCD projection pad on overhead projector

Remote controller   Barcode reader   Printer   Flat-bed scanner

FIGURE 6-9

Some equipment used with microcomputers in schools.

shield of a flight simulator just after a right or wrong move comes uncannily close to the real thing. Now there are increasing chances for children to experience a huge variety of educative and motivating settings in interactive ways.

There are some problems with computer use too, though most are temporary and solvable. Despite noticeably improved software programs, many you'll find in schools are mediocre. Some neglect science process and present information in bookish ways that slight the computer's potential. And software made for one machine may not work in another. Expense is another concern. What can the school budget afford for the extensive hardware and software now available and soon to be developed?

Another drawback of some elementary science software is a lack of accompanying hands-on experiences. This is more likely with older and stand-alone materials. In contrast, the software now integrated into the comprehensive multimedia science programs of major publishing companies usually provides for concrete activity, often before *and* after computer instruction.

The "magic" that lets us work the microcomputer as a tool—to efficiently find data, to reconstruct and show data in different ways, to produce original or graphic materials—is the greatly simplified software now available. Once written in baffling technical language, the newer software allows us to give directions to the machine in plain English: stop, go, print, and so on. Even so, nearly everyone needs some extra guidance and practice to creatively apply this remarkable tool. If you're new to computing, it's easy to feel overwhelmed by the sheer quantity of unfamiliar technology and methods employed. But the good news is, there's plenty of help around to get you up to speed.

If you are new to a school, ask colleagues and the principal what machines and help are available at the school and district levels. Both in-service workshops and informal, person-to-person arrangements are common. And don't be surprised to meet pupils with considerable expertise at microcomputing. By the sixth grade, some children have had several *thousand* hours of experience with these machines at home and school. They can be invaluable aides to other pupils and you.

Consider, too, joining a computer-user group for your school's brand of machine. Colleagues and computer dealers typically can give details. In many cities, you can find groups composed entirely of teachers. Elsewhere, they may be a section of a larger group. You may find, as I have, that teachers in user groups are among the most enthusiastic and creative appliers of microcomputers in education. It's surprising how many problems, even budgetary ones, yield to their imaginative solutions.

Software Sources and Reviews

How can you learn what is currently available and worthwhile? The supply of usable science software continues to grow. Software publishers are producing more materials that reflect the best thinking in cognitive psychology and science education. Science textbook publishers (today they are more accurately called multimedia science program publishers) are integrating software titles into text units and chapters. Some also develop their own software for that purpose.

There are numerous publishers of software. Rather than contacting each, an easier way to find what's accessible is to inspect the catalog of a distributor of products from many companies. Two large distributors are:

Educational Resources
1550 Executive Drive
Elgin, IL 60123
1-800-624-2926

Cambridge Development Laboratory, Inc.
The Science Shop
214 Third Avenue
Waltham, MA 02154
1-800-637-0047

Comprehensive education software catalogs may also be obtained from the two main manufacturers of school microcomputers:

Apple Computer, Inc.
20525 Mariani Avenue
Cupertino, CA 95014

IBM Corporation
Education Software, Dept. 779
1 Culver Road
Dayton, NJ 08810

You can find in-depth evaluations of educational microcomputer products in *PRO/FILES,* published by the EPIE Institute, P.O. Box 839, Water Mill, NY 11976.

Another comprehensive guide to current software is *Microsift Courseware Evaluation,* published by the Northwest Regional Educational Laboratory, 300 S.W. 6th Avenue, Portland, OR 97204.

Find further reviews and many suggestions for using classroom computers and related materials in these magazines:

The Computing Teacher
University of Oregon
1787 Agate Street
Eugene, OR 97403

Electronic Learning
P.O. Box 3021
Southeastern, PA 19398

Media & Methods
1429 Walnut Street
Philadelphia, PA 19102

Science and Children
1742 Connecticut Ave., N.W.
Washington, DC 20009

Technology & Learning
2451 East River Road
Dayton, OH 45439

Appraising Software: What to Look For

You can do a good job of appraising science software for yourself with just a handful of criteria, posed as questions:

1. Is the program compatible with your objectives? (If not, there is no need to consider it further.)

2. Does the program teach important and transferable knowledge or processes? (Look for basic, durable material that children can apply in their lives.)

3. Can the learning happen better through other means? (Hands-on activities may be

more suitable. The clear, full-color illustrations in videotapes, films, and filmstrips may serve better than the computer's fuzzy graphics. The program may consist largely of reading matter at an inappropriate level.)

4. Does the program make good use of the computer's special features? (The pupil continually interacts with the program by making decisions instead of simply pushing a key to keep it going. Responses regulate the difficulty and speed of learning. Responses are recorded when appropriate.)

5. Is the program "user friendly"? (Look for a supportive, encouraging tone, clear directions, easy operations.)

6. Does a helpful, nontechnical teacher's guide accompany the program? (Look for warm-up suggestions, hints on operating the program, supplementary concrete activities.)

7. Does the program fulfill its stated objectives? (You can find out by consulting others who have tried it with children or by trying it yourself. There are probably no other reliable ways.)

SCIENCE PROJECTS

I once had a withdrawn, listless boy in my fifth-grade class who did not come to life until he built a simple, working model of the human lung. He impressed the class and me with a good oral report and demonstration of his project. It was then that I began to appreciate the possibilities of this kind of experience.

A *project* is an organized search, construction, or task directed toward a specific purpose. It's ordinarily done by one person, or a small team of two or three persons, with minimal guidance from the teacher. A project

may clarify, extend, or apply a concept—and cause children to use science processes along the way. Most projects require a lot of independent effort. So they are less appropriate for primary-level children, who usually lack the skills and perseverance needed to operate largely alone.

The need for projects most often arises during a regular instructional unit. But projects may also begin with interests expressed by pupils or from a desire to have a science fair. Our job is to provide some realistic project choices, give deadlines for completing the projects, tell how they will be presented, and check at times for progress.

Providing the right set of choices is the most demanding of these functions. Children need some background and guidelines to proceed smoothly. How to begin? Probably the easiest way is to use the investigations and activities in Part II of this book. With some practice, you can move beyond these experiences into an almost unlimited world of possibilities. Let's get down to specifics.

Using Investigations for Projects

Investigations that you might use with the whole class or in learning centers often present one or two extra open-ended opportunities to go beyond the basic investigation. For example, in "Wheel-Belt Systems," page 405, a follow-up question says, "What wheel-belt systems can you invent?" In "Mealworms and What They Do," page 491, a final question is, "What are some questions about mealworms you'd like to investigate?" In "The Filtering of Polluted Water," page 619, the last questions ask, "Would more or other materials work better? How else could you improve your filter?"

These are the times to either have everyone continue with the investigation or to invite pupils with individual interests to pursue projects. Reports of projects can be presented later to the whole class and the materials placed on a science table for other interested pupils to manipulate. *Since everyone has some background, these further investigations become enriching extensions of familiar concepts and processes.*

You can also use for projects investigations that the class has not seen. Again, make them part of a topic under study in a unit. This makes them more understandable. Because most investigations are broad, let a team of two or three volunteers cooperatively divide the project. Assign a good reader to the team so it is less likely to continually need your help. Just show the team the investigation as printed (minus the "Teaching Comments" section).

Create additional projects by converting closed-ended experiences into open-ended investigations as shown in Chapter 3.

Using Activities for Projects

The activities of Part II also give many possibilities for projects to enrich units or meet pupil interests. But to ensure a good match between pupil and project requires some understanding of your pupils and the kinds of activities that are available.

Some activities are short-range, straightforward demonstrations of concepts or procedures. These are noticeably closed-ended and give exact guidance to pupils. Some examples are

What happens to water [pressure] with depth? (p. 617)

How high can water flow compared to where it comes from? (p. 617)

How can you show that air takes up space? (p. 626)

How can you tell if air weighs anything? (p. 627)

Activities like these make especially suitable projects for less able pupils and those who lack experience.

Some activities give longer-range and more open-ended experiences. They may call for changing some variables or keeping records of observations for a time. Some examples are

How can you make a "nerve tester" game? (p. 361)

In what places are seeds in soil? (p. 436)

How can you measure changes in air pressure? (p. 642)

What does the moon look like from day to day? (p. 669)

Different persons and places are tested in the first pair of activities, and records are kept in the second pair. Such activities make good projects for children who have the interest and patience for a more sustained experience and a willingness to keep good records.

Some concrete activities may be extended and enriched afterward by consulting authority in various forms:

How are the colors made in comic strips? (p. 227)

What happens when your eyes tire from seeing one color? (p. 238)

How can you raise crickets? (p. 492)

Which foods have starch? (p. 546)

A local newspaper office and an eye doctor are possible authorities in the first pair of activities, along with reference materials. A local pet shop owner and a nutritionist, or reference materials, might be suitable for the second pair. Projects like these allow children to extend their interest through applying interviewing and reference skills to answer real needs. Some pupils have poor skills? Pair each with an able one, or give extra help.

Reporting Projects

Children at all elementary levels do better at oral than written reports. But for either kind, some structure aids their understanding of the projects. Here is a form that makes sense to children, with traditional terms stated at the right.

What did I want to find out?	Problem, hypothesis
What materials did I need?	Materials
What did I do?	Procedure
What did I find out?	Findings, conclusions

The first three steps are best stated in the past tense for *reporting* projects, and present tense for *guiding* them. If you want a distinct hypothesis in experimental projects, this might be stated as, "What did I think?"

The simplified form usually works well for *both* observational activities (in which one observes properties of objects and events) and experimental activities (in which one changes the observed properties).

Is the simplified report form really necessary? Probably yes, if the whole class is involved. Remember, there are significant differences in mental abilities in your classroom. So the simplified version is generally easier *for both the givers and receivers* of reports to understand.

As your pupils gain experience, nourish their independence by continually making the projects less directive and more open-ended. At the same time, remain aware that what they are able to do varies greatly among individuals.

Science Fairs and Invention Conventions

With some history of successful projects, consider having a *science fair* to display them. This is exciting to pupils and excellent for public relations. It is wise to keep it modest at first—perhaps for only your classroom or parents' open house. Display projects on tables next to the walls, with written reports behind mounted on a cardboard or chipboard background. Use the simplified form above for the reports.

Instead of prizes, consider presenting a "Certificate of Completion," perhaps with proud parents looking on, to each child who displays a completed project. This formally recognizes everyone's efforts, but downplays invidious comparisons, which elementary school pupils find hard to handle. Other beneficial side effects may be less heavy-handed participation by some parents, and greater class interest in submitting projects. Of course, differences in pupil achievement will still be noticeable to you for educational purposes.

At another time, you may want to work with a fellow teacher for a combined operation, or even organize a schoolwide fair. For details on organizing schoolwide and other science fairs, see:

National Science Teachers Assn., *Science Fairs and Projects for K–8*. Washington, DC: National Science Teachers Association, 1988.

Van Deman, Barry and McDonald, Ed. *Nuts and Bolts: A Matter of Fact Guide to Science Fair Projects*. Harwood Heights, IL: Science Man Press, T.S.M. Marketing, Inc., 1980.

As part of the modern trend to teach science that children can apply to their lives, some science programs today recommend "invention conventions" as well as typical science fairs. Since technology is science applied to solve practical problems, the idea is to give girls and boys chances to develop "technical" solutions to their everyday problems and interests:

I'm tired of feeding my dog. (Maybe an automatic, gravity-driven feeder would come in handy.)

How can I tell how fast the wind is blowing? (A home-made wind gauge, fashioned from cardboard and wood, could fill the bill.)

I'd like to make a weird toy that rolls uphill by itself. (A hidden, twisted rubber band inside an empty salt box may do the job.)

My little brother Corky keeps sneaking into my room. (Perhaps a "burglar" alarm, fashioned from a buzzer, two flashlight batteries and some wire, will give Corky pause.)

I've heard you can make a stool from newspaper that's so strong you can sit on it. (Rolled-up newspaper makes surprisingly sturdy columns.)

For a wealth of fun-filled ideas and ways to stimulate inventiveness in your pupils, see:

Caney, Steven. *Steven Caney's Invention Book.* N.Y.: Workman Publishing, 1985.

Eichelberger, Barbara and Larson, Connie. *Constructions for Children: Projects in Design Technology.* Menlo Park, CA: Dale Seymour, 1993.

McCormack, Alan J. *Inventor's Workshop.* Belmont, Cal.: David S. Lake Publishers, 1981.

If you are interested in a competitive awards program for projects, consider *Invent America!,* a K–8 student contest with yearly cash prizes for students, teachers, schools, districts, and state departments of education. This is a national program, formed after needs were expressed by the U.S. Patent Office, and U.S. Education and Commerce departments. It aims to stimulate creativity and invention in young people as part of a broad effort to keep the nation competitive in science and technology. The award money is donated by American business and industry, and the program is run by a private, nonprofit foundation.

Teachers get sample lesson plans, examples of how to manage the program, ideas for working with parents and community, suggestions for displaying the inventions, and examples of how schools have benefited from using invention programs.

Free materials are available from the U.S. Patent Foundation, 1331 Pennsylvania Avenue N.W., Suite 903, Washington, DC 20004.

HOME/SCHOOL COOPERATION

Common sense and research tell us that pupils do better in school when their parents take an active interest in their studies.[2] While parents want to help their children succeed, they may not know how to go about it, especially when the subject is science. How can you help parents nurture their children's efforts, and how can they support your science teaching?

Recall that in the last chapter I mentioned that your school's science program might include copy masters of letters to parents, concept summaries, and activities that parents and children could do together. Many newer programs include such materials. The letters periodically announce a new unit of instruction, briefly describe it, and state some things parents might do to complement lessons. The concept summaries, often in several languages, inform parents about ideas they might discuss with their children and reinforce with experiences outside of school. The activities usually relate to the unit being studied and feature everyday materials.

Doing and discussing concrete activities with their children is a good way for parents to cultivate science interests and achievement. To further these objectives, some teachers keep at hand fifteen to thirty shoe box kits containing activities that pupils can check out and take home. Kits are easy to prepare when you get parents to help. Here's a way to do so.

Inspect Part II of this book or other science source book for activities and investigations that might enrich your regular science program. Be sure that only free or very low cost materials are needed. Select any number of these and make one copy of each. (Activities usually work better than investigations for parents because they are shorter and less likely to need teaching expertise.) Write a different identification number on each sheet, from one to whatever total you have. Pick one activity, get the materials, and put

---

[2]N. L. Gage and David C. Berliner, *Educational Psychology,* 3d ed. (Boston: Houghton Mifflin, 1984), p. 117.

them in a shoe box. Trim the margins of the activity sheet with scissors and tape it to the *inside lid* of the shoe box. Boldly mark with crayon or felt pen the activity number on top of the lid and both ends of the box.

During Parents' Night or similar meetings early in the school year, briefly introduce your science program—what topics pupils will study, some materials they'll work with, and so on—then show your shoe box kit and give its purpose. Pass out the duplicated activity sheets, have parents examine them, and then ask for volunteers to make the kits. Encourage the volunteers to do the activities with their children, discuss the results together, and have these pupils bring the completed kits to school for checkout by others.

Some teachers like to have parents experience first hand a few children's activities across the curriculum. This puts them in better touch with their children's work than talk alone, and sets up a delightfully informal and enthusiastic meeting. For a science activity that is a good icebreaker, try "How Useful Are Your Thumbs?" on page 522 in this text. A former student teacher of mine did this activity with parents just before requesting shoe box kits from them. Her score: 27 parents, 27 kits.

As mentioned in Chapter 5, remember that parents are also typically willing to supplement your science supplies with discardable items from around the home and with very low-cost materials. Some will volunteer to assist at science learning centers, especially at the primary-grade level. Others may volunteer their expertise in science or technology as tied to what your pupils are studying. But for these things to happen, parents need to hear details from you about what's needed.

Parents are usually more concerned about their children's progress in reading than in any other subject. Point out to them that research consistently underscores the value of parents reading aloud with their children, sharing books, and discussing concepts that come up in the reading.[3] Show them several kinds of science trade books available—biographies, diaries, expositions, and so on—that correlate with upcoming units. Pupils may check out these books from several sources—school or district or public library. If your school has a newer multimedia science program, yet another source is the supply of science-related literature books that typically accompanies these programs.

Show parents examples of useful articles from a newspaper, news magazine, *National Geographic,* or other sources they might share with their children who, in turn, might share the information at school. Explain that this material is easier to understand and remember when it relates to topics and concepts being studied at school. Stress the need to discuss the articles with the children, since they are seldom written in an age-appropriate style. When articles are from a morning newspaper, harried parents who commute to work may not have time to immediately discuss them. Suggest that these be clipped and discussed later. When this happens, pupils are more likely to share at school news that makes sense to them and their classmates. Mention, too, some titles of science periodicals for children. (See listing on page 687.) They contain excellent current material, are more age-appropriate, and will help pupils learn what to look for when scanning newspapers and other publications.

Mindless television-watching is a sore subject with parents, but the fact is that some of the best science programs ever produced are available to children on TV. Ask parents about science programs they have liked sharing with their children. *National Geographic* specials, *Wild Kingdom, Nova* (some subjects), and *3-2-1-Contact* are examples of shows that grownups and kids can enjoy together and discuss to some degree. If program hours are inconvenient, they might be taped and

---

[3] *What Works—Research About Teaching and Learning* (Washington, DC: U.S. Department of Education, 1986).

viewed at another time. Also, encourage your pupils to watch for upcoming shows and announce them to classmates.

Probably some parents and children already will have visited a local natural history museum, zoo, observatory, bird refuge, botanical garden, and so on. Ask parents about these experiences and suggest additional places recommended by seasoned colleagues and school district publications. A school catalog may describe and list places for families to visit at different grade levels or for certain units of instruction. And if *you* intend to take your class on study trips to these places, a parents' meeting is a good time to drum up volunteers to accompany the class.

You probably realize that I've mentioned more things to inform parents about than you'll have time for in one introductory meeting, especially if you discuss other subjects. Periodic newsletters, a classroom newspaper, individual conferences, and further parent–teacher meetings all present more chances to reach them. The content of your message is far more important than its forum. However it's delivered, please remember this: When you give parents specific ways to help their children study science and support your efforts, everyone gains.

SUMMARY

Teachers often complement their whole-class teaching with individual and small group experiences to meet the wide range of abilities and interests in their classes. Three common ways to do this are to use learning centers, microcomputer centers, and projects.

A classroom learning center is a place where one or several pupils at a time can do activities independently through materials and directions found at the center. The center may be organized so pupils can choose at least some of the activities they do and work at their own pace and learning level. Open-ended experiences usually serve best for these purposes. Many of the investigations in this book can be directly converted into learning centers.

A microcomputer center can be set up and run much like a regular learning center. Microcomputer programs are available in three broad instructional formats: tutorials, which teach small chunks of material in sequential lessons; games, which use a chance-taking setting and appealing reinforcers for pupil responses; and simulations, in which pupils respond to situations that approximate real events. Videodiscs, controlled by either the computer or hand-held remote controls, greatly expand the range of audio-visual materials available for instruction. Computer-assisted instruction is ideally suited for individualizing instruction in science, but may neglect hands-on experiences. This problem is remedied in several ways.

A science project is an organized search, construction, or task directed toward a specific purpose and ordinarily carried out by one to three pupils. The need for projects often arises in instructional units through interests expressed by pupils. Both investigations and activities in this book may be converted into science projects. However, some are more demanding than others. Knowing a pupil's abilities and what the project demands are important in arranging a suitable match.

Parents can complement what their children learn about science at school by participating with them in various out-of-school experiences. These might include doing science activities at home, reading and discussing trade books, viewing selected TV programs, and visiting museums or other community resources. Parents are also frequently willing to volunteer their assistance at learning centers, to make shoe box kits, to provide some low cost materials, and share science-related expertise.

SUGGESTED READINGS

DeBruin, Jerry. *Science Fairs with Style.* Carthage, IL: Good Apple, 1991. (A comprehensive guide for upper-grade projects.)

Dockterman, David. *Teaching in the One-Computer Classroom.* Cambridge, MA: Tom Snyder, 1990. (Describes a variety of ways one to several microcomputers can be effectively used in a classroom.)

Linn, Marcia C. "An Apple a Day." *Science and Children,* Nov./Dec. 1987, 15–18. (Describes a probe-type lab in which pupils learn the difference between heat and temperature using real-time data and graphing.)

Paulu, Nancy and Margery Martin. *Helping Your Child Learn Science.* Washington, DC: U.S. Department of Education, Office of Educational Research and Improvement, 1991. (How parents can whet their children's science interests through home activities. One of a series on different school subjects. Available at $3.25 from OERI Outreach Office, 555 New Jersey Ave. NW, Washington, DC 20208-5570.)

Pearlman, Susan and Kathleen Pericak-Spector. "Helping Hands from Home." *Science and Children* 29(7):12–14 (April 1992). (Parent volunteers make active science more manageable.)

Stone, George K. *More Science Projects You Can Do.* Englewood Cliffs, N.J.: Prentice-Hall, 1981. (A paperback book of many interesting projects for upper elementary and middle school pupils.)

7

How to Organize and Assess
Science Teaching

How do you effectively plan and assess science teaching? This chapter aims to enable you to answer that question for yourself. If it does its job, you'll probably preface your answer with the words, "It depends." Here's why.

The teaching conditions for science education can be quite different from one school district to another. One district will put into your hands an activity-centered program with a kit brim-full of materials for everyone in class. Another might supply a multimedia program, with all the materials and hardware you need to teach science seven days a week. At a third site your school principal may just point to a pile of old textbooks and discretely back out of the door.

Naturally, such diverse conditions require different planning. Further considerations include the teaching and cooperative practices you are able to fashion, given your particular pupils and unique background. As you go through this chapter, you'll see a wide array of practices often displayed by top-notch teachers. How many can you immediately expect to handle, especially if you are new to the game? In baseball talk, a realistic aim for you now may be to hit a string of solid singles and an occasional double. Later, with more chances for practice, you can go for home runs.

To take up these matters and more, we'll begin with descriptions of exemplary activity-centered programs, old and new. Next, we'll consider modern multimedia programs and what help to expect from school district curriculum guides. Finally, you'll see ways to construct and assess your own "multimedia" program, using a science textbook and local resources.

ACTIVITY-CENTERED PROGRAMS

Some science programs center on what children can learn through concrete, hands-on experiences. Textbooks, videotapes, and other secondary sources for learning have little or no place in them. Hands-on science programs got a big boost in the 1960s, when national concern for improved science and mathematics teaching led to many federally supported curriculum projects. More recently, a second wave of major curriculum projects featuring hands-on experiences has moved into the limelight. Let's look at the intentions behind these programs and how they might affect your teaching.

The Old and the New Activity Programs

Many professional scientists of the 1960s saw the science teaching going on then as a shallow and bookish perversion of the disciplines they knew. So a number of them recruited teachers, learning psychologists, and science educators, and went to work on curriculum projects. Three major programs in elementary science emerged after almost 10 years of effort: *Science—A Process Approach* (SAPA), the *Science Curriculum Improvement Study* (SCIS), and the *Elementary Science Study* (ESS). Though each differs in format and stresses different things, the three have much in common:

- Learning begins and proceeds through work with concrete materials from specially designed kits.
- Scope of study is narrower but deeper than in book programs.
- Learning activities are more open-ended than in book programs.
- Pupils use a variety of science processes as they work.
- Each program is supported by recognized learning theory.
- Basic science principles are stressed, with little or no technology.
- Mathematics is often integrated into learning activities.

Most measures show that the three programs well met their objectives.[1] Yet even during their period of greatest use, the three major project programs were only adopted by a minority of school districts. And their use as full-scale packaged programs continues to wane today, though many districts and teachers happily keep some parts to supplement text programs.[2] The weight of tradition, the programs' high costs, extensive in-service requirements for teachers, the back-to-basics movement of the seventies, and other things combined to keep down their adoption.

Today, a fresh lineup of activity-centered programs, most government-aided to some degree, are drawing national attention. Among them are *Science for Life and Living, Full Option Science System, EDC Insights, Science and Technology for Children,* and *The National Geographic Kids Network.* (For individual descriptions of these and other project-developed science programs, please see Appendix B.)

These curricula retain many of the strong features of the earlier programs, build onto others, and introduce new features:[3]

▪ Topics and activities have far more personal and social applications.

▪ More subjects, particularly language arts, are integrated. (Printed materials, or even books, may be used.)

▪ Activities challenge pupils' misconceptions and allow time for pupils to rethink their own ideas (schemata).

▪ Teachers and administrators have more say in the design of the programs.

▪ Ways to help teachers teach the program, and manage the materials, are more prominently featured.

If your school district uses one of these or earlier hands-on programs, you'll find that almost everything you've learned so far in this book will apply. That is because the principles that formed the projects are much like those that guided this writing. What's more, this chapter should further help you fine-tune the program to your exact needs. This should make it easier for you to teach with skill and confidence, once you learn the program's details.

Importance of Science Curriculum Projects

Will more schools adopt the newer hands-on curricula than was done with the older programs? It seems likely, but the impact of government-aided projects goes far beyond the specific programs that come out. Innovations in education are risky business. Few commercial publishers can afford to initiate changes in education. Yet competition makes them eager to take on what is accepted.

Good results from science curriculum projects influence nearly everyone in science education, especially textbook and curriculum writers. This noticeably upgrades the quality of what they produce. How far can this go? In the long run, perhaps the only limits to innovation will be the money and time that schools can commit to the products.

▌ MULTIMEDIA PROGRAMS

For more than fifty years textbooks have dominated science teaching in elementary schools. But accelerating evolution has transformed what was once a read-about-science series of books with few activities, into an integrated multimedia program with many

[1]James A. Shymansky, William C. Kyle, Jr., and Jennifer M. Alport. "How Effective Were the Hands-on Programs of Yesterday?" *Science and Children* 20(5):14–15 (Nov./Dec. 1982).

[2]An updated version of *SCIS*, Delta Education's *SCIS3*, is stimulating new interest and support for this landmark program.

[3]Nancy M. Landes, et al. "What Research Says About the New Science Curricula." *Science and Children* 25(8):35 (May 1988).

activities, videodiscs, software, printed materials, and much more. While printed materials form the center of most multimedia programs, it's also possible to find core instruction focused on the videodisc.

For example, *Windows on Science* (Optical Data Corporation) offers a comprehensive program in the earth, life, and physical sciences on a series of videodiscs with integrated support materials. Lessons begin with a videodisc presentation followed by a pertinent hands-on activity. Pupils next study a leaflet designed and written to further build the concept under study, then write and do extending activities that develop thinking.

Multimedia programs are likely to contain a wide array of products for teaching science:

- Pupil books (several forms)
- Teacher guides
- Activity material kits
- Activity logs (for recordings)
- Videodiscs (applying concepts)
- Videotapes (vicarious field trips)
- Software (problem-solving simulations)
- Concept summaries/glossaries (in several languages)
- Audio tapes (for ESL pupils, concept reviews)
- Teacher anthologies (literature selections)
- Blackline masters
- Posters
- Trade books
- OHP transparencies
- Activity cards (for learning centers and projects)
- Assessment package (detailed evaluation materials)

Even more items could be added to this list, but by now you have the idea: modern publishers offer comprehensive, integrated multimedia programs, not simply textbooks. If you have the chance to teach a complete multimedia program, your biggest challenge may be to learn how to use its many options within the time you have to teach science. You might want to start small—with whatever basic material you can comfortably handle— and then add options one at a time.

How much of a complete multimedia program is adopted by a school district usually comes down to what it can afford and what usable teaching materials are already on hand. Many schools can only buy the core printed materials, which may be found in two forms: pupil books and booklets. The booklets, called *modules* or *units,* are like separately published parts of a whole book—each equivalent to a large chapter or section. Why use them? They make it easier for a school district to customize its curriculum, by choosing from about fifty modules or units that may be available for all the elementary grades. Activity materials are separately packaged by units, to fit whatever titles are selected.

Let's assume that you'll only have pupil books and the teacher edition to work with. Most of the following pages will show you how to work with that condition. Once you learn how to operate successfully within lean times, anything extra that comes your way should make it even easier to do a good job.

An instructional unit in a textbook is often a chapter that the authors write from a framework of generalizations, such as

1. Weathering and erosion wear down the earth's surface.
2. Topsoil is made up of mineral, vegetable, and animal matter.
3. Lava flows and crustal movements build up the earth's surface.
4. Three kinds of rocks are formed as the earth's surface wears down and builds up.

Each of the generalizations may be developed in a separate section of the chapter that is headed by a topical title or question:

1. Weathering and Erosion/What is weathering and erosion?
2. Topsoil/What is in topsoil?

3. The Earth's Changing Surface/How does the earth's surface change?

4. How Rocks Form/How are rocks made?

The authors will also usually write one or more objectives for each section, such as the following.

Pupils will

1. *Define* weathering and erosion and give examples of each.

2. *Infer* the three parts of soil after examining soil samples.

3. *Describe* how lava flows and crustal movements build up the earth's surface.

4. *Explain* how igneous, sedimentary, and metamorphic rocks are formed.

Pupils are expected to meet the objectives through reading the text, doing the activities, and using whatever supplementary materials are available. This is done one section or lesson at a time.

Each section or lesson is likely to have three parts:

1. Introduction. (You prepare pupils to do activities and read.)

2. Developing the idea. (Children do activities and read.)

3. Summarizing and extending the learning. (You help pupils generalize and apply what they have studied.)

The teaching suggestions for lessons, and many additional aids, are found in a teacher's edition of the pupil's textbook. Here's a list of what it's likely to have:

■ Science content background material

■ Lesson objectives

■ Lesson generalizations

■ Materials needed for activities

■ Lesson procedures

■ Evaluation questions and tests

■ Ways to help pupils with special needs

■ Ways to integrate other subjects

■ Model bulletin board

■ Model learning center

■ Enrichment activities

■ Home activities

■ Activity worksheets

The last three items may also appear as ditto masters or in separate pupil workbooks.

Despite this abundance, there are several ways in which a textbook unit can be enhanced. Your district may have a curriculum guide for the purpose, but if it does not, you can do the job yourself. Let's look first at how a curriculum guide can help you get the most from a text unit.

SCHOOL DISTRICT CURRICULUM GUIDES

Years ago, curriculum guides of large school districts were likely to contain comprehensive resource units organized around common science topics. They required enormous effort to assemble and seldom met expectations. As text programs gradually improved, fewer and fewer districts made the effort.

Modern guides typically have two uses: they state the district's policies for science, and they supplement the adopted science program by showing how local resources fit into lessons.

Local Policies

We live in a time of accountability. Seldom now in well-managed districts can a teacher select science topics or units simply from preference or interest. For the most part, this is a good thing. Can you imagine the state of mathematics or reading education if everyone operated solely from personal choice?

Many state departments of education have curriculum standards and guidelines that local districts use in adopting a science program. There may also be state or district achievement tests whose objectives are aligned with the guidelines. District leaders naturally want to see a match between what is taught and what is measured on tests. To help ensure this, the local curriculum guide may point out what text chapters to stress, the best sequence to use, and recommend time periods for different chapters.

The guide is also likely to give district policy on safety, such as what animals are acceptable for classrooms, and field trip requirements. Further statements may cover how to group pupils, order materials, correlate subjects, and other practical matters.

Local Resources

Most school districts accumulate sizable collections of audiovisual materials, trade (library) books, teacher reference books, models, microcomputer software, and the like. Many nearby community resources may beckon for firsthand learning experiences: wildlife sanctuary, water filtration plant, aerospace center, zoo, museum, and so on. There may also be a list of community volunteers who are willing to share their expertise with pupils. How can these resources be best used? This is always a question when a new science program is adopted.

The usual job today of a science curriculum guide committee is to supplement text units: It plugs local resources into appropriate places and suggests further activities when those in the text seem sparse. Notice how this is done on a page from a typical guide (Figure 7-1).

Reading from left to right, let's look at the first lesson: "Living Things Need Energy." It can be found on pupil text pages 48–49. The district's objective is for pupils to be able to compare the roles of producers and consumers. A related activity,

"Plants that animals eat," Copy Master page 26, is a reproducible page from a booklet in the text program, and is designed to promote critical thinking. The last column contains the title of a district film whose length is five minutes.

Note in the resource column symbols "PW" and "SEE." These are for *Project Wild,* an environmental studies activity book widely available in the district; and *Science in Elementary Education,* which is this book. Further resources used by the committee in other units included another activity book and materials from a popular math/science project.

Also not shown on the guide page are resources found in each school's instructional materials center. Trade books that can be used with the unit, for example, can be selected by pupils themselves from the center's collection. In other districts, a collection of trade books on a unit topic may be boxed at a central materials center and delivered to a school when needed.

Not all curriculum guides look alike. And a textbook unit might be more than a single chapter. For example, it can be several chapters united by a topical title:

Unit: Earth and Its Neighbor
>   Chapter 1: Earth in Space
>   Chapter 2: The Moon
>   Chapter 3: Rocketing to the Moon

Still, the basic organization as presented shows how many text authors and curriculum guide committees do their work.

As you might expect, the quality of curriculum guide resource help varies from superior to awful. It's clear that an excellent resource supplement takes care of many instructional problems. But what do you do when the guide at hand is little more than a declaration of good intentions, or when there are no resources stated at all? One answer is, do what a guide committee does, only on a smaller scale.

SCIENCE CURRICULUM EXTENSIONS PACKET

Chapter 3: Food Chains and Food Webs   Grade 4

Lesson	Text Page #	Objective	Related activity	Resource	AV/Media Support	Length
1. Living Things Need Energy	48–49	Compare roles of producers and consumers.	Plants that animals eat	Copy Master p. 26	What do they eat?	5
2. Animals and Their Food	50–53	Classify animals according to what they eat.	Classification of animals	Copy Master p. 28	Animals and their foods, Rev. ed.	10
			Finding out	p. 53	Battle of the bugs, 2nd ed.	11
			Deadly Links	PW, pp. 197–200	Plankton: Pastures of the ocean	10
3. Food Chains	54–57	Show how members of a food chain affect each other.	How do food chain members affect each other?	p. 57	World of plant and animal communities	14
			What is a food chain?	SEE, p. 420	Pond-life food web	12
			Foods from plants	Copy Master p. 29		
4. Food Webs	58–61	Understand the relationship between food chains and food webs.	What did your lunch cost wildlife?	PW, pp. 215–216		
			Oh Deer!	PW, pp. 131–134		

FIGURE 7-1
Page from a curriculum guide.

HOW TO SUPPLEMENT TEXTBOOK UNITS

To supplement a textbook unit, consider these suggestions:

1. Thoroughly read the unit, as shown in the child's text and teacher's edition, to grasp what it is about. (Ordinarily, the teacher's edition includes the pupil material.)

2. Look for places where you can use local resources—field trips, audiovisual materials, kits, trade books, speakers, computer software, and so on. (Have on hand the district's instructional resources catalog to consult.)

3. Look for opportunities to integrate reading, math, language, and other subjects into lessons. (These are often mentioned in the teacher's edition, but you will need to address your group's specific needs.)

4. Look for chances to open-end some concrete activities now present, or add a few. (Have on hand this book or others in the bibliography to consult.)

5. Estimate the total time needed to teach the unit, then fit the text's lessons into the block of available time. (We will detail block planning later in this chapter.)

6. Order district instructional materials for times needed and gather other materials for activities. (Your pupils can help gather everyday things.)

When teaching a text unit for the first time, be sensitive to what you can handle. Just try a few of the enrichment ideas in the teacher's edition and those stated above in items two through four. Follow the suggested lesson procedures as found except for the few places where you have amended the lessons.

As you gain experience and confidence, adopt more of the foregoing suggestions and extra helps in the teacher edition. Continue to add more of your own ideas and local resources. The improved results that come from supplementing the text should please both you and your pupils.

Many teachers are satisfied with teaching from a supplemented text. They often cite convenience and time saved as reasons. Since elementary teachers plan and teach about eight additional school subjects besides science, this is understandable.

Other teachers, though, feel restricted by the book format, even an improved one. Without the publisher's full array of multimedia resources to draw from, they see mostly closed-ended activities that illustrate ideas in the book rather than broad chances for real inquiry. They see relatively short, tightly controlled lessons when they want pupils to ask more questions and pursue strong interests over longer periods of time. These teachers are aware of some ways to augment the book unit, but for them these measures don't go far enough. They want the book to be one tool among several, rather than the main event. What they *really* want is a practical way to design their own multimedia unit, and a format that allows them to work flexibly with their pupils.

Making a unit from scratch is generally impractical for teachers because it demands much time, effort, and expertise. But there is rarely a need for it. You can usually assemble what you want in several hours if you start with a well-organized base. The teacher's edition of almost any modern textbook series can give such a base.

HOW TO MAKE YOUR OWN TEXTBOOK-BASED UNITS

Three main things you need to know to make a textbook-based unit are:

- How to determine which *generalizations* to use.
- How to gather more *activities*, if needed, to teach each generalization.
- How to introduce, or *bridge* into, each generalization's sequence of activities.

Determining Generalizations

The chapters or units of most textbooks are organized around from about 3 to 10 large generalizations. (These may be called "concepts.") Rarely are there fewer or more than this, and the average seems to be about five. The teacher's editions of most books contain outlines with the large generalizations clearly labeled. When this is the case all that is needed next, if the scope seems satisfactory, is to look up a few more activities. In other series, generalizations are sometimes too detailed and should be combined to make a broader statement. For example, take these generalizations:

The faster something vibrates, the higher a sound it makes.

Smaller things vibrate faster than larger things.

The tighter something is, the faster it vibrates.

You could combine them to read:

Speed of vibrations affects pitch; smaller, tighter objects sound higher because they vibrate faster.

These statements are mainly for your guidance as you put together the unit, so their exact form does not matter if they make sense to you and reflect the material.

Make a tentative list of such generalizations. Then go through the text chapter to see if they reflect the main parts of the chapter. Big topical headings and the number of pages devoted to each are the main indicators. Change the generalizations as needed to match what you find, if you want to stick closely to the textbook's contents. Your task is to wind up with the fewest big ideas possible without combining unrelated ideas. Don't worry about losing track of details. Those will come out in the activities.

It is easy to think from looking at these suggestions that you need a long time to decide on the large ideas. This is unlikely. Pick out a chapter in a child's text and carefully read it along with the accompanying section in the teacher's guide. After doing so, with average ability in outlining, you can probably pin down the main generalizations in 10 to 20 minutes on your first try.

Whether you use one or several text chapters as a base for a unit or as the entire program, *it is important to think through their basic organization.* When making a unit, you need to know the generalizations to compile extra activities, but the importance of analysis goes beyond this. It boosts your confidence by providing a sense of direction. It leads to the feeling that, if needed, you can make a few changes and add some children's ideas. It helps you to decide what is important and what is not. In contrast, when merely following the book, you go wherever it goes.

Getting Activities

One advantage in using the book as a base is the assurance that at least some activities are "automatically" available and tied to each generalization. The pupil text contains reading matter, pictures to examine, and other things to do. It is your job, then, to expand its present inventory of activities and take advantage of local resources. The more numerous the activities, the easier it is to select exactly what is most fitting at the time of planning specific lessons.

The teacher's edition should have additional activities. Some programs include the teacher's edition in an expanded teacher's resource package, held together by a three-ring binder. It may include blackline masters and further activities. These sources may give you most of what you need. By arranging their offerings in lessons of your own design, they may better suit your purposes.

Many school districts also provide books and catalogs that contain collections of activities. The following resource books contain hundreds of experiments, demonstrations, and other things to do:

Friedl, Alfred E. *Teaching Science to Children: An Integrated Approach.* 2d ed. New York: Random House, 1986.

Lowery, Lawrence F. *The Everyday Science Sourcebook: Ideas for Teaching in the Elementary and Middle School,* Palo Alto, CA: Dale Seymour, 1985.

Strongin, Herb. *Science on a Shoestring.* Reading, MA: Addison-Wesley, 1991.

Further references can be found in the bibliography.

Having a sourcebook that contains many activities can enable you to find what you want without wasting time, if the generalizations selected are broad, basic ones. Part II of this text can also serve, especially if you want open-ended experiences to meet pupils' individual differences.

How many open-ended investigations should you plan for? That depends a lot on the kinds of pupils you have. Gifted and talented children are able to do, and require, much more open-ended work than other children. At the other extreme, the educable mentally handicapped profit most from direct teaching and narrowly defined activities. A worthy goal is to reserve about 40 to 50 percent of unit time for hands-on science experiences, both closed- and open-ended.

Besides a good activity sourcebook, consult your school's audiovisual catalog and other resource catalogs, if any. Note under each generalization what experiences will help you to teach it. Also, record possible study trips.

Perhaps other local facilities can be used, such as the school building and grounds, and local resource persons. It may be worthwhile to check a free-materials catalog for other possibilities.

Children's trade books may be available on the subject at the school library, district library, or local public library. Beyond the primary grades, encyclopedias are worthwhile for additional information. Further, children can check newspapers and magazines for stories and pictures. Extra reading matter can do much to extend children's learning. It takes care of a practical matter, as well. Because fast readers can devour the regular assignment in the class science text within minutes, they need supplementary reading to be challenged.

Take care not to rush into reading activities. Most of the time reserve these for the end of study of each generalization. Our ability to understand words relates directly to our experiences. Let reading activities reinforce and extend these experiences.

There are many chances in a unit to integrate other subjects besides reading into lessons. Now is a good time to consider them. What do the children need more practice with? Oral language? Applied math? Writing? Other skills? What other activities might children do for enrichment? Paint a large mural on butcher paper? Perform a dramatic play? Sing or make up songs or verses about an interesting animal? If you know your pupils well, chances for subject enrichment and practice of basic skills can easily come to mind. However, don't forget to keep the focus on *science*.

After you have grouped some good learning activities under each generalization, arrange them in some logical teaching order.

The sequence of content in the class textbook can provide the overall direction here. Remember to cluster concrete activities ahead of reading and other second-hand activities when possible.

Does noting activities seem lengthy and time consuming? It does not have to be. Most of your references will be within easy reach on your desk throughout the unit, so write down only as much as you need to plan with. Then, consult your references for details as required.

Determining Bridges (Introductions)

Now that you have located some activities for each generalization, you will need some way to introduce each of these main parts of the unit to pupils and move smoothly into each accompanying set of activities. Some teachers call this phase "bridging" because it takes the children from where they are to the beginnings of where they need to go.

A useful introduction, or bridge, relates to pupils' experiences and present understandings. It stimulates them to use their present schemata as you interact with them. Pupil responses and questions give you some insight into what they already know about the generalization or topic to be studied, including their misconceptions. The last part of the bridge also leads into the first activity in each sequence.

You may want to introduce the children to the entire unit at one time by asking questions based on all the generalizations. However, many teachers believe it is easier and more meaningful to the children to introduce only one section at a time. Of course, a brief statement about the overall unit topic should be made in any case.

Ideas for bridging into each set of activities usually can be found in the textbook or its teacher's edition. Most modern programs reflect the constructivist view of learning, as described by Piaget and later researchers (Chapter 2). They are likely to begin a unit or lesson with an opportunity for the teacher to find out what children already know and

Gen. I. Weathering and erosion constantly wear down the earth's surface. (Class text pages 61–68.)

Bridge
How far down do you think the soil goes? What is beneath the soil? What are some ways rock may get broken up? How might broken up rocks and soil be removed? What does weathering mean? erosion?

Activities

(obs.)	**1.** Define weathering and erosion. Tour school grounds for examples. (Open-ended.)
(exp.)	**2.** Plants break rocks experiment, text p. 63. (Open-ended.)
(infer.)	**3.** Dirt mountain erosion demonstration, Schmidt p. 56.
	4. Films: Face of Earth (15 min.), Work of Rivers (10 min.).
	5. Read text pp. 61–68 and library books. SUMMARIZE weathering and erosion forces.
(classif.)	**6.** Kids find and sort picture examples of forces that bring change. Display. (Open-ended.)
	7. Haiku poetry on forces that change the earth's surface.

(Front of card)

Materials
2. Plaster of paris; bean seeds; paper cups.
3. Shovel; hose. (See custodian.)
4. MP204; MP206 (AV center).
6. *Nat'l Geographic, Arizona Highways* back issues; scissors; construction paper; paste.

Assessment
How many examples of weathering and erosion on the school grounds can you find? Find some examples we did not observe on our first tour. Make a record.

Also use end-of-section questions, p. 68.

(Back of card)

FIGURE 7-2
continued

Gen. II. Topsoil is composed of mineral, vegetable, and animal matter; topsoil is conserved in several ways. (Pages 69–77.)

Bridge
What are some reasons farmers might be interested in erosion? How might they guard against soil erosion? What makes up soil? Let's see for ourselves.

Activities

(classif.)	1.	Small group analysis of soil samples. Sort objects found. (Open-ended.)
(exp.)	2.	Plant seeds in poor and good soil samples, text p. 72. (Open-ended.)
	3.	Introduce six study prints on soil erosion. See "Conserving Our Soil" videotape.
	4.	Read text, pages 69–77, and library books. SUMMARIZE ways to conserve soil.
	5.	Possible visit agent, Soil Conservation Service. (Practice interview and listening skills.)

(Front of card)

Materials
1. Magnifiers; old spoons; sack of good topsoil; newspapers; clean pint milk cartons.
2. Bean seeds; sack each of good and bad soil; milk cartons.
3. SP (set of 6) 117; Vid. 440.1 (AV center).
5. Bill Johnson, Soil Cons. Service, 283-6600.

Assessment
What are some ways you might prevent erosion on our school grounds? Think about the examples you found before. Discuss these ways with two partners. Then give a report.

We don't live on farms. What difference would it make to us if most farm soil erodes?

Also use end-of-section questions, p. 77.

(Back of card)

FIGURE 7-2
continued

Gen. III. Lava flows and crustal movements continually build up the earth's surface. (Pages 77–84.)

Bridge
Does anyone know what a volcano is? What do you think makes a volcano happen? What is an earthquake? Has anyone been where there was an earthquake? Let's find out some surprising ways the earth's surface changes.

Activities

(meas.)

1. Film: Earthquakes and volcanoes (30 min.).
2. Film: Trembling Earth (25 min.).
3. Make clay models of volcanoes, p. 79. Also "seismograph," special project Hone, p. 28. (Art and construction.)
4. Guest speaker with northern California earthquake slides. (Or locate earthquake pictures.)
5. Use maps to locate active volcanoes.
6. Read text, pages 77–84, and library books. SUMMARIZE how mountains are formed.

(Front of card)

Materials
1. MP 254 (AV center).
2. MP 261 (AV center).
3. Two colors of clay; newspapers; rulers; scissors. (Seismograph volunteers, check Hone book for materials.)
4. Orville McCreedy, 286–6147. (Or, past *Nat'l Geographics,* 1989 issues.)

Assessment
Children will construct cutaway models of volcanoes and, using the models, be able to explain how volcanoes may happen.

Also use end-of-section questions, p. 84.

(Back of card)

FIGURE 7-2
continued

Gen. IV. Three kinds of rocks are formed as the earth's surface wears down and builds up.

Bridge
Thank you for bringing so many different rocks. What makes them look different? Which of these might have come from volcanoes? How else might some have been made? Before we find out, let's see how many different properties of these rocks you can observe.

Activities
(commun.)   **1.** Partners do rock description game. (20 questions—lang. develop.)
(exper.)   **2.** Crystal growing activity, p. 91. (Open-ended.)
               3. Read text, pages 85–93, and library books.
(classif.)   **4.** Sort rocks as to basic type, p. 90. (Open-ended.)
               5. SUMMARIZE gen. IV and whole unit.

(Front of card)

Materials
2. Baby food jars; string; paper clips; sugar; hot plate; teakettle; newspaper.
4. Children's rock samples—stress variety; heavy paper sacks; several hammers.

Assessment
Children will be able to control the size of "rock" crystals by varying the cooling rates of hot sugar solutions.

Children will be able to identify some properties of rocks and explain how these are clues to the rocks' formation.

Also use unit test questions, p. 93.

(Back of card)

FIGURE 7-2
continued

activities. These can remind you of what to stress in such activities. Several "open-ended" notes serve the same function. Open-ended activities are often the easiest and best way to meet pupils' individual differences in unit teaching.

Finally, note that there is a specific assessment section for each of the four main parts of this unit. For generalizations I and II, assessments are stated as questions. For III and IV, they are stated as pupil behaviors to observe. Which method do you prefer? Some teachers use both. (Details about objectives and assessment appear shortly in this chapter.)

A fine unit does not spring full blown from its first organization. The more you teach it, the more you will want to modify it. Activities may be strengthened, the teaching order changed, scope increased, and so on. With experience, you can often detect from inspection alone where your first organization will falter with your class. In the meantime, you learn largely from teaching it and noting what happens.

The Planning/Teaching Order

When you *teach* a textbook-based unit as described here, you *reverse* the order in which it was planned. Look at it this way—

In *planning* the unit, you determine:

G eneralizations, then

A ctivities for each generalization, then a

B ridge for each generalization's set of activities.

But in *teaching* the unit, you begin with a:

B ridge, which leads into the first of several

A ctivities, which lead into an understanding of each

G eneralization in your unit.

In other words, this is a GAB–BAG approach to planning and teaching a text-based unit. It turns what may be expository and deductive

textbook lessons into inductive lessons that can be front-loaded with concrete activities before reading and other vicarious learning take place. You don't have to be a science prodigy to teach this way. Nearly everything in the unit comes from others. The specific organization, though, is uniquely yours.

Some Further Considerations in Making Textbook-Based Units

Activity Availability. A Slavic proverb says, "To eat bread, there first must be bread in the basket." The main reason to make a text-based unit is to free yourself from text-bound teaching. But to do so requires first that some appropriate activities are available.

If you want numerous *concrete* activities, there will be few for young children in such topics as heredity, atoms, the earth's interior, space travel, cell structure of living things, animal migration, and so on. An easy way to know the topics for which much *is* available is to check the contents of a recent resource activities book (see page 168). The subject-matter section of this book can also be a guide. Be wary of topics that do not appear in either place.

If you want supporting materials such as AV aids, models, and so on, check early on to see what the district or school instructional resource center offers. When the center offers little or nothing and few concrete activities are available, trying to make a textbook-based unit is apt to be frustrating and unproductive.

Which Format Works Best? An easy way for an argument to start between two science educators is for one to claim a better way of laying out a textbook-based unit. You, too, may want to rearrange or add elements in the format I have presented. My basic format, and three workable variations for you to consider, are listed in Table 7-1. Of the three variations, many of my students like the last one (far right) most. But before you make changes, please read the rest of this chapter for additional perspective.

TABLE 7-1
Four ways to lay out a textbook-based unit.

generalization	objective(s)	generalization(s)	topic or problem
bridge	bridge	objective(s)	objective(s)
activities	activities	assessment	introduction
materials	materials	introduction	activities
assessment (based	assessment	activities	materials
on "constant" objectives)		materials	assessment

LESSONS AND BLOCK PLANS

How is a lesson organized? How do you distribute the lessons of a whole science unit among the daily or other periods available for instruction? We will consider both matters in this section and begin with the parts of a lesson. Let's consult again the completely planned unit (Figure 7-2) on pages 171–175 of this book. It is a realistic model designed to contain both good and improvable features—the kind often developed by a student teacher or beginning teacher.

Notice that this unit is organized around four generalizations. For our purposes, think of each generalization and its activities as a separate subunit, or *one complete lesson*. Therefore, four lessons make up this unit. Although it is customary to think of a "lesson" as a daily planned period, you will find it easier to teach and plan with broader learning segments in mind.

One complete lesson has three phrases:

1. *Introducing* phase: Meaning and purpose for study are established.

2. *Finding out* phase: Children engage in purposeful activities and gradually develop knowledge of concepts and generalizations.

3. *Summary/applying* phase: They summarize, apply, and assess what they have learned.

Seldom in true *unit* teaching will you go through all three phases of the lesson cycle in one daily time period. Developing purpose within a meaningful context may take only a few minutes, but it can take considerably longer. The finding out phase may take several hours. The summary/applying segment may vary from a half hour to an hour or more. Following is your possible role in each of the three phases.

Introducing

When you begin a lesson, you start out with a certain amount of goodwill from the children. Whether it grows or vanishes depends on the interest and meaning worked into the lesson.

An introduction that gets pupils to think about their experiences, or that provides an experience, builds interest and usually reveals what they already know—including misconceptions. It may also provoke some pupil questions that can be added to those you raise in the introduction. Many teachers write these questions on a chart, so they can be addressed during the lesson or rest of the unit. To answer questions may require some planning: how to find out, materials needed, and so on. Much of this can be done before the finding out segment begins.

A key to success in this phase is to connect with children's prior knowledge. To do this, apply the concept or generalization to be learned in a problem that makes sense to them. "How can a small child lift a large adult on a seesaw?" is a challenge they are likely to eagerly try to explain, show on the chalkboard, and demonstrate on the playground. Learning that "The force of a lever can be increased by moving the fulcrum closer to the load" will come in the next phase, after further challenges and activities with levers that look nothing like a seesaw.

You might begin this phase in any of several ways. Interesting challenges can come from applying a concept to everyday events, exploring science materials, from a news event, a short story, a demonstration that works or doesn't work ("How can you get the siphon to work?"), a discrepant event ("What makes the ice cubes sink in one glass of clear liquid and float in the other one?") and so on. What you want is something meaningful to think about that relates to the organizing concepts or generalization.

The beginning part of the lesson, then, is where you pose an understandable problem, listen to learn what pupils already know, probably raise further questions from them, and help pupils plan to find out in an overall sense. When you make a text-based unit, *the introducing phase of a lesson and bridging are the same.*

Finding Out

The next part of the lesson is where children pursue their purposes and challenges you raise for activities you've selected. They do experiments, investigate, see demonstrations, explore sequences and frames of a videodisc, view a videotape or filmstrip, read trade books and the class text, and perform other activities. Notice that I've placed the hands-on activities before the more passive ones. First-hand experiences usually provide the background and vocabulary for better understanding vicarious instructional materials that may follow—videotapes, filmstrips, and books, for example—that explain and reinforce the ideas being studied.

Some science programs make a clear distinction between first- and second-hand activities. They divide the finding-out part of the lesson cycle into two phases: a discovery phase, for first-hand activities only; and a concept development or elaboration phase, for working with instructional materials such as books or videotapes that more fully explain the ideas that pupils began to form during their first-hand investigations. This results in a four-part lesson cycle: introducing, discovering, elaborating, and summary/applying.

Summary/Applying

The last part of the lesson is when, through discussion and other means, you help children build a clearer and more general understanding of the concepts and generalization they are constructing. You want them now to see the forest, after they have lingered long among the trees. This is the time to apply and extend what they have learned and, in the process, assess how well they grasp the big ideas.

You might have pupils read or review the pertinent textbook section just before this phase, so information is fresh in mind. Questions not already answered are addressed now. Children may also give reports and show models or drawings to explain the big ideas. You might ask pupils to define in their own words a concept studied. (What does *erosion* mean to you?) Or have them complete a concept map (see page 186) that shows how concepts they have studied are related. This is the time to bring up new examples of applications, and encourage pupils to find more. These actions can be even more productive if done in cooperative groups, because then pupils will continually interact with others to share and sharpen ideas. You might also give a test in which children need to apply their knowledge. (You'll see more detailed ways to assess learning later.)

All of the preceding actions allow you to assess what children have learned, including misconceptions. At the same time, they induce children to build new knowledge and refine what they have already constructed. This is consistent with the constructivist approach to learning.

How to Make a Block Plan

Before we consider the details of how much time to allow for teaching different parts of a unit, reread the sample unit (Figure 7-2) to get a sense of the following features. First, notice that the topic is a broad one. This is typical of a text-based unit. If you go for more depth by adding activities to those of the text's, something has to give. You have only so much time to teach science. It may be best to downplay or even drop one or two generalizations rather than to skim over the entire unit.

How do you decide which generalizations to cut down or drop? Look for those that offer the least chance for children to have concrete experiences. In our unit example, the third generalization on mountain building offers the fewest concrete possibilities for nine-year-olds. But *volcanoes* and *earthquakes* are part of the mountain-building process! Their spectacular qualities make them highly interesting. Also, your pupils may be living in an area that has occasional earthquakes. In cases like this, you need to use judgment. Probably it would be better to downplay this generalization than to eliminate it. Do you agree?

Please turn now to the block plan for this unit on page 171. It was made by a student teacher. She has selected most of the activities in the unit to teach to a particular class within a given time frame. Given another class or time limit, she might choose to teach fewer or more activities, which would cause her to change the present block plan. Overall, she has done a good job of allocating activities and planning ahead. Notice how she allows lead time to ask children for some common materials.

Can you see any places where you would have planned differently? Probably she will need more time for the summary/applying phase in several lessons, so a few more activities will need to be omitted. If she heeds the children's interests, she may also need more time for the rock-collection activities (1, 4) in generalization IV.

When you have a block plan like this, based on generalizations and organized as suggested, you will probably find that you can soon teach well *without making formal plans for each scheduled science period.* So a block plan can save you much time.

Here are some things to consider when you work on block plans. It is better to reserve large blocks of time for daily study than to schedule science for 20 minutes or so a day, 2 or 3 days a week. A few experienced teachers seem to do much even within short sessions. However, it usually takes too much time to set up and distribute materials in a hands-on program for short periods to work well. Forty minutes is a more practical time period at the primary level, with up to an hour for older pupils.

A daily contact with ideas and activities of the unit gives continuity and reinforcement to learning. It also heightens the child's continuing sense of participation and interest. Notice that the *total* time allotted to science during the year, say 60 hours, need not be greater with large blocks of time for units. While science may not be taught during part of the school year as a result, it still uses the available time more efficiently.

There is an exception to these suggestions about time. When the class grows plants or otherwise waits for slow changes to take place, an every-other-day schedule may be more workable, for example. In most cases, it will be best to let the condition of the objects influence when lessons are taught. Even careful advance planning seldom guarantees that living things will act in predictable ways.

The planning shown in the block-plan example does not mean rigid restrictions have been placed on the time, activities, or sequence involved. Flexibility is really a requirement, rather than an option. If the videotape you requested does not arrive on time or the sun fails to shine for the solar heat experiment, something else needs to be ready. And although a certain amount of time is set aside, it may need to be expanded or cut down, depending on what happens in the classroom. So the block plan you start with may look quite different by the time the unit is completed. How things go from day to day will probably cause you to continually modify the plan.

Should everyone put into block plans what appears in this one? Planning is a highly individual matter. Thirty experienced teachers in one college summer session course were asked to make a block plan for a science unit. Wide differences appeared in the notes they felt were necessary for their own guidance. All but one teacher strongly endorsed the making of a block plan. But few agreed as to exactly what it should contain.

HOW WELL CAN YOU CONSTRUCT SCIENCE UNITS?

Making and teaching a unit is a surer way to become competent than merely reading about it. If you do go ahead, some guidelines can help you judge your unit. Following are some questions you can ask yourself to evaluate your work. They reflect most of the important points so far in this chapter and preceding ones. Look over the list carefully. You may want to omit some questions, add a few of your own, and arrange some order of priority among them. Concentrate at first on what you think is most important. In revisions and in later units, work on other points. It takes a lot of practice to do *everything* well.

1. Is the unit based on a small number of basic generalizations (or problems or topics or themes)?

2. Do the lesson bridges relate to pupils' experiences, provide feedback about their present knowledge, and move smoothly into the first activity of each sequence?

3. Are some open-ended activities included?

4. Can a variety of science processes be used in the activities?

5. Are the activities appropriate for the pupils' abilities?

6. Do reading and other second-hand activities, when used, usually follow concrete activities?

7. Are useful activities from other subject areas integrated into learning sequences?

8. Do pupils *apply* their knowledge in assessments or simply recall it?

9. Does the block plan allot enough time for children to learn what is proposed?

10. Does the block plan anticipate needed materials far enough in advance?

OBJECTIVES AND THE ASSESSMENT OF SCIENCE LEARNING

When you design and teach units and lessons, it is important to keep objectives in mind. In most units, you will want children to achieve both knowledge and process objectives and gain positive attitudes. Usually, the science curriculum guide or textbook manual contains statements of possible objectives. From these sources, you can select those that seem to suit your pupils. Sometimes, though, the stated objectives are not much help. They may be vague or stated in such detail that you lose your overall sense of direction.

This brings up a related issue: Should you rely heavily on detailed statements of objectives written by others? Although these may be helpful, you are likelier to get better results if your mind is organized than if the organization is only on paper.

Knowledge

One good way to ease the load of coping with many objectives is to reduce their number. You can cut down knowledge objectives by working toward concepts and generalizations rather than isolated facts. Some teachers recognize this, but then wrongly conclude that they can bypass the facts and directly teach these abstractions. This is unfortunate because what children know about concepts and generalizations depends much on what they construct from the concrete facts they study.

Take, for example, the primary-level generalization "Magnets attract things made of iron or steel." Children begin their study with concrete materials that bring out a fairly large number of facts. The children learn that a magnet attracts nails and metal coat hangers and that these are made of iron. They find that scissors and some pins are attracted and that these are made of steel. They test other metal and nonmetal objects and discover that these are not attracted.

As pupils learn these facts, vocabulary is introduced by the teacher as needed to label emerging concepts. Words such as *steel, iron,* and *rubber* are used by children as they mentally combine objects made of similar materials. Gradually, they also combine these concepts, and so a hazy approximation of the generalization develops in their minds.

But don't expect children to neatly state the generalization. This may not reveal their true understanding. Stating generalizations properly often requires formal operational thinking. Instead, ask children to demonstrate their knowledge by *applying* it in observable ways. This means they should do more than simply recall some facts. A higher level of understanding is revealed if they can use their knowledge of a generalization to *explain, predict,* or *control* objects and events, preferably those that are new to them. You may recall that this is also how scientists use these abstractions, but of course at more complex levels.

To "explain" is to tell how objects may have interacted to cause or prevent change. Children also explain when they give and justify new examples of a concept.

To "predict" means to forecast, using present information, a future observation of an object or event.

To "control" means to show how an object or event can be changed, or how a change can be slowed, speeded up, or prevented.

In a scientific view, to explain, predict, or control objects and events is *the* performance objective of all knowledge objectives. Consider it a "constant" objective, since it does not change, while individual generalizations do. If you keep this in mind, it becomes easier both to state and keep track of objectives. Notice next how this works.

Suppose your school requires statements of observable performance objectives in lesson plans, or you wish to state them. Here is how you might do so with the magnet example used previously:

Pupils will

- Explain why some objects are not attracted.
- Predict some objects that will and will not be attracted.
- Show how to prevent a magnet from picking up an attractable object.

Suppose a middle-grade unit generalization is "Weathering and erosion constantly wear down the earth's surface." Your stated objectives might be as follows:

Pupils will

- Explain why some rocks weather more than others.
- Predict places where gullies may form.

■ Draw a sketch that shows two ways to slow erosion on a bare hillside.

Suppose in an upper-grade unit on the human body a generalization is "Automatic reflex actions (blinking, reaction to sudden pain, etc.) have survival value." Your stated objectives might be as follows:
  Pupils will

■ Explain why automatic blinking has greater survival value than conscious blinking.

■ Predict two situations that will trigger an automatic reflex.

■ Make a sketch that shows how an injury might prevent a reflex action.

Notice that in the preceding sample objectives, no mention was made of how well a child should do or under what conditions evaluation should take place. Because of the many differences in pupils, we must rely on our judgment in these matters. This is true whether we are concerned with knowledge or process objectives.

For many samples of knowledge-type performance objectives for assessment, see the investigations in Part II of this book. The generalizations for these investigations include objectives typically patterned after the explain-predict-control model.

Science Processes

You can also reduce to manageable size the number of process objectives you work with. Remember, there are only about seven broad processes in most programs: classifying, observing, measuring, inferring and predicting, communicating, and experimenting (COMIC–E). These, too, are "constant" objectives in that we want children to constantly apply them in activities and so become ever more competent in their use. Each of these broad categories of processes can help you to recall a cluster of related subprocesses, if these have been learned reasonably well. To do this, you will want to refer to the list of processes on page 90 from time to time. The investigations in Part II of this book can also furnish many chances to practice the teaching of these processes. Notice that in both places they are stated as observable pupil actions. You can easily convert these statements into performance objectives for your own units, if needed.

Process objectives are assessed by providing a situation that requires the child to use the process. Most teachers appraise these objectives by observing children in action during the regular activity time. But don't expect dramatic changes in a pupil's general ability to apply a broad process from one lesson to the next. This kind of growth requires long periods of time and practice in a variety of subject-matter contexts.

Whenever you plan a science activity, try to think of the broad thinking process involved. Then, decide which specific subprocesses, such as those on page 90, can be used in the activity. As you work with children, ask questions from time to time that generate these actions in the children. (For hundreds of examples, see the marginal notes in the investigations of Part II. Also check the accompanying samples of objectives.)

Scientific Attitudes

Recall from Chapter 4, page 97, that scientific attitudes of children are often shown by their behaviors in four broad categories: curiosity, inventiveness, critical thinking, and persistence. The sample behaviors listed under these categories are the kinds of actions you look for when you appraise growth in attitudes. As with process, good times to do so are during hands-on activities and discussions. Additional opportunities will be described in more detail shortly. Remember, though, that broad attitudes cannot be developed quickly. They are a long-range by-product of the quality of learning activities and general atmosphere of your classroom.

Putting Assessment Into Perspective

"I can show you how to assess pupil achievement in many valid and reliable ways, but I can't tell you what grades to give." An outstanding test specialist began his college class on assessment techniques with those words a long time ago. As a fledgling student of education in that class, I didn't understand at first what he meant. After all, wasn't the *purpose* of assessment to give (teacher) and get (student) grades?

Some test experts see a difference between *assessment* and *evaluation,* even though the two terms now generally mean the same thing. To them, assessment is finding out *what* pupils have achieved. Evaluation is placing a *value* or "grade" on what is achieved.

There are only two basic ways to grade. We can compare a child's achievement to that of others in a defined population and place a value on it. ("Jim got more right than two-thirds of the class on this test—that ought to be an A. But this class didn't do as well as last year's—I'd better make it a high B.") Or we can define and pose some objectives for pupils and place a value on how many objectives were achieved. ("Ann met 7 out of 10 objectives—that deserves an A. But maybe only 9 or more should count as an A. Should I get an opinion from another third-grade teacher?")

The point is that placing a value on achievement (A, B, C or Superior, Good, Fair, etc.) is arbitrary. It depends on who makes the rules and how consistently they are followed. We typically are required to do some type of grading, of course, but this is best done within school district guidelines. Decisions on pupil promotion, retention, remedial instruction, and the like are strongly linked to grades. The lack of a common policy among and within schools in a district only invites trouble. Does teacher consistency in grading mean that grades awarded will be perceived by everyone as "fair"? It definitely helps; but fairness, to borrow from a favorite cliché, is in the eye of the beholder.

This chapter reflects the view that the primary purpose of assessment is to improve pupil achievement. By finding out what and how well students achieve, we can improve our teaching.

Is assessment something you do *to* children or *with* them? Each emphasis reflects a different outlook. Have you ever been asked to do something important without knowing exactly how your performance was going to be appraised? Do you like the feeling? When we work out standards or expectations *with* pupils, they usually achieve more and see the assessment process in a different light. It puts their intelligence to work, so they can better guide their own learning within the limits of their maturity and experience. If you want to maximize your teaching effectiveness, make clear to children what makes up success in *everything* they do in your science program. You'll need then to assess together a broad array of their work, not simply tests.

Even the noblest of intentions must heed the limits of time. In a previous section, you saw some ways to zero in on objectives that are most likely to yield a rich payoff. Using time productively requires making many further judgments. It will help now to see when chances for assessment generally arise.

We have three main opportunities to appraise pupils' abilities: before, during, and after teaching the activities in each lesson. The introduction or bridge of a lesson is a good place to assess pupils' present knowledge, including misconceptions. This is called *diagnostic* assessment. It can be done in a written pretest, but usually the questions you put to the children serve better, because you can follow up what they say.

Appraising pupils' work behaviors during activities is *formative* assessment. This is an apt word, since what we observe helps to shape or form our immediate, responsive teaching behaviors. This quick feedback to pupils, in turn, helps them to form improved learning behaviors.

Finally, when we assess pupil achievement after activities, we practice *summative* assessment. To do so, we can ask questions when we summarize and review previous activities. We can also appraise children's projects or other completed work, and use tests. Let's now examine in more detail ways to assess science achievement.

WAYS TO ASSESS PUPIL ACHIEVEMENT

Publisher's science programs have traditionally been weak on assessment. They are now far better. While some testing of facts and simple understandings is still found, newer programs are likely to offer many chances to appraise broad concepts and science processes, and supply more worthwhile material than you probably will have time to use. So rather than having to *create* assessment tools, you'll typically need to judge which is best to apply.

Teacher guides or packets may provide materials and guidelines for all of these assessment possibilities and more:

- Teacher observation
- Written tests
- Performance tests
- Journal writing/Activity logs
- Concept maps
- Projects
- Portfolios

See now some things that are good to know within each of these chances for appraisal.

Teacher Observation

The job of teaching is inexact at best. We might view it as a series of consecutively developed hypotheses. That is, each thing we do or say is a kind of hypothesis that we are

uncertain will be "accepted" (learned) by the children. If much teaching takes place before feedback shows that learning has occurred, we may make many unwarranted assumptions.

We can observe, and often help pupils stay on track, in whole-class settings, but the most productive times are likely to be in individual and small-group situations. There are many chances for informal teacher–child contacts during the finding out or activity times in lessons. Notice what your pupils say and do when they interact with you, a partner, or other members of a small group. What you observe gives you data for fast self-correction or for assisting individual pupils, if needed.

The quickest way to find out if pupils grasp concepts and processes is to ask questions and listen carefully to responses. By fashioning further questions to follow up responses, you can detect misconceptions and may be able to quickly address them. You can also discover much more about what students are learning.

Time will prevent you from getting around to each pupil in every science period, but there is rarely a need for that. If you have organized your class into cooperative learning or other groups, it's usually enough to check what each is doing and to question individual pupils as warranted. When possible, distribute your questions evenly among individuals and groups over each week or so. This will give you a reasonably complete picture of how all your pupils are doing. To make this a habit, try using a chart on which you place a check after working with someone or a group. Don't be surprised if you overlook many children at first. It often takes a systematic effort to properly sample everyone's learnings.

Written Tests

You'll find a variety of tests in the teacher guides and assessment guides of science programs. Written tests are typically found at ends of lessons or chapters and units. They are designed to assess pupil understanding of science words, concepts, and generalizations; the ability to apply them; and ability to do some critical thinking. Besides objective items, such as multiple-choice questions, most programs now include open-ended or essay questions for pupils at grade three and above.

Paper-and-pencil tests can be another useful tool in assessing learning, but should not be used as the only or main means of appraisal. A big drawback of tests is that the results come too late to affect the way the unit or lessons are taught. The immediate, corrective feedback necessary for effective teaching is absent if we rely on tests alone. Since only limited time is available, it's not always possible to go back and effectively take care of incompletely understood or misconceived material.

Another drawback of written tests is that it's hard to test science processes in that format. The processes are used most often in a context where children manipulate science materials. In other words, they perform some observable actions that demonstrate their ability to apply one or more processes, usually with their knowledge of a concept. Process is better appraised in a *performance test*.

Performance Tests

For a quick reminder of a wide range of operations pupils may demonstrate in performance tests, look at the summary of science processes on pages 90–91. Assessing these operations requires pupils to be placed in contexts that allow them to gather and process data.

In its purest form, a performance test has the child demonstrate operations with concrete materials. For instance, the test may ask a child to *measure* several, irregularly-shaped rocks to find the one with the greatest volume. Besides the rocks, materials might include a wide-mouth, clear plastic cup, spoon, marking pen, and container of water. To demonstrate this process, the child might

partly fill the cup and mark the water level with the pen. Next, she might slowly submerge and remove each rock with the spoon, taking care each time to mark the water level and not spill water. If the process is performed properly, the child identifies the rock with the highest water level as having the most volume and the test item is scored correct.

Another performance test might ask a pupil to *infer* the identity of three unknown leaves by consulting a chart with descriptions of leaves. A variation might ask the pupil to *classify* a half-dozen leaves, by putting them into two or more groups and stating the observable property or properties she used to do so. If the groupings are consistent with the stated properties, the answer is scored correct.

Working with concrete materials is not always necessary. Pupils may classify pictures of leaves or animals, for instance. Or a chart may be supplied that shows data from an investigation, and the child asked to interpret the data and draw a conclusion.

When children are capable writers, some performance tests may be completed entirely with words. For *experimenting*, this problem might appear:

> Suppose you want to find out whether bean plants will grow faster with Fertilizer A than with Fertilizer B. How could you set up an experiment to find out?

Or, the problem could address a specific part of the experiment:

> What variables do you need to control?

In some tests with similar problems, the child needs only to select the best answer from several options supplied in a problem—a form of multiple-choice item, though longer than most.

Performance tests with concrete objects obviously take the most time to set up, but those you are likely to see require only a few and easily found materials. And multimedia programs may offer assessment kits that include everything needed. Directions are clear and scoring uncomplicated.

Even so, some teachers with active, hands-on science programs bypass performance tests. They believe that they get all the assessment data they need by observing children at work and interacting with them during regular activity times and follow-up discussions. This may be possible with a wide array of process-rich activities and systematic observing. But mandated performance tests are becoming more prevalent at school district, state, and national levels. Avoiding them entirely in the regular science program may cause pupils to do less well on such tests.

Activity Logs and Science Journals

You saw earlier (pages 80–81) that recording data from an activity in a notebook or log is usually necessary when observations occur over time. Doing so makes it likelier that pupils will keep track of changes, observe more carefully, and think about what they are doing. Teachers may also ask children to respond in writing to questions in activities, for similar reasons. Notice how often questions appear in the investigations and activities of Part II in this book. This practice is typical of elementary school science. Pupils can appraise their recordings by comparing them with those of other group members. When data conflict, it's only natural for them to pursue reasons.

Today the concept of *writing to learn* is applied in all subjects. It holds much value for science. Many teachers have their pupils keep a science journal, which also may serve for recording data. A journal offers opportunities to improve science learning and practice important writing skills at the same time. Writing requires thinking, which changes with different purposes.

Descriptive writing can be used, among other possibilities, to identify things: "Can you describe an animal (plant, habitat, etc.) so well, without naming it, that your partner can tell what it is?" Or, "Make a chart that shows the properties of these rocks. Can your partner match the rocks to your descriptions?" Assessing these writings is straightforward. If there is a problem, both partners can work to figure out why.

Defining concepts in writing, before and after instruction, enables children to assess for themselves what they have gained from their studies. The questions, "What is soil? What is it made of?" may yield quite different results before and after lessons.

Creative writing also can and should be linked to concepts being studied. If your pupils are writing a story about an imaginary visit to an outer planet, you might ask them to correctly use recently learned words, such as orbit, acceleration, and zero gravity. Cooperative learning groups can judge whether concepts are used correctly and consult with you as needed.

You can also ask pupils at different levels to write summaries of what they have learned in a lesson, give an opinion and defend it, write a persuasive letter, compose interview questions, and do much other writing. Each form can be assessed for clarity, logic, and completeness.

It is important to have your pupils assess their own writing as much as possible, through clear directions and standards. You'll probably want to *sample* their work from time to time, but don't end up *doing* their work.

Concept Maps

One message from researchers in human learning is especially clear: Organization and meaning go together. The better we are able to relate new information to what we already know, the easier it is to remember and use it. Science programs now commonly employ several different graphic organizers to help children construct meaningful relationships among the facts and concepts they learn. The *concept map* is probably the most used organizer. It's also an excellent means to assess conceptual knowledge.

Figure 7-3 shows a simple concept map that pupils might complete after some in-

FIGURE 7-3

A concept map.

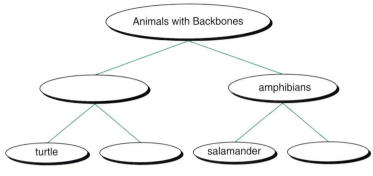

Write these words where you think they belong:

frog   reptiles   lizard

struction on body structures and functions of amphibians and reptiles. Notice that, under "amphibians," pupils need only to supply another example: "frog." On the left, both the larger concept of "reptile" and then "lizard" are needed. Other ways to assess understanding would be to omit all the words now in the map, or have children make their own map.

Pupils often make different concept maps after receiving the same instruction. This happens even when they understand all the concepts in the way you intend. They may simply view relationships among the concepts differently. So it's important for them to regularly compare their maps with partners and interact with you to more fully assess what they have learned.

Projects

It's a good idea to view science projects as normal and regular extensions of concepts and generalizations studied by the whole class. This offers many chances for pupils to take on projects, and they are more likely to do their own work. It also makes assessment simpler, less formal, and more frequent than when projects are reserved for science fairs.

A good project usually requires self-assessment from start to finish. If guidelines are simple, and your comments regarding success are consistent, pupils will develop judgment in assessing their efforts during projects and when reporting them. Let's look again at the simplified project form introduced in Chapter 6, with its first three steps now stated in the present tense, to see how it may further this goal. Questions in parentheses after each step are assessment criteria for you to consider, and for teaching to children when appropriate.

What do I want to find out? (Is the problem clear? Is there enough time to find out? Is it too easy or hard?)

What materials do I need? (What substitute materials can be used, if necessary?)

What do I do? (What exact steps are needed? What's the best order?)

What did I find out? (Does this answer the problem? Is this jumping to a conclusion?)

When you appraise project reports, either written or oral, consider keeping in mind the process acronym, COMIC–E. It can help you to determine if and how children use the processes.

Projects also give many chances for pupils to display the scientific attitudes of *critical thinking* (Are the parts of the report logical? consistent?), *persistence* (Is there evidence that the child overcame difficulties?), *inventiveness* (Was the child resourceful in substituting materials, or otherwise imaginative?), and *curiosity* (Does the child ask further questions, and want to find out more from books, people, or another project?). When you notice behaviors like these and give positive comments, you reinforce them.

As mentioned before, children do better at oral than written reports. But not all oral reports are artfully constructed models of clarity. If I were asked to say only one thing about oral reports it would be this: Encourage children to give them in their own words, with only occasional glances at notes, if possible. It's your best assurance that they understand, and others will comprehend, what they are saying.

Student Portfolios

Would you like to cultivate more self-assessment abilities in pupils? motivate increased effort in learning? show parents tangible and understandable evidence of what their children are learning? If so, consider a *portfolio* for each child. This is a sampling of work over time, collected and stored in a folder. It gives observable evidence of knowledge, processes, and attitudes gained by the child over one or more science units. The work record may appear in any or all of these forms:

- Tests—end of lesson, unit, performance
- Activity log pages
- Project reports
- Book reports
- List of books read, with annotations
- Concept maps, other graphic organizers
- Charts
- Graphs
- Science journal pages
- Creative stories
- Science words learned
- Artwork

These materials may be stored in a standard expandable folder, or a larger folder cut from poster board. Should you have a separate science portfolio? Or is it better to reserve a section for science in a more comprehensive portfolio? Primary-level teachers lean more toward the comprehensive type. Unless some material is sent home periodically or discarded, either type gets overstuffed and hard to store or manage.

Both the child and you should select items for the portfolio. Everything should be dated, so common items in a category can be paired or otherwise put in order by time, and progress observed. Guide children to look for improvements in their work, and to discuss examples they have selected with their groups. Encourage them to pair an original effort with an improved version whenever possible. This can make them more conscious of their progress and help develop pride in work done well. It can also provide incentive for producing more work of good quality.

To help children set goals for themselves, periodically have them review and think carefully about their work samples. This might be done monthly or at the end of a unit. Some teachers ask their pupils to write thoughtful responses to these two questions:

What do I feel good about?

What do I want to improve?

Responses to the second question can make it easy to set goals with children. At the next periodic review, they can examine their portfolios for evidence that the goals were met.

SUMMARY

Teaching that gets good results requires organization. How we organize depends on whether we work with an activity-centered program, a multimedia program, a curriculum guide, or science textbooks.

Activity-centered programs feature hands-on science and use methods compatible with those described in this and other recent books on elementary science education. Typically produced after years of development and try-outs, they offer many rich opportunities for children to learn science through first-hand experiences.

Multimedia programs offer a wide array of materials and methods. They may be organized around a core of books or a set of videodiscs. A complete program offers a wealth of possibilities for first-hand and vicarious learning, but some schools may adopt only part of a program, usually a series of textbooks or the equivalent.

School district curriculum guides are likely to have two uses. They contain local policies for science teaching, and they supplement adopted textbooks with locally available resources.

Modern textbook series offer excellent teaching aids in the teacher editions that accompany pupil books. Still, almost any text can be usefully supplemented by integrating local resources and some open-ended activities.

Some teachers want a more inductive and flexible approach to science than is possible with a textbook format. This can be done, while keeping the benefits of structure and well-written subject matter, by making a textbook-based unit. Its quality, though, is strongly linked to the availability of local teaching resources. The acronym GAB–BAG is an easy way to remember how to make and teach a textbook-based unit.

Lessons ordinarily have an introductory, finding out, and summary/applying phase. In unit teaching, only rarely are all three phases of a lesson cycle completed within a daily science period of 30 to 60 minutes. A block plan is an efficient way to organize what, within a unit, will be taught to a particular class in a given time period. It may change as time and classes vary.

Effective teaching is more likely when we have objectives in mind rather than if they are only on paper. Essentially, we want children to be able to *apply* knowledge and science processes, within a context of appropriate attitudes. The explain–predict–control model for knowledge and the COMIC–E acronym for processes are simply devices to help you keep these "constant" objectives in mind. Assessment of objectives occurs mainly at three times: before activities (diagnostic assessment), during them (formative assessment), and after activities (summative assessment).

This chapter reflects the view that the primary purpose of assessment is to improve pupil achievement. By finding out what and how well students achieve, we can improve our teaching. Pupil achievement can be appraised in many ways, including teacher observation, written and performance tests, journal and activity log writings, concept maps, projects, and portfolios.

SUGGESTED READINGS

Barnes, Lehman W. and Marianne B. Barnes. "Assessment, Practically Speaking." *Science and Children* 28(6):14–15 (March 1991). (An introduction to performance testing.)

Elliott, David, and Kathleen Carter. "School Science and the Pursuit of Knowledge—Deadends and All." *Science and Children* 24(8):9–12 (May 1987). (Points out some of the inadequacies of straight textbook teaching. Shows how to enrich lessons.)

Hein, George (Ed). *The Assessment of Hands-On Elementary Science Programs.* Washington, DC: National Science Teachers Association, 1990. (New assessment approaches for grades K–8 that focus on thinking processes.)

James, Robert K., and Shirley M. Hord. "Implementing Elementary Science Programs." *School Science and Mathematics* 88(4):315–34 (April 1988). (Detailed analysis of what it takes to ensure the fullest and best use of a quality science program.)

Linn, Marcia C. "Free Choice Experiences: How Do They Help Students Learn?" *Science Educa-*

HOW PART II CAN HELP YOU

Part II can help you to apply and learn more deeply the teaching strategies developed in Part I. It reflects the typical subject-matter areas found in children's textbooks and school district science guides. To help bolster your science background, concepts are developed within several major topics in the first section of each chapter. These are followed by *investigations* and *activities* clustered according to the same topics.

The investigations offer opportunities to inquire into a broad topic in open-ended ways.

INVESTIGATIONS

Each investigation is organized as follows:

Title The learning topic is stated briefly for quick reference.

Introduction Several questions or statements are given to arouse children's interest, tie in their former experiences, and sometimes introduce a needed term. This sets the stage for exploring a problem.

Exploratory Problem A broad problem is posed to follow up the introduction. It is stated in a way that requires children to explore concrete materials. (Think of the introduction and exploratory problem as your "bridge.")

Needed Materials needed are listed next. These are mostly the kind easily available at school and home.

Try This Suggestions are made about how to explore the materials or learn some procedure. This is to help pupils build readiness for discoveries, if needed. If it is not needed, move directly to the discovery problems.

Discovery Problems Both broad and narrow questions guide discoveries within several related activities. Marginal notes identify the science processes used in the activities.

Each investigation has a "Teaching Comments" section intended only for you, the teacher; it has these parts:

Preparation and Background Comments tell how to get or prepare needed materials. Some additional information about the topic also is given when useful.

Generalization This is a statement of the science principle that explains the activities.

Sample Performance Objectives Examples of a possible process objective and a knowledge objective are given to help you appraise pupil performance. Because each investigation is ordinarily wide-ranging and open-ended, additional objectives may be stated by you to fit your exact situation.

For Younger Children or *Older Children* One of these headings is found in most of the investigations. Suggestions are made about which activities are most suitable for the children included within either heading. (Also, see the statement shortly on grade placement.)

Before we go on, now would be a good time for you to examine a few investigations. This may help you to apply more easily the following suggestions for using them.

Some Ways to Use the Investigations

What teaching style best suits your needs and those of your pupils? Some teachers say they succeed with a loose, relatively unstructured way of working with their pupils. They pose mainly broad questions with their pupils; narrow questions or helpful hints are supplied only as a last resort. Frequent side excursions by pupils into newly aroused problems or interests are commonplace and welcomed.

Other teachers believe they have more success with a tightly structured, planned progression of activities. They believe their pupils learn more when specific objectives are pursued and carefully appraised. They do not ignore new problems and interests, but these are viewed as less important in helping pupils achieve main learnings.

The investigations of Part II have been planned to suit either teaching style. Here are a few suggestions about how you might use them.

When planning *units,* choose investigations that fit the unit topic or generalizations. Besides giving pupils suitable hands-on experiences, the open-ended nature of the investigations can help you provide for individual differences.

When using *learning centers,* arouse pupil interest by introducing an investigation orally before the whole class. List on the first activity card the remaining material, down to the discovery problems. Then write each of these on a separate activity card. Or simply photocopy the problems and tape them to a card. Audiotaped instructions and teacher aides offer additional possibilities.

For *individual projects* or *small group work,* you might furnish the entire investigation without the "Teaching Comments" section. Children can decide which activities to stress after consulting with you.

For *whole class* work, it is easy to present each investigation as written, or to select parts that seem suited to your situation.

Grade Placement

Since all the investigations have open-ended opportunities, they are suitable for a broad range of learning levels. The activities within each typically range from simple or observa- tional kinds at the beginning to more complex kinds toward the end.

Most of the investigations include some activities appropriate for children of varying abilities and ages, usually 5 to 12 years. You'll find suggestions for working with pupils at either extreme of the age–ability range in the "Teaching Comments" section. In the simpler investigations, suggestions for older children are added. In the more complex ones, suggestions are added for younger children.

Some of the investigations do not include such suggestions. Probably these investigations will be too abstract or otherwise unsuitable for primary-age children.

ACTIVITIES

The activities are usually narrower in scope than the investigations. They are mainly to help children learn concepts and procedures through direct experiences. They may be used independently or to complement investigations and furnish additional projects.

Each activity begins with a question to focus children's attention on some interesting event or procedure. Directions are then given to help pupils observe the event or develop the procedure. Occasionally, some information is given within the directions to help clarify the pupils' experience. Narrow questions are used to focus observations or help children think about what is happening. Broad questions may also be used to help extend the experience or stimulate thinking.

A parenthetical "Teaching Comment" addition in many of the activities presents background or other needed information for you, the teacher.

8

Light Energy and Color

Why does something look larger under a magnifying glass? What makes a rainbow? Why does writing appear backward in a mirror? Children want to know many things about the behavior of light. These and other phenomena are understandable when we learn: (1) how light travels, (2) how it can be "bent," or refracted, (3) the nature of color, and (4) how we see.

[I] THE PATHWAYS OF LIGHT   *Experiences 204*[1]

Imagine reaching for something that is visible in front of you and not finding it there, or shining a flashlight in the darkness and having it illuminate only something in *back* of you. This, of course, is not likely to happen because light travels in straight lines.

It is true that a beam of light can "bend" under certain conditions, such as when going from air into water or glass, and the reverse. (We shall go into this more deeply in the next section.) Scientists also know that light passing through space is attracted and curved by the gravitational fields of massive objects in space. Other than these exceptions, though, light does appear to travel in straight lines.

This property makes many interesting things take place. For example, look at the pinhole "camera" in Figure 8-1. Light from the candle flame shines through a narrow pinhole in the cereal box end. At the other end, an *inverted* image appears on waxed paper taped over the opening. Why? The numerals suggest an answer. If light travels in straight lines, the light going from spot one on the left can only go to spot one on the right, and so on.

Shadows

Because light travels in straight lines, it is easy to block it with different objects. For the same reason, we may easily be able to identify an object from its shadow.

Only objects we cannot see through, such as metal and wood, cast true shadows. These are called *opaque* objects. *Transparent* objects, such as clear glass and cellophane, do not cast a shadow because very little light is blocked by them. *Translucent* objects, such as frosted glass and waxed paper, allow only some light to pass through; not enough light is blocked to produce a true shadow.

Children can learn to make large or small shadows and clear or "fuzzy" shadows. They can do this by varying the distance from the light source to the opaque object and the place where the shadow falls. Shadow exploration is interesting to both young and older children. It can lay the foundation for understanding some important principles of physics in later grades.

Reflections

There are several ways in which we can alter the pathways of light, and some are surpris-

---

[1]Investigations and activities for this section begin on page 204.

FIGURE 8-1
A pinhole "camera."

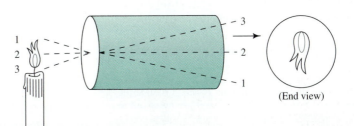

(End view)

ing. For instance, why does a woman powder her nose? Psychological reasons aside, she does it to scatter light reflections.

You know that a ball thrown straight down on smooth, level pavement bounces back up. Try it on rough gravel, however, and its return path is unpredictable. A smooth, shiny surface reflects light rays with very little scattering. But a rough or uneven surface may scatter the rays so thoroughly that reflections may be scarcely visible. What makes makeup powder so effective? Put some under a microscope. Greatly magnified, it resembles gravel!

Of course, even better reflections are possible with mirrors than with noses. Try sprinkling some powder or chalk dust over half of a mirror; leave the remainder clear. Shine a flashlight on both sections of the mirror. Does the powder help to reduce glare? Scattered light rays are called *diffused* reflections. Light rays that are not scattered are *regular* reflections.

The only time we can see something that doesn't glow by itself is when light reflects off it and travels to our eyes. But children typically do not think of light as reflecting off objects, except for mirrors and other "shiny" things. They are more likely to view the visibility of an object as simply another property or condition of the object. So they think they see an object directly rather than the light that reflects from it.[2]

Mirrors

When you deal with flat, or *plane,* reflectors, a special kind of regular reflection becomes possible. If you stand by a mirror and can see the eyes of another person, that person can also see your eyes. No matter from what position or angle you try it, the same results happen if you are close enough to the mirror to see a reflection. The angle at which light strikes a plane reflector (called the angle of incidence) always equals the angle at which it is reflected. In activities designed to help them understand this idea, children can discover this equality of angles.

No attempt is made in this chapter to develop an understanding of curved mirrors. The optical explanations of convex and concave mirrors are beyond most elementary school pupils. But they can note that convex mirrors—those with a bulging center—reduce a wide field to a small area. This is why they are used for rearview mirrors on some automobiles, for example. Concave mirrors—those with a scooped-out center—magnify images. So they are useful for purposes such as cosmetic work or shaving.

If we could not look at our photographs, or double reflections in two mirrors, we would never know how we appear to others. A mirror always produces a reversed image of the observer.

To learn why this is so, study Figure 8-2. In a sense, a mirror image is an optical illusion. Light rays reflect off the mirror into the boy's

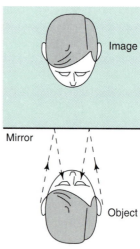

FIGURE 8-2

Why a mirror image is reversed.

[2]Lucille A. Slinger, Charles W. Anderson, and Edward L. Smith. "Studying Light in the Fifth Grade: A Case Study of Text-Based Science Teaching." Paper presented at the annual convention of NARST, Fontana, Wisconsin, April 5–8, 1982, p. 18.

eyes. He stares outward along the lines of the incoming rays. To him, his image appears to be just as far in back of the mirror as he is in front of it.

Here's a puzzler some sharp pupils may wonder about. Light *reflects* off a mirror but it goes *through* clear glass. So why can you sometimes see yourself in a window? We generally think of clear glass as completely transparent to light, yet a small amount does reflect off the surface. Ordinarily, we do not see the reflected light, because it is only a fraction of the rest that passes through. But especially at night, when there is darkness in back of the glass, even dim light striking the surface results in noticeable reflections.

Symmetry

Work with mirrors will enable you to introduce the concept of symmetry to pupils—the idea of balanced proportions in objects and geometric forms. The concept is of value in many fields, including biology, mathematics, and the arts.

A butterfly, for example, has symmetry. If you draw an imaginary line down the middle of its body, the left half is a near duplicate of its right half. A starfish has another kind of symmetry. If you turn its body around on an imaginary axis, a rotational balance is evident.

An investigation in this section takes up the presence or absence of mirror symmetry in letters of the alphabet. Children will be surprised at the ways a mirror can reveal balanced proportions. They can learn to predict which letter shapes will reveal the property of symmetry. Notice in Figure 8-3 that each of these letters is symmetrical. The left and right sides of A are opposite but alike. The remaining letters are different in that the symmetry is vertical—that is, found in the tops and bottoms, but not laterally. A few letters—X, O, I, H—have both lateral and vertical balance. Some, such as L, F, and J, have none at all.

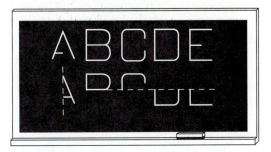

FIGURE 8-3
Symmetry in letters of the alphabet. Dotted lines show how to hold a mirror to reconstruct the original letters.

[2] LIGHT REFRACTION
Experiences 218

Have you ever jumped into the shallow part of a swimming pool only to discover it was deeper than it seemed? Light travels slower in water than it does in air. This results in an optical illusion, even though we may be looking straight down into the water.

Density and Light Speeds

The speed of light changes when it travels into or out of media of different densities. The event is especially curious if the light beam enters or leaves a different medium at a slant. A change in speed may cause the beam to change direction of travel, or to *refract.*

Examples of refraction are all around us. A pencil placed partway into water looks bent. Distant images shimmer through unevenly heated air as we drive along a hot road. The scenery looks distorted through a cheap glass window because its thickness is uneven. Interestingly, the function of an automobile windshield wiper is to restore the rainy outside surface of a windshield to a plane surface. As water is wiped away, the light rays enter the glass at a uniform angle, rather than unevenly.

What happens when light enters or leaves water? Why does it bend? Let's look for a moment into the concept of *density* as it relates to this event. You know that anything in motion will slow down or stop when something is in the way. It is easy to dash across an empty room at top speed. But scatter some people around, and the runner will slow down, bumping head-on into some people, deflecting off others, and so on. The increased population density in the room makes this inevitable. A greater amount of matter takes up the same space.

A similar thing happens with light as it travels through air, water, and glass. Water is denser than air—it has more matter in the same space—and glass is denser than water. When light enters a denser medium, it slows down. The reverse is also true. What makes light "bend" can be understood through an analogy.

Notice Figure 8-4A and B. Sketch A explains why the coin in sketch B appears to be in front of its true location. In the first sketch, the two wheels are rolling freely in the direction shown. But what happens when the leading wheel strikes the sand? The device moves on, but at a slightly different angle. To reverse this, if the device travels upward from the sand along the broken line, one wheel will hit the paved portion sooner. The direction will again change, but in an opposite way.

In sketch B, light bends in a similar direction. As it leaves the water, the light bends slightly toward the horizontal. The observer sights along a stick toward where the coin seems to be. The line of sight seems to be a straight line from eye to coin, but it is not. If the stick is pushed into the water at the same angle at which it is poised—sliding it in the groove formed by a closed book cover may ensure this—it will overshoot the target.

Lenses

People have learned to control light refractions with lenses. Eyeglasses can correct certain vision problems. Magnifying glasses and optical instruments extend the power of sight far beyond that available to the naked eye.

Figure 8-5A, B, and C shows how light refracts when passing through a convex lens. In drawing A, the light rays enter the eye from two opposite slants. (It may help to think of the wheels–axle analogy again.) As the eye follows these slanted rays to the lens, they seem to continue outward, and so they form an enlarged image of the object.

How can we make the object appear even larger? Compare drawings B and C. Notice that the two lenses differ in thickness, although their diameters are the same. Each will bring the sun's rays to a point or focus at

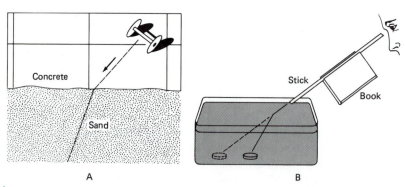

FIGURE 8-4

Light "bends" and changes direction (B) in the same way the wheels change direction (A) when they hit a different surface.

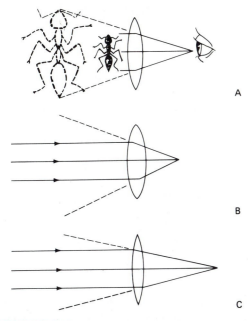

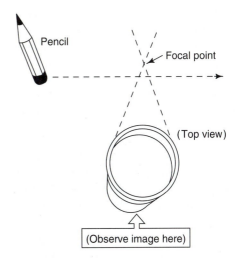

FIGURE 8-6
When an object that is inside the focal length of a convex lens is moved right, its image also moves right. But if the object is *outside* the focal length when moved right, its image moves left

FIGURE 8-5
The shape of a convex lens is what determines how an image is magnified.

a different distance. The distance from the point of focus to the lens is the *focal length.* Notice that the thicker lens has the shorter focal length. By extending the slanted rays outward, you can see why it magnifies more than the lens in C.

A curious thing may happen when we observe a moving object through a convex lens. Figure 8-6 shows the focal point of a small jar of water as light passes through it. (Though the jar is really a cylindrical lens, it acts as a convex lens in this example.) If a pencil is moved to the right *inside* the focal length of the lens, its image will also move to the right. But if it is moved to the right *outside* the focal length, its image will move to the left. The reason is apparent if we notice what happens beyond the focal point. The light rays cross and go to opposite sides.

Convex lenses *converge* light rays, or bring them together, as you have seen. On the other hand, concave lenses cause light rays to *diverge,* or spread out. This causes objects

viewed through them to appear smaller. You can see why in Figure 8-7. The light from the object slants outward toward X and Y as it goes through the lens (remember the wheels-axle analogy). As the eye follows these slanted rays back to the lens, the rays seem to continue inward at a slant and form a smaller image of the object.

Thick drinking glasses and glass eye cups often have concave-shaped bases. Pupils can check if images are smaller by looking

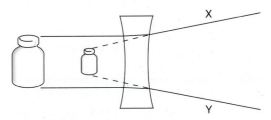

FIGURE 8-7
A concave lens makes objects appear smaller because the light rays diverge.

through them. Perhaps the easiest concave lens to make is simply to leave an air bubble in a small, capped jar of water. An object viewed through the bubble will look smaller, but if viewed through the convex part of the jar, it will appear larger.

Commercial lenses can teach a great deal. Children may learn even more, though, by fashioning their own lenses from a variety of transparent objects, containers, and fluids. A clear glass marble magnifies objects. So does a water drop or drops of other fluids. A small drinking glass with vertical sides (not tapered) magnifies things well when it is filled with water or other fluids. Narrow olive jars make especially powerful magnifiers. However, the best possibilities for controlled study of homemade lenses will happen if you use clear, small plastic pill vials.

[3] COLOR *Experiences 224*

When the ancients saw a rainbow, they were probably inclined to give a magical or supernatural explanation to account for it. Later, people thought that the colors came from the rain droplets through which sunlight passes. It was not until Isaac Newton (1642–1727) performed experiments with prisms that it was realized these colors were the parts of visible sunlight itself.

There are seven universally recognized colors in the visible spectrum of sunlight: red, orange, yellow, green, blue, indigo, and violet. (Many teachers remember these colors and their spectral order through the name Roy G. Biv.) Since indigo is almost indistinguishable from its adjacent colors, it is common to exclude indigo at the elementary level of study.

A prism separates light because each color has a different wavelength and rate of vibration. Red light has the longest wavelength, with about 1,200 waves per millimeter, or 30,000 waves to 1 inch. Violet light has the shortest

wavelength, with about twice that number of waves per unit. As a light beam passes through a prism, the longer waves are refracted least and the shorter waves most (Figure 8-8).

Differences in colors are often compared with pitch differences in sound. A low sound is a result of relatively slow vibrations. Its visual counterpart is the color red. A high sound results from fast vibrations. Its counterpart is violet.

Mixing Colors

There are two basic ways in which we can mix colors, one with colored beams of light and the other with paints or dyes. When light beams of only three primary colors—red, blue, and green—are added together in the right proportions on a white screen, different color combinations occur. These are shown in the overlapping sections of Figure 8-9. When red, blue, and green are used as colored light beams, they are called the additive colors.

Scientists have found that three certain colored pigments can *absorb* these additive colors. That is, if you shine a red or blue or green light on the right pigment, there is almost no color reflection at all. The pigment looks black. Blue light is absorbed by a yellow pigment, and red light by a blue-green pigment called cyan. Green light is absorbed by a purple-red pigment called magenta.

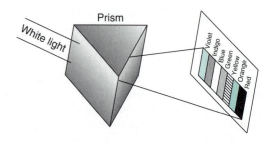

FIGURE 8-8

A prism separates white light into a spectrum of seven colors.

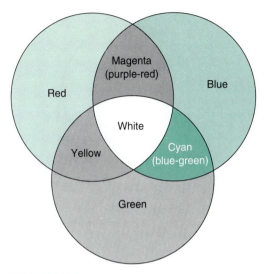

FIGURE 8-9

The additive colors. When beams of red, blue, and green light are added together in the right proportions, the overlapping colors result. Color television is produced by an additive process.

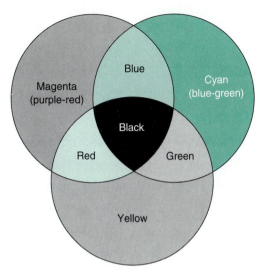

FIGURE 8-10

The subtractive colors. Paints and dyes absorb, or "subtract," some colors from white light and reflect what is left. Note the overlapping colors when the three primary pigments are mixed in the right proportions.

If a *white* light beam shines on these colored pigments, each will absorb, or "subtract," the specific color mentioned above and reflect to our eyes what is not absorbed. We can mix these pigments to get various colors, but the results we get from mixing all three are the *opposite* from mixing the three light beams. This is shown in Figure 8-10.

The foregoing ideas boil down to this: When viewing an object, the color we see depends on (1) the color of light shining on the object and (2) the color reflected by the object to our eyes. Children can do some experiments with colored construction paper and colored light beams to help them understand these ideas and their practical effects. With ordinary materials, it is hard to predict the exact hues that result from the many possible combinations. But at the elementary level, simply discovering the interesting effects of combining colored lights and pigments is highly rewarding.

"Never buy colored clothes at night." We may sometimes hear these words from friends. Is it good advice? Even the best artificial light does not contain the exact colors of sunlight. For this reason, we can't be sure a garment purchased at night will look the same in daylight. For example, most white light bulbs are somewhat deficient in blue. Therefore, a blue garment will look a bit darker under this light than in daylight. Fortunately, most clothing retailers do not depend on natural light—they install lights whose color qualities differ only slightly from sunlight.

Don't be surprised if you find several boys in your class to be at least partly color blind. One male in 12 has the deficiency, contrasted with only 1 in 200 females. Most commonly, reds and greens are seen in shades of gray; other colors are perceived normally. Rarely are all colors seen only in black and white and shades of gray.

Fading

The activity part of this section ends with a brief study of *photochemical* reactions—the changing of light energy to chemical energy when light is absorbed by a colored material. Materials that react photochemically do not just change in appearance. A permanent change occurs in molecular structure. Although this can be annoying when a favorite sweater fades, the phenomenon makes possible many important events, from photography to photosynthesis.

The degree of fading that happens depends on how colorfast a garment is and the amount of light reaching it. In a forthcoming investigation, pupils may explore fading with colored filters of cellophane or plastic and different colored objects.

[4] PERCEPTION AND THE EYE *Experiences 234*

In this closing section of the present chapter, we'll examine how the eye works and apply some ideas met before. Although the eye has many parts, we'll concentrate on three parts directly involved in sight: the *iris, retina,* and *lens* (see Figure 8-11).

Iris

The iris contains pigment that absorbs some colors and reflects others. Because the kind and amount of this coloring matter varies in individuals, some eyes appear brown, some blue, and so on. Two sets of tiny muscles control the size of a small hole (pupil) in the iris. This regulates the amount of light entering the eye.

The eyes of cats have pupils that can dilate far more than ours. This is one reason they see better than humans in near darkness. A dramatic example of this capacity appears when

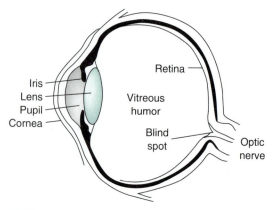

FIGURE 8-11
A simplified eye.

the headlights of an automobile suddenly shine into the eyes of a cat on a dark night. The two shiny round spots we see are the headlight reflections from *inside* the cat's eyes.

Retina

Why is it hard to see when we first walk into a darkened movie theater? Our eyes make a second important adjustment when light varies in brightness. The retina contains two kinds of light-sensitive cells: *rods* and *cones.* Cones are less sensitive than rods and are clustered near the back of the eyeball. They work best in strong light and enable us to see color. Rods are distributed in other parts of the retina and are sensitive to dim light. (To keep rods and cones straight, remember cones and color begin with *C.*)

Chemical changes sensitize either rods or cones under certain conditions. For example, when we walk into a dark theater on a sunny day, it takes several minutes before the rods work well. To achieve optimum sensitivity, up to a half hour may be required.

It is thought that cones are most sensitive to three basic colors—red, green, and blue. According to this idea, we see many colors because the basic colors are seen in various combinations. An activity is provided to apply this theory.

Lens

An eye lens is convex in shape and works like any other convex lens—with one important difference. A muscle permits it to change shape. If a large, close object appears before you, the lens thickens. This refracts light rays entering the eye sharply enough for a focus to occur on the retina. However, light rays from a small or faraway object enter the lens in a near parallel fashion. Only a small refraction is needed to bring the rays to a focus on the retina.

To experience this action, look at a distant object, then suddenly look at something a foot away. Do you feel the tug of your lens muscles pulling the lens? Do you find the near object is fuzzy for the brief instant it takes for the muscles to adjust lens thickness? In a camera, of course, focusing is achieved by moving the lens back and forth.

Eyeglasses

Two of the main vision problems corrected by eyeglasses concern image focus. In *near-sightedness,* the cornea or the lens may be thicker, or the eyeball longer, than normal. This causes an image to focus in front of the retina rather than on it. Notice in Figure 8-12 how the problem is corrected. Sketch A shows a normal eyeball. Sketch B shows a longer-than-normal eyeball and a focal point in front of, rather than on, the retina. In C, a concave lens somewhat spreads out the incoming light rays. This lengthens the focal point just enough to fall on the retina.

In *farsightedness,* the cornea or the lens may be thinner, or the eyeball shorter, than normal. So the focal point is at some imaginary distance beyond the retina. Sketch A of Figure 8-13 shows this happening with a shorter-than-normal eyeball. In sketch B, a convex lens corrects the defect by forcing the light rays to converge at a shorter focal point—on the retina.

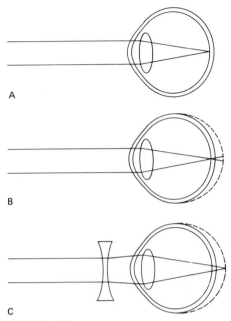

A

B

C

FIGURE 8-12
In near-sightedness an abnormally shaped cornea or eyeball causes an image to focus in front of the retina rather than on it. A concave lens can correct the problem.

Perception

An excellent example of how the brain and eyes work together takes place when we judge distance. Each eye sees an object from a different angle. The closer the object, the more each image appears to be different. We actually see a tiny bit "around" the object. At the same time, we feel our eyes turn inward. With greater distances, the angle gets smaller. The brain interprets this accordingly.

Beyond about 50 yards, we rely mainly on size to judge distance. A small telegraph pole looks far away mostly because we know that telephone poles are large. We also use other clues such as increased haze and the surrounding scene.

Many children don't realize that a movie film flashes only *still* pictures on a screen. The apparent motion of a motion-picture projection results from *persistence of vision.* It takes

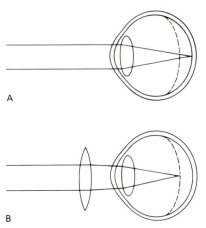

FIGURE 8-13
In farsightedness, the image focuses at some imaginary point beyond the retina. A convex lens corrects this.

about one-sixteenth of a second for an image to fade from our vision after it is withdrawn. By flashing 24 images a second on a screen, a projector creates the illusion of motion.

It took some experience before the present speed of projecting individual motion-picture frames was adopted. Early motion pictures were photographed and projected at much slower speeds. The short, unlighted pause between frames was noticeable. This is how the term *flickers* came about.

It is easy for children to experience the persistence-of-vision effect with pencil and a small pad of paper. For example, children can be guided to draw a pole that falls over. First, an upright pole is drawn on the bottom and center of the first page. On succeeding pages, in the same spot, they draw the pole at successively lower angles, until it is horizontal. A total of about 20 pages is more than adequate. When the pad pages are rapidly flipped over, an animated sequence of a falling pole appears.

Eye Care

Lessons on light energy often present ideal chances to instill in pupils the need to protect and conserve their eyes. Particular care should be taken with sticks, stones, and other potentially dangerous objects. Children should consult a responsible adult when a foreign object is embedded in an eye.

Good lighting is important in reading and studying. Television watching should take place at a reasonable distance from the screen. At night, an extra light will soften the harsh contrast between the screen and surrounding darkness. You might watch for signs of eyestrain or poor vision. The school nurse can decide if medical attention is necessary.

INVESTIGATIONS & ACTIVITIES

SECTION 1
Pathways of Light
[*Background 195*]

■ INVESTIGATION: A Pinhole Camera

Have you ever used a pinhole camera (Figure 8-14)? Light from an object shines through a tiny pinhole at one end. It travels to a waxed-paper screen at the other end. What you see there is called an *image* of the object. What you see may surprise you.

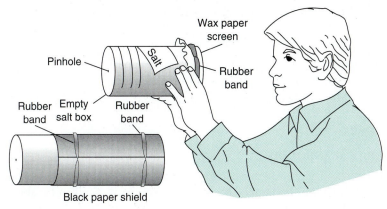

FIGURE 8-14

EXPLORATORY PROBLEM

How can you make and use a pinhole camera?

NEEDED

salt or cereal box   three rubber bands
sticky tape   waxed paper
pin   scissors
black paper

TRY THIS

1. Punch a hole in the center of the box bottom. Use a pin.

2. Remove the box top. Put waxed paper over the box's open end to make the screen. Use a rubber band to hold it.

3. Point the camera at brightly lit objects in or outside a *dark* room. What do you see on the waxed paper screen?

(To use the camera in a *lighted* place, you must shield the screen from the light. Roll black paper into a large tube and fit it around the screen end of the box. Secure with two rubber bands. Press your face against the paper shield's open end to see images on the screen.)

DISCOVERY PROBLEMS

experimenting **A.** How must you move the camera to do these things?
To make the image move right? left? up? down?
To make the image get smaller? larger?
What happens if the camera is still and the image moves? (For example, have person walk from right to left.)

experimenting **B.** How can you make a brighter, sharper image appear on the screen?
What will happen to the image if you
Change the pinhole size?

Line the inside of the box with black paper? white paper?
Use a longer or larger box or a shoe box?
Use paper other than waxed paper for the screen?

experimenting **C.** How can you make a pinhole camera with a larger paper cup? How can a second cup be used as a light shield?

hypothesizing **D.** What other ideas can you think of to try?

TEACHING COMMENT

PREPARATION AND BACKGROUND

Several kinds of boxes will serve for this activity, including milk cartons. If a black paper shield is used, it should be large. The observer's eyes will need to be about 30 centimeters (1 foot) away from the screen to see a sharp image.

Most children will be surprised to find that an upside-down image appears on the screen. You might sketch Figure 8-1 on the chalkboard and invite pupils to think through what happens.

GENERALIZATION

Light travels in straight lines.

SAMPLE PERFORMANCE OBJECTIVES

Process: The child can construct a pinhole camera and show how it works.
Knowledge: The child can explain how the flame image becomes inverted in Figure 8-1.

FOR YOUNGER CHILDREN

With teacher guidance, many primary children will be able to do the exploratory problem and discovery problem A.

■ INVESTIGATION: Shadows

What is a shadow? How can you make a shadow?

EXPLORATORY PROBLEM A

How can you change the length and direction of a shadow?

NEEDED

white sheet of paper   pencil
partner   flashlight
small nail

TRY THIS

1. Put a nail, head down, on some white paper (Figure 8-15).

2. Shine the flashlight on the nail. What kind of a shadow do you see?

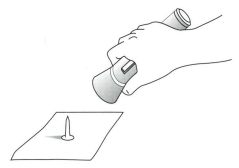

FIGURE 8-15

DISCOVERY PROBLEMS

experimenting   **A.** How can you make a long shadow? short shadow?

experimenting   **B.** How can you shine the light on the nail so there is no shadow?

experimenting   **C.** How can you make a shadow that points left? right?

predicting   **D.** Let your partner turn off the flashlight and point it at the nail. Where will the shadow be when your partner turns on the flashlight again? (The flashlight must be held still.) Draw a line on the paper where you think the shadow will be.

predicting   **E.** Can you tell how long a shadow will be?

predicting   **F.** Can you tell both length and direction at the same time?

EXPLORATORY PROBLEM B

What shadows can you make on the wall with a light projector?

NEEDED

different small objects to make shadows   filmstrip projector

TRY THIS

1. Shine the projector on the wall of a darkened room.

2. Stand between the wall and lighted projector.

3. Make some shadows on the wall (Figure 8-16).

DISCOVERY PROBLEMS

experimenting   **A.** What different shadows can you make?

experimenting   **B.** How can you make a sharp and dark shadow?

experimenting   **C.** How can you make a fuzzy and pale shadow?

experimenting   **D.** How can you make a shadow larger? smaller?

inferring   **E.** What different objects can you identify by just seeing their shadows? In what positions are the objects easy to identify? hard to identify?

FIGURE 8-16

EXPLORATORY PROBLEM C

What kinds of shadows can you make and see outdoors?

NEEDED

outdoor area   sunshine
partner

TRY THIS

1. Go outdoors into the sunshine.

2. Make some shadows on the ground (Figure 8-17).

FIGURE 8-17

DISCOVERY PROBLEMS

experimenting   **A.** Can you and a partner make your shadows shake hands without really touching each other's hands?

experimenting   **B.** How can you make your shadow seem to stand on your partner's shadow's shoulders?

experimenting **C.** How can you make a pale, fuzzy shadow darker and sharper?

experimenting **D.** How should you stand so your shadow is in front of you? in back of you? to your left? to your right?

predicting **E.** Draw a line where the shadow of some object is now. Where do you think the shadow will be in an hour? Draw a second line, then check to see later.

hypothesizing **F.** What are some other things you can try with shadows?

TEACHING COMMENT

PREPARATION AND BACKGROUND

In this investigation, children discover how to predict the lengths and directions of shadows by manipulating a light source. They learn how to make shadows dark and sharp and pale or fuzzy by changing the distance between an object and the light source. They also learn that this affects the shadow's size.

Sunny days may be infrequent in your area. If so, you might begin with Part C whenever the sun shines, and do Parts A and B indoors on cloudy days.

GENERALIZATION

A shadow may be made when an object blocks some light; a shadow may be changed by moving the object or the light source in different ways.

SAMPLE PERFORMANCE OBJECTIVES

Process: The child can manipulate a light source and object to vary a shadow's length and direction.
Knowledge: The child can state how a shadow's darkness and sharpness may be changed.

FOR OLDER CHILDREN

Section B, Problem E can be very challenging if various geometric objects cast shadows from different angles. For example, a cone may look like a disk *or* a triangle.

☐ ACTIVITY: How Many Pennies Can You "Make" with Two Mirrors?

NEEDED

two small mirrors   penny

TRY THIS

1. Fit two mirrors together like two walls joined to make a corner.
2. Place the penny between the mirrors.
   a. How many pennies do you see?

3. Change the mirror angle. Move the mirrors in other ways. Move the penny, also.
b. What is the largest number of pennies you can make? Fewest number?

▪ INVESTIGATION: Mirror Reflections

What are some of the things you can do with a mirror?

EXPLORATORY PROBLEM A

Can you see someone's eyes in a mirror without the other person seeing your eyes in the mirror? (Say the other person is also looking into the mirror.) How can you find out?

NEEDED

small mirror   sticky tape
partner

TRY THIS

1. Tape a mirror flat against a wall at your eye level.
2. Have your partner stand in back and to the right of the mirror.
3. Now you stand in back and to the left of the mirror (Figure 8-18).
4. Move around slowly until you see your partner's eyes in the mirror. Can your partner now see your eyes in the mirror?

FIGURE 8-18

DISCOVERY PROBLEMS

predicting   **A.** What will happen if you or your partner move farther to the side?

predicting   **B.** What will happen if you or your partner move farther back?

inferring   **C.** Is there any spot where you can see your partner's eyes without him seeing your eyes?

EXPLORATORY PROBLEM B

How can you use two mirrors to see over objects taller than you?

NEEDED

two small mirrors   soft clay
meter stick or yardstick

TRY THIS

1. Push a piece of clay into the meter stick near each end.
2. Push a mirror sideways into each lump of clay. Have the mirror surfaces face each other.
3. Fix the mirrors so they look like those in Figure 8-19. When done, you will have a *periscope*.
4. Hold the periscope upright. Look in the bottom mirror. What can you see? You may have to move the mirrors a little to see clearly.
5. Over what tall objects can you see with your periscope?

FIGURE 8-19

DISCOVERY PROBLEMS

experimenting   **A.** How can you use your periscope to see around a corner?

experimenting   **B.** How can you see around a corner with just one mirror on the stick?

EXPLORATORY PROBLEM C

What is the shortest mirror in which you can see your feet and head at the same time?

NEEDED

two small mirrors   sticky tape
meter stick or yardstick   partner

TRY THIS

1. You can use two small mirrors instead of a large, full-length mirror. Have your partner stand at arm's length from the wall.

2. Tape one mirror flat against the wall at your partner's eye level.

3. Hold the second mirror flat against the wall below the first mirror.

4. Move it slowly down the wall. Have your partner say stop when he can see his shoes in the bottom mirror.

5. Tape the bottom mirror flat against the wall.

6. Now your partner should be able to see his head and feet. The top and bottom mirrors are like the top and bottom of a large, full-length mirror (Figure 8-20).

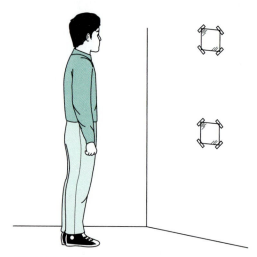

FIGURE 8-20

DISCOVERY PROBLEMS

measuring   **A.** How long is it from the top of one mirror to the bottom of the other mirror compared to your partner's height? Half as long? three-fourths as long? just as long as your partner is tall? Measure and find out.

observing   **B.** Does moving back from the mirror make a difference in the size needed?

experimenting   **C.** Does the mirror size needed depend on a person's height? How could you find out?

predicting   **D.** Can you predict the size of the shortest full-length mirror you'll need to see yourself? Switch with your partner and find out.

TEACHING COMMENT

PREPARATION AND BACKGROUND

When light strikes a mirror at an angle, it is reflected at the same angle in a different direction. That is why if you see someone's image in a mirror, it is possible for that person to see yours. This also explains how periscopes work. Notice in Figure 8-19 that the two mirror angles are identical. For the same reason, a full-length mirror needs to be only about half as long as you are tall.

Check that the mirror is taped *flat* against the wall in the last investigations. If it is not, an error in measurement is likely.

GENERALIZATION

When light travels to a mirror at a slant, it is reflected at the same slant in another direction.

SAMPLE PERFORMANCE OBJECTIVES

Process: The child can construct a workable periscope.
Knowledge: The child can demonstrate positions where two persons should be able to see, at one time, each other's image in a mirror.

FOR YOUNGER CHILDREN

Most primary children should be able to do the exploratory sections of investigations A and B.

☐ ACTIVITY: How Can Ordinary Glass Act Like a Mirror?

NEEDED

one sheet each of white and black paper   classroom
window   sunshine
partner

TRY THIS

1. Face a window where sunshine or bright light is behind you or shines from one side.
2. Look into the window. Have a partner place white paper behind the glass.
   a. How well can you see your image in the window?
3. Do step 2 again, but now use black paper.
   b. How well can you see your image in the window now?
   c. Observe your image in different windows away from school at day and night. Is it easier to see your image when the background behind the windows is light or dark?

(*Teaching Comment:* Not all the light that strikes a transparent window goes through it. A tiny bit is reflected back. When light strikes the white paper, much of it is reflected back through the glass. This interferes with the small amount of light that reflects your image. The black paper absorbs more of the light entering the window. This allows the small amount of light that reflects off the window to visibly produce your image.)

□ ACTIVITY: How Can Two Mirrors Show What You *Really* Look Like?

NEEDED

two mirrors

TRY THIS

1. Look into one mirror. Think of your image as another person facing you.
2. Wink your left eye, then your right.
   a. Which eye does the image blink each time?
3. Get two mirrors. Fit them together in the way that two walls are joined. Move them slightly so half of your face is seen in each mirror (Figure 8-21).

FIGURE 8-21

4. Wink each eye. Touch your left ear. Tilt your head to the right.
   b. What happens each time?
   c. Study Figure 8-21. How can you explain why your right eye appears on the left, like that of a real person facing you?

(*Teaching Comment:* Each mirror reflects half of the image onto the adjoining mirror. This puts it back to normal. A single mirror can only reflect an object backwards. This is why our one-mirror image is not how we look to others.)

□ ACTIVITY: How Can You Relay Light with Mirrors?

NEEDED

three to four small mirrors   sunshine or bright flashlight

TRY THIS

1. Hold a mirror in the light. Reflect the light onto a wall.
2. Pick a "target" on the wall. Reflect the light so it shines on the target.
3. Reflect your light onto another mirror held by a partner. Have your partner try to hit the target.
   a. With how many mirrors can you and some partners relay the light and hit a target? How will you tell if light is being passed from every mirror? Make a drawing that shows how the mirrors were held to hit the target (Figure 8-22).
   b. Have a contest between two or more teams. Which team can hit a target fastest with light passed along from several mirrors? How can you make the contest fair?

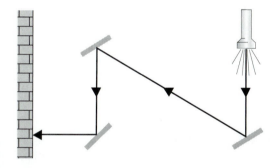

FIGURE 8-22

(*Teaching Comment:* A fair contest will prevent one team from observing and profiting from the mistakes of the other. You can tell if every mirror in a relay is being used by shading each mirror in turn with your hand. The light shining on the target in each instance will disappear. Strong light is needed if more than two mirrors are used. Sunlight is best.)

■ INVESTIGATION: Mirror Balance

Suppose you made a small, simple drawing. Then, you erased half of it. Could you hold a mirror on the drawing so it would seem whole again? Would it depend on the drawing? In what way? Drawings that allow you to do this are said to have *mirror balance.*

EXPLORATORY PROBLEM

How can you find out which things have mirror balance?

NEEDED

paper   small mirror
pencil   ruler

TRY THIS

1. Put the edge of your mirror on the butterfly at line 1 (Figure 8-23). Can you see what seems like the whole butterfly? You can because the butterfly has side-by-side balance.

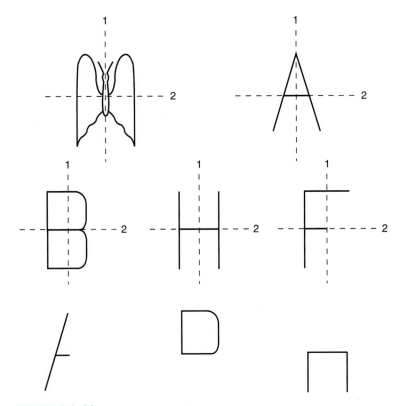

FIGURE 8-23

2. Now put the mirror on line 2. Can you see a whole butterfly now? You cannot because a butterfly's body is balanced only one way.

3. Some letters of the alphabet have balance, also. Put your mirror on line 1 of the capital letter *A*. Can you see what seems like a whole letter *A*? You can because capital letter *A* has side-by-side balance.

4. Now, put the mirror on line 2. Can you see a whole letter *A*? You cannot because a capital letter is balanced only one way.

5. Try your mirror both ways on capital *B*. Notice that you cannot see a whole letter on line 1. But you can on line 2. That is because a capital *B* only has up-and-down balance.

6. Try your mirror both ways on capital *H*. Notice that you see a whole letter both ways. A capital *H* has both side-by-side and up-and-down balance.

7. Try your mirror both ways on capital *F*. Notice that you cannot see a whole letter either way. A capital *F* has no balance.

DISCOVERY PROBLEMS

classifying   **A.** Which capital letters of the alphabet do you think have side-by-side balance? up-and-down balance? both kinds? no balance? Arrange the letters into four groups. Then check each letter with your mirror to see if you put it into the right group.

inferring   **B.** Some words may be made up of only letters from one group. How many words can you think of whose letters have only side-by-side balance? only up-and-down balance? only letters with both kinds of balance?

experimenting   **C.** Use what you know to write secret code words. Notice the half letters in the bottom row of the examples in Figure 8-23. Write a word made up of only half letters like these. Can someone read the word without a mirror? What secret messages can you write?

TEACHING COMMENT

PREPARATION AND BACKGROUND

This is an introduction to mirror symmetry—the idea of balanced proportions in the shapes of objects. The idea is of value in many fields, including biology, geometry, and the arts.

Try to have available small rectangular mirrors with the trim removed from the edges. The trim may obscure part of the reflected drawing or letter. *Caution:* If the mirror edges are sharp, cover them with a strip of cellophane tape.

GENERALIZATION

Some objects have evenly balanced or symmetrical shapes; a mirror may be used to explore an object's symmetry.

SAMPLE PERFORMANCE OBJECTIVES

Process: The child can classify the letters of the alphabet by their symmetry.
Knowledge: The child can draw or identify an object that is symmetrical.

FOR YOUNGER CHILDREN

Find and mount mirror-sized magazine pictures of objects and patterns. Some should, and some should not, be symmetrical. On what place or places in each picture can children put a small mirror to see the whole object?

Have them classify the pictures into two groups—those they can make whole again and those they cannot. Challenge children to use their mirrors to change each picture or pattern. Colored pictures, particularly, are fascinating for young children to explore.

SECTION 2
Light Refraction
[*Background 197*]

■ INVESTIGATION: The Bending of Light

Have you noticed that a pencil appears bent when placed in a half-filled glass of water? How do you think it happens? When light goes through different materials, its speed changes, so it bends one way or another.

EXPLORATORY PROBLEM

How can you bend light?

NEEDED

several small, clear containers filled with water   scissors
sunlight or flashlight   small card

TRY THIS

1. Cut a narrow slot partway up the card, as shown (Figure 8-24).

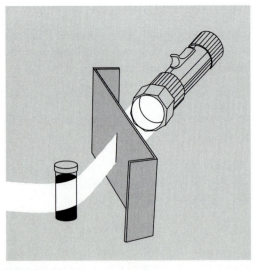

FIGURE 8-24

2. Shine the light through the slot. Direct the beam by moving the card.

3. Direct the beam through the center of the container.

4. Direct the beam through left and right of the center.

DISCOVERY PROBLEMS

observing **A.** In which direction does the beam leave the container each time?

predicting **B.** Suppose you were to direct the beam through two slightly separated containers. Where do you think the beam would come out? Mark this place, then try it.

experimenting **C.** In what different positions can you place the two containers and still predict where the beam will come out?

observing **D.** How will different-sized containers affect the bending of light?

experimenting **E.** Try using more than two containers. How far back toward the light source can you bend the beam?

TEACHING COMMENT

PREPARATION AND BACKGROUND

Clear, narrow plastic pill vials and baby-food jars make excellent cylindrical lenses to bend light. Use only straight-sided containers. The narrower or more sharply curved the water-filled container, the more a light beam is refracted or bent. If there is no sunlight, a flashlight works well when the room light is somewhat dim or if the work area is shielded with a large cardboard box.

GENERALIZATION

Light bends when it goes through different materials at a slant.

SAMPLE PERFORMANCE OBJECTIVES

Process: The child can design a way to change the direction of a light beam with lenses.
Knowledge: The child can predict how a light beam will bend when it strikes one or more lenses at an angle.

□ ACTIVITY: How Can You Hit an Underwater Target if Light "Bends"?

NEEDED

empty plastic cup	cup of water
pencil	straw
book	partner

TRY THIS

1. Pencil a small dot on the middle of the cup bottom inside. This will be your "target."

2. Place the cup on a desk. Look at the dot from an angle. Then, slowly lower your head, so your eyes are just below where you can see the dot.

3. Have a partner slowly pour water into the cup. Hold your head very still.
   a. Does the dot suddenly appear? Where does it seem to be?

4. Empty the cup and repeat step 3 several times. Then give your partner a turn.

5. Now, sight the dot in the empty cup through a straw. Hold the straw close to the cup.

6. Have your partner firmly hold a thin book edgewise under the straw as you aim it. Then let the straw slide down the groove between the outside covers. This will keep you from changing your aim once you decide where the target is.

7. Try hitting the dot from different slants.
   b. How many times are you able to hit the target?

8. Fill the cup with water and repeat steps 5 and 6.
   c. How often do you hit the target now compared with before?
   d. Where must you aim to hit the target from straight above?
   e. Where must you aim to hit the target from a slant?

(*Teaching Comment:* Hitting the target from any angle is easy if one sights into an empty cup. Sighting from directly above the target into a filled cup is also easy. However, when pupils aim toward the target at a slant, they typically overshoot it. Pupils will learn, after some trials, to aim some distance before the target. This compensates for the bending of light as it leaves the water and travels to the eye. For best results, use a low, wide cup.)

■ INVESTIGATION: Some Everyday Magnifiers

How can you make something seem larger? That is, how can you magnify it?

EXPLORATORY PROBLEM

What everyday objects can you use to magnify things?

NEEDED

two pencils	two jars of water (two sizes)
two clear-glass marbles (two sizes)	book
waxed paper	newspaper

TRY THIS

1. Place a piece of waxed paper on a printed page.

2. Dip a pencil tip into some water. Let a drop run off onto the waxed paper.

3. How does the print look through the water drop?

DISCOVERY PROBLEMS

observing

A. Make water drops of different sizes. Which drops magnify the print more?

observing

B. Put the waxed paper on a book. Make a row of drops, each drop bigger than the next. Hold up the book and paper to eye level. Look at the outline of the drops. Which are smaller and rounder? Which are larger and flatter? Which will magnify more?

predicting

C. Get two different-sized clear marbles. Which one do you think will magnify more? How much more? How will you find out?

observing

D. Get a narrow jar of water. Put your pencil inside. Does your pencil look larger? Move your pencil to different places, inside and outside the jar. Where does it look the thickest (Figure 8-25)?

observing

E. Get another, wider jar of water. Will it magnify more or less than the first jar? How can you tell for sure?

inferring

F. What other everyday things can you use as magnifiers?

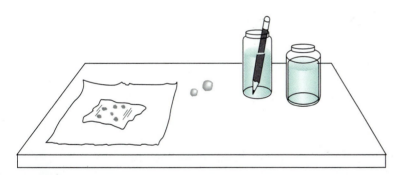

FIGURE 8-25

TEACHING COMMENT

PREPARATION AND BACKGROUND

Any clear, curved, transparent material acts like a lens. That is, light rays that pass through the material are bent. This may cause objects viewed through the lens to appear magnified. Children will enjoy and learn from trials with additional examples of clear glass and plastic materials. Clear, narrow plastic pill vials become especially good magnifiers when filled with water and capped.

The magnifying power of a glass marble may be measured by placing it on narrow-lined paper. The child counts the number of lines seen inside the clear marble. The marble with the fewest visible lines has the greatest magnification.

GENERALIZATION

A clear, curved object may appear to magnify things; a narrow, curved object magnifies more than one of greater diameter.

SAMPLE PERFORMANCE OBJECTIVES

Process: The child can measure the difference in magnifying power of two different improvised lenses.

Knowledge: When shown two water-filled containers of different diameters, the child can predict which will have the greater magnifying power.

FOR YOUNGER CHILDREN

Most young pupils should be able to do all but Discovery Problems C and E.

□ ACTIVITY: How Does an Image Change in a Homemade Convex Lens?

NEEDED

clear plastic vial or baby food jar,   pencil
   filled with water and capped

TRY THIS

1. Place a completely filled vial upright on paper, in sunshine.
2. Notice where the light comes to a point as it goes through the vial. Mark this point with a dot.
3. Look through the vial. Move a pencil slowly in back of the vial from left to right. First do it inside, then outside, the dot.
   a. In which direction does the pencil image move each time?
4. Draw a small arrow sideways on paper.
5. Push over the lens and hold it against the arrow.
6. Look through the lens and slowly raise it.
   b. What happens to the arrow image? How far must you raise the lens for this to happen?
7. Hold the lens sideways, close to your stomach. Look through it at your feet.
   c. How do your feet look? What seems to happen to your feet if you walk forward? Backward?
   d. What rule can you make to explain what happens in steps a–c?

(*Teaching Comment:* The rule is that light rays cross and reverse their positions beyond the focal point of this lens. Therefore, an object's image is reversed when the object is beyond this distance. Use a completely filled vial to avoid an air bubble. A bubble creates a small concave lens within the larger convex lens. Images appear smaller in this lens and do not reverse. Concave lenses spread out rather than converge light rays.)

□ ACTIVITY: How Can You Measure the Magnifying Power of a Hand Lens?

NEEDED

hand magnifying lens   sheet of lined paper
ruler   pencil

TRY THIS

1. Draw two or three evenly spaced lines between the printed lines on your paper. A half sheet of extra lines should be enough.

2. Pencil a small *x* in the middle of the paper where you have drawn lines.

3. Center the *x* in the lens. Move the lens up and down until the *x* looks most clear.

4. Count all the lines you see inside the lens (Figure 8-26).

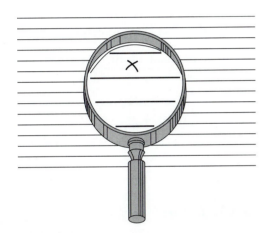

FIGURE 8-26

5. Count all the lines *outside* the lens that are between the first and last lines seen inside the lens.

6. Divide the larger figure by the smaller one. This gives the power of the lens. For example, if the answer is two, your lens makes things appear about twice as large as they are.

   a. What is the power of your lens?

   b. What is the power of other lenses you can try?

   c. How does the power of thicker lenses compare with thinner lenses?

   d. How far above the *x* must you hold different lenses to see it clearly?

   (*Teaching Comment:* Thicker lenses usually magnify more than thinner lenses of the same diameter. The distance from the point of focus to the lens is the focal length. Because they have shorter focal lengths, thicker or curvier lenses must be held closer to the *x* to see it clearly.)

□ ACTIVITY: Why Are Swimming Pools Deeper Than They Seem?

NEEDED

tall jar or glass   water
penny   crayon
ruler

TRY THIS

1. Put a penny into an empty jar. Pretend the jar is an empty swimming pool.
2. Look straight down into the jar. With crayon, mark on the jar's side the level at which the penny appears. Keep looking down as you do this.
3. Fill the jar with water. Do step 2 again.
   a. How far apart are the two marks?
   b. Will others get the same results? Ask several people to do this activity. Will it make a difference if they first mark a filled, rather than an empty, jar?

(*Teaching Comment:* Light travels slower in water than in air. The difference affects our perception of depth.)

SECTION 3
Color
[*Background 200*]

■ INVESTIGATION: How to Mix Colors

Suppose you have two different-colored crayons. How can you use the crayons to make *three* different colors?

EXPLORATORY PROBLEM A

How can you make more than three colors with three different crayons?

NEEDED

white paper   crayons of other colors
red, yellow, and blue crayons

TRY THIS

1. Rub three short, thick lines *lightly* across the white paper. Make one red, one yellow, and one blue.
2. Rub three thick up-and-down lines *lightly* on the white paper, so they cross the first three. Use the same three colors (Figure 8-27).
3. What colors do you see where the lines cross?

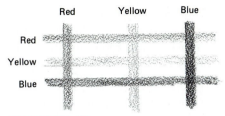

FIGURE 8-27

DISCOVERY PROBLEMS

observing   **A.** How many colors did you make?

experimenting **B.** How many new colors can you make with crayons of other colors? Draw pictures and color them.

EXPLORATORY PROBLEM B

How can you make many colors by mixing water samples of several colors?

NEEDED

four baby food jars   water
red, yellow, and blue food coloring   paper towel
three drinking straws

TRY THIS

1. Fill three small jars half full with water.
2. Put two drops of different food coloring in each jar.
3. Put a different straw in each jar and stir the colored water.
4. Mix a little colored water from two jars into a fourth jar. Use a straw to lift out the liquid from each jar. (See Figure 8-28.)

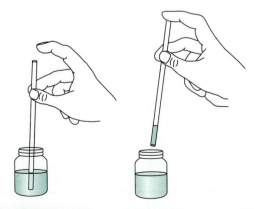

FIGURE 8-28

DISCOVERY PROBLEMS

experimenting
measuring
A. How many new colors can you make by mixing two different colors each time? Use the same volume of each color when mixing colors. Keep a record.

observing
B. What happens when you mix more of one color than another?

inferring
C. Mix a "mystery" color made from two colors. Use more of one color than another. Can someone else figure out how to match exactly your mystery color? Can you match someone else's mystery color? Try many different colors.

experimenting
D. What colors can you make by mixing three colors?

TEACHING COMMENT

PREPARATION AND BACKGROUND

Children will get the best results when combining crayon colors if they rub lightly. However, not all crayons give good results.

When red, yellow, and blue paints or dyes are paired and mixed in the right proportions, we see green, orange, and purple.

Discovery Problem C will be too difficult for some young children unless they are helped. To figure out what a "mystery" color consists of, they will need to know first what two combined colors generally produce the "mystery" color. Then they will have to slowly add more of one color to produce the proper matching shade.

Ordinary tempera paints can serve in place of food coloring, but they lack transparency. Small, clear plastic pill vials make excellent color-mixing containers. Only a few straw "loads" of liquid are needed to fill them to an observable level.

GENERALIZATION

When red, yellow, and blue dyes are paired and mixed, they produce green, orange, and purple. Different shades are produced by mixing different proportions of the colors.

SAMPLE PERFORMANCE OBJECTIVES

Process: The child can infer what combinations of colored liquids produced a new color and the general proportions used.
Knowledge: The child can state how to produce varying shades of mixed colors.

FOR OLDER CHILDREN

You might begin with Discovery Problem B and move quickly to C.

☐ ACTIVITY: How Are the Colors Made in Comic Strips?

NEEDED

colored comic strips from different newspapers   strong hand lens

TRY THIS

1. Study different comic strip pictures with a hand lens.

2. Notice how many colors are made from only a few colors.

3. Notice that some dots may be printed side by side. Or, one colored dot may be printed partly over another.

4. Observe how different shades are made by changing the distance between dots.
   a. What side-by-side colored dots do you see? What colors do they make?
   b. What overprinted colors do you see? What colors do they make?
   c. In what ways are cartoon colors from different newspapers alike? Different?

(*Teaching Comment:* An opaque projector is ideal for analyzing colored comics. Projecting the picture greatly magnifies it and makes the color printing techniques easier to notice.)

■ INVESTIGATION: The Makeup of Colored Liquids

You know that a colored liquid can be made by mixing two or more colors. Most inks and dyes are made in that way. Some of the colors mixed to make another color are surprising.

EXPLORATORY PROBLEM

How can you find out the colors that make up a colored dye or ink?

NEEDED

food coloring (red, blue, green, yellow)   scissors
four toothpicks   baby food jar, half full of water
waxed paper   white paper towel

TRY THIS

1. Cut some strips from a white paper towel. Make them about 10 by 2 centimeters (4 by $\frac{3}{4}$ inches).

2. Put one drop of red food coloring and one of blue on waxed paper. Mix them.

3. Touch the toothpick to the coloring. Make a sizable dot on the middle of one strip.

4. Hold the strip in a small jar that is about half full of water. The colored dot should be just above the water level (Figure 8-29).

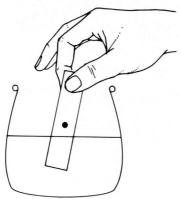

FIGURE 8-29

5. What happens to the coloring as water is soaked up past the colored dot? (This may take a minute or longer.) How many colors appear as the colored dot spreads out?

DISCOVERY PROBLEMS

observing **A.** What colors are in other food coloring samples? How are different brands of the same colors alike or different?

inferring **B.** Try a game with a partner. Mix drops from several food colors, then test them on strips. Keep a record. Remove the tested strips from the jar and let them dry. Can your partner tell which food colors were mixed for each strip? Switch places with your partner. Can you tell what mixed colors were used for your partner's strips?

observing **C.** What colors make up some inks? Also, do different brands of the same colored ink contain the same colors? Get some washable colored inks and test them.

observing **D.** What colors are in some colored fruits and vegetables? Try beets, red cabbage, blueberries, and other examples. Crush a bit of the food in water. Let the colored liquid stand overnight before testing. How are the colors of some foods alike? Different?

TEACHING COMMENT

PREPARATION AND BACKGROUND

The basic process of this investigation is called paper chromatography. The separate pigments that make up the color of a dye are adsorbed at slightly different rates by the paper. This has the effect of spreading out the pigments, which makes them visible. Only washable (nonpermanent) dyes will work.

Blank newspaper strips cut from page edges are sometimes satisfactory for the process. But thick, porous white paper towels are likely to work better.

GENERALIZATION

The colors that make up a dye may be discovered through paper chromatography. Most dyes contain several blended colors.

SAMPLE PERFORMANCE OBJECTIVES

Process: Given the materials, the child can demonstrate how to use paper chromatography to analyze the colored pigments in a dye.
Knowledge: The child can predict the colors blended in several common dyes.

■ INVESTIGATION: How Colored Things Look in Colored Light

Have you ever noticed that clothes colors look different under colored light? You can find out more about this in two ways. You can shine different-colored light on different-colored objects. Or you can look at the objects through colored-light filters—colored sheets of cellophane.

EXPLORATORY PROBLEM

How can you use colored-light filters to find out how colors seem to change?

NEEDED

small squares of different-colored paper   pencil
small pieces of cellophane (green,   white paper
   red, blue)   box of crayons
colored magazine pictures

TRY THIS

1. Put some white paper on a desk top.
2. Look at the white paper through each of three *folded* cellophane filters (a folded filter works better). What color does the paper seem to be each time?
3. Now put a colored square on the white paper. Use the filters again. What color does the square seem to be with each filter? (See Figure 8-30.)

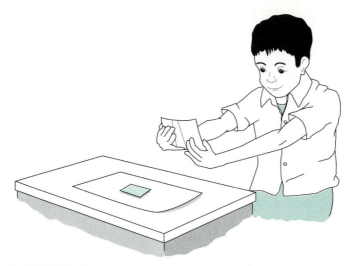

FIGURE 8-30

DISCOVERY PROBLEMS

predicting
communicating

A. Suppose you put one square of different-colored paper at a time on the white paper. How do you think each colored square will look through each filter? Make a chart to record what you think, then see.

Filter Color

Square Color	Red	Green	Blue
Red			
Green			
Yellow			
And so on			

predicting

B. Put a small colored magazine picture on the white paper. How do you think the different colors will look through each filter? Make a record of what you think, then see. Try different pictures. Does practice make it easier to tell how the colors will look?

inferring

C. How can you draw a house with windows that seem to disappear? What color windows will you draw? What color filter must you use for the windows to disappear?

inferring

D. Write the word THAT with four different-colored letters. How can you work it so only HAT or AT appears when you look through a filter?

inferring   **E.** What other words can you use like this? What secret messages can you send to someone? How will the person know what filter to use to read your secret message?

TEACHING COMMENT

PREPARATION AND BACKGROUND

The color of an object varies when we see it through different-colored light filters. This is because some of the reflected color is absorbed by the filter. The same effect happens when only colored light is shown on a colored object. The object may absorb some of the color and reflect the rest to our eyes. However, if the object color and the light color are identical, nothing is reflected; you see black. Only white light (sunlight) is made up of all the rainbow colors. So we can tell the true color of an object only if we view it in unfiltered or white light.

Durable colored-filter holders can be made from large file cards. Cut out a large center portion and tape in place a folded piece of colored cellophane. Two or three thicknesses of cellophane filter light more efficiently than one. Colored acetate, used for report covers, works better than cellophane but may be harder to find.

GENERALIZATION

Colored objects may appear to change colors in colored light or when viewed through a colored filter.

SAMPLE PERFORMANCE OBJECTIVES

Process: The child can demonstrate how to test for the effects of viewing colored objects through light filters.
Knowledge: When given a colored-light filter, the child can draw a colored object that disappears when viewed through the filter.

FOR YOUNGER CHILDREN

With some help, pupils can profit from doing the entire investigation except for Discovery Problems D and E.

□ ACTIVITY: What Colors Make Up Sunlight?

NEEDED

cake pan about half-filled with water   sunshine
mirror   white paper

TRY THIS

1. Place the pan in the sun. Have the mirror face the sun.
2. Hold the mirror upright against the pan's inside rim.

3. Slowly tip back the mirror. Light must strike the mirror below the water's surface.

4. Point the mirror toward a white wall or large sheet of white paper (Figure 8-31).
   a. What colors do you see on the wall?
   b. What happens to the colors if you stir the water lightly?
   c. Try using the light from a filmstrip projector inside the classroom. How will these colors compare with those of sunlight?

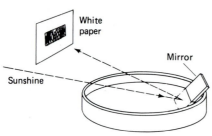

FIGURE 8-31

(*Teaching Comment:* This crude prism does an excellent job of refracting sunlight into its full spectrum of colors. Stirring the water mildly mixes the colors into white light again. The projector light's spectrum will be similar but not identical to that of sunlight.)

■ INVESTIGATION: How Colored Filters Affect Fading

Some furniture stores have display windows that face the sun. These windows may be covered with clear plastic or cellophane that screens or filters the light. This is done to keep the furniture from quickly fading.

EXPLORATORY PROBLEM

How can you find out how fast colored things will fade?

NEEDED

construction paper of several colors, such as white, blue, yellow, red, and black
several pieces of clear and different-colored cellophane or plastic
scissors
cellophane tape

TRY THIS

1. Cut squares of different-colored paper.

2. Cut one smaller square of white paper for each colored paper.

3. Tape one white square in the center of each larger, colored square. (Use only two pieces of tape.) Tape clear cellophane or plastic over each larger square.

4. Do steps 1 through 3 again, cutting the same colors. But now tape a piece of colored cellophane or plastic over each larger square. Use the same color of filter for all (Figure 8-32).

5. Fasten both sets of matched squares to an inside window, facing outdoors.

6. Wait two days before removing the white squares and filters to check what happens.

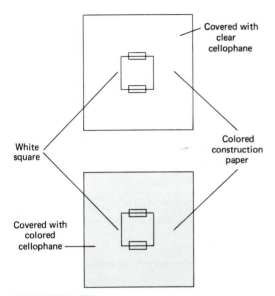

FIGURE 8-32

DISCOVERY PROBLEMS

predicting   **A.** In what order—from least to most—do you think the unfiltered colors will fade? the filtered colors will fade?

classifying   **B.** Arrange the colors in order of fading. How do the results match what you thought?

observing   **C.** What differences do you notice between the unfiltered and filtered colors?

predicting   **D.** What other colored filters can you try? What do you think the results will be?

predicting   **E.** What will be the results if you use windows that face other directions?

experimenting   **F.** How can you test different-colored fabrics? What do you think the results will be?

TEACHING COMMENT

PREPARATION AND BACKGROUND

Pigments that absorb the most light usually fade most. So darker colors are likely to fade faster than lighter colors. Filters that screen out the most light provide the most protection, so darker filters are usually more effective than lighter ones.

If colored fabrics are used, children may be puzzled to find that the results differ somewhat from those gotten with the colored papers. Some fabrics are made more colorfast than others through a chemical-bonding process. In general, however, their order of fading as to color is similar.

GENERALIZATION

Dark-colored objects fade faster than light-colored ones; dark-colored filters screen more light than light-colored ones.

SAMPLE PERFORMANCE OBJECTIVES

Knowledge: The child can predict which colors fade quickest and which colored-light filters are most effective.
Process: The child can order—from least to most fading—a mixed array of colored papers exposed to light.

FOR YOUNGER CHILDREN

With some help, younger pupils typically can do the basic activity ("Try This") and accurately observe differences among and between the filtered and unfiltered samples.

SECTION 4
Perception and the Eye
[*Background 202*]

■ INVESTIGATION: How You See Distance

Suppose you had to see for a while with just one eye. How might this make a difference in telling how far something is from you?

EXPLORATORY PROBLEM

How can you test if two eyes let you tell distance better than one eye?

NEEDED

two pencils	empty soda bottle
ball	partner

TRY THIS

1. Have a partner hold up a thumb at your eye level.

2. Hold a pencil upright, eraser end down, about 6 inches above the thumb. Using both eyes, try to touch the top of your partner's thumb with the eraser. Move the pencil down fairly quickly but gently (Figure 8-33).

3. Have your partner slightly change the distance his or her thumb is from you.

4. Using one eye, try again to touch your partner's thumb. Move the pencil down fairly quickly but gently.

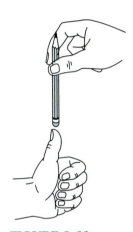

FIGURE 8-33

DISCOVERY PROBLEMS

observing   **A.** In which trial was it easier to touch your partner's thumb?

observing   **B.** Does which eye you close make any difference? How does using two eyes compare with using one? (Be sure your partner slightly changes his thumb position for each trial.)

observing   **C.** Does which hand you use make any difference?

predicting   **D.** Suppose you try to stick a pencil into the opening of a bottle held at your eye level. What do you think will happen if you use two eyes? one eye? Will the eye or hand you use make a difference? (Be sure your partner changes the bottle's distance from you each time.)

observing   **E.** Does the position from where you view the bottle make a difference? For example, suppose you view it with one eye from above the bottle. How does that compare to the results you got in D?

experimenting **F.** Can you catch a ball as well with one eye as with two? How can you find out?

experimenting **G.** How else can you test if two eyes are better than one for telling distance? (For example, you might try to toss a ball several times into a wastebasket placed on a table. When do you do better?)

TEACHING COMMENT

PREPARATION AND BACKGROUND

When we see an object with two eyes, each eye views it from a slightly different angle. So our perception of the object's distance is usually more accurate than if only one eye is used. With faraway objects the advantage decreases. We tend to use size, background, and other clues to estimate distance.

In this investigation, it is important for an object's position to be moved for each trial. Otherwise, muscle memory alone from a preceding trial may allow the child to touch the object. For the test to be valid, the child should not benefit from experience. Also, the pencil should be moved down with some speed, although gently. If done slowly, self-correction becomes too easy.

GENERALIZATION

Two eyes are usually better than one for judging distance.

SAMPLE PERFORMANCE OBJECTIVES

Process: The child can demonstrate a test for distance perception with two eyes and one eye.
Knowledge: The child can predict situations in which distance perception is more difficult with one eye than with two eyes.

FOR YOUNGER CHILDREN

Younger pupils should be able to do most of the investigation with some teacher guidance.

■ INVESTIGATION: Your Side Vision and Color

Suppose you notice an object from the corner of your eye while staring straight ahead. Can you notice it is there *before* you can tell its color? Or can you also tell the color at the same time?

EXPLORATORY PROBLEM

How far to the side can you tell different colors?

NEEDED

four small (5-centimeter, or 2-inch) paper squares of   partner
   different colors
four larger (10-centimeter, or 4-inch) paper squares
   of different colors

TRY THIS

1. Keep your eyes on some object across the room during this experiment.

2. Have a partner stand at your right side, about a step away.

3. Ask your partner to hold up a small colored square opposite your ear. (You should not know the color.)

4. Have your partner slowly move the square forward in a big circle (Figure 8-34).

5. Say "stop" when you first notice the square at your side.

6. Then tell your partner the square's color if you can.

7. If you cannot, have your partner move the square forward until you can tell.

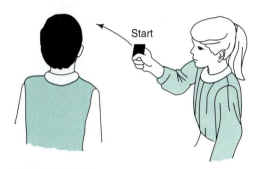
Start

FIGURE 8-34

DISCOVERY PROBLEMS

observing   **A.** Was it as easy to notice the color as the object itself?

observing   **B.** Will it make any difference if you try the test from your left side?

observing   **C.** Will it make any difference if you try different colors? Can you identify some colors farther to the side than others?

observing   **D.** Will it make any difference if you try the larger squares?

experimenting   **E.** What results will you get if you test other people?

TEACHING COMMENT

PREPARATION AND BACKGROUND

The eye's inside lining, or retina, contains millions of cells sensitive to light intensity and color. Most of the eye's color-sensitive cells are clustered at the back of the eyeball near the optic nerve. To see color, some colored light must reach there. When light enters the eye at an angle, this area may not be stimulated. So we can usually detect the presence of an object at our side before we can distinguish its color.

Be sure the children keep their eyes fixed on some far object as they do this investigation, so they can properly test their side (peripheral) vision.

GENERALIZATION

An object at one's side can be noticed before its color can be identified.

SAMPLE PERFORMANCE OBJECTIVES

Process: The child can test different colors to determine the limits of side vision in identifying each.

Knowledge: The child can demonstrate that a colored object will be detected from the side before its color can be identified.

□ ACTIVITY: What Happens When Your Eyes Tire from Seeing One Color?

NEEDED

construction paper—blue, yellow, red   scissors
white paper   watch with second hand
pencil

TRY THIS

1. Pencil an *x* in the center of the white paper.
2. Cut out one small (5-centimeter, or 2-inch) square each of blue, yellow, and red paper.
3. Put the blue square on the *x*. Look at it steadily for 30 seconds.
4. Remove the square and look at the *x*.
   a. What color appears at the *x?*
5. Rest your eyes for a minute or so. Then, try the yellow and red squares in the same way.
   b. What color appears after the yellow square? red square?

□ ACTIVITY: How Can You Tell There Is a Blind Spot in Your Eye?

NEEDED

pencil   ruler
paper

TRY THIS

1. Make an *x* on paper. Make a dot about 5 centimeters (2 inches) to the right.
2. Close your right eye. Look at the dot on the right.

3. Keep looking at the dot. Slowly bring the paper closer to your eye.
   a. What happens to the *x*?

4. Now close your left eye. Look at the *x* on the left.

5. Keep looking at the *x*. Again, bring the sheet closer to your open eye.
   b. What happens to the dot?
   c. Suppose you look between the *x* and dot with both eyes open and bring the paper to your nose as before. What do you think will happen to the dot and *x*?

(*Teaching Comment:* In 5.c., the figures will not disappear. But if pupils stare between the figures and touch the paper to their nose, the dot and *x* will practically converge. This happens because each eye tracks each figure separately. It is an interesting phenomenon, but it is unrelated to the blind spot on the retina, which occurs where the optic nerve is attached.)

SELECTED TRADE BOOKS: LIGHT ENERGY AND COLOR

FOR YOUNGER CHILDREN

Baines, Rae. *Light.* Troll Associates, 1985.

Brockel, Ray. *Experiments with Light.* Children's Press, 1986.

Carle, Eric. *My Very First Book of Colors.* Harper Collins, 1991.

Carroll, Jeri. *The Complete Color Book.* Good Apple, 1991.

Collins, Dorothy. *My Big Fun Thinker Book of Colors and Shapes.* Education Insights, 1983.

Crews, Donald. *Light.* Greenwillow, 1981.

Goor, Ron, and Nancy Goor. *Shadows: Here, There, Everywhere.* Crowell, 1981.

Smith, Kathie B., and Victoria Crenson. *Seeing.* Troll Associates, 1987.

Taylor, Barbara. *Bouncing and Bending Light.* Watts, 1990.

———. *Color and Light.* Watts, 1991.

FOR OLDER CHILDREN

Ardley, Neil. *Science Book of Color.* HarBrace, 1991.

———. *Science Book of Light.* HarBrace, 1991.

Asimov, Isaac. *How Did We Find Out About the Speed of Light?* Walker, 1986.

Cooper, Miriam. *Snap! Photography.* Messner, 1981.

De Bruin, Jerry. *Light and Color.* Good Apple, 1986.

Hecht, Jeff. *Optics: Light for a New Age.* Macmillan, 1987.

Hill, Julie, and Julian Hill. *Looking at Light and Color.* David & Charles, 1986.

Simon, Hilda. *The Magic of Color.* Lothrop, 1981.

Simon, Seymour. *Mirror Magic.* Lothrop, 1980.

Walpole, Brenda. *Light.* Garrard, 1987.

Ward, Alan. *Experimenting with Light and Illusions.* Chelsea House, 1991.

Wilkins, Mary-Jane. *Air, Light, and Water.* Random House, 1991.

Whyman, Kathryn. *Light and Lasers.* Watts, 1986.

9

Heat Energy

The rising cost of fuels has made more people realize that knowing about heat energy has economic as well as scientific value. Actually, it affects many aspects of our lives. This chapter considers (1) what happens when materials are heated and cooled, (2) how materials change state, (3) the difference between heat and temperature, and (4) how heat travels.

[1] EXPANSION AND CONTRACTION
Experiences 250

Question: How tall is the tallest building in the United States?
Answer: I don't know; it keeps changing.

Although answers like this seldom win prizes on television quiz shows, it is a good one. The height of a tall structure may vary a half foot or more, depending on temperature differences when the measurements are taken. Likewise, a steel bridge may change more than a foot in length, and a ship captain may stride a slightly longer deck in southern, in contrast with northern, waters.

Molecules

The molecular theory of matter offers an interesting explanation for these and many other events. To understand molecules, let's look for a moment at a drop of water. If we could subdivide it with an imaginary eyedropper for years on end, eventually we would get to a point where one more subdivision would produce two atoms of hydrogen and one of oxygen. Both are gases and, of course, look nothing like water. From this, we can say that a molecule is the smallest particle of a substance that can exist by itself and have the properties of that substance when interacting with other molecules.

Strictly speaking, only some gases are exclusively made up of molecules. Some liquids and many solids are composed of electrically charged atoms or groups of atoms called *ions*. But as nearly all ionic particles have physical properties very similar to molecules, it is convenient to treat them as such at the elementary science level.

Is there any direct proof that molecules exist? Recently, yes. Pictures of some larger molecules have been taken through powerful electron microscopes. But for the most part, scientists have had to rely on indirect evidence. It is a remarkable tribute to the brainpower of earlier scientists that they were able to forge so powerful a theory from their secondhand observations.

Many early experiments were so simple they may be duplicated today by children. A unit of alcohol added to a unit of water results in slightly less than two units of liquid. When gold and lead bars are clamped together for a long period, there is a slight intermingling of these elements. Solid sugar crystals disappear when stirred into a liquid. Fine powder sprinkled into a water drop may be seen through a microscope of good quality to jiggle and move erratically.

From these and sources of other experiments and observations, the following ideas have been advanced.

Matter is composed of tiny particles that have an attractive force (cohesion) between them.

There is space between molecules. In a solid material, molecules are very close together and are relatively "fixed" in place because their cohesion is greater than that of gases or liquids. Molecules of most liquids are slightly farther apart; their weaker cohesion permits them to slide about and take the shape of a container. Gas molecules are widest apart and have almost no cohesive attraction. Therefore, they can conform to a container's shape or escape from an uncovered container.

Molecules are always in motion, but they come almost to a standstill at absolute zero (−460°F or −273°C). Above this temperature, molecules of solids vibrate in place, whereas liquid and gas molecules move faster and more freely. With increased temperature, motion increases and the molecules move farther apart. The reverse happens when temperature is decreased. This is why most matter expands when heated and contracts when cooled.

Water

If liquids *contract* when cooled, why do some water pipes burst in freezing weather? Although molecular theory states that liquids contract when cooled, we note an interesting exception when water temperature drops toward freezing. Water does contract in volume with decreased temperature until about 39°F (4°C). Then its molecules begin to assemble into a crystalline form that becomes ice at 32°F (0°C). The latticelike arrangement of these crystals takes up more space, about four percent more, than an equal number of free-moving water molecules. This is why water pipes and engine blocks of water-cooled automobiles may burst in winter.

It also explains why a lake freezes from the top down, rather than the reverse. At 39°F (4°C), water is densest and sinks to the lake bottom. Colder water, being less dense, floats to the surface. It freezes into surface ice and traps the heat energy in the slightly warmer water below. Unless the air temperature is extremely cold, this trapped energy is enough to keep the pond from freezing completely.

The importance of this phenomenon to living things can hardly be overestimated. Though it is clear that aquatic life is saved, consider what would happen to the world's climate if bodies of water froze from the bottom up. Because the heat now trapped by ice would escape, ice formation would increase. Gradually, the earth's climate would become colder and eventually fatal to most life forms.

Differences in Cohesion

Different materials vary in their rates of expansion and contraction because their cohesive forces vary. It is easier to tear a paper sheet apart than an equally thin steel sheet because steel molecules attract one another with much greater force. A cohesive disparity is likewise true of alcohol and water. Notice in Figure 9-1 how water bulges above the glass rim when it is overfilled.

The cohesive force of water molecules is greater than that of alcohol. This also explains why equal amounts of heat energy cause alcohol to expand more than water. It is easier to overcome the weaker cohesive force. It tells us also why alcohol evaporates faster than water.

Expansion–contraction and, as we'll see later, changes of state from solids to liquids and gases, are the results of a constant tug of war between heat energy and cohesive force. Which "side" wins depends on which force is the more powerful. Several upcoming activities make the effects of heat energy visible with a solid, a liquid, and a gas: A metal object expands, colored water rises in a homemade thermometer, and a warmed balloon gets larger.

Water   Alcohol

FIGURE 9-1
Surface tension in alcohol and water.

Materials and Safety

Before you try any heat energy activities, a note about materials may be useful. As with all of the activity chapters, this one can be taught with supplies found about the school or home. However, there are several items that should be bought or borrowed to gain the greatest benefit from the activities.

Several small, inexpensive thermometers will be helpful. These should be marked for both the Celsius (centigrade) and Fahrenheit scales, with a full range from freezing (0°C, 32°F) to boiling (100°C, 212°F) points. We'll use both scales, although normally you and the children may find it easier to use the Celsius scale for graphing. Expect cheap thermometers to vary several degrees from each other.

Especially useful will be some glass tubing, a one-hole rubber stopper, and a flask. A candle will serve as a heating source in experiments. It will also be useful to have an electric hot plate.

Some experiences will require use of a lighted candle. Supervise these occasions closely. Probably it will be advisable to handle any burning candle yourself. Never allow a child with long hair or loose, trailing apparel to work by an open flame. Always use a metal tray or other fireproof material to contain a burning or hot substance. Develop standards about not touching a hot plate or other materials at random. All activities in this chapter are safe when you take commonsense precautions.

[2] CHANGING STATES OF MATTER   *Experiences 254*

Sometimes we get so used to our environment it is hard to think of the things about us in new ways. Most everyone knows that air is a mixture of gases. Yet a favorite stunt of science demonstrators at high school assemblies is to grandly pour liquid air from one container to another. Many persons know that carbon dioxide is a gas. Yet is it possible to trip over some or drop it on your toe when it is in the form of dry ice. Steel is certainly a durable solid. But high-temperature tests for possible spaceship uses turn it into vapor.

Temperature

The state of matter at any given moment depends on its temperature. Temperature is a measure of the average speed of molecular movements. When increased heat energy is applied to a solid, its molecules vibrate faster. If the motion is powerful enough to overcome the molecules' cohesive forces, the molecules move farther away, and the solid becomes a liquid. If further energy is applied, the molecules move even faster and farther apart to become a gas. With loss of heat energy, the opposite occurs. The decreased speed of molecules enables cohesive force to be reasserted, thus forming a liquid, then a solid, when enough heat is lost.

Does a solid become a liquid before it becomes a gas? Or a gas, liquid before it becomes a solid? Usually, yes. But a mothball changes to a gas directly; so does dry ice. Frost is an example of vapor freezing directly into a solid state. These phenomena are examples of *sublimation*.

Different substances change state at different temperatures. Adding salt to fresh water lowers its freezing point. Sea water, for example, freezes at 28.5°F (−2°C) instead of 32°F (0°C). Unless the temperature is very low, sprinkling rock salt on an icy sidewalk melts the ice. We add an antifreeze liquid (ethylene glycol) to our automobile radiators to prevent freezing. A heavy salt solution would be even more effective, except for its unfortunate tendency to corrode metal.

What Pressure Does

Pressure also has an interesting effect on changes of state. As a liquid warms, some of its molecules move so fast they bounce off into the air. We recognize this as evaporation. The same thing happens with boiling, except the process is faster. To leave the surface of a liquid, though, molecules must overcome not only the cohesive pull of nearby molecules but also the pressure of air molecules immediately above.

At sea level, a square-inch column of air extending to outer space weighs 14.7 pounds (6.6 kilograms). At the top of a tall mountain there is much less air—and so weight—pressing down. With less pressure, it is easier for liquid molecules to escape into vapor form. So at 90,000 feet (27,000 meters) water boils at room temperature. Astronauts or pilots of high-altitude airplanes wear pressure suits, or are enclosed in a pressurized cabin, to keep their blood from boiling.

Since we normally associate boiling with a temperature of about 212°F, it is important to realize another practical effect of decreased pressure. Boiling point temperature decreases about 1°F for each 550-foot increase in altitude. At a high location, it is hard to cook foods satisfactorily in an open container because of the low temperature at which boiling happens. A pressure cooker is almost a necessity.

The effect of a different kind of pressure is readily observable with ice. Why is it possible to skate on ice, whereas we cannot on other smooth surfaces? The answer is that we do not skate directly on the ice. Our body weight exerts enough pressure through the ice skate blades to liquefy the ice. This furnishes a water-lubricated surface on which we slide. As the temperature drops, however, it takes increasing pressure to melt the ice. It may be difficult to skate at all.

Heat Loss and Gain

Does an iced drink start warming up after the ice has half melted? A change of state always results in the absorption or release of heat energy. It requires energy for the fixed jiggling molecules of a solid like ice to acquire a more freely moving liquid state. Interestingly, until an ice cube melts completely in a container of water, there is no appreciable rise in water temperature. The heat energy absorbed first changes the state of the frozen water, then raises the water temperature once the cube has melted. The next time you have an iced drink, try stirring the liquid until the last bit of ice has melted. You should sense no rise in temperature until after the frozen cubes have completely changed state.

Additional energy is required for liquid molecules to move fast enough and far enough apart to become a gas. Heat is absorbed from whatever accessible substance is warmer than the changing material.

So, if you hold an ice cube in your hand, it removes heat from your body. More heat is required as the liquid evaporates. This is why evaporation has a cooling effect. As the speed of evaporation increases, so does cooling. This is why rubbing alcohol cools your skin more effectively than water. Ethyl chloride evaporates so quickly that it is used by physicians to numb flesh for painless surgery.

Conversely, heat energy is released when a gas condenses to a liquid or a liquid freezes to a solid state. That is because molecular motion continually decreases with each event. It used to be common in rural homes to place tubs of water near cellar vegetable bins. As the water freezes, enough heat is given off to prevent the vegetables (which have a slightly lower freezing point) from freezing.

That heat is absorbed in evaporation and released through condensation is a principle applied in modern electric refrigeration. A liquid refrigerant moves at low pressure into the freezing unit. There it flashes into a vaporous state, cools rapidly, and absorbs heat. As the now slightly warmed vapor leaves the unit, a motor-driven pump compresses the vapor until it has changed to a hot liquid under high pressure. The liquid next circulates in tubes attached to the back of the refrigerator that radiate the heat into the air. The cycle then begins again.

[3] TEMPERATURE AND HEAT ENERGY   *Experiences 257*

You have seen before that the temperature of a material depends on the speed of its molecules. So molecules of a cold substance move slower than those of a hotter substance. The beginning activity of this section gives pupils a chance to observe colored water drops as they spread at different speeds through water samples of unequal temperatures.

Heat Quantity

Although the concept of temperature is understood by many children, quantity of heat is a subtler idea. Consider a white-hot horseshoe just removed from a blacksmith's forge and a large bathtub of warm water. Which contains more heat? Very probably the water. The amount of heat a material contains depends on *how many* molecules it has, as well as how fast they are moving. This is why the owner of a large house pays a larger winter fuel (heat energy) bill than someone who owns a small house, although the same air temperature may be maintained. It also explains why it takes about half as long to bring one liter of water to a boil as two. There are half as many molecules to move.

Heat Capacity

Different materials have different capacities for heat energy. For example, it takes more heat for iron to reach a given temperature than an equal weight of lead. More energy is required to heat water to a given temperature than any other common material, liquid or solid, and water retains this heat longer.

The most important effect of water's high heat capacity is found in weather and climate. Because the earth's oceans and lakes gain and lose heat more slowly than the land, they moderate changes in air temperature throughout the world. The most noticeable effects are found in coastal regions. Summers are cooler and winters warmer there than they are inland.

The Calorie and BTU

Two measures are commonly used to tell heat capacity: the calorie and British Thermal Unit (BTU). A calorie is the quantity of heat needed to raise the temperature of a gram (about $\frac{1}{28}$ ounce) of water 1° Celsius. The caloric value of a food is found simply by burning a dry sample of known weight in a special chamber of a carefully insulated container of pure water. The temperature rise is multiplied by the weight of water in the container. For example, assume 50 grams of water rises 20°C. $50 \times 20 = 1,000$ calories.

To make calculations less cumbersome, a "large calorie" is used in finding heat value of foods. Equivalent to 1,000 small calories, the large calorie is what you see published in diet lists and nutrition recommendations.

The British Thermal Unit is used widely by engineers. Defined as the quantity of heat needed to raise 1 pound of water 1° Fahrenheit, it is also found by multiplying the mass of water by the temperature increase. So to raise the temperature of 5 pounds of water 30°F requires 150 BTU.

Of course, this information is more for you than for the pupils at this level. Yet, it is not too early for many children to grasp the general idea of heat quantity. For this reason, we have included several activities in which children heat different-sized nails, put them in water, and measure the rises in water temperature.

Heat Conservation

Another concept that children can begin to understand is that heat energy is *conserved* when liquids are mixed—that is, not lost but transferred in proportion to the original amount. One liter of warm water has half the heat energy of two liters at the same temperature. Also, if two equal volumes of water at different temperatures are mixed, the resulting temperature is halfway between that of the two samples.

Thermal Equilibrium

In some elementary science curricula, the concept of *equilibrium* is introduced. For example, when water is brought to a boil, its temperature stays at 212°F or 100°C (at sea level) until all the water has evaporated. Because it loses heat energy as fast as it gains the energy, we see a state of dynamic equilibrium—a stable condition that remains until the water disappears.

A second example is seen when something cools. You know that when a jar of hot water is left standing long enough, it loses heat energy to the surrounding air and surface on which it rests. Eventually, the water temperature becomes stable when it reaches *thermal equilibrium* with these interacting objects. The air, of course, is the chief interacting object that influences water's final temperature.

[4] CONDUCTION, CONVECTION, AND RADIATION *Experiences 262*

Until the nineteenth century, it was generally thought that heat was a fluidlike substance (caloric) that could be poured from one material to another. Scientists now realize that heat is a form of energy—energy being defined as the capacity to do work.

Changing Forms of Energy

Many experiments have shown that energy can be changed from one form to another. Our practical experience also shows that this is so. Electrical energy changes to heat in toasters and hot plates; chemical energy yields heat through fires and explosives; mechanical energy (motion) provides the force needed to overcome friction and in the process, heat is released.

Heat, in turn, changes to other forms of energy. Hot fuel turns a generator to produce electricity; gasoline is burned in automobile engines to produce mechanical energy, and so on.

If you put a pan of hot water in a cool room, after a while the water cools to room temperature. But place a pan of cool water in a hot oven, and the water warms to oven temperature. In moving toward thermal equilibrium, as we saw before, heat energy always travels from a place of higher temperature to one of lower temperature.

A misconception of what heat is may interfere with understanding how it travels. Instead of viewing cold as a lesser degree of heat, many elementary school pupils think that cold is distinctly different and the opposite of heat. So it's logical for them to think that "cold" leaves the ice cube in a drink and goes into the liquid, rather than that heat goes from the liquid into the cube, making it melt.[1]

Since heat is felt rather than seen, it may also affect children's understanding of how it travels. By about age eight, they begin to think of heat as something that travels from a source to another place. But before then, for example, they are more likely to view a hot stove or fire as something that instantly makes them warm.[2]

In moving from one location to another, heat energy may travel in one or more of

---

[1]Gaalen L. Erickson. "Children's Conceptions of Heat and Temperature." *Science Education* 63(1):83–93 (1979).
[2]Edna Albert. "Development of the Concept of Heat in Children." *Science Education* 62(3):389–99 (1978).

three ways: by *conduction, convection,* and *radiation.* Let's consider these ways one at a time.

Conduction

If you grasp the metal handle of a hot frying pan, you quickly let go. How is it possible for the heat energy to go from the hot stove grid to the handle? Molecular conduction is responsible. As heat energy enters the pan bottom, its molecules begin to vibrate faster. This motion is passed along, molecule by molecule, up the pan's sides to its handle. Eventually, all the particles are vibrating faster, and you feel the heat.

Of all solids, metals are the best conductors. Their molecules are very close together and transmit heat energy quickly. But each type of metal varies somewhat in conductivity. Copper is the best common conductor, followed by aluminum, steel, and iron. Other solids are comparatively poor conductors, including ceramic materials. This is one reason we use a ceramic cup to hold hot coffee. As any army veteran knows, drinking hot coffee from a metal cup can be a painful experience.

Because molecules of liquids are farther apart than solids, it is reasonable to expect that they conduct heat less efficiently than solids. Our ordinary experiences with bathwater help confirm this thought. When hot water is added to cooler water, it takes a long time for the heat to reach all portions of the tub. For this reason, we stir the water a bit to hasten the process.

Gases are the poorest conductors of all. Their molecules are spread so far apart they do not collide often and regularly enough to pass on increased energy to any appreciable extent. This is why it is possible for frozen-food sections in supermarkets to have open counters. Very little heat energy is conducted downward from the warmer air above the counter.

Convection

Although liquids and gases conduct poorly, it is easy to heat a pan of water quickly to boiling temperature or quickly roast a frankfurter in the hot air over a fire. This means that there must be another, more efficient method of heat transfer in liquids and gases than conduction. To identify it, examine first what happens when air is warmed.

Watch the smoke from burning material. Why does it rise? Is it unaffected by gravity? A clue to its behavior is found when smoke is pumped into an airless vacuum chamber. The smoke particles fall like lead weights. Therefore, smoke does not just "rise"; something must push it up.

When the glowing part of burning material warms the adjacent air, the increased energy agitates air molecules to increased speeds and they spread farther apart. Because now fewer molecules take up a given volume of space, they are lighter than an equal volume of the surrounding air. The lighter air is pushed up with the smoke particles as it is replaced by heavier, colder air. As the mass of lighter air rises, it carries increased energy with it. This is why air near the ceiling is warmer than air near the floor.

When there is an opening for warm air to escape and cool air to flow into a room, a *convection current* is set up. This is what happens when we open a window at top and bottom to freshen the air in a room. It is also the primary cause of winds in the atmosphere.

Similar convection currents are set up in heated liquids. Warmed, expanded water in a pan rises as it is continually replaced by cooler, heavier water until the same temperature is reached in the entire container. Because of the way convective currents move, a heating unit is usually located at the bottom of a hot-water tank and a cooling unit at the top of a refrigerator.

Convection also helps to set up ocean currents. Warm water at the equator is continually being replaced by cold water flowing from the polar regions. Air convection currents form winds that contribute to the distribution of these giant water currents. A third important factor is the earth's rotation. Because water has a high heat capacity, ocean currents are responsible for altering the climates of many countries.

Radiation

A common example of the third method of heat transfer, radiation, is found in the fireplace of a house. This is especially noticeable when the air temperature is low. As you warm yourself in front of the fire, only the portion of your body that faces the fire feels warm. Conduction is poor, because air is the conducting medium. Convection is negligible, because most of the hot air escapes up the chimney. Heat reaches you by radiation.

All vibrating molecules release a certain amount of energy through invisible heat rays called *infrared waves*. These waves largely pass through transparent materials like air and glass but are absorbed by opaque objects, which become warmer as a result. We are aware of radiant energy only when the emitting source is warmer than body temperature. The sun is by far our most important source of radiant energy. In its rays are found visible light, invisible infrared waves, and other forms of radiant energy.

From Solar to Heat Energy

An air traveler who goes from a cold to a tropical climate in a matter of hours usually notices many differences in the new surroundings. Among the most impressive are house colors—largely light pastels and dazzling white. Similar differences can be noted in clothing colors. Although most adults know the basic reason—dark-colored materials absorb more sunlight than light-colored materials—the practical consequences of this fact are most impressive in a tropical climate.

Figure 9-2 reveals why persons in tropical countries find a greater need for lighter colors than those who live farther away from the equator. Light is most intense when it is received from directly overhead. If the same

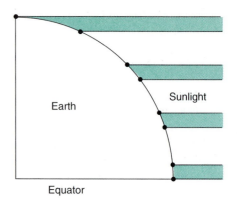

Light is most intense when received from exactly overhead. This explains why people in tropical climates find a greater need for light-colored clothing and buildings than others do.

amount of light is spread out over a larger area, any part of that area receives less light and so less heat.

The changing of solar energy to heat energy is most noticeable when there is an effective way of preventing the heat from escaping. A common example is the temperature rise within a tightly closed automobile parked in sunlight. The rapidly vibrating short waves of sunlight can pass through the windows. When they strike the upholstery they are absorbed, then reradiated as longer, slower-vibrating heat waves. The longer waves are largely unable to penetrate glass, however, so most of the heat stays inside, building up in intensity as sunlight continues to stream in. Because the same thing happens in greenhouses, this phenomenon is aptly called the *greenhouse effect*.

Our atmosphere is also warmed largely by reradiated heat waves. The atmosphere is like a giant glass cover that traps the longer, reradiated heat waves. However, this analogy is not perfect. Fortunately for us, the atmosphere is far less efficient than glass. A substantial amount of reradiated heat escapes into space. Were this not so, the earth's air temperature would become intolerable to life.

Because of the greenhouse effect, air temperatures get warmest in the afternoon rather than at midday. Although the sun is most nearly overhead at midday, the buildup of heat continues for several hours afterward. (We'll consider the greenhouse effect more fully in Chapter 18.)

Solar Heating for Homes.   Solar energy is becoming a popular way to heat water and even entire homes, especially in the sunbelt regions of the south and southwest. Let's examine one way this is done.

A *flat-plate collector* is often attached to, or built into, the house roof. Its purpose is to collect as much solar energy as possible. The collector, made of metal and glass, is positioned to face the sun. The glass is mounted just over a blackened metal plate. Water pipes, also painted black, are attached to the plate. Sunlight is absorbed by the plate and pipes.

Water inside the pipes is heated by conduction. The glass cover contributes to the buildup of heat by trapping the absorbed light energy— the greenhouse effect again (Figure 9-3).

The heated water is stored in a large tank. When needed, pipes circulate it to rooms, where the heat is radiated as needed. Other pipes are connected to hot water faucets in the house.

Notice the three conditions that affect the efficiency of the solar collector. The collector plate and pipes are painted black to absorb sunlight. A clear glass cover admits sunlight but prevents most of the absorbed energy from escaping. Finally, the collector is mounted on a slope that faces the sun. In an upcoming investigation, children can experiment with similar conditions.

Controlling Heat Loss

Knowing how heat travels permits us to control it. We use *insulation* to prevent or retard heat

FIGURE 9-3
A flat-plate solar energy collector.

energy transfer. For example, to retard conduction we use poor conductors. Since air is a poor conductor, materials with air spaces, such as wood and wool, make excellent insulators.

In homes, convection and conduction are reduced by using hollow walls designed to trap the air. Because some convection takes place anyway, many homeowners fill the walls with a light, fluffy material, such as rock wool.

An excellent way to insulate for radiation is to reflect it away, because it behaves like light as it travels. This is why insulating materials in the home may use a shiny foil exterior, particularly in the attic. It explains, also, why silver-colored paint is used on large gasoline storage tanks.

One of the last activities of this section lets children discover, in an open-ended way, the efficiency of many insulating materials.

INVESTIGATIONS & ACTIVITIES

SECTION 1
Expansion and Contraction
[*Background 241*]

☐ ACTIVITY: How Does Heat Affect a Solid?

NEEDED

brass screw and screw eye, each screwed into the eraser end of a separate pencil

small dish and candle
matches

TRY THIS

1. Light the candle and fix it to the dish.
2. Try to pass the screw through the screw eye. This should not be possible.

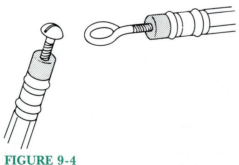

FIGURE 9-4

3. Heat the screw eye in the flame for a minute or so.
4. Try step 2 again.

a. Does the screw head pass through the heated screw eye? If so, keep passing the screw head through the eye. How many seconds go by before you cannot do it?

b. What will happen if you heat the screw but not the screw eye? If you heat both screw and screw eye?

How can you explain what happened in a and b?

(*Teaching Comment:* The screw eye should be slightly smaller than the screw head. Pliers can be used to slightly close or open the screw eye as needed. *Caution:* Supervise burning candle use closely.)

■ INVESTIGATION: Measuring Temperature with a Water Thermometer

Many thermometers use red-colored alcohol or mercury in a closed tube. What happens to these liquids when they get warmer? cooler? You can make a water thermometer that works in much the same way.

EXPLORATORY PROBLEM

How can you make a water thermometer?

NEEDED

small soda bottle	soft clay
small card	plastic straw
sticky tape	crayon
red food coloring	pencil
thermometer	ruler

TRY THIS

1. Fill the bottle almost full with water.
2. Add some food coloring to the water so it is easy to see.
3. Dry the bottle opening with a paper towel. Then put the straw about halfway into the bottle opening.
4. Use clay to stop up the bottle opening and around the straw. Try to get a tight fit, without getting the clay wet.
5. The water should rise about halfway up the straw beyond the clay. If not, move the straw up or down. Then press the clay down tightly again.
6. Put the bottle in the sun. After an hour, lightly mark the water level on the straw with crayon. Then put the bottle in a refrigerator for an hour and mark the level.

7. Measure the distance between the two marks. On a card, mark two dots the same distance and draw evenly spaced lines between. Give each line a number, with the highest on top. Put the column of numbers on the right side of the card.

8. Tape the card to the straw so the top and bottom numbers are even with the two marks on the straw (Figure 9-5).

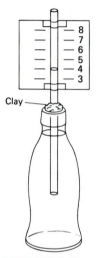

FIGURE 9-5

9. Use your water thermometer to record daily temperatures for a week. You might use a chart like this:

Water Thermometer Readings

Time	M	T	W	TH	F
9:30 A.M.	4	5			
Noon	6	7			
2:30 P.M.	7	7			

DISCOVERY PROBLEMS

measuring   **A.** At what time of day when you measure is it coolest? warmest?

inferring   **B.** During the week what was the coolest morning? noon? afternoon?

predicting   **C.** How closely can you predict the noon temperature from the 9:30 A.M. temperature? the 2:30 P.M. temperature from the noon temperature? Try this for a few days.

communicating **D.** Ask a partner to make another water thermometer. Keep two separate records. How closely do your readings agree with your partner's? If they do not agree, can you figure out why?

measuring **E.** Get a regular thermometer. Measure the temperature with it and your water thermometer. Write the actual temperatures on the left side of the straw card. After a few days, use only your water thermometer to predict the real temperature. Then check the regular thermometer each time. How accurate is your water thermometer? How could you make it more accurate?

TEACHING COMMENT

PREPARATION AND BACKGROUND

A one-hole rubber stopper and glass tube are more reliable than clay and a straw. Wet the tube and stopper before inserting the tube. Hold the tube with a thickly folded paper towel to guard against breakage and use a twisting motion.

Water, especially with this large volume, takes considerable time to gain and lose heat, so readings should be hours apart. Rubbing alcohol responds more quickly to heat and may be substituted.

Children's thermometers will be influenced a bit by changing air pressure and evaporation of water in the straw. To prevent evaporation, put a few drops of light machine oil into the straw top after assembling the thermometer.

GENERALIZATION

Liquids expand when heated and contract when cooled.

SAMPLE PERFORMANCE OBJECTIVE

Process: The child can construct, calibrate, and read a water thermometer.
Knowledge: The child can explain how a liquid thermometer works.

☐ ACTIVITY: How Does Heat Affect Air?

NEEDED

cool, empty soda bottle   round balloon
partner

TRY THIS

1. Snap the balloon opening over the bottle opening.
2. Wrap both hands around the bottle to warm it. Let a partner help, also.
   a. What happens to the balloon? What seems to be happening to the air inside the bottle?
   b. What will happen to the balloon when the bottle cools? Why?

    c. How else can you warm the bottle air? cool the bottle air?

    d. How could you find out if heated air expands by using only a balloon and string?

(*Teaching Comment:* A partly filled balloon may be placed in sunlight. A string may be wrapped around it to compare before and after sizes. A round, moderately sized balloon inflates more easily than the small tubular kind.)

SECTION 2

Changing States of Matter

[*Background 243*]

□ ACTIVITY: How Do Evaporating Liquids Cool Your Skin?

NEEDED

cotton	water
rubbing alcohol	two thermometers
medicine dropper	paper towel
paper clip	

TRY THIS

1. Put a drop of water on your desk with a medicine dropper. Put a drop of alcohol alongside it. (Be sure the dropper is clean before each use.)

    a. Which drop do you think will evaporate faster? (You can spread out each drop a little with a paper clip to make both of them evaporate more quickly.) It takes heat energy for any liquid to evaporate. The faster a liquid evaporates, the more heat it takes away from whatever it touches.

    b. If this is so, which liquid do you think would feel cooler evaporating from your skin?

2. Ask someone to rub one drop of water on the back of one of your hands and a drop of alcohol on the other one. Keep your eyes closed, so you cannot see which hand gets which.

    c. Did you pick the faster-evaporating liquid? Can you pick the same cooler liquid three times in a row?

3. Maybe your skin is playing tricks on you. It is harder to "fool" a thermometer. Soak a small cotton ball in water and another in alcohol. Wrap each around the bulb of a different thermometer. Fan both with a stiff card or paper to help the liquids evaporate.

    d. Which thermometer do you think will be cooler after the liquids evaporate?

▪ INVESTIGATION: The Melting of Ice Cubes

Suppose you have a glass of water. It has the same temperature as the air. Would an ice cube melt faster in the water or air?

EXPLORATORY PROBLEM

How can you find out if water or air will melt an ice cube faster?

NEEDED

thermometer   small plastic bag
water   salt
ice cubes   spoon
two glasses (same)

TRY THIS

1. Measure the air temperature inside one glass with a thermometer.
2. Also measure the temperature inside a glass of water. It should be about the same as the air temperature. If not, let the water stand a while.
3. Find two ice cubes that are the same size.
4. Put one ice cube into the empty glass. Put the other into the glass of water.
5. Compare how fast the ice cubes melt (Figure 9-6).

FIGURE 9-6

DISCOVERY PROBLEMS

experimenting   **A.** How can you make an ice cube melt faster in water? Will stirring the water make a difference? Will an ice cube melt faster in warmer water? Does breaking or crushing the cube make a difference? Does changing the volume of water make a difference?

experimenting **B.** How fast will ice cubes melt in other liquids? Will an ice cube melt faster in salt water? Does the amount of salt make a difference? What other liquids can you try? Can you predict the melting order of ice cubes in them?

TEACHING COMMENT

PREPARATION AND BACKGROUND

The first activity of this investigation requires water of room temperature. Blend warm and cold tap water. Or simply let a glass of water stand for a while.

If you believe your pupils are capable, try asking only the leading broad question in Discovery Problems A and B. Probably the pupils will suggest testing most of the variables posed in the narrow questions that follow.

Some children may find it hard to understand that for each test they will need a paired setup in which only one condition is changed. For example, to test the effect of stirring water on the cube's melting time, two identical ice cubes and glasses of water are used. One is stirred and the other is not. Let the pupils think through this procedure for themselves, as you find possible.

GENERALIZATION

The melting time of an ice cube changes with different conditions.

PERFORMANCE OBJECTIVES

Process: When asked to test a specific variable, the child can set up an experiment in which other variables are controlled.
Knowledge: The child can predict several conditions that will affect the melting times of ice cubes.

FOR YOUNGER CHILDREN

Younger pupils can do the exploratory problem, if they are given water that is at room temperature, and respond to the narrow questions in A and B. But they typically will not control variables unless shown how.

□ ACTIVITY: What Happens to the Temperature of an Iced Drink as the Ice Melts?

NEEDED

two ice cubes   cup of water
thermometer

TRY THIS

1. Put the ice cubes in the water.

2. Take the water temperature once a minute throughout this activity. Stir the water a bit each time.

3. Repeat step 2 until you get the same reading twice. Then answer these questions:
  a. What will happen to the temperature as the ice keeps melting?
  b. When does the water temperature rise again? (A graph can help you keep track.)

(*Teaching Comment:* The ice melting process can be speeded up by heating a metal cup on a hot plate turned to "low." Similar results should happen.)

SECTION 3
Temperature and Heat Energy
[*Background 245*]

☐ ACTIVITY: How Does Heat Energy Affect How Fast Liquids Will Mix?

NEEDED

three clear matching jars or glasses   medicine dropper
blue food coloring   sheet of white paper
hot and cold tap water

TRY THIS

1. Fill one jar with clear hot water and one with cold water. Wait two minutes for the water to settle.

2. Using the medicine dropper, quickly put one drop of coloring into each jar. Hold white paper in back of the jars to help you see.
  a. In which jar does the coloring spread out faster?

3. Ask a partner to empty the used jars and prepare three "mystery" jars. One should have hot tap water, one warm, and one cool.
  b. Using only the dropper test, can you tell which jar is which?

(*Teaching Comment:* The hot water in step 3 should not be so hot that it is immediately obvious or painful to touch.)

■ INVESTIGATION: Heat Energy

Suppose you have two iron nails, one large and one small. Both are heated to the same temperature over a candle flame. Which nail do you think would have more heat energy in it? Or, would both nails have the same heat energy?

EXPLORATORY PROBLEM

How can you compare the amount of heat energy in heated nails?

NEEDED

pie pan
candle and match
two small empty juice cans
pliers or tongs
two small thermometers

soft clay
large and small nail
water
clock

TRY THIS

1. Stick the candle upright in the middle of the pan with clay (Figure 9-7).

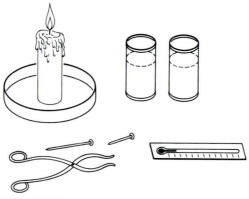

FIGURE 9-7

2. Fill both cans with enough water to cover the nails when they are dropped in later. Check to be sure the water level and temperature are the same in the cans.

3. Light the candle. Use pliers to hold both nails in the flame for three minutes.

4. Drop one nail into each can. Wait one minute. Then stir the water in each can lightly with a thermometer and check the temperatures.

DISCOVERY PROBLEMS

measuring **A.** Which can of water is warmer? Which nail had more heat energy in it?

observing **B.** Maybe one nail was just cooler than the other. Suppose you heated both nails longer to be sure they are the same temperature. Would you still get uneven results?

experimenting **C.** How can you give the *small* nail more heat energy than the larger one?

predicting **D.** Suppose you heated together a large aluminum nail and a large iron nail. Which, if either, do you think would have more energy?

communicating **E.** How can you see what happens to the water temperature for each minute you heat a nail? Make a graph to help.

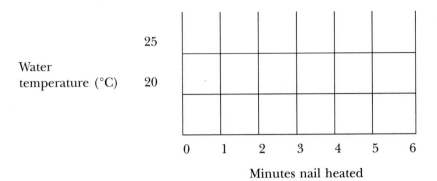

Water temperature (°C)

TEACHING COMMENT

PREPARATION AND BACKGROUND

Be sure to supervise this investigation closely for safety. Caution children to handle heated material only with tongs or pliers. Also, you might prefer to light and extinguish the candle. A hot plate can be used to heat more objects at a time than is possible with a candle.

GENERALIZATION

The amount of heat energy in the same materials depends on their mass as well as temperature.

SAMPLE PERFORMANCE OBJECTIVES

Process: The child can graph and interpret data.
Knowledge: The child can predict that the larger of two heated identical materials will contain more heat energy.

☐ ACTIVITY: How Does the Volume of Water Affect Boiling Time?

NEEDED

hot plate
small, empty pill vial
watch

three small matched cans
water
steel pan

TRY THIS

1. Pour one vial of water into a small, empty can. Pour two vials into another can and three into a third can.
2. Put all three cans into a pan. Place the pan on a hot plate.
   a. How long will it take each water sample to boil? Write down your estimates and turn on the hot plate. Watch and record the times.

b. From what you have seen, how long will four vials of water take to boil? Record your estimate and test it.

(*Teaching Comment:* Observe in item 2b whether pupils start again with a *cold* hot plate. If not, see if they can figure out where they went wrong. Also, can pupils decide what "boil" means? Supervise closely use of the hot plate.)

■ INVESTIGATION: The Mixing of Hot and Cold Water

Have you ever added cold water to cool down hot bath water? Have you added hot water to heat up cool bath water? You can learn to predict the temperatures of a water mixture.

EXPLORATORY PROBLEM

How can you predict the temperature of two mixed samples of water?

NEEDED

large container of hot water   half-gallon milk carton with top cut off
large container of cold water   two thermometers
two small Styrofoam cups   paper and pencil

TRY THIS

1. Fill one small cup with hot water. Take the temperature of the water and record it.

2. Fill another small cup with cold water. Take the temperature and record it (Figure 9-8).

FIGURE 9-8

3. Pour both cups of water into the large carton. Take the temperature of the mixed water and record it.

4. Study your records. Let's say your recorded temperatures are like these:

Hot Water	Cold Water	Mixture
60°C	20°C	40°C

Notice that the temperature of the mixture is halfway between the hot and cold temperatures (60 + 20 = 80, 40 is ½ of 80). Look at the temperature of your mixture. Is it about halfway between the hot and cold temperatures?

DISCOVERY PROBLEMS

predicting   **A.** Suppose you mix *two* cups of hot and *two* cups of cold water. How hot do you predict the mixture will be?

predicting   **B.** Suppose you mix two cups of only hot water. How hot do you predict the mixture will be?

predicting   **C.** Suppose you mix two cups of hot water with one of cold water. Will the mixture be hotter or colder than halfway between the two temperatures? How closely can you predict the temperature of the mixture?

predicting   **D.** Suppose you mix two cups of cold water with one of hot water. Will the mixture be hotter or colder than halfway between the two temperatures? How closely can you predict the temperature of the mixture?

   E. What other mixtures can you make? How closely can you predict temperatures?

communicating   Keep careful records and study them. They will help you to predict temperatures.

TEACHING COMMENT

PREPARATION AND BACKGROUND

The temperature of mixed water depends on the temperature and the volume of each water sample mixed. When the volumes of water samples are equal, the mixture temperature is the average of the sample temperatures. But if the volumes are different, this has to be considered when figuring the average. For example, if one water sample is twice the volume of another, it will have twice the influence on the mixture temperature.

Most children will be unable to grasp this notion mathematically. But repeated manipulative experiences can develop in them an intuitive notion of the range and direction of temperature changes. Of course, classroom predictions can only be approximates. Some heat loss will occur in pouring or mixing the samples and taking temperatures.

Plastic one-gallon milk containers are handy for holding and pouring hot and cold tap water. If hot water is not available, use a teakettle and hot plate. Make sure the hot water temperature does not exceed the capacity of the thermometer used.

Caution: Never heat the water beyond the point that someone can comfortably touch it.

GENERALIZATION

The temperature of mixed water samples depends on the temperature and volume of each sample. The mixture temperature is always somewhere between the high and low sample temperatures.

SAMPLE PERFORMANCE OBJECTIVES

Process: The child can measure water sample temperatures and calculate the average of several samples.
Knowledge: The child can purposefully vary the direction of temperature change (cold or hot) in a mixture by controlling the volume or temperature of added water.

SECTION 4
Conduction, Convection, and Radiation
[*Background 246*]

□ ACTIVITY: How Does Heat Travel in an Iron Rod?

NEEDED

candle and match
metal pan
6-inch square of kitchen foil

straightened wire hanger
wooden clothespin

TRY THIS

1. Light a candle and drip some wax into a metal pan. Make three pea-sized wax balls from the drippings.
2. Attach them in a row near the end of an iron rod. (A straightened wire hanger can serve as the rod.)
3. Fold the foil square twice. Stick the rod through it, as in Figure 9-9. It will shield the wax from the flame.
4. If you put the rod tip over the flame and the rod gets hot, the wax balls will melt a little and drop off. But before you do so, think about these questions.
   a. In what order will the wax balls drop:
      if the rod gets hot from the flame to where it is held?
      if the rod gets hot from where it is held to the flame?
      if the whole rod gets hot at the same time?
   b. What do you think will happen?

FIGURE 9–9

5. Clip a clothespin to the rod to use as a holder. Hold the rod tip over the flame.
   c. How can you explain what happens?
   d. What will happen if you try rods or things made of other metals? Try some
       and see.

(*Teaching Comment:* The shield is to prevent the candle's radiant energy from
reaching the wax. If various metal rods of the same diameter are used, pupils can
discover how fast they conduct heat. A piece of bare copper bell wire will work
better than the iron wire hanger. Of several common metals, copper conducts heat
fastest. That is why the bottoms of steel stove pans are often coated with copper. In
this activity, the weaker the heat source, the closer the wax balls must be affixed to
the wire's end. A clothespin holder is unlikely to be needed, but it does instruct
pupils in a sensible precaution. Supervise closely the use of the burning candle.)

☐ ACTIVITY: What Makes Some Things Feel Colder Even When They Have the Same Temperature?

NEEDED

metal object   newspaper
piece of wood   thermometer

TRY THIS

1. Hold the bulb of a thermometer against any metal object, such as scissors. Find
   its temperature. Do the same with a piece of wood and a folded newspaper.
   They should all be the same temperature. If not, keep them together and wait
   an hour or so.

2. Touch a metal object with one hand and some wood with the other. Compare the metal and newspaper, also.
   a. Which one felt coolest? warmest?
      Some materials conduct heat well and some poorly. Good conductors take away heat quickly from our warm skin, so they feel cool. Poor conductors take away heat slowly. This makes them seem warm because less heat is lost from our skin.
   b. What other materials can you compare at school and home? Make a record of what you find. Share your record with others who test heat conductors.

(*Teaching Comment:* It is assumed in this activity that the temperature of tested materials will be lower than body temperature. If your pupils seem capable, you might invite them to attempt an explanation after problem 2a and withhold for a time the one given.)

□ ACTIVITY: How Do Warm and Cold Water Form a Current?

NEEDED

two matched clear soda bottles   red food coloring
small card   white paper
cake pan or tray   hot and cold tap water

TRY THIS

1. Fill one bottle with cold and the other with hot tap water.
2. Add red coloring to the hot water bottle. Put this bottle on the pan.
3. Hold a card tightly over the opening of the cold water bottle. Turn the bottle upside down and place it carefully on top of the hot water bottle (Figure 9-10).
   a. What do you think will happen if you remove the card? Try it and see. Be careful not to tip over the bottle. Hold white paper behind the bottle to see better.

FIGURE 9-10

4. Empty the bottles and do steps 1 and 2 again, but now put the hot water bottle on top.

   b. What do you think will happen now when you remove the card? How can you explain the results?

☐ ACTIVITY: Where Does Warmed Air Go?

NEEDED

yardstick or substitute	string
two thumbtacks	two matched paper bags
bit of clay	sticky tape
hot plate	

TRY THIS

1. Stick a thumbtack into the middle of the stick near the edge. Tie string to the tack.

2. Hang the stick from the top of a wide table. Use another tack to fasten the loose string end there.

3. Fasten a string to each bag bottom with sticky tape.

4. Hang the bags upside down from the stick ends. Use a tiny bit of clay to balance the stick if needed (Figure 9-11).

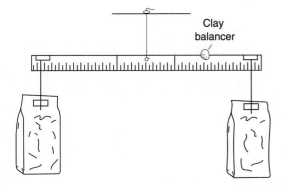

Clay balancer

FIGURE 9-11

5. Place a cold, unplugged hot plate under a bag. (*Caution:* The bag should be at least 30 centimeters or 1 foot above the hot plate since it is flammable.)

6. Plug in the hot plate.
   a. What do you think will happen to the bag when you turn on the hot plate?
   b. What will happen to the bag when you turn off the hot plate?

(*Teaching Comment:* For safety, it's best for you to demonstrate this activity, and to turn off the hot plate as soon as the bag rises.)

■ INVESTIGATION: Solar Energy and Colors

Have you ever felt extra warm when wearing a colored shirt in sunlight? When a colored shirt soaks up sunlight, it does get warmer. But how does the kind of color affect how warm it gets?

EXPLORATORY PROBLEM

How can you compare how warm different colors get in sunlight?

NEEDED

sheets of different-colored construction paper, such as blue, red, green, white
four thermometers
four paper clips
sunshine
partner

TRY THIS

1. Fold the four colored sheets in half. Clip together the open side.
2. Push a thermometer all the way into each folded, clipped sheet (Figure 9-12).

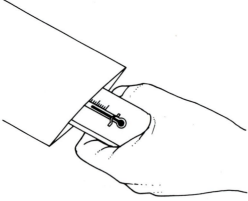

FIGURE 9-12

3. Place the sheets in a row where it is sunny.
4. Wait five minutes. Then check the thermometer temperatures.

DISCOVERY PROBLEMS

predicting   **A.** Before you check, what do you think the warmest to coolest colors will be?

classifying   **B.** Suppose you also tried colored sheets such as orange, yellow, and black. Where would they fit in the order found in A?

observing   **C.** How well can you feel the difference in heat among the colors? Close your eyes. Let a partner help you place your hands on the sheets. Can you feel the hottest and coolest sheets?

measuring   **D.** Will a large colored sheet get warmer than a small one?

measuring   **E.** Suppose you placed *all* the colored sheets in the shade. Would some colors still get warmer than others?

observing
communicating   **F.** How does an automobile's color affect how hot the painted metal gets? What, if any, differences can you tell by touch? How much do others agree with you?

TEACHING COMMENT

PREPARATION AND BACKGROUND

It is possible on extra-bright, hot days for the temperature inside the paper folders to rise quickly. On such days, leave the thermometer tops exposed. Have someone observe and remove any thermometer before it rises near the breaking point.

GENERALIZATION

Absorbed sunlight changes to heat energy; darker colors get warmer than lighter colors.

SAMPLE PERFORMANCE OBJECTIVES

Process: The child can read a thermometer accurately to within one degree.
Knowledge: The child can select which colors are likely to be relatively warmer or cooler in sunlight.

FOR YOUNGER CHILDREN

With some help, younger pupils can detect by touch alone which colors become warmest or stay coolest in sunshine (Problem C).

□ ACTIVITY: How Do Greenhouses and Closed Automobiles Get Warm?

NEEDED

two matched glass jars and cap   two thermometers
two pieces of dark cloth   sunshine

TRY THIS

1. Place each jar on its side. Put a piece of cloth into each. Place a thermometer on each cloth. Cap only one jar.

2. Turn the jars so their tops face away from the sun.

3. Watch the thermometers. Keep a record of any changes each minute. Remove a thermometer before it gets close to its highest temperature, because it can break.

    a. In which jar does the temperature climb faster? How much faster? A graph will help to answer these questions.

    b. How much, if any, difference in jar temperature will there be on a cloudy day?

■ INVESTIGATION: Heating Water with Solar Energy

Some people are using sunshine to heat water for their homes. You too can heat water with sunshine, but in an easier way.

EXPLORATORY PROBLEM

How can you heat water with sunshine?

NEEDED

two small baby food jars with caps   small thermometer
water   tempera paints and brush

TRY THIS

1. Fill two small jars with water and cap them.

2. Put one in the sun and the other in the shade.

3. After 30 minutes, remove the jar caps. Dip a finger into each jar of water. Which is warmer? (See Figure 9-13.)

FIGURE 9-13

DISCOVERY PROBLEMS

measuring   **A.** How much warmer is one jar of water than the other? How can you use a thermometer to find out?

predicting   **B.** Suppose you paint one jar black and the other white. In which do you think water will get hotter in sunshine? How much hotter after 15 minutes? thirty minutes?

predicting   **C.** Suppose you color the water black and white instead of the jars. Which colored water sample do you think will get warmer in sunshine? How much hotter after 15 minutes? thirty minutes?

predicting   **D.** Suppose you leave the top off of one jar. What difference do you think there will be in the water temperatures after 15 minutes of sun? thirty minutes?

predicting   **E.** Suppose you turn a capped jar upside down. What difference do you think there will be in the water temperature after 15 minutes of sun? thirty minutes?

predicting   **F.** Suppose you slant one upside-down jar toward the sun and the other away from the sun. What difference do you think there will be in water temperature after 15 minutes? thirty minutes?

experimenting   **G.** How hot can you get a container of water with 30 minutes of sunshine? Have a race with one or more friends. Try everything you know that may help the water heat up. Make some rules so the race is fair. For example, everyone starts with the same volume of water at the same temperature.

observing   **H.** How are the winning and losing containers different? What rule can
inferring   you make about how to heat water fast with sunshine?

TEACHING COMMENT

PREPARATION AND BACKGROUND

After pupils do the exploratory problem, you may want them to go directly into the open-ended activity found in Discovery Problem G. But if you believe they need more background first, use the present sequence.

GENERALIZATION

Absorbed sunlight changes into heat energy; sunlight may be absorbed and trapped in several ways.

PERFORMANCE OBJECTIVES

Process: The child can measure the temperature differences in several pairs of water samples.
Knowledge: The child can describe several conditions that affect how fast water absorbs the sun's energy.

FOR YOUNGER CHILDREN

Most younger pupils can do the activities if given some help. Because many will be unable to read thermometers, let them compare temperature differences in the paired water samples with their fingers. The average child can detect a difference of as little as 2°F.

☐ ACTIVITY: Where Is It Hottest Around a Lighted Lamp?

NEEDED

table or gooseneck lamp (shade removed)   ruler
small pane of glass   thermometer
watch

TRY THIS

1. Check the room temperature with your thermometer. Then switch on the lamp.

2. Hold the bulb end of the thermometer toward the lamp light. Try the three places shown in the picture (Figure 9-14). Keep the thermometer the same distance from the light each time. Wait for the thermometer to reach room temperature before trying a new place.

   a. How hot does the thermometer get in each place?

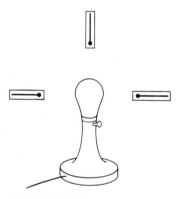

FIGURE 9-14

3. Turn the lamp upside down. Again, hold the thermometer bulb toward the light.

   b. How hot does the thermometer get? How can you explain your results?

4. Set the lamp upright again. Hold a piece of glass between the light and the thermometer. Hold the thermometer in all four places again.

   c. What are your findings now? How can you explain them?

(*Teaching Comments:* Tape the edges of the glass shield with masking tape to avoid a nicked finger. A transparent shield of plastic kitchen wrap will also work. The temperature above an unshielded bulb should be highest because both convection and radiation occur. But convected heat is blocked by a transparent shield, so the temperature above a shielded bulb should be like that found in other positions around the bulb.)

☐ ACTIVITY: How Can You Feel Heat Radiating from People?

NEEDED

partner

TRY THIS

1. Hold the palms of both hands very close to your cheeks.
   a. Can you feel the heat given off by your hands and cheeks?
2. Maybe you are only imagining such heat. Ask a partner to place her or his hands close to your cheeks. Keep your eyes closed so you cannot tell by seeing.
   b. Can you tell when your partner's hands are in place? When they are not? Try this several times both ways. Keep a record of the times you are right and wrong.
   c. How do you think exercise might change the heat energy a person's body gives off? How could you find out?

■ INVESTIGATION: How to Keep Heat In or Out

Most houses have double walls—an inside and outside wall. Packed between the double walls of many houses is *insulation*. This is a light, fluffy material that helps to keep heat in or out. You can work with cans of water and different materials to learn about insulation.

EXPLORATORY PROBLEM

What can you do to see how insulation works?

NEEDED

two small tin cans	hot water
two large tin cans with lids	piece of cloth
kitchen foil	different insulation materials
rubber band	ice cubes
thermometer	

TRY THIS

1. Pour the same amount of hot water into each small can.
2. Cover each small can with the same size of foil. Use a rubber band to hold each cover tight (Figure 9-15).

FIGURE 9-15

3. Wrap one small can with cloth.

4. Put this can into one large can and cap it.

5. Put the other small can into a second large can and cap it.

6. After 20 minutes, remove the 4 can covers. Dip a finger into each small can of water. Which is warmer?

DISCOVERY PROBLEMS

measuring **A.** How much warmer is one can of water than the other? How can you use a thermometer to find out?

experimenting **B.** How hot can you keep a small can of water? Have a contest with a friend. Try different materials, such as sawdust, cotton, wool, rice crispies, puffed rice, torn paper, and so on. Or try your own secret mix of materials. Put the materials between the larger and smaller can walls. Whoever has the warmer can of water after 30 minutes (or longer) wins.

inferring **C.** Can you figure out which single material is the best insulator? Worst insulator? Does how tightly it is packed make a difference?

experimenting **D.** In summer, you want your house to stay cool. Does insulation keep heat out as well as in? Find out. How cool can you keep a small can with an ice cube inside? Have a contest with a friend. Whoever has the larger ice cube after one hour (or longer) wins.

inferring **E.** Are the best materials for keeping the can warm also best for keeping the can cold? If not, which are best?

TEACHING COMMENTS

PREPARATION AND BACKGROUND

Use matched one-pound coffee cans with lids for the larger cans. Small, identical juice cans will fit nicely into the coffee cans. Identical pieces of foil may be used to cap the small cans, so insulating materials do not fall inside. Either hot or warm water from the tap will do for this activity.

In Discovery Problem D, at least an hour may be needed to decide which ice cube has melted more. The cubes may be weighed with a balance before and after the test. If one ice cube is heavier to start, it can be scraped lightly with a knife until a balance is achieved.

GENERALIZATION

Insulating materials may be used to slow the movement of heat energy

PERFORMANCE OBJECTIVES

Process: The child can test which of several heat insulating materials is most efficient.

Knowledge: The child can describe (explain) the contrasting properties of efficient and inefficient heat insulating materials.

SELECTED TRADE BOOKS: HEAT ENERGY

FOR YOUNGER CHILDREN

Ardley, Neil. *Hot and Cold.* Watts, 1983.

Hillerman, Anne. *Done in the Sun.* Sunstone Press, 1983.

Llewellyn, Claire. *First Look at Keeping Warm.* Gareth Stevens, 1991.

Maestro, Betsy. *Temperature and You.* Dutton, 1990.

Oleksy, Walter. *Experiments with Heat.* Children's Press, 1986.

Petersen, David. *Solar Energy at Work.* Children's Press, 1985.

Santrey, Laurence. *Heat.* Troll Associates, 1985.

Wade, Harlan. *Heat.* Raintree, 1979.

FOR OLDER CHILDREN

Adler, Irving, and Ruth Adler. *Heat and Its Uses.* John Day, 1973.

Bendick, Jeanne. *Heat and Temperature.* Watts, 1974.

Cobb, Vickie. *Heat.* Watts, 1973.

Kaplan, Sheila. *Solar Energy.* Raintree, 1983.

Knapp, Brian. *Fire.* Steck-Vaughn, 1990.

Langley, Andrew. *Energy.* Watts, 1986.

Mebane, Robert C., and Thomas R. Rybolt. *Adventures with Atoms and Molecules.* Enslow, 1987.

Scott, John M. *Heat and Fire.* Enslow, 1973.

Whyman, Kathryn. *Heat and Energy.* Watts, 1987.

Yount, Lisa. *Too Hot, Too Cold, or Just Right.* Walker, 1981.

10

Sound Energy

Play a radio loudly and the windows rattle. Watch a parade at a distance and the marchers seem to be out of time with the music. Sing in the shower and suddenly your voice takes on new dimensions. There are few topics that present so many accessible materials and interesting things to explore as sound energy.

In this chapter, we'll consider (1) how sound vibrations are made; (2) how sounds travel in air, water, and solids; (3) how sounds are reflected and absorbed; (4) how the pitch of sounds may change; and (5) how we hear.

[1] SOUND VIBRATIONS
Experiences 284

Every so often in science fiction a sinister scientist invents a machine that can collect and play back all the sounds that have ever been made. At first the scientist uses the machine to help historians find out what King John *really* said at Runnymede, but soon after he offers the enemy military secrets discussed at the Pentagon.

Molecules and Sounds

Of course, all signs show that such a machine could never be invented. Sounds are simply waves of compressed molecules pulsating outward in all directions and planes from a vibrating source.

Consider the air about you. It is composed of tiny, individual molecules of different gases mixed similarly throughout the lower atmosphere. These molecules are rapidly and randomly moving about. A fast vibrating source—hummingbird's wings, bell, guitar string, a "twanged" ruler held on the edge of a desk—compresses billions of these molecules with each back-and-forth movement because the molecules are in the way. Since air

molecules are elastic, they quickly assume their original shape after moving out of the vibrating object's path. But before this happens, they transfer energy to other molecules over a distance.

Please note that it is the *wave of energy* rather than the molecules that may travel a great distance. Each molecule may move less than a millionth of a hair's width, but this is enough to bump the next randomly moving molecule and so pass on the outward movement. Figure 10-1 shows a wave motion resulting from a compression and rarefaction effect on molecules pushed by a vibrating ruler.

A sound fades away when energy behind the original vibrations is used in the transmit-

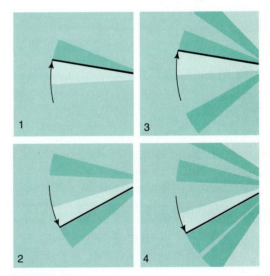

FIGURE 10-1
A vibrating ruler producing sound waves. In 1, the ruler is pushing the air molecules together (compression). Notice the thinned-out space below it (rarefaction). Picture 2 shows the opposite happening, with the first part of the sound wave now moving away. Pictures 3 and 4 show another sound wave being produced. The wave moves outward as the molecules push others in the way, which in turn squeeze other molecules.

ting process. As one molecule bumps another, it uses a tiny amount of energy. As more molecules are bumped, there is less energy available. The sound stops when energy of the randomly moving molecules exceeds the wave's energy. The molecules simply resume their normal helter-skelter movements.

Loudness

How is loudness explained? First, for the moment, let's call it *intensity;* "loudness" is what we actually hear. If our ears are working poorly, a very intense sound may be barely heard. So loudness is a matter of individual perception. Intensity, on the other hand, can be consistently and accurately recorded by a sensitive sound detector in terms of the *decibel,* a unit of measurement in sound. The distinction between loudness and intensity may be too subtle for most children.

You know that shouting requires more energy than whispering. A boost in energy forces any vibrating medium to vibrate to and fro more widely than usual, but in the same amount of time. This compresses molecules more forcefully, so the greater energy is able to move more molecules.

Of course, distance is also a factor in sound intensity. The farther away we are from the source, the weaker the sound. Molecules are pushed less because there is progressively less energy available.

Interestingly, the same mathematical relationship is found in sound loss as in other forms of energy such as light, magnetism, and electricity. Intensity fades with the square of the distance between any sound source and listener. At 20 feet (6 meters), a sound has only one-fourth the intensity it exhibits at 10 feet (3 meters) from the source. With a distance of 30 feet (9 meters), intensity drops to one-ninth of the original sound. At 40 feet (12 meters), only one-sixteenth of the original intensity remains.

Waves

Sometimes the analogy of a water wave is used to teach how sound travels. A pebble is dropped into water, and a circular series of ripples spreads out on the water's surface. This example may be useful to show to your class, but it contains two main defects. Water waves are up-and-down motions that travel at right angles to the line of the waves. These are called transverse waves. Sound waves come from back-and-forth motions that make longitudinal waves. This is the kind of wave you see when a row of dominoes falls, each one striking the next in order. Also, water waves move only horizontally, while sound waves travel outward in all planes. Many science teachers ask students to imagine sound waves as they would a series of rapidly blown soap bubbles, each enveloped within another that is slightly larger, all quickly expanding.

The wave idea is useful to distinguish between sounds and noises. A sound consists of regularly pulsating vibrations; the time interval between each compression and rarefaction is the same. Noise is heard when irregular vibrations are passed on.

Forced Vibrations

If you place the handle of a vibrating tuning fork against a table top, the sound suddenly gets louder. The vibrating fork forces the table top to vibrate with equal speed. This sets in motion many more air molecules than would the fork alone. Try putting a vibrating tuning fork against other objects. Almost any hard object can be forced to vibrate at the fork's natural frequency.

A similar thing happens if you hold a pocket comb against an object and vibrate the comb by running a finger over the teeth ends. Note the decrease in loudness when you vibrate the comb away from the object.

Another example is found with musical instruments such as the guitar and violin. The energy of their vibrating strings forces their wooden sound boxes to vibrate also.

A peculiar example of forced vibrations can occur when a group of soldiers marches over a bridge. If there are enough persons marching in step, the entire structure can be forced to vibrate in time to the step, and the bridge may weaken or collapse. For this reason, a standing military order is, "Break step when crossing a bridge."

Thomas Edison used his knowledge of forced vibrations when inventing the phonograph. He attached a sharp needle to a thin diaphragm that vibrated when sound waves struck it. The needle was placed against a cylinder wrapped with soft tinfoil. As he spoke, he slowly cranked the cylinder around and around. The vibrating needle cut a series of impressions into the metal. To play back his sounds, he placed the needle in the impression first scratched and cranked the cylinder. As it followed the impressions, the needle was forced to vibrate, thus causing the diaphragm to vibrate. Edison could hear his recorded voice!

Sympathetic Vibrations

Have you ever heard windows vibrate in their frames as a low-flying airplane passes overhead? Or noticed dishes faintly rattle occasionally as a loud radio is played? To see why this happens, consider two identical tuning forks. If one vibrates and is held near the other, the second one also begins to vibrate. But with two tuning forks of different pitches, only the struck one vibrates.

When forks are of identical pitch, sound waves arrive at the proper time to set the still fork in motion. Each additional air compression pushes a prong as it starts to bend in from a previous one. Each rarefaction arrives as the prong starts to bend back out. The steady, timed, push-pause-push-pause sets the fork vibrating in almost the same way as you would push someone on a swing.

When forks are of different pitch, the timing is wrong for this to happen. For example, a prong may bend inward properly with a compression, but as it starts to bend back, another air compression may strike it prematurely and slow or stop it. The same thing would happen with a moving swing that is pushed while only partway back on a downswing.

Every solid object has a natural frequency of vibration. If sound waves of that frequency push against an object, it may start resonating—vibrating, sympathetically. (I once had a professor whose deep voice sometimes made part of my chair vibrate.)

Remember that objects vibrate sympathetically only when they have the same natural pitch as the initial sound maker. On the other hand, objects *forced* to vibrate always do so at the frequency of the vibrating object placed against them, regardless of their own natural frequency.

You may have learned that a very loud note sung or played into a thin drinking glass can shatter it through violent sympathetic vibrations; such vibrations have the natural pitch of the glass. However, it is not true that seashore sounds may be detected in shell souvenirs unless someone is listening at the beach. What is heard are only sympathetic or other reflections of nearby sounds.

Properties of Objects and Vibrations

Suppose someone hands you two closed shoe boxes. Inside one is a marble. The other contains a small ruler. Could you tell which box contains which object by tipping them back and forth and listening to the sounds? Of course, you may say. But what allows you to do this?

Every object has certain physical properties that produce "appropriate" vibrations. We expect a round (cylindrical) pencil to roll smoothly and a six-sided pencil to roll roughly.

We assume that a short pencil lying crosswise in a box takes longer to slide and bump against the side than a longer pencil, if the box is tipped from side to side.

Giving children a chance to connect the properties of objects with the vibrations they make causes them to think. A "Mystery Box" investigation appears later in the chapter for this purpose. Another activity allows pupils to explore a variety of objects and make sound effects like those on radio programs.

We'll examine other properties of sound-making in further sections.

[2] HOW SOUNDS TRAVEL
Experiences 289

Watch a parade from afar and band members seem to be out of step with the music they are playing. See a carpenter hammering a nail on a distant rooftop, and you hear the sound as the hammer is lifted instead of when the nail is struck. Note the increasing speed of aircraft, and be assured that protests to the Federal Aviation Administration about sonic booms continue to mount.

Speeds of Sound

The speeds at which sound waves travel lie behind each of the events mentioned. Light travels so fast—about 186,000 miles (297,000 kilometers) per second—that it seems instantaneous to our eyes. But sound is another matter. At sea level and 42°F (6.5°C), sound waves move about 1,100 feet (330 meters) per second in the air—only as fast as a low-powered rifle bullet. Sound also travels in liquids and solids. It moves about 5 times faster in water than it does in air; in steel, sound may travel 15 times faster than it does in air.

Three conditions affect the speed of sound: temperature, density, and the elastic-ity, or "springiness," of the molecules conducting the sound.

Density by itself does not increase the speed of sound. In fact, the speed of sound may decrease with density. But often associated with density is greatly increased elasticity of molecules. When highly elastic, close-together molecules of a solid transmit sound, it travels much faster than in either air or water.

Sounds travel faster when the temperature goes up—about one foot per second faster in air for every one degree Fahrenheit. Have you ever wondered why sounds carry such large distances on certain days? On a cold winter day with snow on the ground, for example, air next to the ground is often colder than higher air. Instead of a sound wave spreading out uniformly and rapidly dying out, the temperature difference causes parts of the wave to travel at different speeds. The upper part begins to travel faster than the lower part and bends back down toward the ground some distance away.

Given the same medium and temperature, all sounds travel at the same speed. If this were not so, it would be hard or impossible to conduct concerts in large auditoriums. The reedy sound of an oboe and the brassy timbre of a trombone always reach your ears at the same time, if they are begun at the same time.

Sonic Booms

When children live where sonic booms often occur, someone may ask what happens when an airplane "breaks the sound barrier." We know that a sound-producing object sends out sound waves in all directions. When the object is set in motion, it continues to send out waves in all directions. But let's continue to increase this object's velocity. As it goes faster, it is harder for waves to travel outward in front of it. When an airplane reaches a certain speed (about 750 miles, or 1,200 kilometers, per hour; this varies greatly with altitude and temperature), air compressions of these sound waves pile up into a dense area of compressed air. This can subject the airplane to severe stresses.

A powerful engine and proper design enable an airplane to wedge through the dense air. But what happens to the compressed air? The tremendous energy is passed on—molecule to molecule—until it hits the earth as a booming shock wave. The shock wave continues on the ground in a wide strip that traces the airplane's flight path. It stops only when the pilot slows the aircraft to less than the speed of sound. Sonic booms that cause the least damage start at very high altitudes. By the time energy in the original area of compressed air is passed on to the ground, much of it has dissipated.

Similar shock waves are formed by an explosion, except they may move out equidistantly in all directions. Very rapid expansion of gases in an explosion compresses the surrounding air. As the shock wave of compressed air moves outward, it may flatten almost anything in its path until the pressure finally dissipates over a distance.

[3] REFLECTED AND ABSORBED SOUNDS
Experiences 296

Sound Reflection

One reason why singing in the shower is so popular comes from the nature of sound reflections. As a sound hits the smooth walls, it bounces back and forth, seeming louder and prolonging the notes a little. This is pleasing to the ear. The smoother the reflecting surface, the better sound reflects. On a very smooth wall, sound reflections bounce off like light reflections from a mirror. The angle of reflection equals the angle of incidence.

Because sound can be reflected, we can direct or channel it in certain directions by using different devices. Open-air theaters often have a large shell-like structure surrounding the stage. (See Figure 10-2.) This enables sounds to be directed toward an audience with reduced energy loss. The same principle is used with cheerleaders' megaphones.

An even more efficient way to conserve sound energy is to enclose it in a tube. Because the sound is kept from spreading out by continual reflections within the encircling wall, such concentrated sound loses energy slowly and may travel a long way. Physicians' stethoscopes and speaking tubes in old apartment houses and ships are some applications. Sometimes children use garden hoses as speaking tubes. These work well, and at surprising distances.

A reverse application of this reflection principle is found in the old-fashioned ear trumpet and in the ears of animals such as rabbits and donkeys. In these cases, sounds are "gathered," or reflected inward. Besides large ears, many animals have the additional advantage of being able to cock them separately in different directions.

Echoes

Since sound takes time to travel and can be reflected, it stands to reason that at a certain distance you should be able to hear a distinctly separate reflection of an original sound—an echo. Most persons need an interval of at least one-tenth of a second to distinguish between two sounds. If the interval is shorter than this, you hear one sound, much like the way your brain interprets separate frames of a motion picture as continuous motion.

If we assume that a sound wave travels at a speed of 1,100 feet (330 meters) per second, in one-tenth of a second it travels 110 feet (33 meters). To hear an echo—a distinguishable, separate sound—we must stand far enough away from a reflecting surface for the sound

FIGURE 10-2
Open-air theaters often have a shell-like structure to reflect sounds to the audience.

wave to travel a total distance of 110 feet (33 meters). Since the sound travels *to* the reflecting surface and *back* to our ears, a distance of 55 feet (16.5 meters) from the surface is adequate to hear an echo. Remember, this distance varies a bit with temperature variations.

Sometimes the combination of a loud sound and many distant reflecting surfaces produces multiple echoes, or *reverberations.* A common example is thunder, which may reverberate back and forth from cloud to earth and among air layers of varying densities.

A few ship captains still use echoes from fog horns to estimate the distance from icebergs or a mountainous coastline. However, the use of radio waves (radar) for this purpose is more typical because it is more con-venient, accurate, and reliable. A difference in temperature at different air levels could result in misleading calculations with sound echoes.

An interesting application of echo detection is found in a United States Navy device called *Sonar.* (The term is coined from the words *SOund NAvigation and Ranging.*) This apparatus sends a sound wave through the water and detects reflections from any direction. The time between an initial sound and its received echo enables a Sonar operator to know the distance of a reflector, whether it is a submarine or an underwater obstruction. Similar devices are used on fishing vessels to detect schools of fish.

A strange use of sound reflections is found in the bat. By listening to reflections of its cries, a bat flying in total darkness avoids collisions and may even catch insects in mid-air. (See Figure 10-3.)

Absorbed Sounds

Have you ever noticed how different sounds seem in a room before and after furnishings are installed? Rugs, drapes, and cloth-covered furniture absorb more sound waves than we may realize. But even a furnished room may have a "hollow" sound if the walls and ceilings are hard and smooth.

Porous acoustical tile on ceilings cuts down sound reflections. So does the use of rough, porous plaster blown on with a compressed-air applicator. Besides absorbing some sound waves, a rough surface interferes with the wave reflection, like the way in which light is diffused when it hits an irregular surface.

Sometimes older children ask, "What happens to a sound when it goes into a porous material?" It appears that sound energy is changed to heat energy. The regular pulsating movements of a wave are broken up into the normal, irregular motions of individual molecules. As this happens, any energy passed into the porous substance is transmitted to other air molecules, thus very slightly raising the temperature. (Temperature is determined by the average speed of molecular movements. The faster they jiggle about, the higher the temperature.)

[4] HOW PITCH CHANGES
Experiences 302

Many pilots of certain crop-dusting airplanes actually rely on sound to gauge the safeness of their air speed. It is hard while skimming low to watch both an air-speed indicator in the cockpit and ground obstructions. Flying speed is estimated by listening to the pitch of sound made by the vibration of the airplane's struts and wires as the relative wind rushes past. Some seasoned pilots can judge their margin of safety to within narrow limits by this method.

Sometimes children fasten small cards against the spokes of their bicycle wheels to simulate a motor sound while riding. As the spokes go around and hit the card, it vibrates and makes a sound. The pitch rises with increased speed of vibrations and lowers with decreased speed of vibrations.

Stringed Instruments

In a stringed instrument, pitch depends on the length, tightness, and thickness of the strings. Shortening a string causes faster vibrations, raising pitch. Lengthening it has an opposite effect. Tightening a string also increases pitch, whereas lessening tension decreases it. A thick string vibrates more slowly than a thin one, and so produces a lower sound.

Why do different instruments—a violin and a cello, for instance—play a note at the same pitch and yet sound different? This is because of the *quality* of tone (timbre) produced by these instruments. Most vibrations

FIGURE 10-3
A bat's ears are well suited for echo ranging.

include more than just simple, back-and-forth movements along a string's entire length. Although there is a fundamental vibration that governs the basic pitch, other parts of the string vibrate at faster frequencies. The combinations of vibrations are different with each string and with various stringed instruments. Together they produce tones of distinctly recognizable qualities.

Wind Instruments

In wind instruments sound is made by a vibrating column of air. The vibrations may be started by a player's lips, as with trumpets and tubas, or by blowing past a reed, as with the saxophone and clarinet.

Pitch is regulated by changing the length of the air column vibrating within the instrument. In a wind instrument such as the saxophone air-column length is changed by opening and closing valves with the fingers. In a trombone air-column length is regulated by pulling or pushing a long, closed double tube, called the slide.

The property of timbre is also present in wind instruments. In this case it is caused by the combinations of additional air vibrations set up within each instrument. Quality of voices is produced in much the same way. This is regulated by the size and shape of air cavities in the mouth and nose.

Homemade Instruments

An interesting way for children to learn about pitch and tonal quality is for them to make their own stringed and wind instruments. Rubber bands of different sizes make pleasant sounds when placed around topless cigar boxes or sturdy shoe box lids. Strong nylon fishing line, fastened on pieces of wood with nails and screw eyes, also works well (see Figure 10-4). When the line is fastened to a screw eye, its tension is adjusted by turning the eye in the appropriate direction. Tuned properly, nylon fishing line sounds somewhat like the string on a regular instrument. Simple tunes can be composed and played on the stringed instruments that children fashion.

Soda straws and bottles make acceptable wind instruments. Interestingly, opposite results in pitch occur with partly filled soda bottles, depending on whether they are used as wind or percussion instruments. That is, if you blow over the tops of soda bottles containing varying volumes of water, the scale

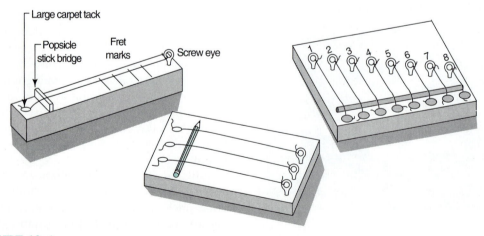

FIGURE 10-4
Children can experiment with pitch and tone by making their own instruments.

may go from low to high, left to right. However, if you *strike* the bottles sharply with a pencil, the opposite happens. The scale will go from high to low, left to right. With blowing, the bottle's *air* mainly vibrates; when striking the bottle, the *water* and glass mainly vibrate.

Mass and Noise

When a noise is made, the amount of mass in the vibrating object usually determines its pitch. A large, dropped wood block sounds lower than a smaller one. When thick paper is torn, it sounds lower than thin paper. A dropped nickel sounds lower than a dime. Both young and older children show interest in this phenomenon.

[5] HEARING AND LOCATING SOUNDS
Experiences 309

The ear must be ranked among the body's most remarkable organs. In our hearing, sound waves are channeled into the ear canal by the outer ear, which acts as a megaphone in reverse. As sound waves collide with the eardrum, this thin membrane of stretched skin begins vibrating at the same frequency as the waves.

Just inside the eardrum are three tiny, connected bones: the hammer, anvil, and stirrup (see Figure 10-5). A vibrating eardrum starts the attached hammer shaking, and this movement is transmitted through the connected bones to the cochlea, or inner ear. This snail-shaped apparatus is filled with a watery fluid and lined with sensitive nerve endings that trail off to the auditory nerve and brain. The transmitted vibrations pass through the fluid and excite the nerve endings. These excitations are converted into electrical impulses that zip to the brain.

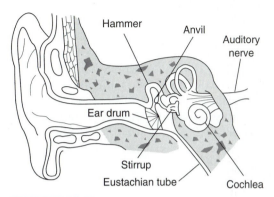

FIGURE 10-5
The human ear.

The Eustachian tube is a narrow opening that leads from the back of the mouth to the middle ear. It equalizes air pressure on the eardrum.

Children should learn some reasonable rules for ear care and safety. A sharp object jabbed into the ear may cause a punctured eardrum. This greatly impairs or prevents eardrum vibrations and results in hearing loss in the affected ear. They should also beware of a sharp blow against the outer ear. This compresses air within the air canal and may cause a ruptured eardrum. Blowing the nose forces air up through the Eustachian tube. If a person is suffering from a cold, hard blowing may force germs up the tube and infect the middle ear.

Hearing Ranges

Although our ears are sensitive to a wide range of pitches, there are limits to what we can hear. Almost no one can detect a sound that vibrates less than about 16 times per second, or more than 20,000 times per second. As we grow older, this range is gradually narrowed.

Hearing ranges in animals often exceed those of humans. A bat may detect sounds that vary between 10 vibrations to 100,000 vibrations per second. A dog's hearing begins at only several vibrations and goes to 40,000 vibrations per second. This is why it is possible to use a "silent" whistle for calling a dog. The sound is simply too high for humans to hear. A cat's hearing is even more remarkable; it can detect sounds up to 50,000 cycles. Sounds that are inaudible to us are called *infrasonic* when they vibrate too slowly and *ultrasonic* when vibrations are too fast.

Locating Sounds

Most people can tell the direction from which a sound comes, even when blindfolded. With two ears, a sound usually reaches one ear just before the other. The slight difference is enough to let the brain interpret the information.

Persons with only one functioning ear can receive similar signals by quickly turning the head slightly on hearing the first sound. When the sound is very short, this may not be possible.

INVESTIGATIONS & ACTIVITIES

SECTION 1
Sound Vibrations
[*Background 275*]

□ ACTIVITY: How Are Sounds Made?

NEEDED

ruler   rubber band

TRY THIS

1. Hold down part of a ruler on a table edge. Let most of it stick out over the edge.
2. Pull down the larger part of the ruler with your thumb. Then quickly slip away your thumb.
3. Notice how the ruler moves up and down as a sound is made. We say the ruler is *vibrating*.
   a. Is there any way you can make a sound with the ruler *without* it vibrating?
4. Take a rubber band. Hold one end firmly in your teeth. Pull the other end gently with one thumb. Do not pull it hard.
5. Stroke the rubber band with a finger. Watch it as it makes a sound.
   b. Does the rubber band move during the sound? after the sound stops?
   c. Is there any way you can make a sound with the rubber band without it vibrating?

□ ACTIVITY: What Makes Your Vocal Cords Work?

NEEDED

vocal cords

TRY THIS

1. Hum softly and feel your throat. Feel your voice box vibrate.
2. Hum with tightly closed lips. Then pinch your nose.
   a. What happens? Why?
3. Breathe out as much air as you can from your lungs. Try to say something *without* taking in air.
   b. What happens? Why?
4. Try to say your name the way a cat or cow makes sounds—while breathing air *in*.
   c. What happens? Why is this hard to do?

(*Teaching Comment:* Air is needed in all these cases to make the vocal cords vibrate. It is hard to speak while breathing in because the normal way humans make sounds is by breathing out.)

□ ACTIVITY: How Can One Vibrating Object Make Another Vibrate?

A. NEEDED

tuning fork

TRY THIS

1. Strike a tuning fork against a rubber heel. (Never against something hard.)
2. As the sound dies, place the handle end against a table top. Notice how the sound gets louder as the table top is also made to vibrate.
3. Try holding the vibrating tuning fork against many different objects.
   a. From which object can you get the loudest sound?
   b. Which object allows you to hear the tuning fork when it has almost stopped vibrating?

B. NEEDED

two matched large soda bottles   one small soda bottle

TRY THIS

1. Blow over the top of one large bottle to make a sound. Blow short, strong tones.

2. Hold the opening of a second large bottle close to your ear, but not touching. Blow short sounds again with the first large bottle.

   a. Do you hear the same note from the second bottle? If you are not sure, have someone else blow short notes on one bottle while you listen with the second bottle.

3. Do steps 1 and 2 again, but this time listen with the small bottle.

   b. Do you hear the same note from the small bottle? Any note?

(*Teaching Comment:* Activity A is an example of forced vibrations. If a tuning fork is unavailable, a sturdy, stiff rubber comb may be used instead. Run a finger down the teeth ends while holding the comb against a surface. B is an example of sympathetic vibrations. If you vibrate one object, a second object may also vibrate if it has the same natural rate of vibrations as the first. No actual touching is necessary. The transfer of energy occurs in the air.)

■ INVESTIGATION: Mystery Sounds

Can you hear something make a sound and tell what it is without looking?

EXPLORATORY PROBLEM

How can you find out if you can identify something by sound?

NEEDED

pairs of small objects that roll (crayons, Ping-Pong balls, marbles, pencils, BBs, small pill vials, etc.)

pairs of small objects that slide (buttons, paper clips, checkers, dominoes, bottle caps, safety pins, etc.)

shoe box with lid

partner

TRY THIS

1. Place one object from each pair of rolling objects on your desk.

2. Give the other rolling objects to your partner. He should put these where you cannot see them.

3. Have your partner put one of his objects in the shoe box. You should not know which one it is.

4. Slowly tip the shoe box back and forth. Listen to the sound (Figure 10-6).

5. Look at the objects on your desk. Which one may be the same as the one in the box? Point to a desk object so your partner knows which one you picked.

6. Look inside the shoe box. Does the object inside match the desk object you picked?

FIGURE 10-6

DISCOVERY PROBLEMS

inferring   **A.** How many of the *rolling* objects can you identify? Which object is easiest to tell? hardest to tell?

inferring   **B.** Suppose your partner holds and tips the box. Can you tell each rolling object just as easily?

inferring   **C.** How many of the *sliding* objects can you identify? Which object is easiest to tell? hardest to tell?

inferring   **D.** Suppose your partner holds and tips the box. Can you tell each sliding object just as easily?

inferring   **E.** Can you identify two rolling objects at the same time? two sliding objects? one sliding object and one rolling object?

experimenting   **F.** What other objects can you try? What do you think will be easy to tell? hard to tell?

TEACHING COMMENT

PREPARATION AND BACKGROUND

This investigation mainly calls for children to make inferences by interpreting data. Try to use objects of about the same weight. This will eliminate weight as a clue. Children will focus on the sounds they hear or vibrations they feel in their fingers as they handle the shoe box.

Objects are paired and one-half displayed to limit the child's choices. It is hard to infer the identity of an object solely from the sound it makes inside a tipped box. More important, we want pupils to use their minds by linking the observable properties of objects to sounds.

GENERALIZATION

An object may be identified by the sounds it makes when interacting with another object.

SAMPLE PERFORMANCE OBJECTIVES

Process: After some practice, the child can infer the identity of several objects from the sounds they make.
Knowledge: The child can describe how the properties of an object are related to the sounds it makes.

FOR OLDER CHILDREN

Older pupils can be challenged by increasing the number and similarity of paired objects to select from.

☐ ACTIVITY: How Can You Make Some Sound Effects for a Radio Program?

NEEDED

two paper cups
thick, unwaxed paper cup
rice or bird seed
cellophane
tape recorder

two wood blocks
fine sandpaper
glue
Ping-Pong ball

TRY THIS

1. Galloping horse: Hold a paper cup in each hand, open end out. Brush one cup against the other in a regular pattern.
2. Squeaky rocking chair: Use a thick, unwaxed cup. Squeeze the cup edge between your thumb and forefinger. Slide them slowly back and forth, back and forth, to make the squeaks.
3. Rain: Pour some rice or birdseed over a Ping-Pong ball.
4. Forest fire: Crumple a large piece of cellophane.
5. Egg frying in a pan: Slowly crumple a small piece of cellophane.
6. Old steam locomotive: Glue sandpaper to two wood blocks about the size of your hands. Slide the blocks together. First, make a long, loud slide forward, then a short, softer slide back. Make the engine go fast, slow, stop, or slowly get closer or go farther away.
7. Sawing wood: Rub the rim of a paper cup back and forth on sandpaper.
8. Practice one or more of these effects with a tape recorder. Then tape and play them for your classmates.
   a. How many effects do they recognize?
   b. How could you improve your sound effects?
   c. What other effects would you like to try?

(*Teaching Comment:* If needed, the audience can be helped to recognize the sounds. Have the audience try to identify the sounds being simulated as they are played. These could be written on the chalkboard, but in a different order than that heard on the tape. This preserves most of the suspense yet limits the range of possibilities.)

☐ ACTIVITY: How Fast Does Sound Travel?

NEEDED

large outdoor space   hammer
partner   piece of wood

TRY THIS

1. Go outdoors to a large, open space.
2. Place a thick piece of wood on the ground. Walk a few steps away.
3. Watch a partner sharply hit the wood once with a hammer.
    a. Do you hear the sound at about the same time the hammer hits?
4. Move farther away. Have your partner hit the wood again. Repeat this pattern several times until you are far away.
    b. When do you hear each sound now? At the same time the hammer hits? Or does each sound appear later and later, *after* each hit?

(*Teaching Comment:* To ensure enough space for this activity, you might suggest two widely separated, familiar reference points at least the length of a football field.)

■ INVESTIGATION: How Sounds Travel in the Wind

How far does your voice carry when you shout into the wind? What happens when you shout downwind? Must someone then be closer, or can they be farther away and hear you?

EXPLORATORY PROBLEM

How can you measure how sounds travel in the wind?

NEEDED

breezy or windy day   meter stick or yardstick
playground   chalk
alarm clock   partner

TRY THIS

1. Put an alarm clock in the middle of a large, open area.

2. Find from which direction the wind is blowing. (You might toss some grass or dust into the air.)

3. Set the alarm ringing. Walk quickly from the clock straight into the wind until you cannot hear the alarm. Mark this place (Figure 10-7). A partner can tell you if the alarm stops before you do.

FIGURE 10-7

4. Rewind the alarm. Do step 3 again, but downwind this time.

5. Measure the distance between the alarm and where you stopped each time.

DISCOVERY PROBLEMS

observing   **A.** What, if any, difference did you find? How did the wind affect the distance at which the alarm was heard?

measuring   **B.** Suppose you walked away from the alarm in a crosswind direction. At about what distance would you not hear the alarm? Estimate this distance and then test it.

hypothesizing **C.** What do you think your results would be on a windless day? a windier day? Do the experiment again under those conditions.

experimenting **D.** Would you get the same overall findings with other kinds of sounds? How could you find out?

TEACHING COMMENT

BACKGROUND AND PREPARATION

If the alarm is very loud, it can be muffled by placing it into a heavy wool sock, or a box, or both. This will, of course, reduce the size of the area needed for the experiment. A small bell can be jingled softly in place of the alarm. If so, children should face away from the bell so they cannot see it being shaken.

Sometimes children will suggest other ways to test wind effects on sound. For example, four pupils could each walk away from the alarm in a different direction. Or, the entire class could walk outward from a tight circle formed around the alarm. In these cases, sensitize your pupils to the possibility of a faulty procedure: Not all children may have equal hearing capacity. After testing and verifying similar hearing ability, either of these two suggestions would be worthwhile to try.

GENERALIZATION

Sound travels farther downwind than upwind.

SAMPLE PERFORMANCE OBJECTIVES

Process: The child can measure with a meter stick the distance between two widely separated positions.
Knowledge: When asked where to stand to speak to a large group outdoors, the child will select an upwind position.

☐ ACTIVITY: How Can You Find Out if Sound Travels Farther in Air or in Wood?

NEEDED

meter stick or yardstick   partner
wristwatch (one that ticks)

TRY THIS

1. Hold a wristwatch tightly against the end of a meter stick.
2. Touch the other end of the stick to a partner's ear. Only you should hold the stick (Figure 10-8).
    a. Can your partner hear the ticking through the wood? If not, move the watch forward on the stick until the ticking is heard.
3. Measure the distance between watch and ear when the ticking is heard.

FIGURE 10-8

4. Next, do not use the stick. Hold the watch in the air at ear level the same distance you found in step 3.

    b. Can your partner hear the ticking now? (If you think your partner is just guessing, remove and then return the watch a few times. Each time, ask if the watch can be heard.)

    c. From how far away can you hear a ticking watch through wood? Try a broomstick, window pole, long narrow board, and other wood things around you.

■ INVESTIGATION: The Vibrations of Metal Objects

Many everyday objects made of metal make beautiful sounds when they vibrate. A metal coat hanger is one example. These things sound much better when you hear them through a solid material than through the air. String is one such solid material.

EXPLORATORY PROBLEM

How can you hear the sounds of a metal hanger through a string?

NEEDED

two matched metal hangers   yarn
several kinds of string   scissors
different metal objects   partner

TRY THIS

1. Cut a piece of string about 60 centimeters (2 feet) long.

2. Loop the middle of the string once around the hanger hook.

3. Wrap several turns of string end around the tip of each forefinger.

4. Gently put the tip of each wrapped finger into an ear (Figure 10-9).

FIGURE 10-9

5. Bend from the waist so the hanger hangs free. Ask your partner to strike a pencil and other objects gently against the metal. You can also make the hanger vibrate by yourself. Sway back and forth until the hanger swings. Then have it hit something that is hard.

DISCOVERY PROBLEMS

communicating   **A.** How can you describe the sounds you hear?

observing   **B.** What happens to the sound if your partner holds one of the strings? both strings?

experimenting   **C.** What kind of string will give the clearest, loudest sound? Cut off equal lengths of different kinds of string and yarn. Test them in pairs. Tie one string end to the hook of one hanger. Tie another to a second matched hanger. Put one string end into each ear. Have a partner first strike one hanger, then the other. When you find the best string, try it with both ears.

inferring   **D.** Does the length of a string affect the loudness? If so, in which kind of string do you notice it most? (You can test pairs of strings as in C.)

observing   **E.** What sounds do other metal objects make? Test things such as old spoons, forks, cooling racks, oven racks, and different-sized cans.

communicating   **F.** How well can you describe sounds so people can understand you? For example, find something you think makes a "spooky" sound. Pair it with an object that does not sound "spooky" to you. Ask someone to test both objects to find the "spooky" one, but now do not say which is which. Can that person pick out the object you think makes the "spooky" sound? If not, try to learn why you disagree.

Do the same thing with objects whose sounds you think are "soft," or "high," or "tinny," or "weird," or "beautiful," and so on. Which words are the hardest to agree on? the easiest to agree on?

TEACHING COMMENT

PREPARATION AND BACKGROUND

Oven cooling racks, barbecue griddles, and other gridlike objects of metal make particularly strange, even eerie, sounds. These sounds come from the overtones produced when the many parts of the object vibrate differently.

Pupils will find in Problem F that some words are more subjective than others. "Spooky" is a matter of opinion. Also, terms such as *high* or *low* are relative, so they may decide to say higher or lower as they contrast the paired objects.

Tightly woven, hard string is more sound-efficient than loosely woven string or yarn. This is especially noticeable as string length goes beyond 45 centimeters (18 inches).

GENERALIZATION

The sounds of a vibrating object may be heard more loudly and clearly through a solid than through air.

SAMPLE PERFORMANCE OBJECTIVES

Process: The child can describe a sound an object makes well enough for another person to recognize the sound when it is made.

Knowledge: The child can select a string, from several different strings, that conducts sounds most efficiently.

FOR YOUNGER CHILDREN

Use the "Try This" sequence and Problem F as general experience activities.

■ INVESTIGATION: A String Telephone

Have you ever used a "string telephone"? It's a handy way to talk to someone far across a large room without shouting.

EXPLORATORY PROBLEM

How can you make a string telephone?

NEEDED

two sturdy paper cups   two paper clips
strong string, about 8 meters (26 feet) long   partner
nail

TRY THIS

1. Punch a hole into the bottom center of each cup using a nail.

2. Put a string end into each hole.

3. Tie each string end to a paper clip. This will keep the string from slipping out of each hole.

4. Stretch the string tightly between you and your partner.

5. Speak into one cup while your partner listens with the other cup (Figure 10-10).

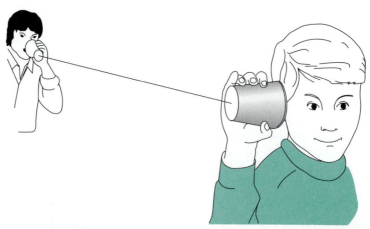

FIGURE 10-10

DISCOVERY PROBLEMS

observing   **A.** Can you hear better through the string telephone than through the air? Whisper softly through the phone. Do it a little louder until your partner hears you. Then whisper to him or her at the same loudness without the telephone.

experimenting   **B.** How can you stop a sound from reaching you on the string telephone?

experimenting   **C.** Suppose two other children have a string telephone. How can you make a party line?

experimenting   **D.** What can you do to make your phone work better? Try containers of different sizes and materials. Try different kinds of string and waxing the string with candle wax.

TEACHING COMMENT

PREPARATION AND BACKGROUND

Holding the string or letting it sag will dampen or stop sounds. So will touching the vibrating cup bottom. For a party line, cross and loop around once the lines of two sets of phones.

Cylindrical cereal boxes (for example, Quaker Oats) and salt boxes work well for string telephones. Metal can bottoms are too thick and rigid to vibrate well. Hard string or waxed string is superior to softly woven string.

Some children might believe the string telephone works like a real one. In the regular phone, sound vibrations are changed into electrical vibrations, or tiny spurts of electricity. These vibrations zip through the wire at almost the speed of light to the receiving phone. This phone changes the electrical spurts back into sound vibrations. Help children to realize that in the string telephone, only sound vibrations are transmitted.

GENERALIZATION

Sound vibrations can travel through string and other solid materials.

SAMPLE PERFORMANCE OBJECTIVES

Process: The child can discover through experimenting at least one way to improve the performance of a string telephone.
Knowledge: The child can explain how sound travels from one string telephone to another.

FOR YOUNGER CHILDREN

Younger pupils can construct and explore how to operate a string telephone. But they are less likely than older pupils to find ways to improve the telephone's performance.

☐ ACTIVITY: What are Underwater Sounds Like?

NEEDED

half-filled aquarium tank or large glass bowl   partner
two spoons

TRY THIS

1. Press an ear against the tank *above* the water level. Listen.
2. Have someone repeatedly hit two spoons together inside the tank, but *above* the water.
3. Again, press your ear against the tank but *below* the water level. Listen.
4. Now have the spoons hit together *below* the water level (Figure 10-11).
    a. How can you describe the difference between the two sets of sounds?
    b. Does sound seem to travel better in water or in air?

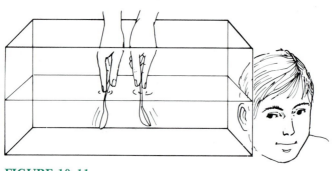

FIGURE 10-11

Reflected and Absorbed Sounds
[*Background 279*]

■ INVESTIGATION: Sounds and Megaphones

What do you do when you want your voice to go far? Do you cup your hands to your mouth? This helps to keep the sound from spreading out, so it travels farther. There's another way to do this. You can make a megaphone.

EXPLORATORY PROBLEM A

How can you make and use a megaphone?

NEEDED

sheet of heavy paper   sticky tape
two partners

TRY THIS

1. Roll up the paper from one corner to make a cone. The small opening should be large enough to speak into.
2. Fasten the two ends and middle with sticky tape (Figure 10-12).

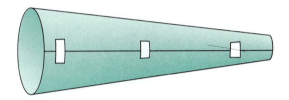

FIGURE 10-12

3. Have a partner stand across the room from you.
4. Point the megaphone toward your partner. Whisper some numbers.
5. Have your partner walk toward you until he hears you, then stop walking.

DISCOVERY PROBLEMS

inferring   **A.** Can your partner hear you without the megaphone? Have him stay where he stopped. Whisper numbers just as before. How can you tell if your partner hears you?

inferring   **B.** Can you send a message to someone without another person hearing? Have a second partner stand to one side of you. He should be as far from you as your first partner. Point the megaphone toward your first partner and whisper numbers. How can you tell if only your first partner hears you?

observing   **C.** How close must someone be to your first partner to hear you whisper?

EXPLORATORY PROBLEM B

How can a megaphone help us to hear better?

NEEDED

two megaphones   sticky tape
windup clock   meter stick or yardstick

TRY THIS

1. Put the clock on a table.

2. Stand where you cannot hear the clock.

3. Put the megaphone to your ear. Point it toward the clock (Figure 10-13).

4. Slowly move toward the clock until you hear it. Then stop.

FIGURE 10-13

DISCOVERY PROBLEMS

observing   **A.** Can you hear the clock without the megaphone at that distance?

predicting   **B.** How much closer will you need to be to hear it?

measuring   **C.** Try two megaphones, one for sending and one for hearing sounds. Lay a megaphone on its side on a table. Tape shut the small end. Put the clock inside. Have the large, open end of the megaphone facing you. Put the second megaphone to your ear. From what distance can you hear the clock with the second megaphone? without the second megaphone?

experimenting   **D.** Will different-sized megaphones make a difference in how far the sound travels? How can you find out?

TEACHING COMMENT

PREPARATION AND BACKGROUND

A megaphone tends to conserve sound energy by reflecting it in a specific direction. This allows sound to travel farther than when it spreads out in all directions. The effect also happens in reverse. The large end of a megaphone can gather sound and reflect it inward. If we listen at the small end, the sound is louder than without the megaphone. More sound energy reaches the ear.

GENERALIZATION

A megaphone reflects sounds in one direction. It may be used to increase our speaking or hearing range.

SAMPLE PERFORMANCE OBJECTIVES

Process: The child can test how a megaphone's size affects its efficiency.
Knowledge: The child can explain in everyday terms how a megaphone works.

■ INVESTIGATION: Echoes

You probably know that smooth, hard walls reflect sounds well. A reflected sound that you hear is called an echo. Sound vibrations take time to travel to a wall and then back to you. When you are at the right distance, you hear the returning sound as a separate sound.

EXPLORATORY PROBLEM

How can you make an echo happen?

NEEDED

meter stick or yardstick   string
large outside wall   scissors
piece of wood   hammer

TRY THIS

1. Find a big wall outdoors in a large area. Try to locate a wall that has no buildings opposite it.
2. Measure a distance of about 25 meters (82 feet) from the wall. (You might cut a 5-meter string to speed up measuring.)
3. Hit a piece of wood once sharply with a hammer. Listen for an echo. If you hear more than one echo, try to find another place (Figure 10-14).

DISCOVERY PROBLEMS

measuring   **A.** How close can you be to the wall and still hear an echo?

measuring   **B.** How far away from the wall can you hear an echo? As you move farther away, does it take less or more time to hear the echo?

observing   **C.** Try another wall. How do the results compare with A and B?

observing   **D.** How many echoes will there be with two reflecting walls? Try to find two facing, widely separated walls. Stand at different distances between them and bang the hammer. How do these results compare with those from a single wall?

FIGURE 10-14

TEACHING COMMENT

PREPARATION AND BACKGROUND

A trundle wheel is even more efficient than a 5-meter string for quick measurements. This device is a wheel with an attached, broomlike handle. The wheel's size is such that when rolled once around on a surface, it travels one meter (or yard, as the case may be).

In B, pupils will probably run out of space before they can fully answer the question. However, they should become aware that increasing the distance also increases the time it takes to hear an echo.

In D, the clearest results should occur with two widely separated, opposing walls.

GENERALIZATION

Echoes may be heard when sounds are reflected over a distance.

SAMPLE PERFORMANCE OBJECTIVES

Knowledge: The child can predict that an echo will be heard later if the distance between the reflecting wall and the observer is increased.
Process: The child can reliably measure the shortest distance at which an echo may usually be heard.

FOR YOUNGER CHILDREN

Use the "Try This" suggestion and Problems A through C as large-group experiences without the measurements.

■ INVESTIGATION: Materials That Quiet Sound

Many people today are trying to cut down unwanted noise. They are putting materials around them that soak up sounds. These materials are called sound insulators. Some materials are better insulators than others.

EXPLORATORY PROBLEM

How can you find out which materials are good sound insulators?

NEEDED

shoe box
windup alarm clock
newspaper
different kinds of cloth

pencil and paper
meter stick or yardstick
aluminum foil
insulation materials of your choice

TRY THIS

1. Wind up an alarm clock. Set the clock to ring within a few minutes.
2. Put the clock inside a shoe box and put on the lid.
3. Wait until the alarm rings. Measure how far away you can hear the ringing (Figure 10-15).
4. Record the distance.

FIGURE 10-15

DISCOVERY PROBLEMS

observing
measuring

A. Suppose you wrap a sheet of newspaper around the clock. From how far away can you hear the sound now? Record and compare this distance with the first one.

predicting
measuring

B. What will happen if you wrap the clock in cloth? Record and compare this distance with the other distances.

experimenting **C.** What insulation materials will work best? Is it possible not to hear any ringing at all? Arrange your materials any way you want. All should fit inside the shoe box. How will you know whether the alarm has gone off?

TEACHING COMMENT

PREPARATION AND BACKGROUND

Loosely woven, soft, fluffy materials absorb sounds well. Hard surfaces reflect sounds. This is why a formerly empty room seems quieter after carpeting, drapes, and upholstered furniture are put in.

Expect some children to have trouble setting the alarm clock. If possible, get one that is easy to set and relatively quiet. Many can be set to go off within two minutes or less.

GENERALIZATION

Loosely woven, fluffy materials are good sound insulators.

PERFORMANCE OBJECTIVES

Process: The child can measure and compare the relative effectiveness of several sound insulating materials.
Knowledge: When shown several new materials, the child can predict which will be a more effective sound insulator.

FOR YOUNGER CHILDREN

Many younger pupils will be unable to measure the hearing distance with a meter stick. Let them measure with different lengths of string or the number of footsteps between them and the clock.

SECTION 4
How Pitch Changes
[*Background 281*]

☐ ACTIVITY: What Happens to Pitch When the Speed of Vibrations Changes?

A. NEEDED
comb   small card

TRY THIS

1. Hold a comb in one hand and a card in the other.
2. Pull the card tip across the teeth of the comb slowly and steadily. Listen to the pitch of the sound—how high or low it is.

3. Do step 2 again, but faster this time. Listen again.
4. Try many different speeds. Listen each time.
   a. What is the pitch like when the vibrations are slow?
   b. What happens to the pitch as the vibrations move faster?

B. NEEDED

bicycle   small card

TRY THIS

1. Turn a bicycle upside down.
2. Crank a pedal around slowly to move the rear wheel.
3. Hold the tip of a card against the spokes as the wheel slowly turns. Listen to the pitch as the card vibrates.
4. Crank the wheel faster and faster. Listen again to the pitch as the card vibrates faster and faster.
   a. What is the pitch like when the vibrations are slow?
   b. What happens to the pitch as the vibrations move faster?

   (*Teaching Comment:* For safety, be sure that fingers holding the card are well away from the spinning wheel.)

■ INVESTIGATION: How to Make a Rubber-Band Banjo

What kinds of stringed instruments have you seen? How are they played?

EXPLORATORY PROBLEM

How can you make a rubber-band banjo?

NEEDED

topless cigar box, or stiff shoe box lid   ruler
eight rubber bands (four thick, four thinner)   pencil and paper

TRY THIS

1. Write the numbers *1* through *8* on the inside of the lid. Use a ruler to space them evenly across the whole lid.
2. Put four thick rubber bands around half of the lid. Space them from numbers *1* through *4*.
3. Put four thinner bands around the other lid half. Space them from numbers *5* through *8* (Figure 10-16).

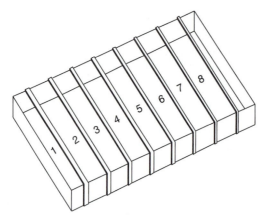

FIGURE 10-16

DISCOVERY PROBLEMS

observing   **A.** Pluck one of the rubber bands. How can you make a soft sound? louder sound?

observing   **B.** Which bands—thick or thin—make the higher sounds? (The highness or lowness of a sound is its *pitch*.)

observing   **C.** What happens to the pitch when a band is shortened? Press down a rubber band halfway across the lid. Pluck the band half nearest you.

observing   **D.** How does tightening a band on the lid affect the pitch? Loosening the band? (Pull the band up or down at the side of the lid.)

classifying   **E.** Can you make an eight-note scale? Tighten or loosen each band in order as needed. Pluck the bands *lightly* so each stays tuned.

observing   **F.** What songs can you play on your banjo? Try some simple songs first: "Mary Had a Little Lamb," "Merrily We Roll Along," "Three Blind Mice," and "Twinkle, Twinkle, Little Star."

communicating   **G.** Can you write songs well enough for other people to play? Write on paper the numbers of the notes to a song. Give the paper to someone, but don't tell the person what song it is. Can someone else play the song on your banjo? If not, how could you improve what you write?

TEACHING COMMENT

PREPARATION AND BACKGROUND

The tightness, thickness, and length of a rubber band (or string) all affect its pitch. Sounds are higher with taut, thin, short strings; they are lower with looser, thicker, or longer strings on any stringed instrument.

The tension of each rubber band may be adjusted by pulling up or down at the side of the lid. Friction between the band and lid will hold the band in place for a while. However, the band will need to be strummed or plucked gently. A sturdy lid is preferable to a flimsy one that bows in the middle.

The last activity (G) can be a challenging one. Children will need to consider sequence and timing within their compositions. Otherwise, the numbers (notes) they write may not communicate well enough for the tune to be recognizable.

GENERALIZATION

Length, tension, and thickness affect the pitch of a vibrating string.

SAMPLE PERFORMANCE OBJECTIVES

Process: The child can communicate to another child a familiar song by using written symbols, such as numbers.
Knowledge: When shown a stringed instrument, the child can predict the relative pitches of sounds the strings make.

FOR YOUNGER CHILDREN

Many younger pupils can discover the factors that affect the pitch of a string. But they will do so less systematically and completely than older children. Many will be able to do Problems A–D.

■ INVESTIGATION: A Soda-Straw Oboe

Have you ever seen an oboe? This is called a reed instrument. When the player blows on the mouthpiece, two flat, thin reeds vibrate. This makes the air inside the oboe vibrate. By opening and closing holes, the player makes different amounts of air vibrate. This changes the pitch of the notes played. You can make an instrument like this from a soda straw.

EXPLORATORY PROBLEM

How can you make a soda-straw oboe?

NEEDED

paper or plastic straws (one smaller to fit inside the larger one)   cellophane tape
straight pin   scissors
                  small paper cup

TRY THIS

1. Pinch the straw end between your thumb and forefinger to flatten it.
2. Snip off the flattened corners with scissors, as in the picture (Figure 10-17). If you have a plastic straw, cut to make a point.
3. Put about 3 centimeters (1¼ inches) of the cut straw end into your mouth. Keep your lips closed but a little loose. Blow hard into the straw. If there is no sound, blow less hard until a sound is made.

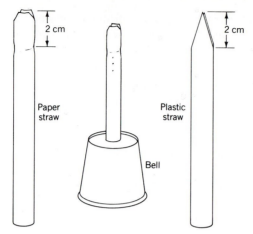

FIGURE 10-17

DISCOVERY PROBLEMS

observing **A.** What happens if you change the length of the straw? Join another straw of the same size to the first straw. To do so, slightly pinch the end of the second straw. Then gently push the pinched end into the first straw. Try adding a third straw in the same way.

observing **B.** What happens if you change the length another way? Try to fit a smaller straw into the larger one. If it is too loose, wrap some cellophane tape around the end of the smaller straw. Slide the second straw up and down as you blow.

predicting **C.** What do you think will happen if you snip off pieces of a single straw while blowing? Try it and see.

experimenting **D.** How can eight people with different-sized straws play a song?

experimenting **E.** How can you make an improved straw oboe? Prepare another straw. To change pitch now, try making a small finger hole in the oboe using a pin. Where is the best place to put the hole? How large should it be? How many holes will work? How can you use a paper cup as a "bell," or flared end, for your instrument? How does this change what you hear?

TEACHING COMMENT

PREPARATION AND BACKGROUND

Paper straws typically work more easily than plastic straws in this activity. If pupils find it hard or impossible to produce a sound, often the cut "reed" is to blame. It may help to press down gently with the lips on the straw just below the flattened part. This will open up the reed slightly and let it vibrate more easily when blown. A plastic-straw reed should be pointed for best results.

A "bell" for the instrument can be made by punching a small hole in the bottom of a paper cup and inserting the straw end into it. It should noticeably increase the loudness of the instrument.

In D, eight straws can be cut to produce a musical scale. A conductor can point to each person to produce the proper note at the right time by reading a numbered "musical score" prepared by pupils.

GENERALIZATION

The pitch of a wind instrument is changed by changing the length of the vibrating air column inside.

SAMPLE PERFORMANCE OBJECTIVES

Knowledge: The child can show at least two ways to change the pitch of a soda-straw oboe.

Process: The child can improve the performance of a soda-straw oboe by testing, observing results, and making changes.

■ INVESTIGATION: A Bottle Xylophone

Do you know what a xylophone looks like? This instrument has a row of different-sized blocks of wood. The player makes sounds by striking the blocks with two special sticks. You can easily make an instrument that works like a xylophone. But instead of wood, you can use bottles of water.

EXPLORATORY PROBLEM

How can you make a bottle xylophone?

NEEDED

eight matched soda bottles   pencil and paper
water

TRY THIS

1. Put different levels of water in each bottle.
2. Line the bottles in a row (Figure 10-18), in any order.
3. Tap each of the bottles lightly with a pencil. Notice how high or low each sound is. This is called *pitch*.

DISCOVERY PROBLEMS

observing   **A.** How much water is there in the bottle of highest pitch? lowest pitch?

classifying   **B.** Can you put the bottles in order from lowest to highest pitch?

FIGURE 10-18

experimenting **C.** What must you do with the bottles to make an eight-note scale?

observing **D.** Can you play a simple song? Put paper slips in front of the bottles. Number them from 1 to 8, for an 8-note scale. Notice the numbers of the notes you play.

communicating **E.** Can you write a song so someone else can play it correctly? Write on paper the numbers of the notes to be played. Use your own made-up song or a known song. Observe how well the song is played.

hypothesizing **F.** How can you improve the way you wrote your song?

predicting **G.** Suppose you blew over each bottle top. Now the air inside would vibrate rather than the water. How do you think that would affect each pitch? Try it and see.

TEACHING COMMENT

PREPARATION AND BACKGROUND

Bottles made of plain glass make clearer, purer sounds than those made of rippled glass. If you or a child can play the piano, children may enjoy playing this eight-note xylophone either as an accompanying or leading instrument. Children may also enjoy singing with the instrument.

GENERALIZATION

An instrument's pitch depends on how much mass vibrates. As mass increases, pitch lowers. With less mass, the pitch gets higher.

SAMPLE PERFORMANCE OBJECTIVES

Knowledge: The child can predict which of two unevenly filled bottles will sound lower when struck.
Process: The child can correctly order an eight-note scale with proportionately filled bottles of water.

FOR YOUNGER CHILDREN

Try the basic activity, plus A and B.

☐ ACTIVITY: How Does Size Affect the Pitch of a Noise?

NEEDED

two different-sized washers, coins, wood blocks, pieces   partner
  of paper, nails

TRY THIS

1. Take a small washer and a large one. Spin them, one at a time, on a table. As each falls over, it will vibrate until it stops. Notice that the smaller, lighter washer makes the higher sound. Is this true of the other pairs of objects, too? Find out by playing a game with a partner.

2. Turn your back so you cannot see. Then have your partner spin each different coin, drop each different wood block, crush each different paper, and drop each different nail separately.
   a. Could you tell in each case which size object was tested first?
   b. Did the smaller, lighter object in every set make the higher noise or lower noise?
   c. Suppose you had *three* different-sized objects in each of these sets. Would you be able to tell the order of testing?
   d. What other objects can you try?

SECTION 5
Hearing and Locating Sounds
[*Background 283*]

☐ ACTIVITY: How Do You Locate Sounds with Your Ears?

NEEDED

eight partners   quiet room
16 pencils

TRY THIS

1. Have your partners sit in a large circle about half the width of the classroom.

2. Sit in the center of the circle. Keep your eyes tightly closed. Listen with both ears.

3. Let each partner, in some mixed order, lightly tap two pencils together once.
   a. Can you tell from which direction the sound comes? Point to the spot each time. Have someone record how often you are right or wrong.

4. Now try step 3 again, but this time listen with only one ear. Hold a hand tightly over the other ear.
   b. Can you locate the sounds as well as before?
   c. Will you get the same results with your other ear?

□ ACTIVITY: How Can You Confuse Someone's Ability to Locate Sounds?

NEEDED

two 60-centimeter (24-inch) pieces of old garden hose

two small funnels

partner

TRY THIS

1. Stick a funnel into an end of each piece of hose.
2. Have a partner put the opposite end of each hose to an ear. Your partner's eyes should be closed.
3. Point the two funnels in different directions while some sound is being made (Figure 10-19).

FIGURE 10-19

4. Ask your partner where the sound comes from each time.
   a. Can you make a sound that comes from the right seem to come from the left?
   b. Can you make a sound made in front of your partner seem to come from the back?
   c. What else can you do to mix up your partner's ability to locate sounds?
   d. Trade places with your partner. What happens to your ability to locate sounds?

(*Teaching Comment:* In the drawing, the child will identify a sound coming from one side as coming from the opposite side. Several children may assist in this activity by making sounds in different locations. A good way to conclude is to repeat several sounds with the listener's eyes *open*. The effect to the listener is typically strange and highly interesting. A few listeners may try to use hose movements felt in their hands as clues to guess directions. You might tell them that in this activity, they are to infer directions only from what they hear. Or, have other pupils hold the hose ends to the listeners' ears.)

SELECTED TRADE BOOKS: SOUND ENERGY

FOR YOUNGER CHILDREN

Allington, Richard L., and Kathleen Cowles. *Hearing.* Raintree, 1980.

Barrett, Sally. *The Sound of the Week.* Good Apple, 1980.

Friedman, Joy T. *Sounds All Around.* Putnam, 1981.

Hughes, Anne E. *A Book of Sounds.* Raintree, 1979.

Jennings, Terry. *Making Sounds.* Watts, 1990.

Lee, J. Douglas. *Sounds!* Stevens, 1985.

Moncure, Jane B. *Sounds All Around.* Children's Press, 1982.

Oliver, Stephen. *Noises.* Random House, 1991.

Spier, Peter. *Crash! Bang! Boom!* Doubleday, 1990.

Wade, Harlan. *Sound.* Raintree, 1979.

Wyler, Rose. *Science Fun with Drums, Bells and Whistles.* Messner, 1987.

FOR OLDER CHILDREN

Ardley, Neil. *Sound Waves to Music: Projects with Sound.* Watts, 1991.

Brandt, Keith. *Sounds.* Troll Associates, 1985.

Kettlekamp, Larry. *The Magic of Sound.* Morrow, 1982.

Knight, David C. *All About Sound.* Troll Associates, 1983.

Knight, David C. *Silent Sound: The World of Ultrasonics.* Morrow, 1980.

Kohn, Bernice. *Echoes.* Dandelion, 1979.

Newman, Frederick R. *Zounds! The Kid's Guide to Sound Making.* Random House, 1983.

Pettigrew, Mark. *Music and Sound.* Watts, 1987.

Riley, Peter. *Light and Sound.* David & Charles, 1987.

Taylor, Barbara. *Sound and Music.* Watts, 1991.

Ward, Alan. *Experimenting with Sound.* Chelsea House, 1991.

Ward, Brian. *The Ear and Hearing.* Watts, 1981.

11

Magnetic Interactions

At the primary level, magnets may be studied more than any other science topic. It is common for young children to have their own magnets and magnetic toys. A few learn something about magnets well before attending school. Older children, too, learn about magnets when they read compasses and become aware of the earth's magnetic field. This chapter considers (1) several kinds of magnets and what they attract, (2) how to make magnets, (3) the field of force that surrounds a magnet, (4) magnetic poles, and (5) the theory and care of magnets.

[I] MAGNETS AND WHAT THEY ATTRACT
Experiences 318

There are many magnets about us for examples in teaching. In kitchens, cloth pot holders containing magnets are placed conveniently on the sides of stoves. Automatic can openers have magnets to hold opened can lids. Cabinet doors remain closed because of magnets. Some women wear magnetic earrings. Beauty operators use magnets to pick up dropped hairpins. Physicians sometimes use them to extract pieces of metal from wounds. Toy stores have many toys that in some way use magnetism.

What Magnets Attract

In nearly all these cases, *the metals attracted to a magnet are iron and steel.* These are the only magnetic metals you and your pupils are likely to use in the classroom. Less well known magnetic metals are cobalt and nickel. Among the more common metals *not* attracted by magnets are brass (an alloy of copper and zinc), aluminum, tin, silver, stainless steel (an alloy of several metals), copper, bronze (an alloy of copper and tin), and gold.

It will help you to know several facts that can clear up some common misunderstandings. For example, a question may arise about the attractable property of so-called tin cans. These are made of thin sheet steel and coated lightly with tin. Although tin is not attractable, steel is. Confusion may also result if some straight pins are attracted by a magnet and other identical-appearing pins are not. Scraping off some silver coating on the nonattractable pins will usually reveal that they are made of brass. Also, although pure nickel is magnetic, the U.S. five-cent piece is largely composed of copper and so should not be used as an example.

Lodestones

Natural magnets are sometimes called "lodestones," or "leading stones," because ancient mariners used them as crude compasses. Lodestones are made of magnetite, an iron ore found in different locations on the earth's crust.

Since only some of these deposits are magnetized, theories have been developed to explain this phenomenon. One such theory holds that lightning may have been responsible. It is thought that electricity discharged into the ore may have arranged many atoms within the ore in a manner like that found in magnets.

Traces of magnetite are common in soils. A magnet dragged along the ground or in a playground sandbox may attract many particles. These particles can be an effective substitute in activities in which iron "filings" are used. For example, if you sprinkle filings on a lodestone, they cluster at the poles. A lodestone may have many poles, but there are always an even number—one south pole for each north pole.

Manufactured Magnets

Artificial magnets are often made of steel and magnetized by electricity. Named for their shape, there are bar, V, U, horseshoe, and cylindrical magnets, to give the more familiar varieties (Figure 11-1). Each of these magnets attracts substances most strongly at the ends, or poles. The U, V, and horseshoe

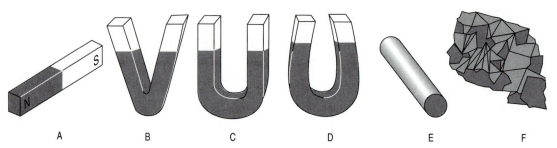

FIGURE 11-1

Magnets: (A) bar; (B) V; (C) U-shaped; (D) horseshoe; (E) cylindrical; and (F) lodestone.

magnets are more powerful than the others when all factors are equal; they are bent so two poles attract instead of one.

Powerful alnico magnets are available at scientific supply houses and in commercial kits. These are made from aluminum, cobalt, nickel, and iron. Alnico magnets are used for home and commercial purposes such as those mentioned at the beginning of this section, as well as for a variety of other purposes.

[2] MAKING MAGNETS
Experiences 323

Magnets made from a relatively soft material, such as iron, usually hold their magnetism only a short time. So they are called *temporary* magnets. Those made from a harder material, such as steel, retain their magnetism far longer. They are called *permanent* magnets. You can make either kind from common materials. Let's see how.

Temporary Magnets

A magnet can be made from an iron nail by stroking it in one direction with one pole of a permanent magnet. Its power increases with the number of strokes you apply. Be sure to lift the magnet clear at the end of each stroke before beginning another. Merely rubbing it

back and forth will usually bring poor results. Within a few minutes after making this magnet, you will notice a marked loss in its power, regardless of how many strokes it has received.

A second way to make a temporary magnet is by holding a magnet very close to any attractable object. For example, if you hold a magnet near the head of a small nail, you may be able to pick up a few tacks or a paper clip with the nail. Move the magnet farther away from the nail head, and the objects typically will fall off the nail. This is called *induced* magnetism.

You can also make a temporary magnet by wrapping an insulated wire around a nail and connecting the two wire ends to a battery. This is an *electromagnet*. Any wire that carries an electric current generates a weak magnetic field around it. Wrapping the wire around the nail core concentrates the field into the core. Disconnect the wire from the battery and the nail is no longer an effective magnet. (A tiny amount of residual magnetism may remain for a while.) We'll take up electromagnets in more detail in the next chapter on electricity.

Probably the handiest soft iron materials available to us for making temporary magnets are nails and wire coat hangers.

Permanent Magnets

It takes longer to magnetize a steel object by stroking it with a magnet than it does an iron one. However, steel may hold its magnetism for years.

A more efficient way to make permanent magnets is by electricity. The steel object is placed into a tube wrapped in wire and attached to a battery or other electrical source. Current is applied for a few seconds to magnetize the object. An upcoming activity shows this method.

Everyday things made of steel include scissors, some knitting needles, sewing needles, screwdrivers, hacksaw blades, and knife blades.

[3] FIELDS OF FORCE
Experiences 327

As children explore with magnets, they can observe that a magnet will attract from a distance. For example, a small nail or paper clip will "jump" to a nearby magnet. They will also see that the attractive force is strongest at the poles. This gives us the chance to introduce the field of force surrounding a magnet.

Inferring the Field

While we cannot see the field directly, its presence may be inferred. Sprinkle iron filings on a sheet of stiff white paper placed over a magnet, and you will see the filings distribute in an orderly way. Their greatest concentration will be at the poles. (See Figure 11-11, page 328.) Theoretically, a magnetic field extends outward to an indefinite distance. For practical purposes, the field ends when we can no longer detect it.

Children can make permanent records of magnetic fields they examine. An upcoming investigation describes how.

Magnetic Transparency

If you hold a powerful magnet against the *back* of your hand, it can attract and move a paper clip in the *palm* of your hand. A magnetic field can also go through many other materials without any apparent loss of power. It seems as if these materials are "transparent" to the field's lines of force. This makes it possible for people to wear magnetic earrings and plumbers to locate iron pipes in closed walls. Also, some wristwatches may be affected unless they are removed beforehand. (Please note.) In fact, the field of force will penetrate any nonmagnetic material children may test.

Materials of iron or steel are considered "opaque" to this force. When they are touched by a magnet, the force passes inside them and back into the magnet.

[4] MAGNETIC POLES
Experiences 332

Suspend a bar magnet from a string in North America and a curious thing happens: It points toward the north magnetic pole. Do the same in South America and it points toward the south magnetic pole. (This assumes no interference from nearby metal deposits or objects.) A magnetized needle placed horizontally on a floating foam plastic chip or slice of cork also points toward a magnetic pole.

To see why this is so, consider the poles of a magnet. When another magnet or magnetized object is held near a suspended or floating magnet, the like poles (north-north or south-south) repel each other. The opposite poles (south-north or north-south) attract each other.

Earth's Magnetism

The earth itself acts like a giant magnet. No one knows why, but there are some theories. One explanation holds that several parts of the earth's interior rotate at different speeds. The resulting friction strips electric particles from atoms. This causes an electric current to be generated that creates a magnetic field. Because the earth's core is supposedly made of nickel-iron, the effect is that of a huge electromagnet buried within the earth.

Recall the discussion before that dealt with magnetic fields of force. When iron filings are sprinkled on paper placed over a bar magnet, they reveal lines of force looping from one pole to another and concentrating at both poles. On a gigantic scale, a similar kind of magnetic field happens with the earth's magnetism. (See Figure 11-2.)

Lines of force from the earth's magnetism run roughly north and south far into space and then loop down to concentrate at the north and south magnetic poles. Therefore, a freely swinging magnet—bar, horseshoe, or any other type with dominant poles—aligns itself parallel to these lines of force. Since lines of force end at the magnetic poles, properly following a compass in the northern hemisphere eventually results in one's arrival at the north magnetic pole. This is located above the upper Hudson Bay region of Canada. If one follows a compass south, the trip ends near Wilkes Land, a part of Antarctica.

Geographic Poles

The north and south *magnetic* poles should not be confused with the north and south *geographic* poles. The geographic and magnetic poles are about 1,600 kilometers (1,000 miles) apart in the north and 2,400 kilometers (1,500 miles) apart in the south. In other words, when a compass points north it does *not* point true north, or toward the north star. Charts must be made for navigators that show the angular variation between true north and the direction toward which a compass points. These charts must be periodically changed, as the magnetic poles are slowly but continually shifting. (See Figure 11-3.)

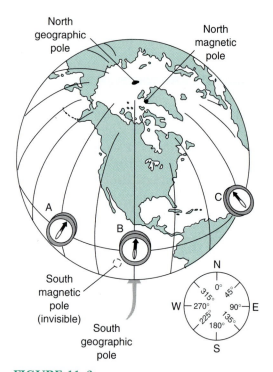

FIGURE 11-3
Note in A, B, and C an angle between the meridian on which the compass is located and the direction toward which the needle points. These differences must be added or subtracted from a compass heading to determine true north. For example, true headings for A, B, and C should all be 0°, or north. Actual readings are 35°, 5°, and 315°. A chart would show the need to subtract 35° from A, 5° from B, and the need to add 45° to C.

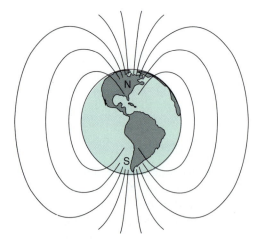

FIGURE 11-2
The earth has a magnetic field that is concentrated at both poles.

Many persons are surprised to discover that a bar magnet or compass points with its *N*, or *north,* pole toward the earth's *north* magnetic pole. Yet it is known that *like* poles *repel* and unlike poles attract. How is this contradiction explained? The answer lies in history. Compasses were used long before reasons for their operation were understood. It became customary to speak of the end of a magnet that points northward as the north pole. It is more accurately called the *north-seeking* pole, and its counterpart the *south-seeking* pole.

[5] MAGNETIC THEORY AND CARE OF MAGNETS
Experiences 334

Although magnetism has been known and used for many centuries, science cannot fully explain it. One theory, when simply explained, can be understood by children. It is based on observations they can make for themselves: Heating or repeatedly dropping a magnet will cause it to lose its magnetic properties. And, although a magnet may be broken into smaller and smaller pieces, each

fragment continues to have a north and south pole. Why?

Magnetic Domains

Scientists believe that there are many tiny clusters of atoms, called *domains,* within potentially magnetic objects. The clusters are normally randomly arranged. But when an object is stroked in one direction, or otherwise magnetized, the domains line up in a single direction. (See Figure 11-4.) Notice that in drawing A, the bar magnet could be broken into many pieces, yet each piece would continue to have opposite poles. Heating a magnet forces the domains into violent motion, and so they are likely to be disarranged as in drawing B. Repeatedly dropping a magnet jars the domains out of line, with the same result.

Standards for Care

Magnets can keep much of their power for years when properly cared for. Storing magnets improperly in the classroom is probably the chief reason why they quickly become weak. A small metal bar, called a *keeper,* should be placed across the poles of a magnet before it is stored. If the regular keeper has been lost,

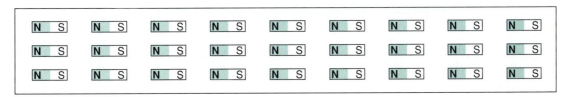

A

B

FIGURE 11-4
A magnetized (A) and unmagnetized (B) steel bar.

a nail can be substituted. Placing opposite poles of magnets together is another effective way to store them. Children can also learn not to drop magnets, which is another common reason why magnets become weaker.

Figure 11-5 shows two charts to help children remember some standards when handling magnets. The first chart is for primary children. The second is suitable for older children.

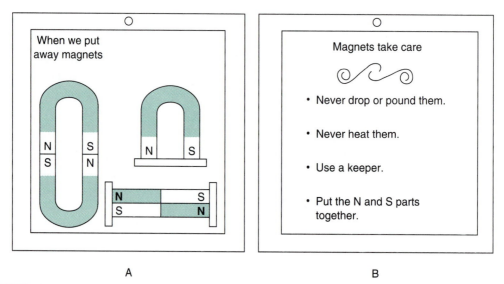

A   B

FIGURE 11-5
Sample charts to help children remember how to handle magnets.

INVESTIGATIONS & ACTIVITIES

SECTION 1
Magnets and What They Attract
[Background 313]

■ INVESTIGATION: Objects Magnets Can Pull

Have you ever played with a magnet? If so, what were you able to do with it?

EXPLORATORY PROBLEM

How can you find out which objects magnets can pull?

NEEDED

two bags of small objects   magnet

TRY THIS

1. Take out the objects from only *one* bag now.
2. Touch your magnet to each object.
3. Which objects are pulled by the magnet? Put these in a group.
4. Which objects are not pulled by the magnet? Put those in another group (Figure 11-6).

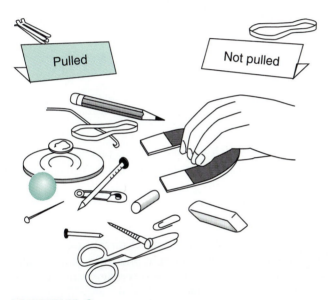

FIGURE 11-6

DISCOVERY PROBLEMS

observing   **A.** How are the objects in the pulled group alike?

inferring   **B.** Can you make a rule about which objects your magnet pulls? Put the objects back into the bag. Put the bag away.

predicting   **C.** Take out the objects from the *second* bag. Which do you think your
classifying   magnet will pull? will not pull? Put the objects into two groups.

inferring   Now use your magnet on the objects in each group. Was every object in the right group?

predicting   **D.** Which objects around the room will your magnet pull? Think, then find out.

observing   **E.** What other magnets can you try? Will they pull the same objects your first magnet pulled?

TEACHING COMMENT

Try to get a variety of attractable and nonattractable small objects for both bags of test materials. Here are some common objects and the chief metals or metal alloys that make them up:

nails ------------------------ iron
wire ------------------------ copper
pins ------------------------ steel (or brass)
screws --------------------- brass (or iron or aluminum)
hair curler ------------------ aluminum
penny ---------------------- bronze

Give children the names of metals as needed to help them generalize about their experience. Of the common materials, only steel and iron will be attracted to a magnet.

GENERALIZATION

A magnet pulls objects made of iron or steel.

SAMPLE PERFORMANCE OBJECTIVES

Process: The child can infer a rule about which objects magnets pick up.
Knowledge: The child can apply the rule to new objects by predicting which will be attracted to a magnet.

FOR OLDER CHILDREN

Older pupils can be challenged by testing solely a variety of metals, especially as used in common objects. If you mix steel and brass straight pins, for example, only the steel will be attracted. Pupils will need to rub off the silverlike coating on the brass pin to discover why it is not attracted. Some can lids are also brasslike in appearance, but they are really made of steel.

Try asking these pupils to bring in some small objects from home that have "surprised" them when tested with a magnet. Challenging their friends to make predictions with these objects will add to everyone's fun and knowledge.

□ ACTIVITY: How Can a Magnet Separate Mixed Materials?

NEEDED

magnet	salt
kitchen plastic wrap	iron filings
plastic spoon	small jar with lid
white paper with turned-up edges	sandbox or loose soil

TRY THIS

1. Put two spoonfuls each of filings and salt into the jar.

2. Cap the jar and shake it to mix the two materials.

3. Pour the mixture onto a white paper "tray."

4. Try using the spoon to separate the filings and salt.

5. Now use the magnet, but first cover the poles with kitchen plastic wrap.

6. To remove the filings from the magnet, remove the kitchen wrap.
   a. Which was easier, step 4 or 5?
   b. Many bits of iron may be found in sand and soils. Cover the magnet's poles again with wrap. Poke the magnet around in a sandbox or loose soil. How many iron bits do you find?

■ INVESTIGATION: The Power of Magnets

Some people say you can tell how strong a magnet is just by looking at it. What do you think?

EXPLORATORY PROBLEM

How can you find out the power of a magnet?

NEEDED

several different magnets   pencil
paper clips   two small pieces cut from a straw
sheet of lined paper

TRY THIS

1. Put a paper clip on two pieces of soda straw, placed on a sheet of lined paper.

2. Make a pencil mark at the front of the clip.

3. Line up an end (pole) of a magnet with the clip. (See Figure 11-7.)

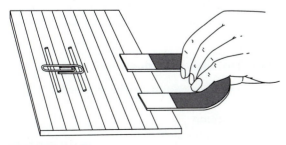

FIGURE 11-7

4. Slowly bring the magnet near the paper clip.

5. Stop moving the magnet when the clip moves.

6. Count the lines between the pencil mark and magnet.

DISCOVERY PROBLEMS

measuring   **A.** Test several magnets. Which is the most powerful? Can you put them
classifying   in order from weakest to strongest?

measuring   **B.** Are both ends (poles) of magnets equally powerful? How can you
find out?

observing   **C.** Do all parts of a magnet pull the clip? Which part of a magnet is
strongest? weakest?

experimenting   **D.** What are some other ways to test a magnet's power? Do you get the
same results?

TEACHING COMMENT

PREPARATION AND BACKGROUND

Most manufactured magnets are made from steel. Named for their shape, there
are bar, V, U, horseshoe, and cylindrical magnets, to give the most familiar kinds.
Some magnets are made from several metals. These tend to be more powerful than
those made only of steel. Try to have several kinds of magnets on hand for this
investigation.

A magnet attracts objects most strongly at the ends or poles. The attractive
power gradually weakens as you go toward the center of the magnet. The center
has very little or no magnetic attraction.

GENERALIZATION

Magnets vary in power; magnets attract objects most strongly at their poles.

SAMPLE PERFORMANCE OBJECTIVES

Process: The children can measure the relative power of several magnets and
arrange them in order from least to most powerful.
Knowledge: The child can describe the parts of a magnet that are likely to be most
and least powerful.

□ ACTIVITY: What Can You Do with a Lodestone?

NEEDED

lodestone
attractable objects
  (pins, tacks, etc.)

small piece of Styrofoam
full glass of water
iron filings

TRY THIS

1. Observe the lodestone carefully.
   a. How can you describe it?

2. Touch the lodestone to some pins or paper clips.
   b. What happens?

3. Sprinkle iron filings all over the lodestone. Notice the places where filings are thickest. These are the poles.
   c. How many poles does your lodestone have? Is it an odd or even number?

4. Put the lodestone on a piece of Styrofoam. Float it in water. Turn the lodestone gently one way, then another, a few times.
   d. Does the lodestone always point one way or in different ways?
   e. How is your lodestone like a made magnet? unlike a made magnet?
   f. How can you describe a lodestone to somebody who has not seen one?

(*Teaching Comment:* This activity leads pupils to make an operational definition of a lodestone. Most pupils will discover that their ability to describe a lodestone will be far more complete and clear in f than in a.)

SECTION 2
Making Magnets
[*Background 314*]

■ INVESTIGATION: How to Make Magnets

Suppose you have an iron nail and a magnet. With these materials, you can make another magnet.

EXPLORATORY PROBLEM

How can you make a magnet?

NEEDED

strong magnet   two matched iron nails
steel straight pins   two screwdrivers (large and small)

TRY THIS

1. Get a large iron nail. Touch it to some steel pins to see if it attracts them.

2. Put one end of the magnet on the nail near the head.

3. Stroke the whole nail with the magnet 20 times. Stroke in one direction only (Figure 11-8).

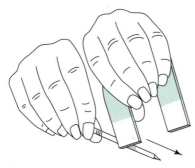

FIGURE 11-8

4. Touch the nail again to some pins. How many pins does the nail attract? Record this number.

DISCOVERY PROBLEMS

observing   **A.** How much stronger can you make your nail magnet? How many pins does it attract after 30 strokes? forty strokes? Record how many pins are attracted each time.

observing   **B.** How strong is the nail magnet after 10 minutes? Compare.

observing   **C.** Test the other nail, to see if it attracts pins. If not, stroke this nail *back and forth,* instead of just one way. How strong is the magnet after 20 strokes? thirty strokes? forty strokes?

predicting   **D.** Suppose you stroke a *small* steel screwdriver one way with a magnet. How many pins will it attract after 20 strokes? thirty strokes? forty strokes? Record and compare your findings with those for the nail.

predicting   **E.** Suppose you stroke a *large* steel screwdriver one way with a magnet. Will you get the same results?

predicting   **F.** How strong do you think both screwdrivers will be after 10 minutes?

hypothesizing   **G.** What other objects can you make into magnets? How strong can you make each one?

TEACHING COMMENT

PREPARATION AND BACKGROUND

An iron or steel object may be magnetized by stroking it with a magnet. A soft iron object that is magnetized, such as a nail, weakens after several minutes. A steel object, such as the shank of a screwdriver, retains its magnetism. However, steel is harder to magnetize. Only a strong magnet is likely to produce significant results. Stroking an object both ways with a magnet is less effective than stroking it in one direction. Use steel straight pins to test the strength of whatever magnets are made. These magnets are likely to be weak, so only small, light objects will be noticeably attracted.

In problems D and E, observe if pupils test each screwdriver for magnetism *before* they proceed. If this investigation is repeated with the same objects, it will first be necessary to *demagnetize* them. To do so, drop the screwdrivers, nails, and pins several times on a hard surface, such as a sidewalk.

GENERALIZATION

Iron and steel may be magnetized by a magnet; steel holds its magnetism longer than iron.

SAMPLE PERFORMANCE OBJECTIVES

Process: The child can infer by comparing data that there is a connection between the number of strokes used to magnetize an object and the object's magnetic power.
Knowledge: The child will say that a steel object should be used if a permanent magnet is to be made.

☐ ACTIVITY: How Can You Magnetize Something Without Touching It?

NEEDED

large iron nail   tacks
strong magnet

TRY THIS

1. Touch the nail to some tacks. Be sure it cannot pick up any before going on.

2. Again, touch the nail to the tacks, but now hold one pole of the magnet just above the nail head (Figure 11-9).
   a. How many tacks does the nail pull?

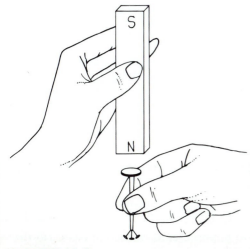

FIGURE 11-9

3. Take away the magnet.

   b. What happens to the pulled tacks? Why do you think this happened?

   c. How does touching the nail head with the magnet change how strongly the nail pulls?

   d. How far apart must the magnet and nail be before no tacks are pulled?

(*Teaching Comment:* The more powerful the magnet, the more likely it will induce temporary magnetism in the nail.)

□ ACTIVITY: How Can You Make Long-Lasting Magnets with Electricity?

NEEDED

thin (number 26 or 28) insulated copper wire   magnet
three D-size flashlight cells   pencil
3- by 5-inch file card   scissors
two steel bobby pins (not magnetized)   tacks
sticky tape

TRY THIS

1. Tightly roll a small file card around a pencil. Fasten it with sticky tape.

2. Tightly wind about 80 turns of thin copper wire in one direction around the tube. Leave 30 centimeters (1 foot) of wire free at each end. Tape the coil ends so the wires stay tightly wound.

3. Strip the insulation from the wire ends with scissors.

4. Remove the pencil from the tube. Put a straightened bobby pin inside.

5. Put three flashlight batteries together as in the picture. (See Figure 11-10.)

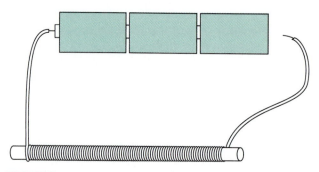

FIGURE 11-10

6. Touch the stripped ends of the wire to opposite ends of the batteries. Do this for no more than 5 seconds.

7. Remove the bobby pin and touch it to some tacks.

    a. How many tacks does the bobby pin pick up?

    b. Suppose you made a second bobby-pin magnet by stroking it with a regular magnet. Could you make it as strong as or stronger than the "electrocuted" bobby pin? If so, how many times would it need to be stroked? Find out.

    c. Magnetize with electricity other things that will fit into the tube. Which objects can be magnetized? Which will hold most of their magnetism over a week or more? Which will not?

Fields of Force
[Background 315]

■ INVESTIGATION: Magnetic Fields

Have you found that some objects can be attracted to a magnet even when the magnet doesn't touch them? That's because around every magnet there is an invisible *field of force*. The magnet pulls on any attractable object within its field. Although the field is invisible, there are ways to tell where it is.

EXPLORATORY PROBLEM

How can you find out about a magnet's field of force?

NEEDED

container of iron filings	two sheets of stiff white paper
four matched bar magnets	with turned-up edges
four matched horseshoe or U	partner
magnets	

TRY THIS

1. Place a bar magnet on a table. Lay a sheet of white paper with turned-up edges over it.

2. Sprinkle some iron filings on this paper tray. Do this over and around where you think the magnet is (Figure 11-11).

3. Observe closely how the filings line up and where they are thick and thin.

DISCOVERY PROBLEMS

inferring   **A.** Ask your partner to observe your magnetic field, but don't tell how you arranged your magnet or what kind it is. Can your partner make one just like it?

inferring   **B.** Have your partner make a magnetic field for you. Can you match it?

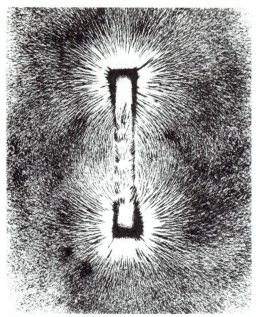

FIGURE 11-11

predicting **C.** Here are more fields for you and your partner to try: How will two bar magnets look with like poles close together? unlike poles close together? How will horseshoe or U magnets look with like and unlike poles close together? First, draw what you predict.

experimenting **D.** What fields can you make with different combinations of magnets, positions, and distances apart?

inferring **E.** What were the easiest fields of force for you and your partner to figure out? hardest fields to figure out?

TEACHING COMMENT

PREPARATION AND BACKGROUND

Pupils should learn that iron filings only crudely show a magnet's field of force. The field extends much beyond where the filings stop.

Permanent inference sheets of magnetic fields can be easily made. These will allow individual pupils to do the activity by trying to match the sheets. To make a permanent record of a field, use plastic spray to fix the filings on a stiff sheet of paper. Hold the spray can far enough away from the sheet so filings are not blown away. For best results, be sure to use fine, powderlike filings and to sprinkle lightly. Let the spray dry before removing the sheet from the underlying magnets.

GENERALIZATION

A field of force surrounds a magnet; it is most powerful near the ends or poles.

SAMPLE PERFORMANCE OBJECTIVES

Knowledge: The child can point out the most and least powerful areas in a magnetic field.

Process: When shown a record of a magnetic field, the child can infer the positions and distances apart of several magnets.

■ INVESTIGATION: If Magnetism Goes Through Objects

Do you think magnetism can be blocked by some materials? If so, which ones? Do you think it can pass through other materials? If so, which ones?

EXPLORATORY PROBLEM A

How can you find out if magnetism can go through materials?

NEEDED

ruler	strong magnet
books	small paper clip
thread	small thin materials to test

TRY THIS

1. Set up your objects as in Figure 11-12. Be sure that the clip does *not* touch the magnet.

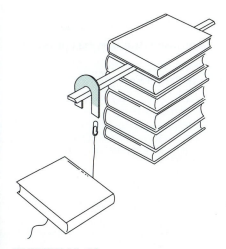

FIGURE 11-12

2. Make the space between the clip and magnet as big as possible, but do not let the clip fall. Slowly pull the thread end to widen the space.

3. Test one of your thin, flat materials. Put it in the space between the clip and magnet without touching them.

4. Does the clip stay up? Then magnetism can go through the material. Does the clip fall? Then magnetism cannot go through the material.

DISCOVERY PROBLEMS

predicting
A. Which of your materials do you think magnetism will go through? Which will magnetism not go through? Put the materials in two piles, then test them to find out.

predicting
B. Will magnetism go through *two* materials put together? Think, then test to find out. (Be sure the two materials can fit between the magnet and clip.)

experimenting
C. Do you think magnetism will go through water? How can you find out?

experimenting
D. What are other ways to test if magnetism can go through your objects?

EXPLORATORY PROBLEM B

How can you find hidden objects with a magnet?

NEEDED

shoe box   small scissors
strong magnet   small and large iron nail
partner   sticky tape

TRY THIS

1. Ask your partner to tape small scissors anywhere inside the box except on the bottom.

2. Then have your partner close the box. You should not know where the scissors are (Figure 11-13).

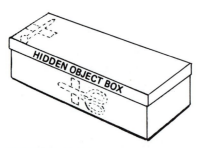

FIGURE 11-13

3. Slide your magnet on the outside of the box. Do not move the box.

4. Stop when you think you have found the scissors. Tell your partner where you think they are.

5. Open the box to see if you are right.

DISCOVERY PROBLEMS

inferring   **A.** Can you find the scissors wherever they are placed in the box? Can you tell how the scissors are pointing each time?

inferring   **B.** Suppose your partner tapes a small nail and the scissors inside. Can you find both? Can you tell which is which?

inferring   **C.** Suppose your partner tapes a small and large nail and scissors inside. Can you find all three objects? Can you tell which is which? Can you tell how each is pointing?

predicting   **D.** What other objects might you find if they are taped in the box?

TEACHING COMMENT

PREPARATION AND BACKGROUND

In Exploratory Problem A, try to provide materials thin enough to pass between the paper clip and magnet. A variety of materials will be useful, such as cloth, flat rubber sink-stopper, paper, glass slide, aluminum foil, wooden tongue depressor or flat popsicle stick, plastic lid, coins, tin-can lid (steel), soft-drink-can lid (aluminum), and the like. *Caution:* Some can lids or other objects are sharp. Cover sharp edges with a narrow band of sticky tape. Use a *powerful* magnet, *small* paper clip, and *thin* thread if possible. This combination will permit a wide gap between the clip and magnet.

In Exploratory Problem B, the child is asked to locate several attractable objects in a shoe box and tell them apart. To do so, one object will need to be much larger than the other.

GENERALIZATION

Magnetism goes through many objects, but not those made from iron or steel.

SAMPLE PERFORMANCE OBJECTIVES

Process: The child can infer the location of a hidden iron object by using a magnet.
Knowledge: Given a magnet and several objects, the child can show that magnetism passes through objects unless they are made of iron or steel.

FOR YOUNGER CHILDREN

Younger children should be able to do most of the activities in this investigation, although with less precision than older children.

SECTION 4
Magnetic Poles
[*Background 315*]

☐ ACTIVITY: How Can You Make a Needle Compass?

NEEDED

two sewing needles   magnet
cork top (thin slice), or Styrofoam chip   water
drinking glass   paper towel

TRY THIS

1. Place a glass on a paper towel. Fill it to the brim with water.

2. Magnetize a needle. Stroke it 10 times, from thick end to point, with the magnet's *S* pole.

3. Scratch a narrow groove in the sliced cork top. Lay the needle in the groove. (This will keep it from rolling off.)

4. Carefully place the cork and needle on the water surface (Figure 11-14).
   a. In which direction does the needle point?
   b. Move the needle gently so it points somewhere else. Wait a few seconds. What happens?
   c. Use your magnet. How can you *push* away either end of the needle with it?
   d. How can you *pull* either end of the needle with the magnet?

FIGURE 11-14

5. Replace the magnetized needle with one that has not been magnetized. Float the cork and needle on the water as before.
   e. What do you think will happen if you try a through d again? Find out.

   (*Teaching Comment:* A glass filled to the brim with water keeps a floating cork centered. With less water, the cork will drift against the glass's sides.)

☐ ACTIVITY: How Can You Use a Compass to Tell Directions?

NEEDED

large, topless cardboard box   partner
large, open area   magnetic compass

TRY THIS

1. Go to a large, open space outdoors. Study the compass. Notice how the needle points. If needed, turn the compass so that the part marked "north" is under the pointing needle.
2. Walk 20 steps toward the north and observe the needle. While walking, try to keep the needle exactly on north.
3. Stop, then turn completely around. Look at the compass. Now "north" is behind you and "south" is straight ahead. The other end of the needle should point south. Walk 20 steps toward the south while watching the needle. Keep it exactly on south. If you do so, you should return to about where you started.
   a. Can you use only your compass well enough to walk somewhere and find your way back? How close will you get? Mark where you are. Put a box over your head so you cannot see around you. Looking at only your compass, walk 300 steps north and then 300 steps south. Have a partner watch out for you.
   b. How well can you do step 3a *without* a compass?
   c. How can you use your compass to walk east or west? Practice these directions as in steps 1 through 3 and then try the box test again.
   d. In what other directions can you walk and return using only your compass?

(*Teaching Comment:* "North" as shown on a compass may vary slightly from true north because of regional magnetic variation. For the purpose of this activity, such variation may be ignored.)

☐ ACTIVITY: Which Needle Is Magnetized?

NEEDED

two matched sewing needles   magnet
partner

TRY THIS

1. Here's a puzzler for you. Magnetize one needle. Stroke it 10 times, from thick to pointed end, with a magnet.
2. Have your partner switch the two needles around while you look away. Now you should not know which one is magnetized.
   a. Using *only* the two needles, how can you find the magnetized one?
   b. If you need help, how can the two drawings help you (Figure 11-15)? (*Clue:* A magnet is very weak at its center part.)

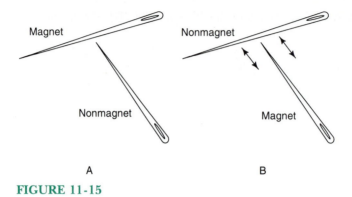

FIGURE 11-15

(*Teaching Comment:* This is a difficult problem for all but abstract thinkers to do unaided. The drawings show how the magnetic needle can be discovered. In drawing A, there is no noticeable attraction when the end of the nonmagnet is held against the center part of the magnet. In drawing B, the needle positions are reversed. The center of the nonmagnet leaps to the pole of the magnet.)

SECTION 5
Magnetic Theory and Care of Magnets
[*Background 317*]

☐ ACTIVITY: How Many Small Magnets Can You Get from a Large Magnet?

NEEDED

iron clothes hanger   tacks
strong bar magnet   side-cutting pliers

TRY THIS

1. Cut a long, straight piece from the hanger with pliers.
2. Stroke it 50 times in 1 direction with 1 pole of a magnet. Stroke it the whole length each time.
3. Touch different parts of the magnetized piece to some tacks.
   a. Which parts pick up the tacks?
4. Cut the piece in half. Do step 3 again with both pieces.
   b. Which parts pick up the tacks now?
   c. Suppose you cut each of these pieces in two. Which parts do you think would pick up tacks?

☐ ACTIVITY: What Are Some Ways a Magnet Can Lose Its Magnetism?

A. NEEDED

magnet
two large matched nails

concrete sidewalk
tacks or paper clips

Test to see how *dropping* a magnet affects its magnetism. (Use magnetized nails so that regular magnets will not be destroyed.)

TRY THIS

1. Magnetize two nails. Stroke each nail its whole length 30 times with one pole of a magnet.

2. Test to see if each nail magnet attracts the same number of tacks. If not, stroke the weaker magnet until it is equally strong.

3. Hold one nail high and drop it on a hard surface. Do this 20 times.

4. Test each nail again. You might record what you find in this way:

	Dropped Magnet	**Other Magnet**
Before	six tacks	six tacks
After	two tacks	five tacks

   a. How did dropping the nail magnet affect it?
   b. What will happen if you drop the second nail magnet?

B. NEEDED

magnet
two large matched nails
tacks or paper clips
pliers or tongs

candle and match
cake pan (to hold candle)
glass of water

Test to see how *heating* affects magnetism.

TRY THIS

1. Again, do steps 1 and 2 in Section A.

2. Use pliers to hold one magnetized nail upright in a candle flame for three minutes.

3. Before testing, dip the nail in water to cool it.

4. Test the two nails. Record your findings as in Section A.
   a. How did heating the nail magnet affect it?
   b. What will happen if you heat the second nail magnet?

   (*Teaching Comment:* Iron nails do not retain magnetism very long. So it is possible that the second, or control, magnet will also be weaker during the posttest. But this change should be slight. If pupils are interested, you might pose two additional problems to give further practice in controlling variables: What is the *fewest* number of times a magnetized nail needs to be dropped to get the same results? What is the *least* amount of time it needs to be heated for the same results? Supervise the candle activity closely for safety.)

SELECTED TRADE BOOKS: MAGNETIC INTERACTIONS

FOR YOUNGER CHILDREN

Freeman, Mae. *The Real Magnet Books.* Scholastic, 1980.

Jennings, Terry. *Magnets.* Watts, 1990.

Kirkpatrick, Rena K. *Look at Magnets.* Raintree, 1985.

Knight, David C. *Let's Find out About Magnets.* Watts, 1967.

Podendorf, Illa. *Magnets.* Children's Press, 1971.

Sacks, Raymond. *Magnets.* Coward-McCann, 1967.

Schneider, Herman, and Nina Schneider. *Secret Magnets.* Scholastic, 1979.

Victor, Edward. *Magnets.* Follett, 1962.

Wade, Harlan. *The Magnet.* Raintree, 1979.

FOR OLDER CHILDREN

Adler, David. *Amazing Magnets.* Troll Associates, 1983.

Adler, Irving, and Ruth Adler. *Magnets.* Day, 1966.

Catherall, E. A., and P. N. Holt. *Working with Magnets.* Whitman, 1969.

Fitzpatrick, Julie. *Magnets.* Silver Burdett, 1987.

Freeman, Mae B. *The Book of Magnets.* Four Winds, 1968.

Santrey, Laurence. *Magnets.* Troll Associates, 1985.

Sootin, Harry. *Experiments with Magnetism.* Norton, 1968.

Victor, Edward. *Exploring and Understanding Magnets and Electromagnets.* Benefic, 1967.

Ward, Alan. *Experimenting with Magnetism.* Chelsea House, 1991.

12

Electrical Energy

Can children learn to appreciate the advantages of a ready source of electricity? One good beginning is for them to count the number of electrical devices we use and then try to devise nonelectrical substitutes for them. By studying activities like those in this chapter, children should also begin to appreciate some of the things that make electrical energy available and the principles that make them work.

We'll consider (1) how electrical circuits are closed and opened, (2) some conditions that affect the flow of electricity, (3) electromagnets, and (4) ways to produce electricity.

[1] CLOSED AND OPEN CIRCUITS *Experiences 349*

Each time we push a button or flip a switch that "turns on" electricity, there is a flow of electrical energy in wires continuously connected from the generating plant to our appliance and back again to the plant. On a smaller scale, much the same thing happens when a battery is connected to a miniature bulb. If there is a continuous connection between the source of electricity and the appliance or device using it, lights go on, bells ring, or motors spin. This continuous connection is called a *closed circuit*. Anytime there is a break or gap in the circuit, the electric flow stops. This condition is called an *open circuit*.

Switches

Regardless of their shape, size, or method of operation, electric switches serve only to open or close a circuit. They offer a safe and convenient way of supplying the flow of electricity when we want it by providing a linkage through which the energy can flow to the connecting wires. In activities of the first section, pupils discover how to make simple paper-clip switches.

Batteries

Much of the work in this chapter calls for the use of dry cells, copper wire, and flashlight bulbs. Size D flashlight cells or number 6 dry cells should be used because they are safe, fairly long lasting, and relatively inexpensive. When fresh, they deliver 1½ volts of electricity, as contrasted with 110 to 120 volts or so supplied in the home. In other words, it would take as many as 80 of these cells connected together to have a force usually supplied by the current found in the home. *Caution the children that house current is dangerous for electrical investigations and should never be used by them for this purpose.*

In this chapter, and in most lessons at the elementary level, three or four connected cells are all that will ever be needed. D-size flashlight "batteries" are preferred over number 6 dry cells because they are cheaper and available from home flashlights. But being smaller, they wear down faster than the larger dry cells. Although individual flashlight cells are commonly called "batteries," and we'll use this term in the activities, it is technically correct to use the term *battery* only when two or more cells are combined.

Bulbs

Because the chapter calls for experiments with miniature bulbs (flashlight-type bulbs), it will be helpful to understand how to use them properly. Miniature bulbs are designed to be used with a loosely specified number of 1½ volt dry cells. Therefore, there are 1-cell, 2-cell, 3-cell, and so on, bulbs. One-cell bulbs are sometimes marked "1.2v," 2-cell bulbs "2.5v," and so forth.

If three dry cells are connected to a 1-cell bulb, it is likely that the thin tungsten filament inside will burn out quickly. So match the bulb with the number of cells used. Too many cells will cause the bulb to burn out quickly; too few will cause it to glow feebly, if at all. A good compromise for this chapter is the 2-cell (2.5-volt) bulb.

Fahnestock Clips

Many unit activities call for the use of commercial-type miniature bulbs and sockets. While several substitutes are possible, these are usually cumbersome and less useful. For maximum ease in using miniature sockets, Fahnestock clips should be fastened to each side of the socket with the screws found there. (See Figure 12-1 for an example.) To connect a wire, simply press down on the springy, open end of the clip and insert the wire end into the exposed half-loop. The wire stays in place when you release the pressure on the clip.

Notice that the large number 6 cell is also supplied with clips rather than the usual binding posts with screw caps. The suggestion to use Fahnestock clips may seem a minor one, but they can save much time and trouble.

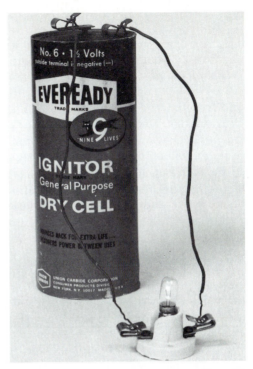

FIGURE 12-1
A number 6 dry cell and two D cells connected in complete circuits.

Wire

The wire you use should also be selected with an eye to convenience. Number 22 wire is excellent for almost every activity. Get plastic-covered solid copper wire, rather than cotton-covered wire consisting of many small, twisted strands. These strands become unraveled at the ends, and cotton insulation is harder to strip off than a plastic covering.

Insulation can quickly be removed with a wire-stripper (Figure 12-2); this device also cuts wires efficiently. With the wire suggested here, scissors may serve almost as well.

Connections

There are several easy ways to connect cells and bulbs, depending on the kinds of materials you have. Figure 12-1 shows how a D-size cell and a number 6 cell can be connected to form a closed or complete circuit. Tape or a wide rubber band will hold the stripped wire ends snugly against the D-cell terminals. The center terminal (positive), recognizable by the bump, corresponds to the center terminal on a large cell. The opposite terminal (negative) is equivalent to the rim-mounted terminal on the large cell. The third arrangement needs only a single wire, with one end touching the negative terminal and the other wrapped around the bulb base. The base touches the positive terminal to complete the circuit. Notice that the wire end wrapped

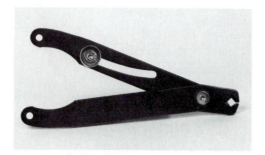

FIGURE 12-2
A wire stripper.

around the bulb base also serves as a bulb holder.

The activities in this chapter have been carefully worked out to help ensure teaching success. However, occasionally something may not go as planned. If this happens, use the occasion as a chance for learning.

Most difficulties with materials in this chapter may be handled by posing one or more of the following questions. By knowing about them in advance, you can help pupils to trace the source of the "trouble."

Bulb: Is it screwed in tightly? burned out? Is there correct voltage?

Dry Cell: Is it in good condition? Is it powerful enough for the circuit?

Connections: Are they secure? Is enough contact being made for the current to flow easily?

[2] SERIES AND PARALLEL CIRCUITS *Experiences 354*

There are only two basic ways to connect electrical devices in a circuit: through series or parallel wiring (Figure 12-3).

Connecting Wires

In series wiring, all of the usable electricity flows through each bulb or appliance. A chief disadvantage of this circuit is obvious to anyone who has had a bulb burn out in an old-fashioned, series-type string of Christmas-tree lights. When one bulb burns out, the circuit is broken and all the lights go out. All the bulbs must then be tested to discover which one needs to be replaced. When flashlight cells are the source of power, adding extra bulbs to a series circuit steadily decreases bulb brightness.

To avoid the troubles of series circuits, most wiring for home and commercial use is parallel wiring. In this kind, electricity flows through a main wire and through branching

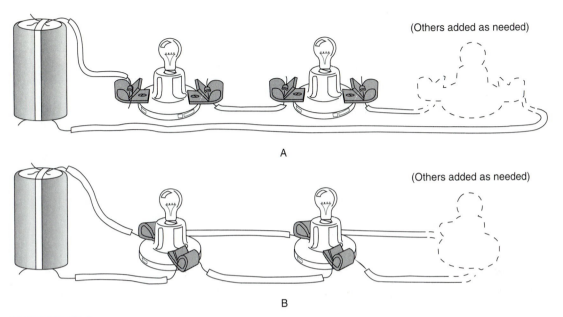

(Others added as needed)

A

(Others added as needed)

B

FIGURE 12-3
Two contrasting circuits: (A) Lights in series, and (B) lights in parallel.

wires connected to it as well, as shown in Figure 12-3B. (In this figure, the Fahnestock clips represent the branching wires.) If a light or other fixture should burn out, no other light or fixture is affected. They receive electricity whether or not the others are in use. And when children make parallel circuits, they will notice no change in bulb brightness as bulbs are added.

Connecting Cells

Cells can also be arranged in series and parallel as shown in Figure 12-4. A wide rubber band can serve to affix wires to flashlight cells, but the cells will buckle where they join unless they are enclosed. A sheet of rolled, stiff paper can be used for this purpose. If children work in pairs, these holders may not be required, as four hands should be able to hold everything together. To keep the cells from rolling, they can be placed in the spine of an opened book.

Note that in the series examples, negative terminals (–) are joined to positive (+)

terminals. In the parallel examples, positives are joined to positives and negatives to negatives.

Voltage

Hooking up cells in series increases the *voltage,* or pressure, behind the flow of electricity. In contrast, arranging several or more cells in parallel makes available a longer lasting supply of current without increasing the voltage. For example, a bulb connected to two cells in series will burn about twice as brightly as when the cells are connected in parallel. However, the bulb will burn about two times longer with the parallel arrangement.

An analogy, as shown in Figure 12-5, can clarify why these differences take place. Cells in series are like connected tanks of water with one mounted higher than the other. The force of the flow is directly related to how many higher tanks are used. In contrast, cells in parallel are like water tanks mounted on the same level. The water flows at about

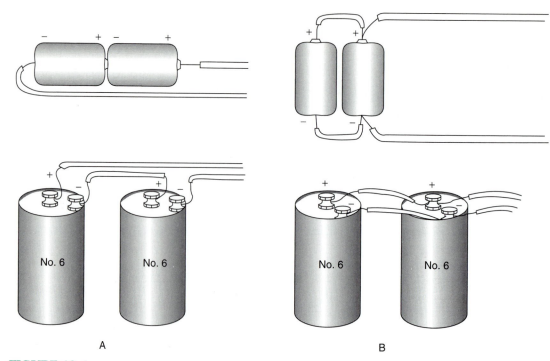

FIGURE 12-4
Batteries arranged in series (A) and parallel (B).

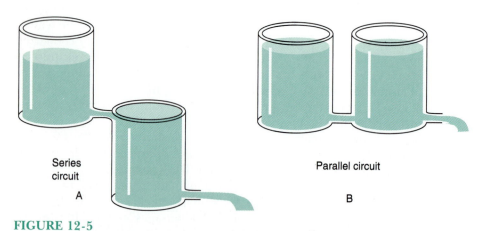

FIGURE 12-5
(A) is twice as forceful as (B), but (B) will flow twice as long.

the same rate as it would with one tank. So in this case, the water supply lasts about twice as long as in the other setup.

In studying circuits, children have many interesting chances to make predictions about which bulbs will light and to make inferences about hidden wires.

[3] CONDITIONS AFFECTING ELECTRICAL FLOW   *Experiences 363*

Conductors

The term *conductor* is usually given to any substance that permits an easy flow of electricity. Metals are by far the best conductors of electricity, and so they are commonly used for wires. Although several of the precious metals are better conductors, copper is most often used, as it is comparable in efficiency and yet cheap enough to produce in quantity.

We often hear the term *nonconductor* for materials such as rubber, glass, plastic, cloth, and other nonmetallic substances. This is misleading, as almost anything will conduct electricity if given enough voltage. These materials are better called poor conductors, or *insulators.*

This is why electricians may wear rubber gloves, and electric wires are covered with cloth, plastic, or rubber. It also explains why appliance plugs are covered with rubber or plastic, and glass separators are used on power line poles to keep apart high voltage lines.

Some poor conductors become good conductors when wet. Pure, or distilled, water is a poor conductor, but when dissolved minerals are added it becomes a fairly good one. Wet human skin is a far better conductor than dry skin. For this reason, it is safer to turn appliances on and off with dry hands.

Resistance

Although metals conduct electricity much better than nonmetals, there is still some resistance in metal wire to the flow of electrons. Of course, the longer the wire, the greater will be the resistance.

You may have experienced the gradual dimming of lights in a theater or adjusted the brightness of dashboard lights in an automobile. The change in both cases may have been caused by a *rheostat,* or dimmer switch. One kind of rheostat increases or decreases the length of wire through which electric current flows, thereby increasing or decreasing the wire's resistance. A simple model is shown in Figure 12-6.

Some metals have so much resistance to the flow of electricity that they glow brightly when there is enough electrical pressure or voltage to force relatively large quantities of electricity to flow in them. Unfortunately, most metals melt or evaporate within a short period of time when hot enough to give off light.

This caused a long search by Thomas Edison for materials to be used as bulb filaments before he was able to find reasonable success. Some of the materials he tried reveal the exhaustive character of the search. Bamboo slivers, sewing thread, even human hair, were carbonized and tested!

Tungsten, sometimes called wolfram, is the metal used in *incandescent* bulbs today. (Any bulb that gives light from a very hot filament is called an incandescent bulb.) With a melting point of almost 3,400°C (6,200°F), tungsten is well able to withstand the temperature caused by the movement of electricity through its highly resistant structure. An inactive gas, such as argon, is pumped into the bulbs to help prevent the burning away of the filament. Still, some of the tungsten evaporates eventually, and the filament separates, breaking the circuit. The ever-darkening appearance of the portion of the bulb next to the filament shows the deposition of the evaporating tungsten.

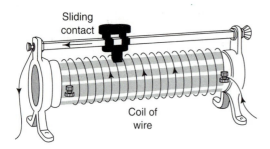

FIGURE 12-6

A simple rheostat, or dimmer switch.

Electric heaters also have wires of highly resistant metal. Most heaters today use nichrome wire, a combination of nickel and chromium.

So far, you have seen that length and composition of wire affect resistance to the flow of electricity. Another factor is the diameter of the wire. An analogy here will help explain why size of wire affects resistance. Imagine part of a large crowd in a sports stadium converging into a narrow passageway. As some of the people begin to enter the passageway, the forward speed of the crowd slackens. At the end of the passageway, the forward pace again picks up.

A thick wire presents a broad pathway for the flow of electricity. A narrow wire constricts the flow. In the "effort" to crowd through the narrow pathway, much friction is created, and the wire grows hot. If thin enough, and when made of material such as tungsten, it can also produce much light as it glows.

Most devices that produce heat—such as heaters, toasters, and electric irons—have relatively thin, long, highly resistant wires. The wires cannot be as narrow in diameter as a light filament—one reason is that they are exposed to the open air and would rapidly evaporate—but they are relatively thin compared to other wires designed to carry a similar voltage.

It would be helpful when teaching electricity to collect some real examples of toasters and heaters for children to observe and take

apart. Discarded electric irons, toasters, and heaters can often be gotten free of charge from electrical repair shops. (It is prudent to cut off the plugs of these devices before examining them, so pupils will not be tempted to plug them in.)

Circuit Hazards

You have seen that when bulbs or appliances are wired into a circuit, they show resistance to the flow of electrical energy. At the place where the energy enters these resistors, a change of energy takes place—some of the electrical energy changes into heat (if it enters a heater) or light (bulb) or sound (radio) or motion (motor). In other words, a significant amount of electrical energy is "used up," or changed.

Suppose, though, there is no resistor connected in the circuit. Because the copper wire has relatively low resistance, a great surge of electricity flows through the wire. The wire now heats up rapidly, even though it normally offers little resistance to a current.

Short Circuits

In house and commercial circuits, intense heating of the wires may come from a "short" circuit. This may happen when two bare wires touch each other, preventing the main supply of current from flowing through the resistor. Since the resistor is largely bypassed, a huge amount of electricity flows.

A common cause of short circuits happens when an appliance cord is placed under a heavily traveled rug. If the insulation between the two internal wires wears away, they may touch and a "short" may develop. A circuit is not necessarily shortened in length for a "short" circuit to occur. The essential thing is that the resistor is bypassed.

Overloaded Circuits

Overloading a circuit is perhaps an even more frequent cause of wires overheating.

Many older houses, for example, were wired when only a few of today's common appliances were widely used. Small-diameter, lightly insulated wires were formerly adequate. But as more and more of today's appliances are plugged in, intense heating occurs that is a potential source of fire.

Fuses and Circuit Breakers

Fuses and circuit breakers protect us from the fire hazard. In some older houses, a screw-in-type fuse contains a narrow metal strip that melts at a fairly low temperature. When a fuse is placed in a circuit, the electricity must travel through the strip. Should the wire heat up dangerously, the strip melts and the circuit opens, thereby shutting off the current.

Occasionally, someone will replace a burned-out fuse with a penny to avoid the "inconvenience" of another fuse burning out. Unfortunately, if the source of the problem is not corrected, the wires may grow so hot that the house may catch fire. An acceptable fuse has two requirements: It must be a good conductor, and it must have a relatively low melting point. A penny meets only the first requirement!

A bimetallic strip circuit breaker is used instead of a fuse in many houses. This consists of two thin, metal ribbons fused together. The ribbons are made of two different metals. When placed in a circuit and heated, the bimetallic strip bends away from one of the contact points, opening the circuit. The bending is the result of different expansion rates of the metals.

Another modern type of circuit breaker works because any wire containing current electricity generates some magnetism. Increasing the supply of current has the effect of increasing the magnetism. When a movable steel rod is enclosed in a coil of wire placed in a circuit, it may be pulled upward as the current (and so magnetism) increases. If the rod is connected to a contact point, its upward movement will result in

the circuit being opened. A spring catch that can be reset by hand prevents the rod from dropping down again. An electromagnetic device that operates this way is called a solenoid.

[4] ELECTROMAGNETS
Experiences 369

In 1820, a professor of physics at Copenhagen made a discovery that opened up for development one of the most useful devices ever conceived—the electromagnet. *Hans Christian Oersted* had believed for years that there was a relationship between magnetism and electricity. Despite much research, Oersted had not succeeded in discovering a useful connection between these phenomena. One day, while lecturing to a class, he noticed that a wire carrying electric current was deflecting a nearby compass needle. Oersted realized immediately that the wire was generating a magnetic field. His later experiments, writings, and lectures helped spread to the world the new concept of electromagnetism.

The telephone, electric motor, and many other tools of modern living had their origin in Oersted's work and related discoveries. Consider some of these devices now.

Electric Bell

An electric bell or a buzzer operates because its electric current is "interrupted," or continually turned off and on. Figure 12-7 shows how this happens. Follow the current as it moves from the battery into the bell. When the current flows around into the two electromagnets, they pull the metal clapper, which rings the bell. The act of moving the clapper breaks the circuit at the contact point, and the electricity stops flowing. The clapper then springs back into place and current flows again to repeat the cycle.

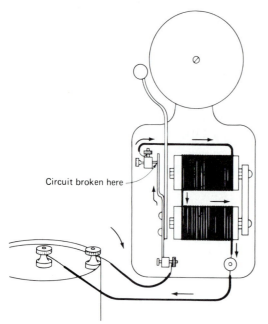

Circuit broken here

FIGURE 12-7
An electric bell or buzzer.

The Telephone

Figure 12-8 shows how the telephone works. Notice the complete, or closed, circuit between the transmitter and receiver. When we speak into the transmitter, a very thin metal diaphragm vibrates from sounds we make. The diaphragm variably squeezes the carbon granules behind it. Loud sounds, for example, squeeze the granules more tightly than soft sounds. This makes the granules conduct variable electrical pulses rather than a steady current.

The electrical impulses rather than the voice itself are transmitted in the wire. So they are able to travel to the other telephone's receiver almost instantly rather than at the much slower speed of sound. As the variable electric current reaches the receiver, it also causes the electromagnets to pull the diaphragm in a variable way. This sets the diaphragm vibrating in the same manner as the first one, and sounds are created.

To summarize, sound energy is used to vary electric energy at one end, which is then used to make sound energy at the other end.

Electric Motor

You may know it is possible to rotate a suspended bar magnet with a second bar magnet. This is because unlike poles attract each other, and like poles repel each other. The suspended magnet is rotated by alternately attracting and repelling each pole. To do this, you twist the bar magnet you are holding so the poles are attracted at first and then repelled. If timed properly, the suspended magnet will rotate smoothly.

You can demonstrate a similar technique with an electromagnet. However, you will not need to twist it to make the suspended magnet rotate.

Figure 12-9 shows how to proceed. First, find the pole on the electromagnet that is the opposite of the bar magnet's nearer pole. It will attract the bar magnet. Next, reverse the way you touch the terminals on the battery. This

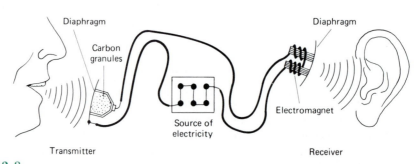

Diaphragm
Carbon granules
Source of electricity
Transmitter
Diaphragm
Electromagnet
Receiver

FIGURE 12-8
A telephone circuit.

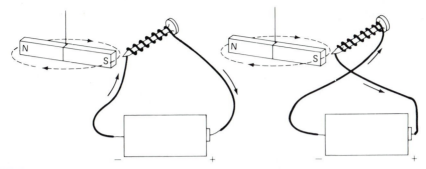

FIGURE 12-9
You can get a bar magnet to spin by alternately reversing the way you touch
the wire ends of an electromagnet to a battery's terminals.

will also reverse the poles on the electromagnet. The nearer pole of the bar magnet will now be repelled. Rotate the suspended magnet smoothly by touching the battery terminals first one way, then the opposite way. (A child can hold the electromagnet in one fixed position while you do this.)

In an electric motor, the electromagnet spins. A device reverses the current automatically, which continually reverses the poles of the electromagnet. The electromagnet spins because it is first attracted to, and then repelled from, another magnet inside. An electric motor is really a spinning electromagnet.

[5] GENERATING ELECTRICITY   *Experiences 372*

Electricity can be generated in several ways. First, we will consider how to produce static electricity, then current electricity, and last, electromagnetic waves that can be sent to various places without wires.

Static Electricity

Not all electricity is useful. Almost everyone has experienced some form of *static electricity:* the crackling sound of hair when it is combed after having been washed and dried; the slight shock felt when a metal door knob is touched after scuffing across a rug; the flash of lightning that briefly illuminates a darkened sky. In each case, an electric charge appears to build up on an object and then stay there (hence, the name static) until a conductor provides a route through which the charge can escape. Although forms of static electricity vary considerably, their causes are similar. To understand these causes, it will be helpful for us to peer briefly into the makeup of molecules and atoms.

We know that most matter is made up of *molecules.* A molecule is the smallest bit of any substance that retains the chemical properties of that substance. If we subdivide the molecule further, it no longer resembles the original substance; we have arrived at the atomic level.

Only two of the particles of which an atom is composed need concern us here: *electrons* and *protons.* Each of these particles has a tiny electric charge that is the opposite of the other. The electron's charge is called a *negative charge* and the proton's charge a *positive charge.*

In their "normal" state, atoms have as many electrons as protons. Because these particles attract each other with equal force, they balance or neutralize each other. The atom is said to be *neutral,* or uncharged. But electrons are easily dislodged or torn away from atoms by rubbing and other means.

When neutral, unlike materials are rubbed together, one tends to lose electrons to the other. For example, when a hard rubber rod is rubbed with a wool cloth, the cloth loses some of its electrons to the rod. This gives the cloth a positive charge and the rod a negative charge. When a glass rod is rubbed with silk, however, scientists have found that some electrons leave the glass and go onto the silk cloth. This gives the silk a negative charge and the glass a positive charge.

Although almost any unlike materials rubbed together will produce some static electricity, the best common materials to work with are hard rubber (comb) and plastic (picnic utensils), and wool, nylon, or other synthetic fabrics.

The basic law of static electricity is *like charges repel and unlike charges attract each other.* Children may discover that identical objects rubbed with the same material will repel each other. If the objects are rubbed with different materials, they will usually attract each other.

What causes lightning? It is produced by friction. A cloud contains varying amounts of dust particles, rain drops, air (gas) molecules, and sometimes ice crystals. When violent currents occur in clouds, these substances rub together in various combinations. If a huge electric charge is built up, it may be attracted by an oppositely charged cloud or the ground. When this happens, we see lightning. (Thunder results when the air through which lightning passes quickly heats up and cools. The rapid expansion and contraction of the air forces air molecules to smash together, which causes loud sounds.)

Current Electricity

Static electricity is both unreliable and hard to manage, so we use current electricity to meet our needs. This generally comes from two sources: batteries and huge power plants of several kinds.

Children are curious about how a battery can "make" electricity. Some think it is stored as water is stored in a tank. What really happens is that chemical energy changes into electrical energy.

This is how an automobile battery works. When two different metal strips—zinc and copper, for example—are placed in an acid, both strips begin to slowly dissolve. However, the zinc dissolves faster than the copper. A surplus of electrons from the dissolving parts of the zinc strip builds up on the rest of the strip, giving it a strong negative charge. Some electrons are also released at the slower-dissolving copper strip, but these go into the acid, leaving the copper strip with a positive charge. If we connect the end of one strip to the end of another strip with a wire, a continuous circuit is set up. Electrons flow from the zinc strip through the wire to the copper strip. If we connect a bulb in this circuit, it lights; a connected starter starts an automobile engine.

Many pairs of dissimilar metal strips, or *electrodes,* can be used to get this effect, and other liquids besides acid can work to release and hold electrons. Such liquids are called *electrolytes.*

A "dry" cell or flashlight battery works in a similar way to the "wet" cell just described. A moist, pastelike electrolyte is used in place of a liquid. The electrodes are most commonly a carbon rod, found in the center of the cell, and a zinc cylinder, which surrounds the paste and rod.

Dry cells are convenient, but they are too weak and expensive for widespread home or commercial use. Mechanical energy—the energy of motion—is by far the main method for generating electricity. Today, most electricity is produced by changing the energy in fuels and falling water.

In hydroelectric power plants, water falls on the blades of huge wheels, causing them to revolve. Other power plants may use oil, coal, natural gas, or atomic energy to heat water into the steam. The steam forces giant turbines to whirl. In both cases, large magnets are spun rapidly inside a wire coil, or the reverse, inducing electrons to flow into the wire.

Current electricity may be generated in additional ways. For example, when sunlight strikes certain light-sensitive materials called *solar cells,* some current is produced. However, these and other promising methods await further advances in technology and lower costs before they are widely adopted.

Producing Electromagnetic Waves

You know that a steady electric current produces a weak magnetic field around a wire. This is why we can make an electromagnet. Long ago, scientists learned that by rapidly varying the electric current in a wire they could change the magnetic field. Instead of a steady field, rapidly vibrating energy waves were given off by the wire. These are called *radio waves.*

At a radio station, music or voice vibrations are changed into a variable electric current. The method is like that used in a telephone transmitter. The vibrating current is strengthened until strong radio waves are given off by the wire carrying the current.

The waves are beamed off in all directions from a tall tower. Some of the waves strike a radio antenna. A weak current begins vibrating in the antenna, and the current is picked up and strengthened in the radio. A connected loudspeaker vibrates and produces sound energy much like a telephone receiver.

About one hundred years ago in Germany, Heinrich Hertz discovered how to produce radio waves by using electric sparks. In an upcoming investigation, pupils can use a flashlight cell and a wire for the same purpose. Brushing a battery terminal with the free end of a connected wire creates tiny sparks (usually visible only in some darkness) and an uneven flow of current. Weak radio waves are produced that shoot outward at the speed of light. The waves are received as static on a nearby radio.

INVESTIGATIONS & ACTIVITIES

SECTION 1
Closed and Open Circuits
[*Background 338*]

■ INVESTIGATION: How to Make a Bulb Light

Have you ever used a flashlight? The electricity to light the bulb comes from one or more batteries. You don't need a flashlight to make the bulb light. You can do it with a single wire and a battery.

EXPLORATORY PROBLEM

How can you light a flashlight bulb with a wire and a battery?

NEEDED

D-size battery   2 wires, 15 centimeters (6 inches) long
two flashlight bulbs   paper and pencil

TRY THIS

1. Remove the insulation from both ends of the wire.

2. Put the bulb bottom on the raised button end of the battery. (See Figure 12-10.)

FIGURE 12-10

3. Touch one wire end to the metal side of the bulb.

4. Touch the other wire end to the battery bottom.

DISCOVERY PROBLEMS

experimenting **A.** How many other ways can you light the bulb? Keep a record of what you do. Make drawings.

predicting **B.** Study each of the drawings in Figure 12-11. Which ways will light the bulb? Which will not? Record what you think. Then find out.

experimenting **C.** How many ways can you light a bulb with two wires? (Use one battery.) Record what you do.

experimenting **D.** How many ways can you light two bulbs with two wires? (Use one battery.) Record what you do.

TEACHING COMMENT

Use number 22 or 24 bell wire, available at most hardware or electrical supply stores. Be sure that the plastic covering is stripped well back from both ends of the wire to ensure good contact. The D-size flashlight cell is most often used, but other sizes also work well.

Probably most children will need a partner when working with two bulbs or wires. It is hard for one pair of hands to connect everything.

Caution: Advise pupils to quickly notice, and discontinue trying a connection, if the wire they use to connect the bulb and battery begins to get warm. This happens when the bulb (resistor) is bypassed and the wire ends touch only the battery terminals—a type of short circuit. A short quickly wears down a battery and, if continued for some time, may make the wire uncomfortably hot.

GENERALIZATION

Electricity flows when there is a complete circuit; there are several ways to light a bulb.

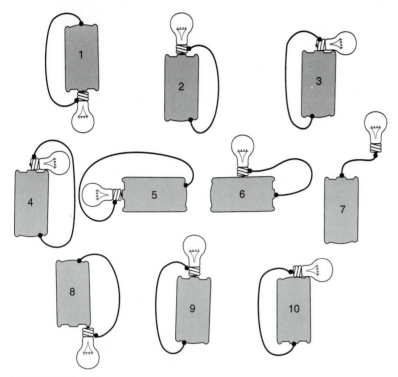

FIGURE 12-11

SAMPLE PERFORMANCE OBJECTIVES

Process: The child can connect a battery and bulb with wire in several different ways to light the bulb.

Knowledge: The child can describe the bulb and battery parts that must be connected for a bulb to light.

FOR YOUNGER CHILDREN

Many younger pupils can do the exploratory activity and, in a limited way, Discovery Problems A and B. However, they may have some trouble in manipulating the materials.

□ ACTIVITY: How Many Bulbs Can You Light with Only One Battery?

NEEDED

flashlight bulbs   D-size battery
bare wire   pencil
scissors   partner

See if you can light more than three bulbs. Use only one or two wires, bulbs without holders, and one battery. Figure 12-12 shows one way to light at least three bulbs.

FIGURE 12-12

TRY THIS

1. Make three single loops in a small bare wire. Bend the wire once around a pencil to make each loop. Screw or push the bulbs into the loops.
2. Touch the connected bulbs to the metal top of the battery.
3. Get a second small bare wire. Touch one end to the battery bottom. Touch the other end to the metal side of one of the bulbs.
   a. How many more bulbs can you light in this way?
   b. How else, using only these materials, can you light more bulbs?

(*Teaching Comment:* About twice as many bulbs may be lighted than shown in Figure 12-12 with this method. Pupils will enjoy a contest to see which team can light the most bulbs at one time. Rules can limit the materials as presently suggested. If the bulb supply is limited, teams can propose models by drawing them on the chalkboard. After an evaluative discussion, models with promise can be tested one at a time.)

□ ACTIVITY: How Can You Make Some Paper-Clip Switches?

NEEDED

flashlight bulb   sticky tape
bulb holder   scissors

D-size battery   two paper clips
cardboard   six paper fasteners
five small wires

TRY THIS

1. Cut a small piece of cardboard. Punch two holes in it and put in two paper fasteners as in Figure 12-13.

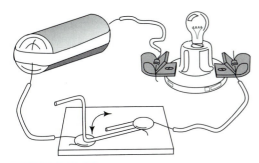

FIGURE 12-13

2. Strip bare the ends of the wires with scissors. Assemble the rest of the materials as shown. Bend a paper clip for the switch.
   a. What happens when you move the switch on and off the paper fastener? How does this switch work in the circuit?

3. Suppose you have a stairway light. You need to control it from both upstairs and downstairs. Make a pair of switches now to control a single light. Do it as in Figure 12-14.
   b. What happens when you move each switch from one paper fastener head to another? What would happen if there was only a single wire between the two switches? How do these switches work?

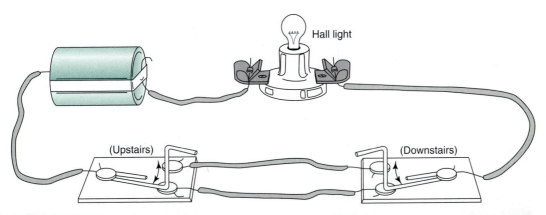

FIGURE 12-14

(*Teaching Comment:* You might suggest that pairs of pupils work the two switches in step 3 in a role-playing way: "I'm downstairs. I want to go upstairs, so I turn on the stairway light from the downstairs switch." For the light to work properly, all connections need to be tight. Be sure the paper fasteners are securely seated and the wires are stripped of insulation where contact is made.)

SECTION 2
Series and Parallel Circuits
[Background 340]

■ INVESTIGATION: Series Circuits

What does the word *series* mean to you? To most people, it means placing things in order, one thing ahead or behind the next one. Electric bulbs may be set up in a series circuit.

EXPLORATORY PROBLEM

How can you set up a series circuit?

NEEDED

three flashlight bulbs   four wires
three bulb holders   two D-size batteries

TRY THIS

1. Remove the insulation from the ends of each wire with scissors.
2. Use two bulbs and bulb holders, two batteries, and three wires. Set up the circuit as shown in Figure 12-15.

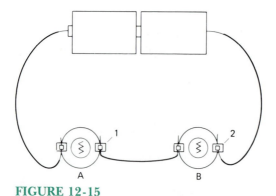

FIGURE 12-15

DISCOVERY PROBLEMS

predicting   **A.** Suppose you remove light A. What will happen to B? If you remove B, what will happen to A?

predicting   **B.** Suppose you disconnect the wire at place 1. What do you think will happen to light A? light B?

predicting   **C.** Suppose you disconnect the wire at place 2. What will happen to light A? B?

observing   **D.** Add another bulb to the series. Use one more wire, bulb, and bulb holder. What, if anything, happens to the lights?

inferring   **E.** How can you explain the results in A through D? That is, how does electricity seem to flow in a series circuit?

TEACHING COMMENT

PREPARATION AND BACKGROUND

If any wire or bulb is disconnected, all the bulbs go out. This is because all of the electricity flows through each connected part in a series circuit. For the same reason, adding more bulbs to the circuit causes all the lighted bulbs to get dimmer. Each resistor cuts down the available flow of electricity.

GENERALIZATION

In a series circuit, all the electricity flows through each connected part.

SAMPLE PERFORMANCE OBJECTIVES

Knowledge: The child can set up a working series circuit with two or more bulbs.
Process: The child can predict the effect on other parts of a series circuit when one or more parts are disconnected.

■ INVESTIGATION: Parallel Circuits

What does the word *parallel* mean to you? To most people, it means placing things side by side. Electric wires are set up side by side in a parallel circuit.

EXPLORATORY PROBLEM

How can you set up a parallel circuit?

NEEDED

three flashlight bulbs   six wires
three bulb holders   two D-size batteries

TRY THIS

1. Remove the insulation from the ends of each wire with scissors.

2. Use two batteries, two bulbs and bulb holders, and four wires. Set up the circuit as shown in Figure 12-16.

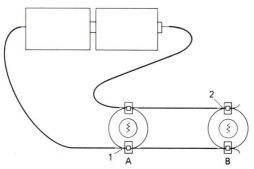

FIGURE 12-16

DISCOVERY PROBLEMS

predicting

A. Suppose you remove light A. What will happen to B? If you remove B, what will happen to A?

predicting

B. Suppose you disconnect the wire at place 1. What do you think will happen to light A? B?

predicting

C. Suppose you disconnect the wire at place 2. What will happen to light A? B?

observing

D. Add another bulb to the circuit. Use two more wires, a bulb, and bulb holder. What, if anything, happens to the brightness of the lights?

inferring

E. How can you explain the results in A through D? That is, how does electricity seem to flow in a parallel circuit?

TEACHING COMMENT

PREPARATION AND BACKGROUND

In a parallel circuit, the wires are arranged to bypass a burned-out or missing light. Therefore, adding more bulbs to the circuit does not noticeably affect bulb brightness. Each bulb beyond the next receives the same flow of electricity. But all bulbs must have the same resistance to burn equally bright.

GENERALIZATION

In a parallel circuit, the electricity flows both to and around each connected bulb.

SAMPLE PERFORMANCE OBJECTIVES

Knowledge: The child can set up a working parallel circuit with two or more bulbs.
Process: The child can predict the effect on other parts of a parallel circuit when one or more parts are disconnected.

■ INVESTIGATION: Hidden Parts of Electric Circuits

Suppose you have a folder like that shown in Figure 12-17. Notice the four holes on the front cover. Each hole has aluminum foil underneath, so each looks the same. Now, look at the back of the front cover. A foil strip goes from hole 1 to hole 3. It conducts electricity like a wire. However, only small pieces cover holes 2 and 4.

Suppose you do not know where the strip is, and you cannot open the folder.

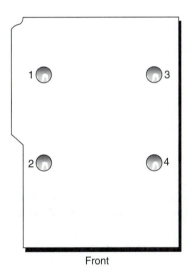
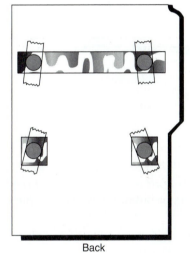

Front   Back

FIGURE 12-17

EXPLORATORY PROBLEM

How can you test for and find the hidden strip?

NEEDED

paper punch   D-size battery
manila folder   aluminum foil
sticky tape   ruler
pencil   scissors
two 30-centimeter (12-inch) wires flashlight bulb

TRY THIS

1. First prepare your own folder. Cut a regular-size folder in half, the shorter way. (Save half for later use.)

2. Punch four holes and cover them with foil as in Figure 12-17. Fasten the foil with sticky tape. Number the holes on the cover.

3. Now prepare your tester as in Figure 12-18. Bare the ends of two wires. Tape the ends to a battery. Bend one of the opposite wire ends into a loop. Wrap the other end around the bulb base and twist it to hold it fast.

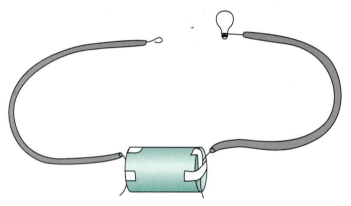

FIGURE 12-18

4. Touch the bulb bottom to the looped end of the other wire. If the bulb lights, you are ready to test your folder.

5. Press the bulb bottom into one hole. Press the wire loop into another hole. Test these pairs of holes; see which completes the circuit and lights the bulb:
1–2   2–3   3–4
1–3   2–4
1–4

DISCOVERY PROBLEMS

A. Suppose you have tested another folder. Here are the results:

Paired Holes	Bulb Lights
1–2	yes
1–3	no
1–4	yes
2–3	no
2–4	yes
3–4	no

inferring

experimenting

Let's say there are two strips connecting holes. How do you think they are arranged? Is more than one way possible? Make drawings of your ideas. Then, prepare a folder and test your ideas.

inferring **B.** Can you test and find out how different folders are "wired"? Have others prepare hidden circuits for you. (You can do the same for them.) Keep a record of your results and what you think. Then, open each folder to check.

TEACHING COMMENT

PREPARATION AND BACKGROUND

In this case, the foil strip conductor is hidden and stretches between two holes. Touching the bulb bottom and the free wire end to the strip completes the circuit, allowing electricity to flow. The free wire end is bent into a loop to avoid gouging the foil.

In Discovery Problem A, three combinations of connections are possible with two foil strips:

```
1|    3          1 \  3          1 \  3
2|___ 4          2 __\ 4         2 |  \ 4
```

Each should be considered correct because each yields identical results.

Abstract thinking ability is required in this investigation. Probably only children in the late concrete stage and formal stage of mental operations can go far with Discovery Problem B. But for those who can, it may be one of the most interesting learning experiences you can offer.

GENERALIZATION

Parts of an electric circuit may be inferred from tests if the wires are hidden.

SAMPLE PERFORMANCE OBJECTIVES

Process: The child can use a circuit tester to connect hidden wires and infer the location of the wires.
Knowledge: The child can explain that a bulb lights when an electric circuit is completed in any of several combinations of connections.

☐ ACTIVITY: How Can You Make an Electric Question Board?

NEEDED

insulated wire	scissors
fourteen paper fasteners	bulb and bulb holder
sticky tape	battery
small file cards	ruler and pencil
heavy cardboard 35 × 45 centimeters	thumb tacks
(14 × 18 inches)	

TRY THIS

1. Use a ruler. Mark seven evenly spaced marks on each side of the board as shown in Figure 12-19.

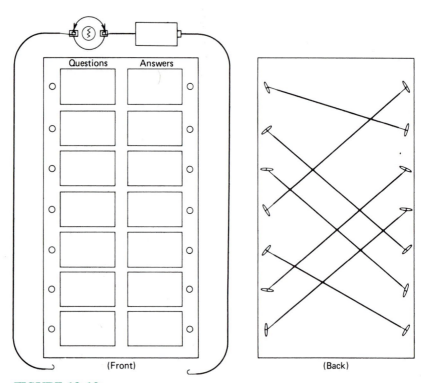

FIGURE 12-19

2. Place the board on the floor. Punch a small hole through each mark with scissors. Stick paper fasteners into the holes.

3. Turn over the board. Cut wires of different lengths to connect pairs of fasteners. Bare the wire ends.

4. Wrap each wire end around a paper fastener and secure it.

5. Make a circuit tester like that shown in Figure 12-19.

6. Touch each end of the tester to the paired fasteners. If a wire is securely connected to each pair, the tester bulb should light. Test each pair, one fastener on each side, as connected.

7. Prepare question and answer cards. Fasten them to the board with thumb tacks at the proper places.

(*Teaching Comment:* For convenience and durability, the paper fastener terminals may be replaced by threaded bolts and Fahnestock clips secured by nuts. This will allow an easy interchange of the wires should pupils quickly memorize positions of the paired terminals. The board is ideal for reviewing questions and answers in science, mathematics, geography, and other subjects.)

☐ ACTIVITY: How Can You Make an Electric "Nerve Tester" Game?

NEEDED

60 centimeters (2 feet) of bare copper bell wire   clay
number 22 or 24 insulated wire   flashlight bulb
sticky tape   bulb holder
heavy cardboard   scissors

TRY THIS

1. Put two lumps of clay on some cardboard as shown in Figure 12-20.

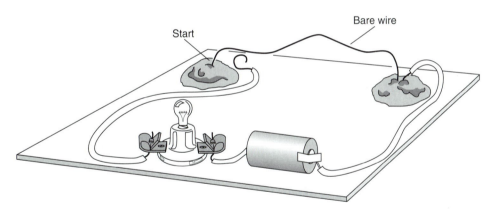

FIGURE 12-20

2. Bend the heavy bare copper wire as shown. Stick each end into a clay lump.

3. Cut three pieces of the lighter insulated wire as shown. Bare the ends.

4. Attach the three wires to the bulb holder and battery. Attach the free end of the battery wire to the end of the heavy wire. Twist it around and push the twisted wires slightly into the clay.

5. Bend the free end of the light bulb wire around a pencil to make a slightly open loop. Touch the loop end to the heavy wire. See if the light goes on.

6. To play the game, carefully place the open loop over the heavy wire so the wire is inside the loop. Move the loop from one end to the other and back without touching the heavy wire. If it touches, the light will go on. The person who lights the bulb least often wins.

a. Who has the steadiest nerves in the class?

b. How does practice help?

c. Is your left hand shakier than your right hand?

d. Are people shakier before or after lunch? What other things might affect how shaky people are?

e. How can you explain this circuit to someone?

(*Teaching Comment:* Any single-strand, somewhat stiff wire will serve for the heavier wire. Even a piece cut from a wire coat hanger will work if the paint is sanded off. To make the bulb light more brightly when the wire is touched, use two batteries in series.)

□ ACTIVITY: How Can You Make a Two-Way Blinker System?

NEEDED

two flashlight bulbs and holders	four large tacks
two small wooden blocks	hammer
thin aluminum pie pan	scissors
sticky tape	6 meters (7 yards) of wire
D-size battery	partner

TRY THIS

1. Cut three short pieces of wire and two equally long wires as shown in Figure 12-21. Bare the ends of all five wires.

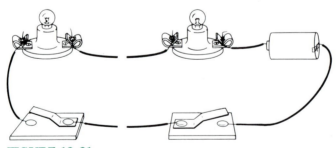

FIGURE 12-21

2. Cut 2 strips 10 centimeters (4 inches) long from the pie pan. Attach the strips, wires, and battery as shown. Use tape to fasten wires to the battery. Use a hammer to pound in the tacks.

3. To send dot-dash signals, press the key a short or longer time. The second key must be held down by your partner while you are sending a message. Both lights will flash on and off as signals are sent.

4. Try using part of the International Morse code to send signals:

A	B	C	D	E	F
.—	—...	—.—.	—..	.	..—.
G	**H**	**I**	**J**	**K**	**L**
— —.	....	..	.— — —	—.—	.—..
M	**N**	**O**	**P**	**Q**	**R**
— —	—.	— — —	.— —.	— —.—	.—.
S	**T**	**U**	**V**	**W**	**X**
...	—	..—	...—	.— —	—..—
Y	**Z**				
—.— —	— —..				

a. What messages can you send and receive?

b. How can you send clearer messages? Talk it over with your partner and then decide.

(*Teaching Comment:* If both lights are dim, add a second battery in series, if only one bulb is dim, replace it with another that matches the bright bulb.)

SECTION 3
Conditions Affecting Electrical Flow
[*Background 343*]

■ INVESTIGATION: Materials That Conduct Electricity

You know electricity can travel through a wire, but how about other materials?

EXPLORATORY PROBLEM

How can you find out which materials conduct electricity?

NEEDED

small wooden objects	pencil
small glass objects	flashlight (D-size) battery
small metal objects	sticky tape
small plastic objects	flashlight bulb
small rubber objects	two 30-centimeter (or 12-inch) wires

TRY THIS

1. Arrange your materials as shown in Figure 12-22, except for the key. Bare both ends of each wire. Be sure the wire is wrapped tightly around the bulb base by twisting the end.

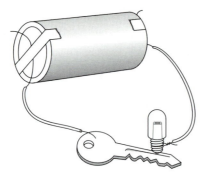

FIGURE 12-22

2. Touch the bulb bottom to the end of the other wire. If the bulb lights, you are ready to test materials.

3. Get some objects to test, such as a key. Touch the bulb bottom to one part. Touch the end of the other wire to another part. If the bulb lights, the object is a conductor of electricity. If it does not light, the object is a nonconductor.

DISCOVERY PROBLEMS

observing

communicating

A. What, if any, rubber objects are conductors? plastic objects? metal objects? wooden objects? glass objects? Make a chart such as the following to record your findings:

Object	Made From	Conductor	Nonconductor
Key	metal	X	
And so on			

observing

B. Some objects are made of several materials. With a pencil you can test wood, paint, metal, rubber, and "lead" (graphite). Which of these will conduct electricity?

observing

C. Look around the room. What other objects can you test that are made of several materials?

inferring

D. Make your conductor tester more powerful. Use two batteries end to end. (Have someone hold them together.) Test some materials again. How do these results compare with your first results?

TEACHING COMMENT

PREPARATION AND BACKGROUND

If the bulb is to operate properly, the wire wrapped around the bulb base should be twisted tightly for good contact. If the wire is insulated, be sure the insulation is stripped well back from the ends of the wires. Use number 22 or 24 wire.

GENERALIZATION

Metals are usually good conductors of electricity; most other solid materials are nonconductors or poor conductors.

SAMPLE PERFORMANCE OBJECTIVES

Process: The child can classify materials as electrical conductors or nonconductors after testing them with an electrical circuit.
Knowledge: Shown new materials, the child can predict which will, or will not, conduct electricity.

□ **ACTIVITY:**   How Well Does Flashlight Battery Electricity Work in "Real" Wires?

NEEDED

D-size battery   flashlight bulb
old extension cord   scissors

TRY THIS

1. Cut the plugs off the cord ends.
2. Separate the wires in each cord end partway. Scrape off the insulation.
3. Attach the bared wires to a battery and bulb as shown in Figure 12-23.

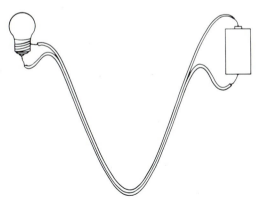

FIGURE 12-23

a. What happens? How are the results like or unlike what you expected?
b. How might shortening the wire affect the light?
c. What results will you get with other wires used for electric appliances? For example, what is the longest wire you can use to light a bulb with one

battery? How does thickness of the wire affect the light? What difference does it make if a wire is a single solid piece or if it has twisted strands?

(*Teaching Comment:* The bulb may not light with some long or thick wires unless two or more batteries are used in series. Caution pupils that experimenting with appliance wires is safe with flashlight batteries but not with house current.)

■ INVESTIGATION: How To Measure Bulb Brightness

Have you noticed that a bulb burns less brightly as a battery wears down? A bulb's brightness can help you know how fresh a battery is.

EXPLORATORY PROBLEM

How can you measure the brightness of a lit flashlight bulb?

NEEDED

two sheets of paper

wire 30 centimeters (12 inches) long

several batteries of the same size (D)

flashlight bulbs

partner

pencil

TRY THIS

1. Have a partner light a bulb with one battery and wire.
2. Tear a small piece from a paper sheet.
3. Hold it tightly against the bulb. Can you see the glow through the paper? (See Figure 12-24.)
4. Tear off another piece of paper. Hold both pieces together tightly against the bulb. Can you still see the glow through the double thickness?
5. Keep adding pieces until you cannot see the bulb's glow.
6. Record the largest number of pieces through which you saw a glow.

DISCOVERY PROBLEMS

measuring

classifying

A. Get some batteries of the same size. How can you compare how strong each is? Can you put them in order from weakest to strongest? Record your findings.

predicting

communicating

B. How many times brighter will the bulb be with two batteries? Three batteries? Add batteries end to end. The raised button end of each battery should face the same way. Record your findings.

measuring

classifying

C. Get different flashlight bulbs. How can you compare how brightly each burns? Can you put them in order from dimmest to brightest? Record findings. Will someone else get the same results?

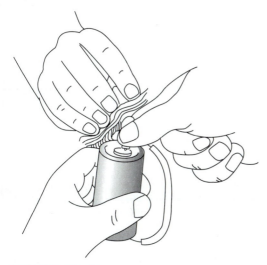

FIGURE 12-24

TEACHING COMMENT

PREPARATION AND BACKGROUND

The corner part of the pages in a notebook or book may be substituted for torn pieces of paper.

Most fresh D-size flashlight batteries can be interchanged and a given bulb will glow with no noticeable difference in brightness. However, as batteries wear down unevenly, the brightness is affected.

Batteries of different sizes may be bought that deliver the same degree of power to light the bulb as a D-size battery. But they will last for a longer or shorter time period, depending on their size. These are known as the number 6, number 912, number 914, AA, and C batteries. If available, let children test these also.

GENERALIZATION

The brightness of a flashlight bulb may vary because of its resistance to electricity and the power of the battery.

SAMPLE PERFORMANCE OBJECTIVES

Process: The child can measure the relative brightness of lighted flashlight bulbs.
Knowledge: When shown a lighted bulb that glows dimly, the child can explain that one reason for the dimness may be the weakness of the battery.

☐ ACTIVITY: How Long Will a Flashlight Battery Light a Bulb?

NEEDED

D-size battery	flashlight bulb and holder
sticky tape	two wires with bare ends

TRY THIS

1. Attach one wire to each end of the battery with tape.
2. Attach the free ends of the wires to the bulb holder. Be sure the bulb lights.
   a. How long will the battery light the bulb if used steadily? Keep a time record.
   b. Here are more things to test if you have more batteries. How long does a battery last if you give it "rest" periods? Does one brand of battery last longer? Do cheaper batteries last as long as expensive ones? Does battery size make a difference?
   c. What are some other things about batteries you might test?
   d. How can you test how long a bulb might last?

□ ACTIVITY: How Can You Make a Dimmer Switch?

NEEDED

graphite, or "lead," about 7 centimeters   circuit tester
  (3 inches), from a pencil   sticky tape

TRY THIS

1. Tape each end of the graphite to a table top.
2. Touch the bulb base of the tester to the graphite. Touch the wire end just next to it. The bulb should light.
3. Slowly, move the wire end of the tester along the graphite. Move it first away from the bulb, then back again as in Figure 12-25.

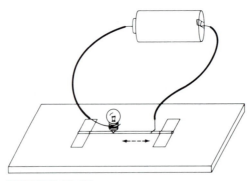

FIGURE 12-25

   a. What happens to the bulb brightness as the graphite connection gets longer? shorter?
   b. Where have you used dimmer switches at home or elsewhere?

(*Teaching Comment:* Graphite from either a mechanical or a cut-apart wooden pencil may be used. Graphite is resistant to electricity. If the tester bulb does not light, try adding one or two more batteries in series.)

☐ ACTIVITY: How Does a Fuse Work?

NEEDED

three D-size batteries	small piece of heavy cardboard
three short wires	two all-metal tacks
flashlight bulb and holder	foil from a gum wrapper
scissors	

TRY THIS

1. Prepare the fuse. Cut a piece from the gum wrapper about 4 centimeters (1½ inches) long and 0.5 centimeters (³⁄₁₆ inches) wide. Leave the paper attached to the foil. Cut a V-shaped nick in the middle of the piece, so there is barely any foil left.

2. Bare the ends of the wires. Also, bare a small section in the middle of two wires.

3. Set up the materials as shown in Figure 12-26.

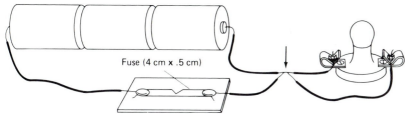

Fuse (4 cm x .5 cm)

FIGURE 12-26

4. Holding the insulated part of the wire, touch one bare wire part with the other. This makes a short circuit.
   a. What happens to the fuse? to the wires? to the light?
   b. Why do you think it is important to have a fuse in a house current?

SECTION 4
Electromagnets
[Background 345]

▪ INVESTIGATION: Electromagnets

Suppose you have some wire, a large nail, and a flashlight battery. With these materials you can make a magnet—an electromagnet.

EXPLORATORY PROBLEM

How can you make an electromagnet?

NEEDED

pencil	box of paper clips
2 meters (about 6 feet) of wire	partner
large iron nail	two flashlight batteries

TRY THIS

1. Get a large nail. Touch it to a paper clip to test the nail for magnetism. The nail should be free of magnetism to start.

2. Bare the wire ends. Wrap the wire tightly around the nail. Leave about ½ meter (1½ feet) of wire free at both ends.

3. Have your partner touch the bare wire ends to a battery. (See Figure 12-27.) Touch the nail end to some paper clips. How many paper clips does your electromagnet pick up?

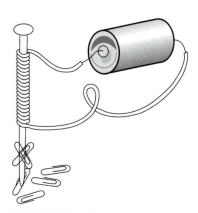

FIGURE 12-27

4. Have your partner move one wire away from the battery. What happens? (Note: do not leave the battery connected for more than 10 seconds each time.)

DISCOVERY PROBLEMS

observing   **A.** Which end of your electromagnet will pick up more clips?

experimenting   **B.** How can you change the strength of your electromagnet? Make a
communicating   record of what you try and the results.

predicting   What will happen if you wrap more wire around the nail?

predicting   What will happen if you take away the iron nail?

predicting   What will happen if you switch a pencil for the nail?

predicting   What will happen if you use an aluminum rod instead of the nail?

predicting   What will happen if you use two batteries end to end?

observing   **C.** Can an electromagnet attract anything a regular magnet cannot attract?

TEACHING COMMENT

PREPARATION AND BACKGROUND

Use number 22 or 24 bell wire insulated with plastic. Strip off some insulation at both ends so good contact can be made with the battery. The regular D-size flashlight battery works well. Be sure to advise children that the wires should be held to the battery no more than about 10 seconds without interruption. Otherwise, its power will be drained quickly. A 3- to 4-inch iron nail should be adequate for the core of the electromagnet. If possible, get a similar-sized rod of aluminum. It will present an interesting contrast if used in place of the nail.

Most of the materials attracted to an electromagnet fall when the electromagnet is disconnected from the battery. One paper clip or other light item may remain. This shows that there is some magnetism left in the nail.

GENERALIZATION

Electricity flowing through a wire acts like a magnet; its magnetic power can be increased in several ways.

SAMPLE PERFORMANCE OBJECTIVES

Process: The child can state at least one hypothesis about how an electromagnet's strength may be increased.
Knowledge: The child can demonstrate how an electromagnet works.

FOR YOUNGER CHILDREN

Some primary pupils will have trouble manipulating the materials. However, with help they should be able to do the Exploratory Problem and Discovery Problems A and C.

□ ACTIVITY: How Does an Electric Buzzer Work?

NEEDED

small, thick wooden block
thin steel pie pan
tinner's snips
two nails, one 6 centimeters (2½ inches),
   one 7 centimeters (2¾ inches)

3 meters (10 feet) of enameled
   magnet wire, number 22 size
hammer
two D-size batteries
large tack

TRY THIS

1. Pound the smaller nail partway into the block as shown in Figure 12-28.

2. Cut a 30-centimeter (1-foot) piece from the wire. Remove the insulation from the ends of both wires.

3. Wrap 100 turns of the longer wire evenly around the smaller nail. Leave some wire free at both ends.

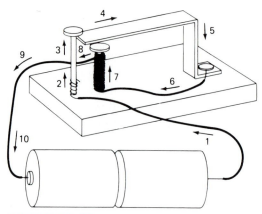

FIGURE 12-28

4. Cut a 2.5-centimeter (1-inch) by 20-centimeter (8-inch) strip from the steel pie pan. Bend it as shown. Attach it to the block with a large tack driven in partway.

5. Wrap two turns from the end of the longer wire around the tack. Now, pound in the tack all the way.

6. Pound in the larger nail where the metal strip ends. Make sure the tip of the strip touches the bottom of the larger nail head.

7. Take the smaller wire. Wrap one end tightly several times around the larger nail.

8. Touch the ends of the two wires to the two batteries placed end to end.
   a. Can you explain how the buzzer works? (For help, study the drawing.)
   b. If it does not work, what needed adjustments can you make?

(*Teaching Comment:* If the buzzer will not work, check all contact points. If the steel strip end sticks to the bottom nail head, the electromagnet is too strong. Use only one battery. If the strip is not pulled, connect two or three batteries in series. Also, bend the strip end down a little and tap down the top nail so the head touches again.)

SECTION 5
Generating Electricity
[*Background 347*]

■ INVESTIGATION: Static Electricity

When you comb your hair on a dry day, does it crackle and stick to the comb? Have you felt a shock when you touched something after crossing a carpet? These are examples of static electricity. You can get static electricity by rubbing different objects together.

EXPLORATORY PROBLEM

What objects can you rub together to produce static electricity?

NEEDED

plastic spoon and fork   paper and pencil
heavy string   rubber comb
piece of wool, nylon   sticky tape
plastic bag

TRY THIS

1. Attach string to the spoon with sticky tape. Attach it where the spoon balances. Hang the spoon from a table edge. Tape the string end to the table.

2. Hold the fork backward. Bring the fork handle near the hanging spoon handle, but don't touch it (Figure 12-29). Notice that probably nothing happens. So far, there is no static electricity.

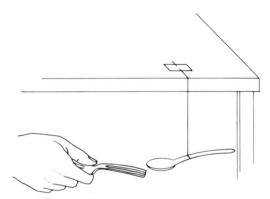

FIGURE 12-29

3. Rub each handle with some wool. Bring the fork handle near the spoon again. Watch what happens.

4. Rub one handle again with wool but the other with nylon. Watch what happens. (Static electricity may have either a positive [+] or a negative [−] charge. When two objects have the same charge, positive or negative, they *repel* or push each other away. When each has a different charge, they attract each other.)

DISCOVERY PROBLEMS

inferring   **A.** Did each object in step 3 have the same charge or different charges? How about in step 4?

observing   **B.** What happens when you rub the handles with different materials?
communicating   Which combinations make the handles repel? attract? Keep a careful record. To do so, you might set up a chart like this:

Fork Rubbed With	Spoon Rubbed With		
	Wool	Plastic	Nylon
Wool	Repel		
Plastic			
Nylon			

predicting   After you complete the first column, can you predict the remaining results?

experimenting   **C.** What results will you get if you substitute other objects for the plastic fork? For example, what happens if you rub a rubber comb with each material?

TEACHING COMMENT

BACKGROUND AND PREPARATION

Almost any plastic items may be substituted for the fork and spoon. The use of a heavy string will keep the suspended object from spinning too freely. Pupils will find that using an unlike material in Problem C will change their findings. Postpone this activity on rainy or especially humid days, as results will be less noticeable.

GENERALIZATION

Rubbing different materials together may produce static electricity. Like charges repel, and unlike charges attract, each other.

SAMPLE PERFORMANCE OBJECTIVES

Knowledge: The child can demonstrate that identical objects rubbed with different materials will develop unlike static charges.
Process: The child can use data on a simple chart to predict new data.

■ INVESTIGATION: A Way to Generate Electricity

Have you ever seen an electric generator in a power plant? Usually, a huge magnet spins and produces an electric current in a coil of wire. You can even produce a current by moving a small magnet in and out of a small coil of wire. But the current will not be enough to light a bulb. To tell that there is a current, you need a current detector, or *galvanometer.*

EXPLORATORY PROBLEM

How can you generate electricity and tell it is being produced?

NEEDED

12 meters (13 yards) of insulated wire   magnetic compass
two strong magnets (one stronger)   scissors
sticky tape

TRY THIS

1. Bare the wire ends with scissors.

2. Coil 50 turns of wire around your hand. Slip off the coil and fasten it in three places with sticky tape. This will keep the coil tight.

3. Wrap 20 turns of wire narrowly around the compass. This will be your galvanometer (Figure 12-30).

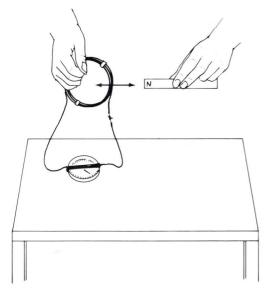

FIGURE 12-30

4. Twist the bare ends of the wire together to close the circuit.

5. Push a magnet end into the coil. See how the compass needle moves. Pull the magnet out of the coil. Watch again how the needle moves. This shows you have generated a current each time. The farther the needle moves, the stronger the current. (However, be sure the magnet is far enough from the compass so it does not *directly* affect it. You want the *electricity in the wires* to move the needle.)

DISCOVERY PROBLEMS

observing   **A.** Does it make any difference if the coil or magnet moves?

observing   **B.** What happens to the needle if you move the magnet faster? slower?

observing   **C.** What difference does it make if you move the magnet's other end?

observing **D.** How does using a stronger or weaker magnet affect the compass needle?

observing **E.** How does changing the number of turns in the coil affect the needle?

experimenting **F.** What is the strongest current you can generate? That is, how far can you make the compass needle move?

TEACHING COMMENT

PREPARATION AND BACKGROUND

By moving the magnet alternately in two directions, the current that is produced also alternates directions. This is shown by the compass needle moving first one way, then the other. The mechanical energy used to move the magnet in this case comes from food the pupil eats.

The teaching strategy of the discovery sequence is to give enough experience for pupils to experiment on their own in F.

GENERALIZATION

An electric current may be generated when a magnet and a wire coil interact. A galvanometer may be used to detect the current.

SAMPLE PERFORMANCE OBJECTIVES

Knowledge: The child can construct a crude galvanometer and use it to detect small differences in electric currents.
Process: The child can generate a stronger electric current by experimenting with several variables.

■ INVESTIGATION: Radio Waves

How close do you live to a radio station? Strong electrical signals, called *radio waves,* are sent out by such stations. Your radio can change these waves into sounds. There are several ways to produce radio waves. One simple way is to use electric sparks.

EXPLORATORY PROBLEM

How can you generate radio waves with electric sparks?

NEEDED

20-centimeter (8-inch) piece of bell wire   sticky tape
two flashlight (D-size) batteries   aluminum foil
small portable radio   meter stick or yardstick
plastic bowl

TRY THIS

1. Bare both ends of the wire. Tape one wire end to the battery bottom.

2. Turn on the radio. Set it between stations, so there is no sound. Turn up the volume.

3. Hold the battery and wire close to the radio. Brush the knob on the battery top with the free wire end. If you hear a crackling "static" sound from the radio, you are generating radio waves (Figure 12-31).

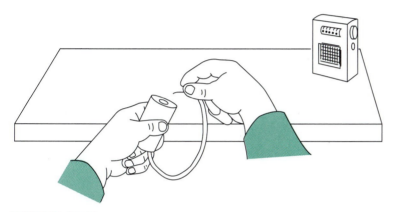

FIGURE 12-31

DISCOVERY PROBLEMS

observing   **A.** Can you notice tiny sparks between the wire end and battery top as they touch? (Probably not, unless the room is fairly dark.)

observing   **B.** From how far will the radio pick up your "broadcast"? Does the way the radio faces make a difference in the distance between it and the battery? in the loudness of the radio static?

observing   **C.** In how many directions will the radio receive your broadcast? Have someone move it around you.

observing   **D.** Broadcast radio waves with two batteries. Have someone hold them end to end as in a flashlight. Do again what you did with one battery. What changes do you notice?

experimenting   **E.** Are both batteries equally strong? How can you find out?

observing   **F.** Can radio waves go through aluminum foil? Tear off a sheet. Have someone wrap it *completely around* the radio, so there are no open places. Generate some radio waves and see.

observing   **G.** What materials will radio waves pass through? Which will block them? Put the radio inside such materials as rubber (boot), glass (large jar), plastic (bag), paper (box), wood (cigar box), cloth, steel (pail), and stone (several bricks).

observing **H.** Will radio waves go through water? Generate radio waves with one battery and wire held under water, in a plastic bowl. Have the radio standing next to the bowl.

experimenting **I.** How can you find out if the waves can go through people?

observing **J.** Tune the radio to a regular station. Will the station's radio waves go through materials your battery-generated waves cannot go through?

TEACHING COMMENTS

PREPARATION AND BACKGROUND

The simple device used in this investigation may generate radio waves that travel less than a meter (3 feet). By putting two batteries together in a series, as in a flashlight, it is possible to increase this distance.

We can hear a portable radio inside a house. This fact may help children realize that radio waves can penetrate many solid materials. On the other hand, automobile radios commonly have outside antennas. This should give children a clue as to what materials cannot be penetrated by radio waves. Faulty findings will often result unless the radio is *completely enclosed* in whatever materials are tested.

One way to test whether radio waves will go through a person is to wrap all surfaces of the radio with foil except for one side. Hold the unwrapped side tightly against your waist. Have someone generate radio waves in back of you. Listen for static.

GENERALIZATION

Radio waves may be generated with a flashlight battery; the waves can pass through most common materials except metals.

SAMPLE PERFORMANCE OBJECTIVES

Process: The child can observe and compare the effects of testing several materials to determine if radio waves will penetrate them.

Knowledge: The child can describe how to increase the range of a flashlight-cell radio-wave generator.

SELECTED TRADE BOOKS: ELECTRICAL ENERGY

FOR YOUNGER CHILDREN

Bailey, Mark W. *Electricity.* Raintree, 1978.

Berger, Melvin. *Switch On, Switch Off.* Harper Collins, 1990.

Bains, Rae. *Discovering Electricity.* Troll Associates, 1981.

Challand, Helen. *Experiments with Electricity.* Children's Press, 1986.

Curren, Polly. *I Know an Electrician.* Putnam, 1977.

Lillegard, Dee, and Wayne Stoker. *I Can Be an Electrician.* Children's Press, 1986.

Taylor, Barbara. *Batteries and Magnets.* Watts, 1991.

Wade, Harlan. *Electricity.* Raintree, 1979.

FOR OLDER CHILDREN

Ardley, Neil. *Discovering Electricity.* Watts, 1984.

Brandt, Keith. *Electricity.* Troll Associates, 1985.

Cobb, Vickie. *More Power to You!* Little, Brown, 1986.

De Bruin, Jerry. *Young Scientist Explores Electricity and Magnetism.* Good Apple, 1985.

Gutnik, Martin J. *Electricity: From Faraday to Solar Generators.* Watts, 1986.

Mackie, Dan. *Electricity.* Penworthy, 1986.

Math, Irwin. *Wires and Watts.* Scribners, 1981.

Provenzo, Eugene F., and Asterie B. Provenzo. *Rediscovering Electricity.* Oak Tree, 1982.

Stanley, Leon R. *Easy to Make Electric Gadgets.* Harvey, 1980.

Taylor, Barbara. *Electricity and Magnets.* Watts, 1990.

Vogt, Gregory. *Electricity and Magnetism.* Watts, 1985.

————. *Generating Electricity.* Watts, 1986.

Ward, Alan. *Experimenting with Batteries, Bulbs, and Wires.* David & Charles, 1986.

Whyman, Kathryn. *Electricity and Magnetism.* Watts, 1986.

Zubrowski, Bernie. *Blinkers and Buzzers.* Morrow, 1991.

13

Simple Machines and How They Work

Imagine a parade of the world's machines— airplanes and tweezers, bulldozers and baby carriages, computers and egg beaters—an almost endless line of inventions, without which we would fare far less well. But perhaps the most remarkable thing about these inventions lies in their construction. All machines, no matter how complex, are made from variations of just six simple machines. These are the inclined plane (ramp), wedge, screw, lever, wheel and axle (windlass), and pulley. We'll consider these machines and the effects of motion and friction on them in this chapter.

Many scientists classify simple machines into only two types: inclined plane and lever. To them, a screw and wedge are only variations of the inclined plane, and a windlass and a pulley variations of the lever.

Our agreement with this idea is reflected in the sequence and emphases within the chapter. The main topics are (1) inclined planes and screws, (2) levers, (3) wheel and axle, (4) pulleys, and (5) motion and friction.

[1] INCLINED PLANES AND SCREWS *Experiences 389*

For any machine to do work, force must overcome gravity, inertia, molecular cohesion (the binding force that holds materials together), and friction. Machines may be used to reduce the force needed to do work, speed up work, or change the direction of a force.

Inclined Planes

Although they may not have thought about it, even small children have had experiences with inclined planes such as climbing stairs, walking up a hill, coasting down a slanted driveway on roller skates, and the like. They know from these experiences that it is harder to climb a steep hill than a gradual hill. Boys

and girls may even unknowingly use the idea that distance may be increased to decrease force, as when a bicycle rider rides diagonally back and forth up a hill. This background of common experiences lets us focus on force/distance relationships fairly quickly when working with inclined planes.

Does an inclined plane or other simple machine make work "easier"? No, if we mean that some part of the total effort is saved. In terms of *work*—force moving a resistance over a distance—it is impossible to get out of a machine any more than is put into a machine. Another way of saying this is: *Effort times distance equals resistance times distance,* or $ED = RD$.

Let's apply this idea to the inclined plane in Figure 13-1.

Suppose we want to push a 50-pound barrel to a height of 5 feet and the inclined plane is 10 feet long. The pushing will take about 25 pounds of force or effort. If we use this figure and the two distances, it can be shown that the total amount of work is the same.

By using the inclined plane: Effort (25 pounds) times Distance (10 feet) = 250 foot-pounds of work.

By lifting straight up: Resistance (50 pounds) times Distance (5 feet) = 250 foot-pounds of work.

This assumes that we are physically able to do the work in both cases. Yet it *is* easier for us to apply less force for a longer distance and time. Muscles get tired quickly from

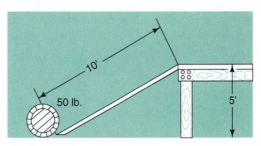

FIGURE 13-1
An inclined plane.

concentrated, heavy work. It is in that sense, then, that a simple machine makes work "easier."

The reduction of force provided by a simple machine is called its *mechanical advantage.* This is found by *dividing the force of the resistance by the force of the effort.* In the foregoing example, the mechanical advantage is

$$\frac{R(50 \text{ pounds})}{E(25 \text{ pounds})} \text{ or } 2$$

In other words, it is twice as easy to lift the barrel with the inclined plane as without it. Or we can say it takes half as much effort.

Pupils can make crude measurements to grasp the force/distance relationship. For instance, a string can be used to compare the length of an inclined plane with the height to which it rises. A rubber band attached to an object may have a ruler held beside it to measure different degrees of applied force in terms of "stretch." Or a spring scale, if available, will be even more effective than a rubber band.

Wedges

A wedge can be thought of as two inclined planes placed back to back. Although the classic use of this machine has waned along with professional rail-splitters and wood-choppers, the wedge principle is employed in many other ways. For example, "streamlining" is a way of better enabling objects to pierce air and water. More speed can be achieved with the same amount of applied force. Paper cutters, knives, pencil sharpeners, nails, needles—all these are everyday wedges used for cutting or piercing functions.

Screws

"The screw is just an inclined plane wrapped around a nail." This is what one child said, and it is a fairly accurate description. We usually think of the screw as a naillike object with a spiral thread that holds together pieces of wood or metal. But other applications of this machine are all around us.

There are spiral staircases, roads that wind around a steep hill or mountain, vises for workbenches, clamps to hold things together, adjustable piano stools, and the adjustable parts of wrenches, to name just a few. Sometimes its appearance is not so obvious, as in propellers for ships and airplanes.

When used to lift things, the mechanical advantage of the screw is the greatest of any simple machine. It is relatively easy for a small person to lift up the front of an automobile with a screw-type jack, and jackscrews employed by house movers actually lift entire houses off their foundations. As with an inclined plane, though, the price paid for such a gain in force is increased distance.

Each time a screw is given a complete turn, it advances into a piece of wood or lifts an object only as far as the distance between its threads. This distance is called *pitch* and is illustrated in Figure 13-2.

The paired drawings show that two screws of similar size, but different pitches, would vary in the number of times turned if screwed into some wood or used to lift something. We expect a steep spiral staircase to take more

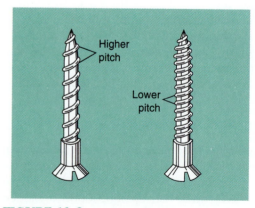

FIGURE 13-2

The pitch of a screw is the distance between its threads.

effort than a longer, gradual one when walking up to the same height. Likewise, the steeper the pitch of a screw, the more force is needed to make it rotate. However, it advances farther and faster than one with a narrower, more gradual pitch.

The mathematical relationships here are identical to those of other simple machines. Mechanical advantage is again found by dividing resistance by effort.

[2] LEVERS *Experiences 392*

No one knows who actually first contrived the lever, but apparently it has been known and used for a very long time. The ancient Greek scientist Archimedes is supposed to have said he could move the world if given a long enough lever, fulcrum, and place to stand. It is widely assumed that primitive people also had knowledge of levers, but probably only in a practical way.

The principles of this simple machine are used in so many ways that a moment's reflection produces surprising examples: The ancient Japanese sport of judo is based on knowledge that the human skeleton is comprised of lever systems. Also, a golfer with long arms may swing the club head faster than a golfer with shorter arms.

Three Parts

The seesaw is a lever familiar to most children. It has three parts: (1) *fulcrum,* or point on which it pivots; (2) *effort arm,* the part on which the force is exerted; and (3) the *resistance,* or load, arm, that part which bears the load to be raised. When the seesaw is perfectly balanced on the fulcrum, the resistance and effort arms will alternate if two equally heavy riders alternately push against the ground to make the seesaw go up and down.

As with other machines, effort times distance (from the fulcrum) equals resistance times distance (from the fulcrum). This is shown in Figure 13-3. The mechanical advantage in this example is two. Another way to calculate the mechanical advantage is simply to divide the effort-arm length by the resistance-arm length. Friction is usually so minor in the lever that it does not need to be taken into account.

Even primary children can arrive at an intuitive understanding of the foregoing "law of levers" if they are given experience with balancing objects. Of course, the mathematics involved is beyond most of them.

Three Classes

Levers are found with parts arranged in three different combinations called *classes.* Children do not need to memorize these combinations or even their examples. But analyzing how everyday levers work can sharpen their observation and classification skills. Notice the three arrangements in Figure 13-4.

Seesaws, crowbars, and can openers are first-class levers. Two levers of this kind are placed together in tools such as scissors and pliers. By varying the effort-arm length, you change the amount of required force or gain in speed and distance. This type also changes direction of movement. You exert force in a direction opposite to which the load moves. If both effort and resistance arms are equal, however, a first-class lever can change only

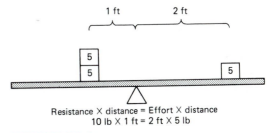

Resistance × distance = Effort × distance
10 lb × 1 ft = 2 ft × 5 lb

FIGURE 13-3
To find the mechanical advantage of a lever, divide the effort-arm length by the resistance-arm length.

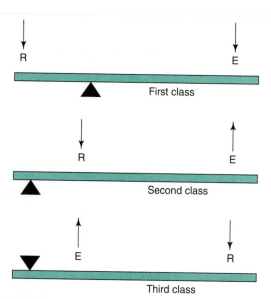

FIGURE 13-4
Three classes of levers; *R* is resistance, *E* effort.

the direction of a force. Neither reduced force nor gain in speed and distance takes place.

Second-class levers are illustrated by the wheelbarrow and post puller. A nutcracker illustrates joined, double levers of this type. Speed or distance are not as likely to be considerations when using a second-class lever as in the previous case.

Should you forget third-class levers, just think of your arm. Your elbow is the fulcrum, your bicep provides the effort at a point just below and opposite the elbow, and your fist represents the load or resistance. Other common applications are found in the broom, baseball bat, fly swatter, and fishing pole, to name just a few. Sugar or ice cube tongs represent double levers of the class. Analysis of this lever reveals that force is traded to get added speed or distance. With a fishing pole, for example, you want to increase the speed of your hands to hook a nibbling fish securely before it can react and get away.

Mobiles

A mobile is a combination of several suspended levers with attached figures. In some mobiles, even the figures may function as levers (Figure 13-5).

When children work on mobiles, they have problems balancing the figures and keeping them from touching. For solutions, they need to think about variables such as figure size and shape, string length, best position for figures, and where to fasten them. This sharpens their thinking skills. Mobiles are also an interesting way to combine artwork with science.

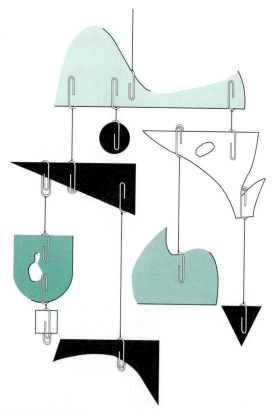

FIGURE 13-5
A tagboard and paper-clip mobile.

[3] WHEEL AND AXLE
Experiences 403

The windlass or wheel and axle is a commonly misunderstood simple machine. Although a windlass looks like a wagon wheel and axle, it is different. We put wheels on a wagon to reduce friction by lessening the surface area that comes in contact with the road. Its axles are stationary. Greater "leverage" is indeed present in a large wheel compared to a small wheel. This is why a large wheel can roll over uneven ground more easily than a small wheel. Still, a wagon wheel and axle combination is not regarded as a simple machine.

In a windlass, the axle and wheel are firmly fixed together. Spinning the axle causes the wheel to rotate; force at the axle is traded off to gain an advantage in speed and distance on the outside of the wheel. By turning the wheel, though, an advantage in force can be gained; speed and distance are then reduced or sacrificed at the axle.

A windlass is really a continuous lever on a continuous fulcrum. Therefore, when a handle is placed anywhere on the wheel, it becomes the end of the force arm. The axle's radius is the load arm. Figure 13-6 shows this idea.

The theoretical mechanical advantage in a windlass is calculated as with a lever. If the effort-arm length is 18 inches and resistance arm length is 2 inches, mechanical advantage equals 9. Because friction is so great with a windlass, however, actual mechanical advantage is found only through dividing resistance by effort.

As with the lever, placing the windlass handle (effort) ever farther away from the axle (fulcrum) decreases needed effort. At the same time, it increases the distance through which the effort is applied.

Understanding the force/distance relationship makes it easy for children to see why a meat grinder needs a longer crank than a pencil sharpener (Figure 13-7), for example, and why a large steering wheel is easier to turn than a smaller one.

Gears, Chains, and Belts

Wheel and axle combinations may be modified to interact with one another by using

FIGURE 13-6
A windlass is a lever.

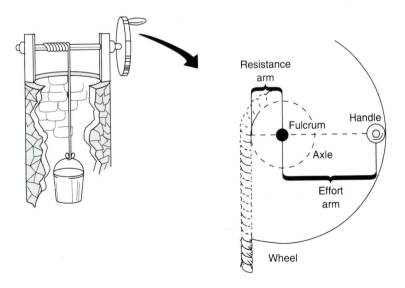

Resistance arm

Fulcrum

Handle

Axle

Effort arm

Wheel

FIGURE 13-7
A pencil sharpener can be used as a wheel and axle.

belts, chains, and toothlike projections on the circumference of the wheel to form gears. The bicycle is a common example of two modified wheels and axles joined by a chain. Because the front gear, or sprocket, is larger than the rear sprocket, one turn of the larger sprocket forces several or more turns of the smaller rear one. Older pupils can find the theoretical mechanical advantage of the larger sprocket by counting and comparing the number of teeth on each sprocket.

In an upcoming activity with spools and rubber bands, children can discover how the speed and direction of rotation of linked wheels can be changed or predicted.

[4] PULLEYS   *Experiences 408*

Pulleys for teaching can be bought through science supply houses. Yet in elementary school activities, two clothesline pulleys or two smaller single pulleys, found in most hardware stores, may work just as well. "Single" pulleys have but one grooved wheel or sheave. Some pulleys have two or more sheaves for combined use with other pulleys in heavy lifting.

Fixed and Movable Pulleys

As its name implies, a *fixed pulley* is securely fastened to some object. A *movable pulley* moves vertically, or laterally, as the case may be, with the load (Figure 13-8).

The pulley's similarity to a lever and windlass is diagrammed in Figure 13-8. As with a windlass, the wheellike arrangement is really a continuous lever.

Observe why a fixed pulley can do no more than change the direction of a force. Like a seesaw whose fulcrum is centered, the effort arm and resistance arm are of equal length. There is no useful mechanical advantage. If one foot of rope is pulled downward, the resistance moves upward one foot. This happens, for example, when a flag is raised on a flagpole.

Notice why a movable pulley offers a theoretical mechanical advantage of two. The resistance arm is only half the effort-arm length. Like a wheelbarrow, this is a variation of a second-class lever. As with similar machines, distance is traded off for decreased effort. We must pull the rope two feet for each foot the load is lifted.

Block and Tackle

By placing a fixed and movable pulley in combination, we are able not only to change the direction of a force but also to decrease the force necessary to lift a load. Such an arrangement is called a *block and tackle* (Figure 13-9). By adding more movable pulleys (or pulleys with two or more sheaves), effort can be reduced even further.

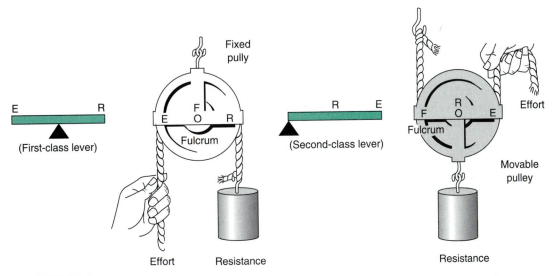

FIGURE 13-8

A fixed pulley offers no mechanical advantage because its effort and resistance arms are equally long. A movable pulley, however, does make work easier because its resistance arm is only half the length of the effort arm.

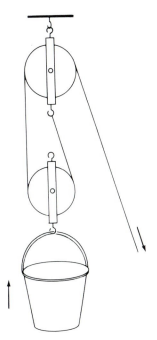

FIGURE 13-9

Block and tackle.

Friction finally limits how far we can go in adding pulleys to reduce effort. It can be partly overcome by greasing or oiling the axle.

Since each rope in a block-and-tackle setup supports an equal fraction of a load, it is easy to know the theoretical mechanical advantage. Two supporting ropes have a mechanical advantage of two, three ropes three, and so on. Because of friction, though, actual mechanical advantage must be calculated through dividing resistance by effort—as with all simple machines.

Pupils may use a rubber band (or spring scale) in the activities to measure differences in the force needed to lift things with pulleys. To attach a rubber band, first fashion a paper-clip hook. Simply pierce or loop the pulley cord at the place where you wish to measure needed force, insert the hook, and then attach a rubber band to it.

As before, a ruler can measure the amount of stretch.

[5] MOTION AND FRICTION *Experiences 411*

Most machines we use are *complex;* that is, they are combinations of simple machines. It is interesting to see how these machines and their parts move.

Three Basic Motions

Some machines have mainly a *straight-line motion.* A few examples are toy or real trains, an upright bicycle (turning requires some leaning), roller skates, and steamrollers.

Some machines or their parts make a repeated forward and back movement called *periodic motion.* The pendulum in a grandfather clock is one example. Others are a swing, a mechanical walking doll, a metronome, and some lawn sprinklers.

A number of machines or their parts make a continuous spinning motion in one direction as they work. This is *rotary motion.* A few examples are the merry-go-round, the turntable on a record player, a rotary lawn sprinkler, and clock hands.

It can be fascinating to examine mechanical toys and other machines. Their parts are designed to produce a particular motion and, in some cases, to change it.

Any moving machine or part continues to produce its designed motion unless another force is applied to alter, reverse, or stop it. When we rotate an older-type telephone dial, for instance, a metal stop prevents us from going beyond one rotation. A spring then returns the dial to its original position. Also, the front wheel of a moving bicycle may be turned by applying a force to the handlebars. But what happens if the force is applied too strongly? Perhaps painful experience has taught you that bicycle and rider will continue in a straight line until road friction finally stops both.

Friction

Accompanying all motion is *friction,* the resistance produced when two surfaces rub together. No surface is perfectly smooth. The tiny ridges in a "smooth" surface, or the larger bumps and hollows in a rough one, catch and resist when the surfaces rub together. The mutual attraction of molecules on the opposing surfaces also adds to the resistance we call friction. Surface pressure is another condition that affects friction. A heavy object has more friction than a lighter one.

Lubricating a surface is effective because the oil or grease fills in the spaces between ridges and bumps. Opposing surfaces mostly slide against the lubricant rather than rubbing against each other.

In many machines, ball bearings or roller bearings are used to change sliding friction to rolling friction. Rolling friction is less than sliding friction because a load-bearing rolling object rolls over tiny surface ridges or bumps rather than catching against them.

Friction reduces a machine's efficiency by robbing some of its power (and so its energy). It also creates heat as surfaces rub and wears out parts. But not all of its effects are bad. Friction also allows us to brake a car or bicycle, walk or run, write on paper, and so on. A frictionless world would create far more problems than it would solve.

INVESTIGATIONS & ACTIVITIES

SECTION 1
Inclined Planes and Screws
[Background 381]

■ INVESTIGATION: Inclined Planes

Is it easier to walk up a steep hill or a low hill? Suppose both hills were just as high but one was twice as long. Which would be easier then? A hill is a kind of *inclined plane.*

EXPLORATORY PROBLEM

How can you measure the force needed to use an inclined plane?

NEEDED

flat board, 60 centimeters (2 feet)   rubber band (or spring scale)
flat board, 120 centimeters (4 feet)   ruler
seven same-sized books   paper clip
roller skate

TRY THIS

1. Lay an end of the smaller board on one book (Figure 13-10).

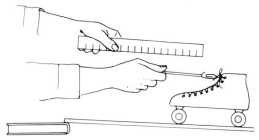

FIGURE 13-10

2. Place a roller skate on the board. Hook a bent paper clip around the tied shoelace. Attach a rubber band.

3. Pull the skate slowly up the board. Measure with a ruler how much the rubber band stretches. (Or measure the pull with a spring scale.)

4. Now make the inclined plane or "hill" three books high. Do steps 2 and 3 again.

DISCOVERY PROBLEMS

measuring   **A.** What was the difference in rubber band stretch in the two trials?

measuring   **B.** How much stretch will there be with "hills" of different heights? Measure also a height of two books, then five and six books. (Do not measure four books now.) Record what you find on a graph such as this:

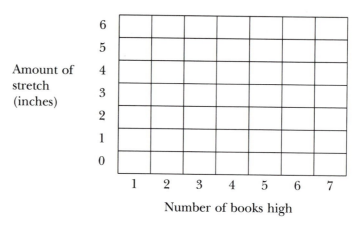

predicting   **C.** Examine your graph data for heights of one, two, three, five, and six books. Can you predict the stretch for four books? Write this down and then test your prediction.

predicting   **D.** Examine your data again. Can you predict the stretch for seven books?

predicting   **E.** Switch this board for one twice as long. Suppose you used one through seven books again. What do you think your results would be? Write down your ideas and then test them.

inferring   **F.** What pictures of different inclined planes can you bring to school?

TEACHING COMMENT

BACKGROUND AND PREPARATION

One long board, rather than two different-sized boards, can be used to demonstrate how changing board lengths affects the force needed to go up a given height. The books may first be placed under the midpoint of the board, and the board tilted. The tilted part beyond the books may be ignored. However, this can confuse some pupils, especially the younger ones. Pairs of boards of almost any lengths may be used, but the larger one should be twice as long as the smaller one.

A spring scale is likely to yield more accurate measurements than a rubber band. A rubber band may not stretch uniformly and, of course, does not indicate force in standard units. Try several rubber bands to select one that stretches easily for heights of one to seven books. If needed, snip and use a single strand.

Two kinds of predicting occur in this investigation. In Problem C, the child predicts *within* the data (interpolating); in D, the child predicts *beyond* the data (extrapolating).

GENERALIZATION

The force needed to go up an inclined plane increases with height and decreases with distance.

SAMPLE PERFORMANCE OBJECTIVES

Knowledge: The child can state that doubling the length of an inclined board halves the force needed to go up a given height.
Process: The child can accurately predict needed force within and beyond graphed data for an inclined plane.

FOR YOUNGER CHILDREN

Try the activity without the graphing of data. Younger pupils generally notice and understand why there are differences in rubber band stretch.

☐ ACTIVITY: How Are the Screw and Inclined Plane Alike?

NEEDED

paper	scissors
ruler	crayon
two pencils	

TRY THIS

1. Cut two different-sized paper triangles as shown in Figure 13-11. Color the edge on the long side of each with crayon. These cutouts are like two inclined planes.
   a. Which inclined plane would be easier to go up? Which would take longer to go up?

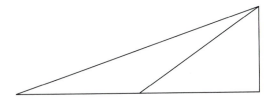

FIGURE 13-11

2. Wrap each paper inclined plane around a pencil as shown in Figure 13-12.
   b. Does each look like a screw? Which would be easier to screw into wood? Which would take longer to screw into wood?
3. Remove the pencil from each paper screw. Stand the loosely wound papers on end.
   c. Do the paper screws now look like spiral staircases? Which would be easier to walk up? Which would take longer to walk up?

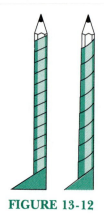

FIGURE 13-12

☐ ACTIVITY: How Tightly Do Nails and Screws Hold?

NEEDED

small pieces of Styrofoam or soft wood   hammer
nail and screw matched for size   screwdriver

TRY THIS

1. Tap a nail halfway into a piece of Styrofoam.

2. Use a screwdriver to turn a screw the same distance into the Styrofoam.

3. Try to pull out the nail and screw with your fingers. If necessary, use the claw end of the hammer to pull them out.

   a. Which was harder to pull out? Which was put in faster?

   b. Which do you think would hold together two pieces of Styrofoam more securely? Try and find out.

(*Teaching Comment:* Styrofoam is easier for children to use than wood. If it is not available, try soft pine.)

SECTION 2
Levers
[*Background 383*]

■ INVESTIGATION: Some Common Levers

Have you used a baseball bat? a seesaw? a house broom? These and many other things we use are examples of *levers.* How levers work can be surprising. Some that look almost alike work differently. Some that look different work the same way.

EXPLORATORY PROBLEM

How can you tell in which ways levers are alike and different?

NEEDED

Real or picture examples of levers in everyday things:

canoe paddle	crowbar
paper cutter	baseball bat
seesaw	post puller
house broom	can opener
wheelbarrow	tennis racket
golf club	boat oar

TRY THIS

1. Figure 13-13 shows a fishing pole in action. Notice how this lever is used. The tip carries the load or resistance (R). The opposite end, which is held, moves very little. This is the fulcrum (F). To pull up the resistance takes effort (E). This happens *between* the fulcrum and resistance.

2. Study the three smaller drawings in Figure 13-13. Levers can be grouped into three classes, depending on how they are used. Each group has a place for the fulcrum, resistance, and effort. But notice that the order in each group is different. This is a good way to tell them apart.

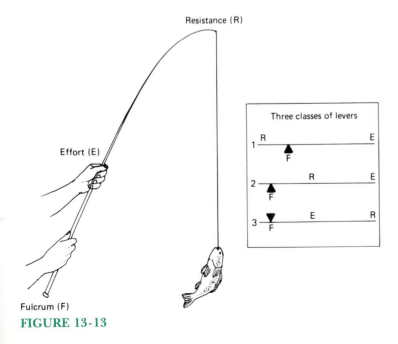

FIGURE 13-13

DISCOVERY PROBLEMS

classifying **A.** In which group does the fishing pole belong?

classifying **B.** Examine real or picture examples of many levers. Use them, or think of how they are used. In which group does each belong? Here's a way to record what you find:

Lever	1. RFE	2. FRE	3. FER
Fishing pole			✔
Paper cutter			
And so on			

inferring **C.** Which of these levers are really alike?

classifying **D.** Examine the bottom half of your arm—the forearm. It is a lever, also. In which group does it belong?

inferring **E.** Play a game with some friends. Think of a common lever. Can they find out what it is by asking questions? You can answer only yes or no. If they get stuck, act out the way it is used. (A good way for them to begin is to find out the load-fulcrum-effort order.)

classifying **F.** What other real or picture examples can you find? In which group does each belong?

TEACHING COMMENT

BACKGROUND AND PREPARATION

It is the *internal* order of resistance-fulcrum-effort that counts in classifying levers. So there is no difference between R-F-E or E-F-R, for example. A few pupils may need help with this idea.

It is not important for children to memorize the internal order of each class. But it is worthwhile for them to develop skill in observing and classifying likenesses and differences in objects.

In Problem D, the part played by the upper arm muscle (biceps) in moving the forearm may be confusing. The actual pull on the *forearm* is just below and opposite the elbow on the inside.

The examples in this and the next investigation are basically levers. It is instructive to have pupils also analyze the parts that help each tool work. The paper cutter, for example, uses a knife (wedge) in combination with the lever.

GENERALIZATION

Levers may be grouped by where places on each are used for the resistance, fulcrum, and effort.

SAMPLE PERFORMANCE OBJECTIVES

Knowledge: The child can demonstrate where to place a lever on a fulcrum to reduce effort.

Process: The child can classify examples of levers into three groups by how they work.

□ ACTIVITY: How Can You Improve a Lever-Type Can Opener?

NEEDED

lever-type can opener   empty can

two rulers   sticky tape

TRY THIS

1. Place the can opener against the can rim. Lift up on the handle so the tip of the can opener punctures the can.
   a. Suppose you made the handle longer. How might that change the force needed to puncture the can?

2. Tape two rulers to the can-opener handle (Figure 13-14). Grip the end of this longer "handle." Puncture the can again.
   b. What do you notice? How does lengthening the handle change the force needed to open the can?

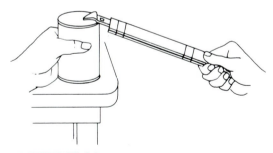

FIGURE 13-14

■ INVESTIGATION: Some Common Double Levers

Have you used scissors? This tool is an example of a double lever that has cutting parts. We use many tools that are mainly double levers. How many can you name or describe? Some that look almost alike work differently. Some that look different work about the same way.

EXPLORATORY PROBLEM

How can you tell in which ways double levers are alike and different?

NEEDED

pliers	lemon squeezer
sugar tongs	tweezers
nutcracker	tin snips

TRY THIS

1. Figure 13-15 shows a pair of scissors. Notice how the parts are used, especially the cutting parts. When you cut something, it resists being cut. So each part that does this work is called the *resistance* (R).

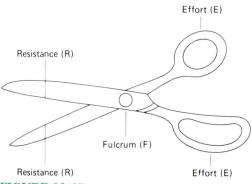

FIGURE 13-15

2. Notice where the two parts of the scissors join and pivot. This is the *fulcrum* (F).

3. See the handles. To cut something requires force or effort, so each of these parts is called the *effort* (E).

DISCOVERY PROBLEMS

observing   **A.** All tools that are double levers have parts for the resistance (R), fulcrum (F), and effort (E). But they are not always in that order. Examine some real or picture examples of double-lever tools. Which tools are arranged differently? How many different arrangements do you find?

classifying   **B.** You can classify these and other double levers by how the three parts are arranged. In which group will each fit? Here's a way to record what you find:

Double Lever	1. RFE	2. FRE	3. FER
Scissors	✔		
Pliers			
And so on			

inferring   **C.** Can you name any parts of your body that work like a double lever?

inferring   **D.** Play a game with some friends. Think of a tool that is a double lever. Can they discover what it is by asking questions? You can answer only yes or no. If they get stuck, act out the way it is used. (A good way for them to begin is to find out the resistance-fulcrum-effort order.)

classifying   **E.** What other real or picture examples of double levers can you find? In which group does each belong?

TEACHING COMMENT

BACKGROUND AND PREPARATION

In classifying double levers, as with single levers, it is the *internal* order of the resistance-fulcrum-effort that counts. So there is no difference between R-F-E and E-F-R, for example.

The thumb and forefinger often act as a double lever. Some children may also incorrectly name the mouth. In this case, only the jaw moves.

GENERALIZATION

Double levers may be grouped by how places on each are used for the resistance, fulcrum, and effort.

SAMPLE PERFORMANCE OBJECTIVES

Knowledge: The child can explain where the places are on double levers for the resistance, fulcrum, and effort.
Process: The child can classify examples of double levers into three groups by how they work.

■ INVESTIGATION: A Balance Board

Have you ever played on a seesaw? Where do you sit to balance someone heavier than you? lighter than you? You can make a small balance board now. It can work like a seesaw. With it, you may find some surprising ways to balance things.

EXPLORATORY PROBLEM

How can you make a small balance board?

NEEDED

two rulers   ten large washers or pennies
crayon   masking tape
rubber band   two thin same-sized books

TRY THIS

1. Cover a ruler the long way with a strip of masking tape.
2. Measure along the strip with another ruler. Mark the tape into eight equal parts. (On a 12-inch ruler, the marks should be 1½ inches apart.)
3. Fasten a crayon tightly to the middle of the ruler. Use a rubber band.
4. Put the attached crayon between two books as shown in Figure 13-16.

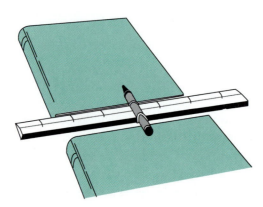

FIGURE 13-16

DISCOVERY PROBLEMS

experimenting **A.** How can you balance two washers? Put one on each side of the crayon.

experimenting **B.** Move each washer to a different place on each side. How can you make them balance again?

experimenting **C.** How can you balance two washers on each side? Try the washers two ways, side by side and piled. In what ways can you balance three washers on each side?

experimenting **D.** In what ways can you balance one washer with two washers? three washers with six washers?

predicting **E.** Study the drawings in Figure 13-17. Which setups will balance? Record what you think. Use your balance board to find out. Hold the board level each time until all the washers are in place. Then, let go and observe what happens.

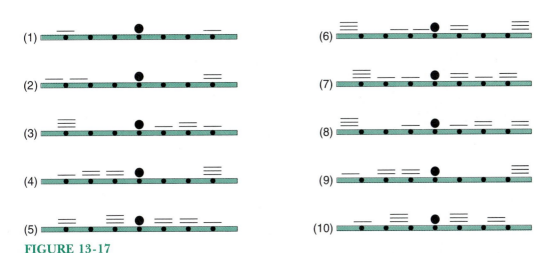

FIGURE 13-17

TEACHING COMMENT

PREPARATION AND BACKGROUND

Any crayon-sized cylindrical object may be used for the pivot or fulcrum. Make sure the crayon is tightly attached to the ruler. This may require doubling the rubber band several times. A suspended ruler is more stable than one placed on top of a fulcrum. Use two *thin* books to make the ruler less tippy.

The secret to balancing objects every time is to understand the "law of levers." The distance (from fulcrum) times the weight of objects on one side must always equal the distance times weight on the other side. Because there are many ways to vary one factor and compensate with the other, working with a balance can be challenging and interesting. Be sure to have identical steel washers or pennies for the activities. Even pennies may vary slightly in mass. For identical pennies, use only those dated from 1982 on.

GENERALIZATION

Objects may be balanced on a board by adding or taking away weight or by changing their distance from the fulcrum.

SAMPLE PERFORMANCE OBJECTIVES

Process: The child can balance an unequal number of washers on a board by distributing the washers differently on each side.
Knowledge: The child can explain that on a balance board objects may be balanced by adding or taking away weight or by changing their distance from the fulcrum.

FOR YOUNGER CHILDREN

Try using a board about the length of a meter stick or yardstick to start off. A small wooden block may be used as the fulcrum. Suggest to pupils that they try to balance a variety of objects on the board. Wooden play blocks are excellent for this investigation.

One activity may be especially interesting. After many different objects are piled and balanced on the board, challenge pupils to take away two objects at the same time (one on each side) and keep the balance.

A pegboard beam balance is also useful for young children. They can suspend washers from paper-clip hooks hung on the pegboard. This will allow them to do most of the problems in this investigation.

□ ACTIVITY: How Can You Make a Balance Board for People?

NEEDED

strong board, about 1.5 meters   brick
   (5 feet) long   people of different weights

TRY THIS

1. Put the brick under the center of the board.

2. Have someone stand by each end of the board. They can help people get on and off. Otherwise, the board may swing around at these times.
    a. Choose two persons; one should be heavier than the other. Using the board, how can you tell who weighs more?
    b. How can the board be balanced with only one person on it?
    c. How can the board be balanced with three people on it? four? five?
    d. When the board is centered on the brick fulcrum, which two people can stand on the ends and be balanced? which four people?
    e. Will it make any difference if the two persons at one end trade positions? If the two persons at both ends trade ends?

■ INVESTIGATION: The Making of a Mobile

Notice the balanced group of objects in Figure 13-18. This is a *mobile.* The word means "something that moves." Even a tiny breeze can move the objects. They may almost seem to be alive!

What kind of mobile objects would you like to make? Fishes, birds, butterflies, balloons, and airplanes are all fun to do. You can even use cutout letters of your name.

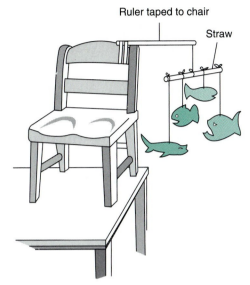

Ruler taped to chair

Straw

FIGURE 13-18

EXPLORATORY PROBLEM

How can you make a mobile?

NEEDED

plastic soda straws   tagboard
thin knitting yarn   sticky tape
paper clips   ruler
scissors   crayons or paints and brushes

TRY THIS

1. Cut some strings of yarn 20 to 30 centimeters (8 to 12 inches) long.

2. Tie one end of each string to a paper clip.

3. Decide what kind of objects to hang. Then, cut three or four objects from tagboard.

4. Set up a place to hang your mobile. Tape a ruler to a chair. Put the chair on a table.

5. Hang the objects from a straw with yarn. Loop the yarn once around the straw. Make half a knot. Then, pull the yarn tight. Clip the paper clip to each object in the usual way.

6. Try to balance the objects. Slide the yarn on the straw. Change where each object is clipped if needed.

DISCOVERY PROBLEMS

experimenting **A.** How can you make a mobile with more straws and objects? It will help to draw your mobile on paper first. Start with a few materials. Add more later. Think about these things:

hypothesizing What can you do to balance your objects?

hypothesizing How can you keep the objects from touching?

hypothesizing How big should each object be? What shape? Where should each be placed?

hypothesizing How long should each string be? Where is it best to clip the string on each object?

B. How can you color your objects with crayons or paints?

TEACHING COMMENT

PREPARATION AND BACKGROUND

Making mobiles is an interesting way to combine artwork with valuable learnings about balance.

Use acrylic four-ply knitting yarn or similar yarn for this investigation. It is inexpensive and readily available. A four-ounce package will serve more than an entire class, if desired. The cut strings may be saved and used indefinitely. Be sure the yarn strings are tied to the *single-wire end* of each paper clip. The yarn will hold fast if looped just once and pulled tight (a half knot). A tightly pulled half knot will also hold the yarn on the straw. Yet you can still slide it on the straw as needed. The yarn is easily removed. Just hold the straw and pull the yarn firmly. The single loop will become undone and slip off.

GENERALIZATION

For mobile objects to balance, we consider variables such as object size and shape, weight, string length, best positions for the objects, and where to fasten them.

SAMPLE PERFORMANCE OBJECTIVES

Process: When shown a simple unbalanced mobile, the child can infer which variable or variables need attention.
Knowledge: The child can explain how to make a mobile.

FOR OLDER CHILDREN

Older pupils typically want to make more complex mobiles than younger children, although their introduction to mobiles may be similar. Invite them to use common, but light, three-dimensional objects for mobiles: bottle caps, empty milk cartons, straightened wire hangers, different-sized autumn leaves, plastic lids or containers, and so on. Encourage them to use *several tiers* of straws from which to suspend objects that balance and can move without touching.

SECTION 3
Wheel and Axle
[*Background 385*]

☐ ACTIVITY: How Does Size Affect the Turning of a Wheel?

NEEDED

broomstick   partner

TRY THIS

1. Have your partner firmly hold the center of the stick with hands together. She should try to prevent you from turning it.
2. Face your partner. Put your hands just outside your partner's hands.
3. Slowly twist the stick around like the spokes on a small wheel.
4. Move your hands near the ends of the stick.
5. Slowly twist the stick like the spokes on a large wheel.
   a. When was it easier to turn the "wheel"?
   b. Will your partner get the same results? Switch places and see.

(*Teaching Comment:* A few words in advance from you can prevent this activity from becoming a wrestling match. Stress that the child holding the center of the stick should moderately resist each time.)

☐ ACTIVITY: How Does a Screwdriver Handle Make Work Easier?

NEEDED

screwdriver with round handle   masking tape
piece of soft wood   screw
hammer

TRY THIS

1. Tap in the screw so it sticks into the wood.
2. Hold the screwdriver below the handle at the steel shank. Try to turn the screw.
3. Now hold the handle. Again, try to turn the screw.
   a. Which was easier?
   b. Maybe your hand slipped on the smooth steel shank. Probably it did not slip on the handle. What will happen if you wrap tape around both parts and try again?
   c. Which is easier this time?

4. Look at the screwdriver on end from the steel tip toward the handle. Notice the difference in width between the steel shank and the handle.
   d. Why do you think it is easier to turn a screw using the handle rather than using the shank?

□ ACTIVITY: How Does an Eggbeater Work?

NEEDED

hand-powered eggbeater   crayon

TRY THIS

1. Examine all the gears and how they are connected.
2. Turn the handle slowly. Observe how the gears turn each other.
   a. How does the one big gear make the two little gears turn?
   b. Notice what happens as you turn the handle: The big gear circles vertically or straight up. What makes the two small gears circle horizontally or sideways?
   c. Why do the two small gears go in opposite directions?
   d. Why do the small gears turn faster than the large gear?
   e. How many turns does each small gear make to each turn of the large gear? Mark each gear in one place with crayon to help you count.
   f. How many teeth does a small gear have? large gear have? Divide the larger number by the smaller number. How does this answer help to explain what you found in Problem e?

■ INVESTIGATION: Wheel-Belt Systems

Have you ever noticed how bicycle gears turn? The two gears are connected by a chain. When you push one gear around, the other moves, also.

A gear is just a wheel with teeth. There are many ways to connect wheels. Often, they are connected with belts. Several connected wheels are called a *wheel-belt system*. You can make your own wheel-belt system with spools and rubber bands.

EXPLORATORY PROBLEM

How can you make a wheel-belt system?

NEEDED

four empty sewing spools   four finishing nails
crayon   board (about the size of this page)
four rubber bands   hammer

TRY THIS

1. Pound four nails into the board as shown in Figure 13-19.

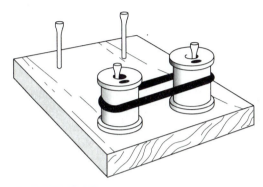

FIGURE 13-19

2. Make one crayon dot on the rim of each spool.

3. Put a spool on each of two nails.

4. Place a rubber band around the two spools.

5. Turn one spool. Watch the other spool turn also.

DISCOVERY PROBLEMS

predicting   **A.** How will the spools turn when connected in different ways? Notice the drawings in Figure 13-20. Each set of spools starts with the left spool. An arrow shows how each is turning. Another spool in the set has a question mark. It is next to a dot on the spool rim. See how the spools are connected.

  Will the dot on the rim turn left or right? Make a record of what you think. Then, use your wheel-belt board to find out.

predicting   **B.** Notice the Figure 13-21 drawings. How should the spools be connected to turn in these ways? How many different connections can you think of? Make drawings of what you think. (Do not cross any rubber bands more than once.) Then, use your wheel-belt board to find out.

experimenting   **C.** What wheel-belt systems can you invent? Make up and trade some problems with friends. Fix your board so you can use more spools.

TEACHING COMMENT

PREPARATION AND BACKGROUND

Part of an end piece from a discarded vegetable crate is ideal for the wheel-belt system base. Be sure that only finishing nails are pounded into the wood. These nails have small heads, allowing the spools to slip easily over them.

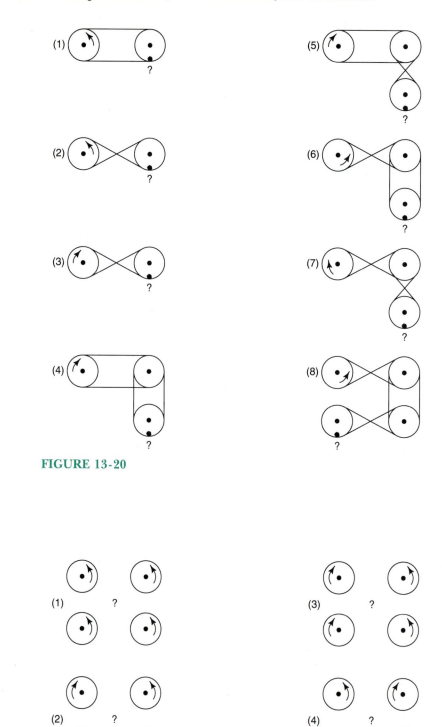

FIGURE 13-20

FIGURE 13-21

Note that this investigation deals only with the direction the spools turn. By using different-sized spools, children also can study how size governs the speed of turning. Because much slipping will happen with the rubber bands, the size–speed relationship cannot be determined accurately. Children can get the idea better by inverting a bicycle and studying the relative turnings of the large gear and the small gear.

GENERALIZATION

A wheel-belt system can be used to change the direction of a force.

SAMPLE PERFORMANCE OBJECTIVES

Process: When shown a two-, three-, or four-wheel-and-belt system, the child can predict the direction each wheel will turn.
Knowledge: The child can point out some everyday examples of wheel-belt systems or their equivalents.

FOR YOUNGER CHILDREN

Many primary pupils work well with wheel-belt systems. But use fewer spools than with older children.

□ ACTIVITY: How Do Bicycle Gears Affect Speed?

NEEDED

10-speed bicycle   chalk

TRY THIS

1. Observe the different-sized gears or sprockets on the rear wheel. Notice that all are smaller than the large pedal sprocket. See how a chain connects the large sprocket with a smaller one.
2. Adjust the chain so it is on the largest of the small gears.
3. Turn the bicycle upside down. Face the chain side.
4. Move the near pedal around. Notice how the rear wheel turns.
   a. How many times does the wheel turn compared to the pedal? Chalk a spot on the rear tire. Crank the pedal around one full turn. Count the turns made by the chalked wheel.
5. Adjust the chain so it is on the smallest rear gear. (You may have to set the bicycle upright to do so.)
   b. Crank the pedal one full turn. How many times does the rear wheel turn now?
   c. How does changing the rear gear size affect how fast you can go?

(*Teaching Comment:* Ten-speed bicycles have two different-sized front sprockets. When the smaller one is used, it causes the pedals to revolve faster. This decreases the forward speed, but allows less force to be used. For simplicity, use only one front sprocket in this activity.)

SECTION 4
Pulleys
[*Background 386*]

■ INVESTIGATION: How Pulleys Work

Many people use *pulleys* to help them work. Have you used a pulley to raise and lower a flag on a flagpole? Painters and roofers use pulleys to haul supplies up and down. Sometimes people work with only a single pulley, but often two or more are used together.

EXPLORATORY PROBLEM

How can you set up one or more pulleys to lift a load?

NEEDED

two single-wheel pulleys	sticky tape
rubber band or spring scale	book
strong cord	ruler
broom handle or stick	scissors
paper clip	

TRY THIS

1. Make a place to hang the pulley. Lay a stick over the backs of two separated chairs. Use tape to keep it from sliding. Loop and tie cord around the stick. Hang a pulley from the loop.
2. Set up a single pulley as shown in Figure 13-22A. This is a *fixed* pulley. Use a book for the load. Pull the cord *down* to lift the load. Practice a few times.
3. Now set up the pulley differently, as shown in Figure 13-22B. This is a *movable* pulley. Pull the cord *up* to lift the load. Practice a few times.

DISCOVERY PROBLEMS

observing **A.** What differences do you notice in using both pulleys?

measuring **B.** Which takes less force to lift the load, the fixed or movable pulley? How much less? To measure, hook a rubber band to the pull cord with a paper clip. Measure the stretch with a ruler. (Or, use a spring scale.)

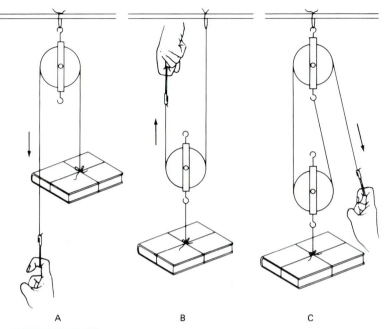

A   B   C

FIGURE 13-22

measuring   **C.** How far must you pull the cord to lift the load 1 meter (3 feet) with each pulley? Measure length of pull from where the cord leaves the pulley.

predicting   **D.** See Figure 13-22C. It shows a fixed and movable pulley working together. This is a *block and tackle*. Which do you think takes less force to lift a load, a single fixed pulley or a block and tackle? How far must you pull the cord with each to lift the book 1 meter (3 feet)? Predict and then measure to answer each question.

predicting   **E.** Compare the block and tackle with the single movable pulley.
measuring   Which do you think takes less force to lift a load? How far must you pull the cord with each to lift the book 1 meter (3 feet)? Predict and then measure to answer each question.

observing   **F.** What examples of pulleys can you find in the classroom? school? How do they work?

observing   **G.** What other pulleys can you collect and try? How do they compare with the three pulleys of this investigation?

TEACHING COMMENT

BACKGROUND AND PREPARATION

If a spring scale is used, be sure the load does not exceed its capacity.

   If you plan to do this investigation in a whole group setting, consider placing the broomstick holder and supporting chairs on a table. This will help pupils to get a clearer view.

Watch for pupils who cannot believe their data in Problem E. Many will be surprised that the advantage with this block and tackle over the movable pulley is solely one of convenience.

GENERALIZATION

A fixed pulley changes the direction of a force. A movable pulley reduces force needed to lift a load.

SAMPLE PERFORMANCE OBJECTIVES

Knowledge: The pupil can set up a block and tackle to lift a load.
Process: The child can measure the difference in force applied, and distance a rope is pulled, with a single and fixed pulley.

FOR YOUNGER CHILDREN

Let younger pupils experience the basic activity and manipulate the block and tackle. Measurements, especially with a spring scale, are better reserved for later grades.

□ ACTIVITY: How Can You Make a Broomstick "Pulley"?

NEEDED

broomstick sawed in half   two partners
5 meters (16 feet) of strong rope

TRY THIS

1. Have two partners face each other and stand about 1.5 meters (5 feet) apart. Each should firmly hold a broomstick.
2. Tie a rope tightly to one stick. Loop it once over the other stick as shown in Figure 13-23.

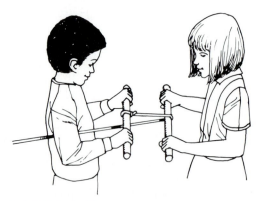

FIGURE 13-23

3. Try to pull your partners together. Pull smoothly, not jerkily, on the rope. They should try to stay apart.

    a. What will happen if you try two, three, and four loops of rope? Loop the rope around a stick one more time for each trial. (You will pull from an opposite direction each time.)

    b. When is it easiest to pull your partners together?

    c. Compare the distance you pull the rope with one loop and the distance you pull with four loops. When do you pull it farther?

(*Teaching Comment:* To avoid a struggle, caution pupils to use moderate effort and resistance. After about four turns of rope, increased friction on the sticks will exceed the benefit gotten from additional turns. Two sturdy metal or plastic pipes could be substituted to reduce such friction. As with a pulley, force in this activity is gained by trading off distance.)

SECTION 5
Motion and Friction
[*Background 388*]

☐ ACTIVITY: How Do Machines and Their Parts Move?

NEEDED

magazine pictures of different machines   toy machines

Some machines move mostly in a straight line when they work, such as a locomotive and roller skates. Some machines or their parts go back and forth, such as a grandfather clock and swing. Some machines or their parts go around, such as a merry-go-round and bicycle wheel.

TRY THIS

1. Find pictures of machines and machine parts in magazines.

2. Cut out and group the pictures by how the machines or their parts seem to move.

    a. Which machines or parts move mostly in a straight line?

    b. Which go back and forth?

    c. Which spin or go around as they work?

    d. Which machines do all of these things? some of these things?

    e. How do some toy machines and their parts move?

3. Look for real examples of machines working. Watch how they and their parts move. Make a record of what you find out.

    f. What machine can you make up and draw? How will your machine or its parts move? What work will it do?

■ INVESTIGATION: Pendulums

Have you ever seen an old-fashioned grandfather clock? One kind has a long weighted rod underneath that swings back and forth. The swinging part is called a *pendulum.* You can keep time with your own pendulum made with a string.

EXPLORATORY PROBLEM

How can you make a string pendulum?

NEEDED

thin string, about 1 meter (or yard) long   paper clip
meter stick or yardstick   clock or watch with second hand
pencil   sticky tape
three heavy washers   graph paper

TRY THIS

1. Tape a pencil to a table edge so it sticks out.

2. Bend a paper clip into a hook shape. Tie one string end to the hook.

3. Loop the free end of the string once around the pencil. Tape the string end to the table top.

4. Put two washers on the hook (Figure 13-24).

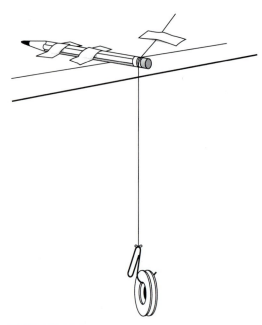

FIGURE 13-24

5. Move the washers to one side and then let go. Each time the washers swing back to that side, count one swing. Be sure the string does not rub against the table edge.

DISCOVERY PROBLEMS

measuring

A. How many swings does the pendulum make in one minute? Have someone help by observing the second hand on a clock. Then you can count the swings.

hypothesizing

B. Do wide swings take more time than narrow swings? Suppose you let go of your pendulum far to one side. What difference might that make in the number of swings it takes in one minute?

hypothesizing

C. Does the amount of weight used change the swing time? What might happen if you use a one-washer weight? a three-washer weight?

hypothesizing

D. Does the length of string used make a difference in swing time? (Measure length from the pencil to the end of the washers.) What might happen if you use a short string? longer string?

experimenting

E. How can you get your pendulum to swing 60 times in 1 minute?

inferring

F. Suppose you had a grandfather clock that was running slow. What could you do to its pendulum to correct it? What if it was running fast?

communicating

G. How well can you predict with your pendulum? Make a graph such as the one shown in Figure 13-25.

Try several string lengths for your pendulum. Count the swings for each length. Let's say you find that a 20-centimeter string swings 65

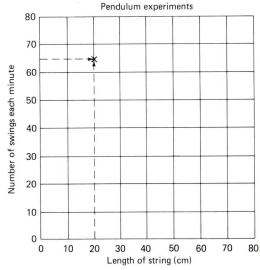

FIGURE 13-25

times in 1 minute. Make a mark on your graph where lines running from these two numbers meet. (See the graph.) Make marks for three or four other string lengths and their swings. Then draw a straight line between the marks.

predicting   Suppose you know the length of a pendulum, but you have not yet tried it. How can you use your graph to predict its number of swings?

predicting   Suppose you know the number of swings of a pendulum, but you have not yet measured its length. How can you use your graph to predict the pendulum's length?

experimenting   How can you make your predictions better and better?

TEACHING COMMENT

PREPARATION AND BACKGROUND

The timing of events is possible with a pendulum because its to-and-fro motion recurs with near-perfect regularity. Through manipulating variables, children can discover that the *length* of the weighted string affects the swing rate, or period, of a pendulum.

Be sure your pupils realize that one complete swing consists of the swing out *and* return movement.

Should washers be unavailable, substitute other small, uniform weights. You can hang a small paper cup from the hook and put marbles, dominoes, or checkers, and the like inside. Some pupils may need help constructing the graph. However, they should be able to follow through on the predicting part after becoming familiar with its construction. The way to more accurate predictions with graphs is to increase the valid data one works with.

GENERALIZATION

A pendulum is any object that swings regularly back and forth; its length affects its swing rate.

SAMPLE PERFORMANCE OBJECTIVES

Process: The child can accurately predict the swing rate of a pendulum for one minute by using graph data.
Knowledge: The child can state how to increase and decrease the swing rate of a pendulum.

FOR YOUNGER CHILDREN

An easy way for younger pupils to see the effect of manipulating a variable is to set up two identical pendulums to start. When both are set to swinging, they should perform in the same way. Thereafter, change only one variable at a time with one pendulum—weight or width of swing or length—so its performance may be contrasted with the unchanged pendulum. This strategy can keep the investigation concrete and understandable from the beginning through Problem D or E.

■ INVESTIGATION: Friction

Suppose someone asks you to slide a wooden box across the floor. On what kind of floor surface would it be easiest to start the box sliding? hardest? When an object catches or drags on a surface, we say much *friction* is present. If it slides or moves easily, little friction is present.

EXPLORATORY PROBLEM

How can you find out about the friction of different surfaces?

NEEDED

two same-sized wooden blocks
thumb tack
thin rubber band
paper clip
sheets of sandpaper, waxed paper, kitchen foil,
   construction paper

ruler
sticky tape
three wide rubber bands
two round pencils

TRY THIS

1. Place a wood block on a wood table. Fasten a rubber band to it with a thumb tack.
2. Hook the rubber band with an opened paper clip. Hold the rubber band end over the end of a ruler. (See Figure 13-26.)

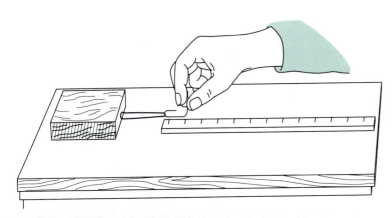

FIGURE 13-26

3. Pull the rubber band very slowly. Observe where the rubber band end is over the ruler. How far does the band stretch before the block moves? Read the ruler to the nearest whole number. Always make the reading *before* the block starts to slide.

DISCOVERY PROBLEMS

measuring   **A.** How much will the rubber band stretch if you pull the block a second time? third time? Record the results and the average for the three trials like this:

Surface Tested	Stretch for Each Trial (CM)	Average Stretch (CM)	Predicted Stretch
Wood	11 15 13	13	

measuring

predicting

    B. How much will the band stretch if the block is placed on other surfaces? Tape a small piece of kitchen foil to the table and place the block on it. Test this and other surfaces such as sandpaper, waxed paper, construction paper, and so on. (To prepare a rubber surface, wrap three wide rubber bands around the block.) Try to predict first how far the band will stretch each time. Record the results.

measuring   **C.** How much will the band stretch if the block is placed on its side? if a second block is put on top?

measuring   **D.** How much will the band stretch if two round pencils are placed under the block?

experimenting   **E.** How can you make the most friction between the block and surface? least friction? (Use more materials if necessary.)

TEACHING COMMENT

Two identical wooden play blocks can be used for this investigation, or cut 2 4-inch squares from a 2-inch by 4-inch piece of wood. A *thin* rubber band works best to pull with. To make it even stretchier, cut and use it as a single strand. If available, a spring scale may be used to compare results. There should be little relative difference, although the spring scale may be calibrated in ounces or grams. *Caution*—make sure the tack that holds the rubber band to the block is secure before the band is pulled.

GENERALIZATION

Friction between two surfaces depends on the force that presses the surfaces together and the materials that make up the surfaces; some surfaces have more friction than others.

SAMPLE PERFORMANCE OBJECTIVES

Process: The child can measure with a ruler how much a rubber band stretches to test the friction between a wooden block and the surface on which it rests.

Knowledge: The child can predict that a smooth surface will have less friction than a rougher one.

FOR YOUNGER CHILDREN

Younger pupils may not be ready to use a ruler for measurements. Instead, they may mark a piece of paper, in place of a ruler, to show the rubber band's relative amounts of stretch. Before this is done, allow time for them to play with and become familiar with the different materials.

☐ ACTIVITY: How Do Ball Bearings Affect Friction?

NEEDED

large metal screw cap from a glass jar   book
six or more matched marbles

TRY THIS

1. Place the book on the metal cap. Try to turn the book so it and the cap turn together. But do not touch the cap. Also, try to move the book and cap forward without touching the cap.
   a. What happens?
2. Stick marbles under the cap, as many as will fit. Be sure the cap does not touch the table. Try step 1 again.
   b. How does this trial compare with the first one? How do ball bearings affect friction?
   c. Where can you find examples of ball bearings in everyday things?

SELECTED TRADE BOOKS: SIMPLE MACHINES AND HOW THEY WORK

FOR YOUNGER CHILDREN

Barton, Bryon. *Machines at Work.* Harper & Row, 1987.

Gibbons, Gail. *Tool Book.* Holiday House, 1982.

Kiley, Denise. *Biggest Machines.* Raintree, 1980.

Lampton, Christopher. *Sailboats, Flag Poles, Cranes: Using Pulleys as Simple Machines.* Millbrook Press, 1991.

Lauber, Patricia. *Get Ready for Robots.* Scholastic, 1987.

Rockwell, Anne, and Harlow Rockwell. *Machines.* Harper & Row, 1985.

Robbins, Ken. *Tools.* Macmillan, 1983.

Wade, Harlan. *Gears.* Raintree, 1979.

Wade, Harlan. *The Lever.* Raintree, 1979.

Weiss, Harvey. *The World of Machines.* Raintree, 1983.

Wilkin, Fred. *Machines.* Children's Press, 1986.

Wyler, Rose. *Science Fun with Toy Cars and Trucks.* Messner, 1988.

FOR OLDER CHILDREN

Adkins, Jan. *Moving Heavy Things.* Houghton, 1980.

Baines, Rae. *Simple Machines.* Troll Associates, 1985.

Barrett, N. S. *Robots.* Watts, 1985.

Brown, William F., and Mary G. Brown. *Experiments with Common Wood and Tools.* Macmillan, 1984.

Fleisher, Paul and Patricia Keeler. *Looking Inside: Machines and Constructions.* Macmillan, 1991.

Gardner, Robert. *This Is the Way It Works.* Doubleday, 1980.

Hellman, Hal. *The Lever and the Pulley.* Lippincott, 1971.

James, Elizabeth, and Carol Barkin. *The Simple Facts of Simple Machines.* Lothrop, 1975.

Jupo, Frank. *The Story of Things (Tools).* Prentice-Hall, 1972.

Lefkowitz, R. J. *Push, Pull, Stop, Go: A Book About Forces and Motion.* Parents, 1975.

Taylor, Barbara. *Force and Movement.* Watts, 1990.

Weiss, Harvey. *Machines and How They Work.* Harper & Row, 1983.

14

Plant Life and Environment

"Chances for open-ended experiments are greater with plants than with any other area of elementary school science."

That is what one longtime teacher said, and I agree. At the same time, there is more need for planning ahead and keeping track of activities so that they may be interrelated. Living things take time to grow, and growth rates can seldom be exactly predicted. The best time for plant study, if you want both outdoor and indoor activities, is the spring.

There are many kinds of plants and plant-like organisms. The simplest forms lack roots, stems, and leaves. Mosses have stems and tiny leaflike parts, but they are rootless. Ferns and their kind resemble the most complex plants, except in reproduction.

The most complex and familiar plants we see are those that produce seeds, of which there are two basic groups. One group is composed of the *gymnosperms*. These plants are flowerless; they develop seeds attached to open scales or cones. Evergreens such as pine, hemlock, spruce, juniper, fir, and redwood are examples. There are about 600 species.

The second and far larger group (about 250,000 species) is composed of the *angiosperms*, or flowering plants. These form their seeds in closed compartments or cases within the flower.

In this chapter, we'll give most of our attention to the flowering plants. We'll consider (1) seeds and ways they grow, (2) how new plants can be started from plant parts, (3) how environmental conditions affect plants, (4) how plant parts work, and (5) how plants respond to their environment. A brief, final section (6) takes up the tiny plantlike organisms called *molds*. As before, common materials are used for the investigations and activities.

[I] SEEDS   *Experiences 431*

"Where do seeds come from?" is a question curious children may ask when they study flowering plants. Seeds are produced in a central part of the flower called the *ovary*. As the ovary ripens, its seeds become enveloped either by a fruity pulp, a pod, or a shell, depending on the kind of plant.

Pears and peaches are fruits whose pulp we eat. Beans, peas, and peanuts are examples of seeds enclosed in pods. When we "shell" string beans, lima beans, peas, or peanuts, we are removing these seeds from their pods. Walnuts, pecans, and coconuts have hard outer shells.

Seed Parts

Seeds come in many different shapes, colors, and sizes. Still, they have three things in common: a protective seed cover, a baby plant (embryo), and a food supply that nourishes the seed as it pushes up through the soil and grows into a young plant. In some plants, such as the bean and sweet pea, the food supply is in two seed "leaves," or cotyledons (Figure 14-1). In other seeds, such as corn and rice, there is only a single cotyledon.

Growth Stages

What happens when a seed grows into a young plant or seedling? For an example, look at Figure 14-2. In A, the seed swells from moisture in the soil. The coat softens and

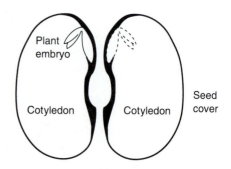

FIGURE 14-1

Parts of a bean seed.

FIGURE 14-2
From seed to seedling.

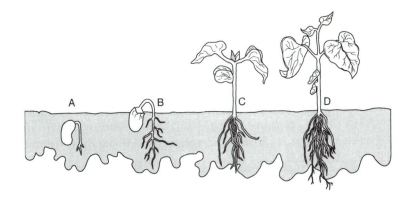

splits. A tiny root and stem emerge. In B, the upper part of the stem penetrates the soil surface and lifts the folded cotyledons out of the seed cover. In C, the cotyledons and tiny plant leaves unfold. Roots deepen and spread. In D, roots become more extensive. The cotyledons are smaller and shriveled. Nearly all the food supply is consumed. The plant begins to make its own food through photosynthesis within its maturing leaves. In a short while, the shriveled cotyledons, then useless, will drop off the growing plant. This growth process, from seed to seedling, is called *germination*. The total time from A to D is about 14 days in a bean plant.

Many pupils are surprised to find that seeds and recently sprouted seedlings placed in the dark grow faster for a time than those placed in the light. However, the plants will be spindly and pale. Light energy seems to partly inhibit rather than stimulate healthy growth in many sprouting seeds until photosynthesis takes place.

Survival Conditions

Some flowering plants produce thousands of seeds a year. If they all grew into plants, before long there would scarcely be room on earth for anything else. Fortunately, a variety of factors enables only a small percentage of wild seeds to grow. Seeds are destroyed by birds, insects, bacteria, and other organisms.

And unless proper conditions of moisture, temperature, and oxygen are present, seeds remain dormant. After several years in a dormant state, all but a few kinds of seeds lose their potential ability to germinate. These few, however, may not lose this ability for hundreds or even thousands of years.

Weeds are everywhere about us. What makes them so prolific? Perhaps you have noticed that weeds appear at different times during a growing season. This is because growth requirements of moisture, temperature, and oxygen vary greatly among different kinds of seeds. Of course, this has great survival value. Conditions are never such that all seeds in the soil die at one time.

How Seeds Travel

We know that people plant seeds in gardens. But they do not plant weeds in fields and vacant lots. Nor do they plant seeds in many other places where plants grow. Where do these seeds come from? This question is sometimes raised by thoughtful children.

Pupils can learn that seeds travel in several ways. Some are scattered through the actions of animals and people. The sharp hooks or barbs on the cocklebur, burdock, and beggar tick cling to clothing or animal fur (Figure 14-3). Birds eat fleshy fruits but may not digest the hard seeds. The seeds pass out of their bodies some distance away. People

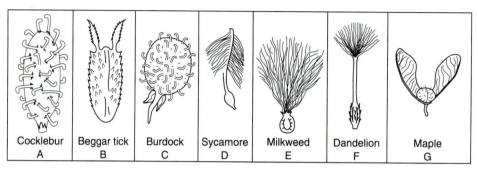

FIGURE 14-3
Some common seeds.

throw away fruit pits, watermelon seeds, and so on. The wind blows many seeds. Some have "parachutes," such as the goldenrod, milkweed, and dandelion. The maple tree seed has "wings." Water can carry seeds from place to place because many seeds float. The capacity of seeds to disperse widely and in different ways is another survival feature.

An excellent time to collect many seeds without cost is in the fall. Pupils will be happy to help.

Sprouting Seeds

It is much cheaper to buy seeds (the kind you eat) at a grocery store than at a seed store, even though a smaller percentage will grow. Some easy-to-grow seeds are kidney beans, lima beans, pinto beans, whole green peas, and yellow peas.

To ensure that only live, healthy seeds are planted, treat them to prevent mold and sprout them before planting. Here is how.

Soak the seeds in water for several hours to soften them. Then remove the seeds and drop them into a mixture of one part liquid bleach to eight parts water. Take out the seeds immediately after immersing them.

To sprout the treated seeds, first soak several paper towels in water. Fold and place them in an aluminum pie pan or dish. Place the treated seeds on top of the wet towels. Then cover the pan with clear plastic wrap to prevent the water from evaporating.

Inspect the seeds every day. Within several days to a week, many bean or pea seeds will have parts sticking out of the seed cover. These sprouted seeds are alive. They are likely to grow into plants if planted while moist and cared for properly.

Containers and Soil

Many improvised containers can be used for germinating seeds and growing seedlings—plastic and paper cups, milk cartons with tops cut off, and cottage cheese cartons. All should be rinsed clean. In some experiments, water glasses permit better observation. Seeds may be planted next to the glass. If black paper masks the roots from light, they may grow a little faster.

All containers may be filled with garden soil, sand, sawdust, or vermiculite—an inexpensive insulating material made up of fluffy bits of mica. Only the garden soil will have minerals needed for healthy growth of plants beyond the seedling stage.

The other "soil" materials let more air circulate around the seed cover and plant roots. They are also more porous and so they are harder to overwater. Plants rooted in these materials may be more easily removed, examined, and replanted without serious root damage.

Small holes punched in containers will aid good drainage. Any water runoff can be caught in a saucer placed below. If holes cannot easily be made, as with a glass jar, include an inch of gravel in the jar bottom before adding soil. Water only when the soil surface feels slightly dry.

Instruct pupils to plant seeds only slightly deeper than their length. But always follow instructions on the seed package for seed store varieties. Since it takes energy to push through the soil, a small seed planted too deeply runs out of food before it reaches the surface. Also, keep the soil somewhat loose so air can get to the roots.

Keep plants by the brightest window in your room. On long weekends or short vacations, cover growing plants with plastic bags. This keeps them from drying out quickly and partly protects them from cold temperatures.

[2] VEGETATIVE REPRODUCTION
Experiences 436

Many people think that only seeds produce new flowering plants. Yet some of the most useful and interesting ways to grow new plants are through the propagation of roots, stems, and even leaves. This is called *vegetative reproduction.*

Roots

Consider the orange-colored tap root of the carrot plant—the part we eat. A carrot plant is usually grown from seed in the spring and harvested some months later. If left in the ground, however, all parts above the soil surface die as the weather becomes cold. No growth occurs during this time. As warmer weather approaches, tender shoots grow from the tap root and emerge into sunlight. These grow into stems and leaves. Some time thereafter, flowers and seeds are produced. Like a seed, a tap root provides the food

energy needed for shoots to emerge and grow. Parsnips and beets are other examples of tap roots that grow in this way (Figure 14-4).

New plants may be grown from tap roots in the classroom by embedding them in moist sand or garden soil. A favorite method of many teachers is to cut off all but the top quarter of a tap root and imbed it in a small bowl containing a layer of pebbles and some water. At least half of the root cutting is above water to assure a sufficient oxygen supply. When sufficient foliage and roots have emerged, cuttings are planted in garden soil for full growth.

A sweet potato is another example of an enlarged root that can propagate a whole new plant. It may be grown in a similar way, described in a forthcoming activity.

Stems

Most ground-cover plants, such as grass, strawberry, and ivy, spread quickly after planting. Each sends out stems or runners that

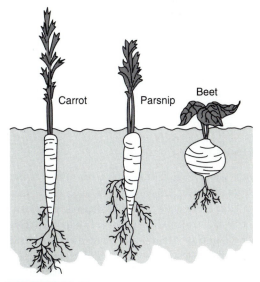

FIGURE 14-4
Carrots, parsnips, and beets have tap roots.

take root, push up shoots, and develop into new plants. These lateral stems may spread above ground, as in the strawberry plant and Bermuda grass, or below ground, as in quack grass. The most persistent weed grasses are of the underground-stem variety, as frustrated lawn growers will testify.

New plants may be propagated from stem cuttings of the geranium and begonia. Other common plants whose stems grow independently are the coleus, oleander, philodendron, and English ivy. Dipping the ends of stem cuttings in a commercial hormone preparation may start root growth in half the usual time.

Sometimes on opening a bag of white potatoes, we find some of them beginning to sprout. Usually, this happens when the potatoes are left undisturbed for a time in a dark, warm place. White potatoes are swollen parts of underground stems, called *tubers*. The dark spots, or "eyes," are buds, from which shoots grow.

Farmers today seldom, if ever, use potato seeds in growing crops. Instead, they cut potatoes into several bud-bearing parts and plant these. Each bud grows into a new plant that produces more potatoes.

Occasionally, we see shoots growing from onion bulbs stored in the home pantry. Bulbs, too, are modified stems. All contain thick, fleshy leaves wrapped tightly around a small, immature stem. Tulips and gladioli are typical flowers that may be grown from both bulbs and seeds.

Leaves

Even some *leaves* may develop into whole plants. Suggestions follow for using an African violet, echeveria, and bryophyllum plant.

Use a fresh African violet leaf with attached petiole (leaf stalk). Put the stalk into an inch of water in a drinking glass. For better support of the leaf, use a card with a hole punched in it placed across the glass

rim. Insert the leaf petiole through the hole and into the water. After roots begin to grow, plant the leaf in rich soil.

An echeveria leaf will usually root by merely laying it flat on dry sand. It is a thick leaf that contains much food and water. After it roots, water sparingly. Like most desert plants, this one thrives in semiarid soil.

The bryophyllum leaf is sometimes sold in variety stores under the name "magic leaf." This title is only a slight exaggeration. To propagate, pin it down flat on damp sand with several toothpicks or straight pins. Tiny plants should grow from several of the notches around the leaf rim. A variation of this method is to pin the leaf to a curtain! When some plantlets start growing, cut them out with scissors and plant them in damp sand so they root.

Why Vegetative Reproduction?

Sometimes children ask, "If plants can grow from seeds, why are the other ways used?" There are several reasons. All of these methods result in whole plants in far less time. Also, some things cannot be grown from seed— seedless oranges, for example. In this case, branches of seedless oranges are grafted onto an orange tree grown from seed.

But the most important reason is quality control. We can never be sure of the results when we plant seeds of some plants. Vegetative reproduction carries the assurance that the new plants will be very much like the parent plant. If large, healthy potatoes are cut up and planted, for instance, we probably can harvest near-identical specimens.

All the foregoing methods of vegetative reproduction are asexual. In other words, reproduction does not require involvement of plant sex organs. Certain lower animallike forms also can reproduce themselves asexually. In another section, we will discuss sexual reproduction in flowering plants; that is, how fertile seeds are produced.

[3] ENVIRONMENTAL CONDITIONS

Experiences 440

Plants grow and flourish only when the environment provides proper amounts of minerals, water, light, temperature, and, more indirectly, space. Because the classroom is an artificial habitat, or home, for plants, pupils will need to furnish the conditions the plants need to survive.

Growth Conditions

Children will find that soil-watering requirements for plants are like those for germinating seeds. Overwatering causes the plant to die of oxygen deprivation or disease. Underwatering usually results in a droopy, malnourished plant. The absence of vital soil minerals and extremes in temperature also have a weakening, or even fatal, effect on plants.

Crowding of plants is harmful to growth largely because competition deprives individual plants of enough of what they need for good growth. Even the hardiest plants develop to less than normal size under crowded conditions.

Green plants need light energy to manufacture their own food, but not necessarily sunshine. Electric lights may be substituted.

Many commercial flower growers take advantage of this fact to regulate the growth rates or blooming times of their flowers to coincide with different holidays. Plants generally grow faster when exposed to light for increased time periods. But overexposure retards growth and delays normal blooming times.

Light color is also a factor in speed of growth. You remember that white light is composed of several different colors. Each color has a different wavelength. At different stages of growth, from seedling to adult plant, wavelengths of certain colors stimulate more growth than others. But generally, of all single colors, red seems to stimulate seedlings to grow most nearly in a normal way. Exposure to white light usually results in the best overall growth patterns.

Three Habitats

Even the casual observer can notice that different kinds of plants live in different habitats. Cacti are unlikely to be found in woodlands, and ferns do not ordinarily live in deserts. It may be hard for us to take pupils directly to different habitats. It is possible, though, to bring several habitats to the classroom in miniature form.

The *terrarium* is a managed habitat for small land plants and, if desired, several small animals likely to be found with the plants. Three basic kinds are the woodland, marsh, and desert terrariums. Almost any large glass or plastic container will do for the basic structure. An old aquarium tank is usually best, but a large pickle jar turned on its side will also do. The container should be thoroughly cleaned before use.

To make a *woodland terrarium*, cover the bottom of the container with a 2.5-centimeter (1-inch) layer of pebbles, sand, and bits of charcoal mixed together. This layer will allow drainage, and the charcoal will absorb gases and keep the soil from turning sour. Add to the bottom layer a second layer about twice as thick, consisting of equal parts of rich garden soil and sand mixed together with a bit of charcoal. Sprinkle the ground until moist, but do not leave it wet, as molds may develop.

Dwarf ivy, ferns, liverworts, and lichens are ideal plants. Partridge berry and mosses provide a nice ground cover, if desired.

After a week or so, the plants should take hold, and a few small animals can be introduced. A land snail, earthworms, a small land turtle, a salamander, or a small frog are suitable for a miniature woodland habitat. A little lettuce will feed the snail or turtle; earthworms get nutrition from the soil. Food for frogs and salamanders might include small live insects, such as mealworms, flies, sow bugs, ants, and the like. A small, shallow dish pressed into the soil can serve as a water source.

Keep the terrarium covered and out of the sunlight to avoid the buildup of heat. A glass sheet loosely fitted to permit air circulation will help keep high humidity inside, reducing the need to water the soil. Here, too, water will evaporate from the soil, condense on the underside of the glass cover, and fall as "rain" in a miniature water cycle.

To make a *marsh terrarium,* the soil must be more acidic and damper than in the previous terrarium. Cover the container bottom with pebbles. Add to that a 6-centimeter (3-inch) layer of acid soil and peat moss mixed in about equal parts. These materials can be bought at a plant nursery.

Suitable plants are the Venus's-flytrap, sundew, pitcher plant, mosses, and sedges.

Some appropriate animals include frogs, toads, small turtles, and salamanders. Again, press a small, shallow dish of water flush with the soil surface for the animals. Keep this terrarium covered and in a cool part of the room.

To make a *desert terrarium,* cover the container bottom with about 3 centimeters (1½ inches) of coarse sand. Sprinkle this lightly with water and an equally thick layer of fine sand on top. Get a few small potted cacti or other desert succulents. Bury these so the pot tops are flush with the sand surface. Sprinkle plants lightly with water about once a week.

Suitable animals are lizards, including the horned toad. Push a partly buried dish into the sand for their water source. Mealworms and live insects will do for food. Place a stick and a few stones in the sand on which the animals may climb or rest. This terrarium may be left uncovered and in the sun.

[4] PLANT PARTS AND FUNCTIONS   *Experiences 446*

Children are usually surprised to learn that, besides fruits and vegetables, all the meat they eat has originally been derived from green plants. Flesh-eating animals depend on plant-eating animals. This is true in the ocean as well as on land. Everything alive basically depends on food synthesized from raw materials in the leaves of green plants.

The plant itself depends on the proper working of its several parts to produce this food. In this section, we'll examine how these parts work. Let's begin with plant roots.

Roots

The experience of weeding a garden makes us very conscious of one function of roots—they anchor the plant. We also know that food storage in roots enables the plant to survive when food making cannot occur. Another function of roots is the absorption of soil water.

Plants that are transplanted sometimes grow poorly for a while, or even die. This is usually due to damage done to tiny, very delicate root hairs that grow from the older root tissue (Figure 14-5). It is the root hairs that absorb nearly all the water, rather than the older fibrous material.

There may be billions of root hairs on a single plant, enough to stretch hundreds of miles if laid end to end. If laid side by side in rows, they would take up the floor area of an average-sized home. Root hairs are so small they are able to grow in the tiny spaces between soil particles and make direct contact with water and air trapped therein.

Growth takes place very largely at the tip of a root. A tough root cap protects the sensitive growing portion as it punches through the soil. Because the soil is abrasive,

FIGURE 14-5
A seedling has many root hairs.

the root cap tissue is continually worn off and replaced by new tissue.

Stems

Water absorbed by the roots goes into the stems, through which it is transported by narrow tubes to all parts of the plant. Dissolved minerals in the water are deposited within the cells of these parts. When water reaches the leaves, some of it evaporates into the air.

Exactly how does this continual movement of water happen in the plant? This has been a mystery until recent times. Modern molecular theory gives an answer.

As you know, molecules that are alike have an attractive force which binds them together (cohesion). These molecules may also be attracted to unlike molecules (adhesion). The thin tubes that transport water in a plant run from root to stem to leaf. Adhesion of water molecules to the tube walls helps to support the tiny water column. Cohesion causes the water molecules to stick together. As water molecules evaporate into the air, they "tug" slightly at the molecules below because of cohesive attraction. Because of cohesion, all the other molecules rise in a kind a chain reaction.

Should an air bubble get into the tube, the chain reaction is broken. The bubble separates some molecules to a distance beyond their effective cohesive attraction.

Leaves

A leaf seems thin and simple in structure from the outside. Yet the intricate mechanisms within it, which produce the world's food supply, have never been fully duplicated by scientists. Inside the leaf cells is a green-pigmented chemical, *chlorophyll.*

Chlorophyll enables a leaf to chemically combine carbon dioxide from air with water to form a simple sugar. The energy needed to power this chemical synthesis in the leaf comes from sunlight, which is absorbed by the chlorophyll. *Photosynthesis,* as the process is called, literally means "to put together with light."

From the sugar leaves manufacture, the plant cells make starch, which may be stored in all parts of the plant. With additional compounds received from the soil and through soil bacteria, plant cells can manufacture proteins and vitamins.

Carbon dioxide is taken up in photosynthesis and oxygen is released as a waste product. But when a plant consumes the food stored in its cells, it takes up oxygen and gives off carbon dioxide as a waste product, as you and I do. Fortunately for us, much more oxygen is released to the air through photosynthesis than is used by plants in oxidizing their stored food. In fact, green plants are the chief source of the world's present oxygen supply.

How do these gases enter and leave the leaf? Thousands of microscopic openings, called *stomates,* may be found in a green leaf. In land plants, these are largely, but not exclusively, located in the leaf's underneath surface. Each *stomate* is surrounded by special cells that regulate the size of the opening (Figure 14-6). Water in the leaf evaporates into the air through the stomates, a process called *transpiration.* Regulation of these openings has great survival value. In dry spells and at night, the stomates stay closed, thereby preventing any appreciable loss of water.

Interestingly, most of the photosynthesis on earth happens in the ocean within uncountable numbers of microscopic algae that float on and near the water surface. We have not yet learned how to use the tremendous food supply this source potentially affords to a hungry world.

Flowers

Many people value flowers because of their beauty. But for flowering plants, flowers have a more vital function. They are the only means by which species can naturally survive. The flower is the reproductive system of a flowering plant. Its two principal organs are the *pistil,* which contains unfertilized egg cells, and *stamens,* which produce dustlike *pollen* cells. (See Figure 14-7.)

FIGURE 14-6
Guard cells (stomates) in a leaf.

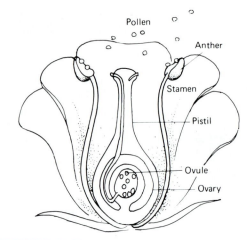

FIGURE 14-7
Parts of a flower.

When a pollen grain lands on the sticky end of a pistil, a tube begins to grow that "eats" its way down to the pistil base, or *ovary.* There, it joins onto an egg cell, or *ovule.* A sperm cell released from the pollen grain travels down the tube and unites with the ovule. Other ovules in the ovary may be fertilized by additional pollen in the same way.

The ovules, now fertilized, begin growing into seeds. The entire ovary begins to swell as a fleshy fruit begins to grow around the seeds. As the ovary becomes larger, parts of the flower drop off. Finally, a whole fruit forms. In the apple, the ovary is enveloped by a stem part that swells up around it. The next time you eat an apple, look at the core end opposite the fruit stem. Quite likely the tiny dried-up remains of the pistil and stamens will be visible.

When examining flowers with children, use single flowers, such as tulips and sweet peas, rather than composite flowers, such as daisies and sunflowers. The centers of these composite types consist of many tiny flowers, each complete with pistil and stamens. They are too small to be readily observed and may be confusing to the children.

Pollination

Self-pollination happens when pollen from a flower's own stamens fertilize the ovules. *Cross-pollination* occurs when pollen from another flower perform this function. However, pollen must be from the same type of flower for fertilization to take place.

Much pollination happens through gravity, as when pollen simply fall from tall stamens onto a shorter pistil. Or pollen may fall from a flower high up on a stem to one lower down. Insects are also primary distributors of pollen. As they sip nectar from flowers, pollen grains rub off onto their bodies. When the insects visit other flowers, these grains may become dislodged. It is interesting to note that bright colored and fragrant flowers are visited by the most insects. Wind is also an important distributor of pollen. In spring, the air contains billions of pollen grains, bringing pollination to plants and hay fever to many people.

Life Cycles

Many garden flowers and vegetables grow from seed, then blossom, produce seeds, and die in one growing season. These are known as *annuals*. Examples are petunias, zinnias, beans, and tomatoes. Those that live two seasons are *biennials*. Examples are hollyhocks, forget-me-nots, carrots, and turnips. Plants that live more than two growing seasons are *perennials*. Trees and most shrubs fit into this classification.

[5] RESPONSES TO ENVIRONMENT
Experiences 454

Adaptation

If you were asked to invent a plant, what adaptive properties would you want it to have for survival value? Whatever your design, it would be wise to have your plant regulate itself to some extent according to its needs.

Assume it has the same needs as other plants. Because it requires water, and water soaks down into the soil, you would want the plant roots to grow downward. But what if there were no water below the roots? You would want roots that could overcome the pull of gravity and grow toward a water source, even if the source were to one side or above the roots.

Because the plant needs light, you would want the stem to be able to grow toward a light source if light became blocked or dimmed. At the same time, it would be desirable to design the leaf stalk to give maximum exposure of the leaf to sunlight. An efficient stalk should be able to grow longer if another leaf blocks its light. It might also turn the leaf perpendicular to the sun's rays as the sun appeared at different positions in the sky.

You would also want to consider the obstructions that the plant might meet in its growth both above and below the ground. It would be helpful for survival if the plant roots and stem could grow around these obstacles to some extent when they touched them.

Of course, there is no need to invent plants like this, as they are now everywhere around you. Most green plants respond to gravity, water, light, and touch. These responses to environmental stimuli are called plant *tropisms*. Let's see why they happen.

Tropisms

Figure 14-8 shows a radish seedling growing on wet blotting paper inside a water glass. The glass has been placed on its side for 24 hours. Notice that the seedling shoot, or stem, is beginning to curve upward, although the root is starting to grow downward. *Both* reactions are responses to gravity.

Why the opposite directions? Check the magnified sections of the seedling. Gravity concentrates plant hormones (*auxins*) all

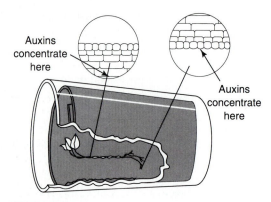

Auxins concentrate here

Auxins concentrate here

FIGURE 14-8
Seedling shoots curve upward and roots grow down almost as soon as sprouting occurs.

along the bottom cells from the beginning of the stem to the root tip. The cells along the bottom of the stem are stimulated by the hormones to grow faster than cells above. Growth of these cells is fastest by the stem tip (left inset). As these bottom cells become elongated, the stem begins to curve upward. Root cells, however, are much more sensitive than stem cells. So the concentration of hormones along the bottom root cells has the opposite effect; it inhibits cell growth. Top cells are least affected and elongate faster, so that the root tip begins to curve downward. Cell growth is fastest by the tip (right inset).

Tropistic responses seem to be the result of plant hormones that concentrate in various parts of the plant. As we have seen, this causes some cells to grow faster than others. Such responses can happen only in growing tissue.

Survival and Environment

The survival of plant (and animal) species is more than a matter of properties the organism inherits by chance. The environment also plays a part because it is continually changing. For example, a long dry spell will favor plants with small bad-tasting leaves and deep roots. Why? Large-leafed plants will lose too much water to survive. Shallow-rooted plants will not be able to tap moisture deep down. Plants with tasty leaves will be eaten first by hungry, thirsty animals.

Organisms that have the capacity to respond to and withstand environmental changes usually reproduce organisms with similar properties. So heredity and environment work together in shaping living things.

[6] MOLDS   *Experiences 456*

In recent years, growing molds has become popular in elementary science programs. It offers pupils many chances to experiment with variables at several levels.

Molds are a subgroup of a broader group of organisms called fungi. Some common examples of other fungi are mushrooms, mildews, puffballs, and yeasts. Molds will grow on a wide variety of animal and plant materials and some synthetic materials.

Tiny, seedlike spores from molds are found in the air almost anywhere. When the spores settle on a substance, they may grow. Molds get the nutrients they need to live from the material they grow on. Unlike the green plants, molds and other fungi cannot manufacture their own food.

Molds may grow under a wide variety of conditions. But those found commonly in classrooms are most likely to thrive when it is dark, moist, and warm.

INVESTIGATIONS & ACTIVITIES

■ INVESTIGATION: Seed Parts

What is inside a bean seed? Can you draw a picture of how it might look inside?

EXPLORATORY PROBLEM

How can you find out about the parts of seeds?

NEEDED

bean seeds   paper towel
corn seeds   glass of water

TRY THIS

1. Soak some bean and corn seeds in water overnight.
2. Open a soaked bean seed with your thumbnails (Figure 14-9).

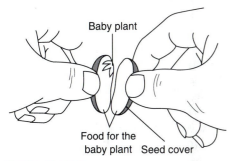

Baby plant

Food for the
baby plant   Seed cover

FIGURE 14-9

DISCOVERY PROBLEMS

observing   **A.** What do you notice about your seed?
                   How many different parts do you find?
                   How does the seed feel to you without its cover?
                   What does the seed smell like?

observing   **B.** Open the corn seed. How is it like the bean seed? How is it different?

observing   **C.** Soak and open other kinds of seeds. In what ways are they alike and different?

communicating   **D.** How well can you describe a seed? Put a seed among three different kinds of seeds. Describe it. Will someone be able to pick it out?

TEACHING COMMENT

PREPARATION AND BACKGROUND

Seeds from flowering plants come in many different shapes, colors, and sizes. But they have three things in common: a protective seed cover, a baby plant (embryo), and a food supply. The food nourishes the sprouted embryo as it pushes up through the soil and grows into a young plant. When its food supply is gone, a green plant can make (photosynthesize) its own food from substances in air, water, and soil if light shines on it. In some plants, such as the bean and sweet pea, the food supply is located in two seed halves or cotyledons. In other seeds, such as corn and rice, there is only a single cotyledon.

GENERALIZATION

Most seeds have a baby plant, food supply, and cover.

SAMPLE PERFORMANCE OBJECTIVES

Process: The child can state several likenesses and differences he or she has observed among different seeds.
Knowledge: When shown a seed he or she has not already examined, the child can predict that it consists of an embryo, food supply, and cover.

FOR OLDER CHILDREN

If possible, let older pupils gather and examine some seeds from evergreen plants such as the pine, hemlock, spruce, fir, juniper, and redwood. They may observe how the seeds are attached to open scales or cones. Have them look up information about the reproductive process of such plants.

□ ACTIVITY: How Can You Sprout Seeds Without Soil?

NEEDED

paper towels   two pie tins or saucers
drinking glass   water
bean seeds

TRY THIS

1. Try two ways to sprout seeds. Soak some seeds overnight.

2. Line the inside of a drinking glass with a wet, folded paper towel as shown in Figure 14-10.

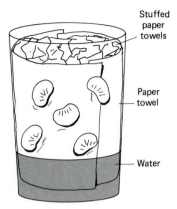

Stuffed
paper
towels

Paper
towel

Water

FIGURE 14-10

3. Stuff a paper towel into the glass. This will hold the other towel against the glass.

4. Stick some soaked seeds between the paper towel and glass.

5. Fill the glass with water up to the lowest seed. The paper towel will soak up the water and keep the seeds wet.

6. Try a second way to sprout seeds. Lay a half-folded wet paper towel on a pie plate or saucer. Put some soaked seeds on top of the towel.

7. Pour some water into the pie plate. This will keep the towel wet. Fold over the wet towel to cover the seeds. Put a second plate on top to keep water from quickly evaporating. Carefully uncover the seeds each day to observe them.
   a. With which way do more seeds sprout?
   b. What differences are there in how fast the seeds sprout? In how fast the sprouted seeds grow?
   c. What other differences, if any, do you notice?

(*Teaching Comment:* Be sure that the water in the glass and plate is below the seeds. Otherwise, the seeds may die from lack of oxygen.)

■ INVESTIGATION: The Growth of Seeds

Where do green plants come from? Have you planted seeds? What did you do?

EXPLORATORY PROBLEM

How can you plant seeds so they may grow?

NEEDED

soil
water
pencil
pie pan

bean seeds soaked overnight in water
paper towel
topless milk carton or paper cup

TRY THIS

1. Poke holes into the carton bottom with a pencil or nail.
2. Put the carton on a pie pan.
3. Fill the carton almost full with soil.
4. Water the soil slowly until water leaks into the pie pan.
5. Poke a hole in the soil. Make it about as deep as the seed you plant is long (Figure 14-11).

FIGURE 14-11

6. Put the seed into the hole. Cover it with wet soil. Tap the soil down *lightly.*
7. Water the soil when it feels dry to your touch, but not more than once a day.
8. Measure your growing plant three times a week. Put a strip of paper alongside. Tear off some to match the plant's height. Date the strips and paste them on a large sheet of paper. What can you tell from this plant record?

DISCOVERY PROBLEMS

experimenting **A.** Try some experiments with more materials. In what kind of soil will a seed grow best? Try sand, sawdust, or soil from different places. Or, mix your own soil from some of these.

experimenting **B.** Will a seed live and grow if you water it with salt water? How much salt can you use?
What else might you use to "water" a growing seed?

experimenting **C.** Will a broken or damaged seed grow?
Will a seed that was frozen or boiled grow?
Will a seed grow if the seed cover is taken off?

experimenting   **D.** Does the position of a seed make a difference? For example, what will happen if you plant a seed upside down?

experimenting   **E.** What other experiments with seeds might you try?

TEACHING COMMENT

PREPARATION AND BACKGROUND

A seed that is soaked before it is planted will sprout faster than one planted dry. But don't leave a seed in water more than overnight. It may die from insufficient air.

GENERALIZATION

Some plants grow from seeds; proper conditions are needed for seeds to sprout and grow.

SAMPLE PERFORMANCE OBJECTIVES

Process: The child sets up an experiment to test a condition that may affect seed growth.
Knowledge: The child describes how seeds may be properly grown into plants.

FOR YOUNGER CHILDREN

Most intuitive thinkers can do the foregoing activities. However, they will be unable to control variables unless guided. Be sure that these children learn right away how to properly plant and care for a growing seed. Then they will see an experiment with another seed as a variation to be compared with their "good" one. This approach makes sense to them. It also ensures that most children will feel successful and encouraged rather than frustrated and disappointed.

☐ ACTIVITY: How Deep Can You Plant a Seed and Still Have It Grow?

NEEDED

six sprouted bean seeds   sticky tape
tall, clear jar with straight sides   black paper

TRY THIS

1. Plant two seeds in soil at the bottom of the jar. Place the seeds next to the glass, so they can be seen.

2. Add more soil. Plant two seeds in the middle of the jar the same way.

3. Add more soil. Plant two seeds near the top of the jar.

4. Wrap black paper around the jar. Remove the paper for a short time to observe the seeds each day. Water the seeds as needed.
   a. Which seeds will have enough food energy to grow to the surface?
   b. What would happen if you planted smaller seeds, like radish seeds?

□ **ACTIVITY:** In What Places Are Seeds in the Soil?

NEEDED

shoe boxes   outdoor places
clear kitchen wrap   small shovel
plastic bags

TRY THIS

1. Line some shoe boxes with plastic bags.
2. Half-fill each shoe box with bare soil from a different place. Record where each place is on the box. Try garden soil, soil where weeds grow, and other bare soils.
3. Water the soil so it is damp. Cover each box with clear kitchen wrap.
4. Leave each in a warm, well-lighted place for several weeks or more.
   a. In which box do you expect seeds to grow?
   b. In which box, if any, did seeds grow?
   c. Will wild plants grow in the exact places from which you took soil? Observe these places from time to time.

SECTION 2
Vegetative Reproduction
[*Background 423*]

■ **INVESTIGATION:** The Growth of a Potato Plant

You do not need seeds to grow some plants. Have you ever seen a white potato stored at home that has grown sprouts? The sprouts grow from the "eyes," or buds, on the potato skin.

EXPLORATORY PROBLEM

How can you grow a potato plant from a white potato?

NEEDED

white potato   nail
soil   pie pan
plastic or paper container   paper towel
water   knife

TRY THIS

1. Punch holes in the container bottom with a nail.
2. Put the container on a pie pan.

3. Fill the container almost full with soil.

4. Water the soil slowly until the water leaks into the pie pan.

5. Cut off a piece of potato that has a bud.

6. Poke a hole in the soil. Make the hole slightly deeper than the potato piece is long. Bury the piece (Figure 14-12).

7. Water the soil when it feels dry to your touch, but not more than once a day.

FIGURE 14-12

DISCOVERY PROBLEMS

experimenting **A.** How big a piece of potato does a bud need to grow into a plant?

hypothesizing **B.** What would happen if you planted a whole potato?

hypothesizing **C.** What would happen if you planted only the tiny bud?

hypothesizing **D.** What would happen if you planted a potato piece that has no bud?

experimenting **E.** What other experiments would you like to try with potatoes?

TEACHING COMMENT

The starchy white part of a potato nourishes potato buds. This is like the food supply of a seed that nourishes the sprouting baby plant. Each bud may grow into a plant with many potatoes.

Use larger-sized containers with this investigation. Clean cottage-cheese cartons and one-gallon milk cartons cut in half work well. You can easily burn drainage holes in the bottoms of plastic containers with a hot nail. (Use a candle flame for heat.)

GENERALIZATION

With some plants a whole new plant may be grown from a part of the plant.

SAMPLE PERFORMANCE OBJECTIVES

Process: The child can design an experiment to test one variable that may affect the growth of a potato bud.
Knowledge: The child can explain that potato pieces require buds in order to grow.

FOR YOUNGER CHILDREN

Most primary children can do this investigation when guided, except for Discovery Problem A. Most are unable to test the size of pieces systematically.

☐ ACTIVITY: How Can You Grow New Plants from Cut Stems?

NEEDED

three clear plastic drinking glasses   soil
sand   water
knife   healthy geranium plant

TRY THIS

1. Cut a strong stem about 13 centimeters (5 inches) long from the plant. Cut just below where leaves join the stem. Trim away all but two or three leaves on top.

2. Stick the cutting into a half-glass of water. Watch for roots to appear.

3. Some cuttings grow roots faster when placed in sand or soil. Make two more cuttings. Plant one at a slant in a glass containing sand. Plant the other the same way in soil. The stem end should be against the glass. In this way, you will be able to see roots start. Keep the soil or sand damp.
   a. In which container does the cutting grow roots fastest?
   b. Does the thickness of a cutting affect root growth? Does the length of a cutting? Plan ways to answer these questions, too.

   (*Teaching Comment:* For safety, handle the knife yourself or closely supervise its use. Pupils might try cuttings from some or all of these plants: begonia, English ivy, willow, coleus, and philodendron.)

☐ ACTIVITY: How Can You Grow Sweet Potato Vines?

NEEDED

sweet potato   wide-mouth plastic drinking glass
three toothpicks   water

Sweet potatoes are the swollen root ends of the sweet potato plant. You can grow beautiful, trailing vines from them indoors.

TRY THIS

1. Place the sweet potato in a glass of water, stem end up. (This end has a small scar where it was attached to the plant.) Stick toothpicks in the sides to support it, if needed. Only about one-third of the sweet potato should be in the water. Keep the water level the same during this activity (Figure 14-13).

FIGURE 14-13

2. Leave the glass in a warm, dark place until buds and roots grow. Then put it in a sunny or well-lighted place.
   a. How long does it take before you see the first growth?
   b. What changes do you notice as the buds and roots grow?
   c. What happens to the sweet potato as vines grow?

☐ ACTIVITY: How Can You Get New Growth from Tap Roots?

NEEDED

two fresh carrots, one small and one large   knife
two low glass jars   gravel

TRY THIS

1. Cut off the top 5 centimeters (2 inches) of each carrot. (You can eat the rest.) Trim away any stems and leaves growing from the top.
2. Put gravel into each jar. Stick each carrot top about halfway into the gravel.
3. Fill each jar with just enough water to cover the bottom. Leave each jar in a warm, well-lighted place. Observe each day.
   a. How long does it take for stems and leaves to grow?
   b. What happens to the tap root part as stems and leaves grow?
   c. Which, if either, carrot top shows more growth?

d. What will happen if you plant the carrot tops in soil?

e. Can you get new growth from other tap roots? Try a beet, turnip, and parsnip.

(*Teaching Comment:* For safety you may wish to cut the carrots.)

SECTION 3
Environmental Conditions
[*Background 425*]

■ INVESTIGATION: How Colored Light Affects Plant Growth

You know that plants need light to grow. But must it be white sunlight? Perhaps plants will grow just as well or better in colored light.

EXPLORATORY PROBLEM

What can you do to find out how plants grow in colored light?

NEEDED

four cellophane or plastic sheets—red,   four topless shoe boxes
   green, blue, and clear   scissors
lawn area   sticky tape

TRY THIS

1. Cut out the bottoms of four shoe boxes. Leave a 2.5-centimeter (1-inch) border on all sides.

2. Cover each cutout bottom with a different-colored cellophane sheet. Fasten the sheets with sticky tape.

3. Place the shoe boxes close together, with cellophane sheets facing up, on a healthy patch of lawn. Lift the boxes once each day for two weeks to observe the grass. Water the grass as needed but do not mow it (Figure 14-14).

DISCOVERY PROBLEMS

observing   **A.** What differences, if any, do you notice each day in the grass under the boxes?

observing   **B.** How do the grass samples compare in height and color?

communicating   **C.** What kind of a record can you make to keep track of what happens?

inferring   **D.** What color seems best for grass growth? worst?

hypothesizing   **E.** What other colors can you test? How will the grass be affected?

experimenting   **F.** How can you test other plants? How will they be affected?

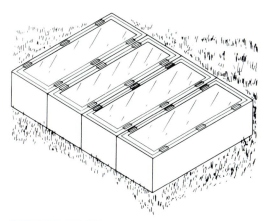

FIGURE 14-14

TEACHING COMMENT

PREPARATION AND BACKGROUND

Other kinds of plants may be tested with shoe boxes as shown in Figure 14-15.

Punch holes in the sides of the box for adequate air circulation. Boxes may be slipped off quickly for observing, measuring, and watering the plants.

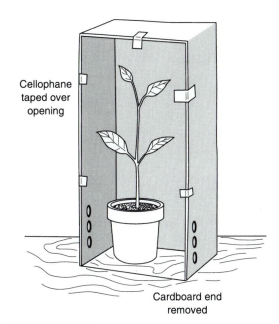

Cellophane taped over opening

Cardboard end removed

FIGURE 14-15

Some children may also like to try growing plants under artificial light. A gooseneck lamp with a 50-watt bulb works well as a light source. If the bulb is left on 24 hours a day, pupils may discover that plant growth slows down.

GENERALIZATION

Plants grow better in natural light than in colored light.

SAMPLE PERFORMANCE OBJECTIVES

Knowledge: The child can name the light colors that are most likely and least likely to help plants grow.
Process: The child can make a record from daily observations of plants and correctly infer from it.

FOR YOUNGER CHILDREN

Try the basic activity and Problems A and B.

■ INVESTIGATION: How Salt Water and Other Liquids Affect Plants

Many places have too little fresh water to grow plants. So some people want to use ocean water. How do you think salt water would affect land plants?

EXPLORATORY PROBLEM

How can you find out what salt water does to plants?

NEEDED

six containers of healthy young radish plants   measuring cup
iodine-free salt   other liquids
teaspoon

TRY THIS

1. Mix a teaspoonful of salt into a half liter (or pint) of water.
2. Water one container of plants with only this salt water. Water a matched container of plants with only fresh water. Observe both sets of plants each day (Figure 14-16).

DISCOVERY PROBLEMS

observing   **A.** What changes do you notice from day to day? Keep a record of what you observe.

experimenting   **B.** Will the plants live if *any* salt is in the water? How much can you use?

experimenting   **C.** How will other plants be affected by salt water?

experimenting   **D.** What other liquids can be used to water plants? How do you think the plants will be affected?

FIGURE 14-16

TEACHING COMMENT

PREPARATION AND BACKGROUND

If ocean water is available, it may be used in place of the salt water mixture. For Problem B, the ocean water may be diluted with fresh water.

GENERALIZATION

When watered with salt water, land plants die or grow poorly.

SAMPLE PERFORMANCE OBJECTIVES

Knowledge: The child predicts plant destruction or poor growth when certain land plants are watered with ocean water.
Process: The child finds through experimenting how much salt water, if any, sample radish plants can tolerate.

FOR YOUNGER CHILDREN

Most younger pupils will be able to do the activities if help is given in matching plants and otherwise controlling variables.

☐ ACTIVITY: How Much Does Fertilizer Help Plant Growth?

NEEDED

bottle of liquid fertilizer	medicine dropper
clean sand	teaspoon
garden soil	six paper cups
sprouted bean seeds	water

TRY THIS

1. Plant two sprouted seeds in each of two cups of sand.

2. Water the seeds in each cup the same way until leaves appear.

3. Prepare a mixture of water and fertilizer. Use the directions on the bottle.

4. Water one cup with the mixture and the other with plain water. Do this for three weeks:
   a. What differences, if any, do you notice in the young plants?
   b. How does garden soil compare to fertilized sand in helping plants grow?
   c. What would happen if you used half-strength or double-strength fertilizer on plants? Plan ways to answer these and other questions you may have.

■ INVESTIGATION: How Crowding Affects Plants

The directions on a seed package say to plant seeds with some space between them. What do you think happens to plants that grow from seeds planted close together?

EXPLORATORY PROBLEM

How can you find out how crowding affects plants?

NEEDED

garden soil	ruler
quart milk carton	paper towel
12 radish seeds	scissors
water	pencil

TRY THIS

1. Cut out one of the carton's long sides.

2. Fill the carton with soil and water it (Figure 14-17).

FIGURE 14-17

3. At one end, plant six seeds close together just under the soil surface.

4. At the other end, plant six more seeds just under the surface. Make sure each is about 5 centimeters (2 inches) apart.

5. Water the soil when the surface feels dry, but not more than once a day. Be careful not to wash loose the seeds.

6. Watch what happens for a few weeks.

DISCOVERY PROBLEMS

observing   **A.** What do you notice about the plants at each end?

measuring   **B.** How do the plants compare in size?

communicating   **C.** How can a record help you to learn how fast the plants are growing?

hypothesizing   **D.** Suppose you thin out a few plants from the crowded end. How might that change the growth of the remaining plants? Does it matter *when* you thin out the plants?

experimenting   **E.** Does crowding affect other kinds of plants? How can you find out?

TEACHING COMMENT

PREPARATION AND BACKGROUND

Crowding of plants is harmful to their growth. Individual plants compete for soil minerals, water, and light. Even the hardiest plants may grow to less than normal size under crowded conditions. Crowded plants are best thinned out early in the growth period. This gives the remaining plants a better chance to achieve full growth.

Radish seeds are good for this activity because they sprout quickly, grow fast, and seldom mold.

GENERALIZATION

Green plants need space to grow properly.

SAMPLE PERFORMANCE OBJECTIVES

Process: The child can make an accurate record of the growth rates of the crowded and uncrowded plants.
Knowledge: When asked to state conditions for proper plant growth, the child includes space as one condition.

FOR YOUNGER CHILDREN

The tiny size of radish seeds make them hard for young children to handle. You may want to substitute larger seeds, such as those from any of the bean groups.

Plant Parts and Functions
[*Background 426*]

□ ACTIVITY: What Are Plant Roots Like?

NEEDED

places where weeds grow	newspaper
small shovel	magnifying glass
pail of water	notebook

TRY THIS

1. Dig up some small weeds from both dry and wet places if possible. Try not to damage the roots. Dig deeply and loosen the soil around the weed. Then slip the shovel under it.

2. Soak the roots in water to remove the soil.

3. Carefully place each plant inside a folded newspaper. Observe the plant roots in class.
   a. Which plants have a single, large tap root with smaller branching roots?
   b. Which plants have branching roots?
   c. Can you see tiny root hairs with a magnifying glass? On what parts of the roots do most appear?
   d. What other differences among the roots do you notice?

■ INVESTIGATION: How Water Rises in Plant Stems

We usually water the *roots* of a plant. How, then, does water in the roots get to the leaves?

EXPLORATORY PROBLEM

How can you use a celery stalk to study how water travels in plant stems?

NEEDED

white celery stalk (fresh, with many leaves)	red food coloring or ink
glass of water	knife
ruler	

TRY THIS

1. Put a few drops of red coloring into the glass of water. This will help you to see how the water moves through the stalk.

2. Cut off the lower end of the stalk at a slant.

3. Put the stalk into the colored water right away (Figure 14-18).

4. Leave the stalk where it will get bright light.

FIGURE 14-18

DISCOVERY PROBLEMS

observing
communicating

A. Check the stalk every hour. How far does water rise in one hour? in more than one hour? Make a record of what you see each time.

observing

B. After a few hours, or the next day, remove the stalk. Cut it across near the bottom. What do you notice about this cutoff part?

observing

C. Cut the stalk the long way. What do you notice? Can you find any long colored tubes?

experimenting

D. Use other stalks for experiments. What can you do to change how fast the water rises? For example:
Does the number of leaves on the stalk make a difference?
Does the amount of light make a difference?
Does wind make a difference?
Will using liquids other than water make a difference?
Have a race with someone to see whose celery stalk wins.

experimenting

E. How can you *prevent* water from rising in the stalk if it stands in water?

experimenting

F. Get a white carnation with a long stem, or some other white flower. How can you make it a colored flower?

predicting

G. Suppose you split the flower stem partway up and stand each half in different-colored water. What do you think will happen to the flower?

TEACHING COMMENT

PREPARATION AND BACKGROUND

Sometimes the water-conducting tubes in a celery stalk or flower stem become clogged. To open the tubes, make a fresh diagonal cut across the stalk or stem base. Immerse *quickly* to keep air bubbles from forming in the tubes. You can eliminate the air-bubble problem by making the cut underwater, but this may be awkward. For safety, supervise the cuts closely, or do them yourself.

Some florists ready their white carnations for St. Patrick's Day by putting the stems in green-colored water.

GENERALIZATION

Stems conduct liquids from one part of a plant to another; light, wind, and the condition and number of attached leaves affect the conduction rate.

SAMPLE PERFORMANCE OBJECTIVES

Process: The child can change the rate at which water rises in a stem by manipulating one variable.
Knowledge: The child can state how to color a carnation after experimenting with celery stalks.

FOR YOUNGER CHILDREN

Most younger children will be able to do the basic investigation up to Problem D. For safety, you will want to do whatever cutting of stalks is necessary.

■ INVESTIGATION: The Properties of Leaves

Have you ever collected different kinds of leaves? There are more than 300,000 different kinds! How can you tell one leaf from another? What do you look for?

EXPLORATORY PROBLEM

How can you describe the properties of leaves?

NEEDED

six or more different leaves   partner
pencil and paper

TRY THIS

1. *Size:* How large is the leaf? Compare their sizes with things everyone knows.
2. *Shape:* What is the shape of the leaf? Some are oval; some are almost round. Others are shaped like a heart, star, or other figure.

3. *Color:* What is the color of the leaf? Most fresh leaves are green, but some are darker or lighter than others. Some leaves have other colors.

4. *Veins:* These are the small tubes that carry liquid throughout the leaf. How do the veins look? In some leaves, they are side by side. In others, the veins look like many Vs in a row with a main center vein. Some leaves have several long veins with Vs. In a few leaves, veins cannot be seen.

5. *Edges:* What do the leaf edges look like? Some are smooth. Some edges are wavy. Other leaf edges look like saw teeth (Figure 14-19).

FIGURE 14-19

6. *Feel:* How does the leaf feel to you? Is it rough? smooth? waxy? hairy? slippery? sticky?

7. *Smell:* What does the leaf smell like? Some leaves may not have a noticeable smell.

DISCOVERY PROBLEMS

classifying   **A.** Play a game with a partner. Sort your leaves into two groups according to one property (shape, veins, and so forth). Let your partner study your groups. Can he or she tell which property you inferring   used to sort your leaves? Try other properties. Take turns with your partner in this sorting game.

communicating   **B.** Play the "I'm-Thinking-of-a-Leaf" game with a partner. Place four or more leaves in a row. Think of just one leaf and its properties.

inferring

Can your partner find out what leaf you have in mind? He must ask you only questions that can be answered by yes or no. Example:
"Does the leaf have veins?" (Yes.)
"Does the leaf have smooth edges?" (No.)
When your partner finds out the right leaf, switch places. How many questions must you ask to discover the leaf your partner is thinking of? The person who needs to ask fewer questions wins.

communicating **C.** How well can you describe your leaves? Can you make a chart that someone else can use to identify them?

Make a chart of all the properties you observe about your leaves. Call your leaves A, B, C, and so on. Try to remember which is which.

Leaf	Shape	Veins	Edges	Size	Feel
A	Like a star	Like Vs	Sawtooth	Medium	Smooth
B					
C					
D					

inferring

Give your completed chart and your leaves to your partner. They should be out of order, so your partner must study your chart to tell which leaf is A, B, and so on.

communicating

Which chart descriptions were helpful? Which confused your partner? How could these be made clearer?

TEACHING COMMENT

PREPARATION AND BACKGROUND

Important: To further the processes of careful observing and communicating, use only leaves that are roughly similar in this investigation. You want different kinds of leaves, but if each is grossly and obviously different from others this will defeat the purpose of the investigation.

It is best to do this investigation with fresh, unblemished leaves. Weed leaves will do. Leaves may be kept fresh for several days by placing them in plastic bags.

GENERALIZATION

Leaves vary in size, shape, color, texture, vein pattern, and other properties; no two leaves are identical.

SAMPLE PERFORMANCE OBJECTIVES

Process: The child can communicate leaf descriptions that enable other persons to identify the leaves.
Knowledge: The child can state at least five of the general properties that can be used to describe leaves.

FOR YOUNGER CHILDREN

Most primary-level children should be able to do Discovery Problem A, and some should be able to do B.

■ INVESTIGATION: How Leaves Lose Water

A plant usually takes in more water than it can use. What do you think happens to the extra water?

EXPLORATORY PROBLEM

How can you find out if water is lost from leaves?

NEEDED

fresh leaf with stalk
four matched, plastic water glasses
knife
two cardboard squares

water
petroleum jelly
paper towel
scissors

TRY THIS

1. Fill one glass almost full with water.
2. Make a small hole in the center of a piece of cardboard.
3. Cover the glass with the cardboard.
4. Take a fresh leaf. Cut off at a slant the tip of its stalk.
5. Quickly put the stalk into the hole in the cardboard.
6. Seal around the hole with petroleum jelly.
7. Put another glass upside down on top of the cardboard.
8. Leave the glass in sunlight for several hours (Figure 14-20).

DISCOVERY PROBLEMS

hypothesizing   **A.** Do water drops form inside the top glass? Where do you think they come from?

experimenting   **B.** Maybe water drops would appear in the glass without the leaf. How could you find out?

experimenting   **C.** What affects how many water drops appear? Leaf size? the kind of leaf? the freshness of the leaf? Does the amount of light affect how many drops appear? How can you find out?

experimenting   **D.** From which side does the leaf give off water? Top? bottom? both sides? How can you use petroleum jelly to find out?

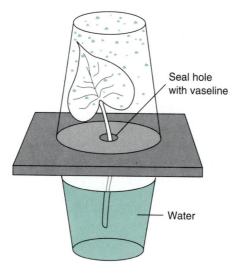

Seal hole
with vaseline

Water

FIGURE 14-20

communicating **E.** Keep a record of what you find. Compare your record with that of
other people.

TEACHING COMMENT

PREPARATION AND BACKGROUND

Many tiny openings, called *stomates,* are found in a green leaf. Gases are taken in
and released through them during the leaf's food-making process. Water, in the
form of water vapor, is also released through the stomates. In this activity, the
released water vapor is trapped by the plastic cover. It then condenses into visible
water drops on the plastic. In land plants, stomates are usually found in the bottom
leaf surface. Water loss varies with weather conditions and the size and kind of leaf.

GENERALIZATION

Plants lose water through tiny openings in their leaves; the amount of water lost
depends on several conditions.

SAMPLE PERFORMANCE OBJECTIVES

Process: The child will arrange a second (control) setup when needed, as in B.
Knowledge: The child can state at least one condition that influences the rate of
water loss in leaves.

☐ ACTIVITY: How Can You Make Leaf Rubbings?

NEEDED

different leaves with thick veins   tissue paper
crayons

TRY THIS

1. Place tissue paper over a fresh leaf.

2. Rub a crayon back and forth. A beautiful vein pattern will appear.

3. Try different colors and leaves.

4. Play a matching game with someone.
   a. Can your partner match each of your patterns with the right leaf? Can you match your partner's patterns and leaves?
   b. How can you use your patterns to make holiday or greeting cards?

☐ **ACTIVITY: How Can You Learn About Plant Buds?**

NEEDED

small branches and twigs from plants   nail
pruning shears or knife   jar of water

TRY THIS

1. Find a low tree or bush with fallen leaves.

2. Look for small branches or twigs that have buds. Observe just above where each leaf was attached to the twig or stem.

3. Cut off a few twigs that have buds. (Ask permission first.)
   a. How are the buds arranged? What patterns, if any, do you notice?

4. Pick apart one or two buds with a thin nail.
   b. How can you describe the buds?
   c. Which of the remaining buds will grow leaves? To see, stick the twig into a jar of water. Change the water every two or three days.

   (*Teaching Comment:* The beginning of spring is a good time to collect twigs for budding.)

☐ **ACTIVITY: What Is Inside of Flowers?**

NEEDED

several flowers   straight pin
newspaper   magnifying glass

TRY THIS

1. Bend back a few flower petals to see inside as shown in Figure 14-7, p. 428.

2. Remove one of the stamens. Pick apart the anther, the part on the end.
   a. Can you see any dustlike pollen? What color is it? How does the pollen look under a magnifying glass?

3. Examine the pistil end.
   b. What does it look like? Is it sticky when touched?

4. Use a pin to carefully slit open the pistil's thicker end.
   c. Can you see any baby seeds inside? What do they look like?

5. Examine other flowers in the same way.
   d. How are other flowers alike? different?

(*Teaching Comment:* Some good choices of flowers for this activity are the tulip, iris, daffodil, lily, rose, gladiola, crocus, and sweet pea. Florists are usually willing to donate unsalable flowers to schools.)

☐ ACTIVITY: How Can You Press and Display Plants?

NEEDED

newspaper	tagboard
heavy books	glue
small whole plants (weeds)	cellophane wrap

TRY THIS

1. Lay out your plants on six sheets of folded newspaper.

2. Cover with six more sheets of folded newspaper.

3. Pile some heavy books on top. The pressed newspaper will soak up the plants' moisture.

4. Change the paper every few days until the plants are dry.

5. Glue the plants to tagboard. Cover them with clear cellophane wrap.
   a. How can you make your display more attractive?
   b. Can you write a story that tells how you found and prepared your plants?

SECTION 5
Responses to Environment
[*Background 429*]

☐ ACTIVITY: How Does Gravity Affect a Growing Plant?

NEEDED

paper towels	soaked radish seed
plastic drinking glass	plastic kitchen wrap

TRY THIS

1. Line the inside of a glass with a wet, folded paper towel.

2. Crumple and stuff some towels inside the lined glass. This will hold the first towel in place.

3. Put a soaked radish seed between the glass and the first towel. The seed should be in the middle of the glass.

4. Pour about 2.5 centimeters (1 inch) of water into the glass.

5. Wait until the seed sprouts, grows leaves, and roots.

6. Pour out what water is left. Cover the glass with kitchen wrap to keep the towel lining moist.

7. Tip over the glass onto one side.
   a. What happens to the upper stem of the plant over the next few days?
   b. What happens to the roots?
   c. What will happen if you tip over the glass onto the opposite side?

☐ ACTIVITY: How Can You Make a Plant Grow Toward the Light?

NEEDED

small and large paper cup   bean seeds
soil

TRY THIS

1. Plant one or two bean seeds in a small paper cup of soil. Water as needed.

2. Wait until leaves appear.

3. Punch a hole into the side of the large paper cup with a pencil.

4. Cover the small cup with the large cup. Uncover briefly when you need to water.

5. Leave the cups in a well-lighted place. Be sure the cup hole faces the light.
   a. What do you notice after a few days?
   b. What do you think would happen if you turned the plant around? (Be sure the cup hole faces the light.)

☐ ACTIVITY: What Happens When a Growing Plant Touches Something?

NEEDED

healthy bean seedling in soil container   books
two rulers

TRY THIS

1. Make two stacks of books. They should be slightly higher than the top of the plant.
2. Put two rulers close together across the stacks.
3. Place the plant under the rulers (Figure 14-21).
    a. What do you think will happen when the leaves touch the rulers?
    b. What can you do to make the plant stem curve twice?

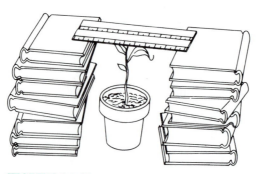

FIGURE 14-21

SECTION 6
Molds
[*Background 430*]

■ INVESTIGATION: How Molds Grow

On what things have you seen molds? How did the molds look?

EXPLORATORY PROBLEM

How can you make a mold garden?

NEEDED

aluminum foil	large pickle jar with lid
sand	baby food jars with lids
water	bread slice
magnifying glass	small pieces of different foods
tissue paper	clay
spoon	medicine dropper

TRY THIS

1. Fill a large glass jar about one-third full with sand.
2. Put the jar down on its side. Shake the jar so the sand settles evenly.
3. Sprinkle some water on the sand to make it damp. Use a spoon.
4. Put different objects that might mold on the sand.
5. Screw the lid on the jar (Figure 14-22). Do not remove it.

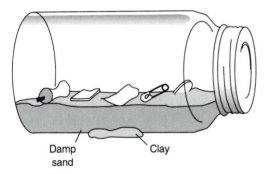

Damp
sand   Clay

FIGURE 14-22

6. Leave the jar where you can observe it each day.

DISCOVERY PROBLEMS

hypothesizing   **A.** On which objects do you think molds will grow? Which will not mold? Which do you think will be covered by molds first? last? Keep
communicating   a record of what you find.

experimenting   **B.** Try some experiments. How can you get a fresh piece of bread to mold? Keep the bread inside a baby food jar. Keep the lid on each jar after starting each experiment, B through F.

experimenting   **C.** Is water needed for molds to grow on bread? If so, how much? Fresh bread may contain some moisture. How can you start with dry bread?

experimenting   **D.** Will bread molds grow better in the dark or light? How about dim light?

experimenting   **E.** How can you *prevent* mold from growing on a piece of bread?

experimenting   **F.** What other experiments would you like to try?

TEACHING COMMENT

PREPARATION AND BACKGROUND

You may prefer to use zip-lock plastic bags instead of baby food jars in B-F. For bread experiments, try to get the white home-baked kind or store bread without preservatives. Commercial bread often contains a mold-inhibiting chemical called sodium propionate. However, in time, this bread can also mold.

The molds or other organisms in this investigation are typically harmless. However, play it safe by having children (1) keep all moldy materials covered, (2) wash their hands if a mold is touched, (3) avoid sniffing molds, (4) avoid growing molds in soil samples, and (5) dispose of all used, still-closed containers in a tightly sealed bag.

GENERALIZATION

Some molds grow well under dark, moist, and warm conditions.

SAMPLE PERFORMANCE OBJECTIVES

Process: The child can set up an experiment to test one condition that may affect mold growth.

Knowledge: The child can state one or more conditions that influence the growth of molds.

FOR YOUNGER CHILDREN

Most primary children can profit from setting up the mold garden and thinking about Discovery Problem A.

SELECTED TRADE BOOKS: PLANT LIFE AND ENVIRONMENT

FOR YOUNGER CHILDREN

Busch, Phyllis. *Cactus in the Desert.* Crowell, 1979.

Challand, Helen. *Plants Without Seeds.* Children's Press, 1986.

Gibbins, Gail. *From Seed to Plant.* Holiday, 1991.

Kirkpatrick, Rena K. *Look at Seeds and Weeds.* Raintree, 1985.

Kuchalla, Susan. *All About Seeds.* Troll Associates, 1982.

Lauber, Patricia. *Seeds: Pop, Stick, Glide.* Crown, 1981.

Miner, O. Irene. *Plants We Know.* Children's Press, 1981.

Moncure, Jane B. *What Plants Need.* Child's World, 1990.

Penn, Linda. *Wild Plants and Animals.* Good Apple, 1986.

Selsam, Millicent E., and Joyce Hunt. *A First Look at Flowers.* Walker, 1977.

Taylor, Barbara. *Growing Plants.* Watts, 1991.

Webster, Vera. *Plant Experiments.* Children's Press, 1982.

FOR OLDER CHILDREN

Bates, Jeffrey. *Seeds to Plants: Projects with Botany.* Watts, 1991.

Cochrane, Jennifer. *Plant Ecology.* Watts, 1987.

Coldrey, Jennifer. *Discovering Flowering Plants.* Watts, 1987.

Conway, Lorraine. *Plants.* Good Apple, 1980.

Conway, Lorraine. *Plants and Animals in Nature.* Good Apple, 1986.

Gallant, Roy A. *Earth's Vanishing Forests.* Macmillan, 1991.

Holley, Brian. *Plants and Flowers.* Penworthy, 1986.

Hogner, Dorothy Childs. *Endangered Plants.* Crowell, 1977.

Lambert, Mark. *Plant Life.* Watts, 1983.

Leutscher, Alfred. *Flowering Plants.* Watts, 1984.

Marcus, Elizabeth. *Amazing World of Plants.* Troll Associates, 1984.

Penn, Linda. *Plant Ecology.* Watts, 1987.

Sabin, Louis. *Plants, Seeds, and Flowers.* Troll Associates, 1985.

15

Animal Life and Environment

Can a gnat have *anything* in common with an elephant?

Despite their enormous diversity, all animals share certain needs and some physical properties. By carefully observing how animals are formed we can place them into groups with common properties. These groups further allow us to learn many of the interesting adaptations of animals without having to study each group member.

This chapter takes up (1) animals with backbones, (2) some animals without backbones, and (3) some interactions of living things with each other and their environment—ecology. But right now, let's briefly consider some ways to keep track of animals.

CLASSIFYING ANIMALS

Of some 1,250,000 different forms of living things, animals make up almost 1,000,000. They run, walk, crawl, fly, slither, and swim. They range in size from microscopic organisms to the blue whale, which may be up to about 30 meters (100 feet) long. Their colors embrace all shades of the spectrum. In almost any way one can imagine, the diversity of animals is truly amazing.

How do scientists keep track of them? A system developed by the great Swedish naturalist Carolus Linnaeus (1707–78) provided the base for modern classification. It takes into account the physical structure of the living thing. Six main categories are used, which range from the general to the particular description of group properties.

For example, let's classify a dog. Parenthetical remarks refer to the general meaning of each category.

Kingdom Animalia (the subject belongs to the animal, not the plant, kingdom).[1]

Phylum Chordata (it has a backbone or a notochord).

Class Mammalia (it is a mammal).

Order Carnivora (it eats meat).

Family Canidae (it belongs to a group with doglike characteristics).

Genus Canis (it is a coyote, wolf, or dog).

Species Canis familiaris (it is a common dog).

Such a system has important advantages to biologists. It is possible to pinpoint most living things and to note relationships that otherwise might be easy to miss. Because the system is accepted by scientists the world over, accuracy of communication is realized.

For elementary school science, however, you will want to work with a simpler classification scheme. The following one should be useful and will fit nicely into any more formal structure the child may develop later in high school and college. Although in this chapter we will not study all the subgroups described, seeing the overall classification scheme should be helpful to you.

We can divide the entire animal kingdom into two huge groups, each with a manageably small number of subgroups.

Animals with Backbones (vertebrates)
Mammals (humans, dog, horse, etc.).
Birds (sparrow, penguin, eagle, etc.).
Reptiles (turtle, lizard, snake, etc.).
Amphibians (frog, toad, salamander, etc.).
Fishes (carp, bass, minnow, etc.).

Animals without Backbones (invertebrates)
Echinoderms Animals with spiny skins (sand dollar, starfish, sea urchin, etc.).
Arthropods Animals with jointed legs: insects (fly, moth, grasshopper, etc.); arachnids (spider, scorpion, tick, etc.); crustaceans (crab, lobster, crayfish, etc.); myriapods (millipede and centipede).
Mollusks Animals with soft bodies (clam, snail, octopus, etc.).
Worms (flatworm, roundworm, segmented worm, etc.).

---

[1]Some scientists have named a third kingdom called protists, which includes single-celled plantlike and animallike organisms. Other scientists have classified living things into five kingdoms: monera (for example, bacteria), protists, fungi, plants, and animals.

Corals and relatives (sea anemone, jelly-fish, coral, etc.).

Sponges (The natural sponges we use are the fibrous skeletons of these animals.)

When young children use the term *animal,* they are inclined to mean mammal, or at best, another animal with a backbone. Yet the five classes of vertebrates—mammals, birds, reptiles, amphibians, and fishes—make up a scant five percent of the animal species in existence.

Animals without backbones make up the rest. Insects, which make up 70 percent of all animals, represent by far the largest class of invertebrates. There are more than 800,000 species. (A species is a group whose members can generally reproduce only among themselves.)

In daily contact and interest, the vertebrates, insects, and several other common animals make up most of the animal world for elementary schoolchildren. Therefore, we will focus mainly on these animals and their fascinating ways in this chapter.

[I] ANIMALS WITH BACKBONES *Experiences 481*

Despite their fewer numbers, the five classes of vertebrates represent the highest forms of life on this planet. We'll begin with the most advanced form, mammals.

Mammals

Look around long enough and you will find animals everywhere: below the ground (mole, gopher, woodchuck); on the ground (humans, giraffe, elephant); in trees above the ground (monkey, sloth, tree squirrel); in the air (bat); and in the water (whale, seal, dolphin). What can such a diverse collection of creatures have in common? All of them are mammals. That is, all have some fur or hair, and all have milk glands. To be sure, you will

not find much hair on a whale—only a few bristles on the snout. And sometimes fur or hair is greatly modified, as with the porcupine's quills. But look closely enough, and if it is a mammal, it has hair.

Both male and female mammals have mammary, or milk, glands. (You can see how the term *mammals* originated.) Ordinarily, of course, only the female produces the milk used in suckling the young.

Another distinction of mammals is their intelligence, the highest of all animal groups. But other unique properties are few and subtle.

Internal Development. Mammals are usually born wholly formed, although growth continues to the adult stage of the life cycle. The embryo develops within the mother from a tiny egg fertilized by a sperm cell from a male of the same species.

During its development, the embryo is attached to the mother by a placenta, or membranous tissue. Water, oxygen, and food pass from mother to embryo through this tissue. In turn, liquefied waste materials flow the other way. These are absorbed into the mother's bloodstream, sent to the kidneys, and eliminated. The navel pit in the abdomen of humans—children call it their "belly button"—is a reminder of this early state of our development.

The two known exceptions to this developmental pattern are the spiny anteater and duck-billed platypus, both of Australia. Each lays eggs. The hatched young, though, are cared for and suckled by the mother as with other mammals.

Warm-Blooded. Mammals are warm-blooded and have efficient hearts with four definite chambers. These properties are shared by only one other group, the birds. Their blood temperatures stay at relatively the same level, whether the air warms or cools. Animals of lesser complexity are cold-blooded. That is, their blood temperature changes as their environmental temperature changes.

It is both an advantage and a disadvantage to be warm-blooded. Vigorous activity is possible within most air temperature ranges. But the body heat of mammals must be conserved, or else death occurs.z

In cold climates, thick blubber or fur performs this function, as does hibernation, and, in some cases, migration. In warm climates, humans perspire. Some animals estivate—become relatively inactive for a period in whatever suitably cool refuge can be found.

Some cold-blooded animals can withstand great cold or heat, but most depend on a narrow temperature range for normal activity or survival. We will go into more detail later with several specific animals.

Although the terms are still relative, it is more accurate to say, "constant-temperatured" and "variable-temperatured" rather than "warm-blooded" and "cold-blooded" when we refer to animals. In hot weather, for example, a "cold-blooded" animal might have a higher body temperature than a "warm-blooded" one.

Teeth. The teeth of mammals are particularly interesting to observe since they seem adapted to specific uses. We can see the four main kinds of teeth by examining our own in a mirror. In front are the chisellike incisors. On both sides of these teeth are the conelike canines. Farther back are the front molars, and last, the back molars. Now note how these teeth are used by several kinds of mammals.

Prominent, sharp incisors are characteristic of gnawing mammals—rats, mice, gerbils, guinea pigs, hamsters, muskrats, beavers, and rabbits. The incisors of these rodents grow continuously at the root and are worn down at the opposite end by gnawing. When prevented from gnawing, incisors may grow so long that the animal cannot close its mouth, and so starves to death.

The flesh eaters (carnivores)—such as cats, dogs, and seals—have small incisors and prominent canines, sometimes called "fangs." Their molars have curved, sharp edges. The canines are useful for tearing meat. The molars are suited for chopping it into parts small enough to swallow.

Plant eaters (herbivores)—such as the horse, goat, and sheep—have wide, closely spaced incisors and large, flat-surfaced molars. Canines do not appear. The incisors work well in clipping off grasses and plant stems. The molars grind this material before swallowing.

You and I are omnivores; in other words, capable of eating both plants and animals. Human teeth include all four types.

Classroom Mammals

The classroom is likely to be a restrictive place for mammals, so it is wise to select those that will fare reasonably well there. It is also important to get an animal that can be used to fulfill some lasting educational purposes. (Most school districts have policies as to what animals are permitted in classrooms. Consult the curriculum guide or school principal for details.)

Some teachers breed white rats or gerbils in the classroom for two months or so each year. This is an interesting experience for youngsters, and it helps them to form a wholesome and intelligent attitude toward reproduction in all animals, including humans.

Experienced teachers often recommend use of white rats and gerbils (Figure 15-1) over common classroom animals such as white mice, hamsters, and guinea pigs. White

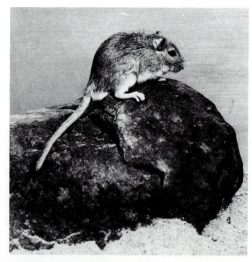

FIGURE 15-1
A gerbil.

mice are good breeders, but they will soon emit a strong and unpleasant odor in the classroom. Mating is less certain with captive hamsters. They also seem more inclined to bite, although this is not so with young, well-handled hamsters. Guinea pigs are a bit large for small classroom cages, and their comparatively long gestation period (63 days after mating) is inconvenient.

Although simple cages for rodents can be homemade from strong screening material, a commercial cage is usually more secure and better suited to the animals' needs. (Never house a rodent in a wood or cardboard container. Remember those incisors!) Rodents are typically quite active and may decline in health unless an exercise wheel is provided. A small, inverted water bottle with tube, affixed to the cage, will present a clean, long-lasting water supply. A commercial cage, like that shown in Figure 15-2, should serve well and last indefinitely. It may be bought at most pet stores and scientific supply houses, as can white rats and gerbils. (In some states, gerbils are banned to prevent a wild pest population from developing.)

Following are some suggestions for housing and caring for a female and male white rat or gerbil.

Cage. Use a commercially produced cage with exercise wheel and inverted water bottle

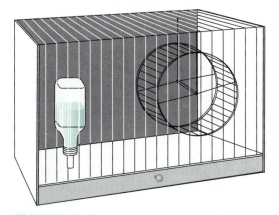

FIGURE 15-2
A commercially produced cage such as this is well suited for housing white rats.

as recommended. Cover the floor with a four-page thickness of newspaper. Scatter a generous covering of sawdust, wood shavings, peat moss, or shredded newspaper over the paper. Remove the floor covering and replace with fresh materials twice a week or more often if odor develops.

The cage should be in a draft-free location, as rodents are quite susceptible to colds. Ideally, the temperature should not fall below 15°C (60°F). However, a deep floor covering usually provides some insulation against the loss of heat energy, since the animals will burrow into it.

Food.[2] Dry pellets for small laboratory animals, including rats, are sold at most pet and feed stores. In addition, feed bits of carrots, lettuce, cheese, and bread. A constant supply of pellets and other nonperishable food may be left in a small, flat container in the cage. However, remove any perishable food within an hour after it has been offered. A fresh bottle of water and tray of pellets should last over weekends, but provisions for feeding will need to be made for longer periods.

Handling. White rats are typically very gentle, likable creatures. They should be handled daily for a short period. This tames them and accustoms them to being around children. If a tiny bit of peanut butter or carrot is offered on the tip of a toothpick, they can be enticed into the children's hands.

Although there is little chance that a white rat will bite if treated gently, caution children to keep their fingers away from the animal's mouth when handling it. (Notify the school nurse immediately if *any* classroom animal should bite a child. Although the bite itself is usually very minor, germs the animal may harbor in its mouth may cause infection unless the wound is promptly treated.)

Breeding. Rats usually breed within a few days. Provide some loose cotton or shredded

---

[2]For food and other requirements of some animals often kept in classrooms, please see Appendix D.

newspaper that the female can use in preparing a nest. Remove the male from the cage after it appears obvious that the female is pregnant. Return the male to the pet store, or give it to the Humane Society.

About three to four weeks after mating, the female will give birth to eight or more young in the nest. Do not disturb the female for ten days after this event. The newborn young will be blind and hairless. They may be weaned gradually to a regular diet after they are about two weeks old. Feed them milk that contains soft bread crumbs for a week and adult food thereafter.

All rats should be given to a responsible source after completion of this activity. Abandoned rodents become wild and add quickly to the local pest population.

During the eight weeks or so of working with this activity, try to have time for frequent, short class discussions about the behavior and habits of the caged rats. Emphasize the birth, appearance, care, feeding, and physical development of the young. You may note rapid day-to-day improvement in children's oral reporting skills as they tell the latest news about their rats.

Use a chart with rotating names for assigning tasks such as replacement of water, paper, and food. Most children are delighted to serve. This may be an excellent opportunity to motivate problem pupils or help them achieve a greater sense of responsibility.

Birds

"A bird is an animal with feathers." This is a primary child's definition, but it really cannot be much improved. Almost all other properties we see in birds may be found here and there among other animal groups, although not in the same combinations. The coloring and construction of birds' feathers vary tremendously, from the luxuriant plumage of a peacock to the scruffy covering of a New Zealand kiwi.

Although we ordinarily think of birds as fliers, chickens and road runners seldom fly,

and some birds—the ostrich, penguin, and kiwi, for example—cannot fly at all.

Food and Heat Loss. "He eats like a bird." How often we have heard a person who eats sparingly described this way. It is hardly fitting. Few other animals possess such voracious appetites for their size. Many birds must eat their weight in food each day just to stay alive.

To see why this is so, examine a small, flying bird closely. Notice that its body volume is relatively small when compared to the large surface area of its skin. As body volume decreases, the relative size of skin surface increases. If this seems unclear, inspect a pint and a quart milk carton. The small carton holds only half as much but clearly has more than one-half the surface area of the larger carton.

A large skin surface area causes heat energy to radiate rapidly away from the body. This is bad when the body volume is small because the heat generating capacity is also small. To generate enough heat energy for normal functioning when heat energy is quickly being radiated away, a high metabolic rate (the rate at which food is oxidized and assimilated) must be maintained. The rapid burning of fuel causes body temperatures in birds of 39° to 43°C (102° to 110°F), the highest of any animal group.

Mammals are also affected in this way. Smaller mammals usually eat more for their size than larger ones. As we travel toward the earth's polar regions, we can observe a general increase in mammals' body size. As body volume increases, the relative size of skin surface decreases. Comparatively less heat energy is radiated away. This has great survival value.

Flight Adaptations. The bodies of most birds are well suited for flight. Inside are several air sacs connected to the lungs. Many bones are hollow, or nearly so, and further reduce body weight. Even a chicken has relatively little marrow in its longer bones. It is said that the great evolutionist Charles Darwin had a pipe stem made from a wing bone of an albatross.

The body of a bird is streamlined and closely fitted with three kinds of feathers. Next to the skin are fluffy, soft down feathers. These contain numerous "dead-air" pockets that help conserve body heat. Contour feathers hug the body closely, and large flight feathers help to propel and steer the bird as it flies.

Most birds continually preen their feathers. This is done by using the bill to press a drop of oil from a gland located just above the tail and then spreading the oil over the feathers. A shiny, waterproof coating results. It is so effective that a duck can float for many hours without becoming waterlogged. If the oil were suddenly removed, a swimming duck would disappear into the water like a slowly submerging submarine.

If you can locate a large, recently molted feather, dip it in water before and after washing it in soap or detergent. Notice how water soaks in after the washing.

The thick white meat or breast section on poultry is partly the result of selective breeding by humans. However, nearly all birds have their largest and strongest muscles in this section because these muscles control the major wing movements.

Senses.   The remarkably keen eyesight of birds has been well advertised. Less known is that they have three eyelids. Two shut the eye, and the third—a transparent membrane—sweeps back and forth, cleaning away dust or other foreign matter without need for blinking. Eyes of most birds are located on the sides of the head. So they must continually cock the head to one side to see directly forward. Their hearing is also acute despite the lack of outer ears. Two small earholes suffice. On the other hand, birds do not appear to discriminate well among various odors or tastes.

Beaks and Feet.   Most birds have horny beaks; their various shapes show great diversity of function. Although all known modern birds are toothless, fossil records indicate that

a variety of toothed birds lived in ancient times. The feet of birds are equally diverse in form. On the legs we find scales, which reveal their evolutionary connection to the reptiles.

Figure 15-3 shows some common structures and functions of birds' bills and feet. The duck's bill is useful for scooping up small fish and plants in water because it is shaped like a shovel. The scooped-up water spills out through the uneven sides of the bill, but the food remains inside. The duck's webbed feet are useful for paddling in water.

The woodpecker's bill is like a large, pointed nail, useful for digging insects out of tough tree bark. (The bills of most other insect catchers are more slender.) Its feet can dig securely into a vertical tree trunk.

The sparrow's bill is small, but strong enough to crack open seeds and some nuts, like a pet canary's does. Its feet are useful for perching because they automatically close around a tree limb. It requires no effort, and

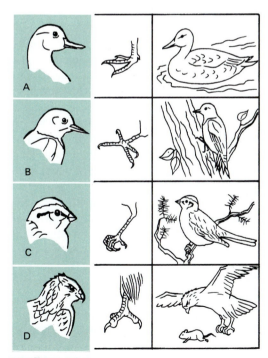

FIGURE 15-3
(A) Duck, (B) woodpecker, (C) sparrow, (D) hawk.

the bird may sleep in this position without danger of falling.

The hawk's bill is like a sharp hook, useful for tearing the flesh from bones of field mice and other small animals it preys on. Its feet are useful for grasping and holding its prey.

Reproduction. As in mammals, sexual reproduction begins with an egg cell fertilized within the female by a sperm cell. However, fertilization is not necessary for an egg to be laid. Many chickens lay an egg every day. We eat these unfertilized eggs.

An egg acquires its hard shell in the lower part of the hen's oviduct, or egg-conducting tube. Glands produce a limy secretion that gradually hardens over a period of hours before the egg is laid. The shell is porous and permits both oxygen to enter and carbon dioxide to leave. In a fertilized egg, this is essential for life in the developing chick embryo.

Chick Hatching. It is fairly easy to hatch chicks in the classroom. To do so, you will need fertilized eggs and an incubator. Get the eggs from a hatchery or farmer. Buy a small incubator from a pet shop or scientific supply house. Although it is possible to make an incubator with a glowing light bulb and insulated cardboard container, few seem to work satisfactorily. It is essential to success that a near-constant temperature of 38° to 39°C (101° to 103°F) be maintained for the 21-day incubation period. Homemade incubators typically fluctuate in temperature well beyond permissible limits.

Fertilized eggs should be turned over twice a day. This keeps the growing embryo from sticking to the shell. A mark placed on the egg will allow you to keep track of egg positions.

In 21 days, or sooner if the eggs have not been freshly laid, the hatching will take place. This process may take several or more hours. Since some hatching may happen at night, it is good to have several eggs. This will increase the chance that a few chicks will hatch during school hours.

Children can observe how a chick breaks out of its shell by using a tiny "egg tooth" on top of its beak. This drops off shortly after the chick emerges. (See Figure 15-4.) The chick will look wet and scraggly until its downy feathers dry. No food is necessary for at least 24 hours, as it will have digested the egg yolk and some egg white before breaking out of the shell. (Many children have the misconception that an egg yolk *is* the undeveloped embryo, rather than its principal food.)

Caring for Chicks. Chicks need constant warmth. This is furnished by a brooder, or warm box. An incubator can be used temporarily if the lid is raised, but it may be too confining after a few days. If the chicks are to be kept for more than several days, use a cardboard box with a shielded, goose-neck lamp shining into it.

Chick feed may be bought at a pet store. Leave some feed and clean water in dishes within the brooder at all times. A fresh newspaper floor cover each day will keep the brooder clean.

Give the chicks to a farmer or hatchery after a week or two. Proper conditions become increasingly difficult to provide in a classroom as chicks get older.

FIGURE 15-4
A chick starts to peck itself out of the egg. Note the egg tooth.

Reptiles

Many children know that snakes are reptiles but are unaware that the term also includes turtles, lizards, alligators, and crocodiles. What do these animals have in common? Typically they have dry, scaly skin. Those with feet have five toes which bear claws. All are lung breathers, which means that even an aquatic turtle will drown if placed underwater for an extended time period.

Cold-Blooded. Reptiles have well developed hearts with three chambers (some have almost four). Unlike mammals and birds, reptiles are cold-blooded. In winter, reptiles in relatively cold climates hibernate below ground; they become unable to move when the temperature drops very low. It is no accident that reptiles are rare in regions beyond the temperate zones and proliferate in the tropics.

Reproduction. In reptiles, reproduction begins with the internal fertilization of an egg, similar to mammals and birds. But the process thereafter is different enough to warrant our attention. All of the turtles and most of the lizards and snakes lay eggs in secluded areas on land. The eggs have tough, leathery covers, and for the most part depend on the sun's warmth for incubation.

Some snakes and lizards retain the egg internally until the incubation period is complete. The young are then born alive. However, the process differs from the development of mammalian young.

In mammals, as was noted, the embryo is attached to the female and nourished directly through a placental membrane. In reptiles, there is no internal attachment. The egg incubates until the growing embryo inside is sufficiently developed to hatch and so leave the female.

Eyes. Turtles and most lizards have three eyelids, as do birds. Snakes have no eyelids. A transparent, horny cover over the eye protects it from injury as the animal moves among sticks and vegetation. Just before a snake sheds its skin—up to several times a year—the transparent eye cover becomes milky in color. Interestingly, the only easy way to tell the several species of legless lizards from snakes is to note whether the eyes blink.

Common Lizards. Children may bring lizards, often swifts, to class. (See Figure 15-5.) In the southwestern United States, it is common for children to bring the gentle and easily tamed horned toad. (The proper name is horned lizard. For a description of true toads, please see pages 468–469.) Nearly all lizards may be housed satisfactorily in a terrarium containing some sand and placed where it is sunny. (*Caution:* Leave the top open to avoid excessive heat buildup.) The anole, or American chameleon—the kind often bought at fairs and pet shops—is more suited to a woodland terrarium. (See page 425 for descriptions of terrariums.)

Chameleons are interesting for children to observe. Like many lizards, they change body color under different conditions of light, temperature, and excitation. However, the color change is greater in chameleons than

FIGURE 15-5
A typical small lizard, the Eastern Fence Swift.

in most other lizards. It is brought about by dilation and contraction of blood vessels in the skin.

Many lizards have fragile tails that break off easily when seized. In some species, the broken-off tail part wriggles about animatedly, thereby often distracting the attention of a would-be captor until the lizard escapes. Lizards can grow back (regenerate) new tails.

Classroom Snake. If possible, try to get a small, tame snake for the children to examine. Let the children touch it and learn that it has dry, cool skin, rather than a slimy coating. Children can learn that nearly all snakes in this country are highly beneficial to humans, and that snakes consume many thousands of destructive rodent and insect pests each year.

At the same time, pupils should learn an intelligent respect for snakes. If poisonous snakes appear locally, show pictures of what they look like. Caution the class never to hunt for snakes unless accompanied by a responsible and informed older person. In the continental United States, only the rattlesnake, copperhead, water moccasin, and coral snake are dangerous to humans.

Amphibians

These are animals that typically spend part of their lives in water and part on land. The main kinds are frogs, toads, and salamanders. Amphibians represent an interesting evolutionary link between fishes and reptiles and have many properties of both groups. If animal life originally began and evolved in the sea, as is generally supposed, it is probable that early amphibians were the first vertebrates to emerge from the water and live successfully on land.

Cold-Blooded. Amphibians are cold-blooded and have hearts with three chambers. Like other cold-blooded animals, they hibernate in cold weather, usually by burrowing in the ground or mud. The adults breathe through lungs, but are also able to absorb some oxygen through the skin. The latter method of breathing is especially useful in hibernation. Still, skin breathing is inadequate for sustained activity, and even a frog will drown eventually if forced to remain underwater.

Frogs and salamanders usually have moist, smooth skins that must remain moist if they are to survive. For this reason, a bowl of water is needed in a terrarium that houses these creatures.

Frogs and Toads. One day a child may show you a small amphibian and ask, "Is this a toad or a frog?" Although it is hard to distinguish between them all the time, a toad usually has dry, rough skin. Its body is broad and fat, and the eyelids are more prominent than those of frogs. Another indicator is where it was caught. Frogs are likelier to live by water, whereas toads are mostly land dwellers (Figure 15-6).

FIGURE 15-6
Toad (left) and frog. Notice the external eardrum, just behind and below the eye.

Can toads cause warts? Many children think they can. The toad's warty-looking tubercles are glands that secrete a fluid that can sicken attacking animals. But the substance cannot cause warts. It may, though, irritate the eyes if they are rubbed after handling a toad. Advise pupils to wash their hands after playing with a toad.

Salamanders.   Less common than frogs and toads are salamanders; chances are that few pupils will have these as pets. Most salamanders have four legs of the same size and long, tubular bodies with tails. Superficially, they resemble lizards and are often mistaken for them. They differ from lizards in several ways: The forelegs of salamanders have four toes instead of five; they have no claws; and typically the skin is smooth rather than rough. (*Caution:* A salamander's skin may secrete a mild poison, so hands should be thoroughly washed after handling it.)

Reproduction.   Perhaps the most striking difference between amphibians and the other groups we have examined is in their means of reproduction. Female amphibians lay their eggs in water or in very moist places on land. Immediately after the eggs are laid, the males fertilize them by shedding sperm over them. Therefore, fertilization is external, unlike that in higher animals.

A single female frog or toad may lay several thousand eggs at one time. The eggs are coated with a thick, jellylike substance that quickly absorbs water and swells in size. This substance protects the developing embryo and serves as a first source of food. Eggs may often be found in ponds in spring. Look for gelatinous clumps (frog) or strings (toad) near grassy edges or where cattails grow.

After one or two weeks, the embryo hatches as a tadpole, or "polliwog," which looks completely unlike the adult. It is only after several months to several years, depending on the species, that tadpoles acquire the adult form. (See Figure 15-7.) This process of changing forms, called metamorphosis, is another distinct departure from the growth and development pattern of higher animals.

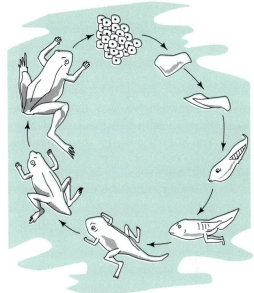

FIGURE 15-7
Metamorphosis of the frog.

In their initial growth stages, tadpoles breathe like fishes—they obtain oxygen from water through tiny gills. So be sure to "age" tap water for at least 24 hours to rid it of chlorine before adding it to the container in which the tadpoles are kept. Use tap water only if pond water is not available.

Fishes

Next to mammals, fishes are the vertebrates that present the greatest diversity in appearance, adaptations, and habits. Certainly, fishes are most numerous, both as individuals and in numbers of species. (When only one species is referred to, "fish" is both singular and plural. "Fishes" means those of several species.) Fossil records show that these creatures were the first animals with true backbones.

Breathing.   Fishes are cold-blooded and have hearts of only two chambers. Only they among the adult vertebrates breathe through gills instead of lungs. Gills are composed of thousands of blood vessels contained in hairlike filaments located in back of the head on both sides. We cannot easily see these filaments on a live fish, as gill covers conceal them.

A fish breathes by opening and closing its mouth. In the process, water is taken in and then forced out of the gill openings. As water passes over the gills, oxygen dissolved in the water filters into the filaments and blood vessels and then circulates throughout the body. At the same time, carbon dioxide passes out of the filaments and is swept away.

One of the advantages in carefully classifying living things by structure is that it enables us to see relationships we might otherwise miss. In fishes, for example, an organ called the "air bladder" appears to be a forerunner of the lung. The bladder is an air-filled sac usually located in the middle of a fish between its kidney and stomach. By compressing and expanding its air bladder, a fish can rise and descend in the water.

In the lungfish, this organ has been modified into a crude lung, enabling it to breathe air directly, in addition to gill breathing. A lungfish typically lives in a muddy pond or marsh, which may dry up in summer. It survives by burrowing into the mud and breathing air supplied through a hole in the mud cover. When its pond fills again with seasonal rainfall, the lungfish resumes the behavior we normally expect of fishes.

The lungfish is found in Africa, South America, and Australia, and it is of no commercial importance. But to a student of evolution, it is a most interesting animal. The lungfish appears to be a clear link between fishes and amphibians in the long evolutionary march of vertebrates from the sea.

Body. The body of a fish is well suited for its environment. Its streamlined contours offer a minimum of resistance to the water. A slimy, mucouslike secretion that exudes between the overlapping body scales further reduces friction and insulates the skin from attack by microorganisms. A large tail fin, wagged from side to side, propels it through the water.

Vertical fins on top and bottom keep the fish on an even keel while it is moving. Two pairs of side fins, one pair near the gills (pectoral fins), and the other pair farther back (pelvic fins), balance the fish when it is stationary. These fins are also used to assist turning, in the manner of oars, and for swimming backward. When held out laterally, they brake the swimming fish to a stop. Pectoral fins correspond to forelegs, and pelvic fins to hind legs, in other animals.

Senses. The eyes of a fish are always open, since it has no eyelids. Focusing is done by shifting the pupil forward and back, rather than by changing the lens shape, as in humans.

So-called flatfish, such as the flounder and halibut, lie on one side. Both eyes are arranged on one side of the head. Because these fish are typically bottom dwellers, this eye arrangement permits greater vision.

Although there are no external ears, fish hear with auditory capsules deep within the head. In many fishes, a lateral line of sensory scales extends along both sides of the body from head to tail. These scales are particularly sensitive to sounds of low pitch. Some expert anglers claim that a fish can hear heavy footsteps (always of other, inexpert anglers, of course) on a nearby bank.

The taste sense appears to be mostly lacking, but a fish is sensitive to smells. Nostril pits on the snout lead to organs of smell just below. The whole body, and especially the lips, seems to be sensitive to touch. In species like the catfish, extra touch organs are found in the form of "whiskers."

Reproduction. In fishes, reproduction is accomplished by either external or internal fertilization of the egg, depending on the species. The female goldfish, for example, lays eggs on aquatic plants. The male fertilizes the eggs by shedding sperm cells over them. Goldfish usually reproduce only in large tanks or ponds.

oxyg
and

Clouc
occur
movii
actioi
matte
growt
practi
carefu

Feedir
aged
be co
quirec
and e
not n
for fe

Cover.
tic wra
For be
open c
cover.
  A tc
cuts dc
tion oi
shows
small w
on the
tank.

As men
ter, the
animals
the largo
insects a
then co
have for
brine sh

Guppies and many other tropical varieties use internal fertilization. The male has a modified anal fin that carries sperm. The fin is inserted into a small opening below the female's abdomen, and sperm cells are released. Fertilized eggs remain in the female's body until the embryos hatch and are "born." Many of the young guppies are eaten by the adult fish, unless sufficient plant growth makes it difficult to detect them.

To raise as many guppies as possible, place the pregnant female (its underside will look swollen) and some plants in a separate container. After the young are born, remove the mother. The young may join the adult guppies safely in about one month.

Try not to be too efficient at breeding guppies, however. Someone good at arithmetic has calculated that a single pair will become three million guppies in a year, assuming all generations and offspring stay alive. A female guppy may produce several dozen young every 4 to 6 weeks at a water temperature of 21° to 27°C (70° to 80°F).

Male guppies differ from the females in several ways. They are about half the size (exclusive of the tails), much narrower in body, and more brilliantly colored (Figure 15-8).

FIGURE 15-8
Male (right) and female guppy.

Children's Aquaria. It is easy for children to set up a number of small aquaria for short-range observations of a week or two. For the containers, they may use large, wide-mouth jars or plastic shoe boxes. One or two goldfish and a few sprigs of water plants per container should do nicely. Tap water can be put into the containers and aged for at least 24 hours before the fish are introduced. A tiny amount of fish food—no more than the fish can eat in a few minutes—should be sprinkled on the water once a day. A more elaborate, long-range habitat for aquatic animals and plants is described next.

Setting up an Aquarium

An aquarium is an excellent source for observing firsthand some examples of ecological principles. In this watery habitat, plants and animals interact with each other and their environment, and reproduction takes place in several ways. It is likewise possible to see a near balance of nature through the interactions, and the consequences when there is an imbalance.

Tank. The materials needed are a tank, some clean sand (not the seashore variety), a few aquatic snails and plants, and several small fish. A rectangular tank of 19- to 23-liter (5- to 6-gallon) capacity serves best for a classroom aquarium. The rectangular shape has less viewing distortion than a bowl. It also permits more oxygen from the air to dissolve in the water because of the relatively greater surface area exposed at the top.

Although it is possible to construct a tank with properly cut glass, tape, and cement, the very high probability of leakage makes this impractical for most beginners.

The tank must be clean. Dirt, grease, or caked lime can be removed by scrubbing thoroughly with salt and water. The salt is abrasive enough to have a scouring effect. Should detergent or soaps be needed, repeated rinsing of the tank is essential. Any

Cake pan

Paper fastener

FIGURE 15-12
A homemade terrarium for butterflies and moths.

in class. Within about eight weeks, children will see larvae hatch from the eggs, feed busily for a time, spin cocoons and pupate, emerge from the cocoons as adult moths, mate, lay eggs, and die. Eggs and specific instructions can be purchased inexpensively from a biological supply house (Appendix C). The mulberry leaves on which the larvae feed are found in most parts of the continental United States.

Another insect with a short (six to eight weeks) life cycle is the greater wax moth. It also may be bought from several supply companies.

Mealworms. The grain beetle (*Tenebrio molitor*) is one of the easiest insects to keep and observe. It, too, undergoes a complete four-stage metamorphosis. This insect has a particularly interesting larval stage, during which time it is called a mealworm. Mealworms shed their skin from 10 to 20 times during the four or five months they remain in the larval stage. The entire metamorphosis takes six to nine months. Cultures of this insect can be bought cheaply at pet stores.

Crayfish and Brine Shrimp

Crayfish, shrimp, lobsters, crabs, water fleas, and sow bugs make up a group of animals called *crustaceans.* Like the insects and other animals with jointed legs, crustaceans have an external skeleton made of a crusty material called chitin. Muscles and other body parts are attached inside to this semirigid exterior. As with insects, crustaceans need to shed their outside covering or molt several times in order to grow.

Unlike insects, which have three body parts, crustaceans have only two: a fused-together head and thorax, and an abdomen. All crustaceans but the sow bug and its relatives live in water. All breathe through gills and have two main pairs of feelers or antennae.

Crayfish. With its hard shell and five pairs of legs, the crayfish looks much like a lobster (Figure 15-13). They are widely found in the United States living in and along the banks of muddy freshwater streams, marshes, and ponds. Children from the Huckleberry Finn era to the present have persisted in calling them "crawdads."

Crayfish are caught with minnow traps, scooped up with small nets, or simply pulled up when they grasp a chunk of fish dangling at the end of a string. Biological supply houses (see Appendix C) also furnish them.

FIGURE 15-13
A crayfish.

Crayfish are found more easily at night, when they emerge from burrows or from between stones to prey on small fish and insects. During the day or night, they may also be caught by flipping over flat stones and quickly grasping them by hand from the rear. They can be safely brought back to the classroom in a plastic bucket loosely filled with wet grass and pond weeds and just enough water to cover the bucket bottom.

Crayfish need a roomy, shallow water habitat. A child's plastic wading pool is suitable for keeping them in a classroom. Their behaviors there give many chances for observing, reporting, and other language activities. Their interactions are particularly interesting to observe, as a recognizable "pecking order" soon emerges. Like other animals brought to the classroom, they should be released unharmed where they were found when the observation period ends.

Details for more observations and care of these animals may be found in the activity section.

Brine Shrimp. Adult brine shrimp are no more than 12 millimeters (½ inch) long (Figure 15-14). However, these animals are crustaceans, just as their distant cousins, the shrimp,

which we eat. Their tiny eggs are found around the shores of salt lakes and salt flats.

Brine shrimp eggs may be hatched in salt water within a wide range of salt concentrations. The eggs are produced in a curious way. The first group of eggs produced by the female hatch inside its body. What emerges are tiny, almost transparent brine shrimp. Any further eggs produced by the same female are released directly into the water. These eggs will hatch only if they are first dried. They may survive for years in a dry condition before being hatched.

The activity section contains details on hatching and caring for brine shrimp.

Snails

Snails belong to one of the largest animal groups—the soft-bodied *mollusks*. Most live in the ocean; they include the squid, octopus, oyster, clam, and many other less familiar animals. Mollusks are divided into three subgroups according to how the foot is attached.

Snails are among the *belly-footed* mollusks (gastropods). They have a single shell and travel on what seems to be their abdomen, but what is really a soft, muscular foot. The foot secretes a mucus, or slime, that reduces friction and protects it from being irritated as the snail moves over different surfaces. The mucus is so effective that a snail may travel over a row of upturned razor blades without injury.

Water, or pond, snails have two stalks, or tentacles, each with a tiny eye at the base. Most are smaller than the land snails, and many breathe through gills.

Land, or garden, snails are lung breathers and have four tentacles. The upper two have primitive eyes at the tips. The lower two carry organs of smell. When threatened, land snails retract their tentacles; water snails do not.

Like the water snail, the land snail has both male and female sex organs. It lays tiny, single eggs, up to about 100 at a time. These may be found in small depressions in the soil,

FIGURE 15-14
Brine shrimp.

often by the base of a plant. The tiny snails that hatch from the eggs eat leaves, as do the adults. The adults live for about five years.

Land snails need a humid environment to be active. When its habitat begins to dry out, a land snail usually attaches itself to some object. A mucous secretion forms and dries over its shell opening. This seal greatly reduces internal water loss. The snail may remain in this inactive state for months until its habitat becomes humid again.

Snails have filelike tongues that shred vegetation into bits small enough to be swallowed. In an aquarium, the tongue of a snail may be observed with a hand lens as it scrapes green algae off the sides of the tank.

For details on investigating land snails, see the activity section.

Earthworms

The earthworm is a segmented worm, the most developed of three broad groups of worms. Its body may have more than 100 segments. The earthworm's peculiar way of eating is what makes it so valuable to farmers and gardeners: It literally eats its way through the soil. The decaying plant and animal matter in the soil is digested as it passes through the earthworm's body.

The eliminated soil is improved in fertility, but the side effects are even more important. The soil is loosened and aerated. Also, mineral-rich soil below the surface is brought up and mixed with mineral-depleted surface soil. The earthworm moves through and on the soil by alternately stretching and contracting its body.

Earthworms are skin breathers. That is, they take in oxygen and release carbon dioxide directly through the skin. For this to happen, the skin must be moist. Handling dries out their skin, so it is important to have wet hands or use a wet file card and spoon if they need much handling.

Find details for earthworm experiments in the activity section.

[3] ECOLOGY   *Experiences 500*

In previous sections, you have seen some ways that animal bodies are adapted to the requirements of their physical environments. In this section, we take up some of the factors that influence the numbers and quality of animal populations. To do so, we will first need to examine some concepts from *ecology*—the study of interactions of living things with each other and their physical environment.

Habitats and Their Dwellers

A *habitat* is the specific environment or place where an animal or plant lives. There are many different kinds of habitats. On land, we see desert, woodland, frozen tundra, farm, vacant lot, and garden habitats, to name just a few. Each contains animals and plants equipped to live in these locations. There are also many freshwater and saltwater habitats with their diverse living things. Some habitats fluctuate between a semidry and a watery condition, as with seashores. Here, too, we see creatures equipped to live and continue their kind.

Populations. Within a habitat, we usually can find a number of organisms of the same kind that live and reproduce there. This is a *population*. A habitat is likely to have more than one population. For example, a "vacant" lot may contain a half-dozen different animal populations: worms, snails, spiders, various insects, and so on. It most likely will contain different plant populations as well: dandelions, alfalfa, clover, various grasses, various weeds, and so on.

Communities. A human community is made up of people with different skills and needs. When groups of these persons interact properly, the community sustains itself. Likewise, a natural community is made up of interacting plant and animal populations. Plants grow when their needs for raw materials are met. Plant eaters eat some of the plants, and animal eaters eat some of the plant eaters.

Food Chains and Webs. The connection between plants, plant eaters, and animal eaters is called a *food chain*. For example, in a freshwater habitat, tiny fish called minnows eat water plants, and they in turn are eaten by frogs.

We can diagram the relationship like this:

water plants ——→ minnows ——→ frogs

The arrows show the direction of food transfer.

Real-life food chains are seldom so simple. Usually more animals are involved, and they eat more than one kind of plant or other animals. For example, we may see something like this:

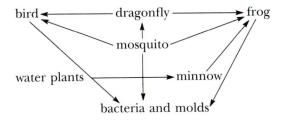

We can classify the organisms in this *food web* into three groups: producers (plants), consumers (animals), and decomposers (bacteria and molds). All three types are usually present in a food web. Consumers are further grouped as *predators* (animal eaters) and *prey* (those eaten by the animal eaters). Most preyed-upon animals are plant eaters.

A large percentage of plants and animals do not complete their life cycles because they are consumed. Those that do complete their cycle finally become food for the decomposers. These organisms are essential to new life because through decay they break down animal and plant matter into minerals, water, and gases. The minerals become part of the soil. The water and gases go back into the air. These elements are used again by growing plants.

Ecosystem and its Energy. To survive, animal and plant communities depend on interactions with the physical environment, as well as with each other. Air, water, enriched soil, temperature, and light all play a part in sustaining life. This web of relationships between a community and its physical environment is called an *ecosystem*. There is no strict agreement as to its size. Some scientists regard the whole earth as one ecosystem. To others, the term may refer to the interactions within a small habitat.

All life in any ecosystem depends on the transfer of energy. You saw how this happens with food webs. But there must be a source to start the energy transfer. That source is the sun. The process that makes the energy usable, of course, is photosynthesis. Even our fossil fuels hold the sun's energy, locked up millions of years ago in buried plant and animal forms.

Biotic Potential

A while back, I jokingly suggested that you not be too efficient at breeding guppies. A single pair might result in three million guppies in a year. A huge reproductive capacity is found in many other living things as well. The greatest increase possible in a population without deaths is called its *biotic potential*. For many reasons no population achieves this potential. Let's look at some of these reasons.

Limiting Factors. Every known organism needs certain environmental conditions to survive. Without certain supplies of air, chemicals, water, light, or proper temperature, for example, living things typically die. If only a certain amount of these factors is present, organisms may barely survive, but not reproduce. Every organism seems to have an optimum range of conditions in which it flourishes. Knowing these conditions is the key to successfully cultivating plants and raising animals.

Physical barriers, disease, and predators also limit populations. Sea plant growth stops at the shores, animals may sicken as humans do, and predators must eat to stay alive.

Adaptations.   Both animals and plants (as we saw in the preceding chapter) have some adaptations that allow many to survive when limiting factors come into play. When winter comes, some birds migrate, some mammals hibernate or grow thicker coats of fur, and so on. At other times, many insects go undetected by predators because their body color blends into their surroundings. Grasshoppers may literally fly on to greener pastures when they run low on food. And sheer numbers in a huge population may allow some members to survive even with a combination of bad conditions.

With less prolific animals, such as birds and mammals, fewer offspring seem to pose a greater risk to population survival. But the lack of numbers is compensated for by an increased capacity to care for their young.

For example, a bird may build a nest for its eggs and feed its young until they are ready to fly. It has the capacity to pick the proper materials from its environment to do so and assemble them in a way that suits the function. For some mysterious reason, the bird does not have to learn this task from older birds. It does the intricate job properly the first time.

So-called instinctive behavior is a common property of animals. A spider does not have to learn how to make its complex web. Nor does an ant have to learn to choose between a solution of high-energy sugar water and an artificial sweetener of little caloric value. There are many such examples in nature.

Such adaptations bring about a dynamic balance in population sizes. Limiting factors reduce populations, but adaptive behaviors counter these factors enough so that sizes stabilize.

The significant exception to the rule, of course, is the human animal. By eradicating most diseases and predators, the human population has grown at a fantastic pace. In the long run, however, limiting factors will exact their toll unless we, too, live in ways that make ecological sense.

Pollution.   The problem of environmental pollution is that it introduces another limiting factor into ecosystems. Pollution usually happens faster than organisms can adapt to the changes introduced. The result is a decline in at least some of the populations subjected to the pollution. The populations most likely to decline are the more complex forms of plant and animal life, including humans. Those less likely to decline are the primitive plants and animals, the decomposers, and their kin.

Material Cycles

Scientists refer to the earth as a closed ecosystem. That is, almost no new raw materials enter or leave the system. Because an ecosystem ultimately depends on its raw materials, it is essential to life that these materials are never used up. Fortunately, they never are. The materials basic to life are used over and over in a kind of cycle. Consider next three important cycles.

Carbon Dioxide–Oxygen Cycle.   Living things need oxygen to convert stored food into energy. As a by-product, they give off carbon dioxide. This is true of plants as well as animals. Fortunately, plants also need carbon dioxide to photosynthesize. During this process, the plants take in carbon dioxide and give off much oxygen. You may recall that decomposers also release carbon dioxide as they work.

So decomposers and animals give plants carbon dioxide, and plants give living things oxygen. The process is continual and may be diagrammed like this:

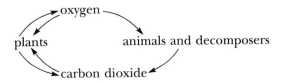

There is another side to this gas exchange that is important to realize. An essential part of living cells is the element carbon. Plants get the carbon they need from the food they make during photosynthesis. Animals get carbon from the plants they eat or from animals that eat plants.

Nitrogen Cycle.   Another cycle occurs with the element nitrogen. It, too, is an essential part of living cells. There is plenty of nitrogen in the air, but neither plants nor animals can use it in a gaseous form. How can it be converted into a form living things can use?

The basic way this is done in nature is through bacteria attached to the roots of plants such as clover, beans, alfalfa, and peas. The bacteria combine nitrogen with other elements to make chemical compounds called nitrates. Plants absorb the nitrates as they grow. Animals eat the plants and so get the nitrogen they need. When the animals die, decomposers convert the nitrogen into a gaseous form again as part of the decaying process.

This process is also continual and may be diagrammed like this:

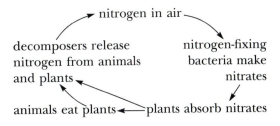

Water Cycle.   As you may know, water on the earth's surface continually evaporates, condenses at some altitude in the sky, and falls again as rain, hail, or snow. Living things need water to transport chemicals to cells and remove waste materials from cells. Plants release water through transpiration, a process whereby water vapor passes out mainly through leaves into the air. Animals release water through exhalation, perspiration, and in waste products. The released water goes into the air and becomes part of the water cycle.

Seen in this way, it is possible that a trace of the water that sustains you today may once have done the same for a dinosaur, or perhaps fell on Julius Caesar's Rome.

INVESTIGATIONS & ACTIVITIES

SECTION 1
Animals with Backbones
[*Background 461*]

□ **ACTIVITY:**   **What Can You Observe About a Bird?**

NEEDED

canary or other pet bird in cage

TRY THIS

1. Look carefully at the bird's eyes. Look for eyelids. Also notice where the eyes are on its head.
   a. Can the bird blink?
   b. What will the bird need to do to see something held in front of it?
2. Look for "ears" or tiny openings in the sides of the head. Can they be seen?
   c. How does the bird respond if you tap two pencils in back of it?
3. Notice its bill. Watch how the bird uses it to eat.
   d. How does the bill help it to eat seeds?
   e. How does the bird drink water?
4. Notice that it has different-sized feathers.
   f. Where are the largest feathers? What might they be used for?
5. Watch the bird preen, or spread oil on its feathers with its bill.
   g. How does it do this?
6. Look carefully at its feet.
   h. How many toes does each foot have? How does the bird use its feet?
   i. What else can you find out about the bird by observing?

(*Teaching Comment:* Most caged pet birds are vulnerable to sudden drops in temperature during cold weather. Be sure some heat is provided if the bird is kept overnight in the room.)

□ ACTIVITY: What Bones Make Up a Chicken Skeleton?

NEEDED

boiled, stripped-clean chicken bones   tray or newspaper

TRY THIS

1. See the drawing of a chicken skeleton in Figure 15-15. Notice the different kinds of bones for each of its parts.
2. Examine the chicken bones brought from home.
   a. Can you find the leg bones?
   b. Which are the large back and breast bones?
   c. Which are the rib bones?
   d. Which are the wing bones?
3. What other bones can you find? Can you tell what they are?
   e. Which bones seem to be missing?

(*Teaching Comment:* The head bones and feet are usually not provided with store-bought chickens.)

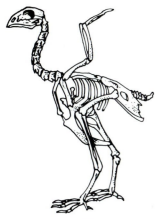

FIGURE 15-15

☐ ACTIVITY: How Can You Keep and Observe a Small Snake?

NEEDED

garter snake or other small,
  harmless snake
large glass tank
branched stick and rocks

wire mesh screen
small pan of water
sand
several mealworms or earthworms

TRY THIS

1. Cover the tank bottom with about 5 centimeters (2 inches) of sand.

2. Push down a small pan of water so it is even with the sand surface.

3. Add a sturdy branched stick and some rocks to the tank.

4. Put the snake inside.

5. Cover the tank with a screen that overlaps. Turn it down on all sides. Use two books to weigh it down.

6. Watch the snake from time to time. Handle it no more than twice a day. (Hold it just behind the head. Support the body with your other hand.)
   a. What are its eyes like? Can you see eyelids? Does it blink?
   b. How does its skin feel?
   c. How does it move? climb?
   d. How does it drink?
   e. How does it take its food? Put a mealworm into the cage and watch.
   f. What else do you observe about the snake?

(*Teaching Comment:* Small, harmless snakes are often found in grassy fields, near small streams, and in lush gardens. They should be caught only with a responsible adult present who can identify the very few poisonous varieties. A small snake can be transported in a cloth sack tied at the top. Small, harmless snakes may also be sold at pet stores. Some snakes will not eat in captivity. After several weeks, they should be returned to their original habitat.)

☐ ACTIVITY: How Can You Raise and Observe Tadpoles?

NEEDED

pond water with some water plants and green scum (algae)

plastic shoe box or aquarium tank

sloping rock for tank

hand lens

frog or toad eggs

fish food

small net

TRY THIS

1. Put the tadpole eggs and pond water into the tank. The water should have a few plants and green scum (algae) for the tadpoles to eat.

2. Place a large, sloping rock into the tank. It should rise out of the water at one end. When the tadpoles grow legs, they can crawl onto the rock.

3. When the tadpoles grow legs, sprinkle some dry fish food into the tank twice a week.

4. Every two weeks replace the old pond water with fresh pond water. Use a small dip net to transfer the tadpoles.
   a. Use a hand lens to observe the tadpoles. When can you see these things happening:
      Tiny tadpoles with gills hatching from the eggs?
      Tiny tadpoles sticking closely to the water plants?
      Bodies and tails getting longer?
      Hind legs starting to grow?
      Gills disappearing?
      Front legs developing?
      Tails shrinking?
   b. What else can you notice about tadpoles?

(*Teaching Comment:* It is likely that the school semester will end before the tadpoles grow into adults. If so, let some responsible children take the tadpoles home or release them where the eggs were found.)

▪ INVESTIGATION: How to Train Goldfish

Have you trained a dog or other pet to do something? Many animals can learn to respond to some signal. You can even train goldfish.

EXPLORATORY PROBLEM

How can you get goldfish to respond to a lit flashlight?

NEEDED

two goldfish in tank   fish food
flashlight

TRY THIS

1. Shine the flashlight into a corner of the tank. The fish should not swim toward the light.
2. Each day, sprinkle a little food near the same corner of the tank. At the same time, shine the flashlight on the food. (Figure 15-16.) Watch the fish swim toward the lighted food.

FIGURE 15-16

3. Do this for at least four days in a row.
4. The next feeding time just shine the light.

DISCOVERY PROBLEMS

observing   **A.** How do the fish act now when only the light is used?

observing   **B.** How many times will the fish respond if only the light is used? (Do not skip more than two feeding days.)

experimenting   **C.** How can you train the fish to respond to an *unlit* flashlight?

experimenting   **D.** How can you train the fish to respond to a sound?

observing **E.** What differences, if any, are there in the behavior of the two fish?

experimenting **F.** How will other fish, such as guppies, respond to training?

experimenting **G.** Are some fish "smarter" (more quickly trained) than others? How could you find out?

TEACHING COMMENT

PREPARATION AND BACKGROUND

If the fish do not respond, try extending the training period. Also, make sure the fish are fed only sparingly. Should more fish and containers be available (plastic shoe boxes will serve), small groups can pursue different discovery problems.

Children enjoy telling others about training animals. Reporting their attempts and successes allows many chances for oral and written language development.

GENERALIZATION

Animals can be conditioned to respond to signals.

SAMPLE PERFORMANCE OBJECTIVES

Knowledge: The child can describe how to condition a fish to respond to a signal.
Process: The child can determine through experimenting whether some fish learn more quickly than others.

FOR YOUNGER CHILDREN

Try the basic activity and Problems A and B.

□ ACTIVITY: How Do Temperature Changes Affect a Fish?

NEEDED

goldfish in small bowl of water
watch with second hand
pitcher of ice water
thermometer

TRY THIS

1. Notice how the fish's gills open and close. This is called a gill beat.
   a. How many gill beats does it make in one minute? Take the water temperature and record it.
2. Slowly pour ice water into the bowl. Do not lower the temperature more than about 10°C (15°F) below the starting temperature. Observe the gill beats again.
   b. How many beats does the fish make in one minute now?
3. Wait long enough for the water temperature to rise again to the first reading.
   c. About how many gill beats a minute do you think the fish will make? Watch and find out.

▪ INVESTIGATION: Making Casts of Animal Tracks

When animals walk in mud or on damp ground, they leave tracks. By examining these tracks closely, we may be able to tell many things about an animal. A large, heavy animal may leave deep, large tracks. A track of a running animal may be pushed up a little at one end. Each kind of animal leaves a different track.

Many animal tracks are interesting to study and keep, but rain can wash them away. There is a way you can save them. You can make a cast of an animal track.

EXPLORATORY PROBLEM

How can you make a cast of an animal track?

NEEDED

place with damp dirt	paper towel
thin cardboard	scissors
old plastic bowl	sticky tape
plaster of paris	newspaper
stick for mixing	water
petroleum jelly	flat-bladed, dull knife

TRY THIS

1. Have someone in your class make a shoe print in the damp ground. (It will be more fun if you don't know who that person is.)

2. Make a low wall around the shoe track with cardboard. Tape it closed.

3. Spread petroleum jelly thinly on the inside surface of the wall. This will keep the plaster from sticking to it.

4. Mix plaster of paris and water in a bowl. Go easy on the water. Make the mixture like a thick milkshake. Pour about 2.5 centimeters (1 inch) of the mixture into the wall (Figure 15-17).

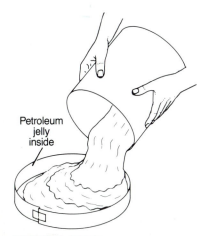

Petroleum
jelly
inside

FIGURE 15-17

5. Wait about an hour for it to harden. Remove the cast from the shoe print and take off the cardboard. Notice that the cast is an opposite or raised model of the shoe print. To make a model that looks like the real shoe print, you must make a second cast, or *mold.*

6. Spread petroleum jelly thinly over the top of the first cast. Place it on newspaper. Put a cardboard wall, also coated thinly with petroleum jelly, around the cast. Tape it closed.

7. Pour about 2.5 centimeters (1 inch) of plaster mix into the wall. Wait again an hour for it to set.

8. Remove the wall. Carefully slip a knife between the two casts to separate them. Clean off the petroleum jelly with a paper towel. The second cast should now look like the original shoe print.

DISCOVERY PROBLEMS

inferring **A.** What can you tell from the cast of the shoe print? Was it made by a girl or boy? How large or heavy might the person be? What kind of shoe was worn? Check by looking at different persons' shoes. Last, you can see if anyone's shoe fits the mold.

inferring **B.** Make a cast of a track from an animal that does not wear shoes. What bird or other animal do you think it might be? How large or heavy might it be? Was it walking or running?

observing **C.** Where can you find the most animal tracks around your school? home?

classifying **D.** What kind of a collection of animal track casts can you make?

TEACHING COMMENT

PREPARATION AND BACKGROUND

If plaster of paris is in short supply, you might have pupils begin with a small animal track rather than a human footprint. Caution children not to spill plaster on their clothing. However, small spills may be brushed off after drying.

Almost any large discardable container will serve to mix the plaster and water. But a plastic container can be bent to pour the mixture more neatly into a narrow form.

GENERALIZATION

We can infer some things about an animal from its tracks.

SAMPLE PERFORMANCE OBJECTIVES

Knowledge: The child can make a negative and positive cast of an animal track.
Process: The child can infer several properties of an animal from its tracks.

[*Background 473*]

SECTION 2
Some Animals without Backbones

■ INVESTIGATION: Mealworms and What They Do

Have you ever seen a mealworm? You can buy them at a pet store to feed to lizards and fish. It's fun to observe mealworms and what they do.

EXPLORATORY PROBLEM

How can you find out about mealworms and what they do?

NEEDED

mealworms	spoon
three rulers	small card
shoe box lid	small jar of bran
magnifier	cotton swab
rough paper towel	ice cube
straw	black sheet of paper

TRY THIS

1. Put a mealworm in an upturned shoe box lid (Figure 15-18).

FIGURE 15-18

2. Use a spoon and card to move it to where you want.

3. Use a hand magnifier to see it more clearly.

DISCOVERY PROBLEMS

observing   **A.** What do you notice about the mealworm? How many legs does it have? How many feelers on its head? What is on its tail end? How many body segments, or parts, does it have?

inferring   **B.** Put it on a rough paper towel, then on a smooth surface. On which does it seem to travel easier?

observing **C.** Put a few more mealworms in the shoe box lid. Observe how they look and act. In what ways can you tell different mealworms apart?

experimenting **D.** In what ways can you get a mealworm to back up? Which way is best?

observing **E.** Suppose you place them on a slant. Will they go up or down? Does the amount of slant make a difference?

measuring **F.** How far can a mealworm go in half a minute?

observing **G.** Which food do they seem to like best? Try cornflakes, flour, bread, crackers, and other foods.

hypothesizing **H.** Suppose you put two mealworms into a narrow straw, one at each end. What do you think will happen when they meet?

experimenting **I.** Do mealworms like moisture? How could a cotton swab be used to find out? How else might you find out?

experimenting **J.** Will a mealworm move to or away from a cold place? How could an ice cube be used to find out?

experimenting **K.** Will a mealworm move to a dark or light place? How can black paper be used to find out?

predicting **L.** Which way will a mealworm go each time (Figure 15-19)?

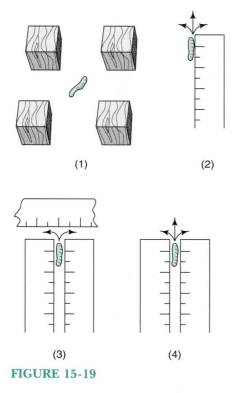

FIGURE 15-19

experimenting   **M.** How can you get a mealworm to go in a straight line for at least 10 centimeters (4 inches)? No fair touching it!

hypothesizing   **N.** What are some more questions about mealworms you would like to investigate?

TEACHING COMMENT

PREPARATION AND BACKGROUND

Mealworms are the larval stage of the grain beetle, an insect often found in rotting grain or flour supplies. They may be bought cheaply at pet stores and are fed to a variety of small animals, including some fishes.

Mealworms can be kept in a closed glass jar containing bran or other cereal flakes. Punch small holes in the jar lid for air. A potato or apple slice can be added to provide extra moisture. When the old bran looks powdery, dump out everything, then wash and dry the jar. Put back into the jar fresh bran and the live, healthy-looking mealworms. In this way, you should be able to maintain a mealworm culture for many months.

It is possible to observe the entire life cycle—egg, larva, pupa, and adult beetle—of this interesting creature in six to nine months. The children will notice quickly how a mealworm sheds its skin as it grows larger. Only the egg stage is hard to observe, because the eggs are tiny. This animal is harmless to handle at all stages.

Children usually try a variety of interesting methods to influence a mealworm's behavior. To make it back up, they may try touching it, blowing light puffs of air through a straw, making a tapping sound, or using a flashlight, heated nail, or cotton swab soaked in vinegar, ammonia, or water. To test for moisture preference, they may stick one moist and one dry cotton swab into a container of bran and mealworms. Whatever methods they use, try to get them to treat these animals humanely. While gentle touching is all right, direct contact with heat or chemicals may be harmful to mealworms.

GENERALIZATION

Some behaviors of an animal are inborn, and some are influenced by its environment.

SAMPLE PERFORMANCE OBJECTIVES

Process: The child can test the preferences of mealworms as to temperature, light, food, and moisture.
Knowledge: The child can state the apparent preferences of mealworms as to temperature, light, food, and moisture.

FOR YOUNGER CHILDREN

Younger pupils should be able to do most of the activities in the investigation, although with less precision than older children.

□ ACTIVITY: What Can You Find Out About Grasshoppers?

NEEDED

dead grasshopper
live grasshopper
paper towel
capped glass jar containing grass,
   a few twigs, and leaves

hand lens
filmstrip projector
pencil
tweezers

TRY THIS

1. Put a dead grasshopper on a paper towel. Examine it closely with a hand lens.
   a. How many large body parts does it have?
   b. How many eyes? legs? Which pair of legs do you think are the main ones for jumping?

2. Examine the mouth parts. Use tweezers and a pencil point to help.
   c. How can you describe the mouth parts?

3. Spread open the wings. Use tweezers to help.
   d. How many wings does it have? How do they compare in size? How are they arranged?

4. Look carefully on both sides of the abdomen for small breathing holes.
   e. How many do you find? How are they arranged?

5. Catch a live grasshopper and put it into a jar. Put it in some grass, leaves, and twigs. Close the jar with a cap that has a few small holes punched in it.
   f. How does the insect's color compare to the materials in the jar?
   g. What does it eat? How does it chew?
   h. What will it do if you tap the jar sharply? (Do this only once or twice.)

6. Hold the grasshopper's middle (thorax) between your thumb and forefinger. Put it in front of a projector shining on a screen. See the large shadow outline of the insect's abdomen. Watch the shadow get larger and smaller as the insect breathes.
   i. How many breaths does it take in a minute?
   j. What else can you find out about grasshoppers?

□ ACTIVITY: How Can You Raise Crickets?

NEEDED

several male and female crickets
custard cup or small dish
paper towel
dry oatmeal or bran
hand lens

plastic shoe box
screen top for shoe box
dry soil
raisins

TRY THIS

1. Put about 5 centimeters (2 inches) of dry soil into the container.

2. Fill the custard cup with soil. Sprinkle water on it until it is all damp. Bury it in the dry soil so the damp soil is even with the dry soil. (This is where the female can lay eggs.)

3. Scatter some pieces of torn paper towel around the container. (The crickets can hide underneath when they need to.)

4. Scatter some dry oatmeal and a few raisins at one end.

5. Put no more than three or four crickets inside the container. Cover it with a screen large enough to bend down at the sides.
   a. How do the crickets act? How do they use the pieces of toweling? How do the females lay eggs? How do the crickets eat? move about?
   b. What happens when cricket eggs hatch? What do the young (nymphs) look like? What do they look like as they get older? Use a hand lens to help you see.
   c. What else can you observe about the crickets?

(*Teaching Comment:* If children are unable to catch crickets in fields, they may often be bought at fish-bait stores. The female may be recognized by a long slender "tail," or ovipositor, through which it deposits eggs in damp soil. From egg to adult takes about six months. Adults live about three months.)

▪ INVESTIGATION: Crayfish

Have you ever caught a crayfish? You can find them under rocks or in the mud of a freshwater pond or stream. Some people catch them with a small chunk of fish or meat tied to a string. When the crayfish grabs the bait, it is slowly pulled out of the water. Usually, the animal hangs on. Other people just sweep the mud with a net to catch them. Crayfish are interesting to observe.

EXPLORATORY PROBLEM

How can you find out more about crayfish?

NEEDED

four healthy crayfish	three small plastic flower pots
child's wading pool	gravel
ice cube tongs (scissors style)	pliers

TRY THIS

1. Cover the bottom of a plastic wading pool with gravel.

2. Break off an opening in each of three flower pots. Make each large enough for a crayfish to go through.

3. Put the pots upside down in different places on the gravel.

4. Pour only about 2.5 centimeters (1 inch) of water into the pool. Let it stand for two days to lose the chlorine. Or, use pond water.

5. Use tongs to place the crayfish in the pool. (See Figure 15-20.)

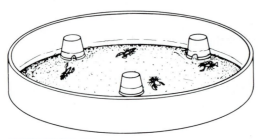

FIGURE 15-20

DISCOVERY PROBLEMS

observing   **A.** Where are the eyes on a crayfish? Can you make the eyes blink without hurting them?

observing   **B.** How many legs does each animal have?

observing   **C.** What are some ways you can tell them apart?

experimenting   **D.** How can you find out if they like the dark or light?

experimenting   **E.** How strongly does a crayfish claw "pinch"? You can use a pencil or rolled piece of clay to find out. Are the pinch marks different for each animal? How so?

observing   **F.** Which crayfish go into the flower pot shelters? How do the crayfish prevent others from getting into a shelter? How do they get another crayfish out?

inferring   **G.** Does any single crayfish seem to be "boss"? How can you tell? What will happen if you remove that crayfish?

observing   **H.** What else have you noticed about crayfish? What else can you learn?

TEACHING COMMENT

PREPARATION AND BACKGROUND

Crayfish need not be fed if kept less than about three weeks. Otherwise, feed them at three-week intervals with small chunks of fresh or canned fish, meat, or earthworms. Place them in a separate container, such as a plastic shoe box, during feeding. This will help to keep the pool uncontaminated. Empty and rinse the container after each feeding.

Crayfish have strong claws, so they should be handled carefully. They can be grasped between thumb and forefinger if approached from the rear. Hold the body just above the thin walking legs. To avoid accidental pinches, you might let pupils use tongs to handle the animals. Tiny nail-polish markings can be used to identify the animals, if needed.

At the end of the investigation period, the crayfish can be returned to their natural habitat.

GENERALIZATION

Some behaviors of a crayfish are inborn; some are affected by its environment.

SAMPLE PERFORMANCE OBJECTIVES

Knowledge: The child can state the apparent preference of crayfish as to darkness and light.
Process: The child can test the preference of crayfish as to darkness and light.

FOR YOUNGER CHILDREN

Younger pupils should be able to do the investigation. But expect less precision and the need for more supervision.

■ INVESTIGATION: Brine Shrimp

Have you ever visited a salt lake? If so, maybe you have seen *brine shrimp.* These small animals lay tiny eggs. You can find out many interesting things about brine shrimp, but first you will need to hatch the eggs.

EXPLORATORY PROBLEM

How can you hatch brine shrimp eggs?

NEEDED

vial of brine shrimp eggs	tap water
noniodized salt	magnifier
plastic teaspoon	small babyfood jars
measuring cup	small package of brewer's yeast

TRY THIS

1. Let a cup of tap water stand overnight. Then mix four teaspoons of salt into it.
2. Pour the water into several babyfood jars. Use one jar now (Figure 15-21). Cap and save the other jars for later use.
3. Take just a tiny pinch of eggs from the vial. Sprinkle them on top of the water.
4. Observe the eggs closely a few times each day. Use a magnifier to see better.

FIGURE 15-21

DISCOVERY PROBLEMS

observing   **A.** When do you first notice changes in the eggs? What changes do you see?

observing   **B.** When do you first notice tiny brine shrimp? How do they look to you? Can you describe what they are doing?

observing   **C.** What changes do you notice as the brine shrimp grow? Observe them each day.

observing   **D.** Do brine shrimp ever seem to rest or sleep? How can you find out?

observing   **E.** How long does it take for a shrimp to start growing?

experimenting   **F.** How long can you keep a brine shrimp alive?

experimenting   **G.** Do newly hatched shrimp go where it is light or dark? How about month-old shrimp? How can you find out?

observing   **H.** How can you tell which brine shrimp are female?

experimenting   **I.** Will brine shrimp eggs hatch in fresh water? In water with twice as much or more salt than you first used?

hypothesizing   **J.** Suppose you hatch many shrimp eggs in one jar and only a few in another. What do you think will happen as the shrimp grow?

hypothesizing   **K.** What else would you like to investigate about brine shrimp?

TEACHING COMMENT

PREPARATION AND BACKGROUND

Brine shrimp are sold at pet stores for fish food. The eggs may be hatched in salt water. About four teaspoons of salt per cup of water work well for both hatching and growth. But the shrimp may hatch within a wide range of salt concentrations. Be sure to use either noniodized or marine salt.

About six weeks are needed for the shrimp to reach maturity under the best conditions. A water temperature of about 27°C (80°F) is ideal. Children will be able to distinguish female from male adults most easily by the females' egg pouches.

It is harder to keep brine shrimp alive for a lengthy period than to hatch them. Some precautions will help. Have pupils make a crayon mark on their jars at the beginning water level. Be sure any evaporated water is replaced by aged tap water containing the proper salt concentration. The water should stand for at least 24 hours to allow the chlorine to escape. Put a tiny pinch of baking soda in each shrimp container once a week to neutralize the acid that builds up. Above all, do not overfeed the shrimp. A tiny pinch of yeast once a week is adequate to grow the bacteria on which they feed.

As with other long-range observational activities, this one is ideal for motivating artwork and language experiences.

GENERALIZATION

Brine shrimp will hatch and grow from eggs, stay alive, and reproduce when conditions are like those of their natural habitat.

SAMPLE PERFORMANCE OBJECTIVES

Process: The child can observe and describe several developmental changes in newly hatched brine shrimp over a two-week period.
Knowledge: The child can state several environmental conditions that are favorable for maintaining live brine shrimp.

FOR YOUNGER CHILDREN

Younger pupils should be able to do this investigation through Problem C.

■ INVESTIGATION: Snails and What They Do

Have you ever seen a snail? If so, where? Many water snails live in and around the edges of ponds. Land snails can be found in gardens, lawns, and around damp soil. They are easiest to find early in the morning or at night. Land snails are usually larger than water snails, so they are easier to observe. What they do is full of surprises.

EXPLORATORY PROBLEM

How can you find out about land snails and what they do?

NEEDED

live land snail	small stiff card
wide-mouth glass jar containing some damp soil	magnifier
	spoon
aluminum pie plate	ruler
sheet of black paper	piece of lettuce
paper towel	small paper cup of water

TRY THIS

1. Put a snail on a pie plate.

2. Use a spoon and card to move it where you want.

3. Use a magnifier to see it more clearly (Figure 15-22).

FIGURE 15-22

DISCOVERY PROBLEMS

observing   **A.** What do you notice about the snail? How does it move? How can you describe its head? shell? other parts?

observing   **B.** How many stalks (feelers) do you observe on its head? Which seem to have eyes? Which seem to be used for feeling?

observing   **C.** What happens when you gently touch the two longer stalks? the two shorter stalks? How close can you get before the stalks move?

experimenting   **D.** How can you get the two longer stalks to move in different directions?

observing   **E.** What happens when you tap the snail's shell gently?

observing   **F.** Try to put the snail upside down on its shell. Can the snail right itself? If so, how?

observing   **G.** Put the snail on a piece of black paper. Observe the silver trail it makes. How far does the snail go in one minute?

communicating   **H.** How well can you draw an animal? Make a drawing of your snail. Show it to someone who does not know you are studying snails. Can that person tell it is a snail?

communicating   **I.** How well can you describe an animal? Write a description of your snail without saying what it is. Show the description to someone who does not know you are studying snails. Can that person tell it is a snail?

observing   **J.** Give the snail some lettuce to eat. Observe its mouth parts with a magnifier. How does it eat?

experimenting   **K.** What foods does your snail seem to like best? Circle your snail with bits of different foods. Which does the snail go to first? What happens when you try this several times? How long should you wait between each trial? Why?

experimenting   **L.** Will a snail go to the dark or light? Put your snail in the pie pan. How can you use a sheet of black paper to find out?

experimenting   **M.** Will a snail go where it is dry or wet? How can you use a paper towel to find out?

hypothesizing   **N.** What other experiments would you like to try with snails? What other kinds of snails can you find to try?

TEACHING COMMENT

PREPARATION AND BACKGROUND

Land snails can be found where there is plenty of vegetation and moisture. They seem to prefer cool, shady places, especially under leaves, logs, and rocks. Early morning is probably the easiest time to collect snails, when leaves are heavy with dew. If collected in a dry "resting" condition, place them on a water soaked paper towel to reactivate them.

Several collected snails may be kept in one glass jar. The jar top should have some holes punched into it for air. Place an inch or two of soil inside and keep it damp. For extra moisture, sink a bottle cap flush with the soil surface and fill it with water. Leave a small piece of lettuce inside for food. Keep the jar in a shady place. After several days, the jar will need to be cleaned.

Try to have a number of snails available for observation and experiments. Even when treated gently, this animal needs a rest period between activities.

GENERALIZATION

Some behaviors of an animal are inborn, and some are influenced by its environment.

SAMPLE PERFORMANCE OBJECTIVES

Process: The child can test the preferences of a snail as to light, food, and moisture.
Knowledge: The child can predict places where land snails are likely to be found.

FOR YOUNGER CHILDREN

Younger children should be able to do most of the observational activities, although with less precision than older children.

□ ACTIVITY: What Are Some Behaviors of Earthworms?

NEEDED

aluminum pie pan   six earthworms
black paper   sticky tape
scissors   plastic spoon
paper towel

TRY THIS

1. Find out if earthworms will go to a wet or dry place.

2. Fold a dry paper towel. Tape it to one-half of the pan. Fold and tape a wet towel to the other half of the pan. Leave a small space between the two towels.

3. Put the earthworms on the wet side. Watch what they do. Then, put them on the dry side and watch.
   a. Which side do the earthworms seem to like better?

4. Find out if earthworms will go to a dark or light place. Place a wet towel on the pan. Cover one-half of the pan with black paper.

5. Put the earthworms in the middle of the pan and watch.
   b. Which side do the earthworms seem to like better?

(*Teaching Comment:* Earthworms can easily be found on the soil after a rain. They are also found at night or early morning in damp soil and under leaves. They can be kept for extended periods in a large glass or plastic container half-filled with humus-rich soil. Occasionally, mix some corn meal into the soil surface to supplement their diet. The soil should be kept damp but not wet. Keep the container in the coolest part of the room.)

SECTION 3
Ecology
[*Background 478*]

□ ACTIVITY: What Living Things Can You Find in Some Small Habitats?

NEEDED

sunny, dry place   meter stick or yardstick
damp, shadowy place   string

TRY THIS

1. Go to a sunny, dry place. Measure a spot one meter (or one yard) square. Put a string around this spot.

a. What animals do you find living inside, on, or near the surface? How many of each? What kinds of plants, if any, do you find in the habitat? Record what you find.

2. Go to a damp, shadowy place. Again, put a string around a one-meter (or one-yard) square area.

  b. What and how many animals are living here? What and how many plants?

  c. How do the animals and plants differ in the two habitats? How are they alike?

☐ ACTIVITY: What Is a Food Chain?

NEEDED

six cards with one of these words or pictures on   six persons
  each: sun, plant, insect, toad, snake, hawk   six pins

Plants need the sun to grow. Many insects eat plants, many toads eat insects, many snakes eat toads, and many hawks eat snakes. This is one example of a food chain. See what happens when a food chain is broken.

TRY THIS

1. Each person should pin a card to her or his clothes.

2. Stand in line and hold hands in this order: sun, plant, insect, toad, snake, hawk.

  a. What animal would die if there were no snakes to eat? (The snake person should drop hands now.)

  b. What animals would die if there were no toads to eat? (The toad person drops hands.)

  c. What animals would die if there were no insects to eat? (Insect person drops hands.)

  d. What animals would die if there were no plants to eat? (Plant person drops hands.)

  e. What would happen if there were no sun to let plants grow?

(*Teaching Comment:* Be sure to point out that these animals might eat a wider variety of food than is shown in this simple chain. However, the basic idea of interdependence is valid. This can be clarified further by making more food chains. Older children can connect two or more food chains to make a more complicated food web. Run strings between and among individuals in the web to show the intricate interrelationships involved.)

■ INVESTIGATION: How Color Protects Animals

If you were an insect that lived in the grass, what enemies might you have? How might having the right color protect you from being eaten by birds and other animals?

EXPLORATORY PROBLEM

How can you test if color affects the chances to survive?

NEEDED

brown and green construction paper
scissors
half-cup of bird seed
jar

lawn area
bare dirt area
set of food colors

TRY THIS

1. Cut out 100 same-sized pieces of green paper and 100 of brown paper. Make each piece about the size of your thumbnail.
2. Have someone scatter 50 pieces of each color on a lawn area.
3. Pretend the paper pieces are insects and you are a bird. Try to find as many pieces as you can in one minute. Let some partners help you (Figure 15-23).

FIGURE 15-23

DISCOVERY PROBLEMS

inferring **A.** How many pieces of each color paper did you find? Which color would be better if you were a lawn insect?

experimenting **B.** Suppose you were an insect that lived in a bare dirt area. Which color would be better? What could you do to find out?

experimenting **C.** How could colored seeds be tested with real birds? Mix a few drops of food coloring with water in a jar. Drop in the seeds to color them.

observing **D.** Observe closely insects on different plants. How are their colors like those of the plant? Different?

observing **E.** How are other animals protected by their skin colors? Find in books and magazines colored pictures of animals in their natural habitats.

TEACHING COMMENT

PREPARATION AND BACKGROUND

Try to have the colors of the construction paper match as closely as possible the lawn and bare dirt areas.

For the bird-seed activity, allow several hours between scattering the seeds and locating the surviving seeds. Make sure pupils realize that they may not be able to locate all the surviving seeds. How can they increase their chances of locating survivors? They may decide to enclose groups of seeds with string or to try other methods.

GENERALIZATION

Survival chances increase when an animal's color matches its surroundings.

SAMPLE PERFORMANCE OBJECTIVES

Process: The child can design a test of survival for colored seeds in different locations with real birds.
Knowledge: The child predicts smaller survival chances when an animal's color is unlike its surroundings and greater chances when its color is similar.

FOR YOUNGER CHILDREN

Try the basic activity. Be sure children understand the analogy of people representing birds and bits of colored paper representing insects.

■ INVESTIGATION: Ant Responses to Sweeteners

Some people do not use sugar because it has high-energy value and may be fattening. They may use an artificial sweetener, which has very little energy value. Many people cannot tell the difference between the two. You probably know that ants and some other insects are attracted to sugar. But what attracts them? Is it the sweetness or something else?

EXPLORATORY PROBLEM

How can you test ant responses to real and artificial sugar?

NEEDED

one or more artificial sweeteners   sugar
two small matched bottle caps   water
two paper cups   teaspoon

TRY THIS

1. Mix one bottle cap each of sugar and water in a cup. Use a spoon to stir. Pour the mixture into one cap until it is full (Figure 15-24).

FIGURE 15-24

2. Do the same with sweetener and water. Use a second cap and cup. Remember to rinse the spoon clean before you stir again.
3. Place both caps close together where there are ants. Mark which cap contains the sugar. Watch what happens.

DISCOVERY PROBLEMS

observing   **A.** What do you notice? Which mixture attracts more ants?

observing   **B.** What will happen if you test the sweetener by itself?

observing   **C.** What will happen if you test it with different kinds of ants?

observing   **D.** What will happen if you test different sweeteners?

experimenting   **E.** How can you find out how other insects will act toward artificial sweeteners?

inferring   **F.** Keep a record of your findings. Look it over. How do the responses of these animals help them to stay alive?

TEACHING COMMENT

PREPARATION AND BACKGROUND

You may want to check where pupils put the caps. They should be equally accessible to the ants.

GENERALIZATION

The ability to respond to a high-energy food can help an animal to survive.

SAMPLE PERFORMANCE OBJECTIVES

Knowledge: The child states that insects are more likely to be attracted to sugar than to low-energy sweeteners.
Process: The child designs ways to test responses of several different insects toward sweeteners.

FOR YOUNGER CHILDREN

You might have younger pupils first try themselves to discriminate between light solutions of sugar water and sweetener water. Afterward, they can also try to "fool" some ants or other insects. Younger pupils typically will show less understanding of the concept of survival value than older pupils.

■ INVESTIGATION: The Fright Distances of Wild Animals

One difference between wild and tame animals is how easily they are frightened. How close have you come to a wild bird before it flew off? How about other wild animals?

EXPLORATORY PROBLEM

What are the fright distances of some wild birds?

NEEDED

wild birds	different kinds of bird food
handkerchief	(bread crumbs, seeds, bacon
meter stick or yardstick	bits, etc.)

TRY THIS

1. Go where there are some wild birds.
2. Sprinkle some bread crumbs on the ground at different distances from you.
3. Watch where the birds pick up the crumbs each time. Measure the closest distance the birds "dare" to come near you (Figure 15-25).

DISCOVERY PROBLEMS

measuring   **A.** What is the fright distance of these birds? Is every bird in this group frightened at the same distance? Are other kinds of birds frightened at another distance?

hypothesizing   **B.** What would be the fright distance if you tried other foods?

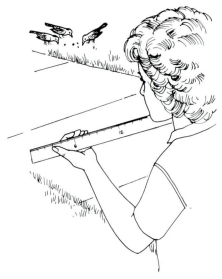

FIGURE 15-25

hypothesizing **C.** Suppose you go to the same place and drop crumbs each day for a week. What do you think the fright distance of the same birds would be then?

measuring **D.** How close can you get to different birds without food? Slowly walk toward each perched bird until it flies away. Measure the distance between you and the perch place each time.

experimenting **E.** How do different sounds and noises affect fright distance? Different movements?

experimenting **F.** What are the fright distances of other wild animals? Find squirrels,
communicating chipmunks, and other animals. Make a record of what happens.

TEACHING COMMENT

PREPARATION AND BACKGROUND

Pupils can usually notice differences in bird species, but they often have trouble communicating what they see. A simple bird identification book can help.

If possible, let children repeat this activity over several days. They will discover that birds and other wild animals typically decrease their fright distances if the same, harmless stimulus is presented each time.

Caution children never to touch wild animals that approach humans and never to feed them by hand. Such animals are abnormal and may be ill.

GENERALIZATION

Fright behavior is an inborn property of wild animals that helps them to survive. Fright distance may decrease when animals become used to objects or events.

SAMPLE PERFORMANCE OBJECTIVES

Knowledge: The child can state that fright distances vary with different species of wild animals.

Process: The child can measure fright distances of animals under several conditions and draw proper inferences from the data.

■ INVESTIGATION: Bird Nests

Have you ever seen a bird nest close up? Birds do not have to learn how to make nests. This is an inborn behavior. A nest is used to lay and hatch eggs in. The hatched chicks stay there until they grow up enough to fly. The materials used for the nest may come from many different things. Sometimes the materials birds use are quite surprising.

EXPLORATORY PROBLEM A

How can you find out more about how some birds make nests?

NEEDED

several unused bird nests   pencil
tweezers

TRY THIS

1. Look for unused bird nests in trees and large bushes. The best time for this is in winter.
2. Collect several nests. Ask a responsible adult to help you do so.
3. Bring the nests to class.

DISCOVERY PROBLEMS

observing   **A.** What is the size and shape of each nest? How is each made?

observing   **B.** How are the nests alike? different?

observing   **C.** What materials were used to make the nests? Use tweezers and a pencil to help you pick apart the nests.

inferring   **D.** Make a list of the materials (Figure 15-26). Which seem to come from where the birds live? Which, if any, seem to come from far away? (Keep this list for use next spring.)

inferring   **E.** What kind of bird probably made each kind of nest? Get some bird books from the library. See if they can help you find out.

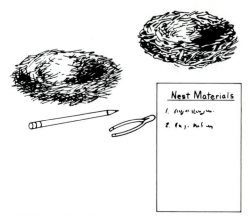

FIGURE 15-26

EXPLORATORY PROBLEM B

Given choices, what materials will some birds pick to make nests?

NEEDED

60-centimeter (2-foot) cardboard square	thread
large nail	aluminum foil
scissors	different strings
different-colored yarn	different cloth pieces
	paper strips

TRY THIS

1. Do this activity in early spring, when many birds build nests.
2. Punch many holes in the cardboard with a large nail. Wiggle the nail in each hold to make it larger.
3. Cut narrow pieces of cloth, paper, and foil.
4. Cut small pieces of string and yarn.
5. Thread these materials partway through the cardboard's holes. Label under each hole what is there.
6. Tack the cardboard to a tree where other trees and bushes grow.
7. Check the board each day to see what is missing.

DISCOVERY PROBLEMS

observing **A.** Which materials were taken first? Replace these materials right away. Will they be taken again before other materials? Check again to see.

experimenting **B.** How can you change the picked materials to make them less attractive? You might cut longer pieces of yarn, for example, or cut wider cloth strips. How can you make the unpicked materials more attractive?

observing   **C.** What will happen if you move the board to another place? How will your findings compare with those before?

observing   **D.** Make a list of the materials selected. How does it compare with the list of nest materials you made in the winter?

TEACHING COMMENT

PREPARATION AND BACKGROUND

Bird's nests are usually abandoned by winter and are rarely used again. So winter is a good time to collect nests. In the unlikely event that eggs are found, the nest should be left undisturbed. The materials-selection board is best placed off the ground on a tree trunk or low limb away from traffic. However, it should be visible and accessible to the children.

GENERALIZATION

Birds use materials from the environment to build their nests; the ability to build nests has survival value.

SAMPLE PERFORMANCE OBJECTIVES

Knowledge: The child can describe the kinds of materials local birds are likely to use in nest building.
Process: The child can compose two listings of findings and compare them for similarities and differences.

SELECTED TRADE BOOKS: ANIMAL LIFE AND ENVIRONMENT

FOR YOUNGER CHILDREN

Aaseng, Nathan. *Meat-Eating Animals.* Lerner, 1987.

Aaseng, Nathan. *Prey Animals.* Lerner, 1987.

Cousins, Lucy. *Country Animals.* Morrow, 1991.

Day, Jenifer. *What Is a Mammal?* Golden Books, 1986.

Dreyer, Ellen. *Wild Animals.* Troll Associates, 1991.

Freedman, Russell. *Tooth and Claw: A Look at Animal Weapons.* Holiday, 1980.

Pfloog, Jan. *Wild Animals and Their Babies.* Western, 1987.

Penn, Linda. *Young Scientists Explore Animal Friends.* Good Apple, 1983.

Priestly, Anne. *Big Animals.* Random House, 1987.

Stone, Lynn M. *Marshes and Swamps.* Children's Press, 1983.

Sutton, Felix. *The Big Book of Wild Animals.* Putman, 1983.

Urquhart, Jennifer C. *Animals That Travel.* National Geographic, 1982.

Wildsmith, Brian. *Animal Homes.* Oxford, 1991.

Wozmek, Frances. *The ABC of Ecology.* Davenport, 1982.

FOR OLDER CHILDREN

Bright, Michael. *Pollution and Wildlife.* Watts, 1987.

Dean, Anabel. *Animal Defenses.* Messner, 1978.

Dean, Anabel. *How Animals Communicate.* Messner, 1977.

Earthbooks Staff, *National Wildlife Federation's Book of Endangered Species.* Earthbooks, Inc., 1991.

Fichter, George S. *Poisonous Animals.* Watts, 1991.

Flegg, Jim. *Animal Builders.* Newington, 1991.

Gallent, Ray A. *The Rise of Mammals.* Watts, 1986.

Grossman, Shelly, and Mary L. Grossman. *Ecology.* Wonder, 1981.

Leon, Dorothy. *The Secret World of Underground Creatures.* Messner, 1982.

Maynard, Thane. *Animal Inventors.* Watts, 1991.

Penny, Malcolm. *Animal Evolution.* Watts, 1987.

Pringle, Laurence. *Home: How Animals Find Comfort and Safety.* Macmillan, 1987.

Sabin, Francene. *Ecosystems and Food Chains.* Troll Associates, 1985.

Sanders, John. *All About Animal Migrations.* Troll Associates, 1984.

16

Human Body and Nutrition

By any measure, the human body is a masterpiece of organization. It is composed of millions of tiny *cells,* many of them differing in shape, size, and internal makeup according to the work they do.

Groups of cells that work together are *tissues.* Examples are the connective tissue that holds the body together, muscle tissue, nerve tissue, blood tissue, and epithelial (skin) tissue. When tissues work together, they are called *organs.* Examples are the lungs, heart, stomach, and eyes. Organs that work together are *systems.*

We'll consider several body systems in this chapter: (1) the skeletal and muscle systems, which support and move the body; (2) the nervous system, which controls the body; (3) the circulatory and respiratory systems, which move the blood and permit breathing; and (4) the digestive system, which fuels the body by breaking down foods into simpler forms. A final section (5) examines *nutrition,* the makeup of foods and how they affect the body.

[1] SKELETAL AND MUSCLE SYSTEMS
Experiences 522

It is hard to imagine how the human body would look without bones. It has more than 200 joined into a skeletal framework that gives the body its overall shape and support. The bones are not all individual, unique pieces that fit together. Rather, there are groups of bones, all well fitted for their specialized work.

Groups of Bones

The main part of the skull consists of eight relatively flat bones joined together into the characteristic helmetlike shape. In children, the joints between the bones are movable.

This allows the bones to grow as children get older. As adults, their skull bones will have grown together into a solid, curved surface with immovable joints. The only head bone we can ever move voluntarily is the jawbone. Chewing and normal conversation depend on this movement.

The skull is joined to a stack of oval and irregular small bones called the *vertebrae,* or spine. The vertebrae permit bending and twisting motions. In between each small bone is a pad of tough, elastic tissue called *cartilage.* The cartilage pads keep the spinal bones from grinding or hitting together as we move. As we age during adulthood, the pads continue to compress, making us shorter. Between 40 and 70, for example, we may lose an inch or more in height.

The spinal bones also have holes in them. This allows the bundle of nerves that make up the spinal cord to run through the length of the protective vertebrae. Side holes in the vertebrae permit nerve branches from the spinal cord to go out to other parts of the body.

Many children think that standing up "straight" means having a straight backbone. This is not so. Although the vertebrae are stacked in a column, the column is curved in a shallow *S* form. This permits better balance than a vertical backbone.

Attached to the backbone are 12 pairs of ribs. The top 10 pairs curve around and join the breastbone in front. But if you feel your two pairs of bottom ribs, you may notice that they are not joined in front. For this reason, they are called "floating ribs."

The ribs form a flexible cage that protects the heart, lungs, and other organs. The cartilage that fastens the ribs is somewhat elastic, and the ribs are bendable. This is why the chest can expand and contract as we breathe.

The *hipbones* are fastened at the other end of the backbone. With the bottom of the backbone, they form a large and open shallow bowl in front. The bowl helps to support the body and protects some of the organs below the waist. The lowest parts of the hipbones are used for sitting.

The *long bones* of the arms and legs are the levers that allow us to walk, run, and throw. These bones are strong but also light for their size, because they are mostly hollow inside. If they were solid, the increased weight would slow us down considerably. Long bones are thicker at the ends than in the center section and fit the ends of adjoining bones.

Composition of Bones

A soft material called *marrow* is found inside many bones, particularly the long bones. There are two kinds of marrow. *Red* marrow is found at the ends of the bones; these are the sites where red blood cells are manufactured. *Yellow* marrow is stored inside the middle of the bones and is mainly composed of fat.

A newborn baby's skeleton is composed mostly of soft cartilage. As the baby grows, its body continually replaces the cartilage with calcium and other minerals from digested food, so the skeleton continually hardens. Children's bones typically are softer than those of adults because they contain more cartilage. This makes their bones less likely to break under stress. Some cartilage never changes to bone, like the ears, tip of the nose, and several other places.

Movable Joints

A rigid skeletal framework would be of little use. The reason we can move is because many bones are held together by movable joints. Tough, thick cords of elastic tissue, called *ligaments,* make up the material that joins bone to bone.

We have several different kinds of movable joints, and each allows different movements. Hinge joints allow us to bend the elbow, knee, and fingers. Notice that the movement is in only one direction.

The thumb is particularly interesting. It has only two hinged joints, yet we can move the thumb so it opposes any finger. A third joint up near the wrist makes this movement possible.

A ball-and-socket joint at the shoulder allows rotary motion of the arm. A similar socket connects the upper leg bone at the hip, but movement in this case is more restricted. Other kinds of joints allow wrist, head, foot, and other motions. In all, we have six different kinds of movable joints.

Muscles

Under the skin, and inside the body, are about 600 muscles, two-thirds of which are *voluntary* muscles. These muscles are connected to bones, and we can move them on command. Some muscles, such as those that move food through the intestines and those that make the heart beat, cannot ordinarily be controlled. These are the *involuntary* muscles.

Muscles can only pull; they work in opposite pairs. This is easiest to see with the jointed leg bones. If you swing a leg forward, muscles in the front part of the thigh and hip contract and pull the leg forward. If you swing the leg back, muscles in the back part of the thigh and hip contract and pull the leg back.

Tendons

Muscles are attached to bone and cartilage by the *tendons.* These are tough, white, twisted fibers of different lengths. Some are cordlike; others are wider and flat. Tendons are enclosed in sleeves of thin tissue that contain a slippery liquid. This permits them to slide back and forth without rubbing.

Tendons are strong and unstretchable. Some that are easy to observe are found inside the elbow and back of the knee. One of the strongest and thickest tendons in the body is the Achilles tendon. It is located just above the heel of the foot. Also easy to observe are the tendons that pull the finger bones as you wiggle your fingers. If you try this and touch the forearm with the opposite hand, you will notice that muscles in the forearm, not muscles in the hand, mainly move the fingers. Children are usually surprised by this.

Makeup of Muscles

How do muscles work? Why do they get tired? Why does exercise make us warm?

A microscope reveals that voluntary muscles are made up of bundles of fibers, each about the size of a human hair, but far stronger. Like the entire muscle, each fiber shortens as it pulls and lengthens as it relaxes. The number of fibers that work depends on how heavily the muscle is strained. Also, not all the fibers work simultaneously. Each is rapidly and continually switched on and off by the nervous system as the muscle works. This allows each fiber some rest and greater overall endurance for the muscle.

The energy to move a muscle comes from a form of sugar called *glycogen*. It is found inside the muscles' cells. About a fourth of the energy released by this sugar goes into moving the muscle. The rest is released as heat. The faster a muscle is used, the more heat is produced. This is why heavy exercise makes us warm.

Sooner or later, heavy exercise fatigues the muscle. Not only is the supply of glycogen consumed, but waste products build up in the cell faster than they can be removed. As the waste products build up, the muscle fibers work more and more slowly.

[2] THE NERVOUS SYSTEM
Experiences 524

Nerves

What happens inside the nervous system when we sense an object and react to it? The central part of the nervous system is composed of the brain and spinal cord. Nerves connected to the brain and spinal cord branch out in ever-smaller tendrils to all parts of the body.

When nerve endings are stimulated in some sense organs, ordinarily an electrical message is zipped through sensory nerves from the receptor to the spinal cord and then to the brain. In turn, the brain flashes back a message along motor nerves, which control muscles. The time between when the brain receives a signal and when it returns a command to the muscles is called one's *reaction time*.

Quick Reflexes

A curious thing happens, however, when a quick reflexive action is required. The brain is bypassed until the reflex action happens. For example, if you should touch a finger to a hot stove, the electrical impulses travel from the finger to the spinal cord. But instead of the signal going to the brain, the spinal cord itself flashes a signal along the motor nerves, which immediately activate muscles to jerk the hand away. Meanwhile, the spinal cord also sends impulses to the brain that cause you to feel pain. The sensation, though, is felt *after* you have already reacted to the danger. This, of course, has survival value.

Brain

The brain is the control center of the body. Instead of a single mass, it is made up of three parts: the *cerebrum*, the *cerebellum*, and the *medulla*. Each has a different job.

The cerebrum is the brain's largest part. It consists of two halves that occupy the top portion of the skull. This is the part that governs the conscious, rational processes and receives signals from the senses. The cerebrum also controls the body's voluntary muscles.

The cerebellum is a far smaller part and is located below and behind the cerebrum. It governs perception of balance and coordinates the voluntary muscles.

The medulla adjoins the top of the spinal column at the base of the skull. It governs the involuntary muscles used for digesting food, coughing or sneezing, breathing, pumping blood, and the like.

Learning

How successfully we adapt to the environment often depends on our ability to learn. We learn in several different ways. At the lowest level is trial-and-error learning. This is how we learn to do handwriting or hit a golf ball. The brain works in combination with the senses and muscles to provide corrective feedback.

Learning increases when we organize the data we deal with. Recognizing patterns, outlining, and drawing diagrams are some ways we improve learning. Learning also increases when we associate something we do not know with something we do know. Using memory devices to learn names or to remember spelling words are examples. Reasoning and problem solving are at the highest levels of learning.

The Senses

We receive most of the sensations our brains turn into perceptions through five organs: the eye, ear, nose, tongue, and skin. How do they work? Let's look at each in turn.

The Eye. In the eye, as in the other sense organs, are the tiny nerve endings of neurons, or nerve cells. The retina, or back section of the eyeball, contains two kinds of light-sensitive neurons: rods and cones. The cones are clustered in and around the center of the retina and are sensitive to color. The rods are distributed outside the cones and are sensitive to light, but not color. The nerve endings of both rods and cones join into a bundle called the optic nerve, which leads to the brain. (Additional details and activities on the eye may be found in Chapter 8, "Light Energy and Color.")

The Ear. The ear has three parts: outer, middle, and inner. The first two parts pass on sound vibrations to the inner ear, located deep inside the skull. The inner ear contains the cochlea, a spiral passage shaped like a snail's shell. Inside are sound-sensitive nerve endings and a liquid. When vibrations move into the inner ear, the cochlea's liquid vibrates and stimulates the nerve endings. This instantly transmits electric impulses to the auditory nerve, which then zips them to the brain. At that point, we hear. (Additional details and activities on hearing may be found in Chapter 10, "Sound Energy.")

If you have ever been seasick, you can probably blame your inner ear. It has an intricate part that controls our sense of balance. The part consists of three tubes, formed in half circles, called the semicircular canals. The tubes contain a thin liquid and are arranged in three different positions relative to each other. These positions correspond to the three ways we move our heads: up and down, sideways tilt, and the turning motion. Each motion of the head sloshes the liquid in one of the canals, stimulating nerve endings inside. The impulses are flashed along a branch of the auditory nerve that leads to the cerebellum rather than to the large cerebrum.

One seasickness theory states that the several motions felt in the inner ear conflict with what we see. This is especially so below deck. The sensory conflict triggers the body reaction.

The Nose. The nose has nerve endings in the nasal cavity that are sensitive to chemicals. When breathed into the nose, the chemicals dissolve in the moist film of mucous that covers a membrane in the nasal cavity. There nerve endings are stimulated to send signals to the sensory nerves and brain. Continual exposure to one odor causes the nerve cells to become insensitive to that odor. Yet other odors may be detected very well at the same time.

Nerve cells of the nose seem to sense only four primary odors: burnt, rancid, acid, and fragrant odors. Some scientists think that every other odor may simply be some combination of two or more of the four primary odors.

The Tongue. Exactly what we taste is an individual matter, even though our tongues are similarly constructed. The tongue contains clusters of nerve cells in the tiny bumps we call taste buds. Taste buds are sensitive to four flavors: sweet, sour, salty, and bitter. Most buds are clustered in the tip, on the edges, and in the back of the tongue. The tip tends to be sensitive to sweet and salty flavors, the sides to sour flavors, and the back to bitter flavors. However, the exact places vary with people. The taste buds clump into small mounds called papillae. These are connected to a sensory nerve that leads to the brain.

Do you remember how tasteless food is when a head cold causes a stuffy nose? It is easy to confuse the sense of taste with that of smell. As we eat, the odors given off by the food stimulate the sense of smell. So both organs work together.

Sometimes the sense of smell dominates. For example, let a pupil chew a tiny piece of radish while you hold a small fresh piece of apple or onion by the pupil's nose. The child will generally believe he is eating the apple or onion.

The Skin. Our skin contains no fewer than five different kinds of nerve endings, which are sensitive to pressure, touch, pain, heat, and cold. These nerve endings are positioned at various depths in the skin. Pressure, for example, is felt much deeper in the skin than touch.

Our nerve endings are also scattered unevenly. The lips and finger tips have many more endings clustered together than other places such as the back of the neck or arm. This is why they are so sensitive. An investigation in the activity section enables children to discover some sensitive and insensitive places on their skin.

[3] THE CIRCULATORY AND RESPIRATORY SYSTEMS Experiences 538

The Circulatory System

It would be difficult to design a better system than the human blood system for the same function. Blood is the vehicle that transports food, chemicals, and oxygen to all parts of the body. It picks up wastes from the cells and moves them through organs whose job is to remove them. Blood also protects the body.

The liquid part of blood is a clear, yellowish substance called *plasma*. In the plasma are three kinds of solid materials: *red cells, white cells,* and *platelets.* The red cells are most numerous and give the blood its characteristic color. They carry oxygen from the lungs to the body's cells and carbon dioxide from the cells back to the lungs. White cells are larger and move about freely among the body's cells, attacking and consuming disease germs. Platelets also have an important function. They help to make the blood clot wherever the body is injured and bleeding.

Blood moves in the body because it is pumped by the heart, a powerful muscle about the size of one's fist. It pumps blood by alternately contracting and relaxing. Oxygen-poor blood flows into one side of the heart. Squeezing motions pump this blood into the lungs, where it receives oxygen. The oxygen-rich blood then flows back into the opposite side of the heart from where it is pumped to the rest of the body.

In a sense, the circulatory system is really a combination of two interconnected networks of tubes of various sizes. One network sends the blood from the heart to the lungs and back again to the heart. The other sends blood from the heart to the rest of the body and returns it to the heart.

Oxygen-rich blood flows from the heart to the body through thick tubes called *arteries*. Arteries branch out all over the body, getting progressively narrower until they become extremely fine *capillaries*. Capillaries may be as narrow as one-fiftieth the diameter of a human hair and are threaded throughout the cells. Digested food and oxygen pass through the capillaries into the adjacent cells. Capillaries also take up carbon dioxide and other waste products from the cells. The waste-carrying capillaries join into progressively larger tubes called *veins*, which carry blood back to the heart. The entire trip takes about 15 seconds.

Respiratory System

Body cells use oxygen to oxidize, or "burn," food. This process releases energy. Carbon dioxide and water vapor are by-products of this process, just as they are when a candle burns inside an inverted jar. A candle goes out when the oxygen supply is diminished. Likewise, oxidation of food requires a steady supply of enough oxygen. The job of the respiratory system is to replace the carbon dioxide and water vapor in our blood with oxygen. Let's see how this is done.

As we breathe in air through the nose, it passes through hollow nasal passages above the mouth where it is warmed and filtered. Hairlike, moving cilia inside the passages catch dust and airborne particles. These particles are swept to the mouth and coughed up or swallowed. The membrane lining the passages is coated with mucus, which also traps airborne materials.

The air then moves through the voice box or larynx and down into the throat. Two tubes are found there. One tube channels food into the stomach and is called the *gullet*. A second tube, the *windpipe*, is located in front of the gullet. It goes to the lungs. A flap of tissue covers the windpipe automatically when we eat or drink. This usually prevents food or liquids from entering the windpipe.

The windpipe shortly divides into two tubes called *bronchi*. One bronchus is attached to each lung. In the lungs, the bronchi split into progressively smaller branches of tubes. Each of the tiniest tubes ends in a tiny air sac. Since there are many thousands of these sacs, the lungs have a soft, spongy appearance.

Each sac swells like a tiny balloon when we breathe air into the lungs. Surrounding each sac are many capillaries. Oxygen from breathed-in air in the sac passes through the sac's thin wall into the capillaries. Carbon dioxide and water vapor in the capillaries pass the opposite way into the air sacs. These gases then move up through the branched tubes and are exhaled.

Your pupils may read that body cells use oxygen to "burn" digested food and that carbon dioxide is one by-product of the process. But don't be surprised if most still assume that the air they breathe out is the same as the air they breathe in.[1]

To show them the difference, you might get some limewater from a drugstore, two identical balloons and small glass jars, and a bicycle tire pump. (Limewater is an indicator for carbon dioxide.) Pour limewater into each of the two jars until half full. Have a child fill one balloon with the pump and the other using lung power. Release the air from one balloon under the limewater surface of one jar, then do this with the second balloon and jar. The limewater exposed to the lung air should turn milky; the other should stay about the same.

Breathing. Children typically believe that the act of breathing in forces the lungs to draw in air and expand. This is not what happens.

[1]Joel J. Mintzes. "Naive Theories in Biology: Children's Concepts of the Human Body." *School Science and Mathematics* 84(7):548–55 (1984).

Breathing in occurs because of unequal air pressure. Examine the process yourself.

Notice what happens when you take a deep breath: The chest cavity enlarges. It enlarges because rib muscles contract and pull the ribs up and outward. At the same time the *diaphragm*, a thin sheet of muscle between the chest and the abdomen, pulls downward. This further enlarges the chest cavity. Enlarging the chest cavity reduces the air pressure inside the lungs. So the stronger outside air pressure forces air into the air passages and lungs.

When we breathe out, the diaphragm relaxes and moves upward. At the same time, the rib muscles relax, and the ribs move down and inward. This reduces the size of the chest cavity, which forces air out of the lungs.

[4] THE DIGESTIVE SYSTEM *Experiences 544*

We can eat food, but when is it inside the body? The answer to this seemingly simple question depends on whose point of view we take.

Most people would say that food is inside the body once it is swallowed. To biochemists, however, any food still within the 9-meter (30-foot) digestive tube they call the *alimentary canal* is considered outside the body. This underlines the uselessness of foods we eat until they are digested—that is, chemically broken down and dissolved into a form that can be used in the cells. The digestive system (Figure 16-1) is marvelously suited to this function. Let's see how it works.

The Mouth

The digestive process begins when we start chewing food. Our front teeth (incisors and canines) cut and tear the food. Back teeth (molars) crush it into small particles. At the same time, saliva pours into the food from six salivary glands in and near the mouth. Saliva softens the food and begins the chemical

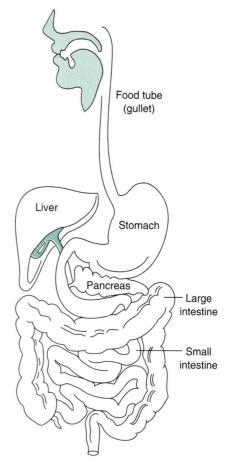

FIGURE 16-1
The digestive system.

breakdown of starches. A gradual, sweetening flavor is experienced when we chew starchy foods such as cooked potato, soda cracker, or bread. The saliva contains an enzyme called ptyalin that reduces large starch molecules into simple sugar molecules. (An enzyme is a chemical that brings about or speeds up chemical reactions without being changed itself.) Besides ptyalin, several other enzymes in the body's digestive system help break down food into usable form.

The Food Tube

Swallowed food passes into the esophagus, or food tube. It is squeezed down into the stomach by regular, wavelike contractions of smooth muscles that surround the esophagus. Similar muscles are located all along the alimentary canal. Because it is muscle action (peristalsis), not gravity, that moves the food inside the canal, it is possible to eat and swallow while standing on our heads.

The Stomach

Peristaltic motions continue in the stomach. The food is churned slowly in gastric juices secreted from the stomach lining. Several enzymes and diluted hydrochloric acid break down most of the proteins. Digestion of starch stops because acid prevents ptyalin from working. Some fats are broken down, but for the most part, fats go through the stomach undigested.

The stomach's hydrochloric acid is powerful indeed. (Remember the television advertisement in which hydrochloric acid burns holes in a handkerchief?) Why doesn't this corrosive liquid digest the stomach itself?

Only in recent years have researchers pinpointed the reason. A small amount of ammonia—this is an alkali or base—is secreted in the lining of the stomach. It effectively neutralizes acid next to the lining without interfering with the acid's digestive action elsewhere in the stomach. We use the same principle of neutralizing an acid when we drink seltzer or soda water to settle a "sour" stomach.

The Intestines

After about two to six hours in the stomach, depending on what and how much has been eaten, the partially digested food materials are pushed into the small intestine. Here, glands within intestinal walls produce digestive juices with enzymes that begin working on the food. Additional digestive juices are secreted into the intestine from small tubes connected to the liver and pancreas.

Throughout the small intestine, peristaltic motion continues as digestive juices complete the breakdown of carbohydrates into simple sugars, proteins into amino acids, and fats into fatty acids and glycerine. At various portions of the small intestine, the sugars and amino acids are absorbed into blood vessels within its lining. Digested fats are first absorbed into the lymph system and then later transported into the blood stream.

Nondigestible material or waste, composed chiefly of cellulose, passes into the large intestine. Much of the water contained in waste material is absorbed into the intestinal walls. The remaining substance is eliminated from the body.

Food products dissolved in the blood are distributed to cells after they are processed by the liver. In the cells, these products are oxidized, changed into protoplasm, or stored as fat.

[5] FOOD AND NUTRITION   *Experiences 546*

We may eat hundreds of foods combined in thousands of ways. But nutritionally speaking, there are four kinds: sugars, starches, fats, and proteins. Some persons would add three more: vitamins, minerals, and water. These seven nutrients may be combined into three groups:

1. Foods for energy—sugars, starches, and fats.
2. Foods for growth and repair of cells—proteins.
3. Food for regulation of body processes—vitamins, minerals, and water.

Carbohydrates

If we heat table sugar in a test tube, the sugar gradually turns black, and water vapor is driven off. The black material is carbon. The water is formed as hydrogen and oxygen atoms given off by individual sugar molecules combine. Heat some starch, and again carbon and water appear. Both sugar and starch are *carbohydrates,* a name that means "carbon and water."

Although sugar and starches are composed of the same elements, these elements may appear in various combinations and form relatively small to large molecules. "Simple" sugar molecules, for example, are the smallest carbohydrate molecules. They may be found in grapes and many other fruits. When two simple sugar molecules become attached, a complex sugar is formed, such as table sugar. A starch molecule is nothing more than a long chain of sugar molecules tightly attached to one another.

In digestion, carbohydrates are broken down into simple sugars. Only in this form are these molecules small enough to pass through cell membranes into the cells, where they "burn" and release energy. The "burning" is a result of *oxidation,* a process in which oxygen chemically combines with fuel—in this case, sugar—and releases heat energy. (Rusting is a form of slow oxidation; fire is very fast oxidation.) The oxygen comes from the air we breathe.

Fats

Analysis shows that fats are also composed of carbon, hydrogen, and oxygen. However, fat molecules have relatively fewer oxygen atoms than carbohydrates. Because they are oxygen "poor," fat molecules can combine with more oxygen atoms and yield about twice as much energy as carbohydrates.

Foods rich in carbohydrates and fats provide our principal source of energy. But when we eat more than we need of these materials, the cells store any excess in the form of fat. Fat storage does not occur uniformly throughout all body cells, as every figure-conscious person knows.

Proteins

The proteins are extremely complex, large molecules. A single molecule may contain thousands of atoms. Like the preceding nutrients, proteins are made up of carbon, hydrogen, and oxygen. But proteins also contain nitrogen, and typically, sulfur. Proteins are the main source of materials (amino acids) needed for growth and repair of body cells. Excess proteins can be oxidized in cells and so provide energy.

Although all animal and some plant foods (mainly beans, peas, nuts) are rich in proteins, no single plant source contains sufficient amino acids for complete growth and repair of body cells. However, a *combination* of legumes and grains—beans and rice, for example—can furnish all the needed amino acids.

Vitamins

Certain vitamins are essential to health because they regulate cell activities. These substances are not digested or used directly but rather permit biochemical processes to take place. Without proper vitamins, the body may suffer from several deficiency diseases, such as scurvy, rickets, and anemia. A balanced diet is usually all that is needed to prevent them. But, particularly in the last decade, scientists have found clues that vitamins may play a larger role than previously thought in achieving optimal health and preventing some chronic diseases, such as cancer, decline of the immune system in the aged, heart disease, eye degeneration, and others. This is why some nutritionists recommend a daily multivitamin as "insurance." However, most researchers see the need for more evidence before they can recommend large doses of vitamins aimed at specific diseases or conditions.

Minerals

Several minerals are essential because they help to regulate cell activities. In addition, some minerals are incorporated into body tissue. Calcium and phosphorus form the hard portions of our bones and teeth. Milk is especially rich in these two minerals. Iron and copper help form red blood cells. A proper amount of iodine is needed in the thyroid gland for normal oxidation to take place in cells. Salt is often iodized to prevent goiter, an iodine deficiency. Some minerals cannot be used by cells unless specific vitamins are present. Most fruits and vegetables are rich in vitamins and minerals.

Water

There are many reasons why water is essential to life and good nutrition. It changes chemically to form part of protoplasm. Water is the chief part of blood. It cools the body and carries away accumulated poisons. It is important to digestion and excretion. About two-thirds of the body itself is composed of water.

Besides drinking water directly, we take in much water in the food we eat. For example, celery is about 95 percent water, and fresh bread is about 35 percent water. Pupils can learn how to find the percentage of water present in a food in an upcoming investigation.

Choosing a Healthful Diet

A century ago many Americans were likely to suffer from undernutrition, but today the problem is often the opposite. Most of us eat too much, particularly of foods rich in fat, such as meat and dairy products. This increases the risk of heart disease, stroke, and diabetes, and may also increase the incidence of certain types of cancer. Nutritionists today recommend that we eat far more grains, fruits, and vegetables than has been customary in the American diet.

Many children and adults realize that they must eat a variety of foods to have a proper or "balanced" diet, but are unsure of its makeup. To help us select a healthful combination of nutrients, the U.S. Department of Agriculture has published a "food pyramid," with guidelines for five groups of foods (Figure 16-2).

Notice that grains, at the base, get the most servings, while fats, oils, and sweets are

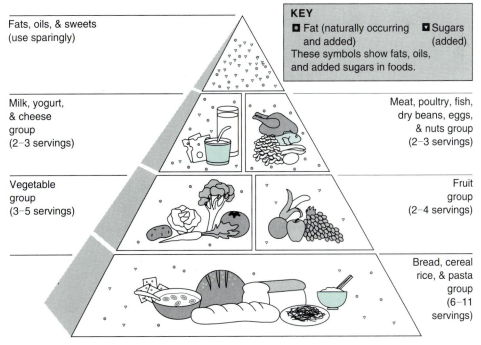

FIGURE 16-2
Food guide pyramid.

to be used only sparingly. In the dairy group, many nutritionists recommend that only non-fat or low fat products be served. In the meat group, they suggest lean rather than well-marbled meat, skinless poultry, and egg whites rather than whole eggs.

Of course, the pyramid is only a general guide. Size of servings and the number of calories we need to eat depend on our size, age, health, and lifestyle.

INVESTIGATIONS & ACTIVITIES

SECTION 1
Skeletal and Muscle Systems
[*Background 512*]

☐ ACTIVITY: What Happens When Minerals Are Removed from a Bone?

NEEDED

narrow jar and cap   vinegar
two clean matched chicken bones

TRY THIS

1. Put one bone in the jar. Leave the other one outside.
2. Fill the jar with enough vinegar to cover the bone.
3. Cap the jar and wait five days.
4. Remove the bone from the jar and rinse it with water.
   a. Compare the bones. In what ways are the two bones different? How easily does each bone bend? How are the bones still alike?
   b. What difference would it make if your bones had no hard minerals? What foods are rich in minerals?

☐ ACTIVITY: How Useful Are Your Thumbs?

NEEDED

paper clip   pencil and paper
tape

TRY THIS

1. Make a list of some things you can do now with one or two hands.
   a. Which do you think you cannot do without thumbs? Which might you do less well? Which might you do as well?
2. You might record what you think on a chart. You can make a check mark first for what you think, and then an *X* for what you find out.

| Can Do with Thumbs | Without Thumbs: | | |
	Can't Do	Do Less Well	Do as Well
Pick up paper clip	✔	X	
Tie shoelace			
Write my name			
Shake hands			
Button a shirt			
Etc.			

✔: I think.   X: I found out.

3. Ask someone to tape your thumbs to your hands.
4. Try doing the things on the list without using your thumbs.
   b. What surprises, if any, did you find? How do your thumbs help you?

☐ ACTIVITY: How Can You Observe Some of Your Tendons Work?

NEEDED

book

TRY THIS

1. Hold a book in your right hand as your arm hangs down. Place your left hand inside where you bend your right elbow.
2. Lift your right forearm and the book up and down. Feel the stringy tendons move. Try to trace the tendons to the muscles that make them work.
   a. To which muscles do they seem connected?
3. Stand on one leg. Lift the lower part of your leg up and down. Place a hand inside where you bend your knee. Feel the stringy tendons move and trace them.
   b. To which muscles do they seem connected?

4. Spread out the fingers of one hand. Move your fingers as if you were drumming on your desk. See and feel the tendons move under the skin. Trace the movement.
   c. To which muscles do they seem connected?

□ ACTIVITY: What Happens When You Overwork Your Muscles?

NEEDED

pencil and paper   watch with second hand

TRY THIS

1. Open one hand all the way, then quickly close it to make a tight fist.
2. Open and close it just like that for one minute without stopping. Do it as fast as you can.
3. Count and record what you are able to do during the first and last 30 seconds.
   a. How do the first half and the last half figures compare?
   b. What difference might it make if you change hands?
   c. If you went slower, would you be able to make more fists in one minute?
   d. Can you make as many fists in a second trial? If not, how long must you rest in between to do so?

SECTION 2
The Nervous System
[Background 514]

■ INVESTIGATION: Eye Blinking

When do your eyes blink? Do they blink when something suddenly comes near them? Eye blinking can protect your eyes. Have you also found that your eyes blink at other times? Regular eye blinking wipes your eyes clean and keeps your eyes soft and moist.

EXPLORATORY PROBLEM

How much can you control your protective eye blinking?

NEEDED

clear kitchen wrap   sticky tape
tissue paper   scissors
large file card   partner

TRY THIS

1. You will need to make an eye shield. Cut out the center of a large file card. Leave at least a 2-centimeter (or 1-inch) border.

2. Stick a double layer of clear kitchen wrap to the border with tape.

3. Hold up the shield to your eyes. Look at your partner through the clear wrap (Figure 16-3). Let him *gently* toss a tiny wad of tissue toward it.

FIGURE 16-3

DISCOVERY PROBLEMS

observing   **A.** Do your eyes blink each time the wad hits the shield? Can you stop your eyes from blinking?

communicating **B.** Are you able to control your eye blinking with practice? If so, how much practice? Keep a record.

observing   **C.** Trade places with some other people. How does their protective eye blinking compare to yours?

observing   **D.** How often do a person's eyes blink the regular way? Secretly observe the number of times someone blinks for one minute. Compare the blinking rates of different people. Do their blinking rates change
inferring   when they know you are observing them?

observing   **E.** How often do some animals blink their eyes? Which animals can you observe?

TEACHING COMMENT

PREPARATION AND BACKGROUND

Blinking is an automatic reflex act that children like to investigate. Many children find it hard to prevent the protective blinking reaction when the wad is tossed at the shield. This is good, because the reaction has survival value. Regular blinking, of course, is easily controllable when we are conscious of the act. The rate varies widely among persons and is influenced by a variety of factors.

GENERALIZATION

Eye blinking is a protective reflex action that is partly controllable. The rate of blinking varies among different people.

■ INVESTIGATION: Your Reaction Time

Have you ever had to stop fast when riding your bike? The time between when we sense something and then act is called our *reaction time*. What people would you expect to have fast reaction times? slower reaction times?

EXPLORATORY PROBLEM

How can you find out about your reaction time?

NEEDED

ruler   paper
partner   pencil

TRY THIS

1. Have your partner hold up a ruler just above your open thumb and forefinger. The ruler's lowest marked number should be facing down. Keep your eye on this ruler end.

2. Have your partner drop the ruler without warning. When you see it drop, close your fingers quickly and catch the ruler (Figure 16-4).

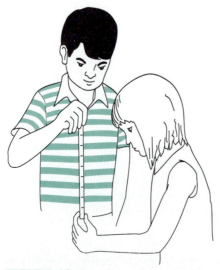

FIGURE 16-4

3. At what number did you catch the ruler? Read the closest whole number just above your two closed fingers. This is your reaction time number.

DISCOVERY PROBLEMS

hypothesizing

A. What persons in your class may have faster reaction times than yours? slower reaction times? Test these people and your partner.

communicating

Keep a record.

inferring

B. Will you react to a sound faster than to what you see? Have your partner make a sound just as he drops the ruler. Your eyes should be closed. Catch the ruler when you hear the sound. Compare this reaction time number with the one made when you saw the ruler drop.

inferring

C. Will you react to a touch faster than to sound or sight? Your eyes should be closed. Your partner can touch your head lightly when he drops the ruler. Catch the ruler when you feel his touch. Compare this reaction time with the other times.

experimenting

D. Does the time of day affect your reaction time? Does practice make a difference? Does which hand you use make a difference? How can you find out? What other ideas would you like to try?

TEACHING COMMENT

PREPARATION AND BACKGROUND

For meaningful comparisons, it is important that pupils do the test in the same way. Suggest the need for uniform procedures if they do not. A common variable that needs to be controlled is the distance the two fingers are held apart. The ruler's width may be used to separate the fingers uniformly. Then, the ruler should be turned so it parallels the separated fingers. *Caution:* It is important that the ruler be turned before it is dropped. You want the flat part of the ruler, *not* the ruler edges, to be pinched by the two fingers.

GENERALIZATION

People have different reaction times. The sense signal people react to also makes a difference in their reaction times.

SAMPLE PERFORMANCE OBJECTIVES

Process: The child can measure relative differences in reaction time of people by using a dropped ruler.
Knowledge: The child can state several variables that may influence a person's reaction time.

▪ INVESTIGATION: How Practice Improves Learning

Suppose you learn to do something one way, and then someone says you must learn to do it in another way. Why might this be hard to do? How might learning to draw or write backward be a problem? How might practice help?

EXPLORATORY PROBLEM

How can you learn to do mirror drawing or writing?

NEEDED

small mirror   paper
clay   pencil
book   ruler
watch or clock with second hand   graph paper

TRY THIS

1. Draw a triangle on paper, no larger than the one in Figure 16-5.

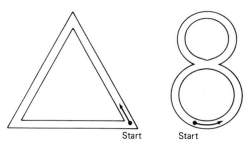

FIGURE 16-5

2. Arrange the paper, a mirror, and a book as in Figure 16-6. Use two pieces of clay to hold up the mirror.

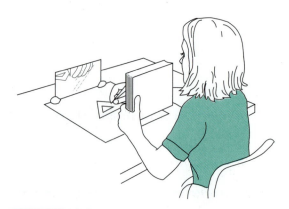

FIGURE 16-6

3. Sit so you must look into the mirror to see the triangle.

4. Place your pencil point on the triangle corner at "start."

5. Observe a watch and notice the time.

6. Draw a line inside and around the whole triangle. Look at the mirror to see what you are doing. Keep the line between the triangle's inside and outside borders. If you go beyond the borders, stop drawing. Start again from the place where you left the border.

7. When you complete the drawing, check the time again. Record in seconds how long it took for this first trial.

DISCOVERY PROBLEMS

measuring **A.** How will practice affect the time needed to draw around the triangle? How much faster will your second trial be? third trial? fourth trial? Make a record like this of what you find out:

Number of Trials	Time to Finish (Seconds)
1	160
2	140
3	100
4	70

communicating **B.** Make a graph of your findings. Notice how to do this on the graph in Figure 16-7. Suppose it took 160 seconds to finish the first trial.

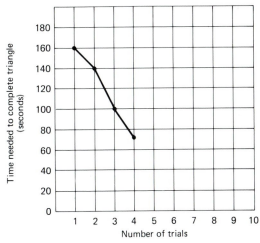

FIGURE 16-7

Put your finger on 1 at the bottom. Follow the line up to and opposite 160. A dot is placed where the two lines cross. Check to see how the other figures are recorded. See how a line has been drawn from one dot to the next. This line is called a *curve*. The graph tells about learning, so the line may be called a *learning curve*.

predicting **C.** Study your own learning curve. How fast do you think you can draw the triangle after six trials? seven trials? eight trials? nine trials? ten trials? Record your findings on your graph and complete your learning curve.

inferring **D.** How does your learning curve compare to those of others? Do some people learn mirror drawing faster than others? If so, how can you describe them?

predicting **E.** Try a mirror drawing of another figure, such as a large 8 (Figure 16-5). What shape will your learning curve be for this figure? Will people who learned fast before learn fast again?

hypothesizing **F.** What other problems about learning mirror drawing can you investigate?

TEACHING COMMENT

PREPARATION AND BACKGROUND

You may have to help some pupils with the line graphs if they lack experience. Also, expect some pupils to have trouble deciding how many seconds it takes to draw completely around each figure.

GENERALIZATION

An earlier learning may interfere with a later learning. Proper practice can improve one's performance.

SAMPLE PERFORMANCE OBJECTIVES

Process: The child can record data accurately on a graph.
Knowledge: The child can predict when an earlier learning is likely to interfere with later learning.

FOR YOUNGER CHILDREN

This investigation is too abstract for young children in its full form. But if the exploratory problem is presented as a hand–eye coordination activity, young pupils will enjoy it.

■ INVESTIGATION: How to Make a Tongue Map

Can you tell by taste if a food is sweet, salty, sour, or bitter? On your tongue, you have tiny taste buds. These allow you to taste differences among foods. Only on some parts of your tongue can you tell certain tastes. Which part do you think lets you sense a salty taste? sweet taste? sour taste? bitter taste?

EXPLORATORY PROBLEM

How can you find out which tongue parts let you tell different tastes?

NEEDED

four cotton swabs
four small jars of liquids (salty, sweet, sour, bitter)

one small paper cup
water
paper and pencil

TRY THIS

1. Pour a tiny bit of salty liquid into a paper cup.

2. Dip a cotton swab into the poured liquid.

3. Spread the salty liquid over your whole tongue. Throw away the swab.

4. Close your mouth and wait about a minute.

5. Try to notice where on your tongue you feel the salty taste.

6. Drink some water before you taste another kind of liquid. Rinse out the paper cup before pouring in another liquid.

DISCOVERY PROBLEMS

inferring   **A.** Study Figure 16-8. Each number shows the main tongue part you may have for a certain taste. On which part do you sense a salty taste? sweet taste? sour taste? bitter taste?

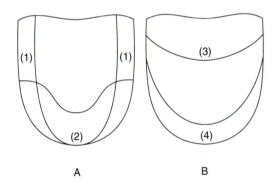

A   B

FIGURE 16-8

observing   **B.** Does pinching your nose make a difference in what you taste?

observing   **C.** Can you tell more than one different taste at one time? If so, which tastes?

inferring   **D.** Get some sweet and sour solid foods and taste them. Where on your tongue do you sense the sweet taste? sour taste? How do your findings compare with those from tasting sweet and salty liquids?

inferring   **E.** How do other people's findings compare to yours? How are they alike? different?

TEACHING COMMENT

PREPARATION AND BACKGROUND

With most people the areas marked (1) on Figure 16-8 are sensitive to sour substances. Sweet substances are usually sensed in area (2), bitter substances in (3), and salty substances in (4). Notice that these areas overlap to some degree. Also, it is common for the areas to vary in many children.

Use four jars of about one-half liter (one pint) capacity to contain the four liquids. Mix into water about one-half of a teaspoon of salt in one jar and one teaspoon of sugar in another. Ordinary white vinegar can be used for the sour substance and plain quinine water for the bitter substance.

GENERALIZATION

Salty, sour, sweet, and bitter tastes are sensed on different and overlapping places on the tongue.

SAMPLE PERFORMANCE OBJECTIVES

Process: The child can test and infer which places on the tongue are sensitive to the four basic tastes.
Knowledge: The child can predict which tongue areas will be sensitive to solid foods that are salty, sweet, sour, and bitter.

FOR YOUNGER CHILDREN

Younger children may need first to learn what the four basic tastes are. They might next taste substances and label them sweet, sour, salty, and bitter. Then, with a little help, most of these children should be able to do the Exploratory Problem and Discovery Problem A.

■ INVESTIGATION: Your Sense of Touch

What can you tell about an object by touch? What are some small objects you might know just by touching them?

EXPLORATORY PROBLEM

What objects can you match just by touch?

NEEDED

cloth blindfold
matched pairs of small objects
partner

open cardboard box (with a
  hand-sized hole cut in each side)

TRY THIS

1. Put a blindfold on your partner. Or, your partner's eyes should be closed. He should not see what you are doing.

2. Put two small, unlike objects inside the box, which should be upside down.

3. Place another small object outside the box. It should match one of the objects inside. Let your blindfolded partner feel it.

4. Next, have your partner feel the objects inside the box. Can he tell which one matches the outside object? (See Figure 16-9.)

FIGURE 16-9

5. Take turns with your partner in playing this game. Use different objects each time. Later use as many objects each time as you can.

DISCOVERY PROBLEMS

observing   **A.** Which objects are hard to tell apart? Which are easy? What makes
inferring   them easy or hard to tell apart?

classifying   **B.** Can you use touch to put objects in order by size? by roughness? Which objects?

experimenting   **C.** Is it easier to tell what an inside object is if you can see the outside objects? How can you find out?

experimenting   **D.** Is it easier to tell what an inside object is with two hands than with one? How can you find out?

TEACHING COMMENT

PREPARATION AND BACKGROUND

Many small objects around the classroom and home may be used in this activity. Among objects easily paired are these: chalk, pencils, leaves, erasers, crayons, nails, coins, washers, rubber bands, cloth of various sizes and textures, paper, foil, and toy figures.

Size, texture, shape, hardness, and, to a minor extent, weight will be the properties used by children to identify objects by touch.

GENERALIZATION

Several properties of an object can be discovered by touch.

SAMPLE PERFORMANCE OBJECTIVES

Process: The child infers the identities of objects and matches them by touch.
Knowledge: The child describes the properties that can be used to identify an object.

FOR OLDER CHILDREN

Try a challenging variation that stresses communication skills. One child holds an object behind him and describes its properties to a partner. The partner touches the several objects inside the box and selects one that matches the description. The described and selected objects are then compared to see if they are identical.

To make the task harder, make the differences among the objects less obvious. Also, put more objects inside the box.

■ INVESTIGATION: The Sensitivity of Your Skin

Suppose you could not tell if something was touching your skin. How might this change your life?

EXPLORATORY PROBLEM

How can you find out how sensitive your skin is to touch?

NEEDED

ruler   paper and pencil
partner   paper clip

TRY THIS

1. Open up and then bend a paper clip into a U shape.
2. Push the two points together so they meet.
3. Touch the points lightly to the palm of your partner's hand. His eyes should be closed.
4. Ask your partner if he feels two points or one.
5. Separate the two points a short distance. Ask again if he feels two points or one (Figure 16-10).
6. Keep repeating this action. Each time, move the two points farther apart until your partner feels two points. Then, measure the distance between the two points with a ruler.
7. Switch with your partner so you can have your skin tested.

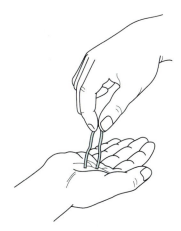

FIGURE 16-10

DISCOVERY PROBLEMS

observing
measuring

A. Where on your skin can you feel the two points soonest? Let your partner measure and make a record such as this one:

communicating

Body Part	**Distance Between the Points**
Finger tip	
Palm of hand	
Back of hand	
Back of neck	
Lips	

inferring
classifying

Look carefully at your completed record. Which seems to be the most sensitive place measured? In what order should the places go if arranged from least to most sensitive?

inferring

B. How does your record compare to those of other people? Are some people more sensitive than others? If so, which people? Are certain places on people's skin more sensitive than others? If so, which places?

TEACHING COMMENT

PREPARATION AND BACKGROUND

Many of our nerve ends are found near the skin surface and are distributed unevenly. Typically, our fingertips are more sensitive to touch than other body parts. This is because a high concentration of nerve endings is located there.

It is important that children who are being tested keep their eyes closed. Otherwise, their perception of touch may be altered by what they see. *Caution:* Supervise closely to ensure that the paper clip points are touched *lightly* to the skin.

GENERALIZATION

Some places on our skin are more sensitive to touch than other places; also, some people are more sensitive to touch than others.

SAMPLE PERFORMANCE OBJECTIVES

Process: The child can measure and compare skin sensitivity at several places on the body.

Knowledge: The child can predict which places on a person's skin are more likely to be sensitive to touch.

FOR YOUNGER CHILDREN

Most primary pupils should be able to do the exploratory section of this investigation and contrast the sensitivity of a fingertip with the palm of the hand.

■ INVESTIGATION: Your Sensitivity to Temperature

Suppose you have two containers of water. One is slightly warmer than another. Could you tell by touch a temperature difference in the water? Does it depend on how much of a difference there is?

EXPLORATORY PROBLEM

How can you find out the smallest temperature difference you can feel?

NEEDED

two cups half-filled with water (one water   paper and pencil
    sample should be warm)   partner
thermometer (one you can get wet)

TRY THIS

1. Dip a finger into each cup. It is probably easy now for you to tell which cup of water is cooler and which is warmer (Figure 16-11).

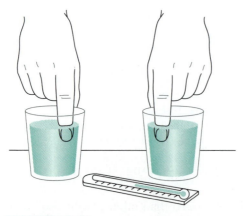

FIGURE 16-11

2. Let your partner pour a little of the cooler water into the warmer water. You can probably still easily feel the temperature difference.

3. Have your partner continue to reduce the temperature between the two cups. He can do this by pouring a little water back and forth between the cups. Keep feeling the water in both cups each time.

4. Stop when you can just barely tell there is a temperature difference. Make sure you are not just imagining this. Close your eyes and let your partner switch around the cups a few times. Tell your partner which cup is cooler or warmer each time. Always keep your eyes closed when the cups are switched.

5. Put the thermometer into each cup for at least half a minute. What is the difference between the two readings?

DISCOVERY PROBLEMS

experimenting   **A.** What is the smallest temperature difference your partner can feel? Get some more warm and cool water and find out.

experimenting   **B.** Are some people more sensitive than others? Are blonds more sensitive than brunettes? Are people with thin fingers more sensitive than those with thicker fingers? Are toes more sensitive than fingers?

hypothesizing   **C.** What questions would you like to investigate?

TEACHING COMMENT

PREPARATION AND BACKGROUND

The beginning temperature difference between the two water samples should be obvious. But it need not be a wide one. If you do not have access to a hot-water tap, warm some water on a hot plate. Or, draw two half-cups of tap water and slip an ice cube into one for several minutes.

Children will need the ability to read thermometers to do this investigation. The average child can detect a temperature difference as little as 1.5°C (3°F). Some pupils will detect an even smaller difference. Eyes are closed for each test.

GENERALIZATION

People differ in their sensitivity to temperature.

SAMPLE PERFORMANCE OBJECTIVES

Process: The child can measure and compare the abilities of different people to detect small differences in water temperature.
Knowledge: The child can state the approximate range of children's differences in detecting water temperature.

□ ACTIVITY: How Can Your Sense of Temperature Be Fooled?

NEEDED

three small bowls of water—one cool, one warm, one hot

TRY THIS

1. Put the three bowls in a row, warm water in the middle.

2. Put your left hand in the cool bowl and right hand in the hot bowl. Leave them there for about a minute.

3. Quickly remove your hands and stick them into the center bowl.
  a. How does the water feel in your left hand? right hand?
  b. Do the sense signals from each hand match? Why or why not?
  c. Suppose you try the experiment again, but switch the end bowls. How might this change what you feel? How *does* it feel?

(*Teaching Comment:* Check the hot water to be sure it is not painful to touch. The cool water may be cooled further with ice cubes for greater contrast. Pupils should realize that our ability to sense temperature is relative. It depends on what we have become used to.)

SECTION 3
Circulatory and Respiratory Systems
[*Background 516*]

■ **INVESTIGATION: People's Pulse Beats**

Your heart pumps blood through long tubes in your body called arteries. Your arteries are very elastic. They stretch, then shrink, slightly each time the heart pumps more blood through them. These tiny movements are called *pulse* beats. You can tell how fast your heart pumps by feeling your pulse beats.

EXPLORATORY PROBLEM

How can you feel and measure how fast your pulse beats?

NEEDED

watch or clock with second hand   paper and pencil

TRY THIS

1. Press on the inside part of your wrist with four fingers. (See Figure 16-12.)

2. Find where you can best feel your pulse.

3. Count how often your pulse beats in one minute while sitting. The number of pulse beats in one minute is your pulse rate.

4. Record your pulse rate on paper.

FIGURE 16-12

DISCOVERY PROBLEMS

experimenting   **A.** How does what you do change your pulse rate? For example, how does standing affect it? lying down? exercise?

experimenting   **B.** How do your pulse rates compare before and after eating?

observing   **C.** Where else on your body can you feel your pulse? Is the pulse rate there the same as at the wrist?

experimenting   **D.** How do the pulse rates of different people compare? For example, how do the pulse rates of boys and girls compare? How do adults and children compare? How do young and old adults compare? Does how tall a person is make a difference in pulse rate? Does how heavy a person is make a difference?

hypothesizing   **E.** What else do you notice about people, or what they do, that might affect pulse rates?

observing   **F.** How do you think the pulse rates of dogs, cats, and other animals compare with those of humans? How can you find out?

TEACHING COMMENT

PREPARATION AND BACKGROUND

The pulse may also be felt quite easily on each side of the throat just under the chin.

The pulse rate usually slows with age and size. Also, boys have slightly slower rates than girls. Seven-year-olds average around 90 beats per minute, which is almost twice the rate for the very aged. Athletic training also reduces the rate because it develops a larger, stronger heart. These factors similarly influence animal pulse rates, particularly size. An elephant, for example, has a very slow pulse rate.

There are several opportunities to make useful graphs in this investigation. For example, how long does it take for the pulse to return to a resting rate after exercise? What is the effect of eating on the rate? Also, watch for chances to control variables and make operational definitions: What is a tall, young, old, heavy, or tired person? If we are testing for age, how can we control height and weight?

GENERALIZATION

One's pulse rate is a measure of how fast the heart beats in one minute. A variety of conditions may affect it.

SAMPLE PERFORMANCE OBJECTIVES

Process: The child can accurately measure his pulse rate.
Knowledge: The child can describe several conditions that influence the pulse rate.

■ INVESTIGATION: The Volume of Air You Breathe

How much air do you breathe in a single breath? How big a container do you think you would need to hold it?

EXPLORATORY PROBLEM

How can you find out how much air you breathe?

NEEDED

large bowl or pail, placed in a sink
1 gallon (or 4 liter) plastic or glass bottle with cap
rubber tube
paper sheet
pencil

masking tape
string
ruler
partner

TRY THIS

1. Stick a strip of tape down the side of the bottle.
2. Mark the strip into 10 equal parts.
3. Partly fill a large bowl or pail with water.
4. Fill the bottle with water and cap it.
5. Put the bottle, upside down, into the bowl.
6. Remove the cap while the bottleneck is underwater.
7. Put one end of the tube into the bottle. (You may have to tip the bottle a little. Have someone hold the bottle so it does not go far over.)
8. Wrap some paper around the other end of the tube (Figure 16-13).

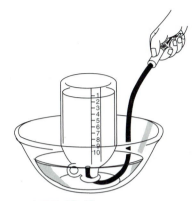

FIGURE 16-13

9. Take a regular breath. Then blow out the air through the tube. Quickly pinch the tube shut when you finish blowing. Observe how much water is forced out of the bottle. This tells you how much air you blow out.

10. Refill the bottle before each time you try a breath test.

DISCOVERY PROBLEMS

measuring **A.** By what tape mark is the water level for a regular breath? Make a record, so you can compare it to other marks.

measuring **B.** How much more air can you hold when you breathe deeply? Take a deep breath. Blow out all the air you can. Compare the new and old marks.

measuring **C.** How much air can other persons blow out in one breath? (Wrap a fresh paper around the tube end each time someone new blows through it.)

communicating **D.** Make a graph of your findings. Use each person's chest size, or height, or weight for one part of your graph. Use their water level mark for the other part, as in Figure 16-14.

predicting **E.** Can you use your graph to predict more findings? For example, will two persons who weigh the same get the same results? Will two people with the same height or chest size get the same results?

hypothesizing **F.** What else do you notice about people that might affect how much air they can hold? For example, do athletes have more lung space communicating than others? But first, what is an "athlete"?

TEACHING COMMENT

PREPARATION AND BACKGROUND

A child can measure chest sizes with string. For good hygiene, a fresh, small slip of paper should be wrapped around the tube end each time it is used.

A typical plastic one-gallon container has curved sides and some space for the bottle neck. Therefore, to divide it accurately into 10 parts requires more

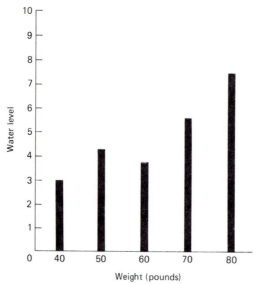

FIGURE 16-14

mathematics than is presently suggested. Interested, able pupils can use a measuring cup to calculate the total number of ounces (or milliliters) in the bottle, and divide by 10. Then they can fill the bottle a tenth at a time to make each mark.

GENERALIZATION

The volume of water displaced by "lung" air is a rough measure of lung capacity. People's lungs vary greatly in air capacity.

SAMPLE PERFORMANCE OBJECTIVES

Process: The child can construct a graph that shows the relationship of weight (or other measurable property) to lung capacity.
Knowledge: The child can explain how the volume of the displaced water is associated with lung capacity.

FOR YOUNGER CHILDREN

Younger pupils will enjoy and profit from making rough comparisons of their lung capacities.

■ INVESTIGATION: How Fast People Breathe

How many breaths do you take each minute? Does everyone breathe equally fast? What conditions may affect how fast people breathe?

EXPLORATORY PROBLEM

How can you find out how many breaths you take each minute?

NEEDED

watch or clock with second hand   pencil and paper

TRY THIS

1. Count one breath each time you breathe *out* while sitting.
2. Observe the time on a clock. Count the number of times you breathe out in one minute (Figure 16-15).

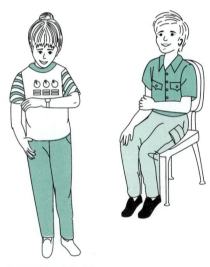

FIGURE 16-15

3. Record the number on a piece of paper.

DISCOVERY PROBLEMS

measuring   **A.** How fast do you breathe after exercise? Bend and touch your toes or do some other easy exercise for one minute. Then count your breaths for one minute.

measuring   **B.** How fast do other people breathe while sitting? Compare people
communicating   who are different in weight, height, and sex. Tell them how to count their breaths. Keep time for one minute. Record each person's name and how fast each breathes.

measuring   **C.** How fast do other people breathe after exercise? Record your findings.

predicting   **D.** Can you predict how fast some people will breathe? Study your records and observe the people. What are the people like who are slow breathers? faster breathers? Perhaps other people who are like them will also be fast or slow. Pick a few people you have not tested before and find out.

hypothesizing **E.** What else about people, or what they do, might affect how fast they breathe?

TEACHING COMMENT

PREPARATION AND BACKGROUND

The main purpose of this investigation is to help children record and think about data. Children will discover a variety of breathing rates, but reasons for these differences will be inconclusive at their level of understanding. You might mention that there is no single proper breathing rate for everyone. What is natural for one person may not be for another.

GENERALIZATION

People have different breathing rates; exercise affects one's breathing rate.

SAMPLE PERFORMANCE OBJECTIVES

Process: The child can compare two sets of breathing data and note likenesses and differences.
Knowledge: The child can predict the approximate average breathing rate of several classmates who are in sitting positions.

SECTION 4
The Digestive System
[*Background 518*]

□ ACTIVITY: How Do You Swallow When Drinking or Eating?

NEEDED

small cup of water

TRY THIS

1. Sip a small amount of water, just enough for about one swallow.
2. Swallow it while standing up. Notice that the water goes *down* your throat and *down* into your stomach.
   a. Do you need gravity to swallow water?
3. Sip about one swallow of water again. Hold it in your mouth.
4. Bend over so your mouth is lower than your stomach. Swallow the water.
   b. What happened? Is gravity really needed, or is it just helpful, when swallowing?

□ ACTIVITY: How Does Changing a Starch into a Sugar Help the Body Use Food?

NEEDED

two small jars or glasses
starch
sugar

teaspoon
sugarless soda cracker
water

TRY THIS

1. Bite off a piece of sugarless cracker and chew it for at least one minute.
    a. How does the taste of the cracker change as you chew it? A soda cracker is made up mostly of starch. The saliva in your mouth starts changing the starch into a sugar. It is changed the rest of the way in your small intestine. Before food can be used by your body cells, it must be in a *dissolved* form. Does changing a starch into a sugar help it to dissolve? Find out for yourself.

2. Half-fill two small jars with water.

3. Put a teaspoon of sugar in one jar and one of starch in the other. Mix each for a minute.
    b. Which food dissolves? Will more stirring make the undissolved food dissolve?

    (*Teaching Comment:* Pupils will need to know that when a material dissolves it is no longer visible. The solution looks clear.)

□ ACTIVITY: What Do Human Cells Look Like Under a Microscope?

NEEDED

microscope or microprojector
glass microscope slide and cover slip
medicine dropper

flat toothpick
iodine
tweezers

TRY THIS

1. Put a small drop of water on a microscope slide.

2. Get a flat toothpick. Using the blunt end, gently scrape some skin cells from inside your cheek. Spread out the whitish, scraped material in the water drop.

3. Dip a toothpick end in iodine. Touch it to the water drop. This will stain the cells so you can see them better. Use tweezers to cover the drop with a cover slip.
    a. What do you think these cheek cells will look like? Draw what you think and then observe the cells by focusing the microscope.

4. Measure the size of the cells. Take a hair from your head. Carefully, lift up one end of the cover slip. Lay the hair across the stained cells. Replace the slip.
    b. How large are the cells compared to the hair?

(*Teaching Comment:* It is instructive to contrast skin cells with plant cells. To do so, slice an onion ring and peel off a bit of thin skin from one of the inside layers. Lay it in a water drop on a slide and stain it with iodine. Cover with a cover slip. Leaves of elodea, a common aquarium plant, are also thin enough for cell study. No stain is needed. See Figure 16-16.)

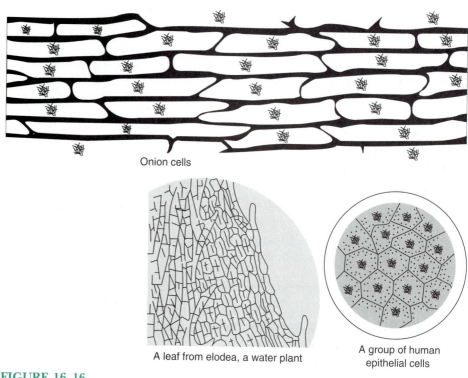

Onion cells

A leaf from elodea, a water plant

A group of human epithelial cells

FIGURE 16-16

SECTION 5
Food and Nutrition
[*Background 519*]

☐ ACTIVITY: Which Foods Have Starch?

NEEDED

iodine

medicine dropper

tiny pieces of foods, such as white bread, rice, macaroni, cheese, potato, cereals, etc.

piece of white chalk

cornstarch

teaspoon

waxed paper

TRY THIS

1. Place a bit of cornstarch on waxed paper. Crush a small piece of white chalk next to it with a spoon.
2. Put one drop of iodine on each. Notice how the cornstarch turns purple-black. The chalk should look red-brown. When a food turns purple-black, it has starch.
3. Test your food samples with the iodine. Crush each sample first with the spoon. Wash it off each time.
   a. Which samples seem to have starch? Which do not?
4. Try the starch test on part of an unripe banana. Then test part of a very ripe banana. Taste a little of each.
   b. What difference do you notice? When does a banana seem to have more starch? When does it seem to have more sugar?

□ ACTIVITY: Which Foods Have Fats?

NEEDED

brown paper bag
small pieces of different foods, such as bacon, olive,
   margarine, bread, apple, cheese, etc.

drop of oil
drop of water

TRY THIS

1. Spread a drop of oil on the brown paper. Fat is mostly oil.
2. Spread a drop of water alongside it. Allow it to dry.
3. Hold up the paper to the light. Notice the difference in the two spots. Fat shows as a shiny, oily spot.
   a. Which foods do you think have fat?
4. Make a list and then test the foods you can. Rub hard each small piece into the brown paper.
   b. Which made an oily stain? How do your findings compare with what you thought?

■ INVESTIGATION: Juices and Vitamin C

Do you drink orange juice? Orange juice contains a nutrient called vitamin C. It can help to keep you healthy. However, not all orange juice contains the same amount of vitamin C. And other juices may contain vitamin C, also.

EXPLORATORY PROBLEM

How can you find out how much vitamin C juices have?

NEEDED

vitamin C indicator liquid
medicine dropper
clean baby food jar
small samples of juices (fresh orange, frozen orange,
  lemon, apple, etc.)

crayon
ruler
white unlined paper
spoon

TRY THIS

1. Mark a small jar about 1 centimeter (½ inch) from the bottom.
2. Pour indicator liquid into the jar to the mark. Put the jar on white paper.
3. Now, test some fresh orange juice or other juice. Add juice to the blue liquid one drop at a time. Use a medicine dropper (Figure 16-17).

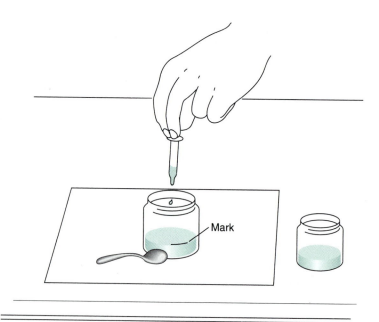

Mark

FIGURE 16-17

4. Count the number of drops you put in. Stir the blue liquid with a spoon, as you add drops.
5. Watch for the blue color of the indicator liquid to disappear. When it is no longer blue, the test is over. Record the number of drops you put in.
6. Rinse clean the indicator jar, spoon, and dropper before each new test.

DISCOVERY PROBLEMS

inferring   **A.** Does orange juice made from frozen concentrate have as much vitamin C as fresh juice? Compare the drops needed for the indicator liquid to lose its blue color. The *fewer* the drops, the more vitamin C is present.

hypothesizing
communicating

B. What are some other juices that may have vitamin C? What fruit or vegetable juices can you test? Keep a record.

experimenting

C. What are some conditions that may make vitamin C disappear? For example, does light destroy vitamin C? Does heat affect vitamin C? Does keeping the juice in an open or closed container make a difference? Does how old the juice is make a difference? How can you find out?

hypothesizing

D. What other conditions might affect the vitamin C of juices?

TEACHING COMMENT

PREPARATION AND BACKGROUND

You can prepare a gallon (or 4-liter) container of vitamin C indicator liquid as follows. Mix a heaping teaspoonful of cornstarch in a cup of cold water. Boil this mixture in a pan for about two minutes. Suck up the mixture in a medicine dropper and squirt it into a gallon container of water. Ten droppers full will be all you'll need. Clean the dropper. Then squirt one dropper full of iodine into the container and cap it. Shake the container a few times until the mixture looks uniformly blue.

The indicator liquid will keep several days. After that, it may lighten in color and become useless. The best color seems to be royal blue—between light and dark blue.

GENERALIZATION

Fruit and vegetable juices may contain different quantities of vitamin C.

SAMPLE PERFORMANCE OBJECTIVES

Process: The child can demonstrate a comparative test of two juices for vitamin C content.
Knowledge: After conducting tests of common juices, the child can predict which untested juices are likely to be high in vitamin C.

■ INVESTIGATION: The Liquid Content of Foods

You get liquids into your body in two main ways. One way, of course, is by drinking water and other liquids. The other way is by eating solid foods that contain liquids. Some solid foods are mostly liquid, although they may not seem so. Even some dry-looking foods may contain liquids.

EXPLORATORY PROBLEM

How can you find out how much of a solid food is liquid?

NEEDED

balance
10 paper clips
small food samples (such as apple, bread, orange,
    potato)

waxed paper
knife

TRY THIS

1. Put a small, identical piece of waxed paper into each cup of a balance (Figure
   16-18).

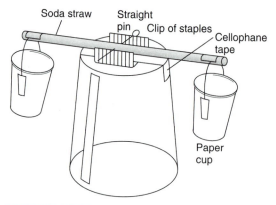

FIGURE 16-18

2. Cut a slice from some food sample. Put it into one of the balance cups.
3. Put 10 paper clips into the other balance cup.
4. Take away some food until the balance is level. Now the food weighs the same
   as the 10 paper clips.
5. Remove the food and waxed paper. Let the food dry for at least five days in
   some sunny place.
6. Put the dried food and same waxed paper into the balance cup. The other cup
   should still contain 10 paper clips and waxed paper.
7. How much liquid has the food lost? To find out, remove some paper clips until
   the balance is level. Did you remove three clips? Then three-tenths of the food
   was liquid. Did you remove five clips? Then five-tenths was liquid, and so on.

DISCOVERY PROBLEMS

inferring
classifying

A. How much liquid do different foods contain? Keep a record.
Arrange your findings in order—foods with least to most liquid.

experimenting

B. How much liquid in a food dries in *one day?* Write what you think
may be so for each different food. How can you find out? How might
the weather affect drying time?

experimenting

C. Where can you put foods so they will dry fastest? Have a food drying
race with some friends.

TEACHING COMMENT

PREPARATION AND BACKGROUND

A sensitive balance is needed for this investigation. If you do not have one, it may be easily made. Get a straw, straight pin, cellophane tape, string, two paper cups, and a drinking glass. You will also need a small clip of stuck-together staples or part of a small card folded into a U shape. The sketch shows how these materials may be assembled. (See Figure 16-18.) To correct any slight imbalance, place a bit of clay on the straw somewhere near the pin.

Some foods contain a surprisingly high percentage of liquid. For example, celery is about 95 percent water. Fresh bread is about 35 percent water. If your pupils have studied percentages, you might use 100 small units, such as pins, rather than 10 paper clip units to calculate liquid loss.

If the weather is rainy, food samples may be oven dried. You can also put the samples on kitchen foil and position a lighted gooseneck lamp about 30 centimeters (1 foot) away. Leave the lamp on during the whole school day. Two or three days may be required for drying, depending on humidity conditions, lamp intensity, and food samples.

GENERALIZATION

Most solid foods contain some liquid; the amount varies greatly among foods.

SAMPLE PERFORMANCE OBJECTIVES

Process: The child can measure the fraction of liquid in a food by drying it and using a balance.
Knowledge: The child can predict approximate percentages of liquids in common foods.

■ INVESTIGATION: Some Properties of Powdered Foods

You eat many different white powders. Cake is made with baking powder. White bread is made with white flour. Cornstarch helps to make gravy. You can even make milk by mixing powdered milk with water.

If you take a quick look at most white powders, they seem alike. But each is really different in several ways.

EXPLORATORY PROBLEM

How can you tell one white powder from another? (*Do not* use taste for this investigation.)

NEEDED

white powders (such as baking powder,
   baking soda, white flour, powdered
   sugar, cornstarch, powdered milk)
small jar of iodine solution
small jar of white vinegar

small jar of water
three medicine droppers
teaspoon
paper towel
magnifier

TRY THIS

1. Put less than a quarter-teaspoon of one powder on a paper towel. Only a little is needed (Figure 16-19).

FIGURE 16-19

2. Observe it carefully through a magnifier. How does it look?
3. Feel the powder with your fingers. How does it feel?
4. Put a drop of water on the powder. What happens?
5. Put a drop of iodine solution on the powder. What happens?
6. Put a drop of vinegar on the powder. What happens?

DISCOVERY PROBLEMS

observing
communicating

A. How does this powder compare to other powders? Test a few more powders. Record what you observe on a chart such as this:

Powder Tested	How It Looks Magnified	How It Feels	Reaction to Water	Reaction to Iodine	Reaction to Vinegar
Cornstarch					
Flour					
Baking soda					

inferring

B. Which test or tests seem most useful to tell apart the powders? least useful?

inferring   **C.** Can you identify an unknown powder? Ask someone to put a quarter-teaspoon of powder on a fresh paper towel. You should not know what powder it is, but it should be one recorded on your chart. Make some tests and use your chart to identify it.

inferring   **D.** Can you identify two unknown powders mixed together? Have someone choose two chart powders and mix them. Do the rest as in Problem C.

hypothesizing   **E.** What other ways can you test white powders? What other powders can you test?

TEACHING COMMENT

PREPARATION AND BACKGROUND

Any material has certain physical properties that may be used to identify it. By performing certain tests, children may learn some of the different properties of similar-looking powdered foods as well as other powders.

Small baby food jars make excellent containers for the powders and test liquids. For the iodine solution, mix two medicine droppersful of iodine in a half-full baby food jar of water.

Children may try additional tests such as heating the powders and mixing them with water. A small cup can be formed from kitchen foil and held over a candle flame with a spring clothespin holder. (Supervise closely for safety.) Only a tiny amount of powder need be heated. A powder may also be mixed in water in a clear glass jar and then compared with other water-powder mixtures.

Caution pupils not to taste powders. Explain that some powders they should not eat may get mixed with some powdered foods in this investigation. For example, some nonfoods they may want to test are powdered detergent, white tempera paint powder, crushed white chalk, talcum powder, alum, scouring powder, tooth powder, and plaster of paris.

GENERALIZATION

A material may be identified by tests to reveal its physical properties.

SAMPLE PERFORMANCE OBJECTIVES

Process: The child can infer the identity of several powders by interpreting recorded data.
Knowledge: The child can describe several different physical properties of at least two common powdered foods.

FOR YOUNGER CHILDREN

Younger pupils can do this activity well with fewer tests and powders. For example, have them observe two powders and make perhaps two tests—how they look magnified and feel. They can then receive an "unknown" powder and try to match it with one of the two powders tested.

SELECTED TRADE BOOKS: HUMAN BODY AND NUTRITION

FOR YOUNGER CHILDREN

Adler, David A. *You Breathe in, You Breathe out.* Watts, 1991.

Berger, Melvin. *Why I Cough, Sneeze, Shiver, Hiccup, and Yawn.* Harper & Row, 1983.

Bishop, Pamela R. *Exploring Your Skeleton.* Watts, 1991.

Hoover, Rosalie, and Barbara Murphy. *Learning About Our Five Senses.* Good Apple, 1981.

Hvass, Ulrik. *How My Body Moves.* Viking, 1986.

Kindersley, Dorling. *What's Inside My Body?* Peter Lang, 1991.

Parker, Steve. *Eating a Meal: How You Eat, Drink and Digest.* Watts, 1991.

Penn, Linda. *The Human Body.* Good Apple, 1986.

Sattler, Helen R. *Noses Are Special.* Abingdon, 1982.

Showers, Paul. *You Can't Make a Move Without Your Muscles.* Crowell, 1982.

Sproule, Anna. *Body Watch: Know Your Insides.* Facts on File, 1987.

FOR OLDER CHILDREN

Allison, Linda. *Blood and Guts: A Working Guide to Your Own Little Insides.* Little, Brown, 1976.

Behm, Barbara. *Ask About My Body.* Raintree, 1987.

De Bruin, Jerry. *Young Scientists Explore the Five Senses.* Good Apple, 1983.

Gabb, Michael. *The Human Body.* Watts, 1991.

Galperin, Anne. *Nutrition.* Chelsea House, 1991.

Harlow, Rosie and Gareth Morgan. *Energy and Growth.* Watts, 1991.

Klein, Aaron E. *You and Your Body.* Doubleday, 1977.

Parker, Steve. *Nerves to Senses: Projects with Biology.* Watts, 1991.

Rayner, Claire. *The Body Book.* Barron, 1980.

Rutland, Jonathan. *Human Body.* Watts, 1977.

Simon, Seymour. *About the Foods You Eat.* McGraw-Hill, 1979.

Taylor, Ron. *How the Body Works.* EMC Publications, 1982.

Walpole, Brenda. *The Human Body.* Messner, 1987.

Ward, Brian R. *Diet and Health.* Watts, 1991.

Wilson, Ron. *How the Body Works.* Larousse, 1979.

Wolf, Donald, and Margot L. Wolf, eds. *The Human Body.* Putnam, 1982.

Wong, Ovid. *Your Body and How it Works.* Children's Press, 1986.

Zim, Herbert S. *Your Skin.* Morrow, 1979.

17

The Earth's Changing Surface

Shifting sand dunes, eroding hillsides, weeds growing on an asphalt playground, muddy water running in gutters—there is evidence all around us that the earth's surface is changing.

This chapter examines some of the forces that wear down and build up the earth and their products—rocks and soil. Four sections take up (1) weathering and erosion, (2) soil and its makeup, (3) the building up of the land, and (4) how rocks are formed.

[1] WEATHERING AND EROSION *Experiences 569*

Perhaps the only permanent feature about the earth's surface is the continuous process of change it reveals. The forces that weather and erode the land are powerful and ceaseless.

Strictly speaking, *weathering* refers to the breaking down of rocks into smaller parts through the action of agents such as plants, chemicals, frost, and changes of temperature. *Erosion* includes weathering plus the process of transporting weathered material from one location to another, as in the action of running water, wind, and glaciers.

Plant Actions

It is hard for some children to realize at first that plants break down rocks. After all, rocks are "hard" and plants are "soft," they reason. But plants weather rocks in several ways.

Growing roots may wedge deeply into a cracked rock and force it apart. As dry plant seeds absorb water, they swell with surprising force and may perform a similar wedging function. Tiny flat plants called *lichens* grow on bare rock (Figure 17-1). Acids released by these plants decompose and soften the rock. Larger plants may then follow in a long succession, each contributing to the rock's destruction.

FIGURE 17-1
Lichens play a part in weathering rock.

Chemical Weathering

Oxygen and water in the air combine with rock surfaces to produce "rust." Reddish soils, for example, usually contain oxidized iron compounds.

Falling rain picks up a small amount of carbon dioxide in the air and forms carbonic acid. Although it is well diluted, this substance slowly wears down limestone. Older limestone buildings and statuary have a soft, worn look from the dissolving effect of acidic rainwater. This is especially noticeable in England and in several areas in the northeastern United States, where coal burning has been prevalent. Abnormal quantities of sulfur dioxide released into the air increase the acidic content of rain and hasten weathering. (We will consider acid rain again in the next chapter.)

Rainwater that percolates into the ground may encounter a limestone formation and dissolve some of it, so forming a cave. This is how the Carlsbad Caverns of New Mexico, Luray Caverns of Virginia, and Mammoth Caves of Kentucky were formed. Because the surface appearance of a rock is somewhat altered by chemical weathering, we must often chip or break it to note its natural color.

Expansion–Contraction

Frozen water also contributes to weathering. Many rocks are relatively porous. Water, you may remember, is one of the few substances that expands in freezing. As absorbed water expands, bits of rock are broken off. In addition, ice may wedge apart cracked rocks.

Stones placed around campfires are sometimes cracked because rocks conduct heat poorly. The difference between a hot surface and cooler interior may produce strains that cause parts to flake off. But some of this *exfoliation,* as it is called, may be from expansion owing to release of pressure. Rocks formed underground are subjected to great pressures. When they finally appear on the surface, because of erosion or other means, there may be a tendency for these rocks to "unsqueeze" slightly, thus starting some cracks.

Running Water

Moving water is no doubt the most erosive force on earth. Abrasive, waterborne rocks and particles have gradually formed the Grand Canyon over millions of years. Millions of tons of soil daily wash from banks and hills over the world into streams and are eventually carried into the ocean. Ocean waves ceaselessly pound huge cliffs and boulders into sand.

Water running down hills usually forms gullies. As the slope angle increases, water moves more swiftly, so hastening erosion. Rain splashing on near-level fields has a different erosive effect. Broad sheets of soil wash off into lower places without obvious gullying.

The force of gravity is a powerful eroder even without water. Landslides and rocks that break off and tumble from cliffs are common examples of its force at work. Gravity may also cause land on slopes to gradually but continually creep downward.

Wind Erosion

The effect of wind erosion became dramatically apparent to millions of Americans in the Dust Bowl years of 1934–35. Prairie lands originally covered by a grassy sod had been broken up for agriculture. A combination of dry weather and marginal farming practices resulted in the most destructive dust storms ever seen in the United States.

Glacial Erosion

Glaciers also contribute to land erosion. Huge snow deposits build up when snowfall exceeds the melting rate. Gradually, some of the underlying snow compacts into ice and the glacier flows slowly downhill, as in the case of mountain valley glaciers.

Continental glaciers are much larger, ranging to thousands of square miles in size. At one time, a large part of North America was buried under snow and ice. Today, much of Greenland and Antarctica are covered by such glaciers. Gravity forces these glaciers to spread out as more and more snow piles on top.

When glaciers move, they scour the land under their tremendous weight, scooping out basins and leveling hills. As they melt, huge deposits of soil and rocks are left at the sides and leading edge. Effects of glaciation may be seen in many parts of our country, particularly in New England and the north central states (Figure 17-2).

Although some activities on weathering and erosion can be conducted in the classroom, it is better to use local resources outdoors. Signs of weathering and erosion are

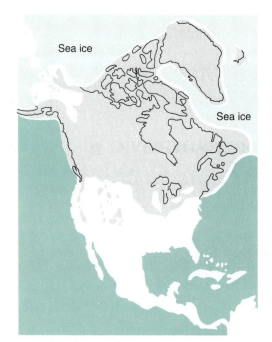

FIGURE 17-2
About 11,000 years ago, glaciers advanced deeply into what is now the northern United States.

everywhere. Pupils are usually delighted to help look for them.

[2] SOIL AND ITS MAKEUP
Experiences 579

Many children understand that weathering and erosion can wear underlying rock into small particles. But they often do not realize that there is more to productive soil than just rock particles. It is not until decomposed plant and animal matter is added (or manufactured chemicals applied) that the soil becomes productive enough to support agriculture (Figure 17-3).

Humus, as this organic matter is called, supplies plants with nitrogen, phosphorus, potassium, and other essential elements. The

FIGURE 17-3
A soil profile, or cross section, 3 feet (0.9 meters) deep. Subsoil becomes coarser and contains less humus with depth.

decomposition of organic material is done by soil bacteria. Acids released in decomposition also dissolve other minerals in the soil particles. Humus retains water well and so keeps soil from drying out rapidly. The darkish color of humus-laden soil absorbs sunlight efficiently, and so it is warmer than light-colored soil. This speeds up plant growth and reduces seed failure.

Earthworms, you may recall, are important to soil for several reasons. They help break up the soil, which permits air, as well as water, to reach the plant roots. Root cells die unless they absorb sufficient oxygen. And, as earthworms eat through soil, they mix it and leave castings that contain rich fertilizing ingredients.

Soil Makeup

The composition of soil is easily studied if you mix some earth in a water-filled jar and allow the jar to stand several hours. Gravity causes the several materials to settle in order. Heavier, coarser particles like pebbles settle first, followed by sand, silt, and clay. Any humus present floats on the water surface.

The best soil for most plants is *loam*, composed of sand (30 to 50 percent), silt (30 to 50 percent), clay (up to 20 percent), and abundant humus. Silt and clay have small particles that retain water well. Having been eroded from rocks rich in certain minerals, they contain elements plants need for healthy growth. Coarser sand particles make soil porous, so enabling air and water to reach plant roots. A soil composed of sand or clay alone lacks the moderate degree of porosity that seems best for watering plant roots.

Soils differ greatly in their degree of acidity and alkalinity. Strawberry plants thrive in acidic soil. Many grasses grow well in alkaline or basic soils. Clover does best in soil that is neither basic nor acidic, but neutral. To conserve soil minerals and fit proper crops to the soil, farmers may conduct tests to find the soil's chemical content. An upcoming activity will show pupils how chemically prepared *litmus paper* may be used to find whether a soil is basic, acidic, or neutral.

Soil Conservation

One of the reasons erosion is a fearsome enemy of the farmer is the time required for good soil to form. It may take up to 500 years for a single inch of good topsoil to be produced by natural means. With a rapidly multiplying world population, topsoil conservation is a serious concern.

Some of the things farmers do to preserve topsoil are shown in Figure 17-4. Each is directed toward a specific problem. *Contour plowing*, for example, is used when plowing hilly land. Plowing straight up or down a hill will cause gullies to form during rain or irrigation. Plowing around the hill reduces gully erosion. *Strip cropping* alternates a row crop that has much bare soil exposed, such as corn, with a ground cover crop, such as clover. This reduces wind erosion. A *tree windbreak* will also help if the field is located where a strong wind usually blows from one direction. *Terracing* may be used to prepare relatively flat areas for growing crops on steep slopes. *Check dams* of stones or logs may be used to slow down water in a stream or prevent a gully from widening.

Perhaps the greatest advance of this century in conserving farm topsoil is a recently adopted practice called *residue management*, which does away with the plow. Even the best plowing practices bare soil to water and wind erosion. Now, many farmers leave the residue or stubble from harvested crops in place to hold soil and moisture. Tractor-pulled machines gouge places for seeds, which then sprout and grow through the decomposing residue. Besides minimizing erosion, the method actually rebuilds the precious topsoil.

[3] BUILDING UP OF THE LAND   *Experiences 585*

Careful geological studies show that the powerful forces of weathering and erosion should have long ago worn down the earth's surface to a low-lying plain. Then why are there mountains? Part of the answer is seen in volcanic activity.

Magma

Fiery molten rock from deep underground, called *magma*, thrusts up through weak spots and cracks in the earth's crust. When this material reaches the surface, it is called *lava*.

Sometimes the accumulation of magma and high-pressure gases is so great that the molten rock shoots up to the surface in a spectacular eruption. This can happen under the ocean, as well as on land. The Hawaiian Islands are the eroded tops of volcanoes, as are the Azores in the Atlantic Ocean.

Sometimes magma may quietly ooze up through great cracks in the crust and spread out over the ground. Large parts of the Pacific Northwest are covered with hardened lava beds to depths of thousands of feet. Similar lava flows have occurred in Iceland.

Several types of magmatic activity are not directly visible until erosion has worn away parts of the crust. Magma may stop flowing and cool before it reaches the surface. Or, it may push up part of the crust, thus forming a dome, or *laccolith.* Erosion of the surrounding crust makes the dome more prominent (Figure 17-5).

Where does heat energy for volcanoes originate? There are several theories, one of which we will look at now. Some scientists think that radioactive rocks are responsible in some places. One radioactive element is uranium, which continually shoots off helium atoms and changes to lead. In the process, a tiny amount of heat energy is generated. If many rocks of this type become concen-

FIGURE 17-4
Some ways of preventing erosion: (*a*) contour plowing, (*b*) strip crops, (*c*) terraces, (*d*) check dam, (*e*) tree windbreak.

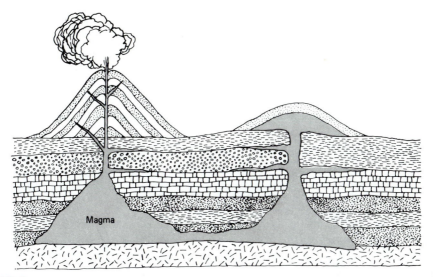

FIGURE 17-5
A volcano and a laccolith.

trated, it is conceivable that they could bring about enough heat energy to melt rocks.

(The known rate of decay of uranium into lead is useful in finding the age of rocks. Since the rate apparently never changes, scientists can figure age by noting the ratio of remaining uranium to lead.)

Earthquakes and Faults

Earthquakes happen when the crust breaks under the strain of its deforming forces. Parts of the crust may move horizontally, diagonally, or vertically along a huge crack, or *fault*. Over a long time, *block mountains* may develop through tilted or vertical movements along a fault line. This seems to be how the Sierra Nevada range was formed.

Other mountains seem to be made through *folding*. Immense forces push parts of the crust into giant wrinkles. The Appalachians are an example.

Plate Theory

How does modern science explain such major changes in the earth's crust? When we look at a world map, certain land masses of the earth, while far apart, seem to fit together like pieces of a jigsaw puzzle. The east coast of South America and the west coast of Africa are examples. Could it be that these and other continents were once joined?

Many modern earth scientists infer this. They think that the earth's thin crust was once solid, but now is fragmented into six to eight immense "plates" and several smaller ones that fit in between. The plates drift on the earth's fiery mantle of molten rock some 100 kilometers (60 miles) or so below. The continents float on the plates like passengers on rafts. Plate edges do not necessarily coincide with the edges of continents. According to *plate tectonics theory*, the plates continually pull apart, collide, grind edges, or partially slide under each other.

Ocean floors, for example, form when two plates drift apart. Magma pushes up from the mantle and fills the ever-widening gap between the plates. When one plate pushes into or under another, folded mountains and block mountains may be formed. A plate edge that thrusts downward under another melts into the fiery mantle below. Some of the magma that results thrusts up through weak spots in the solid crust to form volcanoes. Earthquakes may happen as plates slide past each other in opposite directions. The great friction between the two massive plates may cause the movements to temporarily stop. However, stresses build up until the crust suddenly fractures and the plates grind onward.

Plate movements are surprisingly fast—up to 20 centimeters (8 inches) a year in some locations—given the approximate 5-billion-year age of the earth. Apparently the force needed to move the rigid plates comes from convection currents in the molten mantle below.

Note the correlation between regions of earthquake and volcanic activity in Figure 17-6. Many scientists infer that these active regions reveal some boundaries of the huge, drifting plates.

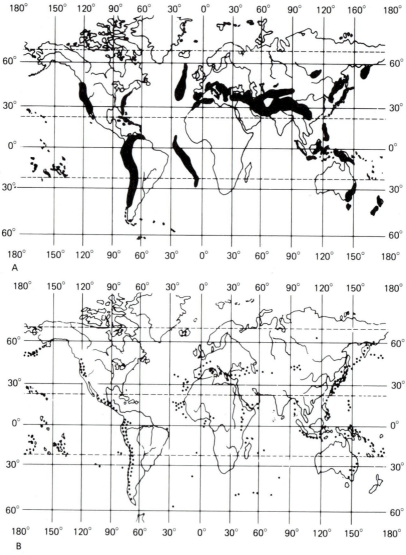

FIGURE 17-6

Earthquake (A) and volcano (B) regions of the world.

[4] HOW ROCKS ARE FORMED   *Experiences 587*

"What are rocks made of?" children often ask. Rocks are made up of *minerals*—natural inorganic materials that make up most of the earth's crust. Some minerals are composed of a single element, such as copper or carbon. A beautiful diamond is an example of almost pure carbon formed under enormous pressure underground. Other minerals are compounds of two or more minerals, such as mica or quartz. The chemical makeup of a mineral is the same anywhere it is found on earth. A pure copper or quartz sample is as recognizable in Asia as in North America.

Geologists have developed many ways of identifying minerals. These may include observing its color, hardness, luster, how it splits along a plane, how it breaks, its density, its crystal structure, and how it reacts to chemicals. Children can observe some of these things, too, as you will see in a later investigation.

Just as a word may be made up of one or more letters of the alphabet, rocks may be composed of one or more minerals. But there are far more known minerals—about 2,000—than letters of the alphabet. Most are seldom seen. Fewer than 100 minerals make up the bulk of the earth's crust.

Usually, rocks are given the same name—granite, for example—when they contain essentially the same minerals. Some samples, though, may contain a greater proportion of one or more of the minerals than other samples. So not all granite samples look alike, nor do many other rock samples given a certain name.

Although there are many minerals, rocks are formed in just three ways. Knowing how they are formed and being aware of several common examples in each case can simplify rock study and make it more meaningful to children.

Sedimentary Rocks

Sediments from eroded rocks are the raw materials for new sedimentary rocks. The sediments are usually moved and deposited by rivers into coastal trenches and basins. Some rivers deposit sediments into large lakes. Sand, clay, silt, pebbles, and stones are common sedimentary materials. Sediments gradually collect layer upon layer where they are deposited, which makes the layers press harder and harder on the lower sediments. The enormous pressure, plus chemicals dissolved in the water, cement the sediments together. Sand particles become sandstone, mud or clay becomes shale, and pebbles and rocks and sand combine to form conglomerate.

Not all sediments come from eroded materials. Limestone and chalk are examples of rock formed on the ocean floor from the compressed skeletons and shells of billions of ocean animals, including clams, mussels, and corals. Some sedimentary rock may also form from previously dissolved chemicals that deposit out of solution when the water can no longer hold them.

Igneous Rocks

A second way rocks are formed is through the cooling of magma or lava. These are igneous rocks (the word *igneous* means "formed from fire"). A common example of igneous formation happens in domes, or laccoliths. Magma squeezes under a surface rock layer, slowly cools, and becomes solid. When the surface rocks erode away, the underlying rock is exposed. Granite is the most frequently found rock of this kind. Its large crystals reveal that it cooled slowly.

Lava that is blown from a volcano or that flows out of cracks in the crust cools quickly. So it has small crystals or no visible crystals. The light, spongy rock called pumice and the black, glassy rock called obsidian are examples.

Metamorphic Rock

Sedimentary and igneous rocks may undergo severe pressure and heat as parts of the crust move, fold, thrust deeper under the ground, or are buried under lava flows. This may cause physical and chemical changes in the rocks, making them metamorphic rocks (the word *metamorphic* means "changed in form"). Sedimentary rocks such as limestone become marble, sandstone may become quartzite, and shale becomes slate. Igneous rock such as granite changes to gniess (pronounced "nice"), soft coal changes to hard coal, and so on.

Metamorphic rocks are harder than the original rock material. They often have compression bands of different colors. Usually, crystals are small. Still, it is easy to confuse metamorphic rocks with igneous rocks.

Table 17-1 shows 12 kinds of rocks children can use to become acquainted with the three basic types. They are fairly distinctive and easy to obtain. Some, and perhaps all, of these rocks may be included in specimens pupils bring to school. If not, they may be gotten from local rock collectors, museums, and science supply companies.

Fossils

The remains, or signs, of animals or plants in rock are called fossils. The most likely rocks in which fossils are found are sedimentary. Occasionally, fossils are found in partly metamorphosed sedimentary rocks, but pressure and heat usually destroy fossils.

Fossils are formed in different ways. When some animals died, they were covered by sediments. The soft body parts decomposed,

TABLE 17-1
Igneous, sedimentary, and metamorphic rocks.

Igneous Rocks	Description	How Formed
Pumice	Grayish, fine pores, glassy, frothy, light, floats on water.	From rapid cooling of frothy, surface lava containing gases.
Volcanic Breccia	Consolidated fragments of volcanic ash, such as glass, pumice, quartz.	From being exploded high into the air from a volcano and settling.

TABLE 17-1
continued

Igneous Rocks	Description	How Formed
Obsidian	Black, glassy, no crystals.	From very rapid surface cooling of lava.
Basalt	Dark, greenish-gray, very small crystals, may have some holes.	From rapid cooling of lava close to the surface. Escaping gases form holes.
Granite	Coarse crystals, white to gray, sometimes pinkish.	From slow, below-surface cooling of molten rock (magma), as when domes are formed.

TABLE 17-1
continued

Sedimentary Rocks	Description	How Formed
Conglomerate	Rounded pebbles, stones, and sand cemented together.	From loose materials compacted by pressure of overlying sediments and bound by natural cement.
Sandstone	Sand grains clearly visible, gray, yellow, red.	From sand compacted by pressure of sediment, bound by natural cement.
Shale	Soft, smells like clay, fine particles, green, black, yellow, red, gray.	From compacted mud bound by natural cement.
Limestone	Fairly soft, white, gray, red, forms carbon dioxide gas bubbles when touched with acids.	From dead organisms that used calcium carbonate in sea water in making body parts; from evaporation of sea water containing calcium carbonate.

TABLE 17-1
continued

Metamorphic Rocks	Description	How Formed
Marble	Different, mixed colors, may have colored bands, medium to coarse crystals, fizzes if touched with acids.	Formed when pure limestone is subjected to intense heat and pressure.
Slate	Greenish-gray, black, red, splits in thin layers, harder than shale.	Formed when shale is subjected to intense heat and pressure.
Quartzite	Very hard, white, gray, pink, indistinct grains, somewhat glassy.	Formed when sandstone is subjected to intense heat and pressure.

but teeth and skeletons remained, preserved by hardened layers of sediment. In other cases, even the skeletons disintegrated, but before they did, mineral-laden water infiltrated into the bones and replaced bone with minerals. This left a perfect cast replica of the skeleton in many cases. Some trees have left casts in a similar way. This is how specimens of the Petrified Forest in Arizona were formed. Additional fossils have been discovered frozen in ice, found in tar pits, and other places.

The so-called *fossil fuels*—coal, oil, and natural gas—were formed from the remains of plants and animals millions of years ago. Huge masses of organic matter in swampy forests were covered by mud, silt, and other sediments. Gradually, the sediments formed into stony layers. Pressure and heat from immense crustal movements caused physical and chemical changes in the buried organic matter. Some formed into seams of coal trapped between shale and slate. Some deposits changed into thick, black oil and natural gas, often trapped between layers of folded rock.

Rock Cycle

The same processes that formed rocks in the past continue today. Over many thousands of years, rocks change their forms. Even so, there is much evidence that the same mineral materials are used over and over in a kind of rock cycle. Figure 17-7 shows what seems to happen.

All three kinds of rocks erode when exposed on the earth's surface. The resulting sediments, under pressure, form into rock cemented with water-borne chemicals. When these rocks undergo further pressure, torsion, and heat, they metamorphose. The metamorphic rocks turn into magma when heated further. When the magma cools and hardens, it becomes igneous rock. Some of it may metamorphose if folded or twisted or heated again. Some erodes. The cycle continues.

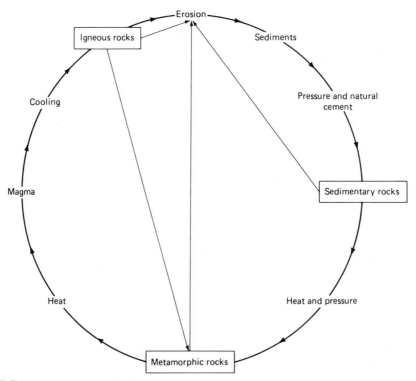

FIGURE 17-7
The rock cycle.

INVESTIGATIONS & ACTIVITIES

SECTION 1
Weathering and Erosion
[*Background 556*]

☐ ACTIVITY: How Can Seeds Break Up Rocks?

NEEDED

two small topless milk or juice cartons   moist soil
plaster of paris   stick
bean seeds

TRY THIS

1. Soak some bean seeds in water overnight.
2. Plant them in a small carton half-filled with moist soil.
3. Mix some plaster of paris and water in a second carton. Make the mixture like a thick milk shake.
4. Pour the plaster mixture lightly over the soil. Make the cover about 0.5 centimeter (¼ inch) thick.
   a. Will the growing seeds be strong enough to break through the hard cover? If so, how long do you think it will take?
   b. If the seeds do break through, how thick a plaster cover will beans go through?
   c. What examples can you find of plants breaking up rocks and other hard materials? Look for plants growing in cracks in rocks, sidewalks, asphalt, and other paved surfaces.

■ INVESTIGATION: How Weathering Breaks Down Minerals

Over time, gases in the air can cause a chemical change in many different minerals in rocks. The process is called *chemical weathering*. A rock that is chemically weathered becomes loose and easily crumbled. Something like this happens when iron or steel breaks down as it rusts. You can learn more about chemical weathering by making things rust.

EXPLORATORY PROBLEM

How can you make an iron nail rust?

NEEDED

plain iron nails
container of wet soil

container of dry soil
steel wool

TRY THIS

1. Rub the nail with steel wool for a few seconds. This will take off any chemical that may have been put on to prevent rusting.

2. Get a container of wet soil. Bury the nail just under the surface. Dig up the nail each day to see if, or how much, it is rusting. Put the nail back in the same way each time. Keep the soil damp (Figure 17-8).

FIGURE 17-8

DISCOVERY PROBLEMS

observing   **A.** When does rust first appear? How quickly is the whole nail covered with rust?

hypothesizing   **B.** Will a nail rust more quickly on the wet soil's surface than below it? What do you think?

hypothesizing   **C.** What would happen if you put a nail in water?

hypothesizing   **D.** What would happen if you buried a nail in dry soil?

hypothesizing   **E.** Will a piece of steel wool rust faster than a nail? What do you think? (Each strand of steel wool is very thin. So much more of this metal is exposed to the air than with a nail.) Keep a record that describes any changes happening over several weeks. Will it easily crumble? If so, how long might it take?

experimenting   **F.** What are some other materials that might rust? In what other ways can you get them to rust? How can you prevent materials from rusting?

TEACHING COMMENT

PREPARATION AND BACKGROUND

Make sure that any steel wool used is the soapless variety. Plastic margarine or cottage-cheese containers are handy to hold soil for this activity. Soil may be dried, if needed, by spreading it on a newspaper and exposing it to sunlight.

Oxygen chemically combines directly with many minerals, as in the rusting process. Carbon dioxide also produces chemical weathering, but indirectly. It dissolves in rainwater to form a weak acid called carbonic acid. This attacks limestone and cementing materials that hold minerals together in some rocks.

GENERALIZATION

Gases in the air may cause chemical weathering in rocks. Rust is an example of chemical weathering.

SAMPLE PERFORMANCE OBJECTIVES

Process: The child can experiment and determine which among several variables are likely to produce rust.
Knowledge: The child can identify several conditions that are likely to produce chemical weathering.

FOR YOUNGER CHILDREN

Younger children should be able to do Try This, Discovery Problem A, and the first question in Discovery Problem F.

☐ ACTIVITY: How Do Mineral Deposits (Stalactites and Stalagmites) Form in Caves?

NEEDED

Epsom salt	two small paper cups
thick, soft string	large paper cup
spoon	two small stones
thick wash cloth or piece of towel	

TRY THIS

1. Fill a large paper cup three-fourths full with water. Dissolve as much Epsom salt in it as you can.

2. Pour the solution into the two small paper cups.

3. Tie a small stone to each string end to weigh them down. Put one string end into each small paper cup. Have the string sag between cups.

4. Place the cups on top of the wash cloth. Leave at least 4 centimeters (1 ½ inches) between the cloth and string. Allow a few days for mineral deposits to form on the string and cloth (Figure 17-9).

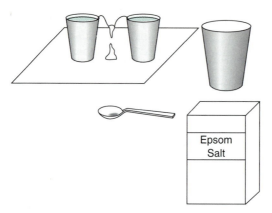

FIGURE 17-9

In a real cave, water with dissolved minerals in it drips from the cave ceiling to the floor. The water leaves minerals behind as it evaporates at both places. Little by little, the mineral deposits build up to look like "icicles" of stone. Those that hang down are called *stalactites*. Those that point up are *stalagmites*. (To remember them, think of *C* for ceiling and *G* for ground.)

a. In your model where is the stalactite? stalagmite?

b. How does your model work compared to the real thing?

☐ ACTIVITY: How Does Freezing Water Break Up Rocks?

NEEDED

several porous or cracked rocks   freezer
bag

TRY THIS

1. Leave some rocks in water for several hours. Use cracked rocks and those that soak up water. Sandstone and limestone are good to use.

2. Put the rocks in a bag. Place the bag in a freezer overnight. Examine the rocks the next day.

a. What, if anything, happened to the rocks?

b. How can you explain your results?

c. If some rocks broke, maybe the cold alone did it. How can you experiment to be more sure that freezing water broke the rocks in this case?

(*Teaching Comment:* Porous rocks may be detected by placing some rocks in water and looking for those on which bubbles form. Pupils can be more sure that freezing water cracked their rocks by placing in the freezer another bag that contains similar, unsoaked rocks.)

☐ ACTIVITY: What Happens When a Rock Heats and Cools Quickly?

NEEDED

candle and match   pliers
clear glass marble   glass of water

TRY THIS

1. Use pliers to hold a marble in a candle for a minute. Hold it above the flame a bit so it does not get black.

2. Quickly put the marble into a glass of water.

3. Take out the marble and examine it.
   a. How does the marble look?
   b. How is this like what happens to rocks that rim a campfire?
   c. Many rocks may crack when rain falls on a forest fire. Why do you think this happens?

(*Teaching Comment:* For safety, supervise open-flame activities closely. Rocks used to contain a camp-fire get very hot from the fire. Often, such fires are doused with water. The sudden cooling may crack some of the rocks. Surface rocks are also heated in forest fires. Rain may have a similar cooling effect.)

☐ ACTIVITY: How Much Water Will a Sandstone Rock Soak Up?

NEEDED

balance   sandstone rock
clay   empty paper cup
medicine dropper   paper cup of water

TRY THIS

1. Place a sandstone rock on one side of a sensitive balance. Place an empty paper cup on the other side. Put bits of clay into the cup until the rock balances.

2. Remove the rock and let it soak under water in a cup overnight.

3. Remove the rock from the cup. Put the rock on the balance again, as in step 1.
   a. How many water drops will it take to balance the rock? Use a medicine dropper to add water to the paper cup on the balance that contains the clay. (This will show how much water the rock soaked up.)
   b. How quickly does a sandstone rock soak up water? Use another rock. Place the rock in water. Take it out and balance the rock each hour to find out how quickly it soaks up the water. Keep a record or make a graph. How will you know when the rock has soaked up all the water it can hold?

□ ACTIVITY: How Does an Acid Change Limestone?

NEEDED

small limestone rock or seashell   paper clip
baby food jar of white vinegar

TRY THIS

1. Open the paper clip. Scrape the outside of the rock or shell.
   a. How easily can you make a mark in the rock?
2. Place the rock or shell inside a small jar of vinegar. Observe it for a few minutes.
   b. What, if anything, do you notice? (Use both eyes and ears.)
3. Cap the jar and wait overnight. Then, take out and scrape the rock or shell again.
   c. How, if at all, has the surface changed?
   d. What do you think will happen if the rock or shell is kept in vinegar for a week?

(*Teaching Comment:* Vinegar is a weak acid. When a calcium carbonate such as limestone or a seashell is placed in it, a chemical reaction occurs. This softens the object's surface. Small bubbles appear in the vinegar and a faint fizzing sound may be heard. These actions may be observed more easily if the stone or shell is crushed. This permits more of the material to come into contact with the acid.)

□ ACTIVITY: How Does Weathering Change a Rock?

NEEDED

several different weathered rocks   thick paper bag
soft paper towel or facial tissue   hand lens
empty egg carton   hammer

TRY THIS

1. For safety, to break open a rock, put it into a thick paper bag. Hold the bag against a cement curb or sidewalk. Hit the rock a few times with a hammer through the bag.
2. Look at the weathered and fresh rock surfaces with a hand lens.
   a. How are they different? alike?
3. Make a weathered rock display. Take two of the larger pieces of the rock. Wrap one piece in tissue or soft towel so only the weathered part shows. Wrap the other so only the fresh surface shows. Place them in opposite spaces in an egg carton. Do this with other broken rocks, also, until you fill the carton.
   b. What will happen if you shift the rocks around so the samples are not opposite one another? How many of the rocks will your friends be able to match? If someone shifts them for you, how many will *you* be able to match?

■ INVESTIGATION: Soil Erosion

After a rain have you noticed how water has carried away, or *eroded,* soil? Splashing raindrops and running water are responsible for much soil erosion. But not all places with soil erode, and some places erode much more than others.

EXPLORATORY PROBLEM

How can you test to see what affects soil erosion?

NEEDED

two throwaway pie pans   soil
two matched, plastic sauce dishes   measuring cups
two small matched juice cans   meter stick or yardstick
a small- and a medium-sized nail   hammer

TRY THIS

1. Punch 10 holes in the bottom of 1 juice can with a small nail. Use a medium-sized nail to punch 10 holes in the second can. Both cans should be open at the top.

2. Fill a sauce dish level and to the brim with soil. Put the dish into a pie pan to catch any spilled material.

3. Place a meter stick or yardstick upright behind the dish. Hold the small-hole can 60 centimeters (24 inches) above the dish.

4. Have someone pour a half-cup of water into the juice can. When the can stops "raining," observe the soil and pie pan (Figure 17-10).

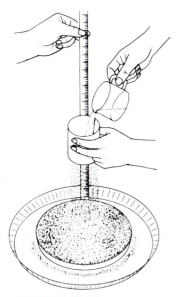

FIGURE 17-10

DISCOVERY PROBLEMS

observing **A.** What, if any, signs of erosion can you observe?

observing **B.** How will a heavier "rain" affect erosion? Fill a second saucer with soil. Use the medium-hole can for rain. Compare the results with the first trial.

observing **C.** How will loose soil erode compared to tightly packed soil? Prepare two saucers and find out. (Use only one can for the "rain" in Problems C through E.)

observing **D.** How will tilted soil erode compared to level soil?

observing **E.** How will covered soil erode compared to bare soil? Cover the soil in one dish with several leaves.

inferring **F.** What are some conditions that seem to reduce soil erosion? That seem to increase soil erosion? What examples can you find outdoors that show some or all of these conditions?

TEACHING COMMENT

PREPARATION AND BACKGROUND

All of the preceding conditions are important in affecting soil erosion. But all are not easy to produce reliably with small-scale soil testing. The sizes of materials suggested—sauce dish about 13 centimeters (5 inches), half-cup of water, small juice can, and so on—are likely to bring satisfactory results. Finding actual samples of erosion, as in Discovery Problem F, is important to achieving full understanding.

GENERALIZATION

Rainfall, soil cover, degree of incline, and compactness affect soil erosion.

SAMPLE PERFORMANCE OBJECTIVES

Process: The child can locate several outdoor examples of soil erosion and infer the conditions that influenced the examples.
Knowledge: The child can state several conditions that affect soil erosion.

■ INVESTIGATION: Wind Erosion

What happens to loose soil on a windy day? The moving of soil or rocks from one place to another is *erosion*. Soil erosion by wind is a big problem in some places.

EXPLORATORY PROBLEM

How can you find out about wind erosion around you?

NEEDED

two rulers	sticky tape
crayon	scissors
small, empty milk carton	open unpaved area outdoors
sand or soil	large sprinkling can
windy day	

TRY THIS

1. Make a wind erosion recorder. Cut two narrow slots on top of a small milk carton. (See Figure 17-11.)

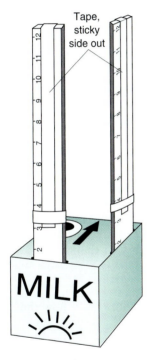
Tape, sticky side out

FIGURE 17-11

2. Stick two rulers through the slots.
3. Fill the carton with sand or soil to make it heavy.
4. Cut two 45-centimeter (18-inch) strips of sticky tape.
5. Put one strip evenly over the top of each ruler, *sticky side out*. Fasten the strip ends to each ruler with tape.
6. Draw an arrow on the carton top with crayon.
7. Place your recorder where the wind is blowing loose soil. Point the arrow north. Leave the recorder for 30 minutes. Notice how bits of windblown soil collect on the sticky tape.

DISCOVERY PROBLEMS

observing
inferring

A. Examine the sticky tape on all four sides. Which side has the most soil? From which direction did the wind blow most?

hypothesizing

B. Where do you think there is the most wind erosion around the school? least wind erosion? Make more recorders. Put one in each place and find out. What reasons can you give for what you find?

experimenting

C. What difference in wind erosion is there between grass-covered and bare soil? How can you find out?

experimenting

D. What difference in wind erosion is there between dry and damp soil? How can you find out?

classifying

inferring

E. Collect windblown soil bits each day for a week with your recorder. Change the sticky tape each day. Can you arrange the strips in order from most to fewest soil bits? On what day was there the most wind erosion? least erosion? Can you tell from which main direction the wind blew each day?

hypothesizing

F. When during the day is there the most wind erosion where you live? How can you find out? What else can you discover with your recorder?

TEACHING COMMENT

PREPARATION AND BACKGROUND

Some children may not realize at first that some variables need to be controlled in this investigation. If two areas are to be tested—one grassy and one with bare soil, for example—two identical recorders must be exposed to wind within equal areas at the same time. When possible, let pupils discover this for themselves.

GENERALIZATION

Soil erosion by wind depends on how hard the wind blows and how the soil is protected from the wind.

SAMPLE PERFORMANCE OBJECTIVES

Process: The child can place in order, from most to fewest soil particles, tape strips collected during a given time for one week.
Knowledge: The child can state several soil conditions that contribute to wind erosion.

□ ACTIVITY: How Do Glaciers Change the Land?

NEEDED

throwaway aluminum pie pan   freezer
stones and pebbles   place with bare soil

TRY THIS

1. Put some rocks and pebbles in a pie pan. Spread them about halfway around the pan's inside edge as shown in Figure 17-12.

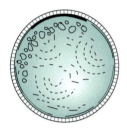

FIGURE 17-12

2. Put some water into the pan, but let the tops of the rocks stick out of the water.

3. Leave the pan in a freezer overnight.

4. Remove your frozen glacier model from the pan. Turn it over so the rocks sticking out are underneath.

5. Place the model flat on some bare dirt. Push it so the stones are forward. Press down at the same time. Push it in a straight line for about 60 centimeters (2 feet).

6. Let your model stay and melt at the end of that distance. Come back to this place several hours later after it has melted. Observe carefully everything that has been left behind.
   a. How can you tell the direction in which the "glacier" moved?
   b. How can you tell how wide it was?
   c. How can you tell where the forward part of the glacier stopped and melted?

SECTION 2
Soil and Its Makeup
[Background 558]

■ INVESTIGATION: The Makeup of Soils

What are some things you eat that grow in soil? How is soil important in your life? What do you think makes up soil?

EXPLORATORY PROBLEM

How can you find out what makes up soil?

NEEDED

two bags of different, fresh soils spoon
three glass jars with caps newspaper
water three sheets of white paper
magnifying glass paper cup

TRY THIS

1. Spread newspaper on a table or desk. Put a sheet of white paper on top.
2. Pour some soil from one bag onto the white paper. What is the color of the soil? (See Figure 17-13.)

FIGURE 17-13

3. Spread out the soil with a spoon. Use a magnifier to see better. What animals or animal parts do you see? (Put live animals in a paper cup.) What plant or plant parts do you see? Animal and plant materials in soil are called humus.
4. Feel the soil between your fingers. Rough soil has more large-sized rock bits or particles than smooth soil. Use a magnifier. Can you find three sizes of rock particles? Which size makes up most rock particles in your sample?
5. Sort the different humus and rock materials into layers. Here is how. Fill a glass jar half full with the soil you are observing. Fill the rest of the jar with water. Shake the jar and then let it settle for an hour. Where does the humus settle? How much is there? In what order do the different-sized rock particles settle? How much is there of each size?

DISCOVERY PROBLEMS

observing

inferring

A. How good a soil detective are you? Can you tell which two soil samples are from the same place? Have a partner pour some soil into three white sheets. Two soil samples should come from one bag and one soil sample from the other bag. (Do not look while this is done.) Try to identify the two soil samples from the same bag. Observe color, humus, and rock particles. Do the shake test, also, if needed.

observing

B. What is the makeup of soil from different places? Get samples of different soils around school and home. How are the soil samples alike and different? How does deeper soil compare with surface soil from the same place? How many soil samples can you match as in Discovery Problem A?

inferring

TEACHING COMMENT

PREPARATION AND BACKGROUND

The two bags of soil in the first activity should come from two very different locations. Make sure the materials in each bag of soil are fairly evenly distributed. Otherwise, it will be hard to match soil samples that come from the same bag. Discarded glass coffee or peanut butter jars make good shake-and-settle-containers for soils. Jars should be washed clean outdoors, not in a sink; soil clogs plumbing.

GENERALIZATION

Soil is made up of humus and rock particles; different soils may be identified by the kinds and amounts of these materials.

SAMPLE PERFORMANCE OBJECTIVES

Process: When shown three samples, two of which are the same, the child can observe similarities and differences and match the proper pair.
Knowledge: The child can describe the materials that make up soil and can explain that soils look different because these materials vary in kind and amount.

FOR YOUNGER CHILDREN

Most primary pupils do well in this activity. However, they are less systematic than older pupils in how they observe soil materials and need more help in locating soil samples.

■ **INVESTIGATION: How Water Sinks into Different Soils**

Some of the rain that falls on soil runs off it into streams. Some rain also soaks into the ground. This water can help crops grow. If water sinks deep below the surface, it may be pumped to the surface for many uses. How fast water soaks into soil depends on several conditions. You can find out some for yourself.

EXPLORATORY PROBLEM

What can you do to test how fast water sinks into soils?

NEEDED

two matched cans, one with both ends
  removed
different outdoor places with soil

watch with second hand
water

TRY THIS

1. One can should be open at both ends. Scratch a mark sideways on the can's side 2.5 centimeters (1 inch) from one end.

2. Go to a place with soil outdoors. Use your foot to press the can into the soil up to the mark.

3. Have the second can filled with water. Pour the water into the first can without spilling any (Figure 17-14). With a watch, check how long it takes for all the water to sink in.

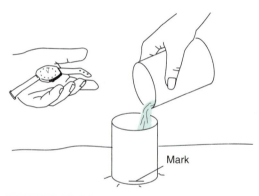

Mark

FIGURE 17-14

DISCOVERY PROBLEMS

measuring **A.** How much time is needed for the water to sink into the soil?

measuring **B.** Compare the sink times of different soils. How will soil with grass compare to the same kind of soil without grass?

measuring **C.** How will sandy soil compare with sticky soil?

measuring **D.** How will hard-packed soil compare with loose soil?

measuring **E.** How will soil that is usually in the sun compare with soil that is usually in the shade?

measuring **F.** How will soil on a hill compare with soil that is on a flat surface?

inferring **G.** What are some things about soil that seem to make water sink in quickly? slowly?

TEACHING COMMENT

PREPARATION AND BACKGROUND

A steel can is likely to hold up better than an aluminum can for this activity. Some hard soils may require an adult's weight to push the can down to the mark.

GENERALIZATION

Permeable soils tend to be loosely packed and composed of coarse mineral particles with little or no humus.

SAMPLE PERFORMANCE OBJECTIVES

Process: The child can measure and compare the permeability of several different kinds of soils.
Knowledge: The child can explain the conditions that are likely to be found in highly permeable soils.

FOR OLDER CHILDREN

To make this investigation into an experiment for older students, start with Discovery Problem G. Then, after discussing hypotheses, ask, "How can we find out?"

■ INVESTIGATION: Soil Chemicals

Plants will grow well only in soils that suit them. Plants that live in forests and moist habitats usually have soils that contain *acid* chemicals. Vinegar is one example of an acid. Plants that live in sandy or desert areas usually have soils with *alkaline* chemicals. Baking soda is one example of an alkaline material. Many soils are neither acid nor alkaline. These are *neutral* soils. You can test to see what kinds of soils are around you.

EXPLORATORY PROBLEM

How can you find out if a soil is acid, alkaline, or neutral?

NEEDED

neutral, or distilled, water   red and blue litmus paper
soil samples   three baby food jars

TRY THIS

1. An acid liquid turns blue litmus paper red. An alkaline liquid turns red litmus paper blue. A neutral liquid leaves each color of litmus paper unchanged. Touch a strip each of red and blue litmus paper to the water you will be using. Touch only a small part, so you can use the strip again. Both colors should stay unchanged to show the water is neutral. If it is not neutral, use distilled water.
2. Half-fill a baby food jar with soil from a well-fertilized garden.
3. Pour neutral water into the jar until it is almost full.
4. Cap and shake the jar for a half-minute. Then let it settle for at least 10 minutes.

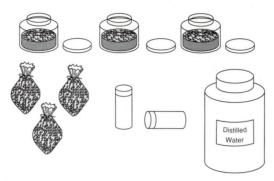

FIGURE 17-15

5. Uncap the jar. Touch a strip each of red and blue litmus paper to the soil water. Observe the strips.

DISCOVERY PROBLEMS

observing **A.** How would you label this soil? What is your reason?

observing **B.** Make other litmus tests. How does a light-colored soil compare to a dark-colored soil?

observing **C.** How does a surface soil sample compare with one that is 30 centimeters (1 foot) or more beneath it?

hypothesizing **D.** Where can you find acid soils around you? alkaline soils? neutral soils? What is growing in each of these soils?

TEACHING COMMENT

PREPARATION AND BACKGROUND

The soils available to you may not be acid or alkaline enough for litmus paper to change colors. If so, you might want to add a spoonful of vinegar or baking soda to some of the soil water samples. You'll want to inform the pupils, of course, but it will be more interesting if you don't tell them exactly which samples are affected.

GENERALIZATION

Soils may contain chemicals that make the soil acid, alkaline, or neutral. Some plants are best suited to each kind of soil.

SAMPLE PERFORMANCE OBJECTIVES

Knowledge: The child can predict the likelihood of a soil being acid, alkaline, or neutral from observing the plants it supports.
Process: The child can test soils with litmus paper to determine which are acid, alkaline, or neutral.

SECTION 3
Building up of the Land
[Background 559]

☐ ACTIVITY: What Makes a Volcano Erupt?

NEEDED

carbonated soft drink in small bottle   lever-type bottle-cap opener

Fiery-hot melted rock, called *magma,* can be found deep underground. Sometimes magma oozes up to the surface through giant cracks in the earth. In other cases, the magma is trapped where there are no cracks. If enough magma mixes with enough high-pressure gases underground, great pressure may build up. The gas pressure may make the magma shoot up, or erupt, through a weak spot in the earth's crust. This is called a *volcano.* You can make a model volcano with a carbonated soft drink.

TRY THIS

1. Take the soft-drink bottle outside where you can spill its contents.
2. Shake the bottle about 20 times. This will mix the gas that is inside with the liquid.
3. Point the bottle away from people. Place a lever-type opener over the bottle cap. Quickly flip off the cap.
   a. What happens to the contents?
   b. Compare your model to a volcano. What in the model is like magma? What is like the high-pressure gases mixed with the magma? What is like the weak spot in the earth's crust?

(*Teaching Comment:* The bottle's contents will erupt more spectacularly if kept at room temperature rather than chilled.)

☐ ACTIVITY: What Happens When Magma Pushes up Without Breaking the Earth's Crust?

NEEDED

box lid or tray   large, round balloon
sand or dry soil

When rocks melt underground, they form a thick fiery-hot liquid called *magma.* Hot gases and steam, released when the rocks melt, mix with the magma and build up great pressure. This forces the magma to squeeze into cracks or weak places under the earth's crust. Magma may push up and bend rock layers above without coming to the surface. This can make a *dome mountain*. You can make a model of one.

TRY THIS

1. Spread a thin layer of sand or soil in a box lid or tray.

2. Lay a balloon on the sand. Let its neck stick out over the lid's side.

3. Cover the balloon with about 5 centimeters (2 inches) of sand or soil. Make the "land" surface level.

4. Slowly blow air into the balloon so it is partly filled.
   a. What happens to the land surface?
   b. What in the model is like the magma?
   c. What is like the layers of rock above the magma?

(*Teaching Comment:* A large, round balloon is recommended. Small balloons are hard to inflate, and the weight of the soil will make this even harder to do. A small plastic bag may also be easily inflated if its opening is tightly wrapped around the end of a drinking straw and fastened with sticky tape.)

□ ACTIVITY: How Does Mountain Folding Produce Heat?

NEEDED

wire coat hanger   wax candle

When land is pushed from two sides, it may move up and fold. When a solid material bends, there is much friction. This makes the material hot. You can see this with a wire coat hanger.

TRY THIS

1. Hold the hanger near the ends as shown in Figure 17-16.

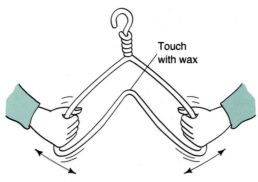

Touch with wax

FIGURE 17-16

2. Push the hanger together so it bends and pull it back again. Do this very fast about 20 times.

3. Have someone touch a candle to where the hanger bends most.
   a. What happens to the candle wax where it touches the wire?
   b. How was the hanger movement like that of a folding mountain? unlike?

(*Teaching Comment:* The land is pushed into a fold, but is not pulled out of the fold as was the hanger. The land movement is very, very slow, whereas the hanger movement had to be fast to build up heat.)

SECTION 4
How Rocks Are Formed
[*Background 563*]

■ INVESTIGATION: The Properties of Rocks

Have you ever heard the saying, "It's as hard as a rock"? Does this mean all rocks are equally hard? What do you think?

EXPLORATORY PROBLEM A

How can you find out the hardness of different rocks?

NEEDED

penny   six different rocks
large iron nail   partner
glass baby food jar   pencil and paper

TRY THIS

1. Study this hardness scale. It can help you to group your rocks.

Hardness Scale	Rock Test
Very soft	Can be scratched with your fingernail
Soft	A new penny will scratch it. A fingernail will not.
Medium	A nail will scratch it. A penny will not.
Hard	It will scratch glass. A nail will not scratch it.

2. Test each rock according to this scale.

3. Keep a record of how hard each rock is. One way is to give each rock a different letter—A, B, etc. Write the letter on a slip of paper. Then put the rock on the slip (Figure 17-17). Record each rock's letter and hardness on a sheet of paper.

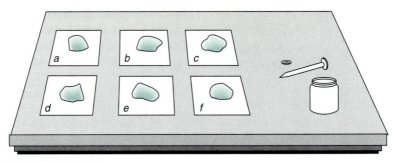

FIGURE 17-17

DISCOVERY PROBLEMS

observing **A.** Will someone else who tests your rock agree with you? Let your
classifying   partner test your rocks. They should be on the lettered paper slips.
Have her record each rock's letter and hardness. How much is this
record like yours? Are there differences? Why?

classifying **B.** How can you put your six rocks in order from softest to hardest?
(*Hint:* How can scratching one rock with another help?)

observing **C.** What other rocks can you test for hardness? How much will
classifying   someone else agree with you if they test the same rocks?

EXPLORATORY PROBLEM B

What other properties of rocks can you observe and describe?

NEEDED

same materials as in Exploratory Problem A   vinegar
piece of white tile   new partner
paper cup

TRY THIS

1. *Color:* What is the color of the rock? Some rocks have several mixed colors. The
best way to decide color is with a streak test. Rub the rock on the rough side of
some tile. What color is the streak? (Figure 17-18.)

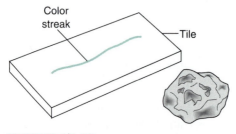

FIGURE 17-18

2. *Feel:* How does the rock feel to you? Is it rough? smooth? soapy? What else?

3. *Layers:* Does the rock seem to be made up of flat layers pressed together?

4. *Holes:* Does the rock have many small holes in it?

5. *Fizz:* If the rock is placed in a small cup of vinegar, do many tiny bubbles appear?

6. *Fossils:* Can you see tiny parts of sea shells or other such materials?

7. *Heaviness:* How heavy does the rock seem for its size? Light? medium? heavy?

8. *Other Properties:* What other properties of your rocks can you observe?

DISCOVERY PROBLEMS

classifying **A.** Play a game with a partner. Sort some of your rocks into two groups according to one property (use color, or feel, etc.). Can a partner tell which property you used to sort them? Try other single properties; take turns with your partner.

observing
communicating **B.** Play the "I'm-Thinking-of-a-Rock" game with a partner. Place four or more rocks in a row. Think of just one rock and some of its properties. Can your partner find out what rock you have in mind? She must ask you only questions that can be answered by yes or no. Example: "Is it a rough rock?" (Yes.) "Does it have holes?" (No.)

When your partner finds the right rock, switch places. How quickly can you discover the rock your partner is thinking of? The person who needs to ask the fewer questions wins.

communicating **C.** How well can you describe your rocks? Can you make a chart that your partner can use to identify them?

Make a chart of all properties you observe about your rocks. Call your rocks A, B, and so on. Try to remember which rock is which.

Rock	Hardness	Color	Feel	Layers	Holes
A	Medium	Gray	Smooth	No	Yes
B					
C					
D					

Give your completed chart and rocks to your partner. The rocks should be out of order, so he or she must study your chart to tell which rock is A, B, C, and so on.

inferring Which chart descriptions were helpful? Which confused your partner? How could these be made clearer?

TEACHING COMMENT

PREPARATION AND BACKGROUND

Only about 30 minerals make up most common rocks. So you will observe some of the same minerals many times in different rocks.

A main intention of this investigation is to sharpen how children observe, classify, and communicate. There is no attempt to teach the technical content of identifying rocks and minerals. Yet some interested, capable children may become motivated enough to learn such material. There are many library books on collecting and identifying rocks to help them.

If you cannot get pure mineral samples, ask pupils to bring in large, different-looking rocks. To break up a rock, put it into a heavy paper bag for safety. Hold the bag against a hard surface and smash the rock with a hammer. Small broken pieces of white porcelain tile may be obtained free by teachers at many stores where tiles are sold. The unglazed back of the tile is used for the color streak test. To make rock identification harder, omit the property of color.

GENERALIZATION

Rocks vary in hardness, color, texture, and other properties.

SAMPLE PERFORMANCE OBJECTIVES

Process: The child can classify rocks on the basis of hardness by using a simple hardness scale.
Knowledge: The child can state several properties by which rocks can be described.

FOR YOUNGER CHILDREN

Most younger pupils should be able to sort rocks by color and by "either–or" categories: smooth–rough, heavy–light, holes–no holes, and so on. Some also should be able to perform hardness tests. To put their rocks in order by hardness, they may try to scratch one rock with another. The harder rock scratches the softer one. Also, by rubbing each pair over some white paper and noting the color of the fallen material, children may discover which is the harder rock.

■ INVESTIGATION: Crystals and How They Grow

It is interesting to see the crystals that make up some rocks. Most crystals are formed underground when melted minerals collect and grow in size as they cool. You can learn more about crystals and how they "grow" by making some yourself.

EXPLORATORY PROBLEM

How can you grow crystals?

NEEDED

glass or ceramic saucer   string
hand lens   hot water
table salt   cup
alum (potash)   spoon
borax

TRY THIS

1. Stir as much salt into a half-cup of hot water as will dissolve.
2. Pour the salt solution into a saucer. Put a small string in the solution. Leave part of it outside so you can pick up the string later (Figure 17-19). Put the saucer where it will not be disturbed.

FIGURE 17-19

3. Wait several days until most of the salt solution has evaporated. Carefully pour off what is left. Then give the crystals forming on the saucer bottom and string a day to dry.
4. Examine the dry crystals with a hand lens.

DISCOVERY PROBLEMS

observing   **A.** How do the salt crystals look? Study their shape, size, and how they stick together.

observing   **B.** What do alum and borax crystals look like? Prepare crystals from these materials as you did from salt. Study the crystals carefully with a hand lens.

inferring   **C.** Have someone place before you strings of crystals prepared from salt, alum, and borax. Can you tell which is which without being told?

observing **D.** How, if at all, does quickness of cooling affect crystal size? Prepare two solutions of alum in separate saucers. Put one in a refrigerator so it will cool fast. Put the other where it will cool slowly. Examine each solution the next day.

TEACHING COMMENT

PREPARATION AND BACKGROUND

Use a microprojector if you want your whole class to observe and discuss together the properties of different crystals.

Alum (potash) is sold in drugstores, rather than in grocery stores. Sugar is another substance from which a solution may be prepared for crystal growing. However, it often attracts ants. All solutions should be very heavy or saturated for good crystals to form.

A solution that cools quickly forms small crystals. This is like molten rock that cools relatively quickly at or near the earth's surface. A solution that cools more slowly has time to form larger, coarser crystals. This is like molten rock that cools slowly deep underground.

GENERALIZATION

Crystals may form from molten rock or may be grown from mineral solutions. The size of crystals depends on how fast the molten rock and solutions cool.

SAMPLE PERFORMANCE OBJECTIVES

Process: Through observing, the child can determine enough properties of three common minerals to identify them when they are unlabeled.
Knowledge: The child can explain that crystal size depends on the cooling rate of either molten rock or a mineral solution.

☐ ACTIVITY: What Minerals Can You Find in Sand?

NEEDED

sheet of white paper   hand lens
small jar of sand   magnet

TRY THIS

1. Spread a small amount of sand on white paper.
2. Using a hand lens, separate the grains of sand so you can see a few at a time. How many different-colored minerals can you find?
3. Using a pencil tip, push a number of black grains of sand into a group. What, if any, differences do you notice among them?

4. Which, if any, sand grains are attracted to a magnet?

5. Is all sand alike? Get another sample from a different place. How is this sand like and unlike the other sand?

(*Teaching Comment:* Different-colored grains or crystals usually indicate the presence of different minerals. There may be several minerals of similar color. Black crystals may be hornblende, mica, or magnetite, for example. Crystals of similar color may be separated by differences in size and shape. Also, a magnet will attract magnetite, separating it from the other crystals.)

SELECTED TRADE BOOKS: THE EARTH'S CHANGING SURFACE

FOR YOUNGER CHILDREN

Booth, Eugene. *Under the Ground.* Raintree, 1985.

Branley, Franklyn M., *Earthquakes.* Crowell, 1991.

Butler, Daphne. *First Look Under the Ground.* Gareth Stevens, 1991.

Harris, Susan. *Volcanoes.* Watts, 1979.

Ingoglia, Gina. *Look Inside the Earth.* Putnam, 1991.

Leutscher, Alfred. *Earth.* Dial, 1983.

McNulty, Faith. *How to Dig a Hole to the Other Side of the World.* Harper, 1979.

Podendorf, Illa. *Rocks and Minerals.* Children's Press, 1982.

Roberts, Allan. *Fossils.* Children's Press, 1983.

Schwartz, Linda. *My Earth Book.* Learning Works, 1991.

Sipier, Paul. *I Can Be a Geologist.* Children's Press, 1986.

Williams, Lawrence. *The Changing Earth.* Wright Group, 1986.

Wyler, Rose. *Science Fun with Dirt and Mud.* Messner, 1987.

FOR OLDER CHILDREN

Bramwell, Martyn. *Planet Earth.* Watts, 1987.

Challand, Helen. *Volcanoes.* Children's Press, 1983.

Fordor, R. V. *Earth in Motion: The Concept of Plate Tectonics.* Morrow, 1978.

_____ . *Chiseling the Earth: How Erosion Shapes the Land.* Enslow, 1983.

Gallant, Roy A. *Our Restless Earth.* Watts, 1986.

Lampton, Christopher. *Earthquake.* Millbrook Press, 1991.

Lauber, Patricia. *Volcanoes and Earthquakes.* Scholastic, 1991.

Lye, Keith. *The Earth.* Millbrook Press, 1991.

Marcus, Elizabeth. *All About Mountains and Volcanoes.* Troll Associates, 1984.

Nixon, Hershell H., and Joan Lowery Nixon. *Glaciers: Nature's Frozen Rivers.* Dodd, 1980.

Rickard, Graham. *Geothermal Energy.* Gareth Stevens, 1991.

Ruthland, Jonathan. *The Violent Earth.* Random House, 1987.

Rydell, Wendy. *Discovering Fossils.* Troll Associates, 1984.

Selden, Paul. *Face of the Earth.* Children's Press, 1982.

Watson, Nancy, et al. *Our Violent Earth.* National Geographic, 1982.

Williamson, Tom. *Understanding the Earth.* Silver Burdett, 1985.

Winner, Peter. *Earthquakes.* Silver Burdett, 1986.

18

Water, Air, and Weather

It's easy to take clean air and water for granted. And why not? For most of us, all we need do is breathe easily and turn on a faucet. But experiences of recent years with pollution and water shortages are making people lose their complacency.

In this chapter, we examine some properties of water and air, the importance of a clean supply of both, and some concepts basic to understanding weather, organized under three headings: (1) water, (2) air and its properties, and (3) weather. There are many chances for thought-provoking experiences within these topics.

[I] WATER   *Experiences 608*

Our need for water commands our attention in both direct and indirect ways. Water is vital to life. You saw in another chapter how water transports chemicals to cells, removes waste materials, and performs other vital functions. Although humans may survive for weeks without food, water is needed within a few days. Bathing, cooking, recreational activities, and so on also require water.

Agriculture consumes enormous volumes of water for irrigating plants in rain-poor regions. Industry, too, is a huge user of water. The manufacture of paper, steel, rubber, chemicals, and other products continually requires more water.

Even our future energy resources depend, in part, on having adequate water. For example, coal in the western United States would be most efficiently transported if crushed and sent through pipes after being mixed with water. The extraction of oil from shale rock also requires much water. It is unlikely that there is now enough water in the right places to meet all such needs.

Because water has so many uses, it is important to understand its properties. Let's look at some now.

Some Properties of Water

Water is an excellent solvent. In fact, more substances dissolve in water than in any other common liquid. Some other properties of water basic to our discussion are its molecular attraction, how it exerts pressure, and how it flows.

Molecules and Water.   You may recall from an earlier chapter (Chapter 9, "Heat Energy") that there is an attractive force between molecules called cohesion. In a solid, the spaces between molecules are relatively small. So a solid material sticks together, or coheres, well enough to maintain its own shape. Molecules of a liquid are farther apart. Their weaker cohesion causes them to slide about and assume the shape of a container. The cohesion of gas molecules is weaker still since these molecules are even farther apart.

Cohesion of water molecules is central to the process of evaporation. Heat energy must overcome water's cohesive force, as well as the force of air pressing down. If this could not happen, evaporation could not take place. The sun, of course, is the chief source of heat energy. When we spread out a water puddle to make it dry faster, the sun's energy overcomes the cohesive force of more water molecules at one time. So the rate of evaporation increases.

Because water takes the shape of its container, we can use water to measure the volumes of irregular objects, inside or out. Several investigations in the experiences part of this chapter help pupils to learn this skill and discover the cohesive properties of water.

Pressure.   The weight of water gives it pressure. The deeper the water, the more pressure. This is one reason a dam is built with a thicker base than top. At any depth, the pressure is exerted in all directions and planes.

Pressure is also involved when something floats. For an object to float, opposing balanced forces work against each other. Gravity pulls down on the object, and the water pushes it up. The key to floating is the object's size relative to its weight. If it is light for its size, it has relatively high volume. That is, it presents a large surface area for the water to push against. This is why a ship made of *steel* floats. The water displaced by an object that is light for its size pushes up as forcefully as gravity pulls the object down.

An object floats higher in the ocean than in fresh water because ocean water has more minerals dissolved in it—especially salt. Therefore, a cup of ocean water weighs more than a cup of fresh water. Having more weight, it pushes back with greater force on any object that displaces it. This allows a ship to carry a heavier cargo in salt water than fresh water.

Water Flow. Gravity is the force that moves water in nature. Water cannot flow higher than its source unless some other force is more powerful. To store their water supply, some towns and small cities pump water into a large tank mounted on a tower. Water then flows by gravity through all pipes connected to the town tank. In some places, buildings are constructed that are taller than the tower. Pumps are installed in the buildings for water to reach the higher floors.

Clean, Adequate Water

Will there be enough water for enough people in enough places in the foreseeable future? A dependable answer to this question seems impossible now. But we can survey what it takes to get a clean and adequate supply of water, beginning with some sources of water.

Sources. A look at a globe tells us there is no shortage of water. About 71 percent of the earth's crust is covered with it. Most, though, is in the oceans and is too salty for either land plants or animals. So our immediate sources of fresh water are found elsewhere, in lakes, rivers, reservoirs, and beneath the land surface as groundwater.

Groundwater comes from rainwater that is absorbed into the soil and porous rock. It continues to sink until it reaches a layer of solid, nonporous rock. As more rainwater soaks into the ground, more of the below-surface section becomes saturated. The upper limit of the saturated section is called the *water table*. The table profile often corresponds roughly to that of the surface. When the surface dips below the water table, we see a lake or spring. Groundwater in a location does not always come from rainwater sinking from directly above. Groundwater may percolate through ground and porous rock diagonally or horizontally for some distance before it stops.

To construct a water well, a hole is drilled or dug to some depth below the water table. This helps to ensure a steady supply of water should the water table lower during dry spells.

Ocean water is the main source of evaporating water on earth. So the oceans are the basic source for fresh water. When salt water evaporates, the salt is left behind. Air currents carry the water vapor far inland. There it condenses and falls as rain, hail, or snow.

Over the long run, the water cycle gives what should be a steady supply of groundwater and other water. But several factors today make it hard to find usable fresh water in many places. Increased uses for water, as mentioned earlier, is one reason. Another is pollution.

Pollution. Many cities continue to dump partly treated or raw sewage into nearby rivers or lakes, from which drinking water is often drawn. As a result, purification of water is getting harder and more expensive. Factories, too, often discharge wastes into accessible waters. Another major source of pollution is agriculture. Chemical fertilizers and pesticides wash off the land into streams and bays.

An overload of fertilizers or sewage in a lake or other body of water causes an abnormally large population of algae to grow. The algae block sunlight from reaching aquatic plants under the water's surface; so the plants, as well as the animals that feed on them, die. Dead material piles up on the lake bottom. The overcrowded algae also die in time, and the decomposers take over. Eventually, the oxygen supply in the water is largely depleted and the decomposers die, too. They are replaced by bacteria that can live without oxygen. What was once a source of clean water and a complex community of living things is a silted, near-dead putrescent swamp. A reversal can occur through natural changes of the land surface and a gradual succession of ever-higher forms of life, but this may take centuries or longer.

In recent years, much publicity has been given to a particularly ominous threat to the nation's water supply—hazardous waste dumps. At such sites, poisonous chemicals may leak from storage containers and percolate down through the ground, contaminating groundwater, nearby streams, and lakes. Drinking or swimming in the water, and eating fish whose organs have accumulated the poisons, have been linked to severe health problems, including brain damage, cancer, and birth defects in children born to exposed parents.

Acid Rain. Many waste products are discharged into the air as well as on the ground and into bodies of water. These, also, may end up polluting our water and other natural resources. The burning of fossil fuels in factories, power plants, and automobiles releases sulfur and nitrogen oxides into the atmosphere. When water vapor is present, these gases are converted into sulfuric acid and nitric acid. The rain that falls from a polluted region can be as acidic as vinegar.

Acid rain—including acid sleet, hail, and snow—is contaminating water supplies, killing trees, fish stocks, and corroding water systems. Its effects are easily noticeable where there are large concentrations of coal-burning power plants, heavy industry, and automobiles. But even more damage may result far beyond these places. Winds aloft,

especially the prevailing westerlies in our country, sweep the pollutants into large, distant regions. The northeastern United States and adjacent Canadian area have been most affected.

Some progress has been made in reducing the pollutants through the use of chemical filters in industry and pollution control devices for automobile exhaust systems. But large-scale improvements in industrial pollution bear a daunting price tag. Especially nettlesome is the answer to the question: Who pays? When suspected sources of pollution are hundreds of miles away, and thousands of jobs or millions of utility bills are affected, an acceptable answer becomes highly complicated.

Conservation. It seems inevitable that people will need to change certain water-use habits. Many habits were fostered when regional populations were small, pollution was less severe, water uses were fewer, and resources were more abundant. Conservation, or wise use, of water resources is becoming more common because more persons now are aware of the consequences if it is not practiced.

Stricter laws to protect water supplies are continually enacted. More attention is being given to the recycling of industrial wastes and the safe storage of long-lasting, harmful chemicals. Bare slopes are being planted to protect watersheds. Fertilizers and pesticides are being used under more controlled conditions in agriculture. People are learning to use less water in more situations without wasting it. An important by-product of water conservation is energy conservation. A significant amount of the nation's energy is used in pumping water and heating it.

Future Water Supply. It's possible that even increased conservation measures will fail to meet future needs for water. Where will more usable water come from? Just as some scientists are looking for ways to directly tap the sun's energy, others are investigating methods for directly converting ocean water to fresh water.

One way to remove salt from ocean water is to distill it. The water is heated, changed to a vapor, and condensed, much like in the water cycle. Another method freezes ocean water. The ice that forms at the surface is mostly fresh water. It is removed and melted. There are many other methods now being used and explored. At present, all are too expensive for widespread use. If more economical means can be found, the direct conversion of ocean water to fresh water could bring major changes in many dry regions of the world and in the world's food supply.

[2] AIR AND ITS PROPERTIES   *Experiences 620*

Air has many of the properties of water and may contain much water in gaseous form. However, air also has some unique properties. To better understand some of its specific features, let's first take an overall look at where our immediate air supply comes from: the atmosphere.

The Atmosphere

Space exploration has made us more aware of how dependent we are on our atmospheric environment. Without an air supply, humans cannot survive for more than minutes. Although we may travel in comfort thousands of kilometers across the earth's surface, an ascent of only 5 kilometers into the sky may require special oxygen apparatus.

How far out does the atmosphere extend? No one knows exactly, but meteorologists have identified four roughly separable layers of differing properties: the troposphere, stratosphere, ionosphere, and exosphere (Figure 18-1).

Troposphere.   The troposphere extends to a height ranging from 8 kilometers (5 miles) at

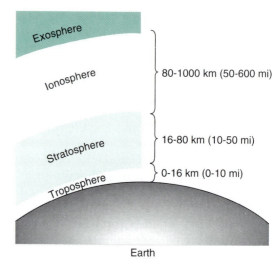

FIGURE 18-1
The atmosphere has several layers.

the poles to about 16 kilometers (10 miles) at the equator. This is the region where practically all weather conditions take place.

Why the difference in altitudes? Tropospheric air is coldest at the poles and so weighs more per unit than warmer, equatorial air. Also, the earth spins on its axis. The fastest speed of rotation, about 1,600 kilometers (1,000 miles) per hour, is at the equator. This offsets the earth's gravitational pull to some extent. The speed of rotation decreases as distance to the poles decreases, just as a person who runs on an inside track can slowly jog along, while someone on an outside track must run swiftly just to keep abreast. As the rotational speed slows, gravity has an increasing effect. In the troposphere, stable air temperature steadily decreases with altitude.

Stratosphere.   Just above the troposphere is the stratosphere, which reaches to about 80 kilometers (50 miles). This is the layer airlines use on some routes for long-range cruising. The cold, thin air is remarkably smooth and clear because vertical movements of warmed air and atmospheric dust particles are largely confined to the layer below. Air travelers may note some pale clouds of ice crystals above cruising altitude, but these are infrequent.

Between the lower reaches of the stratosphere and the troposphere are found winds that vary greatly in force and direction. Most interesting are the *jet streams,* rivers of high-velocity air several kilometers high and more than 150 kilometers wide. They range to thousands of kilometers in length and tend to flow from west to east. A pilot may increase the speed of a plane several hundred kilometers per hour by locating and staying within a jet stream.

In the stratosphere, at an altitude of 16 to 48 kilometers (10 to 30 miles), is a layer of *ozone* that absorbs much of the sun's harmful ultraviolet radiation. The layer is largely composed of molecules that have three atoms of oxygen, rather than the usual two. Certain chemicals released into the atmosphere, called *chlorofluorocarbons* (CFCs), collect unevenly in the ozone layer and destroy the ozone molecules. This greatly reduces the layer's capacity to block ultraviolet rays and so more get through to the earth's surface at various places.

Excess radiation increases the risk of skin cancer, eye damage, and immune system impairment. It can also reduce crop yields and disrupt ocean food chains. International agreements in force require the phasing out of CFCs, widely used in refrigerants, air conditioners, industrial cleaning solvents, and manufacture of some plastics. They are being replaced by less harmful but more expensive chemicals.

Ionosphere.   Beyond a height of about 80 kilometers (50 miles), the stratosphere gradually blends into the ionosphere. In this region are ions—electrically charged particles formed when air molecules are hit by high-energy solar and cosmic rays. These harmful rays are largely absorbed at and below this level. Auroras are sometimes visible. Meteors burn to ashes from friction as they strike scattered air molecules.

The ionosphere is an invaluable aid to radio communication on earth. The earth's surface is curved, but radio waves travel in straight lines. One way of overcoming this problem has been to transmit radio waves to the ionosphere, where they are reflected downward to other points on earth. Since solar "storms" frequently disturb the ionosphere and disrupt communication, this has not proved to be a completely satisfactory solution. Radio and television signals reflected from communications satellites are helping to solve this problem.

Exosphere.   The exosphere begins at about 1,000 kilometers (600 miles) and extends to an undetermined distance. A few air molecules have been detected beyond where the ionosphere adjoins the exosphere and it is probable that others are scattered thousands of kilometers beyond. For practical purposes, this region may be considered the beginning of interplanetary space.

Although scientists estimate the entire weight of our atmosphere at an enormous 4.5 quadrillion metric tons, more than half of all air molecules are concentrated below a height of 5.6 kilometers (3.5 miles). The combination of this enormous pressure and the unimaginably small size of air molecules results in the presence of air in practically everything on or near the earth's surface. Air is found in most soils, water, and even in some rocks. Consider now more effects of this pressure.

Air Pressure

Because the average weight of air is about 1 kilogram per square centimeter, or 14.7 pounds per square inch, at sea level, there are tons of air pressing against the human body. Why, then, are we not crushed? There are two basic reasons. As with water, air at a given level presses with equal force in all directions. Because there is a counteractive force for every force, the pressure is neutralized. Counteractive pressure also takes place in our bodies. Air molecules are so tiny that they dissolve in the blood stream, besides occupying space in our lungs and other body cavities.

Unlike free air, the air in our bodies lags somewhat in building up or reducing counteractive back pressure as atmospheric pressure changes. Have you noticed your ears "pop" while rising quickly in an elevator of a tall building? This happens because air pressure in the inner ear tends to remain the same while the outside air pressure decreases with increased altitude. The result is an uncomfortable outward pushing sensation behind the eardrums. A slow elevator gives more opportunity for inner ear pressure to be adjusted through the Eustachian tube, which connects the inner ear to the nasal passages and mouth.

A similar but much more dangerous situation is faced by deep-sea divers. As they descend into the water, air is pumped under increasing pressure into the diving helmet and suit to counteract increasing water pressure. After working for 20 to 30 minutes, the diver's circulatory system contains an abnormal amount of air. If the diver ascends rapidly to the surface, a region of much lower air pressure, air in the blood may expand and form bubbles. This causes a very painful and possibly fatal condition known as "the bends."

The lag in adjusting to outside atmospheric pressure may also be why some persons complain of aches and pains just before rainy weather. Outside air pressure usually lessens before a storm. If the body's blood pressure remains the same, the blood will now press outward a little more forcibly than usual against body joints and tissues. It is possible that the slight extra pressure may cause discomfort.

Makeup of Air

There are so many references to the earth's "ocean of air" that it is easy for us to get the impression that pure air is a uniform compound, such as pure water. Actually, the air we breathe is a mixture of several separate and distinct gases, of which the three most important to survival are oxygen, nitrogen, and carbon dioxide.

Oxygen makes up about 21 percent of the air, and nitrogen 78 percent. Oxygen is essential to us because it combines readily with sugars in our body cells and releases heat energy. Oxygen is also essential to burning.

Nitrogen is essential to survival because it is necessary for plant growth. It also dilutes the oxygen we breathe. Continual breathing of pure oxygen speeds up metabolic processes to the point where the body cannot get rid of waste products fast enough to survive. The small amount of carbon dioxide in the air, about $\frac{3}{100}$ of 1 percent, is needed for photosynthesis in green plants. Besides these gases, there is less than 1 percent of such gases as argon, krypton, helium, neon, radon, and xenon. All these atmospheric gases are remarkably well mixed by winds up to a height of 8 to 10 kilometers, or 5 to 6 miles.

But this is not all we breathe. As hay-fever sufferers know, there are other substances mixed in the air. Besides the troublesome pollens, there are dust, smoke, salt particles, water vapor, chemicals, spores, bacteria, and viruses.

The Reality of Air

Because pure air has no taste, color, or odor, its study for children, especially primary level pupils, has an elusive quality not present in many other areas. So it is usually good to begin with activities that bring out the tangibility of air. Like other material objects such as automobiles, houses, books, and people, air is a real thing. Children can feel it and see it move things in the form of wind. A blown-up balloon or a soap bubble shows that air takes up space.

A slowly falling parachute demonstrates that air resists motion. A can that is crushed when some inside air is removed shows that air has weight. Sipping liquid through a straw shows this, also. Since many children are confused about how a straw works, consider it for a moment.

When we sip some air out of a straw, the air pressure in the straw is reduced. Since the atmosphere now has more relative pressure, it presses down on the liquid's surface and pushes it up inside the straw's space once occupied by the air.

If you are skeptical, try the following experiments. Place two straws in your mouth, but leave one *outside* the pop bottle or glass. You will find it is now practically impossible to drink the liquid. Why? Air traveling inward through the outside straw restores the pressure in your mouth and drinking straw to normal. For the second experiment, fill a flask with water and seal it tightly with a one-hole stopper containing a glass tube. No matter how hard you sip, no water goes up the tube. There is no air pressing down on the water. With a *two*-hole stopper, though, normal drinking is possible. Air pressure is exerted through the second hole.

As with drinking straws, the events we associate with "suction" are really due to removing or reducing air pressure from one part of a device. Air pressure on all other parts then pushes and performs the work. In vacuum cleaners, for example, the motor whirls a reversed fan that reduces air pressure at the cleaning nozzle. The surrounding air then *pushes* dirt particles into the nozzle. A plumber's force cup, or "suction" cup, works in a similar way. By pressing down on the pliable rubber cup, most of the air inside is forced out. Air from all other sides pushes against the cup's exterior and holds it fast to whatever surface it has been pressed.

For further ways to show the reality of air through its properties, see the experiences section.

[3] WEATHER   *Experiences 632*

Weather is the condition of the lower atmosphere at a given time and place. If you have been rained on while expecting a sunny afternoon, you know how quickly it can change. Weather changes happen because changes in temperature, moisture, pressure, and other variables alter the way air "behaves." We'll examine some of these variables next, one at a time.

Causes of Winds

At early morning off an African coast, hundreds of fishing boats point out to sea as a fresh land breeze fills their colorful lateen sails. The boats return in the afternoon with sails taut from a sea breeze blowing in the opposite direction. You have probably experienced a similar shift of winds at the seashore or by a large lake. How does this happen? (See Figure 18-2.)

Temperature Differences.   You may recall from the heat energy chapter that warmed air expands and is pushed up by denser, colder air that rushes in and replaces it. Winds are caused by the unequal heating and cooling of the earth's surface. During the day, solar radiation is absorbed by the sea and land. The land heats up much faster. One reason is that sunlight penetrates only a short distance below the land's surface, but penetrates more deeply into water. Another reason is the higher heat capacity of water.

After a short period of sunlight, air immediately above the earth is heated by the ground and begins expanding. Cooler, heavier air from the sea rushes in and pushes the lighter air upward. The reverse occurs at night and until the following morning. During this period, the land cools quickly and stays cool, while the sea remains relatively warmer. As air warmed by contact with the water expands,

Day   Night

FIGURE 18-2
Winds are caused by unequal heating and cooling of the earth's surface.

it is pushed upward by cooler air rushing in from the cooler land.

These air movements are not confined to land and sea settings. The same basic air movements take place between any surfaces that have a temperature difference. As temperature differences increase, the resulting wind force increases. This is one reason why a large fire is so destructive. It sets up a powerful, localized wind that fans and spreads the flames.

Prevailing Winds. The world's prevailing winds are caused by the same unequal heating of the earth's surface on a grand scale. But the earth's rotation adds a factor. If the earth did not rotate, heavy, cold air at the poles would simply flow due south and north, and push up warmed, expanding equatorial air. The rotation (named the *Coriolis effect*) results in a wind deflection to the right in the northern hemisphere. A deflection to the *left* occurs in the southern hemisphere.

You can see why this happens with a globe and some chalk. Rotate the globe from west to east. While it is moving, draw a line from the North Pole due south toward the equator. Note that the line curves to the right. Draw a line from the South Pole and the curve is reversed. (We will return to the Coriolis effect in a later section.)

Winds Aloft. Detailed understanding of wind patterns requires much more background than can be given here. For example, we have briefly discussed jet streams. There are, however, other winds aloft. It is possible for an airplane pilot to meet a wind blowing from one direction at one altitude and another blowing from another direction higher up. You will not want to explore this subject in detail at the elementary level. Still, it will be worthwhile to help pupils learn that wind direction aloft may differ from surface wind direction.

To calculate winds aloft, meteorologists use measuring instruments to observe small, helium-filled balloons as they rise to various altitudes. A cruder method is to observe cloud movements with a *nephoscope,* a circular mirror marked with the points of a compass. Properly aligned, this instrument can show children the direction of cloud movement as the cloud reflection moves across the mirror.

Air Temperature

In parts of Southern California and Mexico, it is sometimes possible in winter to observe snowy mountain peaks while lying on a warm, sunny beach. Children are curious about conditions like this ("Aren't the mountain peaks closer to the sun?"). Most adults know that air is colder at higher altitudes. But why?

Temperature and Altitude.   One reason air is colder at higher altitudes is the varying distance of air molecules from the earth's surface. Air molecules closest to the earth are warmed more easily by conduction and heat waves radiated from the earth's surface than those farther away.

Second, as we get closer to sea level, more and more molecules are piled up. This increased weight compresses the air. With reduced space for movement, there is more energy exchange among molecules as they collide. So the heat energy in the denser molecule "population" is concentrated into a relatively low, dense layer.

There is also a third reason. As warmed air is pushed up, it expands and cools as it meets lower air pressure with the increased altitude. Whatever heat energy is contained in the original air parcel is dissipated throughout an ever larger volume.

The combined effect of these causes makes pushed-up air cool about 2°C for each 300 meters, or 3.5°F for each 1,000 feet. As pushed-down air is compressed, the opposite happens.

Temperature and Pollution.   As you saw, the atmosphere is a gigantic greenhouse that slows the loss of heat received from solar radiation. Fortunately, the earth loses and gains about the same amount of heat each day. A narrow temperature range enables life to continue. Since the Industrial Revolution, though, conditions have been developing that may upset this delicate balance.

Most scientists think the lower atmosphere is gradually becoming slightly warmer through increased carbon dioxide from the burning of fuels such as coal and oil. As light waves from the sun warm the earth's surface, heat waves going from the surface into the atmosphere are partly blocked by carbon dioxide. Some of the heat energy cannot escape into space. This causes the atmosphere to lose slightly less heat than it gains from solar radiation. Recent data seem to support a global warming trend.

Yet a few scientists say it is also possible that the trend may be reversing. To them, the data suggest that the earth's atmosphere is cooling very gradually. In recent years, there has been a large increase in air pollution throughout the world. The greater number of suspended pollutants in the air may be causing more and more sunlight to be reflected away from the earth *before* it reaches the earth's surface. If true, this could overcome the effect of the increased carbon dioxide.

Although not everyone agrees about what is happening to the air temperature, a definite trend in either direction could bring trouble. An average increase of a few degrees could turn huge, fertile land areas into semi-deserts, and an average temperature drop of 4° to 5°C could launch another ice age.

Evaporation and Humidity

Many children understand in a limited way the concepts of evaporation and humidity. But they don't grasp how the two are related. This section can help you deal with their conceptions.

Evaporation.   In an earlier chapter, you saw that heat and atmospheric pressure affect an evaporating liquid. Increased heat energy increases the speed of molecules. Additional speed enables molecules to overcome the cohesive forces of nearby molecules, and greater numbers leave the liquid's surface than before. Any decrease of atmospheric pressure also affects evaporation because it tends to "take the lid off." The counterforce of air molecules pressing down on the surface of an evaporating liquid becomes weaker, and more evaporation takes place. This is a reason mountain climbers must be especially watchful of dehydration.

It is easy to see why increasing a liquid's surface area increases the rate of evaporation. There is greater exposure to the air above and a higher probability of more molecules escaping. This is why you have to add water more often to a rectangular aquarium than to a fish bowl of equal volume.

The wind, too, speeds up evaporation. When air just above the surface of an evaporating fluid becomes quickly saturated, the wind blows it away and replaces it with drier air.

Humidity. Another factor influencing evaporation is *humidity*—the amount of moisture already present in the air. On humid days, we feel sticky and uncomfortable because our perspiration evaporates very slowly. We may turn on an electric fan to feel more comfortable. Moving air from a fan cools us because it speeds up evaporation of perspiration from the skin.

Without an evaporating liquid, *a fan has no cooling effect at all.* You can see this by putting a thermometer in front of a whirling electric fan. There is no difference in the before and after readings. But dampen some cotton and stick it to the thermometer bulb. The rapidly evaporating water will now cause a noticeable drop in temperature.

The moisture content of air changes considerably from time to time. The capacity of air to hold moisture depends on its temperature—warm air holds more moisture than cooler air. The percentage of moisture in air at a certain temperature, compared to all it could hold at that temperature, is called its *relative humidity*. During a period of low relative humidity, our skin moisture evaporates more quickly than it can be effectively replaced. This results in dry, chapped skin.

One reason we have more colds in winter may be directly related to the relative humidity of air in our homes. The cool air of winter holds comparatively little moisture. As it is warmed by heaters, it expands and becomes even drier. Unless the home heating system is equipped to give additional moisture, the air becomes increasingly dry. The protective mucous film that coats the delicate nasal membrane evaporates, and we become more open to infections.

Relative humidity is often measured with a wet-and-dry bulb thermometer apparatus called a *hygrometer.* Two identical thermometers are placed next to each other. The bulb of one instrument is enclosed in a wet cotton wick that is immersed in water. The wet-bulb thermometer is fanned rapidly until its reading steadies at some lower point. As water evaporates from the wick, it is continually replaced by water traveling upward through the wick by capillary action. Any difference in thermometer readings is translated into the percentage of relative humidity by consulting a reference table.

Condensation

Dew. Many mornings we see dew drops glistening on lawns, parked automobiles, spider webs, and other surfaces. When the ground cools during the night, its temperature may fall below that of the surrounding air. As the surrounding air loses some heat energy, its molecules slow down. Water vapor molecules in the air slow enough to be attracted to, and condense on, a cool nearby surface. The same thing happens when water droplets form on a cold pop bottle or cold water pipe.

Remember, relative humidity varies with air temperature. Any parcel of air containing some water vapor becomes saturated if cooled enough. The loss of heat energy slows down molecular speed and reduces the range of molecular movement. The attractions of water molecules for one another now draw them together into visible drops.

Dew Point. The temperature at which condensation takes place is called the *dew point*. In very humid air, as in a steamy shower room, water vapor condenses on walls and mirrors although they may be only several degrees cooler than the air. Comparatively dry desert air may have to be cooled much more before reaching its dew point.

A forthcoming activity calls for observation of dew on the outside of a shiny metal can containing ice cubes and water. If low humidity exists in the classroom, very little or no moisture may collect on the can unless the can temperature can be reduced. To do so, just add a few spoons of salt to the water. This will cause the ice cubes to melt faster and so reduce the temperature even more.

By substituting dry ice (frozen carbon dioxide), the can temperature will drop below freezing. Condensation will occur in the form of frost. This is what happens in the freezing compartment of refrigerators, causing the need for periodic defrosting. Below-freezing temperatures also produce frost in place of dew on the ground.

Fog.   We may see fog when the surface temperature is low enough to cool air that is a short distance above the ground to its dew point. In this case, water vapor condenses on tiny specks of airborne dust and remains suspended.

Sometimes fog results from the unequal cooling of land and water. Such fog is common over a lake in summer. Cool air from the land flows over warm, moist air just above the lake. As the warmer air cools to its dew point, condensation occurs and we see fog. Fog can be considered a low cloud.

Clouds and Cloud Types.   Clouds at higher altitudes are formed in several ways, but all involve a parcel of air that is cooled to its saturation, or dew, point. In one method, wind may blow moist air up a mountain slope. As the air rises, it expands because of decreasing air pressure, cools, and condenses on airborne dust particles. If the dew point is below freezing, tiny ice crystals may form.

Sometimes air is pushed aloft when two huge air masses merge. The cooler, heavier air mass will push under the warmer, lighter mass. Again, expansion, cooling, and condensation take place.

A third method of cloud formation happens when heat from the ground develops convection currents. The affected air near the ground becomes increasingly heated and is pushed up by heavier, cooler surrounding air. The rising air finally cools and its moisture condenses.

When enough moisture is present, the tiny, constantly moving droplets within a cloud collide from time to time and form larger drops. These may fall as rain. In freezing temperatures, ice crystals collect and fall as snow.

Knowing the air temperature and its dew point can enable you or upper-grade pupils to roughly calculate cloud heights. Here is how it is done. Suppose the outdoor air temperature is now 88°F. Stir a thermometer around in a metal can of ice water. At the exact instant water droplets occur on the can, read the temperature of the immersed thermometer. This is the dew point. Say it reads 74°F, which makes a difference of 14°F between the two figures. Rising air cools at about 3.5°F for each 1,000 feet of altitude. Dividing 14 by 3.5 gives a quotient of 4. Multiply this figure by 1,000. The bases of nearby clouds should be about 4,000 feet above you. (With metric measures, use 2°C for 3.5°F and 300 meters for 1,000 feet.)

Although experts have invented more than 200 cloud classifications, even young children can be taught to recognize three basic cloud forms. *Cirrus* clouds are high, wispy formations of ice crystals. *Cumulus* clouds are white, fluffy, and usually associated with clear visibility and fair weather. *Stratus* clouds are lower, darker formations that appear as a dense layer. These clouds may blanket the entire sky and precipitate rain within a short time. (See Figure 18-3.)

Water Cycle.   You can see that condensation is the opposite of evaporation. Together, they form the water cycle. Powered by the sun, an immense but finite volume of water over the earth constantly evaporates, condenses, and falls without apparent end.

Air Masses and Cyclones

At one time, it was thought that air pressure over any one point was always the same. We

FIGURE 18-3
Three basic cloud forms: (*a*) cirrus,
(*b*) cumulus, (*c*) stratus.

now know otherwise. Huge masses of air are continually on the move over the earth, bringing changes in pressure and weather.

Air Masses.   An air mass is a huge volume of air that picks up distinctive temperature and humidity conditions from the surface under-neath. These conditions are fairly uniform throughout the mass, which may cover thousands of square kilometers or miles.

An ocean air mass is typically moist. Air over land is drier. Air near the polar regions is cold, while that near the equator is warm. So four different kinds of air masses are possible: cold and dry, cold and moist, warm and dry, and warm and moist. Figure 18-4 shows the origins of four kinds of air masses that often move into the continental United States.

Cold air is heavier than warm air. Dry air is heavier than moist air. Just as water flows from a high point to a lower one, air flows from a region of relatively high pressure to one of lower pressure. But because of the earth's rotation, the flow is not in a straight line.

Cyclones and Anticyclones.   The Coriolis effect causes air masses and the general circulation of air to move in gigantic spirals called *cyclones* and *anticyclones*. (Cyclones should not be confused with tornadoes—small violent, twisting air currents that come from a mixture of super-heated and cold air.) A cyclone is a larger area of relative lower pressure with the point of lowest pressure in the center; it is also called a *low*. An *anticyclone* is a large area of relatively high pressure with the highest pressure in the center; it is also called a *high*.

In the northern hemisphere, air movements spiral counterclockwise toward the center of a low. In a high, they spiral clockwise away from the center of highest pressure. These movements are reversed in the southern hemisphere. Highs and lows may move hundreds of kilometers a day. A typical pattern of movement in the United States is from west to east.

Lows often bring bad weather. This is because cold or dry heavier air moves in and pushes up warm or moist lighter air. The moisture condenses when the air rises to its dew-point altitude and falls as rain or snow.

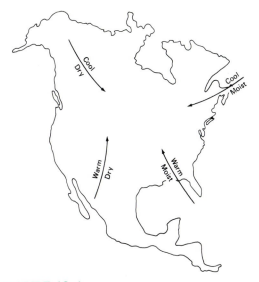

FIGURE 18-4
Four common air masses.

Highs usually bring more pleasant weather. As cool or dry heavier air spirals downward from the center of a high, it warms about 2°C (3.5°F) for each 300 meters (1,000 feet) loss of altitude. As it warms, the mass of air is able to hold more and more moisture without it condensing. The result is usually clear, sunny weather.

Measuring Pressure. Highs and lows are detected by noting changes in cloud, temperature, and wind patterns. However, the most important changes observed are those in air pressure. An instrument used for measuring air pressure is the *barometer.* There are two kinds.

In a *mercurial* barometer, a glass tube about 90 centimeters (36 inches) long and closed at one end is filled with mercury and inverted into a dish of mercury. While some of the liquid runs out, a column of about 76 centi-

meters (30 inches) remains. This tells the force of air pressing on the liquid's surface. As air pressure increases, the column rises higher into the vacuum above. The reverse takes place with reduced pressure.

Since mercurial barometers are easily broken and cumbersome, most weather observers use the *aneroid* barometer (Figure 18-5). This consists of a thin, flexible, metal box from which air has been largely removed. As air pressure presses on it with varying degrees of force, the box moves in and out accordingly. A cleverly linked leverage system transfers these movements to a movable needle on a dial.

Because air pressure also changes with altitude, aneroid barometers are used in many airplanes to indicate altitude. This is done by merely changing the dial to read in a unit of height rather than one of pressure. Such a barometer is called an *altimeter.*

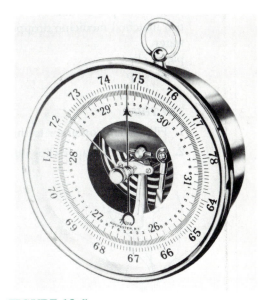

FIGURE 18-5
Aneroid barometer.

of the stick. How does the print look now? Try drops of soapy water and alcohol, also.

inferring   **E.** Can you match up a liquid with its drop print? Can you tell from how high each drop fell? Ask a partner to make drop prints as you did. Do not watch as the prints are made.

hypothesizing   **F.** What other liquids can you test? How do you think they will compare with your first liquids?

TEACHING COMMENT

PREPARATION AND BACKGROUND

Any liquid has the property of cohesion—the tendency for its molecules to stick together. The cohesion of water is strong compared with some other liquids. This is why water forms a bulge that rises above the rim of an overly full glass. Soap weakens the cohesive power of water, so the bulge of slightly soapy water is noticeably lower. That of alcohol is lower still; its cohesion is relatively weak. This is one reason it evaporates so fast.

By manipulating the suggested liquids, children can develop a beginning awareness of their differences. In later schooling, they can learn the theoretical principles behind their early observations.

Try to supply three small, identical, clear plastic vials. Drugstores dispense pills in such vials, so they are easily gotten. Two identical medicine droppers also are needed to compare drop size. A dropper should be cleaned each time a different liquid is used.

GENERALIZATION

Some liquids seem to stick together more strongly than others.

SAMPLE PERFORMANCE OBJECTIVES

Process: The child can observe and compare the relative sizes of drops of water, soapy water, and alcohol.
Knowledge: The child can predict the relative sizes of drops of two liquids after first observing how high each bulges in the filled container.

FOR YOUNGER CHILDREN

Most younger pupils are successful in manipulating the materials and making keen observations. They probably will not be able to count well enough to do Discovery Problem C.

■ INVESTIGATION: How Much Water Bottles Hold

Bottles, jars, and other containers have many different shapes. Sometimes it is hard to tell if one holds more than another.

EXPLORATORY PROBLEM

How can you find out which of two different-shaped containers holds more water?

NEEDED

five small, different-shaped containers   small funnel
plastic bowl of water   large jar with straight sides
small plastic pill vial   five rubber bands

TRY THIS

1. Fill one small container with water.
2. Pour the water from this container into a large jar.
3. Mark the water level by ringing the jar with a rubber band. Then empty the jar (Figure 18-8).

Rubber
band

FIGURE 18-8

4. Fill another small container with water.
5. Pour this water into the large jar. Compare the new water level with the rubber-band marker. Which of the two small containers holds more water?

DISCOVERY PROBLEMS

measuring   **A.** How else can you tell if one container holds more than another?

classifying   **B.** How can you put the five containers in order, from smallest to largest?

inferring   **C.** Pick two different-shaped containers. Fill one with water about halfway up. Suppose you were to pour this water into the second container. How far up do you think the water would rise? Ring the second container with a rubber band to mark your estimate. Then find out. Try this with other containers, also.

measuring

predicting

D. Use a small plastic vial to fill a container with water. How many vials of water does it hold? Can you predict how many vials of water each of the other containers will hold?

predicting

E. Ring an odd-shaped container with a rubber-band marker about halfway up. Can you predict how many vials of water are needed to reach it? Try this with the marker at other places on the container. Try other containers, also.

inferring

F. What other odd-shaped containers can you find for harder predictions?

TEACHING COMMENT

PREPARATION AND BACKGROUND

The foregoing activities may help young pupils learn to *conserve* the volumes of liquids or pourable solids, such as rice or sand. That is, the child may be helped to realize that a given volume of a liquid stays the same, even though its surface level may change when poured into different-shaped containers. Notice in several activities how the child must compensate for the irregularity of a container's shape to properly estimate how much it will hold.

Small bottles or jars—180 to 360 milliliters, or 6 to 12 fluid ounces—may be filled quickly. Vitamin and olive bottles, and mustard and small pickle jars, often come in this size range. If such containers are used, a plastic pill vial will be handy for measuring and pouring water. A funnel will help prevent spills. The large jar used in the exploratory activity should be larger than any other container.

GENERALIZATION

The volumes of different-shaped containers may be compared in several ways; the same volume of water may rise to different levels in different containers.

SAMPLE PERFORMANCE OBJECTIVES

Process: The child can measure and order, from least to most capacity, a set of five containers.

Knowledge: When shown two irregularly shaped bottles containing the same volume of water but different water levels, the child can explain that one reason for the difference in levels may be the bottle shapes.

FOR OLDER CHILDREN

Older pupils may perform the preceding activities much more accurately. Let them calibrate the large glass jar in the exploratory activity. Have them place a strip of masking tape the long way on the side of the jar. Let them pour water into the bottle from a small container whose volume is known, such as a measuring cup, and make a pencil mark on the tape for each desired interval.

■ INVESTIGATION: How to Measure Volume with Water

Rocks and other solid objects have many different shapes. Sometimes it is hard to tell which of two different-shaped objects is larger; that is, takes up more space. (The amount of space an object takes up is its volume.)

EXPLORATORY PROBLEM

How can you compare the volumes of small solid objects?

NEEDED

five small, different-shaped rocks   ruler
oil base modeling clay   large jar with straight sides
small lead fishing sinker   water
masking tape and pencil   fork or spoon

TRY THIS

1. Fasten a strip of masking tape on a jar the long way.

2. Half-fill the jar with water.

3. Put one rock into the jar. Mark the water level on the tape with a pencil.

4. Remove the rock with a fork or spoon.

5. Put a second rock into the jar. Compare the new water level with the pencil mark (Figure 18-9).

FIGURE 18-9

DISCOVERY PROBLEMS

classifying   **A.** How can you put the rocks in order from smallest to largest?

inferring   **B.** Make a clay ball the size of some rock. Where will the water level be if you put it into the jar? Mark the tape to show your estimate, then find out.

inferring **C.** Suppose you form the same clay ball into another shape. Where do you think the water level will be? Try many different shapes.

inferring
observing **D.** Suppose you break the same clay piece into two parts. Where do you think the water level will be? What happens to the water level when you break the clay into more than two parts?

inferring **E.** Will a heavy clay ball make the water level rise higher than a lighter one? Make two clay balls the same size, but have a lead weight in the middle of one ball. Try each ball and find out.

measuring **F.** How much larger is one rock compared to another? With a ruler and pencil, make evenly spaced marks on the jar's tape strip. Call each pencil mark one "unit." Compare the difference in water-level units before and after a rock is put in the jar. How much difference in units is there between your smallest and largest rock?

predicting **G.** Get other small objects. How well can you predict the volume of each in units?

TEACHING COMMENT

PREPARATION AND BACKGROUND

This investigation may help some of your pupils learn to conserve volume as measured by displaced water. That is, the space an object takes up is determined by its overall surface, rather than shape, weight, or number of parts. Probably most of your pupils will not be stable conservers of this concept for several years. Use oil base modeling clay to prevent dissolving in water.

Notice that arbitrary units, based on ruler markings, are used for Problems D through F. If you have a small graduated container marked in milliliters or ounces, it may be used instead to calibrate the large jar. The measurement principle remains the same.

GENERALIZATION

The volumes of different-shaped solid objects may be compared by the water each displaces.

SAMPLE PERFORMANCE OBJECTIVES

Process: The child can measure the difference in volume between two rocks by using "water-level units."
Knowledge: The child can explain that the volume of water an object displaces is determined by the volume of space the object occupies.

FOR YOUNGER CHILDREN

The Exploratory Problem and Problems A through D may be used as readiness experiences.

▪ INVESTIGATION: Things That Float in Water

Can you tell just by looking whether something will float in water? What kinds of objects float? What kinds of objects sink?

EXPLORATORY PROBLEM

How can you find out which small objects will float?

NEEDED

plastic bowl	salt
bag of small objects to test	ruler
oil base modeling clay	spoon
large washers	paper towels
kitchen foil, 15 centimeters (6 inches) square	

TRY THIS

1. Half-fill a plastic bowl with water.
2. Empty the bag of small objects on your desk. Put those you think will float into one group. Put those you think will sink in another group.
3. Place all the objects from one group into the water. Observe what happens, then remove the objects. Do the same thing with the other group of objects.

FIGURE 18-10

DISCOVERY PROBLEMS

inferring **A.** How many objects did what you thought? What are the objects like that floated? sank?

experimenting **B.** What can you do to sink the objects that floated?

experimenting   **C.** What can you do to float the objects that sank?

experimenting   **D.** In what ways can you get a piece of foil to float? sink?

experimenting   **E.** How can you make a foil boat?

experimenting   **F.** How many washers can your foil boat carry? What can you do to make it carry more washers?

experimenting   **G.** How can you get a piece of clay to float?

inferring   **H.** Make a clay boat the same size as your foil boat. Which do you think will carry more washers?

measuring   **I.** Can you make two foil boats that will carry, from the first try, exactly the same weight? two clay boats that will carry the same weight from the first try?

experimenting   **J.** What can you get to float in salt water that cannot float in fresh water?

inferring   **K.** Can you find anything that will float in fresh water and sink in salt water?

TEACHING COMMENT

PREPARATION AND BACKGROUND

Children can develop some understanding in this investigation about the buoyancy of different objects in water and how the density of water affects buoyancy. You might also want children to explore liquids other than water.

A bag of small objects to test for floating might include a wooden checker, pencil, key, marble, plastic objects, pieces of leather, rubber eraser, and small toy figures. The children can bring in much more. Any clay should be the oil-based kind, such as Clay-cene or Plasticine, that does not dissolve in water.

Uniform objects other than large washers may be used to measure the weight-carrying capacity of children's boats. Identical marbles, pennies, or small pieces of ceramic tile work well. To avoid rust, be sure all steel washers are dried before they are stored.

GENERALIZATION

Objects that are light for their size float; adding salt to water makes floating easier.

SAMPLE PERFORMANCE OBJECTIVES

Process: Through measuring, the child can construct two near-identical boats with near-identical weight capacities.
Knowledge: When shown some new objects, the child can predict which will float.

FOR YOUNGER CHILDREN

Activities A through G have been done successfully by primary pupils. The other activities that involve careful measuring and counting will be difficult and are not recommended.

☐ ACTIVITY: What Happens to Water Pressure with Depth?

NEEDED

tall, empty milk carton   nail (or sharp pencil)
sink   water

TRY THIS

1. Punch a nail hole in the carton's side, halfway up, from the inside out.

2. Punch another hole above it and a third hole below it, from inside out.

3. Cover all three holes tightly with three fingers. Fill the carton with water. Keep it in the sink.
    a. If you take away your fingers, what do you think will happen?

4. Remove your fingers quickly from the three holes.
    b. What happened? In what part of the carton was the water pressure the greatest?

    (*Teaching Comment:* Sometimes the torn edges of the holes will impede the flow of water. Punching the holes from the inside out makes this less likely.)

☐ ACTIVITY: How High Can Water Flow Compared to Where It Comes From?

NEEDED

rubber tube, 1 meter (or 1 yard) long   container of water
funnel that fits the tube   sink

TRY THIS

1. Stick the funnel end tightly into a tube end. Do this activity in a sink.

2. Hold up the funnel. Have someone pour water into it.

3. When water comes out of the tube, pinch it off.

4. Have someone fill the funnel with water. Keep the tube end pinched off.
    a. How high will you be able to hold the tube end and still have water come out? Higher than the funnel? as high? lower?

5. Let go of the tube end. Try holding it at different heights.
    b. What did you find?

☐ ACTIVITY: What Happens to the Water Table When Water Is Taken from Wells?

NEEDED

large, deep glass bowl   small paper cup
sand or loose soil   plastic bowl
can open at both ends   crayon

TRY THIS

1. Put a small amount of sand in the bottom of the bowl. Then place the can upright in the center.

2. Fill in the space around the can with sand. Make the sand almost as high as the can.

3. Slowly pour water into the bowl. Stop when it reaches halfway to the sand surface. This is the water table. Mark its level on the glass outside the bowl (Figure 18-11).
   a. Where is the water level inside the can "well"?

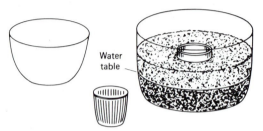

FIGURE 18-11

4. Remove some water from the well with a small paper cup.
   b. What happens to the water level inside the well? What happens to the water table?

■ INVESTIGATION: The Filtering of Polluted Water

Most cities have water treatment plants to clean, or *purify*, their drinking water. The unclean water is first pumped to a large settling tank, where it stays for a while. Some of the dirt and other polluting particles in the water settle to the bottom. The cleaner water on top then goes into a filtering tank, which has thick layers of sand and gravel. Sometimes there is a layer of charcoal between these layers. As the water filters through, still more polluting materials are left behind.

It's not easy to clean polluted water, even by filtering. You can find out more about this yourself.

EXPLORATORY PROBLEM

How can you clean polluted water by filtering?

NEEDED

cut-off pint milk carton	clean sand
charcoal briquette	cotton
small glass jar	nail
jar of soil water	small paper bag

TRY THIS

1. Punch some holes with a nail in the bottom of a cutoff milk carton.

2. Spread some cotton inside on the carton bottom. Add some clean sand.

3. Put crushed charcoal on top of the sand. (To crush charcoal, put a briquette into a small bag. Pound it with a rock.) Then add another layer of sand.

4. Place the filter on top of a small glass jar.

5. Pour some *clean tap water* into your filter. (This will pack the materials more tightly together.)

6. Prepare a jar of soil water. Put a handful of soil into a jar of water and mix. Let the water settle for a half hour.

7. Pour some soil water from the top of the jar into the filter. Watch the filtered water trickle into the small jar (Figure 18-12).

FIGURE 18-12

DISCOVERY PROBLEMS

observing   **A.** How clean is the filtered water compared to the soil water?

observing   **B.** How clean would the water get with fewer filtering materials? with just one filtering material?

observing   **C.** Will your filter remove ink or food coloring?

observing   **D.** Does the order in which you have your filter materials matter?

experimenting   **E.** Would more or other materials work better? How else could you improve your filter?

TEACHING COMMENT

PREPARATION AND BACKGROUND

Caution pupils not to drink their filtered water. They should know that a chemical is added to filtered water in city water plants to kill germs that survive filtering.

Your pupils may enjoy having a contest to determine the best filter. They may need to be reminded that everyone should filter samples of the same polluted water.

GENERALIZATION

Some water pollutants may be removed by filtering the water through layers of different permeable materials.

SAMPLE PERFORMANCE OBJECTIVES

Process: The child can experiment to find ways that improve the efficiency of a simple water filter.
Knowledge: The child can make a water filter with simple materials that removes larger particles from polluted water.

☐ ACTIVITY: How Can You Distill Water?

NEEDED

teakettle	small can, open at one end
salty water	food coloring
aluminum pie plate	hot plate

TRY THIS

1. Put some salty water into a teakettle. Add several drops of food coloring.
2. Put the teakettle on a hot plate and turn it on.
3. Place a small can loosely over the teakettle spout. Place the pie pan under the can.
4. When the kettle steams, collect the water drops as they drip from the can. Turn off the hot plate. Wait until the collected water cools and then examine it.
   a. Can you taste any salt? Can you see any food coloring?
   b. What does distilling water do to impurities in the water?

(*Teaching Comment:* Caution—be sure that the can is loosely placed over the teakettle spout, so the spout remains open. Steam must be free to leave the teakettle, condense inside the can, and fall into the pie pan.)

SECTION 2
Air and Its Properties
[*Background 598*]

■ INVESTIGATION: Where Air Can Be

Air is found everywhere on the earth. Air can go into tiny places. But can air get inside everything? What things do you think have some air inside? do not have air inside?

EXPLORATORY PROBLEM

How can you find out what things have some air inside?

NEEDED

plastic bowl half-filled with water	cracker
piece of brick, leather, soft wood	stone
sand	coin
several kinds of fabrics	orange peel

TRY THIS

1. Put a piece of brick into a bowl of water (Figure 18-13).

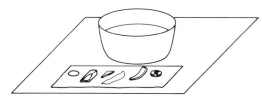

FIGURE 18-13

2. Watch for tiny bubbles on the brick. These are air bubbles. This shows there was some air inside the brick.

3. Put a coin into the water. You will probably see no bubbles. This shows the coin probably had no air inside.

DISCOVERY PROBLEMS

observing   **A.** Does a piece of cloth have air in it? Do some kinds of cloth have more air in them than others?

observing   **B.** Does leather have air in it? Can a soft piece of wood have air in it?

observing   **C.** Does a cracker have air in it? does an orange peel?

observing   **D.** Can a stone have air in it? Try several different kinds.

experimenting   **E.** Does sand have air in it? How can you find out?

inferring   **F.** What else do you think might have air in it? What else might not have air in it?

TEACHING COMMENT

PREPARATION AND BACKGROUND

Some soft materials show dramatically that they contain air if squeezed under water. Soft pine, balsa wood, and leather are examples. Pliers or tongs may serve as squeezers, if needed.

The spaces between sand or soil particles commonly contain much air. Surface air bubbles may easily be seen if water is poured into a small jar with sand inside.

(While water also usually contains air, the volume is small compared to that found in the spaces between sand particles.)

GENERALIZATION

Air can be found almost everywhere. Most porous materials contain some air.

SAMPLE PERFORMANCE OBJECTIVES

Process: The child can infer which objects are likely to contain air by observing their physical properties.
Knowledge: The child can describe the properties of objects that contain or do not contain some air.

FOR OLDER CHILDREN

Older children can be challenged to detect if water contains air. They may look for bubbles in the water that rise to the surface and break. This can be seen in standing water, but is more quickly observable as water becomes heated.

Also, let them boil some aquarium water in a teakettle to remove most of the air. After the boiled water cools again to the aquarium temperature, a goldfish may be placed in the water. Have them compare the more rapid gill movements of the fish with those observed before in the aquarium. Return the fish to the aquarium after several minutes to avoid harming it.

■ INVESTIGATION: Soap Bubbles

Have you ever blown soap bubbles? If so, how big was your biggest bubble? how small was your smallest bubble?

EXPLORATORY PROBLEM

How can you blow soap bubbles?

NEEDED

paper cup of bubble liquid	soda can with ends removed
bendable plastic straw	paper cup half full of water
small piece of cardboard	liquid detergent or soap
scissors	glycerin
6-inch thin wire	spoon

TRY THIS

1. Cut the straw end into four parts. Use the end that bends.

2. Push back the four parts as shown in the drawing (Figure 18-14).

3. Bend the straw into a *J* shape.

4. Dip the cut end into the bubble liquid.

5. Put the other straw end into your mouth and blow gently.

FIGURE 18-14

DISCOVERY PROBLEMS

observing **A.** What different kinds of bubbles can you blow? How big a bubble can you make? how small?

observing **B.** How many bubbles can you blow with one dip of your pipe? How few?

observing **C.** What do you see when you look at a bubble? when you look through a bubble?

predicting **D.** What will happen if you catch a bubble in your hand? What will happen if your hand is soapy?

experimenting **E.** How can you make a bubble floating in air stay up? Move to your left? right? up? (*Hint:* How might a piece of cardboard help you?)

experimenting **F.** Bend pieces of wire into loops and other shapes. Dip them into the liquid and blow. What kinds of bubbles do they make?

experimenting **G.** Make extra-large bubbles. Take a soda can that has no top or bottom. Dip one end into bubble liquid. How big a bubble can you make?

experimenting **H.** Can you make a better bubble liquid? Mix a capful of liquid detergent or soap in a half-cup of water. How does it work? Will adding some glycerin make bigger bubbles? How much works best?

TEACHING COMMENTS

PREPARATION AND BACKGROUND

Use either a commercial bubble-blowing liquid or prepare your own from liquid detergent. Many teachers have gotten excellent results from Dawn or Joy liquid detergent. Both products are made by Procter and Gamble. A 1-part detergent to 16-parts water mix works well. Add some glycerin (sold at drugstores) for even bigger bubbles. Mix thoroughly.

This investigation is done best outdoors. However, when pupils try to steer their bubbles in a certain direction by waving a piece of cardboard, a near-windless condition is needed. On a windy day this activity can be done indoors in a more limited way. Pupils can discover that a bubble stays up best if the cardboard or hand is waved rapidly from side to side *over* the bubble. This decreases the air pressure over the bubble and so the surrounding air rushes in, holding up the bubble. Likewise, for lateral motion, a bubble will "follow" a waved cardboard.

GENERALIZATION

A soap bubble is made up of air inside and soap outside; big bubbles have more air inside than small ones. Moving air can make soap bubbles move.

SAMPLE PERFORMANCE OBJECTIVES

Process: When given the materials, the child can vary the mixture of a bubble liquid to produce larger bubbles.
Knowledge: The child can explain that a large bubble contains more air than a smaller one.

FOR OLDER CHILDREN

Older pupils enjoy and profit from an experimental approach to this investigation. Have them test the relative effectiveness of several commercial or their own bubble preparations: Whose makes the biggest bubbles? Whose bubbles last longest? Let them change the proportions of your prepared mixture or substitute other ingredients. For example, adding glycerin to bubble mix makes giant, long-lasting bubbles.

Invite them to compare several kinds of commercial bubble pipes and plastic rings ("wands") for making bubbles. Or, encourage them to invent their own devices. Challenge them to land soap bubbles inside a designed target area outdoors. To do so, they will have to consider wind velocity, the height from which they release bubbles, and bubble sizes.

■ INVESTIGATION: Parachutes

How does a parachute help someone who jumps from an airplane? What makes a parachute fall slowly? You can learn more about real parachutes by making small ones.

EXPLORATORY PROBLEM

How can you make a small parachute?

NEEDED

thin plastic (clothes cover)   sticky tape
thin cloth (scrap cotton)   scissors
string   modeling clay

TRY THIS

1. Cut a square the size of a handkerchief from thin plastic.
2. Cut a small hole in the center of the plastic.
3. Cut four strings the same size.
4. Tie one string end to each corner of the plastic.
5. Tie the other string ends together in a knot.
6. Shape a small ball of clay around the knot (Figure 18-15).

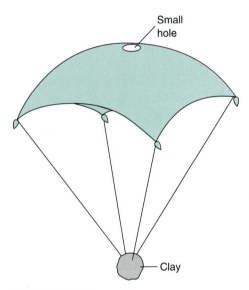

FIGURE 18-15

DISCOVERY PROBLEMS

observing
A. Try out your parachute on the playground. Drop it from the top of the play slide. Then, roll it up loosely and throw it into the air. Which way works better?

hypothesizing
B. Suppose you cover the hole with sticky tape. What difference might this make?

hypothesizing
C. Suppose you make the hole larger. What difference might this make?

hypothesizing
D. Suppose you add more clay to the ball. What difference might this make?

experimenting **E.** How can you make a parachute that will fall slower than the one you have now? How will you compare them so it is fair?

experimenting **F.** How can you get a small and large parachute to fall equally fast?

experimenting **G.** What is the smallest parachute you can make that will work?

experimenting **H.** What other materials can you use to make parachutes?

TEACHING COMMENT

PREPARATION AND BACKGROUND

Learning about parachutes allows children to thoughtfully manipulate several variables. In doing so, they learn to think of air as a tangible, material substance.

The thin plastic clothes bags dry cleaners use are excellent material for chutes. *Caution:* Remind pupils that a plastic bag should never be placed over the head.

Notice that Problem E asks the child to compare the performance of two parachutes in a fair way. Many children will realize correctly that both must be dropped at the same time and from the same height. Fairness is a concept children often apply when variables need to be controlled.

GENERALIZATION

A parachute is built to catch the air as it falls; it can be changed to fall faster or slower.

SAMPLE PERFORMANCE OBJECTIVES

Process: When comparing the performance of two model parachutes, the child drops them from the same height at the same time.

Knowledge: The child can describe how to make a model parachute fall faster or slower.

FOR OLDER CHILDREN

Older pupils can construct parachutes with improved performance. In addition, they may invent rubber-band launchers (slingshot type, for example) to zip a rolled-up parachute into the air. Ask them to predict the effect of wind drift on their parachutes. Some may be able to predict direction and distance well enough to hit a named target area.

☐ ACTIVITY: How Can You Show That Air Takes Up Space?

NEEDED

large, deep glass bowl   water
two small glasses   paper towels

TRY THIS

1. Fill the bowl three-fourths full with water.

2. Hold a glass with the open end down. Push it straight down into the water.

3. Put a second glass in the water sideways, so it fills with water.

4. Now tip the first glass. Try to "pour" the air up from the first glass into the second glass (Figure 18-16).

FIGURE 18-16

    a. What happens to the water in the higher glass?
    b. What happens in the lower glass?
    c. How can you get the air back into the first glass?
    d. Suppose you put a crushed paper towel in the bottom of a glass. How could you put the open glass underwater without getting the towel wet?

(*Teaching Comment:* If no air bubbles are lost in the process, the air may be transferred from one glass to the next indefinitely. Because air is lighter than water, the air-filled glass will always need to be below the water-filled glass during the transfer.)

□ **ACTIVITY: How Can You Tell If Air in a Balloon Weighs Anything?**

NEEDED

two matched balloons	scissors
meter stick or	sticky tape
yardstick	string

TRY THIS

1. Hang a meter stick evenly from a doorway or other place. Use a string and tape.

2. Attach a string loosely to each of the two deflated balloons.

3. Tape each string to an *end* of the stick. Be sure the stick is level after the balloons are hung. If not, place a partly open paper clip on the stick where needed to balance it (Figure 18-17).

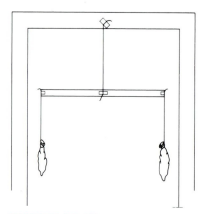

FIGURE 18-17

    a. What will happen if you blow up one balloon and rehang it?
    b. In what ways can you make the stick level again? The strings must stay at the ends of the stick.

(*Teaching Comment:* Be sure the balloon strings are always affixed to the stick *ends* to help assure balance. In b, the deflated balloon can be blown up like the inflated one. Or, the inflated balloon may be slowly deflated by puncturing it at the neck with a pin.)

☐ ACTIVITY: How Can You Tell If Air Pressure Works in All Directions?

NEEDED

plastic cover from a cottage cheese container   small drinking glass
sink

TRY THIS

1. Fill a drinking glass with water.

2. Press a plastic cover over the top of the glass.

3. Turn the glass upside down over a sink.
    a. What will happen if you let go of the cover?
    b. What will happen if you tip the glass in all directions?
    c. What will happen if you use a half-full glass?

(*Teaching Comment:* Pupils should learn that the contents of the glass—water, or air and water—exert less pressure than the air outside. Tipping the glass in all "directions" (planes) shows that the pressure is exerted in all planes. A plastic cover is superior to cardboard because it does not soak up water.)

☐ ACTIVITY: How Does Air Pressure Help You to Use a Soda Straw?

NEEDED

glass of water   two soda straws

TRY THIS

1. Put two straws in the water. Sip some water through the two straws.

2. Now pull one straw out of the water while still having both straws in your mouth.
   a. Suppose you sip again on the two straws. What do you think will happen?
   b. How can you explain what happens?

(*Teaching Comment:* The two straws should be close together in the child's mouth in both parts of the activity.)

■ INVESTIGATION: Air Needed for Burning

What are some ways you can stop a candle from burning? How important is air for a candle to keep burning?

EXPLORATORY PROBLEM

How long do you think a candle will burn inside a closed jar?

NEEDED

small candles	metal pie pan
matches	pencil and paper
modeling clay	paper towels
four different-sized wide-mouth glass jars	graph paper
clock or watch with second hand	measuring cup

TRY THIS

1. Stick some clay to the middle of a pie pan.

2. Stand a candle upright in the clay.

3. Light the candle. Put the used match in the pan.

4. Pick up your next-to-smallest jar. Put it upside down over the candle (Figure 18-18).

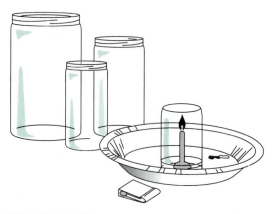

FIGURE 18-18

5. Look at a clock that has a second hand. How long does it take for the candle to go out? Record this time.

6. Remove the jar. Move a wad of several paper towels in and out of the jar a few times. This will clear out the bad air inside.

DISCOVERY PROBLEMS

measuring
communicating

A. How long will the candle burn a second time? a third time? Be sure to remove the bad air after each trial. Record the trial times and the average time like this:

Jar Size	Time for Each			Average Time	Predicted Time
Smallest					
Next smallest	30	34	32	32	—
Next to largest					
Largest					

measuring
predicting

B. How long do you think the candle will burn in the smallest jar? in the next-to-largest jar? Write your predicted times on the chart. Use three trials for each jar. Record the trial times and the average times on your chart. Compare the average and predicted times.

observing
predicting

C. How much larger than the other jars is your largest jar? Compare your jars and then study your chart. How long do you think the candle will burn in the largest jar?

communicating   **D.** You can make better predictions. Get different jars. Use a measuring cup to discover how much water each jar holds. Find out burning times for the smallest and largest jars. Then make a graph. Mark the average burning times of the smallest and largest jars. Draw a light line in between.

predicting   How closely can you predict the burning times for other jars? Find the jar size column on the bottom of the graph. Follow the column up until you reach the drawn line. Then, look straight across to the left at the burning time. (See Figure 18-19.) How will recording more jar times make it easier to predict more accurately?

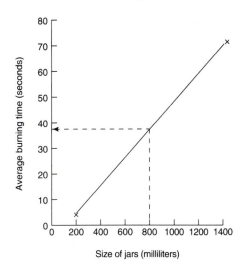

Candle burning experiments

FIGURE 18-19

hypothesizing   **E.** What difference will it make in burning times if you change the candle? For example:
Does candle size make a difference?
Does the flame's closeness to the jar top make a difference?
Will two candles die out twice as fast as one?

observing   **F.** Does the shape of the jar make a difference in burning times? Compare pairs of matched jars with different shapes and find out.

experimenting   **G.** How can you make a candle burn longer in a *small* jar than in a larger jar? Can you think of several ways?

TEACHING COMMENT

PREPARATION AND BACKGROUND

A candle flame dies out in a closed container after it uses a certain percentage of the oxygen in the air. The flame burns longer in a large jar than in a smaller one because of the larger oxygen supply.

Provide at least four different-sized wide-mouth glass jars with straight sides for the investigation. You might try half-pint, pint, quart, and half-gallon sizes, or 200-, 400-, 800-, and 1,600-milliliter sizes. These exact capacities are not critical.

If you wish to stress the graphing activity in Problem D, you might begin with it and continue through the sequence. If you believe your pupils are not ready for it, omit this activity. If many points are plotted on this graph, the line drawn between them will resemble a curve rather than a straight line. Use this finding to demonstrate that using more data allows more accurate predictions. More than four jars will be needed to do Problem D.

Caution: Some schools restrict the use of matches or an open flame to responsible adults. In any event, it is wise to closely supervise their use.

GENERALIZATION

A flame needs air to burn; how long a flame burns depends, in part, on how much air it has.

SAMPLE PERFORMANCE OBJECTIVES

Process: When given minimal data, the child can construct a graph to predict the burning times of candles in different-sized containers.
Knowledge: The child can explain why a candle will burn longer in a large closed container than in a smaller one.

FOR YOUNGER CHILDREN

Supervise this investigation closely and omit the measuring and graphing activities. It is simpler to compare pairs or sets of jars in each activity than to time each candle-burning event. When done this way, most of the activities should be interesting and understandable. Only you should handle burning materials.

SECTION 3
Weather
[*Background 601*]

□ ACTIVITY: How Fast Does Soil Heat and Cool Compared to Water?

NEEDED

two matched glass jars   sunshine
soil   water

TRY THIS

1. Fill one jar with soil and the other with water.

2. Leave the jars in a shady place for an hour.

3. Touch the soil and water surfaces to see if both are about the same temperature. If not, wait a while. If they are, then put both jars in the sun for an hour.

4. Touch both surfaces again.
   a. Which feels warmer, the soil or water surface?
   b. Which will cool faster if you put both back in the shade?

(*Teaching Comment:* This activity is useful when teaching how the unequal heating of the earth's surface causes winds.)

□ ACTIVITY: How Can You Make a Wind Vane?

NEEDED

pencil	straight pin
clay	ruler
straw	construction paper
scissors	square piece of cardboard
glue	bead

TRY THIS

1. From construction paper, cut two end pieces for the straw as shown in Figure 18-20.

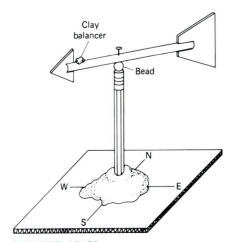

FIGURE 18-20

2. Cut a notch in each end of the straw. Fit and glue the end pieces in the notches.

3. Stick a pin through the straw. Wiggle the pin a little to make a loose fit. Then stick the pin end into the eraser end of a pencil. Put a bead between the straw

and the eraser so the straw may swing freely. Use a tiny piece of clay to help balance the straw if needed.

4. Draw a line upright in the center of a square piece of cardboard. Draw a second line sideways through the center. Mark the four main directions—N, S, E, W—near the edges of the square.

5. Put a lump of clay in the center of the square. Push the pencil upright into the clay.

6. Go outdoors. Line up the *N* on your marked square with north. Watch the way your wind vane points into the wind.
   a. From what direction is the wind blowing?
   b. What will be the wind direction at different times of the day? Make a record of what you find out for a week. What pattern, if any, can you see during the day? from day to day?

☐ ACTIVITY: How Can You Tell the Directions of Winds That Are High in the Sky?

NEEDED

cardboard, 20 centimeters (8 inches) square   ruler
small mirror   crayon
scattered clouds in the sky

TRY THIS

1. Draw a line upright in the center of a cardboard square. Draw a second line sideways through the center.

2. Mark the four main directions—N, S, E, W—near the edges of the square.

3. Place a small mirror where the two lines cross (Figure 18-21).

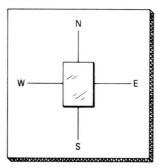

FIGURE 18-21

4. Take the cardboard and mirror outdoors when scattered clouds appear.

5. Put the materials on the ground. Line up the *N* on the square with north.

6. Watch the reflections of clouds in the mirror. Notice how they move across the mirror in a certain direction. This shows how the wind is blowing at the cloud level.

   a. From what direction is the wind overhead moving?

   b. How does the overhead wind direction compare with the surface wind direction? (Notice blowing smoke, leaves, flags, or wind vanes on the land surface.)

   c. What will be the wind direction overhead at different times of the day? Make a record of what you find out for a week or more. What pattern, if any, can you see during the day? from day to day?

   (*Teaching Comment:* Some pupils may notice that scattered high clouds may move in a different direction than middle or low clouds. Also, winds aloft may come from a different direction than surface winds. This happens often and shows why knowledge of winds aloft is important to airplane pilots. The instrument made in this activity is a *nephoscope.*)

■ INVESTIGATION: Evaporation

Many persons hang wet clothes on a clothesline. After a while, the clothes are dry. What do you think happens to the water? When water disappears into the air, we say it *evaporated.* You can find out more about evaporation by drying wet paper towels.

EXPLORATORY PROBLEM

How can you get a paper towel to dry? How long will it take?

NEEDED

plastic bowl of water   piece of cardboard
paper towels   two aluminum pie plates

TRY THIS

1. Put a paper towel underwater to soak it.

2. Bunch the wet towel in your fist. Squeeze out all the water you can.

3. Open the towel and lay it on a pie plate (Figure 18-22).

4. Leave the plate on your desk. Check the time.

5. Every so often feel the towel to see if it is dry. Check the time again when it is all dry.

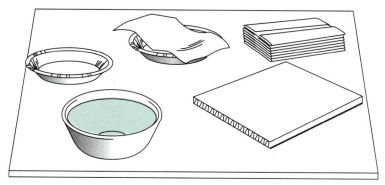

FIGURE 18-22

DISCOVERY PROBLEMS

predicting **A.** Suppose you put one wet towel where it is shady and cool, and another where it is sunny and warmer. Which wet towel do you think will dry first?

communicating **B.** What can you do to show that a dried-out towel is completely "dry"? How many others agree with you?

predicting **C.** Suppose to make it windy, you fan one wet towel with cardboard. You do not fan a second wet towel. Which towel do you think will dry first?

predicting **D.** Suppose you spread out one wet towel and leave another bunched like a ball. Which towel do you think will dry first?

predicting **E.** Suppose you leave one wet towel on top of a plate. You leave a second wet towel under another plate. Which towel do you think will dry first?

experimenting **F.** Play a game with a friend. Who can dry a wet paper towel faster? How can you make the game fair?

experimenting **G.** What is the longest you can keep a wet paper towel from drying?

TEACHING COMMENT

PREPARATION AND BACKGROUND

The foregoing sequence gives several chances for children to manipulate conditions that affect the evaporation rate of water. The last two activities encourage them to manipulate these conditions creatively. Discovery Problem C calls for fanning one wet towel with cardboard to simulate a windy condition. Clipping the towel to the pie plate with several paper clips will keep it from blowing off the plate.

GENERALIZATION

Wind, heat, and an uncovered and spread-out condition all help to make a wet paper towel dry faster.

SAMPLE PERFORMANCE OBJECTIVES

Process: The child can vary and control at least one condition to increase the drying rate of a wet paper towel.

Knowledge: The child can state at least one condition that will change the drying rate of a wet paper towel.

FOR OLDER CHILDREN

Invite older children to do the activities with more precision. For example, they might attempt to predict the drying times in each of the activities.

Have them calculate the drying *rate* of a wet towel or sponge by using a beam balance. Let them suspend a wet towel from one end of the beam, and clay or another object on the other end to achieve a balance. Then, as the towel dries and lightens, the beam will begin to tilt up. Pupils can add water to the towel with an eyedropper, one drop at a time, to keep the beam level.

Ask questions such as, How many drops evaporate in one minute? Does spreading out the drops you add make a difference in the evaporation rate? Will half of a wet towel have half the evaporation rate of a whole towel? and so on. If you do not have a beam balance, just suspend a meter stick or dowel from a string. Your pupils will be delighted at the dramatic effect of the evaporation rate. It takes only a few minutes, under usual conditions, for it to be noticeable.

▪ INVESTIGATION: Relative Humidity

Can you remember times when the air has felt very dry? very moist, or *humid?* The amount of moisture, or water vapor, in the air often changes. Warm air can hold more moisture without raining than cold air. The percent of moisture now in the air compared to what it can hold at the present temperature is the *relative humidity.* You can make an instrument to measure the relative humidity. It is called a *hygrometer.*

EXPLORATORY PROBLEM

How can you make a hygrometer?

NEEDED

two matched Fahrenheit thermometers
narrow cotton strip or thick cotton shoelace
quart milk carton

cardboard
two rubber bands
paper clip

TRY THIS

1. Fasten two thermometers to the sides of an empty milk carton. Use rubber bands to hold them in place.
2. Take a pencil. Punch a hole in the carton under one thermometer.
3. Put about 2.5 centimeters (1 inch) of water into the carton. Close the top with a paper clip. This will keep the water from evaporating quickly.
4. Wet a strip of cotton with water.
5. Stick one end of the strip through the punched hole into the water inside. Fasten the other end to the bulb of the thermometer above (Figure 18-23).

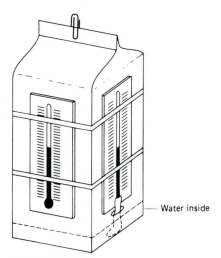

— Water inside

FIGURE 18-23

6. To use your hygrometer, fan the thermometers with some cardboard for three minutes in a shady place. Read the temperatures of each thermometer.

7. Use the relative humidity table (Figure 18-24) to find the percent of moisture in the air. At the left, mark the wet bulb temperature lightly with pencil. At the top, lightly mark the dry bulb temperature. Move one finger across the row and another down the column from the marked spots. Notice the percent of relative humidity where your two fingers meet.

Dry bulb temperature (°F)

Wet bulb temperature (°F)

	56	58	60	62	64	66	68	70	71	72	73	74	75	76	77	78	79	80	82	84
38	7	2																		
40	15	11	7																	
42	25	19	14	9	7															
44	34	29	22	17	13	8	4													
45	45	38	30	24	18	14	10	6	4	3	1									
46	55	47	40	33	26	21	16	12	10	9	7	5	4	3	1					
48	66	56	48	41	34	29	23	19	17	15	13	11	9	8	6	5	4	3		
50	77	67	57	50	43	36	31	25	23	21	19	17	15	13	12	10	9	7	5	3
52	88	78	68	59	51	44	38	33	30	28	25	23	21	19	17	16	14	12	10	7
54		89	79	68	60	53	46	40	37	34	32	29	27	25	23	21	19	18	14	12
56			89	79	70	61	54	48	45	42	39	36	34	31	29	27	25	23	20	16
58				90	79	71	62	55	52	49	46	43	40	38	35	33	31	29	25	21
60					90	80	71	64	60	57	53	50	47	44	42	39	37	35	30	26
62						90	80	72	68	65	61	58	54	51	48	46	43	41	36	32
64							90	81	77	73	69	65	62	59	56	53	50	47	42	37
66								90	86	82	78	74	70	66	63	60	57	54	48	43
68									95	91	86	82	78	74	71	67	64	61	55	49
70											95	91	86	82	79	75	71	68	61	56
72													96	91	87	83	79	75	69	62
74															96	91	87	83	76	69
76																	96	91	84	76
78																			92	84
80																				92
82																				

Percent of relative humidity

FIGURE 18-24

DISCOVERY PROBLEMS

measuring   **A.** What is the relative humidity now?

hypothesizing   **B.** How, if at all, might relative humidity change from day to day? How, if at all, does it change?

observing   **C.** How well can you sense by yourself that the air is drier or moister from day to day? Use your hygrometer to check how well you do.

measuring   **D.** How does the relative humidity outdoors compare to that indoors?

hypothesizing   **E.** What would you expect the relative humidity to be outdoors on a rainy day? Measure it in some partly sheltered place and see.

inferring   **F.** How do your relative humidity measurements compare with those of the local weather bureau?

TEACHING COMMENT

PREPARATION AND BACKGROUND

When no difference appears between the wet and dry bulb temperatures, the relative humidity is 100 percent. This condition is unlikely to be recorded outdoors unless there is dense fog or rain.

Pupils may notice a marked difference between indoor and outdoor readings. This is most likely in winter. As the room is heated, the air is able to hold more moisture, so the relative humidity goes down.

GENERALIZATION

A hygrometer can be used to measure the relative humidity. This is the percent of moisture air holds compared to what it can hold at a given temperature.

SAMPLE PERFORMANCE OBJECTIVES

Process: The child can measure the relative humidity by using a hygrometer and consulting a table.
Knowledge: The child can describe conditions when high and low humidity are likely.

☐ ACTIVITY: How Can You "Collect" and See the Water Vapor in the Air?

NEEDED

clean, shiny can   thermometer
ice cubes

TRY THIS

1. Half-fill the can with water. Add five or six ice cubes.
2. Put a thermometer inside the can of ice water.

3. Watch for tiny drops on the can's sides. When they first appear, take the water temperature and record it. (This is called the *dew point*. It tells the temperature at which water vapor will change from a gas to a liquid and *condense* on objects.)
   a. At what temperature was the dew point?
   b. Will the dew-point temperature be different in a smaller or larger container?
   c. Can an ice-water mixture get colder than the dew point?
   d. How, if at all, will the dew-point temperature change from day to day?

▪ INVESTIGATION: Solid Particles That Pollute Air

Have you ever tried to see through, or breathe, smoky air? Smoke you see is made up of tiny, unburned solid particles from whatever made the smoke. There are many other solid particles, and gases, too, that dirty, or *pollute,* the air.

EXPLORATORY PROBLEM

How can you find out what solid particles are polluting the air?

NEEDED

small white file cards or stiff paper   hand lens
clear, sticky tape   graph paper

TRY THIS

1. Fasten three strips of tape, sticky side up, the long way on a file card.
2. Leave the card, sticky side up, on a table or other flat place outdoors. Tape down two corners of the card so it does not blow away.
3. Pick up the card after one day. Use a hand lens to examine the particles that collected on the tape. Stick a small piece of graph paper under the middle of the tape (Figure 18-25). Count the number of particles in one square.

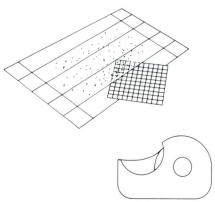

FIGURE 18-25

DISCOVERY PROBLEMS

measuring   **A.** How many particles are inside one square? How can you estimate the number of particles on the rest of the card? (*Hint:* First, see if the particles are evenly spaced.)

observing   **B.** What different kinds of particles do you see? Where do you think they came from?

hypothesizing   **C.** In what different places can you collect more samples? Which place do you think will have the most air pollution? the least? (Write the location of each place tested on the card used.)

experimenting   **D.** How does height affect the number of particles collected? How could you find out?

experimenting   **E.** How does time affect the number of particles collected?

experimenting   **F.** How does wind affect the number of particles collected? (You might shield one card from the wind without covering it.)

observing   **G.** What, if any, air particles can you find indoors? How does what you find compare with findings from outdoors?

TEACHING COMMENT

PREPARATION AND BACKGROUND

When children compare the number of airborne solid pollutants in different places, they can be guided to control several variables. For instance, the tapes should be placed at about the same height and exposed at the same time and for the same time period. It is also important for pupils to realize that many airborne pollutants, especially the gases, are not detectable by their tape test.

GENERALIZATION

There are many solid pollutants in the air; the amount found changes with a variety of conditions.

SAMPLE PERFORMANCE OBJECTIVES

Process: The child can estimate the total number of pollutants on the test tapes by counting the number of particles in several representative squares, averaging them, and multiplying by the number of squares exposed.

Knowledge: The child can describe some conditions that change the number and variety of solid pollutants in the air.

FOR YOUNGER CHILDREN

Younger pupils can leave tapes exposed in different places and make rough comparisons of their findings.

□ ACTIVITY: How Can You Measure Changes in Air Pressure?

NEEDED

glass jar   balloon
rubber band   scissors
straw   file card
glue

TRY THIS

1. Make a *barometer.* Cut out a large part of a balloon. Stretch it tightly over the jar opening. Use a rubber band to hold it fast.

2. Pinch one straw end flat. Cut a point with scissors at this end.

3. Glue the straw's other end to the center of the stretched balloon.

4. Fasten a file card to a wall. Place the barometer by it. Have the straw pointer centered on the card and almost touching.

5. Make a mark on the card where the straw points each day for a week (Figure 18-26).

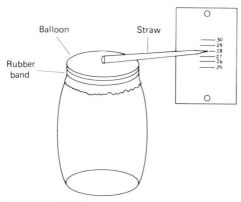

Balloon   Straw

Rubber
band

30
29
28
27
26
25

FIGURE 18-26

   a. On what day was the air pressure the highest? lowest?

   b. When, if at all, was there no change in air pressure?

(*Teaching Comment:* Increased air pressure pushes down harder on the balloon diaphragm. This makes the straw pointer go up. Decreased air pressure causes the higher pressure inside the jar to push up on the diaphragm, so the pointer goes down. The movement can be increased a bit by gluing a piece of matchstick under the straw at the jar rim. You might challenge pupils to calibrate their barometers. They can note the daily barometric pressure in the newspaper or phone the weather bureau. After a week or so of recording the official pressure next to their own recordings, they may be able to predict roughly the official pressure from their own barometers. Place this kind of barometer where it will have the least change of temperature. Otherwise, the air in the jar may expand and contract so much that the effects of changing air pressure will be obscured.)

SELECTED TRADE BOOKS: WATER, AIR, AND WEATHER

FOR YOUNGER CHILDREN

Ardley, Neil. *Working with Water.* Watts, 1983.

Branley, Franklyn M. *Air Is All Around You.* Harper & Row, 1987.

Eden, Michael. *Weather.* Merrimack, 1982.

Gibbons, Gail. *Weather Forecasting.* Macmillan, 1987.

Greene, Carol. *Caring for Our Air.* Enslow, 1991.

———. *Caring for Our Water.* Enslow, 1991.

Kirkpatrick, Rena K. *Look at Weather.* Raintree, 1985.

Leutscher, Alfred. *Water.* Dutton, 1983.

Llewellyn, Claire. *First Look in the Air.* Gareth Stevens, 1991.

Lloyd, David. *Air.* Dial Books, 1983.

Martin, Claire. *I Can Be a Weather Forecaster.* Children's Press, 1987.

Palazzo, Janet. *What Makes the Weather?* Troll Associates, 1982.

Pluckrose, Henry. *Think About Floating and Sinking.* Watts, 1987.

Seixas, Judith S. *Water—What It Is, What It Does.* Greenwillow, 1987.

Smeltzer, Patricia, and Victor Smeltzer. *Thank You for a Drink of Water.* Winston, 1983.

Swallow, Su. *Air.* Watts, 1991.

Webb, Angela. *Water.* Watts, 1987.

Webster, Vera. *Weather Experiments.* Children's Press, 1982.

FOR OLDER CHILDREN

Arnov, Boris. *Water: Experiments to Understand It.* Lothrop, 1980.

Branley, Franklyn M. *Water for the World.* Harper & Row, 1982.

Bright, Michael. *Polluting the Oceans.* Watts, 1991.

Cosner, Sharon. *Be Your Own Weather Forecaster.* Messner, 1982.

De Bruin, Jerry. *Young Scientists Explore the Weather.* Good Apple, 1983.

Dickinson, Jane. *Wonders of Water.* Troll Associates, 1983.

Flint, David. *Weather and Climate.* Watts, 1991.

Ford, Adam. *Weather Watch.* Lothrop, 1982.

Frevert, Patricia. *Why Does the Weather Change?* Creative Education, 1981.

Gallant, Roy A. *Rainbows, Mirages, and Sundogs.* Macmillan, 1987.

Jeffries, Lawrence. *Air, Air, Air.* Troll Associates, 1983.

Kiefer, Irene. *Poisoned Land: The Problem of Hazardous Waste.* Atheneum, 1981.

Miller, Christina, and Louise Berry. *Acid Rain.* Messner, 1987.

Pollard, Michael. *Air, Water, and Weather.* Facts on File, 1987.

Riley, Peter D. *Air and Gases.* David & Charles, 1986.

Seymour, Peter. *How the Weather Works.* Macmillan, 1985.

Smith, Henry. *Amazing Air.* Lothrop, 1983.

Snodgrass, M. E. *Environmental Awareness: Water Pollution.* BSP Publications, 1991.

Steele, Philip. *Wind: Causes and Effects.* Watts, 1991.

Walpole, Brenda. *Water.* Watts, 1987.

Ward, Alan. *Experimenting with Surface Tension and Bubbles.* David & Charles, 1986.

19

The Earth in Space

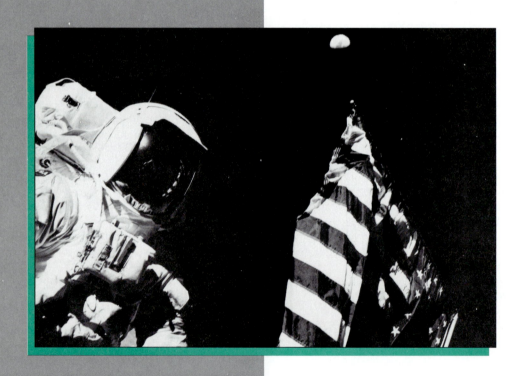

The sky's the limit.
What goes up must come down.

Even tricycle riders today smile at these clichés. Television, magazines, and space missions have given children a beyond-the-earth outlook unknown to most previous generations.

But few children learn outside of school the basic ideas and physical laws that give meaning to the motions of objects in space. We'll concentrate on several of these ideas and laws in this chapter as we examine: (1) how the earth's motions in space cause time and seasonal changes; (2) how the relative motions of sun, earth, and moon bring about moon phases, eclipses, and tides; (3) size and distance in the solar system and beyond; and (4) how gravity and the laws of motion affect the movements of planets, satellites, and rockets.

[1] TIME AND SEASONS
Experiences 658

Because the earth is so large compared to the size of a person, it is hard at first to visualize the earth's motions in space. One remedy is to make the earth small compared to a person. That is what a globe model of the earth does.

Globe and Shadows

If you put a globe in the sun, the sunlight shines on one-half of the globe, as it does on one-half of the earth. If you position your town or city so it is upright, and north on the globe faces north, the globe will face the sun as the earth does.

How will you know this is so? You can test it. Stick a small nail through a piece of sticky tape and fasten the nail head down to your town on the globe. Be sure the nail is vertical.

(You may have to prop up the globe base with a book or two.) Then look at the nail's shadow. You'll find it identical in direction and proportional to shadows of other objects around you. Leave the globe in place during the day, and the nail shadow will move and change length like the other shadows do as the earth rotates. Or, if you want a preview of what shadows the earth objects will make, you can rotate the globe and watch the nail's shadow.

Rotation and Time

Most upper-grade children know the earth rotates, but few can tell in which direction. Since the sun apparently rises in a generally eastern direction and sets in a generally western direction, with opposite shadows, at least some good thinkers will figure this out for themselves. Only a west-to-east rotation does this.

Figure 19-1 shows how persons on the east coast of the United States move into the sunlight. To them, it looks as though the sun is rising from the horizon and climbing higher as time goes by. Six hours from the

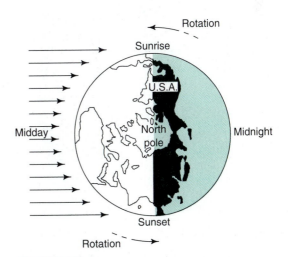

FIGURE 19-1
The apparent motion of the sun is caused by earth's rotation.

time they first observe "sunrise," the sun is closest to being directly overhead. This is *midday*—the exact middle of the daylight period. Gradually, they continue to rotate counterclockwise. Shadows grow longer. Around 6:00 P.M., it is almost twilight, and the sun appears to sink into the western horizon. The next 12 hours they spend in darkness, until once again the sun appears to rise. A complete rotation takes 24 hours, or one complete day.

Of course, most of the time people in New York (or elsewhere) do not have equal parts of daylight and darkness. You know that summer days are longer than winter days, for example. We shall take up why shortly.

Expect some trouble with the term *day* because it has two meanings—the hours during which it is light and the time for one complete rotation. You might use the terms *complete day* and *daylight* to separate the two; this should eliminate confusion.

Time Zones

It would be extremely inconvenient to judge time by where the sun is overhead. Every location a few kilometers east or west of another location would have a different noon time as the sun reached its midday position, for example. Though this was not a problem in the days of slow-moving transportation, it became intolerable when railroads were established.

The problem was solved in 1833 by creating four standard time zones in the United

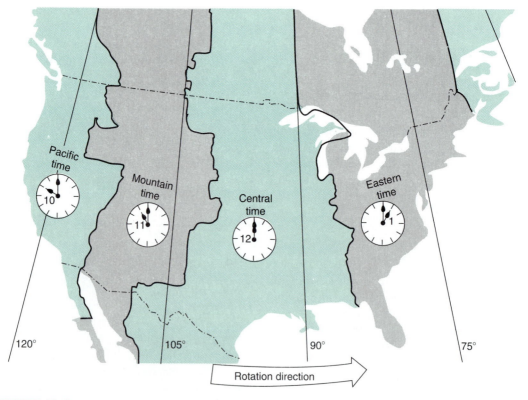

FIGURE 19-2
The continental United States has four time zones.

States. Figure 19-2 shows those in use today in the continental United States. We set our watches ahead going eastward and back going westward. The entire globe is now divided into 24 time zones, 15° apart. (The 15° separations came from dividing 360°—the earth is a near sphere—by 24 hours.)

The practical effect of having the same time zone for three cities hundreds of kilometers or miles apart is shown in Figure 19-3. Notice that only one city can experience midday at a given moment, although it is noon at all three cities.

Seasons

Persons in New York on any December 21st experience about 9 hours of daylight and 15 hours of darkness. Six months later, the reverse happens. An even greater difference is found at a higher latitude, such as near Seattle,

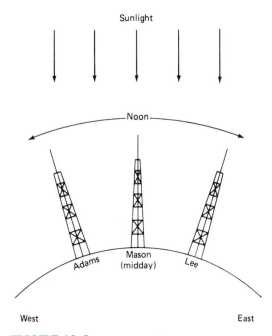

Sunlight

Noon

Adams   Mason (midday)   Lee

West   East

FIGURE 19-3

Midday at one city and noon at three cities in the same time zone. (Not to scale.)

Washington (50th parallel). To see why, first examine Figure 19-4.

Notice that the earth's axis is tilted 23½° from the plane of the earth's orbit around the sun. As the earth revolves about the sun, its axis continues to point in the same direction—toward the north star. Check the winter position. Because of the tilt, the northern hemisphere is in darkness longer than it is in daylight. You can see this by checking the length of the parallels of latitude shown. In the summer position, you see the reverse. Now the same latitude is exposed to sunlight for a much longer period. At the "in between" periods—spring and fall—day and night periods are more nearly equal.

Also observe that the southern hemisphere has opposite conditions to those in the northern hemisphere. While New York shivers in December, the beaches in sunny Rio de Janeiro are crowded with swimmers and sun bathers enjoying their summer.

However, besides the increased length of the days, there is another reason why summers are warmer than winters. The sun's rays are more nearly overhead during summer than at other times. Note the words *more nearly overhead*. Because the earth's axis is tilted, at noon the sun can never be completely vertical (at a 90° angle) north of the Tropic of Cancer or south of the Tropic of Capricorn.

If you ask pupils to explain why it is warmer in summer than it is in winter, don't be surprised if one replies, "The earth is closer to the sun." This is entirely logical, even though it is wrong. In fact, the opposite is true. The earth's path (orbit) around the sun is a slightly elongated circle, or ellipse, as are nearly all the orbits of celestial bodies. In winter, we are almost 5 million kilometers (3 million miles) closer to the sun than in summer. But because this distance is small compared to the average distance, about 150 million kilometers (93 million miles), the effect is negligible.

FIGURE 19-4

The seasons. Outside figures as viewed from above. Note the unequal periods of daylight at the 50th parallel except on March 21 (spring equinox) and September 23 (fall equinox).

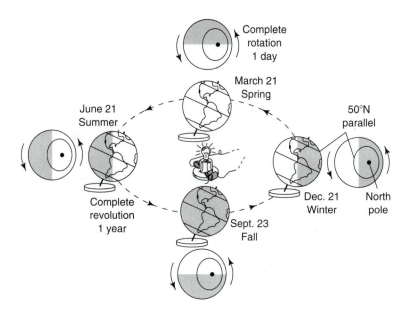

[2] INTERACTIONS OF THE MOON, EARTH, AND SUN   *Experiences 668*

Why does the moon seem to change its shape? Why does the ocean have tides? What causes eclipses? Children are curious about these things. This section presents some ways the sun, earth, and moon interact. We'll consider moon phases first.

Moon Phases

You know that the moon, like our earth, receives and reflects light from the hot, glowing sun. Also, the moon revolves around the earth in about 28 days. Study Figure 19-5 for a moment. The drawings on the right show the earth and moon as seen from far out in space. The drawings of the moon on the left show how it looks to us when the moon is in each of eight different positions.

Imagine standing on the earth in the center of this illustration. Look at position 1. This is the *new moon* position. The moon's face is now dark to us. Slowly, the moon moves on in its orbit. At position 2, we see a *new crescent moon;* at position 3, a *first-quarter moon.* At position 4, we see a *new gibbous moon;* one side is now almost fully illuminated. At 5, there is a *full* moon. The other positions reverse the sequence of phases—old gibbous, last quarter, old crescent—until once more there is a new moon.

As the moon moves from the new to full positions, more and more of it appears to be shining; it is said to be *waxing.* But from full to new moon positions, less and less of its lighted part is visible from earth, so it is said to be *waning.* Try the moon phase investigation on pages 670–671. Compare the phases you see with those in Figure 19-5.

Tides

The interaction of sun, moon, and earth also results in tides. How do they happen? The law of universal gravitation, first formed by the great eighteenth-century philosopher and scientist, Sir Isaac Newton, provides much of the answer. Briefly stated, *every object in the universe attracts each other; the force of this*

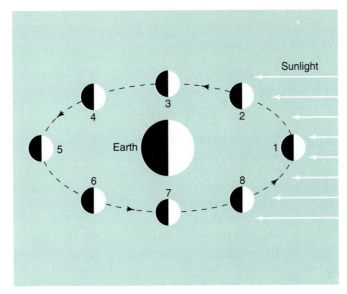

FIGURE 19-5
Moon phases as seen from the earth (left).

attraction depends on the mass of each object and the distance between them. ("Mass" is the amount of matter that makes up the object.)

As shown in the Figure 19-6, the mutual attraction between earth and moon causes the ocean to bulge at position 1. This is a *direct high tide.* An *indirect high tide* appears at 3 because it is most distant from the moon, so gravitational attraction is weakest here. (We will add a refinement to this statement shortly.) Also, the land surface is pulled slightly away from this region. Positions 2 and 4 have

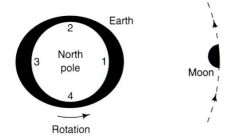

FIGURE 19-6
Mutual attraction between earth and moon causes ocean tides.

low tides because these are areas of weak attraction that furnish the extra water making up the high tides.

What causes the tide to rise and fall? Put yourself in position 1. As you rotate on the earth toward 2, the tide will seem to ebb, or fall. You experience a low tide. Moving from 2 into 3, you gradually come into the bulge. It seems as though the tide is "coming in." You experience a high tide. Rotating onward, you have another low tide before once again arriving at the direct high-tide area. In other words, the oceans tend to bulge continually in the moon's direction, and opposite point, as the earth rotates. While the oceans rotate with the land, of course, the effect of the continual bulges creates the illusion that the tides are moving in and out independently.

Since the earth's rotation takes about 24 hours, high tides happen about every 12 hours. (Remember, there is one direct and one indirect high tide simultaneously.) Six hours elapse between low and high tides. Actually, these times are a little longer because the moon itself moves some distance in its orbit while the earth rotates. Because the tidal bulge moves in alignment with the moon as it advances, the earth must rotate an extra 52 minutes each 24 hours before it is again in the direct high-tide zone.

Twice monthly, unusually high and low tidal ranges occur called *spring* tides. High tides are very high and low tides are very low. (Incidentally, there is no connection between "spring" and the season. Perhaps the name arose because these tides appear to "spring up" so fast.) A week later, there is much less variation from high to low tides. Tides during this period are called *neap* tides.

Figure 19-7 shows how these tides take place. When the sun and moon are aligned *(a)*, the sun's added gravitational attraction causes very high spring tides. This happens when the moon is in either the full or new moon phase. Because the sun is so far away, its tremendous mass adds only one-third to the force of gravitational attraction. When the sun and moon pull at right angles *(b)*, we have neap tides. This happens when the moon is in its first- and last-quarter phases.

Interestingly, besides water tides, there are also huge atmospheric tides and tiny land tides. All happen through the same interaction of sun, moon, and earth. Accurate measurements show that some land portions of the earth rise and fall more than 30 centimeters (one foot) with the tides.

Eclipses

Causes of eclipses are seen in Figure 19-8. Both earth and moon cast conelike shadows.

When the moon is in position 1, the tip of its shadow barely reaches the earth. Persons in this small, shadowy area see a *solar eclipse*. A total eclipse is never more than 272 kilometers (170 miles) across. Sunlight is cut off except for a whitish halo, called the *corona*. The shadow moves quickly over the ground, because both the earth and moon are in motion. Sunlight is never blocked for more than eight minutes.

In position 2, the moon is eclipsed when it revolves into the earth's large shadow. Practically everyone on the earth's dark side can see a *lunar eclipse*, which may last for two hours before the moon revolves out of the earth's shadow. There are several partial lunar and solar eclipses each year.

Notice that eclipses can happen in the full and new moon positions. Why, then, don't they occur every few weeks? The reason is that the moon's plane of orbit is tilted about 5° from the earth's orbital plane around the sun. This usually causes the moon to pass above and below positions required for eclipses.

A 5° tilt would be only a minor deviation from the earth's orbital plane in Figure 19-8, hardly enough to make a difference. But in proper scale, this small deviation is quite significant. With a scale of 2.5 centimeters to 1,600 kilometers (1 inch to 1,000 miles), the earth's diameter is 20 centimeters (8 inches), and the moon's is 5 centimeters (2 inches). Their distance apart is 6 meters (20 feet). This is seldom realized by children. The sun's

Sun   Moon   Earth

A

Moon

Sun   Earth

B

FIGURE 19-7
The sun also affects tidal flows.

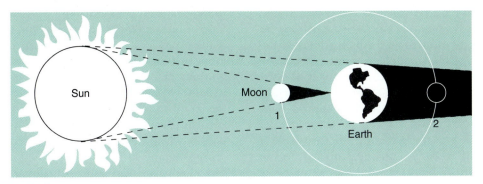

FIGURE 19-8
Causes of solar (1) and lunar (2) eclipses.

diameter and distance at this scale are even more surprising. Imagine a sun model 22 meters (72 feet) across, 2.4 kilometers (1½ miles) away!

The Earth-Moon System

We normally think of the moon revolving around the earth, but strictly speaking, this is not quite the case. The gravitational attraction of these two objects is such that they are locked together in a revolving system that has a common center of mass (barycenter). To see why this is so, look at Figure 19-9.

The large ball of clay represents the earth, and the small one is the moon. A short wire joins the two to simulate their gravitational attraction. If you suspend system A from the middle with a string, the much heavier earth goes down and the moon goes up. The same thing would happen if a heavy adult and a small child got on a seesaw with the fulcrum in the middle. In B, the balance is improved but much the same thing happens. In C, though, a balance is found. If you spin each model system with a twisted string, A and B will wobble and sway unevenly; but C revolves uniformly and simulates the motion of the earth-moon system.

Now for the refinement on the cause of indirect tides, as promised earlier. In any spinning system such as this, there is a tendency for the two objects to fly apart. The

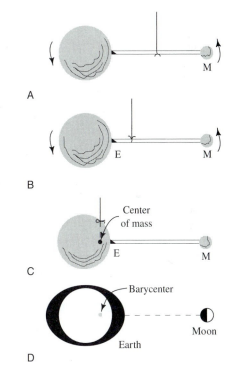

FIGURE 19-9
The earth-moon system has a common point of balance, or center of mass, called the barycenter. (Distance not to scale.)

gravitational attraction between the two prevents this from happening. In D, the side of the earth facing the moon is strongly attracted to the moon. The water moves more easily than the solid earth, so it flows strongly toward the near side and becomes a high tide. The earth's opposite side is attracted less because it is farther away. So the tendency of this far side of the spinning system to fly apart is countered only weakly by the weakened gravitational pull. The result is an indirect high tide.

Our model is imperfect in several ways. The earth's mass is about 80 times greater than the moon's. Also, the distance scale is wrong. If we were to use the proper scale, our short wire connector would need to be at least several feet long.

The Moon's Orbit

From an earth reference position, it is natural to regard the moon as revolving in a circular path around the earth (or, more accurately, the barycenter). But motion is relative to the observer. If we could see the moon's path from far out in space, it would not look circular. Instead, it would weave in and out in a shallow, alternating pattern along the earth's orbit. (See Figure 19-10.) Since the sun is in motion, a similar pathway is woven by the earth. Is it wrong, then, to say the moon *revolves* around the earth, and the earth around the sun? Not at all. It is just another way of looking at the same set of facts.

[3] THE SOLAR SYSTEM AND BEYOND   *Experiences 676*

Planets

The earth is one of nine planets revolving around a medium-sized star, the sun. How did the solar system begin? Scientists are not sure. One prominent theory holds that the sun and planets may have been formed from an enormous swirling cloud of dust and gases. Slowly, gravitational attraction caused these materials to come closer together. The speed of rotation increased more and more. As rotating dust and gas particles rubbed together, much friction and heat developed. A large mass in the center became so hot that it formed into the sun. Gradually, most of the remaining materials spread out as a result of their spinning and began revolving around the sun. They slowly shrank and cooled into nine separate masses, which became planets. (See Figure 19-11).

Mercury is the closest planet to the sun. It rotates very slowly, only two-thirds around to one complete revolution around the sun, which takes only 88 days. Its small mass results in a surface gravity too weak to retain an atmosphere. As might be expected, Mercury is hotter than any of the other planets.

Venus, next in order from the sun, is enveloped in a dense atmosphere of mostly carbon dioxide. This reflects sunlight so well that, except for the sun and moon, Venus is the brightest object in the sky. Its surface temperature, too, is very high.

After the earth is *Mars.* It has an unusual reddish appearance and polar ice caps that advance and recede with the seasons. It is more like the earth than the other planets, but its very thin atmosphere and severe weather make it unlikely that living things are on this planet. In 1976, two remotely controlled space vehicles landed on Mars, but their instruments detected no forms of life. Two tiny natural satellites, or moons, revolve speedily around Mars.

Moon's orbit

Earth's orbit

FIGURE 19-10
The earth and moon orbits drawn to scale.

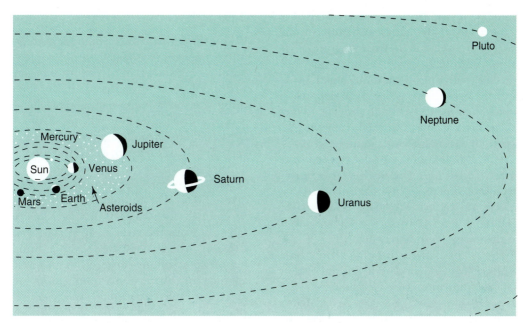

FIGURE 19-11
The solar system. (Not to scale.)

Between Mars and the next planet, *Jupiter,* is an unusually large gap containing several thousand irregularly shaped chunks of stone and metal called *asteroids* (tiny "stars"). Some astronomers think these may be the remains of a planet that came too close to huge Jupiter and disintegrated under its powerful gravitational attraction. Ranging from about 1.6 to 800 kilometers (1 to 500 miles) in diameter, they are invisible to the unaided eye.

Of the *outer planets,* as the five beyond Mars are called, *Jupiter* and *Saturn* are by far the largest. Jupiter's diameter is 11 times greater than that of the earth. Saturn is conspicuous because of its many rings, believed to be composed of ice particles. *Uranus* and *Neptune* are nearly the same size, about three and one-half times the earth's diameter. *Pluto* is so small and distant that it was not discovered until 1930. Its orbital plane is tilted sharply from those of other planets, and its orbit is so elliptical that at times the planet is closer to the sun than Neptune. All

the outer planets but Pluto have moons. All are so distant from the sun it is probable that at least some of their atmospheric gases are frozen.

Ancient sky-watchers were so puzzled by the changing appearance of the planets that they named them "wanderers." Long ago all such objects were thought to be stars, which ordinarily seem fixed in space. We realize now that their differences in brightness and position from time to time occur because they revolve at different distances and speeds in their orbits around the sun.

Comets and Meteors

Comets are huge, unstable bodies apparently composed of gases, dust, ice, and small rocks. A few are briefly visible as they occasionally sweep near the sun and far out again in immense, highly elliptical orbits. They have so little mass that the pressure of sunlight causes a long streamer, or "tail," to flow from the comet head always in a direction opposite the sun. Like the planets, comets may have originated from the gases and dust of the solar nebula over 4 billion years ago.

Most children have seen "shooting stars." These are fragments of rock and metal, probably from broken-up asteroids and parts of comets, that hurtle through interplanetary space at high speeds. Although most are no larger than a grain of sand, some weigh tons. It is estimated that billions of such *meteors,* as they are called, plunge daily into the earth's atmosphere and burn into extinction from the heat of air friction. The few that do penetrate to the earth in solid form other than dust are called meteorites.

Is there any danger of being struck by a meteorite? Not much. There are only a few instances of anyone ever being injured. One such event happened in 1954. An Alabama woman was grazed by a 10-pound meteorite that crashed through her roof. In 1982, a 6-pound meteorite smashed through the roof of a home in Connecticut. But no one was injured.

Size and Distances

By far the most difficult ideas in astronomy for children to grasp are the distances and sizes of objects in space. It would be helpful to their thinking if a large section of the playground could be used for scaled distance activities. Yet even a very large area can be inadequate to demonstrate both distance and size on the same scale. At 2.54 centimeters to 12,000 kilometers (1 inch to 8,000 miles), for example, Pluto would need to be located about 11 kilometers (7 miles) away!

Distances are even more astounding as we move beyond the solar system. Now, the kilometer or mile is too tiny as a unit of measurement for practical purposes. You will want to acquaint pupils with the light-year, defined as the distance a beam of light travels in one year. At 300,000 kilometers (186,000 miles) per second, this is almost 9.5 trillion kilometers (6 trillion miles).

The Stars

When we view the stars, some seem to group into a pattern, or constellation. People commonly think such stars are about the same in size and distance from the earth. But the only thing stars in a constellation typically share is a common direction. If we could view constellations from other angles (we can, very slightly, as the earth orbits the sun), most constellation patterns would disappear.

The light from the nearest star, the sun, takes about eight minutes to reach the earth. In contrast, a distance of 4.3 *light-years* separates us from the next nearest star, *Proxima Centauri.* These stars have over a hundred billion companions clustered in an immense aggregation of stars and filmy clouds of gas and dust called the *Milky Way galaxy.* The shape of our galaxy is like a pocket watch, with a thickened center, standing on end (Figure 19-12). It is thought to be about 100,000 light-years long and 12,000 light-years thick. The galaxy seems to be slowly rotating about its center, where the stars are most thickly concentrated.

Our galaxy is but one of millions more strewn throughout space at incomprehensible distances, containing further stars beyond reliable calculation.

[4] GRAVITY AND THE LAWS OF MOTION
Experiences 681

It is a good idea when teaching astronomy units to avoid getting involved in the technology of satellites and space vehicles. Although this is where the "glamour" is, space technology is intricate and continually changing. It is better for lasting understanding to focus on the principles behind technological innovation. The basic scientific laws that govern motions of natural and

FIGURE 19-12
The Milky Way galaxy.

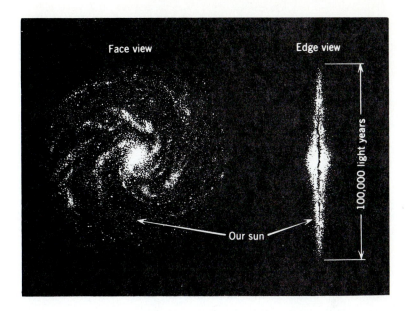

artificial satellites, planets, and rockets are the same.

This does not mean we should avoid references to rocket design, propulsion systems, and so on. The motivation and interests of children are broad and should be recognized. And the products of technology may furnish a perfect setting through which we can teach principles. It merely suggests where to place the emphasis.

Causes of Orbits

Nobody knows what caused the planets to begin moving, but the reason they keep moving is readily understandable: There is almost nothing in space to stop them. But why do they circle the sun? You have already been introduced to Newton's law of gravitation. Equally important to understand is Newton's law of *inertia*. Briefly stated, *any object at rest or in motion remains at rest or continues in motion in a straight line unless acted on by some outside force.*

Anyone who has ever tried to push a heavy, stalled automobile knows how hard it is to move a heavy body at rest. It has much inertia. Anyone who has ever tried to stop a heavy,

rolling automobile by pushing against it knows how difficult *this* is. A body in motion has the inertia of motion (momentum). The more momentum it has, the harder it is to stop it.

Figure 19-13 shows how the laws of gravitation and inertia combine to keep objects in

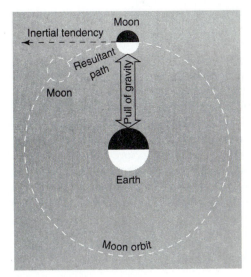

FIGURE 19-13
A balance between gravity and inertia keeps a satellite in orbit.

orbit. Although a natural satellite, the moon, is shown in this case, the same laws operate with all bodies that orbit other bodies in space.

If the moon were unaffected by our earth's powerful gravitational force, it would follow a straight path owing to its inertial momentum. Because it is affected, the moon follows a path that is a result of each factor countering the other.

A common example of this countering effect happens when a ball rolls swiftly off a table. Instead of falling straight down, the ball's inertia of momentum keeps it going nearly sideways for an instant until gravity forces it to the floor. The resultant path of its fall is an arc.

In our illustration, gravity and inertia are equally powerful. If this were not so, the moon would either be drawn into the earth or pull away from it. This is what happens to an artificial satellite that moves too slowly or too fast. Clearly, getting a space satellite into a sustained orbit is tricky business. Its velocity and angle of entry into orbit must be calculated closely. Since perfection in these matters is nearly impossible, most orbits are markedly elongated (elliptical).

Because gravity weakens with distance, the speed of the orbiting body must be slower as the distance from its parent body increases. This is necessary in order to maintain balance of the two forces. At 35,680 kilometers (22,300 miles) from the earth, for example, the proper orbital speed for a satellite results in one complete orbit each 24 hours. Because this is the period of the earth's rotation, a satellite positioned above the equator always stays in the same relative position. With several of these satellites properly spaced, television and radio signals are relayed to any place on earth.

Zero Gravity

When astronauts circle the earth in a satellite, they have no sensation of weight. This is because the pull of gravity is balanced exactly by the counteracting inertia of motion. We sometimes experience this *weightless*, or *zero gravity*, condition on earth for an instant when an elevator starts rapidly downward or an automobile goes too fast over the crown of a steep hill.

In one science lesson not long ago, a bright child asked her teacher an astute question: "If we would be weightless in an orbiting satellite, why wouldn't we be weightless on the moon?" The teacher had her reconsider the law of gravitation, especially the part that says ". . . this attraction depends on the *mass* of each object and the distance between them."

Because the moon has a much smaller mass than the earth, its surface gravity is only about one-sixth that of the earth's. An 81-kilogram (180-pound) astronaut weighs a mere 13.5 kilograms (30 pounds) on the moon. However, the moon's mass is almost infinitely greater than that of a space vehicle. The tiny mass of a space vehicle has practically no gravity at all.

Since prolonged periods of weightlessness seem detrimental to astronauts' health, attempts are being made to design space vehicles that create a gravitylike condition. This may be done by rotating the vehicle at a carefully calculated speed. The astronauts' inertia gives them a feeling of gravity as they are slightly pressed against the spaceship's interior. An analogy is the small ball that remains stationary on the rim of a roulette wheel until it stops turning.

Rockets

Through the ages, people have always yearned to explore what mysteries lie beyond the earth. But until recently, our technology has not been as advanced as our ambitions. Early devices and inventions designed for space travel included hitching a flock of geese to a wicker basket, hand-cranking propellers attached to hot-air balloons, and festooning a box with crude rockets containing gunpowder. Occasionally, such contraptions were personally occupied by their daring inventors, and some did depart from this earth, although not in the manner intended.

Because space is a near vacuum, no engine that draws oxygen from the air to burn its fuel can serve in a propulsion system. Instead, rocket engines are used; these carry their own oxygen supply. Rockets work because *for every action there is an equal and opposite reaction* (another law of motion by Newton). When a rocket pushes hot gases out of its combustion chamber (action), the gases push back (reaction) and thrust the rocket ahead.

Most rockets today are composed of multiple stages fastened together in a cluster or a tandem arrangement. The main rocket propels all the stages to a point where the rocket's fuel is expended and then it drops off. The remaining stages reach even higher velocities as the process continues, lightening the load each time. The speed of the last stage represents the accumulated sum of speeds attained by each stage. Perhaps future rockets will be efficient enough to reduce or eliminate the necessity for present cumbersome staging techniques.

Problems in Space Travel

Although modern rocketry provides the means to reach beyond the earth, travel for astronauts poses some difficult problems. As the rocket blasts off in a terrifying surge of power, the rapid acceleration pins the astronauts' bodies to the seats with crushing force.

Once beyond the earth's atmosphere, they need oxygen and sufficient pressure to keep their bodies working normally. They need some means of temperature control. Without air conduction of heat energy, the side of the spaceship facing the sun gets very hot, and the dark side grows freezing cold. Because of their weightless condition, the astronauts may eat and drink from plastic squeeze bottles.

To prevent the space vehicle from being burned to a cinder as it enters the atmosphere, the angle and speed of reentry must be exactly right. These are only some of the problems of space travel.

With so many difficulties, why do people venture into space? Although our curiosity is one answer, of course, there are many advantages to be gained from continued space efforts. Some benefits are improved communications, surveys of earth resources, long-range weather forecasting and possible weather control, astronomers' observation posts beyond the annoying interference of the earth's atmosphere, possible solutions to how the universe was formed, improved mapping and navigation, and many more.

Eventually, there will be the most important reason of all. Someday, perhaps three to five billion years from now, the sun's nuclear fuel will be largely depleted. The sun should gradually expand and engulf the inner planets in an unimaginable inferno of extinction before it finally collapses and dies out. Perhaps by then our descendants, whoever they may be, will have found a comfortable haven among the stars.

INVESTIGATIONS & ACTIVITIES

SECTION 1
Time and Seasons
[*Background 645*]

■ INVESTIGATION: The Way the Earth Rotates

Each day, the sun seems to follow a pattern in the sky. It seems to rise in one direction, move across the sky, and then set in the opposite direction. But the sun is relatively still. We know that it only seems to move because the earth rotates. In which direction does the earth rotate? You can find out for yourself by using a globe and then the earth itself.

EXPLORATORY PROBLEM

How can you find out the direction in which the earth rotates?

NEEDED

globe	sunshine
small nail with large head	hammer
sticky tape	stick, 1 meter (or 1 yard) long

TRY THIS

1. Get a small nail. Push the nail point through the sticky side of a small piece of tape. Fasten the nail head down to the place on the globe where you live.
2. Take the globe, hammer, and stick out in the sunshine. Pound the stick upright into the ground.
3. Notice the shadow made by the stick. Position the globe so the nail is upright and makes a shadow exactly in the same direction. (You may have to slip a book under the globe's base to keep the nail upright.)
4. Rotate the globe from west to east as shown in Figure 19-14.

DISCOVERY PROBLEMS

observing   **A.** What happens to the nail shadow if you rotate the globe a little from west to east? Make a record of the direction and length of the shadow.

observing   **B.** What happens to the nail shadow if you rotate the globe a little from east to west? Make a record.

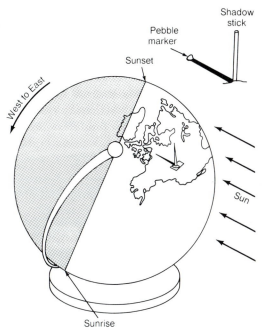

FIGURE 19-14

observing

C. Put a pebble marker at the tip of your stick's shadow. Look at the shadow again 5 minutes later. In which direction did the shadow move?

inferring

D. In which direction does the earth rotate?

inferring

E. Notice other shadows around you. How does their direction compare to the direction of the stick's shadow? How does that help you with Problem D? Where will their shadows be in an hour? In 3 hours?

TEACHING COMMENT

PREPARATION AND BACKGROUND

Some pupils may need to be shown directions outdoors and on the globe. You might help them to understand that north always runs from where they are to the north pole. South runs from there to the south pole, and so on.

For the best shadow, the stick needs to be reasonably upright. A plumb bob, made of string to a piece of chalk, can help pupils align the stick if needed. Or substitute a tetherball pole for the stick. The nail, also, should be upright. If needed, something can be slipped under the globe base to make the nail vertical.

Perhaps you can borrow briefly some globes from other teachers. If so, you might want to do this activity with your entire class divided into small groups.

GENERALIZATION

Daily shadows on earth move from west to east; this shows that the earth rotates the same way.

SAMPLE PERFORMANCE OBJECTIVES

Process: The child can infer from globe and shadow data the direction of the earth's rotation.
Knowledge: The child can explain why the sun seems to rise in the east and set in the west.

■ INVESTIGATION: A Shadow Clock

Before people had clocks, one way they told time was by watching shadows on sunny days. You can do that, too. But now you can use a clock to check how well you can keep time using shadows.

EXPLORATORY PROBLEM

How can you keep time with shadows?

NEEDED

large, blank file card   pencil
nail   clock or watch
sunny day

TRY THIS

1. Lay the card in a sunny place. Put the nail, pointing up, in the center of the card. Trace a small circle around the nail head. If the nail falls over, be sure to replace it inside the circle.
2. Each hour you can, trace the nail shadow with a pencil, and then check a clock. Record the hour by the tip of the pencil tracing (Figure 19-15). It is all right to carry your shadow clock back and forth, but always put it back in the same way and place.

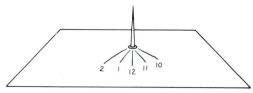

FIGURE 19-15

3. Plan to check your shadow clock on the next sunny day.

DISCOVERY PROBLEMS

observing   **A.** Check the shadow clock each hour, or when you can. Notice where the shadow is. How well can you keep time by the hour?

observing   **B.** Can you tell the right time on the half hour? Can you tell when it is 15 minutes before the hour? fifteen minutes after the hour?

observing   **C.** How long will your shadow clock keep the right time? a week? longer than a week?

observing   **D.** Do the nail shadows slowly change? If so, how?

inferring   **E.** Compare a regular clock with a shadow clock. What are some advantages and disadvantages of each?

TEACHING COMMENT

PREPARATION AND BACKGROUND

It is essential that pupils align their shadow clocks exactly the same way each time. Otherwise, their pencil recording may not coincide with additional shadows. A chalk outline or piece of tape to align an edge can be a helpful reminder.

Within a week, or sooner, observant children will detect a difference in the shadow alignments. This happens because the tilted earth continues to move around the sun. The same event is responsible for changes of seasons.

GENERALIZATION

It is possible to keep track of the time in a general way with a shadow clock. It gets less accurate as time goes on.

SAMPLE PERFORMANCE OBJECTIVES

Process: Within several days the child observes discrepancies between the first shadow and following shadows made by a shadow clock.
Knowledge: The child is able to make and estimate the approximate time with a shadow clock.

FOR YOUNGER CHILDREN

Try the basic activity. But have younger children record shadows for only one or two times: "How can the shadow clock tell us when it's time for lunch?" "Time to go home?" and so on. (Taping paper over the classroom clock will add interest.)

■ INVESTIGATION: Midday Where You Live

Have you learned to tell time with a shadow stick? If so, you know that shadow lengths change during the day. The shortest shadow is always found at the middle of the day, or *midday*.

Can you predict when the midday shadow will appear here today? You may say "noon," but it may be earlier or later. You don't have to check shadow lengths for hours to be sure. You can learn a faster way.

EXPLORATORY PROBLEM A

How can you tell exactly when midday will happen here?

NEEDED

today's newspaper	hammer
long stick	meter stick or yardstick
sunshine	clock or watch
pebbles	

TRY THIS

1. Find the weather section in today's newspaper. Read the times of sunrise and sunset for today.

2. Figure out how long the sun will appear in the sky here today. When half of that time has gone by it will be midday. (For example, suppose the sun rises at 5:00 A.M. and sets at 6:00 P.M. This means it is in the sky for 13 hours. Halfway between, it will be midday. Half of 13 hours is 6 hours and 30 minutes. Add that to the sunrise time. Midday would be 11:30 A.M.)

3. Pound a shadow stick upright into the ground outside.

4. Observe shadow lengths when you think it will be midday. Also, do this starting 15 minutes before and ending 15 minutes after you think it will be midday. Mark the tip of the shadow with a pebble each time.

DISCOVERY PROBLEMS

predicting   **A.** When do you think it will be midday here today?

measuring   **B.** When does the shortest shadow appear?

EXPLORATORY PROBLEM B

How many places do you think can have midday at the same time? How can you find out?

NEEDED

globe	sticky tape
four small nails with large heads	sunshine

TRY THIS

1. Tape a nail head down on the globe where you live. Tape a second nail just left, or west, of the first one. Tape a third nail just east, or to the right, of the first one.

2. Just before midday, take the globe outside to a sunny place. Point the globe's north pole toward the north. Adjust the globe so the middle nail is upright. (You may have to prop a book under the globe's stand to keep the nail upright.)

3. Exactly at midday observe the shadows of the three nails (Figure 19-16).

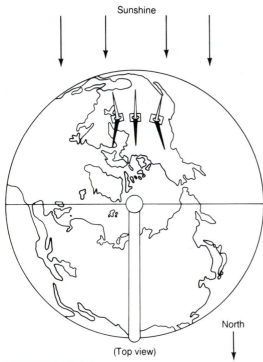

Sunshine

North

(Top view)

FIGURE 19-16

DISCOVERY PROBLEMS

observing   **A.** Which nail shadow points exactly north?

predicting   **B.** Which shadow will next point north? Watch the shadows very slowly change directions as the earth rotates from west to east. (If you cannot wait, just rotate the globe west to east.)

predicting   **C.** Suppose a nail is taped south of where you live. How will its shadow compare with the first nail's shadow?

predicting   **D.** Suppose a nail is taped north of where you live. How will its shadow compare?

inferring   **E.** When it is midday where you live, in which directions is it also midday? in which directions is it not midday?

TEACHING COMMENT

PREPARATION AND BACKGROUND

In Part A, the longer the shadow stick, the more easily pupils will be able to detect differences in shadow length. A weighted string can be held briefly alongside the stick to make sure it is vertical. If possible, use a flagpole or tetherball pole as the shadow stick.

Part B should show that when it is midday at any point, it is also midday at points north or south of it, but not east or west.

GENERALIZATION

It is midday at any point where half the daylight is over. When it is midday at any point, it is also midday at points north and south of the point.

SAMPLE PERFORMANCE OBJECTIVES

Process: The child can find the times of sunrise and sunset in the newspaper and calculate the time of midday.

Knowledge: The child can explain that midday happens on all points of a north–south line when the sun is at its highest anywhere on the line.

☐ ACTIVITY: Where on Earth Is It Night and Day Now?

NEEDED

globe   small nail with large head
sunlight   sticky tape
black paper or cloth

TRY THIS

1. Take the globe to a sunny place. Put a large sheet of black paper under it. (This will help you to see more easily the shadowy half of the globe.)

2. Push a nail through the sticky side of a bit of tape. Tape the nail head down to the place on the globe where you live.

3 Point the top end of the globe toward north. Turn the globe so the nail is straight up. (You may have to slip a book under the globe base to keep the nail upright.)

4. This should now make the globe's position just like the earth's position in the sun. Check the shadows of things around you to see if they are like the nail's shadow.
   a. Which part of the earth has night? Look at the half of the globe that is in shadow.
   b. Which part has day?
   c. Where is it sunrise now? sunset? (Rotate the globe a little from west to east if you are not sure.)

□ ACTIVITY: Where on Earth Is the Sun Exactly Overhead Now?

NEEDED

globe   sticky tape
two nails with large heads   sunshine
tweezers

TRY THIS

1. Tape a nail head down to the place on the globe where you live.
2. Point the north pole of the globe north. Then position the globe so the nail points straight up. (You may need to slip some books under the globe base to do so.)
3. Check the nail shadow to be sure it is like other shadows around you.
4. Objects directly under the sun do not cast a shadow. Use tweezers to hold and slide a second upside-down nail over the globe.
   a. Is there any place where the nail has no shadow?
   b. Can the sun be exactly overhead at more than one place at a time?

   (*Teaching Comment:* On a sphere, only one point can be vertical to the sun at one time. It will be somewhere between the Tropics of Cancer and Capricorn.)

□ ACTIVITY: How Can You Tell Directions with a Watch?

NEEDED

watch   sunny day
pencil   paper

TRY THIS

1. Push a pencil upright into the ground.
2. Place a watch flat on the ground. Place paper under it to keep it clean.
3. Move the watch so the hour hand points away from the pencil and is in the center of the pencil's shadow. Notice that the hour hand now also points away from the sun. (*Caution:* Never look directly at the sun. It can harm your eyes.)
4. Look at a point halfway between the hour hand and the numeral 12 on the watch. That point is north.

   How important is it that the pencil be upright? Do steps 2 through 4 with the pencil slanted. What difference, if any, does it make?

□ **ACTIVITY:** How Warm Is Slanted Sunshine Compared to Direct Sunshine?

NEEDED

cardboard   two matched thermometers
black paper   stapler
scissors   books

TRY THIS

1. Cut two same-sized pieces of cardboard.
2. Staple black paper to each piece. Staple a pocket for each thermometer as shown in Figure 19-17. Slip a thermometer in each pocket.

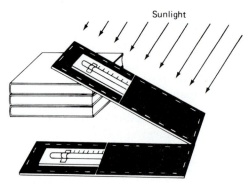

FIGURE 19-17

3. Lay one thermometer flat in the sun. It will get slanted sunshine. Prop up the other thermometer with some books so the sun strikes it directly.
4. Look at each thermometer carefully. Be sure neither thermometer rises so high that it breaks. After a few minutes, take out the thermometers and check the temperatures.
   a. Which has the higher temperature?
   b. Which seems to give more heat, slanted or direct sunshine?

   (*Teaching Comment:* Your pupils may be unsure about how high they must prop up the direct-sunlight thermometer. You might have them tape a nail head down to the cardboard. They then can tilt the cardboard until the nail no longer makes a shadow, indicating relatively vertical sunlight.)

■ **INVESTIGATION:** Why We Have Seasons

Suppose you could see the earth from outer space as it circles the sun each year. This would help you to understand why we have seasons. But you might have to wait a long time to do that. You can use a globe and light to find out now.

EXPLORATORY PROBLEM

How can a model earth (globe) and sun (lighted bulb) be used to show seasons?

NEEDED

tilted globe	unshaded table lamp
small nail with large head	pencil and paper
sticky tape	ruler

TRY THIS

1. Get a tilted globe. The earth rotates on a make-believe pole. The pole's north end always points toward the North Star as the earth circles the sun. (That is why globes are tilted.)

2. Label one wall "north." (You will need to keep the globe tilted toward that wall.)

3. Tape a nail head down to the place on the globe where you live.

4. Set up the globe and lamp as you see in Figure 19-18. Darken the room.

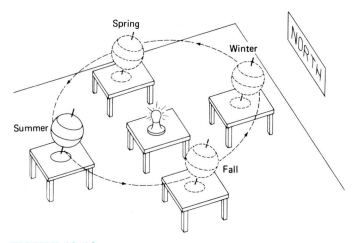

FIGURE 19-18

5. Begin at the summer position. Center the nail in the "sunshine" and point the north pole toward north. Look at the nail shadow where you live. Measure and record how long it is. Notice how much daylight there is east and west of where you live.

6. Repeat step 5, at each of the other three positions.

DISCOVERY PROBLEMS

observing   **A.** During what season do you see the shortest shadow where you live? the longest shadow where you live? (A short shadow shows strong, direct sunshine. A long shadow shows weak, slanted sunshine.)

inferring **B.** When is the longest period of sunshine where you live? When is the shortest period of sunshine? (The longer the sun shines, the warmer it gets where you live.)

inferring **C.** During which seasons will the periods of daylight and darkness be about the same?

inferring **D.** Where and when north of you is it possible to have 24 hours of darkness? twenty-four hours of daylight? When and where can this happen south of you?

TEACHING COMMENT

PREPARATION AND BACKGROUND

If four globes are available, all four can be set up and used at the same time with four groups of pupils. Each group can rotate to a new position after a few minutes for observation and measurement. The best place from which to observe the amount of daylight and darkness at one's latitude is just above the globe's north pole.

GENERALIZATION

The earth's tilted axis and revolution about the sun cause seasonal changes.

SAMPLE PERFORMANCE OBJECTIVES

Process: The child can measure and compare shadow lengths and contrasting areas of daylight and darkness on the globe.
Knowledge: The child can explain that without a tilted axis and the earth's revolution around the sun there would be no seasons.

SECTION 2
Interactions of the Moon, Earth, and Sun
[*Background 648*]

☐ **ACTIVITY:** **Where Will the Moon Be from Time to Time?**

NEEDED

day or night moon   pencil and paper

TRY THIS

1. Find the moon in the sky. Line it up over some tall tree or some other object.
2. Come back 30 minutes later to the same spot. Find the tree you used before.
   a. Where is the moon now compared with the treetop? Notice its direction and height.
   b. Where do you think the moon will be 30 minutes from now? an hour from now? later still?

3. Pick out some tall objects that might be under the moon at these times. Draw them and where you think the moon might be, so you do not forget. Then come back later to check.

   c. How close did you come to predicting the moon's position?

☐ ACTIVITY: How Far Does the Moon Move Each Full Day in Its Path Around the Earth?

NEEDED

day or night moon   paper and pencil

TRY THIS

1. Observe the moon several days or nights in a row. Do this at the same time. Line up the moon over some tall objects. Stand in the same place each time.

2. Make an outline drawing of the tall objects. Draw where the moon appears above them and date the spot each time.

   a. After a few times, can you predict where the moon will be? Lightly pencil a place on your paper and then find where the moon really is.

   b. Suppose you have cloudy weather. Will you be able to predict the moon's position when it is clear? Can you tell where it may have been when the weather was cloudy?

☐ ACTIVITY: What Does the Moon Look Like from Day to Day?

NEEDED

day or night moon   paper and pencil

TRY THIS

1. Draw neat circles in a row on paper. To do so, trace around a coin or other round object.

2. Look at the moon each day for several weeks. Draw inside a circle what you see each time and date each circle.

3. When you cannot see the moon, leave a circle blank, but date it, also.

4. After several weeks, look carefully at your drawings.

   a. What pattern of shapes do you see?

   b. How can your pattern help you to draw the right shapes in the dated, blank circles?

■ INVESTIGATION: Moon Phases

Have you ever watched the moon over one or two weeks? If so, you know its shape seems to go through changes, or *phases*. You can predict what phase will show when you understand why the moon's appearance changes. Working with a *moon model* can help. A ball can be the moon, and your head can be the earth. Light from a bright window can be the sun.

EXPLORATORY PROBLEM

How can a model be used to show moon phases?

NEEDED

white ball (tennis or volleyball)   bright window
daytime moon

TRY THIS

1. Draw all the classroom shades except for one bright window.
2. Hold the ball above eye level and face the window (Figure 19-19). See the dark or shadowy side of the model. This is a *new moon*. (A real new moon cannot be seen from the earth.)

FIGURE 19-19

3. Turn the model moon to the left. Stop when you are sideways to the window. This is a *first-quarter* moon. The moon has gone a quarter, or one-fourth, of the way around the earth.
4. Make another quarter turn to the left. Stop when your back is to the window. Now all of the moon facing you is lighted by the sun. This is a *full* moon.

5. Move a quarter turn left until you are sideways to the window. This is a *last-quarter* moon. Compare it to the first-quarter moon. Notice that the opposite part shines now.

6. Move the last quarter turn to your left. This is the new moon again. From one new moon to the next takes about four weeks.

DISCOVERY PROBLEMS

inferring   **A.** Figure 19-20 shows eight moon phases out of order. Using your moon model, can you figure out the correct order? Start with the new moon.

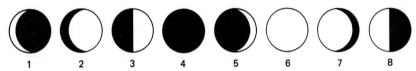

1   2   3   4   5   6   7   8

FIGURE 19-20

observing   **B.** Go outside in the sun. Point your model toward the real moon. Notice where the sun shines on the real moon. Notice where it shines on the model. How does the real-moon phase compare to the model phase?

experimenting   **C.** How can you move your model in the sun to make other phases? (*Caution:* Never look at the sun. It may harm your eyes.)

predicting   **D.** Observe the moon now and then for a few days. Notice how its appearance changes. Keep a record. Can you predict what it will look like in a week? two weeks? Draw what you think, and then find out.

TEACHING COMMENT

PREPARATION AND BACKGROUND

If a bright window is unavailable, use the light from a filmstrip projector in a dark room. To do Problem B, a daytime moon must be visible. Consult the detailed weather section of your local newspaper for moonrise and moonset times during a period when a daytime moon is visible.

GENERALIZATION

Moon phases appear because one-half of the moon is lighted by sunshine as it revolves around the earth.

SAMPLE PERFORMANCE OBJECTIVES

Process: The child can predict an upcoming sequence of moon phases after observing the moon for a week.
Knowledge: The child can demonstrate with a ball and sunshine how moon phases occur.

☐ ACTIVITY: Is a Low Moon Larger Than a High Moon?

NEEDED

low full moon   paper clip

TRY THIS

1. Open the paper clip into a V shape.
2. Hold the clip straight out at eye level. Sight through the V at a low, full moon. Bend the tips of the V so the moon just fits inside.
3. Wait until the moon is higher in the sky and seems smaller. Then, measure again the moon's size as in step 2.
   a. What, if any, difference do you find?
   b. What do you think the moon's size will be later? Check again and see.

☐ ACTIVITY: What Do Shadows Show About the Moon's Surface?

NEEDED

handful of clay   slide projector
pencil

TRY THIS

1. Shape a handful of clay into a ball for a model moon.
2. Pinch parts of the clay to make low and high mountains.
3. Use both ends of a pencil to make some different-sized craters.
4. Smooth parts with your fingers to make some smooth plains.
5. Darken part of the room. Turn on a slide projector.
6. Stick the moon on the end of a pencil. Hold it at arm's length. Turn it slowly in the bright light. Look carefully at the shadows.
   a. What differences, if any, can you see in crater sizes?
   b. What differences can you see in mountain sizes? Can you pick out the highest mountain? lowest mountain?
   c. How many smooth plains areas can you pick out?
   d. If someone else has also made a model moon, switch models. What can you tell from the other moon's shadows? What can the other person tell about yours?

☐ ACTIVITY: Why Can We See Only One Side of the Moon from Earth?

NEEDED

partner

TRY THIS

1. Have your partner's head be the moon. You can be the earth.

2. Let your partner circle you, but face you all the time.
   a. Were you able to see the back of the "moon"? Did your moon rotate one time (face all four walls) as it went around the earth? (This is what the real moon does.)
   b. Could you see the back of the moon if it did not rotate?

3. Have your partner circle you again, but without rotating. That means your partner should face only *one* wall while circling you.
   c. Were you able to see both sides (halves) of the moon this time?

■ INVESTIGATION: An Earth-Moon Model

Astronauts have now walked on the moon several times, so it is easy to think that the moon is close to earth. However, the moon is far away. One way to show its distance is to make a scale model.

EXPLORATORY PROBLEM

How can you make a scale model of the earth and moon?

NEEDED

basketball	string
tennis ball	ruler
scissors	clay

TRY THIS

1. You will need a large ball for the earth and a smaller one for the moon. The earth is about four times as wide as the moon. Measure the width of a ball by putting it between two books. Use a ruler to find the distance between the books. A basketball is about four times wider than a tennis ball.

2. The moon is about 30 earth widths away. Or, it is 10 times farther away than the distance around the earth. Wrap a string 10 times around the basketball. Cut off what is left.

3. Stretch the string between the "earth" and "moon" (Figure 19-21). This scale model shows sizes and distance compared to the real earth.

DISCOVERY PROBLEMS

measuring   **A.** How can you make a scale model that is half this size?

measuring   **B.** Suppose you had a ball 10 centimeters (4 inches) wide to use as the earth. How large would the moon need to be? How far apart should the earth and moon be? (*Hint:* check steps 1 and 2 again.)

FIGURE 19-21

measuring **C.** Suppose you had a ball 5 centimeters (2 inches) wide to use as the moon. How large would the earth need to be? How far apart should the earth and moon be?

measuring **D.** Suppose you wanted your whole model to be no longer than a meter stick or yardstick. How large would you make your earth and moon? How far apart would you place them? (You might make clay balls to help you think.)

TEACHING COMMENT

PREPARATION AND BACKGROUND

The sequence is designed to help children reason without getting into the mathematics of proportion. After these experiences, most pupils should have a realistically scaled view of the earth-moon system. With mathematically advanced pupils, you might proceed directly with figures they can scale: earth diameter 12,800 kilometers (8,000 miles), moon diameter 3,200 kilometers (2,000 miles), and average distance between them 384,000 kilometers (240,000 miles).

GENERALIZATION

Relative sizes and distance in the earth-moon system may be shown in a scale model.

SAMPLE PERFORMANCE OBJECTIVES

Process: Given one measure, the child can derive the two other measures needed to make a scale model of the earth-moon system.
Knowledge: The child can make a scale model of the earth-moon system.

■ INVESTIGATION: Eclipses of the Sun and Moon

Sometimes the earth, moon, and sun are in a straight line in space. Then, something interesting may happen: The moon may block off, or eclipse, the sunlight, or the earth may block, or eclipse, the moon. You can learn how eclipses work with a model of the sun, moon, and earth.

EXPLORATORY PROBLEM

How can you use a volleyball, a tennis ball, and a projector to show eclipses?

NEEDED

volleyball or basketball   filmstrip projector
tennis ball   sticky tape
string

TRY THIS

1. Set up the materials as shown in Figure 19-22. Put a basketball or volleyball on a table. This will be the "earth."

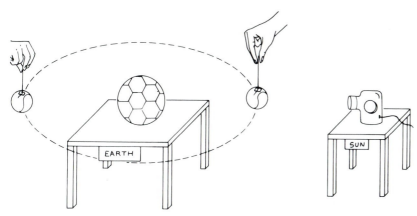

FIGURE 19-22

2. Fasten a short string to a tennis ball with sticky tape. This will be the "moon."
3. Darken the room. Turn on the projector "sun." Point it toward the earth.
4. Holding the string, move the moon around the earth. Notice the shadows made by the moon and the earth.

DISCOVERY PROBLEMS

observing **A.** At what position does the moon make a shadow on the earth? (This is an eclipse of the sun.)

observing **B.** How much of the earth is covered by the moon's shadow?

observing   **C.** At what position does the earth make a shadow on the moon? (This is an eclipse of the moon.)

observing   **D.** How much of the moon is covered by the earth's shadow?

inferring   **E.** Would more people on earth be able to see a sun eclipse or a moon eclipse? Why?

inferring   **F.** Move the moon around the earth again, but now have it go just above or below the earth. Do you see eclipses now? Why or why not?

TEACHING COMMENT

PREPARATION AND BACKGROUND

Some pupils may wonder why there are not a solar eclipse and a lunar eclipse every month. You might use Problem F to help them understand that the plane of the moon's orbit around the earth is somewhat tilted. Also, the two bodies are relatively much farther apart than in the model, so usually the moon's shadow misses the earth, and the earth's shadow misses the moon. The distance between the two bodies also means that the moon's shadow on earth in solar eclipses is much smaller than found in Problem B.

Caution children never to look at the sun during a solar eclipse. The sun can injure their eyes.

GENERALIZATION

A lunar eclipse happens when the earth's shadow falls on the moon. A solar eclipse happens when the moon's shadow falls on the earth.

SAMPLE PERFORMANCE OBJECTIVES

Process: The child can infer from observing a model whether a solar or lunar eclipse is more likely to be viewed from the earth.
Knowledge: The child can describe the relative positions of the sun, moon, and earth during a lunar eclipse and solar eclipse.

SECTION 3
The Solar System and Beyond
[*Background 652*]

■ INVESTIGATION: Size and Distance in the Solar System

The solar system is huge. You cannot make a model that shows both size and distance at the same time. It would be too big to fit in the classroom or playground.

But you can make a scale model of part of the system—the sun and earth. It can help you to understand more about distance and size in the solar system.

EXPLORATORY PROBLEM

How can you make a scale model of the sun and earth?

NEEDED

yellow construction paper   clay
meter stick or yardstick   straight pin
sticky tape   playground
scissors

TRY THIS

1. Make a clay ball 1 centimeter (⅜ inch) wide for the earth.

2. The sun is 108 times wider than the earth, so cut out a circle 108 centimeters (43 inches) wide from yellow construction paper. (You may need to tape some sheets together.)

3. The sun is about 150 million kilometers (93 million miles) from the earth, so the 2 models will need to be about 116 meters (383 feet) apart.

4. Practice taking giant steps. Try to make each step a meter (or yard) long. Then step off the sun-earth distance on the playground (Figure 19-23).

FIGURE 19-23

5. Have someone hold up the model sun at one end. Hold up your tiny model earth, stuck on a pin, at the other end. (Are you surprised at how far away the sun is? Get ready for more surprises.)

DISCOVERY PROBLEMS

measuring **A.** The planet Jupiter is five times farther away from the sun than the earth. How far away (meters or feet) would Jupiter be with your model?

measuring **B.** Uranus is almost 18 times farther from the sun than the earth. How far away would Uranus be with your model?

measuring **C.** Pluto, the farthest planet, is more than 39 times farther away. How far would Pluto be with your model?

measuring **D.** The largest of the solar system's nine planets is Jupiter. It is 11 times wider than the earth. How large would Jupiter be with your model?

measuring **E.** The smallest planet is Pluto. It is only about one-third as wide as the earth. How large would it be with your model?

TEACHING COMMENT

PREPARATION AND BACKGROUND

A large circle may be drawn with a pencil tied to a string. Its radius with the present sun model would be 54 centimeters (21½ inches).

Many pupils will enjoy being challenged to extend their solar system model on a local map. Pluto will need to be placed several kilometers or miles away!

GENERALIZATION

The large distances among planets in the solar system make it difficult to scale planet sizes and distances together in a model.

SAMPLE PERFORMANCE OBJECTIVES

Process: The child can measure and calculate size and distance in constructing a model of the solar system.
Knowledge: The child states that either size or distance may be scaled in a partial solar system model, but not both, if the model is to fit into a classroom.

☐ ACTIVITY: How Fast Do Stars Seem to Move?

NEEDED

soda straw   clear night sky
tape   watch

TRY THIS

1. Look up and toward the south on a clear night. Look through a straw at some bright star. Steady the straw against a fence or other object.

2. Center the star in the straw opening. Then tape the straw to the fence.

3. Watch the star seem to move from the straw's center to its edge.
   a. How long does this take? Remember that the sun seems to move toward the west. (If you are facing south, that is to your right.) Does the star also seem to move west? Do the other stars?
   b. Do some stars seem to move faster than others? How could two straws be used to find out? How could the up-and-down edge of a building be used to find out?

   (*Teaching Comment:* Many pupils will not realize that the stars seem to move for the same reason the sun seems to move—the earth rotates.)

■ INVESTIGATION: Constellations

Most people have seen the group, or *constellation,* of stars called the Big Dipper. The stars make a pattern that looks like an old-fashioned water dipper. There are many more constellations of stars. But while they seem to make a pattern, they may be very different in size and millions of kilometers from each other. Seen from another angle, they may not look at all like constellations. You can find out more about what constellations are like by making a model.

EXPLORATORY PROBLEM

How can you make a model of a constellation?

NEEDED

cardboard box	aluminum foil
scissors	black thread
black paint or paper	sticky tape

TRY THIS

1. Cut off the top and one side of a cardboard box.

2. Cover the side and back inside with black paint or paper.

3. Snip different-sized pieces of black thread to hold your "stars."

4. Make different-sized stars from pieces of foil. Wrap each piece around a thread end. Squeeze each into a ball shape.

5. Ask someone to use tape and hang your stars in some pattern different from the one shown in Figure 19-24. (Notice that in the front view, this constellation looks like a *W,* but from the side it looks like an upside-down *V.* If the box's side

was as long as the playground, you could put the stars even farther apart. Then you would see no pattern at all from the side.)

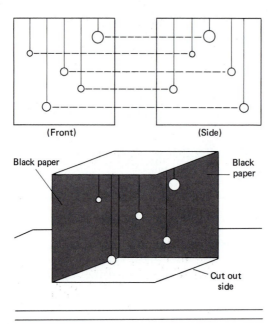

FIGURE 19-24

DISCOVERY PROBLEMS

observing   **A.** Look at the constellation your partner has made from the front view from 15 steps away. Can you draw its shape?

observing   **B.** At what distances from you are the stars? Which is closest, next closest, and so on? Record what you think from left to right.

inferring   **C.** What do you think the constellation looks like from the side? Draw what you think.

observing   **D.** Ask your partner to twist the box around very slightly. How, if at all, does this help you to tell distances and the side pattern? How much more must the box be twisted around to tell?

inferring   **E.** Play a game with your partner. Each person hangs a different constellation. How many stars can you order properly by distance from you? How many side patterns can you tell from front patterns?

TEACHING COMMENT

PREPARATION AND BACKGROUND

It is essential that pupils first view the constellation model directly from the front and from some distance. Otherwise, the activity may be less effective. The foil balls may quickly be suspended, and shifted as needed, by affixing each thread end to the box top inside with a bit of tape.

You might tell the children that a constellation pattern will always look about the same from the earth during their lives because the stars are so far away. Even so, if astronauts ever travel someday among the stars, they may want to learn new patterns to guide them.

GENERALIZATION

Stars of a constellation share a common direction, but they may vary greatly in size and distance from each other.

SAMPLE PERFORMANCE OBJECTIVES

Process: The child can infer a "side" pattern of stars by observing the constellation from a slight angle. (The degree of skill is related to the size of the angle needed to make a correct inference.)

Knowledge: The child states that the pattern of a constellation depends on the position of the observer in space.

SECTION 4
Gravity and the Laws of Motion
[*Background 654*]

☐ ACTIVITY: Why Doesn't the Sun's Gravity Pull the Near Planets into the Sun?

NEEDED

strong string, 2 meters (6 feet) long	partner
rubber ball	watch with second hand
sewing thread spool	outdoor place

TRY THIS

1. Tie one end of the string tightly to the ball. Slide the other end through the hole of a sewing spool.
2. You will be the "sun." The ball "planet" will revolve around you on the string. Hold the spool in one hand. Whirl the planet by moving the spool around. Hold the string with your other hand to keep it from slipping through the spool (Figure 19-25). (You could mark the string below the spool to easily see any slip.)
3. Feel how the ball pulls on the string. Have someone count the number of times your planet circles the sun in 15 seconds. Try to keep the string length above the spool the same.

FIGURE 19-25

4. Try it a second time. Keep the string length the same as before, but now pull harder on the string below the spool. This increases the pull of "gravity" on your planet.
   a. If the planet is to stay at the same distance, what must happen to its speed?

5. Have someone count again the number of orbits your planet makes in 15 seconds.
   b. How do the first and second counts compare? What do you think makes it possible for the closer planets not to be pulled into the sun?

☐ ACTIVITY: What Makes a Rocket Work?

NEEDED

sausage-shaped balloon	sticky tape
string, 6 meters (20 feet) long	paper clip
soda straw	five pennies

TRY THIS

1. Thread one end of the string through a straw. Fasten that end low on a table leg. Fasten the other end high on a wall. The string should be tight.

2. Blow up the balloon. Fold over the small, open end and fasten it with a paper clip.

3. Fasten the balloon to the straw with tape (Figure 19-26).

4. Hold the balloon near the floor end of the string. Quickly remove the paper clip and let go.
   a. What happens to the balloon?
   b. How can you explain what happens?

5. Have a contest with teams of classmates to see whose balloon rocket can lift the most weight to a "space station." Tie one end of each string to a light fixture or other high place. Fasten pennyweights to each balloon with sticky tape.

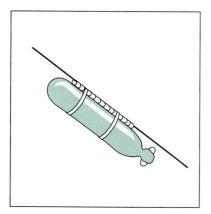

FIGURE 19-26

Make some fair rules: The lower end of each string and rocket must touch the floor when the rocket is released. Each team gets two turns; the first is for practice. Observe carefully what the best rockets look like during the first trial. Use this information to prepare for the second trial. No team can change its rocket once the second trials begin.

To win, here are some things to think about.

a. How much air should be in the balloon? (If it breaks, you're out of the contest.)
b. How long should the straw be? How should it be attached to the balloon?
c. Should the string be upright or at a slant? What kind of string is best?
d. How many pennies should be stuck on the balloon? Where is it best to put them for balance?

(*Teaching Comment:* When air rushes out of the balloon, there is an equal and opposite push inside, so the balloon moves. In a rocket engine, burned fuel forms hot gases that push out the open back of the engine. An equal and opposite push inside moves the rocket forward.

If you have several balloons, your whole class can enjoy activity 5. Divide the class into teams. The object is to solve the problem by deciding on the best combination of variables. You might have to ask the custodian for a ladder to tie strings to some suitable, high up "space station.")

___

□ **ACTIVITY: How Does Having More Than One Stage Make a Rocket Go Faster?**

NEEDED

bicycle
chalk
meter stick or yardstick

playground
ball

A space rocket is usually made of two or three sections, called *stages*, fitted together. Each stage has its own rocket. After a rocket blasts off and gains some speed, a stage drops off and the rocket of the next stage takes over. You can see for yourself why this boosts the speed of the rocket. You can use a bicycle and ball to find out.

TRY THIS

1. Go to a clear, paved place where you can ride a bicycle. Mark a line on the paved surface with chalk.

2. Sit on a bicycle at the line. Have someone balance you. Throw a ball straight ahead *with an underarm motion* as far as you can. Do it without straining or losing balance. Have someone mark where the ball first lands.

3. Pump your bicycle to a fairly fast speed and then coast to the line. As you cross it, throw the ball again the underarm way without straining or losing balance. Have someone mark again where the ball lands.
   a. Which time did the ball travel farther?
   b. Which time did the ball travel faster?
   c. How is this like what happens to a two-stage rocket?

(*Teaching Comment:* As underarm throw is safer than an overarm throw because it has little or no effect on the rider's balance. You might bring out an additional reason why a rocket stage is discarded: It no longer contains fuel, and so it is useless mass. By discarding it, the remaining mass is smaller and requires less force and energy to reach a faster speed.)

SELECTED TRADE BOOKS: THE EARTH IN SPACE

FOR YOUNGER CHILDREN

Bendick, Jeanne. *Artificial Satellites: Helpers in Space.* Millbrook Press, 1991.

———. *Comets and Meteors: Visitors from Space.* Millbrook Press, 1991.

Branley, Franklyn M. *The Moon Seems to Change.* Harper & Row, 1987.

———. *The Planets in Our Solar System.* Harper & Row, 1987.

———. *Rockets and Satellites.* Harper & Row, 1987.

———. *The Big Dipper.* Harper & Collins, 1991.

———. *What Makes Day and Night.* Harper & Row, 1986.

Calmenson, Stephanie. *My Book of the Seasons.* Golden Press, 1982.

Fradin, Dennis. *Spacelab.* Children's Press, 1984.

Friskey, Margaret. *Space Shuttles.* Children's Press, 1982.

Gorey, Edward, and Peter Neumeyer. *Why We Have Day and Night.* Capra Press, 1982.

Hamer, Martyn. *Night Sky.* Watts, 1983.

Jackson, Kim. *The Planets.* Troll Associates, 1985.

Jay, Michael. *Planets.* Watts, 1987.

FOR OLDER CHILDREN

Adams, Richard. *Our Wonderful Solar System.* Troll Associates, 1983.

Adler, Irving. *The Stars: Decoding Their Messages.* Crowell, 1980.

Alexander, Kent. *The Kid's Book of Space Flight.* Running Press, 1990.

Asimov, Isaac. *Ancient Astronomy.* Dell, 1991.

———. *Projects in Astronomy.* Gareth Stevens, 1990.

Berger, Melvin. *Bright Stars, Red Giants and White Dwarfs.* Putnam, 1983.

Branley, Franklyn M. *Star Guide.* Harper & Row, 1987.

Cabellero, Jane A. *Aerospace Projects for Young Children.* Humanics, 1987.

Couper, Heather, and Nigel Henbest. *The Moon.* Watts, 1987.

Fichter, George S. *Comets and Meteors.* Watts, 1982.

Furniss, Tim. *Let's Look at Outer Space.* Watts, 1987.

Gallant, Roy A. *Once Around the Galaxy.* Watts, 1983.

Gardner, Robert. *Projects in Space Science.* Messner, 1988.

Lauber, Patricia. *Journey to the Planets.* Crown, 1982.

Lewellen, John. *Moon, Sun and Stars.* Children's Press, 1981.

Myring, Lynn. *Sun, Moon and Planets.* EDC Press, 1982.

Richard, Graham. *Spacecraft.* Watts, 1987.

Ridpath, Ian. *Space.* Watts, 1991.

Riley, Peter D. *The Earth and Space.* David & Charles, 1986.

Simon, Seymour. *The Long Journey from Space.* Crown, 1982.

Vogt, Gregory. *Mars and the Inner Planets.* Watts, 1982.

———. *Space Laboratories.* Watts, 1987.

Wood, Robert. *Thirty-Nine Easy Astronomy Experiments.* Tab Books, 1991.

Professional Bibliography

GENERAL SOURCES OF ACTIVITIES

Bybee, Rodger, Rita Peterson, Jane Bowyer, and David Butts. *Activities for Teaching About Science and Society.* Columbus, Ohio: Merrill, 1984. (Activities that relate to social needs and problems.)

DeVito, Alfred, and Gerald H. Krockover. *Creative Sciencing: Ideas and Activities for Teachers and Children.* Glenview, IL: Scott Foresman (Goodyear), 1991. (About 160 activities designed to stimulate creativity.)

Freidl, Alfred E. *Teaching Science to Children, An Integrated Approach.* New York: Random House, 1986. (A large array of hands-on activities for children, including many discrepant events.)

Jacobson, William J., and Abby S. Bergman. *Science Activities for Children.* Englewood Cliffs, N.J.: Prentice-Hall, 1983. (Activities in eight subject areas for primary and intermediate levels.)

Lowery, Lawrence F. and Carol Verbeeck. *Explorations* (3 volumes: *Earth Science, Physical Science, Life Science*). Carthage, IL: Fearon, 1987. (48 process-oriented activities for grades 1–3.)

Strongin, Herb. *Science on a Shoestring.* Reading, MA: Addison-Wesley, 1991. (Easy-to-do investigations with readily-found, inexpensive materials.)

Van Cleave, Janice P. *Science for Every Kid* (5 volumes: *Biology, Chemistry, Earth, Astronomy, Physics*). New York: Wiley, 1989–1991. (Each volume has 101 activities for grade three and beyond, many of which are suitable for science fair projects.)

PERIODICALS (Teachers)

Discover, Time, Inc., 3435 Wilshire Blvd., Los Angeles, CA 90010. (Monthly. Interesting, up-to-date information about developments in science.)

Journal of Research in Science Teaching, John Wiley and Sons, Inc., 605 Third Ave., New York, NY 10158. (Quarterly. Scholarly articles on research and practice.)

Natural History, American Museum of Natural History, Central Park West at 79th St., New York, NY 10024. (Monthly, 10 issues a year. Interesting articles on a variety of natural subjects, including ecology.)

School Science and Mathematics, School Science and Mathematics Association, P.O. Box 1614, Indiana University of Pennsylvania, Indiana, PA 15701. (Monthly, nine issues a year. Includes articles on methods and research.)

Science, American Association for the Advancement of Science, 1515 Massachusetts Ave., N.W., Washington, DC 20005. (Monthly, except bimonthly Jan./Feb. and July/Aug. Accurate, up-to-date nontechnical information about developments in science.)

Science Activities, Science Activities Publishing Company, Skokie, IL 60076. (Ten issues a year. Useful activities for teachers of the upper grades and beyond.)

Science and Children, National Science Teachers Association, 1742 Connecticut Ave., N.W., Washington, DC 20009. (Monthly, eight issues a year. Articles of interest and practical value to elementary school teachers.)

Science Education, John Wiley and Sons, Inc., 605 Third Ave., New York, NY 10158. (Quarterly. Reports of research and essays on the teaching of elementary and secondary school science.)

Science News, Science Service, 1719 N Street, N.W., Washington DC (Weekly. Brief, easy-to-read reports on current findings of scientific research.)

PERIODICALS (Children)

Digit, P.O. Box 29996, San Francisco, CA 94129. (Six issues a year. Computer games, ideas, challenges. Upper elementary.)

Enter, One Disk Drive, P.O. Box 2686, Boulder, CO 80322. (Ten issues a year. Computer games, ideas, challenges from the producers of the Children's Television Workshop. Upper elementary.)

National Geographic World, National Geographic Society, Department 00481, 17th and M Streets N.W., Washington, DC 20036. (Monthly. Articles on environmental features of interest to children.)

Odyssey, AstroMedia Corp., 625 E. St. Paul Ave., P.O. Box 92788, Milwaukee, WI 53202. (Bimonthly. Full-color astronomy and space magazine for children 7 to 13.)

Ranger Rick's Nature Magazine, National Wildlife Federation, 1412 Sixteenth St., N.W., Washington, DC 20036. (Monthly, for children of elementary school age. Interesting stories and

pictures on natural subjects, including ecology. *Your Big Backyard,* also 10 issues, is for preschool and primary-level children.)

Scienceland, 501 Fifth Ave., Suite 2102, New York, NY 10017. (Monthly, eight softcover booklets issued a year. Well-received magazine for children, preschool to third grade.)

Science Weekly, P.O. Box 70154, Washington, DC 20088. (Twenty issues a year. Current science developments for children in grades one through six.)

3–2–1 Contact, Children's Television Workshop, P.O. Box 2933, Boulder, CO 80322. (Ten issues a year. Experiments, puzzles, projects, and articles for children 8 to 14.)

PROFESSIONAL TEXTS

Abruscato, Joseph. *Teaching Children Science.* Englewood Cliffs, N.J.: Allyn & Bacon, 1992. (Methods, activities, and content for elementary school science.)

Blough, Glenn O., and Julius Schwartz. *Elementary School Science and How to Teach It.* New York: Holt, Rinehart and Winston, 1990. (Methods and comprehensive coverage of subject matter content.)

Cain, Sandra E., and Jack M. Evans. *Sciencing: An Involvement Approach to Elementary Science Methods.* Columbus, Ohio: Merrill/Macmillan, 1990. (A methods text organized into six broad units to develop teaching competencies.)

Carin, Arthur A. *Teaching Science Through Discovery.* 7th ed. Columbus, Ohio: Merrill/Macmillan, 1993. (Methods and activities, with emphasis on discovery teaching.)

Esler, William K., and Mary K. Esler. *Teaching Elementary Science.* Belmont, Calif.: Wadsworth, 1989. (Methods and subject matter. Exemplifies and applies three kinds of lessons.)

Gabel, Dorothy. *Introductory Science Skills.* Prospect Heights, Ill.: Waveland Press, 1984. (A laboratory approach to learning science and mathematics skills, and basic chemistry.)

Good, Ronald G. *How Children Learn Science.* New York: Macmillan, 1977. (Research on children's mental development and recommendations for teaching science.)

Harlan, Jean. *Science Experiences for the Early Childhood Years.* Columbus, Ohio: Merrill/Macmillan, 1992. (Everyday science activities for younger children.)

Henson, Kenneth T., and Delmar Janke. *Elementary Science Methods.* New York: McGraw-Hill, 1984. (Methods and activities for elementary schoolchildren.)

Jacobson, Willard J., and Abby Barry Bergman. *Science for Children.* Englewood Cliffs, N.J.: Prentice-Hall, 1987. (Methods and content of elementary-school science.)

Peterson, Rita, Jane Bowyer, David Butts, and Rodger Bybee. *Science and Society: A Source Book for Elementary and Junior High School Teachers.* Columbus, Ohio: Merrill, 1984. (Content and comprehensive methods. Emphasizes science's impact on society.)

Renner, John W. and Edmund A. Marek. *The Learning Cycle and Elementary School Science Teaching.* Portsmouth, N.H.: Heinemann, 1988. (Emphasizes methods that match children's cognitive processes for successful science teaching.)

Victor, Edward. *Science for the Elementary School.* 7th ed. New York: Macmillan, 1993. (Methods, content, and activities. Features an extensive scope of subject matter in outline form.)

Wassermann, Selma, and J. W. George Ivany. *Teaching Elementary Science.* New York: Harper & Row, 1988. (Stresses informal, inquiry-type science experiences for children.)

Wolfinger, Donna M. *Teaching Science in the Elementary School.* Boston: Little, Brown, 1984. (Extensive treatment of the basic, causal, and experimental processes of science. Integrates much research on science teaching.)

Zeitler, William R., and James P. Barufaldi. *Elementary School Science,* New York: Longman, 1988. (Modern methods for teaching science. Contains a variety of illustrative lessons.)

Some Major Project-Developed Programs

This program, developed at Fresno (California) Pacific College, was originally funded by the National Science Foundation to train a group of teachers in the rationale and methods for integrating science and mathematics in Grades 5–8. The classroom testing of written materials produced such positive results, a full-fledged writing project was launched to develop 15 teaching booklets. Materials are now available for K–8.

The rationale for AIMS includes these points: (1) Math and science are integrated outside the classroom and so should also be integrated inside it; (2) as in the real world, a whole series of math skills and science processes should be interwoven in a single activity to create a continuum of experience; (3) the materials should present questions that relate to the student's world and arouse their curiosity; (4) the materials should change students from observers to participants in the learning process; (5) the investigations should be enjoyable because learning is more effective when the process is enjoyed.

For more information, write to AIMS Education Foundation, P.O. Box 8120, Fresno, CA 93747.

EDUCATION DEVELOPMENT CENTER INSIGHTS   Grades K–6

The Education Development Center is in Newton, MA. The program contains 17 activity-based modules that can be used separately within another science curriculum, or as a full curriculum within the life, earth, and physical science areas. Each module is organized around four phases of instruction: Getting Started, Exploring and Discovering, Organizing and Processing for Meaning, and Applying and Extending Ideas. Six major science themes are incorporated into the program: systems, change, structure and function, diversity, cause and effect, and energy. Content and process skills are balanced across the curriculum. Material from other school subjects is integrated into many activities to give an overall understanding of how they normally relate.

The activities, often open-ended, focus on experiences that draw on the urban environment. Playground apparatus, toys, and the pupils themselves may serve as resources for learning science concepts. Instructional materials are designed for both the inexperienced teacher and the veteran who seeks innovative strategies to develop critical and creative thinking in pupils.

An advisory group of teachers from seven major urban areas continually gave feedback to program developers about the quality of learning and assessment activities.

The commercial distributor is Science Kit, Elementary Science Division, 777 East Park Drive, Tonawanda, NY 14150.

ELEMENTARY SCIENCE STUDY (ESS)   Grades K–6

ESS was begun in the 1960s as a curriculum improvement project of the Education Development Center, a nonprofit organization devoted to generating new ideas for education.

The program consists of 56 units of instruction that cover a wide range of science subjects. Each unit has a teacher's manual, and most units have an accompanying kit of materials. No fixed master plan exists for scope and sequence. The developers felt that each school district was best qualified to assemble its own curriculum from the units to meet local conditions.

ESS is intentionally child centered. Activities are designed to reflect the wonder, curiosity, and natural play of childhood. While the teacher guide for each unit suggests an overall structure, the pupils help determine in which directions the activities go and how much time is spent on each

activity. So most classroom procedures are exploratory and open-ended. ESS believes that learning happens best when children are free to use their own styles without overstructuring and premature closing from adults.

Materials are available from Delta Education, Inc., P.O. Box 915, Hudson, NH 03051.

FULL OPTION SCIENCE SYSTEM (FOSS) Grades K–6

This program is designed to serve both regular and most special education pupils in a wide cross-section of schools. Developed at the Lawrence Hall of Science, Berkeley, California, the program features several modules at each grade level that include science lesson plans in the earth, life, and physical sciences, and extension activities in language, computer, and mathematics applications.

The laboratory equipment includes several package options, from complete kits to individual items. Materials assembly directions show how teacher and pupils can gather and construct equipment for many activities. A correlation table tells how to integrate activities with other programs and state department of education guidelines for science.

Much care is taken to have a suitable match between activities and pupils' ability to think at different ages. Further work has been done to make the program easy to instruct and manage. Provisions for preparation time, ease of giving out and retrieving materials, cleanup, storage, and resupply have continually guided program developers.

The commercial distributor of FOSS is the Encyclopedia Britannica Educational Corporation, 310 South Michigan Avenue, Chicago, IL 60604.

NATIONAL GEOGRAPHIC KIDS NETWORK
Grades 4–6

The National Geographic Kids Network is a program that has children gather data on real science problems and then use a computer network to share their data with a scientist and children in other locations. The developer is the Technical Education Resource Center (TERC), in partnership with the National Geographic Society, which publishes and distributes the program.

Each of the instructional units is six weeks long and focuses on a central science problem. Children learn to ask questions and gather data in scientifically acceptable ways. The data are transmitted to an interested scientist who analyzes the data, answers children's questions, and then sends back an overview of all the collected information from cooperating schools.

Curriculum materials include children's handbooks that have background information on the topic of study, teacher guides, and computer software. The software is made up of a word-processing program, data charts, and a computer map of North America, all of which are used to ready and transmit data.

For details, write National Geographic Society Educational Services, 17th & M Streets, Washington DC 20036.

NUFFIELD SCIENCE 5–13
Grades K–8

Science 5–13 is a series of reference and resource publications for the teacher that suggests an open-ended, child-centered approach to elementary science. ("5–13" signifies the age span of the children served.) This program was begun as a curriculum project at the Nuffield Education Foundation of Great Britain.

The basic set of teaching units is com-posed of 20 volumes. Some unit titles are: "Working with Wood"; "Science, Models, and Toys"; "Structure and Forces"; "Children and Plastics"; "Trees"; and "Ourselves." An additional set of six titles in environmental education complements the basic program.

A major contribution of Science 5–13 is how it takes children's beginning experiences with everyday things and freely extends them in many directions. All the while, children's intellectual development is carefully considered.

In the United States, the distributor is Macdonald-Raintree, Inc., 205 W. Highland Ave., Milwaukee, WI 53203.

OUTDOOR BIOLOGY INSTRUCTIONAL STRATEGIES (OBIS)
Ages 10–15

Developed at the Lawrence Hall of Science, University of California (Berkeley), OBIS is designed for use with community youth organizations and schools that want to offer outdoor laboratory experiences. Four activity packets offer a broad selection of interesting, firsthand activities for studying ecological relationships in different environments: desert, seashore, forest, pond and stream, city lots, and local parts.

Each activity card consists of background information for the leader, description of materials needed, what advance preparation may be required, a lesson plan, and several follow-up suggestions. Each activity can be used alone or as part of a developmental sequence.

The commercial distributor is: Delta Education, Box 915, Hudson, NH 03051

SCIENCE FOR LIFE AND LIVING   Grades K–6

The full name for this curriculum is "Science for Living: Integrating Science, Technology, and Health." The developer is the BSCS Group, a nonprofit foundation for science education.

After readiness activities at the kindergarten level, these concepts and skills form the main curriculum structure: order and organization (Grade 1); change and measurement (Grade 2); patterns and prediction (Grade 3); systems and analysis (Grade 4); energy and investigation (Grade 5); and balance and decisions (Grade 6). Children build their own understanding of an integrated world of science, technology, and health as they work through activities that bring out the concepts and skills.

Each complete lesson contains five consecutive phases: (1) An *engagement* activity begins the lesson. Children connect what they know to the present material and reveal their prior knowledge, including misconceptions. (2) *Exploration* follows, in which pupils explore the materials or environment and form a common base of experience. (3) Next, an *explanation* phase gives pupils a chance to describe what they are learning, and the teacher is given an opportunity to state the intended learning. (4) *Elaboration* then provides activities that extend understandings and give further chances to practice skills. (5) The last phase, *evaluation,* allows pupils and teacher to assess what has been learned.

Published materials are available from the Kendall/Hunt Publishing Company, 2460 Kerper Blvd., Dubuque, IA 52001.

SCIENCE AND TECHNOLOGY FOR CHILDREN (STC)
Grades 1–6

The developer of this curriculum project is the National Science Resources Center, established in 1985 by the National Academy of Sciences and the Smithsonian Institution to improve the teaching of science and mathematics in the nation's schools. The project's mission is to significantly increase the number of schools that offer hands-on science programs to children, and to interest more females and minority members in science.

Teaching units include such titles as *Weather and Me* (Grade 1), *The Life Cycle of Butterflies* (2), *Plant Growth and Development* (3), *Electric Circuits* (4), *Microworlds* (5), and *Magnets and Motors* (6). They are designed to focus on easy-to-use materials and integrate science with other areas of the curriculum. Each unit includes a teacher's guide; pupil activity booklet; a description of needed materials; and annotated lists of recommended trade books, computer software, and audiovisual materials.

The developers sought to make the management of materials and activities as practical as possible. In the field testing of units, evaluation procedures monitored how well the units worked under a wide variety of classroom conditions.

For details, contact the National Science Resources Center, Arts and Industries Building, Room 1201, Smithsonian Institution, Washington, DC 20560.

SCIENCE—A PROCESS APPROACH (SAPA)
Grades K–6

SAPA has a unique structure. It uses process skills rather than subject-matter content as the base for its scope and sequence. Subject matter is used mainly as an aid to developing the skills, although much content is presented.

Eight "basic" processes are taught in grades K–3: observing, using space/time relationships, using numbers, measuring, classifying, communicating, predicting, and inferring. In grades 4–6, five "integrated" processes are taught that build on and extend the basic processes: formulating hypotheses, controlling variables, interpreting data, defining operationally, and experimenting. The method used to organize the development of the skills was to identify the process behaviors of scientists, and then to logically break down the behaviors into sequences through which they could be learned by children.

SAPA II, a more recent version of this program, has a more flexible structure than the first edition. Alternate procedures have been provided to allow the teacher more leeway in meeting pupils' individual differences and organizing teaching.

The commercial supplier is Delta Education, Inc., P.O. Box 915, Hudson, NH 03051.

SCIENCE CURRICULUM IMPROVEMENT STUDY (SCIS)   Grades K–6

SCIS is organized on a base of powerful and modern science concepts. Each of 12 instructional units features a central concept, with supporting subconcepts and process skills integrated into the activities.

Lessons have three parts: exploration, invention, and discovery. In the exploratory part, children are given objects to observe or manipulate. At times these observations are guided by the teacher; otherwise, the children observe and manipulate the objects as they wish.

Explorations allow firsthand contact with the material under study and provide a basis for children to use language. At the same time, the need arises for an explanation to make sense out of what has been observed.

This is taken up in the second part of the lesson sequence. After discussion, the teacher gives a definition and a word for the new concept.

This "invention" of a concept sets up the third part of the lesson. Now, the children are given a variety of further experiences within which they discover many applications of the concept. These extend and reinforce their knowledge and skills.

An updated version of this program, *SCIS3*, is available from Delta Education, Inc., P.O. Box 915, Hudson, NH 03051.

UNIFIED SCIENCES AND MATHEMATICS FOR ELEMENTARY SCHOOLS (USMES)   Grades K–8

The USMES project was funded by the National Science Foundation to develop and try out interdisciplinary units of instruction involving science, mathematics, social sciences, and language arts. The units are centered on long-range investigations of real and practical problems geared to the local environment. Twenty-six in all, the units may be used by local school planners to design different curricula to meet their needs but yet commonly reflect a problem-solving approach.

Several kinds of materials are provided for planners and teachers: an introductory guide to USMES, a teacher resource book for each major problem, background papers, a design lab manual (that tells how to set up and make needed apparatus), and a curriculum correlation guide.

More information may be gotten from ERIC, Ohio State University, 1200 Chambers Road, Columbus, Ohio 43212.

Commercial Suppliers of Science Materials and Equipment

(*Note:* The following classifications of suppliers may not be entirely accurate because suppliers often change offerings with business conditions. A current catalog should reveal the full scope of materials for sale in each case. Use school stationery when requesting free elementary-level catalogs. An annual, comprehensive listing of suppliers accompanies each January issue of *Science and Children.*)

General Supplies—Physical and Life Science

Carolina Biological Supply Company
2700 York Road
Burlington, NC 27215

Delta Education, Inc.
P.O. Box 915
Hudson, NH 03051

Edmund Scientific Company
101 E. Gloucester Pike
Barrington, NJ 08007

Frey Scientific Company
905 Hickory Lane
Mansfield, Ohio 44905

Learning Things, Inc.
68A Broadway
Arlington, MA 02174

Life Science Supplies

Carolina Biological Supply Company
2700 York Road
Burlington, NC 27215

Connecticut Valley Biological Supply
    Company
Valley Road
Southampton, MA 01073

Ward's Natural Science Establishment
5100 West Henrietta Road
P.O. Box 92912
Rochester, NY 14692

Balances

Ohaus Scale Corporation
29 Hanover Road
Florham Park, NJ 07932

Microscopes

American Optical Corporation
Eggert and Sugar Roads
Buffalo, NY 14215

Bausch & Lomb, Inc.
1400 North Goodman Street
Rochester, NY 14602

Swift Instruments, Inc.
P.O. Box 95016
San Jose, CA 95016

Microprojectors

Ken-A-Vision Manufacturing Company
5615 Raytown Road
Raytown, MO 64133

Aquaria, Terraria, Cages

Carolina Biological Supply Company
2700 York Road
Burlington, NC 27215

Jewel Aquarium Company
5005 West Armitage Avenue
Chicago, IL 60639

Science Kit, Inc.
777 E. Park Drive
Tonawanda, NY 14150

Kits and Models

Delta Education, Inc.
P.O. Box 915
Hudson, NH 03051

Denoyer-Geppert Company
5235 N. Ravenswood Avenue
Chicago, IL 60640

NASCO Company
901 Janesville Avenue
Fort Atkinson, WI 53538

Science Kit, Inc.
777 E. Park Drive
Tonawanda, NY 14150

Requirements for Various Animals

Food and Water	Rabbits	Guinea Pigs	Hamsters	Gerbils	Mice	Rats
Daily pellets	rabbit pellets: keep dish half full	large dog pellets: one or two				
or grain	corn, wheat, or oats: keep dish half full		1½ tablespoons	or sunflower or 2 teaspoons	canary seeds or oats: 2 teaspoons	3–4 teaspoons
green or leafy vegetables, lettuce, cabbage and celery tops or	4–5 leaves	2 leaves	1 leaf	⅛ leaf or less	⅛–¼ leaf	¼ leaf
grass, plantain, lambs' quarters, clover, alfalfa (or hay, if water is also given)	2 handfuls	1 handful	½ handful	—	—	—
carrots	2 medium	1 medium		—	—	—
Twice a week apple (medium)	½ apple	¼ apple	⅛ apple	⅛ apple or ½ core and seeds	½ core and seeds	1 core
iodized salt (if not contained in pellets)	or salt block		sprinkle over lettuce or greens			
corn, canned or fresh, once or twice a week	½ ear	¼ ear	1 tablespoon ⅓ ear	½ tablespoon or end of ear	¼ tablespoon or end of ear	½ tablespoon
water	should always be available	necessary only if lettuce or greens are not provided				

Food and Water	Water Turtles	Land Turtles	Small Turtles
Daily			
worms or night crawlers or tubifex or blood worms	1 or 2	1 or 2	¼ inch of tiny earthworm enough to cover ½ area of a dime
and/or raw chopped beef or meat and fish-flavored dog or cat food	½ teaspoon	½ teaspoon	
fruit and vegetables: fresh		¼ leaf lettuce or 6–10 berries or 1–2 slices peach, apple, tomato, melon or 1 tablespoon corn, peas, beans	
dry ant eggs, insects, or other commercial turtle food			1 small pinch
water	always available at room temperature; should be ample for swimming and submersion		
	¾ of container	large enough for shell	½ to ¾ of container

Food and water	Goldfish	Guppies
Daily dry commercial food	1 small pinch	1 very small pinch; medium-size food for adults; fine-size food for babies
Twice a week shrimp—dry—or another kind of dry fish food	4 shrimp pellets, or 1 small pinch	dry shrimp food or other dry food: 1 very small pinch
Two or three times a week tubifex worms	enough to cover ½ area of a dime	enough to cover ⅛ area of dime
Add enough "conditioned" water to keep tank at required level	allow one gallon per inch of fish	allow ¼–½ gallon per adult fish
	add water of same temperature as that in tank—at least 65°F	add water of same temperature as that in tank—70–80°F
Plants [for aquaria] cabomba, anacharis, etc.	should always be available	

	Newts	Frogs
Daily small earthworms or mealworms or tubifex worms or raw chopped beef	1–2 worms	2–3 worms
	enough to cover ½ area of a dime enough to cover a dime	enough to cover ¾ area of a dime enough to cover a dime
water	should always be available at the same temperature as that in tank or room temperature	

Reprinted with permission from Grace K. Pratt-Butler, *How to . . . Care for Living Things in the Classroom*, Rev. Ed. (Washington, D.C.: National Science Teachers Association, 1978), p. 11.

Summary of Children's Thinking in Three Piagetian Stages*

Thought Process	Intuitive Thought[*]	Concrete Operational	Formal Operational
Cause and Effect	Logic often contradictory, unpredictable. Events may occur by magic or for human convenience.	Contradictions avoided. Physical objects are linked to show cause and effect. Commonsense explanations may be wrong but logical.	Can separate logic from content. Systematic control of variables possible, plus hypothetical "thought experiments," to test ideas.
Relative Thinking	Egocentric perceptions and language. Little grasp of how variables interrelate. Physical properties viewed in absolute, not relative, ways.	Perceptions of position and objects more objective. Aware of others' views. Some understanding of interrelated variables, when connected to concrete objects and pictures.	Understand relative position and motion. Can define and explain abstract concepts with other concepts or analogies. May temporarily show some egocentricity in propositions.
Classifying and Ordering	Sort one property at a time. Little or no class inclusion. Trial-and-error ordering in early part of stage.	Understand class inclusion principle. More consistent seriation with diverse objects. Can follow successive steps—less discrete thinking.	Can recombine groups into fewer, more abstract categories. Can form hierarchical systems.
Conservative Thinking	Mostly do not conserve. Perceptions dominate thinking. Center attention on one variable and do not compensate. Little or no reverse thinking.	Can reverse thinking, consider several variables and compensate. Conserve most of the Piagetian test concepts.	Conserve all of the Piagetian test concepts, with displaced and solid volume usually last.

[*]Intuitive thought is the last period of the preoperational stage.

Index

ISBN 0-02-341302-6